CACHE Level 3

Child Care and Education

4th Edition

Penny Tassoni

Kate Beith • Kath Bulman • Harriet Eldridge

www.heinemann.co.uk

✓ Free online support
✓ Useful weblinks
✓ 24 hour online ordering

01865 888118

Heinemann

Heinemann is an imprint of Harcourt Education Limited, a company incorporated in England and Wales, having its registered office: Halley Court, Jordan Hill, Oxford OX2 8EJ. Registered company number: 3099304

www.heinemann.co.uk

Heinemann is the registered trademark of Harcourt Education Limited

Text © Penny Tassoni, Kate Beith, Kath Bulman, Harriet Eldridge 2007

First published 2007

12 11 10 09 08 07
10 9 8 7 6 5 4 3 2 1

British Library Cataloguing in Publication Data is available from the British Library on request.

ISBN 978 0 435987 42 8

Edited Caroline Low, Virgo Editorial
Index by Sophia Clapham
Designed by Kamae Design, Oxford
Original illustrations © Harcourt Education Limited 2007
Illustrated by Duncan Mackenzie and Kamae Design
Cover design by Wooden Ark Studio
Picture research by Chrissie Martin
Cover photo/illustration © Jupiter Images
Printed in the UK by Scotprint

Acknowledgements
Every effort has been made to contact copyright holders of material reproduced in this book. Any omissions will be rectified in subsequent printings if notice is given to the publishers.

Websites
The websites used in this book were correct and up to date at the time of publication. It is essential for tutors to preview each website before using it in class so as to ensure that the URL is still accurate, relevant and appropriate. We suggest that tutors bookmark useful websites and consider enabling students to access them through the school/college intranet.

Contents

Acknowledgements

Photo acknowledgements

The authors and publisher would like to thank the following individuals and organisations for permission to reproduce photographs:

Alamy Images / Adrian Sherratt: 34, 248, 488; ... / Bernie Epstein: 56; ... / Carlos Davila: 187; ... / Christina Kennedy: 528; ... / Craig Holmes: 169, 544; ... / David Poole: 207; ... / ePictura: 269; ... / Image Source: 469; ... / Jennie Hart: 582; ... / Janine Wiedel Photography: 170, 428, 554; ... / Malcolm Fairman: 31 (bottom); ... / Medical-on-line: 411 (centre); ... / Mike Abrahams: 404, 448; ... / Mike Goldwater: 519; ... / Photo Network: 31 (top left); ... / Picture Partners: 214

Brand X Pictures: 1, 325, 493

Caroline Low: 338, 466, 468, 577, 594

Comstock Images: 535

Corbis: 150, 463; ... / Andrea Rugg Photography, Beateworks: 283; ... / Baumzartner Olivie: 432; ... / Bettmann: 279 (top left and right); ... / Brand X Pictures: 447; ... / Gideon Mendel: 347; ... / Steffan Kuyler: 497

Department for Education and Skills: 15

Digital Vision: 114, 200, 276, 328, 555

Eyewire: 156, 159, 203, 254

Getty Images / **Photodisc**: 2, 17, 232

Harcourt Education Ltd / Debbie Rowe: 506; ... / Gareth Boden: 143, 270, 335, 453, 483, 597; ... / Jules Selmes: 5, 9, 14, 25, 26, 29 (both), 30 (both), 31 (top right), 32 (left), 55, 62, 88, 100, 105, 113, 119, 137, 140, 145, 166, 168, 172, 175, 181, 184, 191, 198, 205, 219, 227, 230, 233, 264, 274 (both), 280, 285, 305, 309, 320, 350, 360, 364, 365, 368, 373, 378, 379, 386, 390, 464, 475, 494, 500, 512, 513, 516, 526, 530, 563, 570 (top centre, bottom centre and bottom), 580, 581, 592; ... / Malcolm Harris: 197, 247; ... / Mark Bassett: 389; ... / Tudor Photography: 8, 28 (both), 32 (right), 33 (both), 68, 122, 190, 220, 262, 290, 359, 454, 536, 569 (both), 570 (top)

iStockPhoto.com / Elena Kornebaum: 567; ... / Jamie Wilson: 160; ... / Melissa King: 435

Jupiter Images / **Photos.com**: 48

Masterfile / **Jerzyworks**: 80, 134

Penny Tassoni: 545, 546 (both)

Photos.com: 300, 326

Punchstock: 213

Reed International Books Australia Pty Ltd / Lindsay Edwards Photography: 238, 329

Rex Features / Peter Lawson: 480; ... / Phanie Agency: 426; ... / Phanie / Burger: 568; ... / SIPA Press: 259

Science Photo Library: 279 (bottom); ... / Coneyl Jay: 414; ... / Dr. H.C. Robinson: 411 (top); ... / Ian Hooton: 396; ... / Lauren Shear: 420; ... / Maximilian Stock: 456; ... / Michael Donne: 206; ... / Dr. P. Marazzi: 411 (bottom); ... / Samuel Ashfield: 501

Topfoto / **Imageworks**: 403

Authors' acknowledgements

As with many writing projects, this book has required a team approach. I would like to thank Harriet Eldridge, Kate Beith and Kath Bulman, my co-authors for making my life as editor easy. I am also grateful to the Heinemann team who have carried out a lot of work behind the scenes, especially Beth Howard for her support, Louise Perfitt and Shirley Bartlett for their loyalty. I would also like to thank Caroline Low of Virgo Editorial for her thoroughness and patience when working on the manuscript. Thanks must also go to the many tutors and students that I meet who provide me with encouragement as well as important feedback. Finally, I must again thank the Tassoni Team, especially my husband Jean-Michel, for their continued support.

Penny Tassoni

As ever, sincere thanks and amazement at the understanding of Ian in his support during the hours of attachment to my computer. Thanks to all the children I know and see in my work and travels who provide an endless source of inspiration and examples, and to colleagues who share their ideas and views on my work.

Kath Bulman

Kate Beith would like to especially thank Beth Howard at Heinemann and Caroline Low of Virgo Editorial for their support and patience, Penny Tassoni for her humour and friendship and all the children and colleagues who have inspired her over the years, including Emma, Tom, Sam, Katie and Alex.

Harriet Eldridge would like to thank all of her colleagues and the students at Bexhill College for being an inspiration and Penny Tassoni for her continual support. She would also especially like to thank her children, Michael and Sophie, for their cheerful support.

About the authors

Penny Tassoni

Penny Tassoni is an education consultant, author and trainer. Penny trained and worked as an early years and primary teacher before lecturing in a FE college on a range of childhood studies courses. Penny has also worked as the UK Education and Training manager of one of the larger day care nursery chains. She has written over twenty books including the bestselling *Planning Play for the Early Years* as well as the previous editions of the *Diploma in Child Care and Education*. She also writes for various early years publications such as *Nursery World* and *Practical Pre-school*. In addition to her writing, Penny works for CACHE as a revisor for their awards. Penny is an experienced trainer and keynote speaker both nationally and internationally.

Kate Beith

Kate Beith is an experienced early years practitioner, trainer, manager and proud mother of three adult children. She has co-written a number of successful early years books and articles and her work is recognised both nationally and internationally. Formerly a principal of an early years college in the UK, she has been involved in a number of international early years projects and is currently developing a large early years department in a school in South East Asia.

Kath Bulman

Kath Bulman has many years experience in the early years field, including nursing, midwifery and health visting, developing and delivering and examining qualifications. Kath now inspects education and training, including that for early years practitioners delivered by colleges and training providers. As well as four grown-up children and step-children, Kath has an army of nieces and nephews to gain examples and inspiration from!

Harriet Eldridge

Harriet Eldridge trained as a nurse and midwife and worked in both hospitals and community in South London and East Sussex, and as a nurse in Israel. She has also worked with children of all ages in playgroups, parent and toddler groups, parent and baby groups, holiday clubs and a youth club. She now teaches on Childcare and Health courses at Bexhill Sixth form College and is Head of the Childhood Studies, Health and Technology Section. She has co-authored several books for Heinemann.

Introduction

Congratulations on your decision to take a qualification that will enable you to work with children! It is an exciting time to work with children as there are many varied career opportunities that you might in time choose to take. By taking a Level 3 qualification you are well on the way to starting out on a demanding but hugely rewarding career. A Level 3 qualification should open many doors, and with the full Diploma you will be in an excellent position to work in an unsupervised position with children or even to go on and study at university.

About your course and assessment

The CACHE Level 3 course in Child Care and Education is divided into units. The qualification can be taken either as an Award, Certificate or Diploma, depending on the number of units completed.

CACHE Level 3 Award in Child Care and Education

To gain the Award you have to complete:

→ *Unit 1: An introduction to working with children*
→ *Unit 2: Development from conception to age 16 years*

These are both mandatory units.

Assessment

→ Unit 1: a multiple choice paper that is externally assessed
→ Unit 2: an assignment that CACHE has set, which is marked by your tutor

CACHE Level 3 Certificate in Child Care and Education

To gain the Certificate you have to complete Units 1 and 2 plus:

→ *Unit 3: Supporting children*
→ *Unit 4: Keeping children safe*
→ *Unit 5: The principles underpinning the role of the practitioner working with children*

These units are mandatory.

Assessment

You will complete the same assessments as for the Award. In addition:

→ For each of Units 3, 4 and 5, you will have an assignment that CACHE has set. Your tutor marks each assignment.
→ There is also a short answer paper based on a case study that checks your knowledge of Units 3, 4 and 5.

CACHE Level 3 Diploma in Child Care and Education

In order to gain the full Diploma you will need to complete Units 1–5 plus:

→ *Unit 6: Promoting a healthy environment for children*
→ *Unit 7: Play and learning in children's education*
→ *Unit 8: Caring for children*
→ *Unit 9: Development of professional skills within children's education*

These nine units are mandatory. Unit 9 is the practical component and this means that you will need to attend placements and show that you have a range of practical skills.

In addition to completing the mandatory units, to gain the full Diploma you will also need to complete *three* of the following optional units:

→ *Unit 10: Research into child care, education and development*
→ *Unit 11: Care of sick children*
→ *Unit 12: Nutrition and healthy food for children*
→ *Unit 13: Child, family and outside world*
→ *Unit 14: Working with children with special needs*
→ *Unit 15: Developing children's (3–8 years) mathematical skills*
→ *Unit 16: Developing children's (3–8 years) communication, language and literacy skills*
→ *Unit 17: International approaches towards children's education*
→ *Unit 18: Working with babies from birth to 12 months*

- → *Unit 19: Multi-agency working with children*
- → *Unit 20: Children, parent and family needs*
- → *Unit 21: Supporting children with English as an additional language*

This book covers five optional units – Units 11, 12, 14, 16 and 18.

Assessment

You will complete the same assessments as for the Certificate (and Award), but in addition:

- → For each of Units 6, 7 and 8 and for each of your three optional units, you will have an assessment task that CACHE has set. Your tutor will mark each task.
- → For Unit 9, to show your practical competency when working with children, you will need to achieve a grade E or above on your Practice Evidence Records and a pass on your Professional Development Profiles. These are checked by your tutor.
- → To complete the Diploma, you will also have an externally assessed assignment that takes the form of a research task. This will check that you can recall, apply and analyse the knowledge that you have gained in Units 1–9.

Preparing for external assessment

The term 'externally assessed' is used to mean that an examiner employed by CACHE will mark your work.

Multiple Choice Questions (assessment for Unit 1)

In this type of exam you are given a question and then four possible answers. You have to choose the best answer and mark it on the sheet.

Multiple Choice Questions (MCQs) need to be read very carefully. You should read through all the possible answers before making your choice. If you think there are two possible answers, go back to the question and read it again. For example, two toys that are suitable for 2-year-olds may be given as possible answers to the question 'The BEST toy to promote a 2-year-old's fine motor development is...' You will need to decide which toy will best develop the child's fine motor movement.

To help you practise your MCQ technique, some sample questions are provided on the Heinemann website. Go to www.heinemann.co.uk/CACHE and enter the password: 4child

Short Answer Paper (assessment for Units 3, 4 and 5)

In this type of exam you are given a case study to read and then a series of questions that link to the case study. You must then write a short answer to each question.

It is important to read the case study through carefully and to think about how best to answer the questions. A good tip is to look at the first word in the question and the number of marks allocated; doing this will help you to judge how best to tackle a question. For example:

- → *Identify ways in which...* Look to see how many marks are allocated. For example, if there are five marks allocated, you would be expected to make five appropriate points.
- → *Discuss/Consider/Analyse ways in which...* These words at the start of a question indicate that you will need to answer using sentences and in depth. Think about whether you can use an example of a theory in your answer.

To help you prepare for the Short Answer Paper, there is a sample question for you to try at the end of Unit 5 (page 246). It is also worth asking your tutor if they have any past papers or exemplars from CACHE.

Research Task (assessment for Diploma candidates incorporating aspects of all mandatory Units 1–9)

You will be able to complete this task in your own time, but it will be sent off in order to be marked.

The research task is designed to be quite demanding. This means that you must set aside sufficient time in order to be able to complete it. You will need to read the task carefully and the assessment criteria that you will be given. In order to gain a grade E or above, you will have to meet all the grading criteria given for the grade E. This is important to remember as sometimes learners can write a good assignment but forget to cover one of the grade E criteria.

To help you prepare for the research task, there is a sample assignment for you to try at the end of Unit 8 (page 358).

About this book

This book has been specially written to support you through your CACHE qualification, whether you choose to complete the Award, Certificate or Diploma. All the mandatory units are covered in this book and a good choice of optional ones so that you will be in a great position to gain the underpinning knowledge that will be essential for your assignments. The book has been written in a clear and informative way by authors who are well known in the child care and education field. This textbook should support and supplement the teaching that you will receive from your tutors. It also matches the delivery guidance of the qualification and so should be a good tool to aid your study and completion of the assignments.

In each unit you will find a number of learning features, as shown below, which are designed to help you get the most out of your studies.

Key term
A concise definition of important concepts and terms is provided when they are first used in a unit.

In practice
This feature presents a short 'real world' scenario to help you to understand why what you are about to learn is important for working with children.

Did you know?
This feature provides interesting facts or statistics.

Find out!
Suggestions for where to find more information on a particular topic.

Case study
These contain scenarios with a 'real world' feel to help you relate what you have learned to practical situations. Case studies are followed by questions of increasing difficulty.

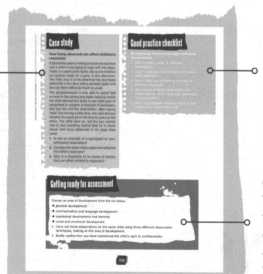

Good practice checklist
These are lists of advice which will help you work towards best practice.

Getting ready for assessment
You will usually find these features at the end of a section or unit. They provide questions and activities which will help you to prepare for your assessment.

We hope that you enjoy your course and using this book. Good luck with your studies!

Penny Tassoni

Unit 1

An introduction to working with children

In this unit you will learn:

1. The range of provision for children

2. Demonstrate an initial understanding of the roles and responsibilities in promoting the rights of children

3. What is meant by professional practice

4. The principles and values that underpin working with children

5. How to develop relevant study and time management skills

Section 1

The range of provision for children

In practice

You have just started your course. Everything seems new. Your tutor is organising your placement and asks you if you have any preference about where you should go. You are not really in a position to answer this as you are not sure what is available in your local area.

By the end of this section you should know about the range of provision that is available for children and their families both locally and nationally.

The range of provision locally and nationally for children

Statutory and independent sectors

There are different types of provision and services for children. Who runs which services can be quite complex to understand but in general services can fall into four categories:

1. *Statutory* – These are services that have to be available by law, i.e. legislation has been passed which requires either the government or local authorities to provide them.
2. *Voluntary* – These are services provided by organisations such as charities where some or all of their funding comes from donations.
3. *Private* – These are profit-making services.
4. *Independent* – These are services that are provided independently of the state and do not rely on government funding. The term 'independent' is usually used in relation to schools. Independent schools may choose not to follow the national curriculum of the country because they do not receive government funding.

Range of provision

Provision and the way that it is provided can change from area to area. The chart below outlines some common provision for children and their families. In Unit 8, you will look in more detail at how the provision might be organised and also funded.

Childcare

Services that take the place of parents so they can return to work or study. Most require parents to pay fees, although funding and tax credits may be available. They include:
- childminders
- nannies
- workplace nurseries
- day care centres
- children's centres (these also provide some health and social services)
- after-school clubs.

Health services

Services that promote children's health and well-being. Most services will be statutory and free. They include:
- health visitor
- family doctor (GP)
- health clinic
- speech and language therapists.

Social services

Services that support children and their families. Most services will be statutory and free. They include:
- social workers
- respite care
- residential care
- home visiting schemes
- foster homes.

Education

Services that provide education for children include:
- nursery schools attached to schools
- infant schools (for children aged 5–7 years)
- primary schools (for children aged 5–11 years)
- preparatory and independent schools (private sector).

Leisure and recreation

These services provide children and their families with leisure and recreational opportunities. Some of these are provided by the local authority and are subsidised, while others are privately owned and run. They include:
- sports centres
- libraries
- parks
- play areas
- holiday clubs
- lessons, e.g. drama, music, dance
- clubs, e.g. gym, football, rugby, karate.

 Find out!

Look at the chart above and research which services are available for children and their families in your area.

Note that local libraries often have notices and guides as to what is available locally.

The implication of funding for the statutory and independent sectors

Some services are free for parents while others are either **subsidised** or charged at full price.

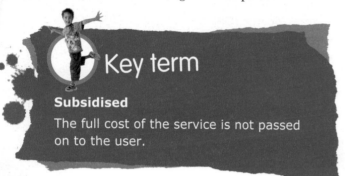

Key term

Subsidised
The full cost of the service is not passed on to the user.

Statutory services are usually free of charge. A good example of this is schools. The government is legally obliged to provide schools for children and to pay money to the local authority or in some cases directly to the school for their running. In the same way, a local authority has a duty in law to support children who are 'in need'. This means that they might pay for respite care or holiday clubs for some children.

Voluntary organisations may also provide some of the statutory services and will be paid by the local authority or government to do so.

Subsidised services

Sometimes local authorities will provide some children's services free of charge or at great subsidy. They may do this because they think it will benefit the community in some way. For example, parents may find that swimming lessons for their children at a local authority swimming pool cost less than those at a privately-run pool. This might reflect the local authority's decision to pay towards the cost of swimming lessons in order to improve the health of children in the area.

Because local authorities have different priorities when spending money, the cost of services to parents may vary from one area to another. For example, music lessons in one area may be free but quite expensive in another. Local spending priorities can also change and this can mean that services are cut.

Some services relating to childcare can cost parents money but can be partly refunded through the tax system, for example parents may claim the cost of the after-school club on a tax form. This is known as a tax credit and is quite complex – the amount of money will depend on the earnings of the parents. This means that the actual cost to parents is not the full cost.

Voluntary organisations may also offer subsidised and in some instances free services. Homestart is an example of a charity that supports parents; it provides volunteers free of charge to assist new parents.

Full price services

Full price services are often 'extra' services and are usually run by the private sector. A dance school, for example, may charge full price for their ballet lessons while a private school will charge full price for their education services.

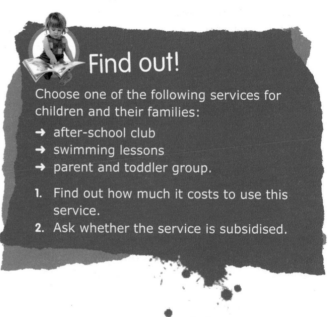

Find out!

Choose one of the following services for children and their families:

→ after-school club
→ swimming lessons
→ parent and toddler group.

1. Find out how much it costs to use this service.
2. Ask whether the service is subsidised.

Section 2

Demonstrate an initial understanding of the roles and responsibilities in promoting the rights of children

In practice

During the first days of your course you have heard about the importance of respecting children's rights. You are not sure what this means or where to find out further information.

By the end of this section you will have an understanding of children's rights and know some basic ideas about how this translates in practice.

The rights of children and how to promote them

One of the most important changes in children's and young people's lives has been the shift in attitudes towards them. Children and young people today are seen not only as having rights but as able to contribute to decisions that affect them. This change in attitudes towards children can be seen in the way that early years practitioners work with them.

There are some basic ways that you can promote children's rights through your practice.

Respect

You will need to treat children and their families with equal concern and respect. This means that you must not have favourites among children or parents.

Building on children's interests and strengths

One of the ways that you can empower children is to help them develop. With young children this can be done by observing them and thinking about their strengths and interests. Activities can then be planned accordingly.

Valuing children

Children need to feel that they are valued by the adults around them. You can value children by listening properly to them and acknowledging their efforts, ideas and interests. You must also listen to their fears and concerns. Laughing at children or making them feel bad about themselves is never appropriate.

Finding out about children's needs

One way in which you can promote children's rights is to understand their needs. When you are qualified you will talk directly to parents, but as a learner you may be told about how best to meet a child's needs. This can be anything from dietary requirements through to care of skin or adapting an activity to suit the child's stage of development.

Legislation that underpins working with children

Children have clear rights that are enshrined by law. In Unit 3 you will look at these in more depth, but it is important that you have some understanding of the key legislation and how you can promote children's rights.

There are many pieces of legislation that enforce children's rights. You need to be aware that legislation varies in the four different countries of the United Kingdom, although children broadly have the same rights.

United Nations Convention on the Rights of the Child

A good starting point is to be aware of the United Nations Convention on the Rights of the Child (UNCRC). The Convention was drawn up in 1989 and gives children and young people under the age of 18 years their own special rights. There are five main strands to this Convention, as shown in the diagram below.

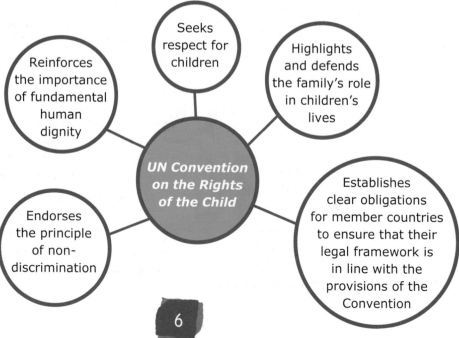

The UNCRC is divided into articles. Below are some of the key articles that might affect your practice with children and young people.

Article 2	The right to be protected from all forms of discrimination
Article 3	The best interest of the child to be the primary consideration in all actions concerning children
Article 12	A child's rights to express his or her views freely; a child's view to be given due weight in keeping with the child's age or maturity
Article 13	A child's right to freedom of expression and exchange of information regardless of frontiers
Article 28	A child's right to education with a view to achieving this right progressively on the basis of equal opportunities

Case study

Refused a place

A nursery school tells a mother that there are no places available. Afterwards the mother finds out that other parents have been given places. She thinks she was refused a place for her child because he has special dietary requirements.

1. Look at Article 28 and use this to explain why the nursery school has acted wrongly.

2. How might mother and child feel as a result of the school's decision?

3. Why is it important for legislation to be in place?

Children Act 1989

As a result of the UK government adopting the UN Convention on the Rights of the Child, new legislation was required. The 1989 Children Act came into affect in 1991 in England and Wales and 1996 in Northern Ireland. The Act attempted to bring together various pieces of legislation. It is wide ranging and covers child protection and parental responsibility as well as inspection of settings. The Act is especially well known for its stance that children's welfare is of paramount importance. The 1989 Children Act also made it clear that children's and young people's views had to be taken into consideration when decisions about their future were being made.

In Scotland, new legislation was brought in under the 1995 Children (Scotland) Act. This Act gave children protection from discrimination as well as ensuring that their welfare was considered of prime importance and their views listened to.

How to value diversity, promote inclusiveness and differentiate activities

As an early years practitioner, you need to be able to meet every child's needs and understand that all children are special and unique. This means that it is not possible or desirable to treat children in exactly the same way, as if they were all robots.

A good example of this is attention. Some children will need more of your attention than others; they may be younger or going through a period in their life when they need additional security and affection. Rationing attention and giving children only an allotted amount would be foolish as this would not be meeting children's individual needs. The focus in the early years sector is therefore to work in ways that are right for individual children. This is quite a challenge, especially in situations when there are large numbers of children.

When considering how to meet children's needs there are three terms which are useful to understand: diversity, inclusiveness and differentiation.

Diversity

Recognising diversity is about understanding that children come from a variety of backgrounds and family structures, and that this is reflected in many ways including the languages they speak, their culture, beliefs and even care needs. While the core needs of children are the same (love, affection, stimulation and physical care), recognising diversity means responding positively to the differences and valuing all people, not just the children and families you feel closest to.

⇧ **Each of these children will have their own needs**

Inclusiveness

The term inclusiveness is often used in relation to children with special needs or disability (see also Unit 14), but the concept should be used in a wider context. Inclusiveness is derived from the verb 'to include'. To include someone means making them feel a part of what is happening. Inclusiveness is therefore about the way you meet a child's or their family's needs in such a way as to not make them feel excluded or a nuisance.

Differentiation

The term differentiation is often used in relation to planning activities with children. Children learn at a different pace and have different interests. This

Think about it

Below are two examples of how a child's dietary need is met. Which approach makes the child feel included?

1. Mark is allergic to strawberries. He watches at snack time as all the other children are given strawberries. He is given a banana instead and is told to sit at a different table in case he touches any of the strawberries. He is alone.

2. Mark is allergic to strawberries. At snack time the children are told that there are two tables. One table is for children who would like strawberries and the other is for those who would like a banana. Mark goes to the banana table with some other children.

makes planning group activities quite a challenge as you should always be trying to meet all children's needs. In practice, this means that plans should show how you intend to change or adapt an activity to meet an individual or group of children's needs.

The case study below shows how a practitioner has found a way of differentiating a maths game for a group of 4-year-olds.

Case study

Maths game

Jim is planning a maths activity. The purpose of the activity is for children to begin to recognise some numbers. He has decided to make it a practical activity because children learn more easily when they are playing games. He decides to work with children in pairs or small groups so that he can give them plenty of attention.

Jim has devised a simple game. The children will throw a dice and then spoon teaspoons of damp sand into a beaker. The number of spoonfuls is to be determined by the number shown on the dice. To make sure that all the children can play the game, Jim has found a way to adapt a dice for the children who find number recognition difficult. He puts some plain stickers onto a dice and writes on this dice the numbers that he thinks they will know. This means that all the children can take part in the game.

1. Would all the children have enjoyed the activity had they all been given exactly the same dice?

2. How did this activity provide a challenge for all children?

3. Find out how your placement differentiates activities.

What is meant by professional practice?

In practice

It is your first day on a placement. You are feeling a little nervous. You are wondering what you should do and how you should act. You are not sure what type of questions you should be asking.

By the end of this section you should have an understanding of what is meant by 'professional' and 'practice' and your role as a learner.

Professional practice is the skills that will be required of you to develop in order to work effectively with children. These include understanding your role and responsibilities, the ability to establish and maintain good relationships with children and colleagues, and communication skills. This section is an introductory section and you might also like to read Unit 9 in order to deepen your knowledge.

Your role and the boundaries and limits of it

In order to find out what you can and cannot do while on placement, you must spend time reading any information that your placement supervisor or tutor gives you. You may, for example, be given some policies when you first arrive at placement. If you find it difficult to read or understand the information, it is important to let your supervisor or tutor know. The four areas that are particularly important when thinking about your role, boundaries and limits are:

→ health and safety
→ managing children's behaviour
→ child protection
→ confidentiality.

Health and safety

Keeping children safe is everyone's responsibility. As soon as possible you should find out about your role in this, even at a basic level, for example shutting doors and gates and what to do if there is a fire alarm. You also need to find out what to do if you spot something that could be unsafe or if you are with children and one of them has an accident. As well as physical safety, you also need to understand and follow your placement's policy on hygiene. This may include wearing a uniform, tying hair back and using resources that have been provided such as disposable gloves.

Managing children's behaviour

It is important that you are aware of your setting's policy in relation to managing children's behaviour. You should find out in what situations you can intervene and how you should do so. It is also important to be aware of your own actions when working with children. There is a careful balancing between playing with children and encouraging them to become over-excited or distracting them when they are meant to be focusing on an activity. It is also important to observe how other staff, particularly experienced practitioners, manage children's behaviour and to notice the 'rules' and conduct that is expected. This is essential as children need to be given similar messages by adults so they can feel secure (see also Unit 9).

Child protection

It is important that you are aware of how to keep children safe from abuse. Every setting will have a child protection policy. You will need to find out whether you need to wear a badge, how to sign in and also in what situations you may work with children. It is normal for settings to insist that you should never be alone with children and you should be aware that this is important for your protection too. You should also be aware of how much physical contact you should give children. Learners often find that children are keen to hug and touch them. While this might be appropriate with young children, it is unlikely to be

Case study

Inappropriate behaviour

Amanda is on placement in a Reception class. The teacher has asked if she can sit with the children at story time. During story time, Amanda keeps talking to one of the children next to her. She also lets this child sit on her knee and keeps tickling her. The teacher becomes quite irritated and finally asks Amanda if she could start tidying up the art area.

1. Explain why the teacher became irritated.
2. Why is Amanda in danger of breaching child protection procedures?
3. Discuss ways in which Amanda could have acted more professionally.

encouraged with older children. It is worth noticing the amount of physical contact that other staff use with children. This will help you determine what is appropriate. If you are not sure what to do, remember to ask your supervisor or tutor.

Sometimes children tell learners things that may raise concerns. It is important that you find out at the start of your placement what you should do and who you should go to if a child tells you something that may point to abuse. In Unit 3, you will look in more detail at your role in protecting children from abuse.

Confidentiality

As a learner on placement, you will find out quite a lot of information. Some of this information will be confidential and must not be shared with friends or others outside of the setting. Examples of confidential information include children's and their families' personal information and that of staff.

A good test as to whether a piece of information is likely to be confidential is to think about whether it is common knowledge or whether you only know it because of your position in the nursery or school. If you are not sure whether information might be confidential, it is worth asking your manager or supervisor.

The characteristics of working in a multi-agency approach

The term 'multi- agency approach' is increasingly used to describe the way that several professionals may be involved in supporting children and their families. There are many benefits for children and families when this type of approach is used as support, advice and childcare can be tailored to ensure some continuity. In practice, this may mean that parents may be able to leave their children in a nursery while in the same building or nearby they attend a parenting class or take a younger baby to the health clinic. A multi-agency approach is also helpful as professionals can share knowledge about the family's needs with each other so that parents do not have to be asked the same questions over and over again. It also means that professionals are aware of each other's role in supporting the family and so conflicting advice or timings of appointments can be minimised.

How to support children and families through the multi-agency approach

With many services coming together in a multi-agency approach, it is essential that everyone working with children and their families communicates well and understands their roles and responsibilities. As a learner on placement, this means that you will need to find out what other professionals are involved in your setting and how this might affect your work.

Working with parents

It is now recognised in the early years sector that relationships with parents are important. Most nurseries, pre-schools and schools have policies relating to the way in which they work with parents. The aim is that parents are seen as valuable partners in their children's care and education. This means that you are likely to meet parents while you are on placement. It is important that while you are courteous and polite at all times, you do not assume the role of a member of staff. You should identify yourself as a learner rather than a member of staff as parents may prefer to pass on information directly to the team. Most settings ask that learners should immediately refer a parent to a member of staff and that learners should not answer any enquiries from parents. You will need to find out how your placement setting expects you to work with parents. It is, however, useful for you to observe how members of staff interact and communicate with parents. You should see that they are friendly and welcoming but remain professional.

How to develop appropriate relationships with colleagues and children

On placement it is important that you work effectively with colleagues and children. The quality of the relationships that you make will affect how much you enjoy and gain from your placement. In Unit 9 you will consider some of the basic ways in which you can help yourself make a good start. They include making sure that you arrive on time and that you are reliable as well as being polite and considerate.

Friendly, but not friends

One of the most important skills is learning how to remain professional while being friendly. The aim of professional relationships with colleagues and children is to be friendly and approachable but to not treat them as though they were family members or close friends. To learn how to do this you might like to think about your tutor's relationship with you. Hopefully, you feel that you can talk to him or her but you might recognise that there still remains a little distance between you.

The importance of professional standards when working with children

You are more likely to develop a good relationship with colleagues and children if you are able to demonstrate professional standards. The spider diagram below shows the standards that are normally associated with working with children.

Caring

Professionals working with children have a duty of care towards them. This means that they need to think about how best to meet children's needs, both physical and emotional. When working with children you are effectively standing in for their parents. You can show that you care for children by the way you talk to them, plan activities and also spend time with them.

Reliable and punctual

Even as a learner you will quickly find that children and staff begin to count on you. They may, for example, plan activities expecting that you will be there to assist or supervise. It is therefore essential that you are reliable and punctual.

Fair and consistent

Children need adults to be fair and consistent. They need to know that they can count on the adults who look after them. This means that even if you are tired or something has irritated you, you are still able to put the children first. Children also need adults to be fair and consistent in terms of managing their behaviour.

Respectful and thoughtful

While working with children and their families, you are likely to meet many people. It is essential that you can show respect and courtesy to everyone. You also need to be thoughtful and responsive to others' needs.

Patient

Working with children is a demanding career. While it can be exciting and certainly not boring, it can also be tiring and much patience is required. Children need you to be patient and calm when you are with them.

Hardworking

All practitioners working with children need to pull their weight and work hard. While there are some aspects to the work that are good fun, there are also other aspects that are not so interesting. Work placements are particularly pleased to get learners who are ready to accept all aspects of their role, which may include some tidying up as well as cleaning.

The importance of effective communication skills and how to communicate with children and adults

Most learners find that over the length of the course they develop confidence in their ability to communicate with children and adults. This is a skill and it will be important to learn how to talk to others in a style that is appropriate. In Unit 9 you will look at the importance of communication in settings. As this is an introductory unit, you will focus here on some of the essential skills that you need.

Listening

You will need to become a good listener. This is important for you to be able to follow instructions and take in information. A parent, for example, may ask you to pass on a message, while a child might need you to listen carefully so that you can understand what he or she is trying to say.

Body language

Body language is important because it sends out messages to other people and so makes a difference in terms of relationships and communication skills. Babies, for example, will cry if they sense that the person holding them is not relaxed because they can feel the tension in the person's arms.

You will need to think about how often you smile, how you look interested in what other people are saying and doing, and whether you look as if you are enjoying being on placement. With young children you will also need to make sure that you bend or crouch down so that you are on the same level with them and can make eye contact.

⇧ **Can you identify which is more effective body language and why?**

Section 4

The principles and values that underpin working with children

In practice

In your placement you notice that many of the policies keep referring to values and principles. You have also heard about Every Child Matters and the five outcomes but you are not sure what this is.

By the end of this section you will have a basic knowledge of the principles and values of the early years sector.

The principles and values that underpin working in children's services

It is important to be aware of the principles and values that underpin the early years and education sector. Interestingly, you will find a statement of values at the beginning of the curriculum framework that your country uses to deliver education. This statement of principles and values help practitioners to decide how to work with children.

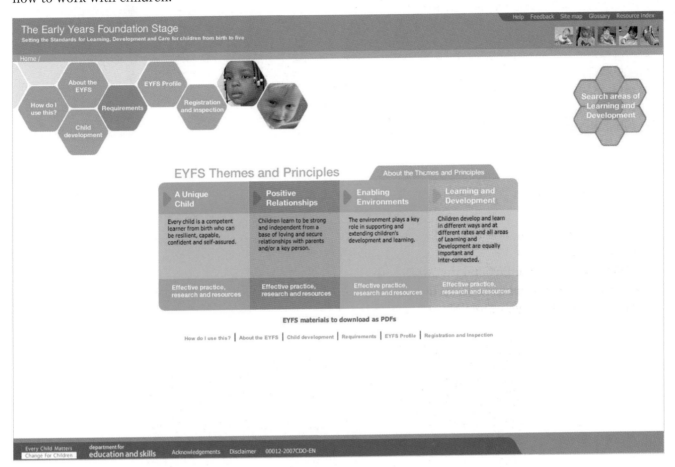

The DfES website for the Early Years Foundation Stage (EYFS) curriculum clearly states its themes and principles

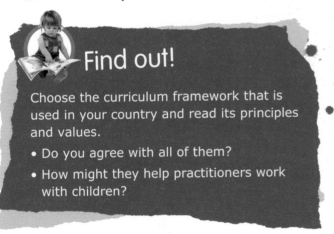

Find out!

Choose the curriculum framework that is used in your country and read its principles and values.

- Do you agree with all of them?
- How might they help practitioners work with children?

In England there are two pieces of legislation that currently shape the values and attitudes of the early years sector: the 1989 Children Act and the 2004 Children Act.

The welfare of children is paramount (Children Act 1989)

A key principle that you should always remember when working with children is that their welfare is paramount. This phrase has its origins in the 1989 Children Act and is well known. The idea is that when decisions are made, the needs and interests of children come first. While the Children Act 1989 principally looked at protecting children, you can adopt this value even in small ways in your work as an early years practitioner.

Think about it

Simon has noticed that one of the children he is working with has some unusual bruises. He is due to go off shift in five minutes. His girlfriend is meeting him from work today. He knows that he should report what he has seen to his supervisor. He is tempted not to say anything as he is afraid that it will make him late.

1. Why might Simon be putting the child in further danger?
2. What should Simon do?
3. Explain why under the 1989 Children Act, Simon would be failing in his duty if he did not say anything.

Every Child Matters

Since 2004, all services in England that work with children and their families are operating with a programme known as Every Child Matters, which has been embedded into law (see also the Children Act 2004). The programme's goal is that every child, whatever their background or circumstances, has the support they need to:
→ be healthy (this includes growing and development as well as emotional and physical well-being)
→ stay safe
→ enjoy and achieve through learning (this includes emotional well-being)
→ make a positive contribution to society
→ achieve economic well-being.

The Every Child Matters programme is particularly important to your work with young children. It is recognised that the first few years of children's lives are critical in their later development. This means you should ensure that the first three strands of Every Child Matters are reflected in your placement's work with children. Practitioners may, for example, plan healthy meals and snacks for children or provide information for parents about vaccination or safety. Enjoy and achieve through learning means that settings have to think about how they organise activities so that all children can learn and benefit.

As part of the Every Child Matters programme, the inspectors of schools and providers of early years care and education, Ofsted, now focus on how individual children's needs are being met. Inspectors consider the following question: 'What is it like to be a child in this setting?'

Case study

Small Hands Nursery

The staff of Small Hands Nursery are thinking about how they organise their snack time. Traditionally they have had all the children eating their snack at the same time. This worked well for the staff but not necessarily for the children: it meant that many children would become bored and restless, as they had to wait for everyone to come to the table and for the snack to be served. After thinking about the values of Every Child Matters, it was decided that the children's needs should come first. The staff looked again at their organisation and decided that snack time would be served in much smaller groups in future. This would mean that children's time would not be wasted.

1. Explain how the principles and values of Every Child Matters have made a difference to this nursery's approach to children.

2. Why is it important for early years settings to have a value system?

Find out!

You can find out more about Every Child Matters by visiting the following website: www.everychildmatters.gov.uk

Section 5

How to develop relevant study and time management skills

In practice

You have been given your first assignment for your course. You want to do well but are not sure about how to go about it. You are also worried that you will waste or run out of time.

By the end of this section you will know how to manage your time and be able to carry out research and evaluate your own learning and study needs.

Your preferred learning style(s) and how to improve your ability to learn

This section will help you to learn about your learning! It is now recognised that everyone has different strengths and needs when it comes to learning new skills or knowledge. This means that most colleges and training providers will ask new learners to take some tests. These test are not exams but diagnostic tools that help tutors work out what type of support you might need.

Learning styles

People appear to process information or new bits of learning in different ways or using a combination of skills. You will need to discover how you learn and study best. The following three categories are often used when talking about learning styles.

→ *Auditory* – processing by listening, for example enjoys being told about things
→ *Kinaesthetic* – processing by doing or moving, for example enjoys practical activities
→ *Visual* – processing by watching, for example enjoys being shown things or remembers information when it is presented using photos, diagrams or other visual means

While you might recognise that you prefer a certain style of taking in information, you might also find that you are good at using all three types depending on the learning situation. Most people will find that a practical skill such as being able to display children's work is learned better when someone shows you (visual) or encourages you to practise the skill yourself (kinaesthetic). It is unlikely that anyone would be able to learn how to display children's work from just hearing about it.

Recognising how you best process information can be helpful when revising or learning for tests. For example, if you know that you can process information through listening, you may prepare some tapes for yourself. If you know that you learn best by doing, you might physically cut up information on bits of paper and make yourself move them around the room. On the other hand, if you are good at remembering information in 'picture' format, you might use a mapping technique (see page 21) or put words and diagrams up in the area where you study.

Relevant study skills

There are many skills that you will need to develop in order to complete this course. The key study skills that you will need are:
→ time management
→ evaluation
→ research
→ referencing
→ presentational skills.

Time management

Being able to complete an assignment or prepare for an exam requires good time management skills. Some capable learners may find that they do not fulfil their potential because their time management skills are weak.

Planning your time

It is important at the start of any assignment or task to be aware of how much time it will take. You may, for example, know that you find reading a little difficult or are someone who has to put ideas down in draft before writing out an assignment. This means that when you are given an assignment, you should work out how much time each part is likely to take you. It is important to be realistic when you do this and to allow for problems, for example there may be delay when printing out your work or difficulty getting hold of books that you need. It is also worth considering that you might be unwell in this period or that something unexpected may crop up. This is why it is usually best to do some work straight away. The example below shows how a task can be divided into steps and how you might also start to consider the complexity and possible difficulties in a task.

Example assignment

Sara and her group have been asked to carry out an observation on a child in placement. They have been told to ask permission from their placement supervisor and then choose one child and look at that child's fine motor skills. Once they have completed the observation, they must then consider how they will use books to work out how the child's skills compares to the normative development. Both the observation and their evaluation of the child's physical skills must be presented in writing. The tutor is expecting around three pages of writing.

The task in the example above can be divided into five different steps.

1. Asking the placement supervisor for permission to observe a child
2. Observing the child
3. Writing up the observation
4. Researching normative development
5. Writing up an evaluation

Possible problems might include:

1. The placement supervisor may not be available.
2. It may not be possible to observe the chosen child.
3. There may not be any books available to research normative development.

Possible difficulty with skills could include:

1. Sara's observation skills may need practising.
2. She may struggle to find the words she needs when writing up the observation.
3. She may find taking notes and choosing the relevant points about normative development difficult.
4. She may find it hard to put her thoughts into words.
5. She may have difficulties with handwriting/typing and/or spelling and punctuation.

Think about it

→ At what time of day do you work best?
→ Do you need to work in a quiet and calm atmosphere?
→ How easily distracted are you?
→ How do you cope with pressure?

Using your time effectively

It is important to learn how to use your time effectively. A good starting point for this is having some knowledge about your own capacity for studying and the way in which you best complete work. Most people find that they work best in 'bursts' of activity rather than sitting down and spending hours at a time revising, writing or researching. Many people also find that they work better when they have set themselves a goal for each 'burst' of activity. Working in structured 'bursts' can also prevent you from becoming distracted or losing motivation. Having a small goal to achieve can also make you feel that you are achieving something.

Think about it

You have been asked to give a presentation on safety and outdoor play for your group. You must also produce handouts for the group and be ready to answer questions.

1. Break this task down into steps.
2. Consider the potential difficulties.
3. Consider what skills are required.

Knowing yourself

It is important to be honest with yourself and think about how you normally work. Some people are best when they work in the morning; others work best in the evening. It is also important to think about the effects of pressure on you. Some people work well when they are under pressure and can juggle more than one assignment or task at once, while others find that the stress causes them to work more slowly or is a distraction.

Case study

A lesson in poor time management

Joy needs to hand in an assignment in three weeks time. She is not worried about it as she thinks she has plenty of time. She listens to the tutor explaining what is required but does not think that she needs to take any notes. She tells herself that she has a good memory.

Two weeks slip by and suddenly Joy realises that she has to complete the assignment in a week. However, she is not too concerned as she is quite good at writing quickly. Another three days slip by. Some of Joy's friends are moaning about how difficult they are finding the assignment. That evening Joy decides to have a look at what she needs to do. She reads the questions and then panics. The task requires quite a lot of research which will mean finding some books and also going on the Internet. She decides to start with some of the easier research. She goes online but quickly gets bored and decides instead to see what is on eBay!

Another two days go by and Joy decides not to think about the assignment. The day before the assignment is due in she decides to work during her break and lunchtime, and through the night, to get the task in. When she goes to the library at break, she cannot find the books she needs – they are already out on loan. She tries using the reference copy in the library but gets quite stressed. By the end of the afternoon she is really worried but manages to get one of the books she will need. When she gets home, she realises that she will not be able to complete the assignment and decides that it is not worth trying now. The next day she stays at home rather than go into the college.

1. Explain how taking notes can be helpful when assignments are handed out.
2. Why is it important to start any reading or research immediately?
3. Discuss what Joy should have done once she realised that she had not managed her time well.

Revising for tests

Learners who do well with tests and exams tend to be 'active' revisers. This means that they do not simply pick up a book or their notes and read them, but do a variety of things that actively engage their brain. The spider diagram opposite shows some useful strategies for revising.

Research

Knowing how to carry out research will help you to complete assignments and tasks and while on placement. It is important to identify the sources for any information that you need to access. Some key sources of information are:

→ websites
→ leaflets and guides
→ books
→ magazines and newspapers
→ libraries.

Websites

Using a website can provide you with quick information about a topic. Some websites also allow you to download publications. It is important, however, to understand that anyone can post information on to a website so you need to be sure that the information is accurate. It can therefore be a good idea to take note of the websites you have used and, if needed, check with your tutor that they are reputable.

Some learners believe that it can be quicker to use a website to look something up than a book, but this is not always the case unless you have a precise address. It is also worth printing out information that you have read on a website if you are short of time, so that you can look at it later.

Leaflets and guides

Leaflets and guides, such as those provided by the National Health Service, can be very useful when researching specific topics such as immunisation or weaning. It is worth noting, though, that they are best used as a starting point – in order to keep the leaflet concise, the information may be fairly basic. It is also important to note the date of publication as information can become out of date.

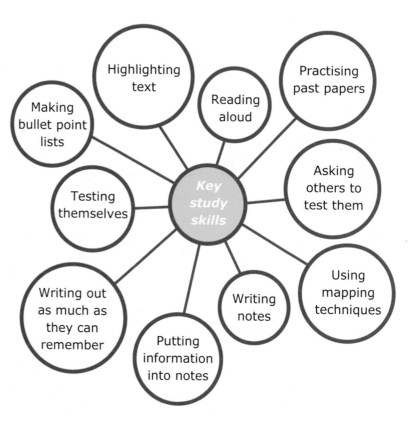

Books

Most tutors will expect you to use books as a major source of information for assignments. Use the contents or index pages to check that a book has the information you are looking for. It is also worth quickly looking at the relevant pages to ensure that there is sufficient information at the correct level for your course. You should also consider whether you are able to read and understand it.

Magazines and newspapers

There are several magazines and newspapers that are produced specially for educational professionals. Articles can be informative and useful if you are looking for different perspectives or ideas for activities. As with leaflets and guides, you should check that the information is up to date.

Libraries

Visiting your college or local public library can be useful. College libraries should have a range of books for your subject area as well as magazines and newspapers. Public libraries may not have so many books in your subject area, but often will order them in if you allow sufficient time. Most libraries also offer Internet access.

Taking notes

It is not enough simply to find information – you need to be able to process it in some way. The most effective way is to take notes.

Taking notes is a skill. You may find at first that you tend just to copy out whole chunks, but the aim is to begin to write notes using your own words. This can avoid you committing plagiarism (see page 22). Some people write notes using bullet points to help them remember and understand what they have read, while others use a mapping technique (see below). It is useful to write on your notes the date and the sources that you have used. This information is needed later on when you have to write a bibliography.

Bibliography

Most essays and assignments require that you should put at the very end of your work details of the sources you have used. This is known as a bibliography. There are many ways of writing a bibliography but essential information to include is:
→ the title of the book
→ the name of the authors
→ the publisher
→ the date of publication
→ the edition.

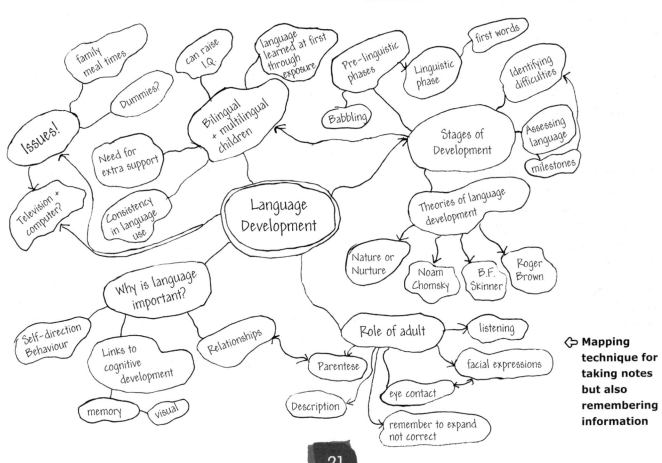

⇦ **Mapping technique for taking notes but also remembering information**

The same information is needed if you use other sources, although for a website you would need to write the website address and link and give the date that you used it.

Department of Health (2003) *Keeping Children Safe*. London: HMSO

Hucker, K. (2001) *Research Methods in Health, Care and Early Years*. Oxford: Heinemann

Meggitt, C. (2003) *Food Hygiene and Safety*. Oxford: Heinemann

Tassoni, P. (2006) *Diploma in Pre-School Practice*, 2nd edition. Oxford: Heinemann

⇧ **Example of a bibliography**

Plagiarism

Plagiarism is when a learner copies text from a book or other source without acknowledging it. Some learners believe that if they simply change a few words in a sentence that this is sufficient, but if the overall feel of the text is similar it is still plagiarism. Sometimes plagiarism is deliberate – a learner knows that he or she has copied material – but at other times it may be unintentional. This is why taking notes in your own words is useful as it will help you avoid plagiarism.

Referencing

When you come to writing an assignment, you might be asked to include references. References show that you have researched and used books or other sources of material. They also show that you can support your writing with some evidence. You should also make sure that your references are relevant to your writing.

There are two types of references: direct and indirect. Examples of each are given below.

While I observed Ayse, I noticed that she enjoyed playing with buttons. I believe she was enjoying the sensory experience and that she was learning about the properties of buttons at the same time. According to Tassoni, 'Children need opportunities to explore both the natural and man-made world. For babies and toddlers, this exploration can take the form of sensory play and heuristic play' (Tassoni, 2006, p.163).

Piaget's work has been the subject of much criticism. Margaret Donaldson suggested that children found it hard to complete the tasks of decentration because

of the way in which the original experiments had been structured. She argues that the context of the experiments misled the children (Donaldson, 1978).

Note how a direct reference contains an actual quote from a book along with the author's name and the date that the book was published. It is also good practice to include the page number as well. Make sure that you copy out any text accurately.

At the end of your assignment you need to write out a list of the books or sources that you have used for reference. This is usually put under a heading of references. As with writing a bibliography, you should include the author, book title, publisher and date of publication. In theory it should be possible for your tutor to read a reference and then, from the information given, go to the book or other source and find the reference. This is why it is important that the date of the book or source is given along with a page number.

Evaluation

One of the skills that you need to develop is the ability to evaluate. During your studies you will need to evaluate what you have observed or read about and your own practice. Evaluation requires you to analyse information and come to an informed conclusion that you can justify. At first many learners find the process of evaluating difficult and tend to describe or explain rather than evaluate.

Presentational skills

As part of your course you might be asked to make a presentation. This may sound daunting but it is a useful skill to learn. The key to making a good presentation is to plan your time carefully and get to know your material thoroughly. If you are working as part of a group, it is worth deciding who will be responsible for which part of the presentation. It can be worth writing this down so that there are no misunderstandings later.

Practising a presentation

Speaking in front of others comes more easily to some people. You will always find it easier if you have practised your presentation beforehand. Think about the key messages that you wish your audience to learn about. Some people find it easier to write notes on to cards so they do not forget what they want to say. It is also worth practising speaking at a slower pace than usual as this makes for a clearer presentation. It is also a good idea to time your presentation so that you can check that you have sufficient material.

Using computer software

Some people find it helpful to produce their presentation using software such as PowerPoint. If you decide to do this, it is worth practising using it. Remember also to back up your presentation and print out a copy of it.

Good practice checklist

Giving a presentation
✓ Prepare carefully.
✓ Decide on your key points.
✓ Think about how best to present these points.
✓ Practise your presentation with a friend.
✓ Remember to speak slowly and clearly.

Think about it

Look at the two examples below. In both, a learner has written about a collage activity carried out with a group of children.
→ Decide which text is an evaluation and which is a description.
→ Discuss the differences between them.

Example 1
The activity went really well. The children enjoyed themselves and Mark used the scissors competently. The children talked about the colours they were using and I encouraged them to feel and discuss the textures.

Example 2
I feel that the activity was successful as the children concentrated and were enthusiastic. They cooperated well and seemed relaxed, often talking to each other. From this I would suggest that the children were enjoying the activity. I saw that Mark was able to use the scissors to cut out on lines that he had drawn for himself. I think this shows that he is now using scissors confidently. While the children talked about the colours they were using, they did not talk about textures – I had to draw their attention to them, although they were keen to touch and use them. This may be linked to their level of vocabulary and could be an area for further work.

Getting ready for assessment

Unit 1 is externally assessed through a multiple choice question paper.

It is a good idea to prepare for this assessment by practising answering multiple choice questions on this unit. You can do this by visiting the website www.heinemann.co.uk/cache and typing in the password 4child. The website provides two example question papers (each containing 25 questions) for the CACHE Level 3 qualification in Child Care and Education. You will get instant feedback after answering each question. If you answer a question incorrectly the feedback will tell you which pages of this textbook to read to learn more about that topic.

Unit 2

Development from conception to age 16 years

In this unit you will learn:

1. How to apply the general principles and theoretical perspectives to all areas of development

2. How to use a range of observation techniques appropriate to different stages of development and circumstances

3. How to assess the development of children and reflect upon the implications for practice

Section 1

How to apply the general principles and theoretical perspectives to all areas of development

In practice

Andreya is 18 months old. Her parents have come to ask you about when she ought to be toilet trained. They are also worried about her speech as she is still babbling although she has a few words. She has bitten her mum on the arm. Mum is worried that she might have inherited a temper from her granddad.

By the end of this section you will know whether Andreya's development is typical and the theories behind this development.

The development of children from conception to age 16 years

Child development is a large area of study with many facets. It looks at the way in which children gain skills and abilities but also processes such as language and thinking. Having a working knowledge of child development is essential when working with children and young people. It will help you to understand children's behaviour, meet their needs and appreciate ways in which you might plan for them.

Factors affecting development

Children's development is not necessarily automatic. There is a range of factors that underpins development, as the spider diagram below shows.

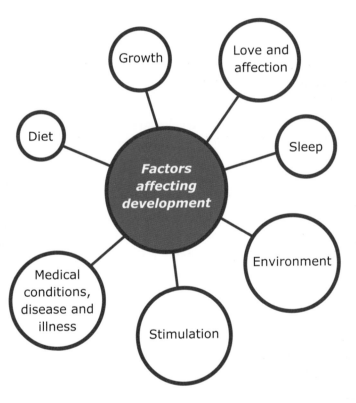

Growth

Growth is extremely important to the development process. Growth is the process by which cells subdivide. This may not sound significant, but in reality growth is responsible for a long list of things that you may take for granted such as height and weight gain and the development of muscles and structures within the brain. A good example of the way in which growth affects development is linked to speech: the growth of teeth in the jaw makes a difference to speech production and the ability to eat.

Diet

What children and young people eat makes a difference to growth and the ability to keep healthy and well. A good diet is now recognised to make a difference to children's ability to concentrate and thus learn. This is one reason why it is currently an important area of debate.

Love and interaction

The emotional care that babies, children and young people receive seems to make a significant difference to their physical well-being, behaviour and learning.

Sleep

Alongside diet, sleep also seems to play a major function in supporting development. Sleep is vital for cognitive function and for growth to take place. Lack of sleep affects children's relationships with others as sleep seems to make a difference to behaviour and control of emotions.

Stimulation

Babies, children and young people need stimulation in order for the brain to develop and to create opportunities to physically use the body. There are many ways in which opportunities for stimulation can be provided. These include play, outings, trying new tastes, meeting others and learning new skills.

Environment

The place in which children grow up can affect their development. This is often linked to economics, with low-income families often having poorer access to housing and local facilities such as sports centres, libraries and parks. This can mean fewer opportunities for stimulation or to practise skills such as riding a bicycle.

Medical conditions and illness

Being ill or having a chronic medical condition can affect development depending on its severity. Some children have to take time off school or are restricted in what they are allowed to do. This can have an impact across all areas of development as, for example, a young child who is not allowed to play with others outdoors will be missing out on opportunities to socialise. The child may also not develop feelings of competency.

Disability

Some children's disabilities will prevent them from accessing the same opportunities as other children and so may affect their development.

Care in pregnancy

Development of children can be affected by what happens during the pregnancy. Exposure to alcohol, nicotine and drugs can have long-term effects on later health and cognitive development.

A holistic overview of development from birth to 16 years

Later in this section you will look at the different areas of development and theories that are relevant to them. It is important before doing this to understand that development is interlinked. Many of the skills that you take for granted actually require that you are competent in several areas. For example, a child who wants to play football will need a range of skills that link to different areas of development. In addition to physical skills, the child will also need cognitive skills so that the ball is strategically placed, social skills in order to play as a team member and communication and language skills in order to interpret what others may be saying.

It is useful when working with children and young people to get a feel of what they might be doing at any given age. The next few pages will give you an overview of development from birth to 16 years.

Babies at birth

Most babies are born at 40 weeks gestation although very few arrive on their due date! Growth and development have been ongoing since conception and by the time babies arrive, they are already able to recognise their mother's voice. Newborns have many survival reflexes that can be clearly seen. First, babies instinctively breathe, cry and suckle. Other reflexes that newborns show will over time disappear and be replaced by conscious movements. Well-known reflexes include the moro reflex, whereby the baby flings out their arms if they sense a sudden downward movement, and the palmar grasp reflex, where babies cling on to fingers tightly. For the first few weeks, babies will develop a pattern of sleeping and feeding, and over time will increase their amount of wakefulness.

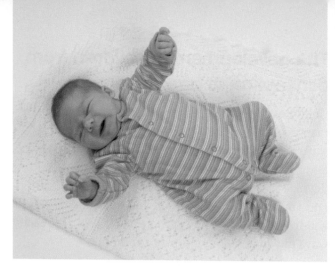

⇧ **Newborn showing moro reflex**

Babies at 3 months

At 3 months the temperament of babies is beginning to show. Some babies will be easy-going while others will need more skill and care as they may find it hard to settle or relax. Babies will show that they enjoy being with others by smiling and making eye contact, and may even protest if they are not being given enough attention.

Physically, babies have developed many skills already although there is still a long way to go. They may manage to hold on to a rattle although controlling it will be difficult. Some of the early reflexes have begun to disappear so babies are, for example, less easily startled. Many babies have already started to recognise key elements in their routine by, for example, showing excitement as they see the bath water. Babies are also showing that they like to play and need adults or older children to play with them. While they recognise their main carers' voices, they are still happy to go to people they don't know.

⇧ **3-month-old baby playing with his fingers**

Babies at 6 months

At 6 months, babies are becoming increasingly strong and may roll over. In the next three months they will learn to become mobile, usually by crawling although some will bottom shuffle or develop a rolling technique. Most babies will also be close to sitting up; initially sitting is supported but by around 9 months is achieved without support. This gives babies new opportunities as they can sit and use their hands to play or touch things.

⇧ **9-month-old baby crawling**

⇧ **6-month-old baby pushing up on his hands**

Over the next few weeks babies will begin weaning and will be introduced to some new tastes. Weaning is a vital step in development as the body now needs a wider range of nutrients, especially iron. While some babies are quick to accept foods from a spoon, others will be slower and patience will be required as foods may be spat out!

The amount of crying should also have decreased, with babies now using their voice to attract attention. They are likely to laugh, coo and make some early babbling sounds and show that they enjoy being with adults. While at 6 months, few babies cling to their main carers; however, over the next two months this usually changes as they begin to have a distinct preference for being with familiar people.

Babies at 9 months

At 9 months, most babies are now clear about who are the main people in their life. They show this by wanting to stay near them and react by crying or turning away from strangers. Many babies will now be crawling or otherwise mobile and they will be extremely active. This opens up new opportunities

as they can now go over to what they can see and thus begin the journey to independence. Babies are usually also able to sit unsupported and this means that they can see something, get to it and sit and then play with it. While babies at 9 months are now able to play independently with toys, they will particularly enjoy being played with especially where games are repetitive. They can now hold and manipulate objects easily and are also starting to pick up small things with a pincer grasp.

Babies are also trying to communicate and over the next few weeks will start to point to things to draw adults' attention. They now understand a few words and will enjoy looking at books. By 9 months, babies should be weaned and may be starting to feed themselves with simple finger foods such as soft bread. Routines such as feeding time and bathing time are now recognised although some babies during a nappy change will try and roll away!

Babies at 12 months

The baby's first birthday reminds us just how many skills they have developed.

→ Most babies will be mobile with some now walking. Others will be able to walk by holding on to furniture in a movement that is sometimes called 'cruising'.

→ Babies will have developed their own personality and their family will recognise their strong likes and dislikes. They will have favourite toys and people. Strangers and unfamiliar faces are likely to be a source of upset and the baby will immediately seek reassurance from those that they know.

→ At birth, babies were passive; now they are truly active and try to be independent. They point to things they want and will try to grab at things they see.

Their physical coordination means they can now hold things and pass them between hands, although they will still have difficulty in, for example, using a posting toy or getting a spoon into their mouth.

In the next couple of months, the main carers should notice that among the baby's tuneful babbling some words will appear. First words are easily produced sounds such as 'baba' or 'dada' and will refer to a person or important object.

⇧ **Baby aged 1 year self-feeding with fingers**

Children at 18 months

There is a significant shift in development at this age. Most babies have now become toddlers and are walking. Their style of walking may be unsteady, with a gait to their style, but being mobile provides them with new opportunities. They are able to see their world from a new angle and to see things that were previously out of sight. As well as being able to walk, toddlers have also learned to climb and have gained increasing control over their hands. These newly developed skills mean that they may be quite determined and may show the first signs of becoming frustrated. Emotionally, toddlers need to be with their main carers and will often check that they are still present even when busy playing.

Children at 2 years

Two-year-olds can find life very frustrating as they are at a crossroads in their development. Frustration is seen in their behaviours as they may bite others and have strong temper tantrums. The source of their anger and frustration is often that they can see what they want and understand what is said, but have not yet developed the skills they need to control their impulses or to express their needs. In terms of fine hand movements they may also know what they want to achieve but struggle to get their hands to

⇧ **Children aged 18 months will begin to show signs of frustration**

manage the task. They may, for example, want to do a jigsaw puzzle but can't quite get the pieces inside. This leads to anger and frustration. Language is a key factor in resolving this and fortunately over the next year children will increasingly develop language. At the beginning of this year they will have many words, but by the end of this year they should be able to put together a simple sentence and use it to express their feelings and desires.

The physical skills of a 2-year-old are now more competent – they can climb on furniture and run, but while doing so will not be aware of any associated dangers. This often leads to adults stopping them and again causes frustration.

While this may seem a negative picture, there are also many positives as well. Two-year-olds can be extremely loving as they now have strong bonds with their main carers and will want to spend time with them. They also show positive emotions such as laughter, pulling faces and trying to amuse adults. They are also keen to be independent and will want to dress or feed themselves. Play is also developing and can provide a good channel for their energies as well as a way in which they can practise skills and be independent. The beginnings of imaginative play can be seen and many 2-year-olds will take out their frustrations on a hapless teddy!

Children at 2½ years

At $2\frac{1}{2}$ years, children are still pushing for independence. They are extremely active and restless so may want frequent changes of activity. Tantrums may still be a feature for some children, but if

↑ **2-year-olds may start to climb**

↑ **2½-year-old playing alongside other children**

language is developing well and adults are thoughtful these will decrease during the next few months. Children at this age still need reassurance from their main carer and will want to spend time with them. Fear of strangers and being left with unfamiliar faces will continue to cause distress and anxiety.

Imaginative play is now a main feature for many children, although playing with toys that promote physical skills such as tricycles and bricks also give enormous pleasure. Hand preference is usually established and children of this age begin to enjoy mark making on a large scale with paints and crayons.

At this age children may start to be interested in other children of their own age, although may not necessarily have the social skills to cope with waiting their turn or the language for cooperative play. This means that children may be playing side by side or copying each other's movements. At around this time, many children will be toilet trained. This gives children enormous confidence.

Children at 3 years

After the storm of the 'terrible twos', most 3-year-olds' development allows them to be calmer and more sociable. They begin to play well with other children of the same age and gradually start to share and learn to take turns. Their language is one reason

for this change as they can now express themselves fairly well. They use questions and have a large vocabulary, although they are not yet fluent. They usually enjoy songs and rhymes and may well sing to themselves. Most of what a 3-year-old says should be intelligible to someone who does not know the child.

Three-year-olds enjoy playing and are now able to play independently although they still enjoy being with adults. Another significant shift is the way in which 3-year-olds begin to cope when separated from their main carer. While still being wary of strangers, most happily leave their main carer for someone they know such as their key worker.

At 3 years, children have again increased their physical skills. They can now pedal and steer a tricycle and enjoy the sensation of speed and control.

↑ **Many 3-year-olds enjoy small world play**

⇪ **4-year-olds singing nursery rhymes**

Children at 4 years

During this year, most children will begin school. This is a huge transition which means that they will be with many more children than before. For most children, this is not a problem as their social skills have developed and they enjoy playing with others. Most children will also have developed one or two close friendships, and although the odd squabble may break out they have usually learned how to do some simple negotiating. This skill does of course link to their overall language development.

Most 4-year-olds are now able to use language well and fairly grammatically, although there will be some speech immaturity and mispronunciations. Most 4-year-olds' behaviour is cooperative, although they do need plenty of reassurance and praise from adults and play activities that interest them.

Physically, children are now able to manage many tasks that give them increasing pleasure and independence. They can, for example, eat with a knife and fork and dress themselves, and are able to catch and throw a large ball. Their hand–eye coordination means that they can draw pictures that are more representational and make things such as a simple necklace using a lace and beads.

Children aged 5–6 years

In previous years, development in all areas has been rapid. From this point through until puberty, development might be described as steady. The key changes that take place are the refinement of existing skills. A good example of this is using scissors – previously children were able to roughly cut out, but in these years children should refine this skill and be able to cut on a line. In the same way, there is increasing coordination of the larger movements so that children can run, swerve and dodge more easily than before, for example when playing games of chase.

Most children will be established in school and, as part of their schooling, will be learning to read and write. This is a long process requiring considerable effort to decode simple words. As well as learning to read and write, children will also be exposed to new concepts, for example learning about number.

Socially, most children in this age group have developed some strong friendships. These are based mainly on shared interests, although it is interesting to note that most children will choose same sex playmates.

⇪ **Children aged 5–6 years enjoying a joke**

Children aged 7–9 years

In this period children make enormous strides in the cognitive development. First, children start to reason and this shows itself in the complexity of their play and their mathematical ability. Games have more complex rules and children understand the need for rules even if they change them to suit the situation. Another interesting advance that links to cognitive development is children's reading and writing skills. Reading for most children becomes easier and they do not have to follow the words using a finger or read aloud. This is a significant change although some children will still need support.

⇑ **Children aged 7–9 years reading**

Children also become more physically skilled which results in them being able to do tasks more quickly, confidently and easily. They may, for, example cut around a shape without effort or draw a simple picture.

Friendships are still important and become more stable, with some children having 'best friends'. Squabbles remain a feature but children are often keen to resolve them.

Most children in this age range will be in school. This has a major influence on their emotional development. For some children, school is affirming and helps them to gain confidence as children from this age onward compare their achievements with those of others.

⇩ **Children aged 10–11 years increasingly prefer the company of their friends**

Children aged 10–12 years

This period in children's lives marks the start of their growing independence. Friendships become more special with children talking more about the characteristics of their friends than their shared interests. This is the start of a process that will see young people confiding more in their friends than in their close family members.

At 10 and 11 years, most children have also gained in confidence. They may feel 'grown up' as they will be the older children in a school. This does not last though, as children are likely to face a major transition as they move from a primary to a secondary school. For most this is an exciting time but also nerve racking. Instead of having a single teacher for most of the day, they need to cope with several changes in a day. The size of the school is also likely to be much larger than their primary school. Children are also expected to be more organised and take on responsibility for following a timetable. These challenges can give children more confidence although some will need additional support and time to adjust.

Cognitively, children's development continues with reasoning and problem-solving skills becoming more sophisticated. Children are also likely to be competent in areas that interest them such as sport, computers or drawing.

During this period, girls' puberty begins with a growth spurt and the first physical changes to the breasts.

Young people aged 13–16 years

During these years, young people have to cope with many changes as they move from childhood towards adulthood. This journey is not necessarily a smooth one as a result of hormones, changing expectations and the desire to be seen as an individual separate from the family unit. Conflicts with parents are often experienced as young people try to make their own mark through fashion and music choices but also behaviour. Friendships, on the other hand, are a source of support and a way of gaining identity. Young people are likely to mix in groups with each group having its own identity, standards and codes of behaviour.

⇧ **Young people express their social identity through their fashion and lifestyle choices**

Young people in this age range start to make decisions that will affect their future and often feel under pressure as a result. In addition to the changes in social identity, young people are also coming to terms with their changing body shape. Puberty is well established for girls but just starting for boys. Changes in physical shape and appearance can affect self-esteem, with both boys and girls worrying about their attractiveness and whether they are 'normal'. Some young people will also begin to take an interest in the other sex and may start to form early relationships.

Nature versus nurture

In child development there has been a long-standing debate as to whether our skills and behaviour are inborn (a nativist perspective) or the result of our experiences (a behaviourist perspective). For a long time this has been known as the nature versus nurture debate. Some of the original theories and philosophies of child development were either heavily nativist or behaviourist.

Today, most people carrying out research into development believe that both nature and nurture are powerful influences on children's development and work hand in hand. A good example of this is brain development: it is clear that babies are born with some key structures already in place, but this in itself is not sufficient for further development – the baby needs to be touched, spoken to and stimulated.

While both nature and nurture are at work, the jury is still out as to whether they have an equal influence across all areas of development or one plays a more significant role. Interestingly, the nature versus nurture debate is not restricted just to scientists and researchers. Expressions such as 'children need to go outside to let off steam' show us that views about how children develop and how to care for them are underpinned by one of the perspectives!

Did you know?

If you talk to parents you may find that they take a nativist perspective especially if they have more than one child. They may notice the differences between their children and ascribe them to genetic influences. Professionals working with children will often favour a behaviourist perspective believing that their work can make a significant difference to children!

Think about it

Look at the following statements. Decide whether they reflect a nativist or behaviourist perspective.

1. 'It's not surprising that she's like that when you think about all that has happened to her.'
2. 'I don't know where she gets it from! None of our family is good at maths.'

Talk to parents about their children. Do they believe that their children will be more influenced by where they are living and what happens to them or their inborn characteristics?

Areas of development

While it is important to gain an overview of development, it is also useful to have a deeper understanding about the types of skills and learning that takes place. To enable this, development is usually subdivided into four sections or areas of development:

1. Physical development
2. Communication and language development
3. Intellectual development
4. Social, emotional and behavioural development.

Over the next few pages you will look at each of these areas of development and some of the theories that are usually associated with them. Before doing this, however, it is worth understanding the type of skills each area of development broadly covers.

Communication and language development

This area is about the ability to talk, understand what others are saying and interpret facial expressions and body gestures. It also encompasses the skills of reading and writing. Communication and language development is linked to cognitive development because more sophisticated communication involves thinking about what others are trying to convey as well as thinking about what you are trying to express.

Areas of development

Physical development

This area of development is physical movements. Walking, drawing and cutting with a knife are all examples of movements that most children will gradually learn. Physical development is closely associated with becoming independent.

Intellectual development

This is a large area of development, also known as cognitive development. It encompasses the way in which we think and learn. Intellectual development is responsible for reasoning and behaviour. It includes understanding of abstract concepts such as time as well as the ability to remember things.

Social, emotional and behavioural development

People are social beings and so need these skills to live together and understand each other. Emotional development is about recognising and controlling emotion and having self-confidence. Social development looks at the skills we need to live alongside others. This area is closely tied to cognitive and language development – children gradually need to use words or body language to express themselves and so need communication skills.

Physical development

The difference between growth and development

→ The term 'growth' refers to the way in which cells subdivide to, for example, allow bones to lengthen.
→ Development refers to the skills that the child masters.

Many aspects of children's development are firmly intertwined with growth, for example babies cannot walk until their bones are long and strong enough to take their weight.

Why physical growth is important

Growth provides the background for development

Physical growth is essential in helping children's development as it makes certain movements possible, for example children's hand movements are linked to the growth of the bones in their wrists. This in turn means that new opportunities for stimulation are available for the child. For example, once a child can walk they can now see their environment from a new height.

Growth affects adults' responses

The size and shape of a child affects the way adults respond to him or her. A tall child may be given more responsibility. Development as a result of growth also affects adults' responses. Adults may, for example, start to expect more of a child once they are able to dress themselves. An example of this with young people is the way in which adults begin to expect them to become more responsible once they show outwards signs of puberty.

Growth can affect self-esteem

As children begin to grow, they often start to feel more capable. Taller children, for example, usually have higher self-esteem. The shape of a child's body can also affect how they feel about themselves. This is particularly true during puberty when body shape changes significantly and self-esteem scores can drop.

Physical growth is not smooth and continuous

The rate at which children grow is not smooth and continuous. The first two years are marked by significant growth, after which children grow more steadily until the onset of adolescence. Interestingly at this point, hands and feet grow before other body parts. This is why teenage boys are often perceived as being ungainly or gawky.

Did you know?

Babies gain in height and weight very rapidly – around 30cm is gained in the first year. By 2 years children have reached half their adult height and will have tripled their birth weight.

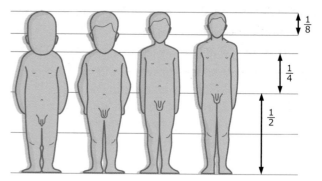

Newborn   2 years   7 years   16 years

⇧ **Body proportions change with age**

Measuring growth

During children's early years and especially the first year, health professionals measure children's growth. Height, weight and head circumference are all noted. Measurements are plotted onto a growth chart which some professionals refer to as a centile chart. There are separate charts for boys and girls, which reflects the fact that boys are usually heavier and taller than girls. Health professionals also have to take into account a child's ethnic background as some races are lighter or shorter than others.

How the growth chart works

Each area has nine bands, known as centiles. A height measurement on the 78th centile means that for every hundred children, only 12 will be this height and taller. Where, for example, a child's height falls above or below the centile bands, the child will be unusually tall or short.

The chart below shows the growth rate curve that children's measurements should be following. While many children will slightly vary, their measurement curve should look similar. Reasons why there might be short-term changes in the rate of curve might include difficulties in feeding because of a cold. Significant variations from the norm growth rate curve are always investigated as there might be an underlying medical reason such as a heart condition or diabetes.

What the growth charts show

→ The growth chart allows health professionals to carry out a **longitudinal** measurement of a child's growth, i.e. a baby's weight gain may show signs of levelling off over a month.

→ The growth chart also helps health professionals to compare rates of growth, for example a child's head circumference may be showing a rapid expansion compared to the rate of height and weight gain. Significant differences in growth rates might indicate that there is an underlying medical problem such as hydrocephalus which is where fluid is collecting in the head.

→ The growth chart also provides **cross-sectional** information about the child in relation to others of the same age. Parents might be interested to find out that their child is taller than most other children of the same age.

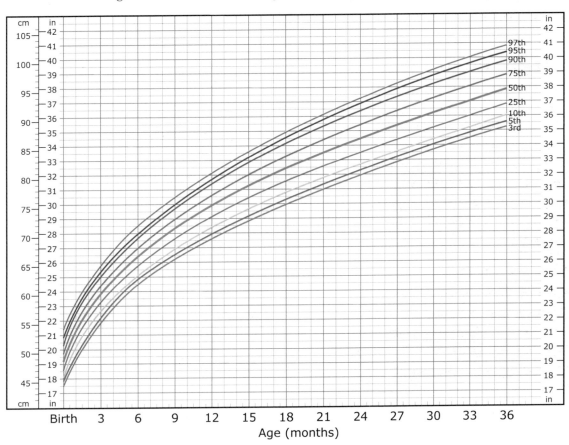

⇧ **Centile chart showing range of growth rates for children**

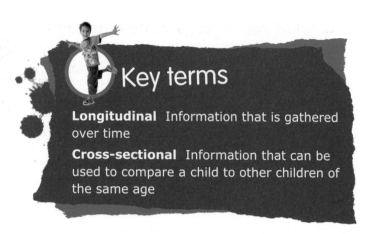

Key terms

Longitudinal Information that is gathered over time

Cross-sectional Information that can be used to compare a child to other children of the same age

What is physical development?

Physical development is the process by which children gain control of their movements. Most children have learned all the basic skills they require by the age of 6 or 7 years. Afterwards, children just become more skilled at using these movements, for example they tend to be able to run faster or use two or more skills at once.

Physical development is important for children's overall development for three key reasons:

1. *It allows new learning to take place.* A baby who learns to crawl can then start to move and explore his or her environment, touching items of interest.

2. *It allows further development to take place.* Once a child has learned one skill, he or she can then build on this skill.

3. *It affects children's confidence and self-esteem.* Children who have learned to ride a tricycle feel good about themselves, while older children who feel that they are no good at skipping may lack confidence.

Fine motor

The term 'fine motor' covers the smaller movements. It can be broken down into two categories:

→ *Fine manipulative skills* – These are small movements that are needed when children write, draw or put together a jigsaw puzzle. You should note that although many fine manipulative activities often involve a degree of hand–eye coordination, hand–eye coordination is actually a separate skill. A feely bag, for example, requires fine manipulative skills but no hand–eye coordination.

→ *Fine motor skills* – These are small movements using the whole hand and wrist, such as twisting a knob or opening a jar.

Gross motor

This broad term covers the large movements. It can be broken down into two categories:

→ *Gross motor skills* – These are whole limb movements used when, for example, a child kicks a ball.

→ *Locomotive skills* – These are movements that children use in order to walk, run and jump.

⇧ **Drawing is a fine manipulative skill**

⇧ **Turning the pages of a book is a fine motor skill**

⇧ **Throwing a Frisbee is a gross motor skill**

⇧ **Running is a locomotive skill**

Coordination

Sometimes children will need to be able to coordinate more than one type of movement or skill at once. For example, in order to skip with a rope, children need to be able to move their arms while jumping. This is what is meant by coordination. There are some specific types of coordination that most children need to develop. These include hand-eye coordination, foot-eye coordination and balance.

Hand-eye coordination

Some activities such as throwing and catching or writing can be done more easily when the eyes guide the hands. Most children therefore learn to coordinate the information received by their eyes and use it to guide their hands. (For children with visual impairment they may learn to coordinate sounds, such as instructions or a bell in a ball, with control of their hands.)

Foot-eye coordination

There are some activities that involve the eyes guiding the feet. Although there are more examples of hand-eye coordination, children also need some foot-eye coordination in order to do the following: climb stairs; run; kick a ball; avoid obstacles.

Balance

The ability to balance comes with age as the body learns to coordinate its movements with the information being received by the central nervous system.

Think about it

List the actions that you have done today, for example eating breakfast, getting dressed, closing the door, turning pages of a book, running for a bus. Consider what types of physical skills were involved, for example fine manipulative, gross motor, etc.

Key principles of physical development

Arnold Gessell, an American paediatrician, identified three principles of physical development, as follows.

1. *Development follows a definite sequence.*
   As you watch children growing and developing, you see a pattern emerging and that certain movements have to be in place before others can follow. For example, the child has to be able to walk before he or she can skip (see also pages 40–1).

2. *Development begins with the control of head movements and proceeds downwards.*
   Babies at first gain control of their head and top of the spine before other parts of their body. This is thought to be a survival mechanism as it is important for babies to be able to turn their head to feed.

⬆ **Babies begin by gaining control of their head movements**

3. *Development begins with uncontrolled gross motor movements before becoming precise and refined.*
   At first the young baby's arm and leg movements are uncontrolled, but some control is quickly gained – first of the arms and then of the wrist and hands. By 6 months most babies are usually able to take an offered toy reasonably easily. As an adult you may have had a similar learning experience if you have learned to use a computer with a mouse. Most people find that at first it is all they can do to keep the mouse visible on the screen before gradually learning more refined movements which allow them to position the mouse accurately.

Physical development is closely linked to the nervous system

The nervous system is the body's information-gathering, storage and control system. Its 'headquarters' is the central nervous system (CNS) which is made up of the brain and spinal cord. Information is sent to the CNS from the sense organs via nerves that fan out through the entire body. As a result of the information, the CNS sends out instructions to muscles (including muscles controlling speech), glands and internal organs.

In some cases you are conscious and in control of these instructions, for example when you are hungry you may decide to peel a banana. At other times instructions are made involuntarily (without conscious thought), for example flinching when you are hurt. When babies are first born they show a number of involuntary movements and reflexes, but as the central nervous system matures it is able to interpret information and remember responses. This means that more voluntary control is gained.

The maturation of the central nervous system takes time, so some functions such as gaining control of the bowel and bladder cannot take place until there is some maturity. This effectively means that while you can encourage children's physical development by praising them and stimulating them, thus helping the central nervous system to remember movements, you cannot 'fast track' children.

Brain development

Maturation of the nervous system is linked to brain growth and development. In terms of physical development, this growth affects the development of gross and fine motor skills. A good example of this can be seen in children between the ages of 6 and 8 years, when there is significant neural growth. This helps children's fine motor skills and improves the fluidity of their movements. It can also be seen in the way that children find handwriting easier and start to enjoy more demanding sporting games.

Measuring motor development

To measure children's physical development, professionals look at the skills that children have acquired. These skills are sometimes referred to as **milestones** and are linked to children's ages. The milestones have been determined by looking at large groups of children's development and considering what the 'norm' for each age is. This means there will always be some variation, with some children showing development that is in advance of the milestones. Significant delays in reaching milestones are likely to be monitored and investigated.

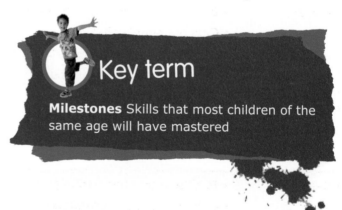

Key term

Milestones Skills that most children of the same age will have mastered

⏷ **Milestones for the development of fine motor and gross motor skills by age**

Age	Developoment of fine motor skills	Development of gross motor skills
3 months	• Watches hands and plays with fingers • Clasps and unclasps hands • Can hold a rattle for a moment	• Lifts head and chest up • Waves arms and brings hands together over body
6 months	• Reaches for a toy • Can move a toy from one hand to another • Puts objects into mouth	• Moves arms to indicate he/she wants to be lifted • Can roll over from back to front

Age	Developoment of fine motor skills	Development of gross motor skills
9 months	• Can grasp object with index finger and thumb • Can deliberately release objects by dropping them	• Can sit unsupported • Is likely to be mobile, i.e. crawling or rolling
12 months	• Uses index finger and thumb (pincer grasp) to pick up small objects • Can point to objects with the index finger	• May stand alone briefly • May walk holding on to furniture (although some children may be walking unaided)
18 months	• Can use a spoon to self-feed • Can scribble • Can build a tower of three bricks	• Can walk unaided • Can climb up on to a toy • Can squat to pick up a toy
2 years	• Can draw circles and dots • Can use spoon effectively to feed with	• Can run • Climbs on to furniture • Uses sit-and-ride toys
2½ years	• May have established hand preference • Can do simple jigsaw puzzles	• Can kick a large ball • May begin to use tricycles
3 years	• Turns pages in a book one by one • Washes and dries hands with help • Holds a crayon and can draw a face	• Can steer and pedal tricycle • Can run forwards and backwards • Throws large ball
4 years	• Buttons and unbuttons own clothing • Cuts out simple shapes • Draws a person with head, trunk and legs	• Walks on a line • Aims and throws ball • Hops on one foot
5 years	• Forms letters; writes own name • Colours pictures in • Completes 20-piece jigsaw	• Skips with a rope • Runs quickly and is able to avoid obstacles • Throws large ball to a partner and catches it
6–8 years	• Is able to join handwriting • Cuts out shapes accurately • Produces detailed drawings • Ties and unties shoelaces	• Hops, skips and jumps confidently • Can balance on a beam • Chases and dodges others • Can use bicycle and other wheeled toys such as roller skates
8–12 years	Fine motor skills become more refined allowing for intricate work such as model making, knitting and typing. Less concentration is required allowing children to talk as they use their hands.	Increased coordination and perceptual skills. These allow children to concentrate on strategies during games such as football or netball.
12–16 years	Ossification of the hands and wrists is completed in the teenage years. It allows for increased strength in hands allowing for movements such as twisting lids off jars.	Increased stamina and physical endurance as lungs and heart develop

Stamina

Stamina is important as it affects how many times a child may complete a movement or how long they may stay at an activity.

Children aged 2–5 years

Toddlers and pre-school children often move and run in short bursts. They find it difficult to go for long walks but will happily run a little and then clamber to sit in a pushchair. The heart rate of toddlers and pre-school children is higher than that of adults as their lungs and heart are smaller.

Children aged 6–11 years

As children's heart and lungs grow they are able to sustain activity levels for slightly longer periods, although the need to rest frequently remains. This means that most 10-year-olds will be able to maintain physical activity for longer periods than 6-year-olds, but both age ranges will still need resting periods. Endurance-type activities such as long distance running for this age range are not usually appropriate because of the developing stamina levels. Boys' and girls' stamina levels are similar, with boys having the slight edge, although there are of course individual differences which are partly dependent on the physical build, weight and exercise levels.

Young people aged 11–16 years

During adolescence, stamina levels increase dramatically. This is because of the growth spurt that takes place as part of puberty. There are marked differences between the stamina, speed and strength of boys and girls: boys are stronger and able to sustain physical activity for longer periods.

Puberty

The process of moving into adulthood is marked by physical changes to the body. It is a complex process involving a series of different hormones which produce a range of chemical interactions. The pituitary gland begins the process by producing hormones that stimulate further hormone production in the testes and ovaries. In boys the key hormone is testosterone, while in girls the key hormones are the estrogens, notably estradiol. These hormones result in changes to the key organs usually referred to as primary sex characteristics. In girls these are changes to the ovaries, uterus and vagina while in boys there are changes to the penis and testes.

As well as primary sex characteristics, hormones also change the physical appearance of boys and girls. These changes are known as secondary sex characteristics and include pubic hair development in both sexes as well as breast development in girls and change in voice pitch in boys. The physical transformation from child to adult usually takes place over four or five years, although as with other areas of development there can be variations.

Puberty in girls

Puberty begins earlier in girls than in boys and follows a definite sequence, although the timing can vary considerably between girls. The starting point is changes in the breasts when the nipples begin to protrude or 'bud'; this is often seen in 10–11-year-olds. This is followed by initial growth of the pubic hair and then a significant growth spurt. The growth spurt is usually followed by the first period known as the menarche. At this point, few girls are fertile and it takes some time before periods become regular and fertility is fully established. In terms of timing, the majority of girls will start their periods between the ages of 11 and 15 years, with 12 to 14 years seen as the 'optimum' time by girls themselves. The physical transformation is often completed by 17 years, although as with all areas of physical development this is only a guide.

Puberty in boys

The start of puberty begins with initial pubic hair growth and genital development. The timing of this varies between boys but is likely to occur at around 11 years. This is followed by a sharp growth spurt alongside continued development of the testes and penis. Growth in terms of height often continues until boys are 18 years old. The voice deepens or 'breaks' after this initial burst of growth and so many boys by 15 years will have a deeper voice. Whiskers also appear on the face towards the end of the process. During puberty, muscle strength increases as a result of testosterone.

Hormone	Gland	Effects
Thyroxine	Thyroid	Rate of growth and brain development. Secreted in significant amounts in first two years of life.
Adrenal androgen	Andrenal	Affects growth especially in girls during puberty. Interacts with other hormones. Responsible for strength in muscles and bones.
Testosterone	Testes	Produced in significant quantities in boys from the age of around 11 years onwards. Responsible for sexual development but also triggers further quantities of growth hormone.
Estradiol	Ovaries	One of the sex hormones in girls. Responsible for breast development, pubic hair and menstrual cycle.
Growth hormone	Pituitary	Responsible for growth and physical maturation.
Gondatrophic hormones	Pituitary	Hormones produced by the pituitary as messengers to the ovaries in girls and the testes in boys. As a result they respectively produce estrogens and testosterone.
Lutenising hormone (LH)	Pituitary	Regulates the menstrual cycle
Follicle stimulating hormone (FSH)	Pituitary	Stimulates the ovaries to produce an ova

Communication and language development

The ability to communicate with others is essential to the ability to socialise. Communication takes many forms including body language, facial expression, pictures and symbols although many communications involve the use of language.

The spider diagram opposite shows some of the ways in which children and young people may use communication skills.

Gaining reassurance and help
'I can't find my apron.'

Predicting and anticipating
'I might get a cat soon.'

Socialising with others
'Let's go together.'

Ways in which communication skills are used

Assertiveness
'It's mine!'

Asking questions
'Why is it raining?'

For self-direction
'I'm doing the head and then the eyes.'

Describing events and objects
'This feels all sticky.'

Giving explanations and instructions
'Now it's time for drinks.'

What is meant by language?

One might think that language is about being able to talk. This is not the case: language is about being able to communicate. Although at first most children will use speech to communicate, it is important not to forget that reading, writing and signing are all ways of communicating with others. Deaf children may use a sign language such as British Sign Language (BSL) to express themselves and to understand others, while children with multiple disabilities may use a computer to write and receive messages.

These are the common features of any language:

→ It is a way of communicating.
→ It has rules that are understood by those using it.
→ It is made up of sounds, gestures and symbols that have meaning for those using it.
→ It allows the user to be creative and expressive, i.e. a user can make up and use his/her own sentences, provided that they fit the overall 'rules' so that others can understand.

For children to learn a language they need to learn the rules – or grammar – of a language as well as the meanings of words. This is a gradual process for children and one in which adults have an important role.

Stages in language and communication development

It is interesting to note that babies and children, irrespective of the country in which they are born, all follow a similar pattern of development. The first year of a baby's life is spent trying to 'tune' in on the language they are hearing and learn the skills of communication, i.e. making eye contact and responding to others' facial expressions and words. This first year is often known as the pre-linguistic phase and is now considered to be vital in children's overall language development.

The chart below outlines the major stages in language development.

⇩ **Stages in language development**

Stage	Age	Features	Comments
Pre-linguistic stage			
Cooing	6 weeks	Cooing	Babies making cooing sounds to show pleasure. These early sounds are different from sounds made later on, mainly because the mouth is still developing.
Babbling (phonemic expansion)	6–9 months	Babies blend vowels and consonants together to make tuneful sounds, e.g. *ba*, *ma*, *da*	Babbling has been described as learning the tune before the words. The baby seems to be practising its sounds, and babies increase the number of sounds or phonemes. This is sometimes called phonemic expansion. All babies, even deaf babies, produce a wide range of sounds during this period. During the past few months babies have also learned some essential communication skills. These include making eye contact, recognising some emotions in others and responding to them.
Babbling (phonemic contraction) Echolalia (repetition of syllables in words, e.g. 'deddedded')	9–10 months	Babies babble but the range of sounds is limited	The range of sounds or phonemes that babies produce becomes more limited and reflects the phonemes used in the language that they are hearing. At this stage it would, in theory, be possible to distinguish between babies who are in different language environments. By 10 months babies can understand 17 or more words. Babies' communication skills have also developed further. They now know how to attract adults' attention by pointing and raising their voice. They can also understand a lot of what is being said to them through word recognition but also by reading faces.

Stage		atures	Comments
Linguistic stage			
First words	Around 12 months	Babies repeatedly use one or more sounds which has meaning for them	The first words are often unclear and so gradually emerge. They are often one sound but are used regularly in similar situations, for example 'baga' meaning drink and cuddle. Babbling still continues.
Holophrases	12–18 months	Toddlers start to use one word in a variety of ways	Toddlers use holophrases to make their limited vocabulary more useful for them. One word is used in several situations, but the tone of voice and the context helps the adult understand what the toddler means. Most toddlers have between 10 and 15 words by 18 months. By this time toddlers have often learned how to get adults' attention and how to make them laugh.
Two-word utterances (telegraphic speech)	18–24 months	Two words are put together to make a mini sentence	Toddlers begin to combine words to make sentences. They seem to have grasped which are the key words in a sentence, for example 'dada gone' or 'dada come'.
Language explosion	24–36 months	A large increase in children's vocabulary combined with increasing use of sentences	This is a period in which children's language seems to evolve rapidly. Children learn words so rapidly that it becomes hard for parents to count them! At the same time the child uses more complicated structures in their speech. Plurals and negatives begin to be used, for example 'no dogs here!'
	3–4 years	Sentences become longer and vocabulary continues to increase	Children are using language in a more complete way. Mistakes in grammar show that they are still absorbing the rules and sometimes misapplying them. Mistakes such as 'I wented' show that they have learned that '-ed' makes a past tense. These types of mistake are known as 'virtuous errors'. By this time, children are able to use their communication skills in order to socialise with others in simple ways. They may, for example, repeat a question if they think they have not been understood.
Fluency	4–6 years	Mastered the basic skills of the language	Children have mastered the basic rules of English grammar and are fluent, although will still be making some 'virtuous' errors.

Stage	Age	Features	Comments
Speech maturity	6–8 years	Mastered the reproduction of most sounds	During this period children's speech becomes clearer as their tongue, teeth and jaw develop. Children begin to use language to get their point of view across to others, although some do this by simply raising their voice! In this period, children's level of language is key to their acquiring the skills of reading and writing.
	8–11 years	Confidence in reading and writing	During this period, children's vocabulary continues to increase. They should also be starting to use language to help them problem solve and reason. Confidence and skills in reading and writing develops.
	12–16 years	Can reason using logic	Young people's speech is fluent, mature and they can use it to argue and negotiate. Young people should be able to read easily and write fairly accurately, but these skills are variable. Where language is developed, young people are able to use it to reason using logic.

Understanding the language development of multilingual children

Children who are learning more than one language at a time tend to be slightly slower in learning to talk and communicate. It is thought that this is because the child has to absorb more than one language system. This early delay in speaking does not affect children's overall language development, provided they are given adequate support.

The process by which young children learn additional languages is through absorption and association. This means that they gradually associate a language with a person or a situation and are able to respond in the language they hear. In the same way that you might use the word 'Ta' with your friends but use 'Thank you' with your lecturers, children learn which phrases to use with non-English speakers and which phrases to use with English speakers.

Although some young children may speak more than one language, it is not until they are older that they start to understand that they are using more than one language. Most children find that it is difficult to use their home language in situations where they are used to speaking in English. This means that if they are asked what the word for saucepan is in their home language, they may not be able to immediately think of the word. This may make them feel that they are failing in some way.

By the age of 8 years, children will understand that they are using more than one language and start to be aware of equivalent words and phrases, for example that saying 'Merci' to their father is the same as saying 'Thank you' to an English speaker.

Children need to master their home language

It is now widely recognised that in order for most multilingual children to achieve, their home language also needs to be supported. Studies have shown that unless a child has mastered one language, he or she will find it difficult to make process in others. This is why in some settings where there are children who have little English, teachers are employed who can carry on supporting the child's home language. Some communities organise after-school activities in order that the child can learn to read and write in his or her home language.

Racism and multilingual children

It is sad that instead of valuing all children who can speak more than one language, the approach often taken in UK society is to value some languages and not others. Society often sees the ability to speak a European language such as French or German as an advantage, whereas speaking Punjabi or Urdu may not be valued in the same way.

Speaking another language is actually part of a child's self-identity, so when a child's home language is not recognised or valued the child is being sent the message: 'We don't care about your family or your culture.'

Emotional and social needs of multilingual children

It is important to recognise that children who are multilingual will have emotional and social needs as well as needs connected with their language development. Common feelings among children who speak more than one language include:

→ *Embarrassment* – Children may feel embarrassed and different from other children. They may pretend that they do not speak another language.

→ *Rejection* – Children may feel that their home language, and consequently their home life, is not important and not valued. This is particularly true of children who speak non-European languages. Staff may stop children from speaking together in their home language.

Helping children who are multilingual

Not mixing languages

To help young children learn which language they should be using, it is important that the people around them stay in one language. For example, an English speaker should not start speaking to them in their home language. This prevents children from mixing up their languages.

Gaps in vocabulary

As children are learning languages by association and absorption, they may find themselves in some situations where they have a word in only one language. For example, a child may know the word for 'bed' in his or her home language as this word is used at home, but not know the word in English. Similarly, children may wish to tell their parents that they have been playing with Playdough but know this word only in English.

If children are unable to find the words and phrases they need to express themselves, there is a danger that they will stop talking about what they are doing. This means they may not tell their parents what they have been doing, or they may never talk about home life in settings. Many settings used to working with multilingual children aim to involve parents in the setting in order to solve this problem. Parents may

Think about it

In pairs, continue this list of words or phrases that are mostly used in school settings: *book corner; assembly; lining up time.*

Now continue this list of words or phrases that are mostly used at home: *pillow case; settee; doorbell.*

U2
1

be asked if they would like to spend some time in the setting or early years practitioners may work with parents to make sure that children learn the English words that are used at home.

The importance of having a multicultural ethos

In many ways, helping children who are multilingual is about creating an atmosphere in which they feel comfortable. Settings that have a good understanding of equal opportunities will be able to do this easily as they will already have activities and materials that promote an understanding of different cultures and languages.

Being sensitive to children's needs

An early years practitioner needs to be sensitive to the needs of individual multilingual children in the same way as those of any other child. It is important that the child does not feel like a 'party turn' because he or she can speak another language. There may be some children who are keen to stand up and sing a song in their home language, whereas for another child this would be embarrassing.

The most useful way of helping children feel comfortable in a setting is to build a good relationship with them. This may mean spending some time playing or talking to the children by themselves and encouraging them to talk about their family. Children can sense when someone really cares for them and this 'caring' is, in the end, the best way to help children value themselves and their culture.

Involving and valuing parents

All children need to see that their parents are liked and valued. If the setting is able to build a relationship with parents, multilingual children will be more likely to value their language.

⇧ **Caring for children is the best way to help them value themselves and their culture**

There are many ways in which this relationship can be established. For example, parents could come in to help or early years practitioners could ask the parents if they would like to see some of the activities that the child has been carrying out.

Intellectual development

Intellectual development is about the way in which you learn to think and reason but also store and process information. It is a large area of development which includes several theories and approaches. Defining stages and sequences for this area of development is especially difficult as there can be wide differences between individual children and young people. The causes of these differences are hotly debated – again, it is possible to return to the nature versus nurture debate. As you will see there is some support that intellectual development may be linked to language and the opportunities that children and young people are given. There is also support for the idea that intellectual development may be linked to inherited ability. All this makes for a fascinating area of study.

Cognitive development and concepts

Most people confuse cognitive development and intelligence. Cognitive development is about the process of thinking, organising information and learning abstract concepts. There is a link between cognitive development and intelligence, although defining what is meant by intelligence is quite difficult.

Measuring intelligence

From the beginning of the twentieth century it was though that intelligence in children could be measured. This was a very attractive idea because if it was possible to know how intelligent a child was, schools could group children according to their potential. The first intelligence tests were developed by two French men in 1905 called Binet and Simon, with the aim of looking to see which children would have difficulty in school. The tests concentrated on measuring vocabulary and mathematical and verbal reasoning.

The Binet–Simon test was revised by an American team of psychologists in the 1930s and became known as the Stanford–Binet test. In the 1950s, Britain's secondary education system was based on the principle of intelligence testing at the age of 11 years. Following an examination commonly called the 'Eleven Plus', children were put into either grammar schools, which followed an academic curriculum, or secondary modern schools, which were supposed to be more practical.

Unfortunately, these tests were found to be measuring not intelligence but children's knowledge and language skills. This disadvantaged children who had potential but whose language skills were undeveloped. Children who did not pass the test often felt that they had failed in some way and in the 1970s testing in this way was phased out.

Today, intelligence testing is treated with much caution and the latest theories of intelligence would suggest that there may be different types of intelligence. This would explain why some people are talented in one area but may have difficulties in other cognitive areas, for example a talented artists might find it difficult to organise and understand their business affairs because they had poor mathematical reasoning.

Find out!

To find out more about the theory of different types of intelligence, you could read about Sternberg's triarchic theory of intelligence, for example in *The Developing Child* by Helen Bee (Longman, 1999).

Think about it

Look at three blue things in the room you are in. They are likely to be different shades.

- How do you know they are blue?

If you had to explain what makes something blue, you would find it difficult. You simply know that blue is blue!

Think about it

1. If there were a perfect intelligence test, do you think that children should be tested?
2. Are there any dangers in testing for intelligence?

What is meant by an abstract concept?

Part of the process of cognitive development involves being able to understand abstract ideas or concepts. An example of an abstract concept is blue.

Colours are examples of concepts. Your brain has learned to categorise and store information which means that you are able to look at a colour and name it.

Concepts that children need to learn

Children need to learn many concepts. Some concepts they will learn just through seeing and experiencing. Other concepts will be learned through being supported by the adults around them. The spider diagram below shows some of the key concepts that children learn during their early years.

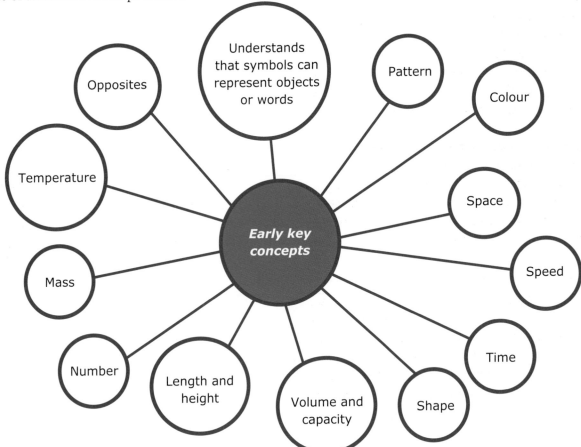

Adults have a key role in helping children learn concepts. In many ways, adults should see themselves as supporters rather than as teachers. The idea of supporting children is sometimes called **facilitating**. This means the adult should be there to provide activities, equipment and encouragement which, in turn, allows children to explore their world. It is generally accepted that young children need to be active in their learning – they need to do, rather than watch!

Key term

Facilitate To provide help

Stages and sequences of cognitive development

It is very difficult to give milestones for cognitive development as children's acquisition of concepts depends on their play experiences and their own individual pattern of development. The chart below attempts to look at some of the stages and areas of learning concepts. It is based on some of the work done by NFER/Nelson, which is often used in devising programmes for children with special education needs.

⇪ **Stages and areas of learning concepts in children aged 0–6 years**

Age	Probable sequence of tasks	
0–1 year	• Looks for an object that has been removed • Places an object in container when asked • Finds an object that has been seen and then hidden	
1–2 years	• Takes out objects one by one from container • Points to parts of the body • Scribbles • Points to a named picture	
2–3 years	• Completes a three-piece puzzle • Copies a circle • Matches textures • Is able to point to big and little, e.g. 'Which is the big teddy?' • Matches three colours • Stacks beakers in order	
3–4 years	• Tells if an object is light or heavy • Is able to repeat a simple story • Matches one to one, e.g. putting a cup with each saucer • Points to long and short objects • Is able to sort out simple objects • Knows primary colours • Names three shapes • Counts ten objects with support	

Age	Probable sequence of tasks	
4–5 years	• Picks up a number of objects, e.g. 'Find me four cubes'. • Names five textures • Names times of day associated with activities, e.g. bedtime, dinner time • Names eight colours • Matches symbols (letters and numbers) • Is able to decide which object is the heavier • Places objects beside, behind and next to • Counts by rote up to 20	
5–6 years	• Counts accurately up to 20 items • Prints own name • Arranges objects in order of size • Names days of week in order • Tells month and day of birthday • Sight reads ten or more words • Predicts what happens next • Points to half and whole objects, e.g. half a cake • Counts up to 100 by rote	

Activities and equipment to help cognitive development

There are some activities and pieces of equipment that can help children's cognitive development. A major part in the thinking process is the ability to classify, store and retrieve information. This means that activities that encourage children to have any of these skills are particularly valuable.

🕯 **Activities and equipment to help promote cognitive development**

Construction toys	Concepts	Cognitive skills
Puzzles • Shape sorters • Tray puzzles • 3-piece puzzles • 12-piece puzzles • 3D puzzles	Children learn about shape and space. They also learn to sort and match. As they become older, trial and error learning will decrease as they start to use reasoning skills to work out the position of pieces.	• Classifying • Attention and concentration
Sorting objects • Buttons • Plastic shapes	Children are able to sort, order and classify objects according to colour, shape or size. Children can be asked to find all the blue cars or all the yellow buttons.	• Classifying • Attention and concentration
Sewing cards *Threading beads*	Children learn about patterns and also colours.	• Classifying • Attention and concentration
Kim's game	This is the game where objects are put on a tray and then one is removed. The children have to work out which object is missing.	• Memory • Attention and concentration

Construction toys	Concepts	Cognitive skills
Construction toys Duplo Lego Wooden bricks Popoids	Children learn about space, shape and structures. They can also experience matching and sorting as well as being encouraged to think about size.	• Classifying • Attention and concentration
Matching games Lotto Pairs Pelmanism Snap	These types of game help children sort and match. Pelmanism can help children's memory as they work out where they have seen a matching card (cards are put face-down; children choose a card and then work out where its partner is).	• Classifying • Memory • Attention and concentration
Feely bags	These encourage children to use their senses to work out what object is in a bag.	• Classifying • Memory • Attention and concentration

Concentration

Concentration is an important skill in order to process and retain information. Concentration requires sustained attention on a particular focus. In order to achieve this some level of arousal is necessary in order to gain attention in the first place.

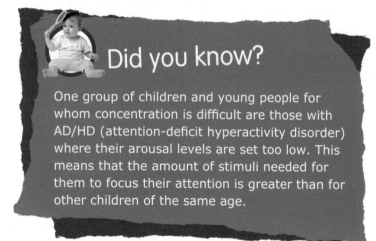

Did you know?

One group of children and young people for whom concentration is difficult are those with AD/HD (attention-deficit hyperactivity disorder) where their arousal levels are set too low. This means that the amount of stimuli needed for them to focus their attention is greater than for other children of the same age.

Babies and young children are able to concentrate but not to the same extent as older children and young people. This is partly because concentration is an active skill that requires us to consciously ignore irrelevant information to avoid becoming distracted. Thus while a baby may stare at a mobile, he or she will stop at the sound of a door opening or when shown another toy.

By the age of 14 years or so, most young people have mastered the skills of concentration, although variables such as tiredness, hunger and interest need also to be taken into account.

Memory

Memory is an important component of the ability to process information. It was not until the 1950s that memory was studied in depth by psychologists; they have since proposed a 'multi-store' model as to how information is coded and retrieved. Theories about the way people store and retrieve information vary, but most psychologists agree that there is a process system to memory. It also seems clear that learning to use and search your memory is a skill that children acquire over time. Thus younger children may find it hard to remember some types of information while older children and young people will find it easier.

Most psychologists agree that memory storage is divided into two components, commonly called short-term and long-term memory.

→ Short-term (or primary) memory is that which people use when remembering a new telephone number for a few seconds before dialling it. An hour later they might not remember it. Short-term memory typically lasts for about 15–20 seconds.

→ In contrast, long-term memory can hold information for a few minutes or for a lifetime, and is seen as having unlimited capacity. This may come as a surprise if you are someone who has difficulty remembering things, but storage capacity is completely different from the process of retrieving information.

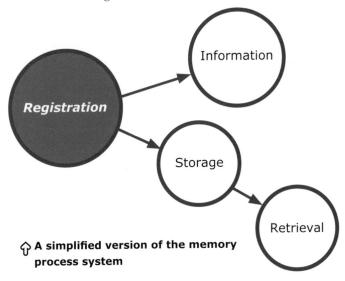

⇧ **A simplified version of the memory process system**

Storing information

In order to be able to retrieve information from either long- or short-term memory, it has to be encoded. With the development of language, maturation and experience, children gradually learn to use some of the strategies below.

→ *Rehearsal.* This is repeating to yourself what you want to remember, for example repeating a telephone number or practising the words and actions to a song. Rehearsal is a strategy that can boost short-term memory capacity. Children start using rehearsal from around 6 years of age, but older children and young people often use it purposefully, i.e. they 'make' themselves repeat information as they realise this is an effective way of remembering.

→ *Clustering or chunking.* This involves grouping pieces of information. For example, rather than remembering a telephone number as 0-0-3-3-5-6-0-6-7-9-9-7, you would remember it in clusters or chunks, for example 00-33-56-06-79-97. In the same way, rather than remember each item that you needed in a supermarket, you could think about all the dairy items you wanted or all the ingredients needed to make a cake.

Children as young as 2 years old can begin to chunk information, and this skill becomes more sophisticated in older children and young people.

→ *Elaboration.* Elaboration means finding connections between things that need to be remembered. If you find a person's name difficult to remember, you might think about one feature of that person to help you. Mnemonics such as 'Never Eat Shredded Wheat' (to remember the points around a compass) are forms of elaboration. Older children and young people are often able to do this purposefully and may use it as a strategy for revision.

Retrieving information and metacognition

As well as storing information you also need to be able to retrieve it. Retrieving information is a complicated process which partly depends on the way in which it was stored. As children develop, they gain more control and skills in 'working' their memories. A young person faced with a question to which they know the answer, but can't quite remember it, may be able to think 'around' the answer and thus eventually find the memory. This is a sophisticated task and is part of a set of skills known as metacognition skills. Metacognition is about the way in which you actively control your thoughts, memory and concentration. A young person may, for example, be aware that a certain passage in a book needs more attention and may re-read it. In this way, the young person has controlled their concentration.

Social, emotional and behavioural development

Social and emotional development often underpins children's and young people's happiness, security and success. It is increasingly being recognised as an essential area that impacts on behaviour and achievement. A starting point for this development begins early on in a child's life as they embark on their first strong relationships – those with their parents. These relationships are usually life-long and, it is now recognised, can form the basis for later life.

Early attachments

⌁ Stages of attachment

Age	Stage	Features
6 weeks to 3 months	Indiscriminate attachments	Babies begin to be attracted to human faces and voices. First smiles begin at around six weeks.
3 months to 7–8 months	Indiscriminate attachments	Babies are learning to distinguish between faces showing obvious pleasure when they recognise familiar faces. They are happy to be handled by strangers and prefer to be in human company rather than left alone – hence the term indiscriminate attachments.
7–8 months	Specific attachments	At around 7 or 8 months, babies begin to miss key people in their life and show signs of distress, for example crying when they leave the room. Most babies also seem to have developed one particularly strong attachment, often to the mother. Babies also show a wariness of strangers even when in the presence of their 'key people'. This wariness may quickly develop into fear if the stranger makes some form of direct contact with the baby, for example by touching him or her.
From 8 months	Multiple attachments	After making specific attachments, babies go on to form multiple attachments. This is an important part of their socialisation process.

Attachment continues

Parents play a continuing role throughout children's and young people's lives. You have seen that attachment is important early on in children's lives, but what about later on?

Interestingly, older children and young people still need the security of their parents, although they do not need to be continually with them. This means that while older children and young people will increasingly spend time with their friends, they will still have a bond with their parents. This is reassuring for many parents who often feel 'pushed' away by their offspring in their teenage years, since young people are likely to spend more time with their friends than with their parents.

Stages and sequences of emotional and social development

Learning to build relationships with others is an important skill that children develop over time. It is a gradual process, but by the age of 8 years most children socialise well and are able to understand the needs of others and act in an acceptable way.

The stages and sequence of emotional and social development of children are outlined below, but as with any area of development children will reach different stages at different times. You should always concentrate on building up a 'picture' of a child rather than thinking about what is 'normal'.

Development from birth to 1 year

Important social skills are learned in the baby's first year. Babies learn some of the skills of socialisation. They learn that making eye contact, smiling and laughing can keep their carer's attention.

The first year is also critical in terms of emotional development. Babies need to develop a strong bond, or attachment, with their carers. In some ways, developing this bond may be instinctive as, at birth, babies are able to recognise the smell of their mother and are quickly soothed when they hear her voice. Babies who have a strong bond or attachment with their primary carer at the end of their first year will be more comfortable when they socialise with others.

⬆ **Babies quickly learn that eye contact can keep their carer's attention**

Age	Stage of development
1 month	Watches primary carer's face
3 months	• Smiles and coos • Enjoys being handled and cuddled
6 months	Laughs and enjoys being played with
8 months	Fears strangers
9 months	• Plays peek-a-boo • Discriminates between strangers and familiar adults
12 months	• Is affectionate towards family and primary carers • Plays simple games such as Pat-a-cake

Development from 1–2 years

During this year, children learn more social skills. They are able to play with their primary carers and are comfortable with other familiar adults. They start to explore their environment but need the reassurance that their primary carer is nearby. At the end of this year, children often start to notice other children and become able to play alongside them.

In terms of emotional development, children are very dependent on their primary carer. They will protest and cry if their primary carer leaves them and it is important that they are left with someone who is familiar to them. Although they are still dependent on their primary carer, they are starting to realise that they are an individual. They recognise and begin to use their own name.

The end of this year also marks a change in many children as they become increasingly aware of what they want. They begin to show anger and frustration if they cannot have their needs met immediately.

Age	Stage of development
15 months	• Begins to explore environment if familiar adult is close by • Begins to use words to communicate with • Has a stronger feeling of being an individual
18 months	• Language is increasing • Points to objects to show familiar adults • Explores environment and shows some independence but still needs familiar adults • Strong emotions, e.g. anger, fear and joy, are shown
2 years	• Plays near other children (parallel play) • Begins to talk when playing (pretend play) • Imitates adults' actions • Strong emotions, e.g. anger, fear and joy, are shown

Development from 2–3 years

This is an important year in a child's life although it is often not an easy one for carers – hence the expression 'the terrible twos'!

Children in the first part of this stage are keenly aware of what they want to do, although they become easily frustrated because their own physical and language skills are not developed enough to meet these desires. They also find it difficult to understand why they cannot have what they see, because they lack the concept of ownership or objects being unsafe. Frustration is often vented through temper tantrums or inconsolable crying. These tantrums and strong feelings lessen as children gradually develop more language and physical skills. Carers working with this age group need to be very sensitive and organised so that children are not often in a position where they can become frustrated.

Children often need their comforter with them during this year to help them feel more secure, especially as many children will also be having their first experience of being separated from their primary carers on entering pre-school settings. This is an important step as children learn to socialise without the backup of their primary carers. The first experiences of separation need to be carefully handled and children entering pre-school settings will need a lot of reassurance from early years practitioners. (See pages 82–3 for more on separation.)

⇧ **Children aged 2–3 years often need their comforter with them**

During this year most children will:

→ move out of nappies
→ have a strong sense of their identity, including their gender and age
→ be happy to leave their primary carer for short periods
→ start taking an interest in other children and playing with them

→ show concern for other children, e.g. telling primary carer if baby is crying
→ start to wait for their needs to be met.

There is a wide variation in the way children progress over the year, so it is hard to put times to these steps.

Development from 3–4 years

This is a more settled year for children. Most of them are happy to leave their primary carers and socialise with other adults and children. The first real friendships start to develop, with children seeking out particular friends. Social skills, e.g. turn-taking, sharing and concern for others, are shown. Emotionally, children still need reassurance from their immediate carers but are more independent and play by themselves for longer periods. They still feel strong emotions, and quarrels and temper tantrums continue to surface at times.

Many children will still be reliant on their comforter, especially when they are unwell or unsure of a situation.

During this year, children will:

→ be affectionate towards family, friends and carers
→ want to help and please primary carers and other familiar adults
→ imitate (in play) actions seen, for example putting a teddy to bed, feeding dolls
→ share playthings
→ play with other children, mostly pretend play
→ show concern for other people, e.g. rub the back of a crying baby.

Development from 4–6 years

In some ways the expression 'I can do' sums up this period of a child's life. Emotionally, most children are feeling confident and express themselves in terms of their achievements, e.g. 'I got a sticker today' or 'Look at me, I can climb this now.' They may start to use words and actions in imitation of other people.

Playing with other children is increasingly important and some children start to make close friendships. At this time, children start to play with children of their own gender which may link to their understanding of gender roles.

Development from 6–8 years

At the end of this period, most children are skilled communicators and their social skills are well developed. This means that they often have stable friendships and are able to share, play and understand others' viewpoints. They become more aware of their abilities and may start comparing themselves to their peers. Some may start losing confidence in certain areas, e.g. drawing or reading, and it is important for adults to support them during this time.

Developing friendships

Although you have looked at the general stages of emotional and social development, you must recognise that friendships are often the source of much happiness and sadness in a child's life. The nature of friendships changes as children grow and become more emotionally dependent on their friends. The chart below outlines the ways in which children develop friendships.

Stages of social interaction

Age	Stage of development
0–2 years	Children notice other children, particularly older ones. By the age of 2 years, children are playing side by side.
3–4 years	By the age of 3 years, children are beginning to play cooperatively and friendship preferences start to emerge. They often play with both genders and friendships are fluid, with the choice of activity being more important to children than who else is involved in the activity.
5–7 years	The first stable friendships begin to emerge. Children actively start to seek the company of their friends. They share willingly with their friends and having a friend starts to become important; they may cry if their friend has not come to school that day. They are starting to choose same-sex friends.
8–11 years	Friendships are based more on compatibility, with children sharing common interests. They have strong same-sex friendships and there are some gender differences between the sexes. Boys tend to gather in larger groups and are more likely to be involved in activities such as sport, while girls often meet in pairs and spend more time sharing confidences.
12–16 years	In this period young people have more friendships and the nature of these friendships change. They increasingly become support networks for young people and help them to forge an identity away from their family unit. Young people are likely to talk more to their friends than to their parents and will often use them for advice and information. Friendships tend to be based on personality and values rather than on interests. The gender split that is seen from 3 years onwards subsides. Group size increases and reaches a peak at around 13 years with young people forming 'crowds' of between 8 and 12 people. Crowds within settings have distinct personas and young people can often tell you about their crowd and others within the setting. From 14 years onwards group size becomes smaller again with many young people at 16 years having just 4 or 5 close friends.

Why are some children more popular than others?

You may already have noticed that some children seem to be more successful in their friendships than others. This is an area that is beginning to be researched more, because it seems that children who find it difficult to play with others are more likely to have problems with their relationships in adulthood. For example, a study by S.W. Duck (1991) suggested that children who were rejected by their peers were more likely to display signs of alcoholism, schizophrenia and delinquent behaviour in later life. It seems likely that if the 'loners' can be detected early on and helped to play with others, bullying and later social isolation can be avoided.

Characteristics of popular and unpopular children

There have been various studies (many by Kenneth Dodge) that have looked at why some children seem to be more popular than others. Below is a list of some of the characteristics that seem to be noticeable in popular and unpopular children.

Popular children:
➜ have good social skills, e.g. being able to join a game gradually rather than demand to take it over
➜ may be physically more attractive (Langlois et al, 1994).

Unpopular children:
➜ are more likely to be aggressive towards their peers
➜ tend to be disruptive in play situations, e.g. knocking over another's work
➜ are more likely to wrongly interpret situations, believing that others are hostile towards them.

Helping children who have difficulties in relating to others

Some children find it hard to form relationships with other children. There are many reasons for this, including children who have been bullied or have not had opportunities to mix with other children. It is vital that adults around them try to help them learn the skills they need, as children who find it difficult to socialise with others can become victims of bullying or potential bullies.

If a child seems to find it difficult to socialise with others, it may be a good idea to carry out a series of observations on the child, to discover the areas in which he or she is having difficulties. You could carry out a time sample over a session to see what areas they seem confident in, for example a child might be able to play alongside children while finding it difficult to share equipment or cooperate with others.

Strategies for helping children

Children who have difficulties in playing with other children can lack confidence. A good starting point is to make them feel good about themselves. You can achieve this by playing with them and praising them when they show social skills that will be attractive to other children, for example waiting for their turn when playing a game or passing you a piece of equipment.

Once the child appears more confident, you can introduce activities with other children, for example a board game for three or four players: you remain a participant in the game but progressively take a less active role. As the child gradually shows the social skills needed to play with peers, you can plan less structured activities until the child is able to join in with the others. In addition, you could teach the child to follow the lead of other children in order to join in their game. Rather than ask children if it is all right to join in, the child could instead imitate what the others are doing.

Seeking further help

It is also important for early years practitioners to refer children on to other services if they feel a child has serious difficulties in cooperating and playing with others. Such difficulties may be signs of a deeper psychiatric or medical problem that may need further investigation.

Observing children's friendships

A sociogram is an interesting way of finding out about children's friendships. It works well with school-age children as younger children tend to have less stable friendships. You simply ask each child in a class to name three of his or her friends, preferably when the friends are not present! You can then see who has named whom. An example of a sociogram is shown later in the unit, on page 96.

In your evaluation consider the following points:

→ Are there any children who were not named?
→ If so, have these children been absent recently?
→ Which children were the most frequently named?
→ Do these children have any siblings in the school?
→ Were these children the oldest ones in the class?
→ Did children show any gender preferences, e.g. boys naming only boys?

It is important to realise that a sociogram gives a good indication of friendship patterns, although it is important to follow up any findings with a recorded observation, for example a time sample at playtime on a child who has not been named. It is also interesting to repeat the sociogram after a few weeks to see which friendships are stable.

The development of self-concept

Who are you? What are you like? These are fundamental questions for children, almost like being able to place oneself on a map. In some ways, the development of **self-concept** is the process by which you gather information about yourself. It is important because self-concept is closely linked with **self-esteem**.

It is useful to understand the difference between the terms used when talking about self-concept.

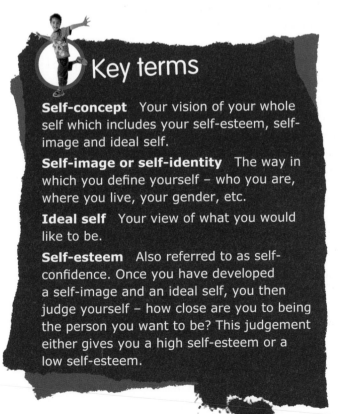

Key terms

Self-concept Your vision of your whole self which includes your self-esteem, self-image and ideal self.

Self-image or self-identity The way in which you define yourself – who you are, where you live, your gender, etc.

Ideal self Your view of what you would like to be.

Self-esteem Also referred to as self-confidence. Once you have developed a self-image and an ideal self, you then judge yourself – how close are you to being the person you want to be? This judgement either gives you a high self-esteem or a low self-esteem.

Developing self image

Children gradually develop **self-image**. The first step for children is to be able to recognise who they are. A well known test to see if children can recognise themselves is to put a touch of red lipstick on a baby's nose and then put the baby in front of the mirror. A child who is beginning to recognise himself will touch his nose rather than the nose in the reflection. Most babies are doing this by the time they are 18 months old.

How self-esteem and self-image are linked

Once you have established what you think you are like – your self-perception – you then consider whether you are happy with the result. Someone with a high self-esteem will be reasonably happy about their self-image, whereas someone with a low self-esteem feels that they are not 'measuring up'. This means that self-esteem and self-image are linked. It is always fascinating to discover that people who appear to have everything may actually have quite low self-esteem – how can this happen?

There has been much research into the process by which people come to make judgements about their self. Based on the research findings, there seem to be three main factors that affect this process, which carries on throughout life. These are:

→ reaction of others
→ comparison to others
→ **ideal self-image**.

Reaction of others

The reaction of others is important in helping children to learn about themselves – children may listen to what their parents say about them or notice how carers talk and treat them. If children perceive that they are wanted, liked and loved, they will have positive self-regard. If they are constantly criticised they will come to the conclusion that they are not good enough or naughty. Children may also link performance to praise, believing they must always achieve if they are going to be liked or loved by their parents and carers. This means you must be careful to make sure that you give children 'unconditional praise', to show them that you like them for who they are as well as giving praise for their achievements and efforts.

People also notice the reaction of others to their achievements. If you are good at a skill that is valued then you are likely to feel positive, but if you are good at a skill which others do not value, it does not become a positive part of your self-image. This becomes an issue particularly when children reach school age, for example a boy who is an excellent dancer will not necessarily have high self-esteem if dancing is not valued by his friends and peers. The reaction of others means that as friendships become more important to children and young people, peer group comments can have a positive or negative effect. Children and young people who have been rejected by their peers are therefore likely to have lower self-esteem scores.

Comparison to others

As children become older they begin to compare themselves to others. They may notice that they are not running as fast as others in their class or that they are not able to read as fluently. The process of comparison helps children to work out 'their place' but it can also lead children to feel that they are not as good as others. As adults people continue to compare themselves to others, for example learners may consider their essay marks, homeowners may look at their neighbour's new kitchen! It is interesting to note that sometimes children who are doing well at school may still have low self-esteem simply because they are comparing themselves to their friends who they may perceive to be doing better.

Did you know?

The beginnings of comparison can be seen in children from around 6 years old. Younger children are fairly egocentric and seem less aware of others in comparison.

Ideal self-image

As part of the process of developing self-esteem, people seem to judge themselves according to their own ideal self. This means that although someone may be attractive and intelligent, they may not necessarily have high self-esteem because they may not live up to their ideal self-image.

Research by Susan Harter (1987) suggests that a child's level of self-esteem is a product of two judgements: what they think they are like and what they would like to be (their ideal self). Where there is a great difference between the self-image and ideal self, children have low self-esteem. It is suggested that the development of an ideal self occurs when children are around 9 years old.

Gender differences in self-esteem

Over time there are gender differences in self-esteem. These are particularly noticeable after adolescence with girls generally having lower scores than boys. This may be a result of the pressure to 'look' good and because feminine qualities may not be as valued by society as masculine ones.

Helping children's self-esteem

It is clear from research, for example Weinberg (1978), that children who have high self-esteem are more likely to fulfil their potential. This means that early years practitioners must help children to develop high self-esteem. This is not as easy as it sounds because once a child has low self-esteem it will take some time and a lot of effort for him or her to feel more confident. Remembering to praise a child from time to time is not enough.

Providing a positive atmosphere

One of the best ways to help children's self-esteem is to provide them with a positive atmosphere. Children need to feel they can experiment, fail and not be criticised. Children who are often criticised or reprimanded gradually develop a feeling that they are not as good as others. Reprimanding children needs to be done carefully so they know that, although their behaviour is inappropriate, they themselves are still wanted.

In a positive atmosphere, children feel that they are special, noticed and valued. This means that a young child can come for a cuddle or an older child can chat to an adult about what they are doing. Settings that only value achievement can make some children feel inferior and, although you must praise children when they are doing well, it is important to consider other children's feelings. Children who are finding it difficult to read may come to the conclusion that they are less important if they constantly hear other children being praised for reading. Ideally, an atmosphere should be created where all children feel included when work or behaviour is being celebrated.

Praise

Children need to be encouraged and praised. It is important that not all praise is directed at achievement. Children can be praised because they are looking happy or have played well with another child. Children from a different cultural background can be praised for sharing their home news with you and a child living in poverty can be praised for helping a younger child. There is a danger that when children are praised only for work or for doing something well, they become afraid of failing or not performing well. This is important because, at some time or another, children will not succeed at a task – such is life – and it is essential that, when this happens, children do not lose their confidence.

Realistic expectations

What adults expect of children can influence not only the way they behave and achieve but also how they come to see themselves. This means that you must make sure that tasks you give children are within their capability. Older children often give up if their first experience of something is failure – especially if they see another child succeed.

You must also be careful about the comments you make. Children need to hear adults saying positive things about them so they come to understand that the adults around them really believe in them.

Look at these common phrases:

→ 'Never mind, you've done your best.'
→ 'Don't worry, I was no good at ... ... when I was your age.'
→ 'Never mind, you can't be good at everything.'

Such phrases are often used to reassure children when they are disappointed. Unfortunately they can be interpreted by children as meaning 'Never mind, you can't do any better.' The outcome may be that some children stop trying because they feel that the adults around them do not expect them to do any better.

Think about it

Yasmin is 5 years old. She is tired at the end of the day and is now in tears because her picture of a dog looks more like a horse.

1. What can you say to make Yasmin feel better?
2. What can you do to make sure that Yasmin does not come to the conclusion that she is no good at drawing?

Being vigilant

It is important that adults working with children look closely for early signs of children losing confidence, for example a child not being as keen to do something as before or a child avoiding a task or situation. If you are able to spot that a child is starting to lose confidence it is easier to support or talk to the child. The task may need to be made easier or the child may need more adult support.

Think about it

Tom is 4 years old. He used to be keen to go outside and play with the tricycles. Lately he often hangs back and watches the others rather than taking a turn. The early years practitioner mentions this to his father and finds out that he had a fall from the tricycle the previous week.

1. How can the early years practitioner encourage Tom to play with the tricycles?
2. Why is it important that the early years practitioner spends some time with Tom?

Providing play materials

It is important to provide children with plenty of opportunities and materials for exploring different roles and learning that people come in all shapes, colours and sizes. Seeing images, books and having stories about children from different backgrounds is important. Some children may not have both parents living together; other children may be using a wheelchair or wear glasses. If you introduce an understanding that everyone is different but still special, children will be more likely to feel supportive rather than hostile to children whose background or needs are different from their own.

⇧ **It is important that children have stories about children from different backgrounds**

Most pre-school settings use home corners and dressing-up areas to help children explore their identity and the role of others. It is considered good practice to stock these areas with a variety of materials, including items from a range of cultures, for example cooking utensils, saris and tunics.

Displaying children's work

Displaying children's work and objects shows children that you value them and can give them a big boost. Paintings, models or anything that a child is proud of can be displayed; children can also bring in objects they like from home. It is good practice to avoid displaying only the 'best' work as this can make some children feel their work is not good enough.

The links between age, stage of development and behaviour

You have now looked at the theories of how children learn behaviour. Early years practitioners also need to understand that learning appropriate behaviour is a gradual process which is linked to children's overall development, although particularly to their language and cognitive development. For example, a 2-year-old will not have the concept of ownership and therefore may often snatch toys.

It is important that early years practitioners have realistic expectations of children's behaviour. You know that if expectations of behaviour are too high, children can feel that they are failing; if expectations are too low, children may not learn appropriate behaviour for their age.

The chart on the following pages looks at children's behaviour in relation to their age and also at the role of the adult. It shows the goals for behaviour. The goals are they types of behaviour that early years practitioners should be encouraging, while remembering that the child will not automatically be able to show this type of behaviour. As with any developmental chart, it must be seen as a guide since children vary greatly in their development. For example, a 6-year-old child with learning difficulties may show behaviour that is normally associated with a 2-year-old.

☝ Goals for behaviour at different ages

Age	Stage of development	Goals for behaviour	Role of adult
1–2 years	• Actively explores environment • Is learning from adults and will copy simple actions • Repeats actions that gain attention • Alternates between clinging and independence • Has no concept of sharing or ownership; will want what is seen	• To play alongside other children (parallel play) • To carry out simple instructions, e.g. 'Can you find your coat?'	• *Good supervision:* children of this age do not understand the dangers around them. • *Distraction:* this is necessary to stop unwanted behaviour; children often forget what they were doing, e.g. if a child wants another child's toy, offer him or her another toy instead. • *Praise:* this should be given to help children understand how to get adults' attention in positive ways and help them develop good self-esteem. • *Being a good role model:* children learn behaviour through imitating those around them.
2–3 years	• Easily frustrated and may have tantrums • Less easily distracted • Copies actions of others • Dislikes attention being shown to other children by carers • Cannot wait for things • Finds sharing difficult • Active and restless	• To wait for needs to be met, for example at mealtimes • To share toy or food with one other child with adult help • To play alongside other children • To sit and share a story for 5 minutes • To say 'please' and 'thank you' if reminded • To follow simple instructions with help, for example 'Wash your hands'	• *Good supervision and anticipation:* children are trying to be independent but lack some of the physical and cognitive skills necessary, which makes them angry and frustrated. Adults need to anticipate possible sources of frustration and support children either by offering help or by distracting them, for example if a child does not want to go out, give him or her a book to look at while getting dressed. • *Praise and encouragement:* this is necessary to help children learn what behaviour adults expect from them. Some unwanted behaviour that is not dangerous should be ignored so that children do not repeat it, hoping for adult attention. • *Consistency:* children are trying to work out what the limits are on their behaviour. Children of this age start to form patterns of behaviour, for example tantrums or whining. • *Being a good role model:* children model their behaviour on others around them. This is especially important at this age as they act out their experiences through play.

Age	Stage of development	Goals for behaviour	Role of adult
3–4 years	• Follows simple rules by imitating other children, for example collects aprons before painting • Able to wait for a short while • Enjoys activities, e.g. painting • Enjoys being with other children • Able to play cooperatively • Enjoys helping adults • Occasional tantrums, often when tired and frustrated	• To follow rules in game when helped by adult, e.g. playing Lotto • To say 'please' and 'thank you' often without reminder • To take turns and share equipment • To follow instructions of adults most of the time, for example 'Shall we put the red bricks away?' • To help tidy up	• *Praise and encouragement:* this is needed to build confidence; it makes children more likely to show desirable behaviour. • *Explanation of rules:* children are more likely to remember and understand rules that are explained to them. • *Good supervision:* although children are able to do many things for themselves, they are still unaware of the dangers around them. Most of the time children will be able to play well together, but squabbles will still break out. • *Being a good role model:* this is central to helping children learn the social skills they will need to resolve arguments and express their feelings. • *Supporting children:* this is necessary so that children can try to resolve their own conflicts, for example 'What do you think we can do to make sure that you all have a turn on the slide?'
4–5 years	• Plays with other children without help from adults • Able to communicate feelings and wishes • Understands the need for rules	• To ask permission to use other children's toys • To comfort playmates in distress • To say 'please' and 'thank you' without a reminder • To tidy up after activities	• *Providing activities and tasks:* these need to be stimulating and allow children to develop confidence. Children of this age are keen to help adults and enjoy being busy. Tasks such as laying the table or getting objects allow children to feel independent. • *Praise and encouragement:* this is needed to make children feel good about themselves. This is important because children often start school at this time. They need to feel they are able to be 'good'. • *Explanation:* this is required to help children remember and understand the need for rules or decisions. • *Being a good role model:* by this you will help children learn social skills, as they are copying what they see. • *Supporting children:* this includes giving them opportunities to resolve potential problems themselves, for example 'I have some drinks here. How do you think we can share them?'

Age	Stage of development	Goals for behaviour	Role of adult
5–8 years	• Has strong friendships • Able to argue back • Copies behaviour of other children, e.g. swearing or spitting • Understands the need for rules and plays games that have rules • Understands the difference between right and wrong • Has many self-help skills, e.g. getting dressed, wiping up spills	• To follow instructions from adults • To apologise to others • To listen to others *From 6 years onwards:* • To work independently and quietly in school settings • To be helpful and thoughtful	• *Praise and encouragement:* this is required so children do not look for other ways of gaining attention. Praise is needed as children become more aware of others and compare themselves critically. • *Explanation:* this should be given so that children can understand the reasons for rules and decisions. Children should also be made to consider the effects of their actions on others. • *Boundaries:* as children become older they are likely to argue back so clear boundaries are needed and have to be enforced. • *Being a good role model:* children are trying to understand more about the adults they are with. Speech and actions are modelled increasingly on adults they admire. • *Providing activities and responsibilities:* this is necessary to help children 'mature' as they learn more about their capabilities. Small responsibilities help children to become independent as well as giving them confidence, e.g. asking them to tidy areas of a setting or pour out drinks for other children.

Think about it

Look at these examples and consider whether these types of behaviour are usual for these ages of children.

1. A 4-year-old snatches a ball from a 2-year-old.
2. Two 6-year-olds share out some biscuits.
3. A 2-year-old has a tantrum when the telephone is moved out of the way.
4. A 7-year-old argues back to an adult.
5. A 5-year-old cries because he has to wait for his turn.

Other areas of development affect behaviour

There is a strong link between the overall development of children and their ability to demonstrate acceptable behaviour. For example, some social skills such as sharing or turn-taking require children to think of others. Where children are delayed in some aspect of their development, they are likely to show behaviour that is not normally associated with their age. Even a slight delay can affect a child's behaviour.

Early years practitioners often find that many children who have a developmental delay are aggressive or have tantrums. This behaviour is often the result of a child's general frustration. For example, the child might see what they want but not have the language to express their needs or the physical strength or mobility to get it. Early years practitioners who work with such children need to be patient and get to know the children well, so that they can understand their needs and, therefore, prevent incidents from occurring.

Differing opinions on development

Nature versus nurture

While most people who are experienced in working with children can observe the stages of development that are outlined above, the reasons behind development are less than clear. There are therefore several theories that look at children's development. Explanations of development generally link to either a biological/genetic explanation or stress the importance of the experiences of the child, including the way that adults have interacted with him or her. The differences in opinions have often been referred to as the nature/nurture debate. While traditionally there were clear-cut differences between theories, now most researchers would suggest that there is interplay between 'nature or nurture'.

Theories of development

Theories of development can help you to understand what you are seeing in terms of children's development. The theories of development described below have influenced practice. Some theories have acted as a springboard for further research and have in this way evolved.

Constructivist approaches to children's learning

Some theories look at the way in which children's intellectual development and language develops from them not being 'taught' but by learning through experiences within their environment. Key constructivists theorists are Piaget and Vygotsky.

Piaget's theory of cognitive development

One of the most influential theories of how children's thinking develops was put forward by Jean Piaget (1896–1980).

Piaget's interest in children's thinking and logic began while working on intelligence tests. He was fascinated by the way that children regularly gave similar but wrong answers to some of the questions. From this he came to the conclusion that children's logic was different to that of adults and began to explore why this was. Using his own children as a basis, he wrote detailed observations about their development. He finally concluded that children were 'constructing' their ideas based on their experiences. This is why the term 'constructivist approach' is used in relation to his theory.

Piaget used the term 'schema' to mean a child's conclusions or thoughts. Piaget felt that children's schemas would change as new pieces of information came to light.

Assimilation	
Child constructs a schema based on what he or she knows	'The lady at the nursery stays there because I always see her there.'

Equilibrium	
The schema remains the same while the child's experiences seem to confirm his or her ideas	'Every day, the lady at the nursery is waiting for me in the room.'

Disequilibrium	
The child has information that seems to cast doubt on the schema or idea. Things do not add up any more!	'I am in a shop, but I can see the lady from the nursery. What is she doing here because she is always at the nursery?'

Accommodation	
Child adapts his or her thinking and constructs a new schema incorporating this new information	'The lady at the nursery doesn't stay there all the time.'

⇧ **The process by which children's schemas form and change**

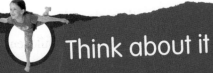

Think about it

See if you can draw a person in under 30 seconds. If you can, this means that you have developed a schema – a quick way of doing something or thinking something that no longer requires much thought.

Try to draw a person again, but this time start with the feet and work your way upwards. This is usually much harder because you have to change your schema about how to draw a person.

Stages of development

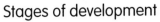

As well as trying to understand how children's thoughts develop, Piaget also looked at stages of children's development. He came to the conclusion that this was also influential in their thinking. He believed that structures within the brain were being developed and the way children thought was also linked to their biological development. (Recent work on brain development now shows that children's brains do actually grow and develop from birth onwards.)

Piaget grouped children's cognitive development into four broad stages and gave ages to each stage, although he did suggest that not all children would reach the final stage. The table below outlines these stages. Note that subsequent work has suggested that Piaget may have underestimated children's development.

Piaget's four stages of cognitive development

Stage	Age	Features
Sensori-motor	0–2 years	The child develops physical schemas as he/she gains control of his/her movements. At around 8–9 months, the baby begins to understand that objects continue to exist even if he or she cannot see them. This is known as object permanence and may explain why most babies begin to protest when their carer leaves the room.
Pre-operational	2–7 years	Children begin to use symbols to stand for things, for example a piece of dough represents a cake. Language is also a way of using symbols (see pages 43–4). Children also show egocentrism – believing that everyone will see the same things as them or have the same thoughts. Piaget felt that children in this stage were easily tricked by appearances, as is shown by his experiments involving conservation (see below).
Concrete operations	7–11 years	Piaget felt that this stage marked a significant change in children's logic. They were less easily deceived by appearances and could apply rules and strategies to their thinking. The term 'concrete' is used because Piaget felt that children were helped in their thinking when they could do and see things in practical ways, for example physically counting out items.
Formal operations	11–15 years	In this stage, children are able to think entirely in the abstract, for example they can multiply numbers in their head or read maps without having to turn the page.

Sensori-motor stage (0–2 years)

This is the first stage of a child's life. It begins at birth with babies using their reflexes to survive. Babies are also very reliant on using their senses in the first two years, especially taste and touch. Babies' first schemas are physical ones with babies learning to repeat and then control their movements.

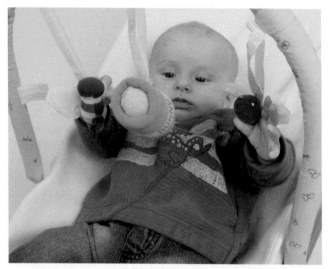

⇧ **Babies' first schemas are physical ones. This baby will repeat this movement before gaining control**

Development of object permanence

One of the tests that Piaget used to show the development of thought in babies was object permanence. In the first few months, a baby will appear to accept the disappearance of an object. Piaget suggested that this is because babies have not learned the idea that an object is still in existence somewhere, even if it is not visible. At around 8 or 9 months, babies seem to develop this concept, and you can test it by taking an object from a baby and hiding it under a cushion near them. The baby should lift up the cushion to find it. Interestingly, if the game is played a few times and the object is put in a new place, the baby at 8 or 9 months will keep looking in the place where it was previously hidden, not the new place. At 12 months, the baby will look in the last hiding place.

Pre-operational stage (2–7 years)

During this stage, children develop their skills at using symbols, i.e. language. Many early years practitioners will find that children in this stage engage in a lot of imaginative play with objects in a representational way, for example sticks become guns, cardboard boxes become cars.

Piaget divided this stage into two further sub-stages – pre-conceptual and intuitive, although there are four main features which run through both of these sub-stages:

→ Egocentrism
→ Centration
→ Animism
→ Conservation

Egocentrism

Children in the pre-operational stage tend to see things from their perspective and thus their logic is different from adults. Piaget called this egocentrism and this is a strong feature of the whole of the intuitive stage.

Centration

As part of the pre-operational stage, Piaget felt that children's thinking was based only on their own experiences and a belief that everyone would have the same experiences as themselves (egocentrism). From this he understood that young children would have difficulty 'decentring'; decentration is the ability to imagine someone else's perspective.

To test children's ability to decentre, Piaget constructed a model of three mountains. Each mountain was a different colour and had a different feature on it. Children could walk around the model and then were asked to sit down on one side of the model. A doll was put on the other side. Children were then show pictures of different views and were asked to choose the view that the doll would have. While 4-year-olds chose the picture that represented the view they could see, 7- and 8-year-olds consistently chose the view that the doll would see.

Case study

A puppet show

Anthony is watching a puppet show. Both puppets are on the stage, a mouse and fox. The mouse hides a ring in a box and then goes off to play. The fox takes the ring and hides it under a hat. The mouse comes back and starts looking for the ring in the box where it was left. Anthony can't understand why the mouse doesn't go straight to the hat. ⇨

1. Why does Anthony think that the mouse should look under the hat?

2. What does this tell you about Anthony's ability to decentre?

3. At what age might you expect Anthony to decentre?

Animism

Many children in the pre-operational stage draw pictures with human faces or believe that inanimate objects such as puppets and teddies, etc. have real feelings. This is thought to be linked to egocentrism as children believe that if they have thoughts and feelings, so must other things.

Conservation

One of Piaget's tests to see which stage children might be in relates to children's ability to 'conserve'. Conservation means understanding that certain things do not change even if their appearance is different. Piaget suggested that young children find it difficult to conserve because they are easily taken in by appearances. He argued that this explains why children come to different conclusions to adults. A 3-year-old may, for example, think that a man wearing a women's dress has become a woman.

The chart below shows some of the tests that are commonly used with children. You might like to try these for yourselves.

⇑ **This child has counted these buttons already. He is counting them again because they have been moved slightly and the child cannot 'see' that this will not affect the overall number**

Concrete operations stage (7–11 years)

This stage marks a great leap in children's logical abilities. They begin to use rules and strategies to help their thinking. Piaget called this the concrete stage because children are helped in their thinking when they can do it in practical ways, for example using counters to find the answer to 15 minus 9.

Children in the concrete operations stage are also able to conserve and decentre, although Piaget suggested that this did not occur uniformly, i.e. a child may understand conservation of mass but not get conservation of number for a few months. Piaget also suggested that children would understand the

⇩ **Examples of Piaget's tests commonly used with children**

Number	Two parallel rows with equal numbers of counters are shown to the child. The counters in one of the rows are then put closer together so that one row appears longer than the other. Children are asked, 'Are there the same number?'
Length	Two pencils of identical length are put side by side. One pencil is then moved diagonally so that its point is no longer alongside the other pencil. The child is asked, 'Are they the same length?'
Volume	Two identical beakers are filled with equal amounts of water. The content of one of the beakers is poured into a narrower but taller beaker. The children are asked, 'Is there the same amount of water?'
Mass	Two equal balls of clay or dough are rolled into two balls. The child is asked to pick them up to check that they are the same. One of the balls is rolled into a sausage shape. The child is asked, 'Is there the same amount of clay in each?'

concept of reversibility. An example of reversibility is where clay that is rolled into a ball and then into a sausage and back into a ball would still have the same mass. In mathematical terms it means that children are able to understand that there is a link between division and multiplication, for example $7 \times 5 = 35$ and $35 \div 7 = 5$.

Formal operations stage (11–15 years)

The main difference between this stage and the concrete operations stage is that children are now able to manipulate thoughts and ideas to solve problems without needing practical props. This means that, in theory, tasks such as map reading can be done without having to turn the map around to work out whether a turning is on the right or left. This is an interesting example of the type of formal operations task as many adults may have difficulty reading maps!

Piaget (1972) suggested that thinking at the formal operations level would not be an automatic step. He thought that in some areas of learning people would not all achieve this level all of the time and in some areas it would depend on the training and experiences that they were given. In the case of map reading, for example, you might be able to manage to read a map without turning it around given enough experience and training.

Another feature of the formal operations stage is that children are able to hypothesise about situations in a realistic way, for example what would you do if someone broke into your home? The ability to hypothesise means that children can speculate on outcomes. This feature of thinking Piaget referred to as hypothetico-deductive reasoning.

How to apply Piaget's theory to practice

Piaget's work suggests that children and young people need enriching opportunities in order to extend and revise their schemas. Piaget also accepted that brain maturation was part of the process. This also means that while opportunities for stimulation are essential, you cannot necessarily 'fast track' children since their cognitive development will affect their logic and thinking process. Thus a 3-year-old is unlikely to be able to achieve complex deductive reasoning. Piaget's approach does, however, mean that you should observe children and young people carefully so that you can provide appropriate experiences to extend their thinking.

Vygotsky's studies of the way children learn

Vygotsky is another theorist who took a constructivist approach to children's thinking, believing that children are active in their learning and thinking. His work was not published in English until the early 1960s, even though his work was known in Russia in the 1920s and 1930s. He believed that children's social environment as well as their experiences is very important. He considered that children were born to be sociable, and through being with their parents and then with their friends acquire skills and concepts. This is a key feature in Vygotsky's work and his emphasis on adults differs significantly from Piaget's in this respect. Vygotsky saw children as 'apprentices', learning and gaining understanding through being with others.

The term 'scaffolding' is often used alongside Vygotsky's theory. This reflects the idea of the child being helped by adults to learn concepts, a strong feature of his work. In support of Vygotsky's work, Wood et al (1976) looked at the ways mothers worked with their children on a construction task. They saw that although techniques varied, mothers were able to encourage their children by either demonstrating or by praising movements that would help the children to complete the task. As with Piaget, Vygotsky also suggested that maturation was an important element in children's development although he felt that adults had an important role in extending children.

Zone of proximal development (ZPD)

Vygotsky felt that adults were able to 'extend' children's thinking and skills by careful intervention. By looking at what a child can currently do and then thinking about what might be within the child's grasp, the adult moves the child to a higher level, as shown in the chart on the next page.

Current level of development	Proximal development achieved with adult intervention and support
This child has good fine manipulative skills and can tie a simple knot in a cord. 	The child can now tie a bow because an adult has taken the time to show him. The child is developmentally ready for this. 

How to apply Vygotsky's theory to practice

There are many ways in which you can apply Vygotsky's theory to practice. Firstly, Vygotsky saw that adults need to be actively involved with children and young people. He also suggested that children and young people tackle problems at a higher level when working as a group rather than individually. In practice, this means that early years practitioners might organise group activities that require problem solving, and they need to interact with children and young people and to encourage their thinking.

Social cognitive learning

This theory looks at the way in which children and young people learn through observing and then imitating in a process called modelling. This is an interesting theory that has been developed over time, principally by Albert Bandura. Originally he called this theory the social learning theory, but has since considered the cognitive elements involved in it. As with the operant condition theory (see page 73), there are no developmental stages, but by considering the cognitive elements Bandura has attempted to explain why some actions are picked up but not others.

Learning through modelling

In the 1960s Bandura was able to show through a classic experiment that children would perform actions they had previously seen an adult do. The experiment involved showing children a film of an adult with a large inflatable doll known as a Bobo doll. Two groups of children watched the adult hitting the doll. The first group was then shown a second adult either ignoring or encouraging the aggressive behaviour, while in the other group the second adult intervened to punish the aggressive behaviour. Afterwards, children were put in a room with the Bobo doll and their responses were noted. The children in the first group replicated the aggressive actions on the doll while the second group showed little aggressive behaviour towards it. This experiment shows that children are influenced by adults' actions.

Cognitive elements

Bandura has explored further the type of cognitive elements required for learning through modelling to take place, particularly memory and retrieval of memory.

Attention

Children and young people need to be interested enough to pay attention and to notice what the adult or other child is doing. In addition, they have to focus on the right elements and avoid distractions or the irrelevant. For example, an adult might stop and blow his nose while logging onto the computer; the blowing of the nose is irrelevant to the process of logging on to the computer. As you have seen earlier, being able to filter out the irrelevant and focus attention is a skill that develops over time.

Encoding and retrieving information

In order to learn the information it has to be encoded into the long-term memory so that it can be retrieved. This may mean visual encoding or, in terms of language-based modelling, a **semantic code**. As you have previously seen (pages 52–3), memory use becomes more sophisticated with age.

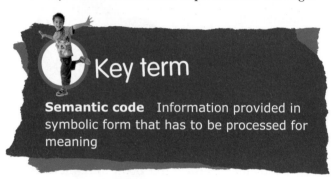

Key term

Semantic code Information provided in symbolic form that has to be processed for meaning

Opportunity to reproduce actions

Children and young people also need to be in the position where they can replicate what they have seen, for example an 8-year-old cannot light a match if no matches are available. A sufficient level of physical skills might also be necessary, for example the 8-year-old needs a particular level of fine motor skills in order to strike a match.

Motivation

Reason and motivation is another key ingredient. Children and young people might find the action itself interesting or there may be a desire to 'become' the person they have watched. They may also have seen that reinforcement, such as admiration of others, results from the action. For example, a 7-year-old may notice in an after-school club that other children laugh at a boy who makes silly sounds and be motivated to try this out.

Views of language development

The nature versus nurture debate appears once more when we look at theories of how children learn language.

Noam Chomsky

Noam Chomsky's work on language is based on the idea that the ability to learn language is instinctive. This is a 'nature' or nativist theory. His theory has been widely accepted as it is comprehensive and, unlike Skinner's ideas (see below), explains why all babies' language development follows a pattern.

Chomsky is famous for suggesting that humans have a Language Acquisition Device (LAD). This is not an actual physical part of the brain but a structure within the brain that allows babies to absorb and understand the rules of the language they are being exposed to. The brain is able to analyse the language and work out the system that the language uses. This is a complex process but explains why children can quickly understand and then use their language creatively and correctly without ever being formally taught or 'knowing' the rules.

The LAD would explain why all babies can learn any language they are exposed to and why all babies follow the same pattern of development even though their IQ may be very different.

Is there a critical period for learning language?

The idea of a critical period is an attractive one. It has been suggested that children who are not exposed to language in the first 10 years of life would not be able to learn to speak. There is some evidence for and against this idea.

Case study

Learning to read

Harry is 5 years old. His older brother is always reading and sometimes reads books to him. Harry's mother will often sit with Harry and spend time sharing a book with him. She gives him plenty of attention during this time, which Harry likes. She knows that Harry can read simple words and has shown him how to break longer ones down into the sounds that make the words up, such as 'care-ful-ly'.

1. Is Harry likely to be interested in learning to read?

2. How might Bandura's theory of role modelling link to Harry's learning to read?

3. Can you think of another theory of learning that might also be influencing Harry's reading?

- Teenagers and adults who have been brain damaged as a result of an accident find it harder to regain language they have lost, whereas children with similar injuries find it much easier. This would support the idea of a critical period.
- Children who have suffered severe deprivation have still managed to acquire some language. One of the most famous of these children is Genie. Genie was 13 years old when she was rescued in 1957. She had spent her childhood in appalling conditions. She was punished for making any sounds and was strapped down. When she was found she could understand a few words but essentially had no speech. Although she made progress in learning to speak, she struggled with the rules of speech. This case and others would cast doubt on the idea of a 'critical period' because speech was gained.

Skinner's operant conditioning theory

This is a 'nurture' theory. Skinner suggests that language is learned mainly because when babies try and communicate their efforts are rewarded or reinforced in some way. For example, a baby may get a smile from a parent if she gurgles, and a toddler saying 'more' and pointing at food will learn that by using language he can get what he wants. Skinner used this idea of reinforcement to explain why babies stop making some sounds – he reasoned that when babies made sounds that parents did not recognise they would not receive any attention, while sounds which were recognisable were noticed and reinforced. He called this process selective reinforcement.

This approach would explain why children speak in similar ways to their parents using the familiar phrases and intonation.

Criticisms of the Skinner's theory

- The theory does not explain why all babies and children follow the same pattern of gaining language. If Skinner's theory was correct, you would expect children's language to develop very differently depending on the amount and type of reinforcement that adults and others give. This is not the case, however, as most children seem to pass through the same stages.
- The theory does not explain why children speak in different ways to the adults around them, for example a toddler saying 'dada gone'. If children learn by imitating what they hear and not having incorrect sounds or sentences reinforced, why do they say things such as 'wented' or 'swimmed'?
- The theory does not explain how children learn the rules of the language in such a way that they are quickly able to make up their own sentences. Learning through imitation and reinforcement would mean that children would only be repeating what they have heard, rather than being able to invent their own sentences.

Vygotsky

Vygotsky suggested that thought and language begin as two different activities. For example, when a baby babbles, the baby is not using babbling as a way of thinking. At around the age of 2 years, language and thinking merge and at this point the child uses language to structure thinking.

Vygotsky also differentiated between two types of speech:

- inner speech, which supports thinking
- external speech, which allows communication with others.

An example of inner speech would be saying either out loud or inwardly 'then I am going to ...' as a way of self-direction. Between the ages of 2 and 7 years, Vygotsky felt that children are not able to use inner speech in distinct ways and therefore their speech is often a blend of the two, with young children often providing a running commentary of what they are doing. Vygotsky referred to this early speech and thought as egocentric.

Think about it

Do you ever talk to yourself when you are busy or have things to remember?

Psychoanalytical theories of social and emotional development

An interesting question that has not yet been fully answered is 'What makes me the way I am?' Everybody is different – some people are outgoing and talkative while others are quiet and reflective. It is generally accepted that childhood experiences will affect personality. This means that, as an early years practitioner, you need to be aware of some of the main psychoanalytic theories of emotional and social development.

The Greek word 'psyche' means spirit or mind, and psychoanalytic theories use the exploration of the mind as the starting point for explaining behaviour and personality.

Two famous psychoanalytic theorists are Sigmund Freud (1856–1939) and Erik Erikson (1902–94). Both of their theories are based on the idea that:

→ behaviour is guided both consciously and unconsciously by the mind
→ personality is formed during childhood
→ children pass through certain stages at certain points in their childhood
→ personality is affected by how well a person copes with each of these stages.

There are many similarities between Freud's and Erikson's theories, but the main differences are:

→ Freud's stages are called psychosexual stages because he put emphasis on the physical pleasures that are associated with each stage
→ Erikson's stages are called psychosocial stages because his emphasis was on the child's exploring relationships.

Sigmund Freud (1856–1939)

Freud is well known because he was the first theorist to consider that people have an unconscious mind. Freud was interested in the way people say and do things without always realising them, for example sucking the top of a pen.

The unconscious mind and moral development

Freud suggested that people have an unconscious mind that is split into three parts:

1. *Id* – this is the part of the mind that represents a person's desires and needs. Freud thought that babies were all id as they are unable to consider other people's needs.

2. *Ego* – this emerges later as children begin to consider the consequences of their actions and also start being able to plan the best way of meeting the powerful id's demands. For example, the id wants a sweet; the ego considers that the best way of getting a sweet is by behaving well.

3. *Superego* – this is the moral part of the unconscious that knows right from wrong – in other words, the conscience.

Freud suggested that in the subconscious mind there is often conflict between the id and the superego – that is, conflict between what a person really wants to do versus what is the right thing to do. For example, if you were hungry and saw a bar of chocolate belonging to someone else on the table:

→ your id would urge your ego to plan how to take it
→ your ego would consider the consequences of taking it
→ your superego would tell your ego that the chocolate belongs to someone else and that you would be punished if you took it.

⇧ **It is surprising how many people feel that this type of dialogue often happens inwardly when faced with temptation**

Freud suggested that gradually children develop all three parts of the unconscious, which would mean that they could gradually make moral decisions.

74

Stages of emotional development

Freud felt that people are driven by the need to satisfy some basic needs and pleasures. He called this drive or energy the libido.

Freud suggested that there were five stages of childhood on which the drive – or libido – concentrated; the table below describes these five stages. The stages link to the physical development of the body. Freud felt that if a person does not pass through these stages satisfactorily, part of their energy or libido would become stuck – or fixated – at that stage. This fixation would affect their behaviour and personality.

↷ **Freud's five stages of emotional development**

Age	Stage	Area of pleasure	Features of stage	Effects on personality and behaviour if fixation occurs
0–1 years	Oral	Mouth	Babies gain pleasure from feeding and sucking. They will also be weaned during this stage.	Behaviour linking to pleasures gained in the mouth, e.g. overeating, smoking, thumb sucking. Also naivety – 'Swallows anything they are told'!
2–3 years	Anal	Anus	Children are learning to control their bowel movements. They learn that adults praise them when they master toilet training and can be angry with them if they do not.	Freud argued that if children were toilet trained too early and were controlled, they would develop 'controlling' habits, e.g. extreme tidiness, meanness, stubbornness. Conversely, if children did not have enough encouragement to become toilet trained, they would become overgenerous and gushing in personality.
4–5 years	Phallic	Genitals	Children explore their body and notice their genitals. They also learn about their gender. Freud felt that girls need to adopt the gender role of their mother, while boys have to separate from the mother and follow the gender role of their father (see also the Oedipus complex below).	Vanity, recklessness
6–12 years	Latent	None	Freud felt that this was a resting period for children in terms of their emotional development.	None
13–18 years	Genital	Genitals	Children are developing into mature adults. If they have passed successfully through the other stages they will be able to make strong relationships with the other sex.	

Oedipus complex

Freud is famous for talking about the Oedipus complex. Freud suggested that boys in the phallic stage are in love with and desire their mother, but unconsciously realise they cannot marry her because of their father's presence. He suggested that boys are not only jealous of their father, they are also afraid of him. (Freud felt that they were afraid of being castrated.) This causes boys a dilemma – should they love their mother and risk their father's anger? Freud felt that most boys resolve this dilemma by deciding to make friends of their father by copying his actions and interests.

Although many people laugh at this idea, it is noticeable that boys of this age do tend to hold on to their genitals when they are worried and start to model themselves on their father!

Freud suggested that a similar complex existed for girls – the Electra complex, whereby girls desire their father.

Criticisms of Freud's work

There have been many criticisms of Freud's work, although his thinking changed the way that people with emotional problems are treated. He concentrated more on the development of men than women, and he is seen as putting too much emphasis on the physical and sexual drives that people have as a way of explaining behaviour. He will always be famous because he was the first theorist to make people aware that some of their actions and reactions are unconscious. For example, the expression 'Freudian slip' is used when someone says something that he or she did not mean to say, such as saying your ex-boyfriend's name to your current boyfriend. According to Freud's theory, this 'slip' would reveal an unconscious desire to be with your ex-boyfriend.

Understanding how Freudian theory may link to practice

Working with children

Freud felt that children need enough time to explore different parts of their body. For example, in the oral stage a baby may wish to suck, even though the baby has finished feeding. Freud felt that stopping children from exploring during the different stages might prevent them from successfully completing that stage.

In the anal stage, when most children are being toilet trained, Freud's theory suggests that children should not be put under too much pressure and that they should not be trained too early.

Observations

You might be able to refer to some of Freud's theories in your observations.

→ Children sucking their thumb – *oral stage.*
→ Small boys clutching their penis – *phallic stage.*
→ A child pushing his father away or stopping his parents from cuddling – *phallic stage.*
→ Children exploring their bodies, e.g. playing doctors – *phallic stage.*

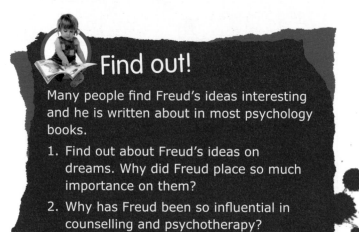

Find out!

Many people find Freud's ideas interesting and he is written about in most psychology books.

1. Find out about Freud's ideas on dreams. Why did Freud place so much importance on them?
2. Why has Freud been so influential in counselling and psychotherapy?

Erik Erikson (1902–94)

Erikson was a student of Freud and there are a lot of similarities between their theories. Erikson accepted Freud's stages of psychosexual development and built on them. One of the main differences is that Erikson felt that the stages of development were linked to cognitive and social development rather than led by physical needs. It is interesting to see that Erikson also believed that the personality continued to develop into adulthood.

Erikson considered that there were 12 stages in the development of personality. He saw each stage as a dilemma and believed that how a person coped with the dilemma would affect their personality.

Erikson's stages of personality development

Age	Dilemma	Stage	Effects on personality
0–1 years	Basic trust versus mistrust	Babies have to decide whether the world and the people around them are safe and friendly or hostile.	If babies do not have their needs met, they may decide their world is a hostile one. This can mean they find it harder to form relationships later.
2–3 years	Autonomy versus shame and doubt	Children are learning to explore their environment and develop some control over their body and bowel movements. They may try to do things for the first time, e.g. dressing.	If children are not given encouragement to explore or are made to feel guilty about toilet accidents, they may feel doubt about themselves. This can mean they will be less independent when older.
4–5 years	Initiative versus guilt	Children are increasingly able to plan and carry out activities. They also need to learn about their gender role – similar to Freud's phallic stage.	Children need to feel they are independent, although they also need to learn what the boundaries of their behaviour are. Too much control may result in fearful, dependent children, whereas a very permissive attitude may leave children without any guilt or conscience.
6–12 years	Industry versus inferiority	In these years, children are comparing themselves to other children.	Children who experience failure and notice that they are not as competent in some areas as their peers, may lose confidence and feel inferior. Children in this stage who meet only with success may become over-confident and lack humility and empathy.
13–18 years	Identity versus confusion	Adolescents need to consider their identity (including their sexual identity) and what they wish to become in the future.	Ideally, at the end of this stage, adolescents have a firm idea of who they are and what they want to do with their life. If they have not worked through this stage they may 'drift'.
19–25 years	Intimacy versus isolation	This age group may be considering whether to live alone or find a partner to settle down with.	Adults must decide whether to form a couple or stay single. If this conflict is not resolved, they may find themselves unable to commit to a relationship.
26–40 years	Generativity versus stagnation	Adults in this stage are often having their own children or are making progress in their careers.	In this stage, adults are trying to make an impact on the future. Most people have children or try hard in their careers. If adults feel they have not left their mark on life, they may feel bitter and resentful.
41 plus years	Ego integrity versus despair	Adults in this stage are thinking more about their mortality.	In this stage, adults are trying to come to terms with themselves and the way they have lived. They may feel satisfied and accepting of themselves or they may feel depressed and bitter.

Understanding how Erikson's theory may link to practice

Working with children

A large part of Erikson's theory suggests that in order for children to go successfully through each stage, they must gain enough confidence. This means that adults working with children need to make sure that they give them enough time to explore and take the initiative as well as giving them plenty of praise.

Think about it

Look at the following situations and see if you can link each situation to a stage of Erikson's theory.

1. A child looking at another child in a way that suggests comparison
2. Babies having their needs met quickly
3. Toddlers having a go at dressing themselves
4. Adults praising children

Albert Bandura's social learning theory

You looked at Bandura's social learning theory on pages 71–2. Here you will consider the theory in terms of how children may develop their personality.

Social learning theory suggests that children model their behaviour on the behaviour of the adults around them. Thus, children who have parents who are visibly generous and kind towards others are more likely to develop these characteristics.

Criticisms of the social learning theory

It is true that children often share characteristics, speech and actions with their parents, but the theory does not explain why some children in the same family develop such different personalities. Neither does it explain why children gradually develop moral codes.

The moral development of children

Jean Piaget (1896–1980)

An important part of socialisation is understanding what is right and wrong. Piaget looked at children's moral reasoning. He was particularly interested in observing children play and the rules that they developed while playing. He also told children stories to examine their reasoning of right and wrong. For example, a tale of one child who broke several plates while helping a parent and a second tale of a child who threw one plate down in a temper. Piaget noticed that young children tended to concentrate on the damage caused when deciding what was naughty rather than whether the act was an accident, saying that the child who had dropped several plates was the naughtier.

Piaget therefore concluded that moral reasoning changed according to children's cognitive development: a child in the pre-operational stage (see page 68) would be able to think only in terms of behaviour being either right or wrong, whether the behaviour would be punished or not; a child in the formal operational stage starts to be able to consider other elements, for example whether an act was deliberate.

Lawrence Kohlberg (1927–87)

Kohlberg's work also looked at how children think about right and wrong. Kohlberg devised a series of tests to find out what children and adults thought about different dilemmas. From these tests he concluded that there were three main stages in children's and adults' moral development, although each stage is divided into two. Kohlberg concluded that not everyone would reach the final stage or even the final level.

Think about it

Have you ever been told that your voice, mannerisms or the way you speak is similar to another family member?

Level	Age	Stages
Pre-conventional	6–13 years	**1.** Obeys rules to avoid punishment.
		2. Behaves well to avoid punishment and to gain reward.
Conventional	13–16 years	**3.** Conforms to behaviour in order to win approval and acceptance of others – 'good girl/boy'.
		4. Being good means doing one's duty and conforming to authority – laws are there and need to be obeyed.
Post-conventional	16 years plus	**5.** Laws need to be obeyed but only if they are fair and the majority of people accept them – some questioning of authority.
		6. We must act according to our own conscience and this should be our guide as to whether to obey authority or not.

Criticism of Kohlberg's theory

There has been some criticism of Kohlberg's work because he mainly used boys in his first studies. Since that time, his work has been used with children in several countries and this has shown that the stages do occur in the order that Kohlberg suggested with relatively few differences between cultures.

Linking theory to practice

Working with children

The work of Piaget and Kohlberg shows that children are not able, at a young age, to tell the difference between right and wrong and often show good behaviour to avoid punishment or to gain reward. This means that concepts such as ownership of objects will not be automatic for children and they will need explanation as to why they cannot have everything that they see. It also means that children will be prone to temptation as they are still developing a sense of conscience, for example they may take another child's biscuit.

Find out!

It might be interesting to test Piaget's and Kohlberg's theories with children. You might consider using a test like the one below to see a child's reasoning.

→ *There was a boy who didn't like his dinner. He threw his dinner on the floor and the plate broke.*

→ *There was a boy who was helping his father to wash up. He knocked over a tray of cups. Fifteen of the cups fell to the floor and broke.*

Was one of the children naughtier than the other?

It is important to tell the tales carefully and not to indicate, through facial expression, what you are feeling. After a child has given his or her answer, carefully record the child's reasons for this answer. It is always interesting to repeat these types of dilemma with children of different ages, to observe how children of different ages are developing.

Theories of attachment, separation and loss

Attachment theory

Attachment theory suggests that children need strong relationships with their primary carers and that this bond or relationship begins in the first few months of a baby's life. For most babies and children, the primary carer will be their mother or father. It is generally accepted that when children do not have a strong bond with a primary carer, they find it difficult to socialise and develop relationships with others. Where a child cannot be with their primary carer, it is important that he or she receives a good quality of consistent loving care.

⇧ **Attachment theory suggests that children need strong relationships with their primary carers**

John Bowlby (1907–90)

John Bowlby was one of the first people to recognise the need of babies and young children for a strong, stable relationship with their primary carers. In the 1950s, Bowlby was asked to study the effect on children of being in orphanages or other institutions. His findings suggested that children who were, at an early age, deprived of a relationship with their primary carers were more likely to have behavioural problems in later life. Bowlby's report 'Child Care and the Growth of Love' (1953) changed many of the childcare practices of the time.

There were three aspects to Bowlby's theory of attachment that have since been developed by other researchers such as Mary Ainsworth.

1. Children who have been separated from their parents are more likely to suffer from psychological problems in later life.

2. Attachment is an instinct in babies. They must form an attachment by the time they are 12 months old as otherwise they may find it hard to develop strong relationships in the future.

3. Babies' and young children's fear of strangers is instinctive. Babies start to fear strangers from the age of 7–8 months. Bowlby wondered if this was a primitive reaction which, in nature, would prevent babies from coming to harm.

Criticisms of Bowlby's work

There are many criticisms of Bowlby's work and it has been superseded by other pieces of research. When looking at the criticisms of his work it is, however, important to remember the political, economic and social climate of the time of his writing.

→ *The role of the mother was over-emphasised*
This has been the major criticism of Bowlby's early work. At the time of writing, women were the traditional caregivers and, after the Second World War (1939–45), the government was keen (for economic reasons) for women to return to their traditional role within the home. Bowlby's later work did emphasise that babies could form an attachment with someone other than the mother.

→ *Attachments to more than one person were not explored*
Bowlby placed much emphasis on the importance of one single attachment. Subsequent research has shown that as children get older, they can develop equally strong attachments to other figures such as their father and siblings (see page 83 for information about multiple attachments).

Who will babies and children form attachments with?

Up until the 1950s, it was generally thought that babies and children automatically formed the strongest relationship with the people who fed them and met their physical needs. This is sometimes referred to as 'cupboard love'!

Several pieces of research have shown that this is not necessarily true (see Harlow's monkeys on page 81). One strong piece of research by Schaffer and Emerson (1964) showed that babies and children can form an equally strong attachment to their father, even when the father is not the main caregiver. Over a period of 18 months, they visited babies at four-weekly intervals and found that most children, by 18 months, protested equally when separated from the mother or father. This piece of research showed that care-giving alone did not automatically mean that a child would form a main attachment.

Linking theory to practice

One of the major concerns most parents have when leaving their baby with a nanny or childminder is that the child will attach to the caregiver and not know who the parent is. Although in theory this is possible, it is unlikely providing that the parents spend time responding to and interacting with the baby. This is the idea behind 'quality time', where the quality of the interaction and responsiveness of the parents is more important that the actual amount of time spent with the child.

Looking at the quality of attachments

There has been some research looking at the quality of babies' early attachments (see below). It would seem that, when babies and children are 'securely' attached, they are able to explore and develop their independence. Children who are attached to their parents, or another figure in their life, such as their key worker, may show the following signs:

→ actively seeking to be near the other person
→ crying or showing visible distress when that person leaves or, for babies, is no longer visible
→ showing joy or relief when that person appears
→ acute awareness of that person's presence, for example looking up at them from time to time, responding to their voice, following their movements.

Babies and children whose attachment is less secure seem to show either indifference or clingy types of behaviour.

Harlow's monkeys

Harlow and Zimmerman (1959) raised rhesus monkeys from birth. The monkeys were put in a cage with two man-made substitute mothers. One mother was a wire mother and the other was covered in terry towelling. Half of the monkeys were fed by the wire 'mother' and the other half were fed by the cloth 'mother'. Harlow and Zimmerman found that regardless of which monkey was feeding them, the monkeys attached themselves to the cloth monkey.

⇧ Harlow's monkeys experiment showed that providing food alone does not mean that attachments will be formed

They clung on to her when they were frightened and they turned to her for comfort. This study showed that providing food alone does not mean that attachments will be formed.

In a development from this study, Harlow and Rosenblum (1963) looked at what would happen if the cloth mothers 'rejected' the monkeys. One group of monkeys was randomly blasted with compressed air by the cloth mother, while monkeys in a second group were not. The monkeys in the first group tended to spend more time clinging to their cloth mother than those in the other group. This seems to show that rejection or abuse made the monkeys insecure and made them try more often to gain some comfort even though there was a chance they would be 'rejected' again.

Mary Ainsworth

The quality of attachments was also looked at by Mary Ainsworth, who is considered, alongside Bowlby, to be a key figure in this area of psychology.

Ainsworth and her colleagues (1979) created a scenario where babies' reactions to being left with a stranger and then reunited with the mother and/or father were measured. This scenario is now widely used to study attachment behaviour, and is known as the 'strange situation'. The strange situation is divided into eight parts with each part lasting about 3 minutes. During the experiment, the baby (1-year-old) has some time alone as well as with a stranger.

The strange situation

1. Parent and baby enter the room
2. Parent remains inactive; baby is free to explore room
3. Stranger joins parent and baby
4. Parent leaves room
5. Parent returns, settles baby and stranger leaves
6. Baby is alone in room
7. Stranger returns and interacts with baby
8. Parent returns again and stranger leaves

Ainsworth and her colleagues were particularly interested in the reactions of the baby to the parent when he or she left or returned, and the way in which the parent interacted with the baby. The categorised the behaviour into three types.

Type A: Anxious-avoidant

The baby largely ignores the parent and shows little sign of distress when the parent leaves, continuing to play. The baby ignores or avoids the parent on his or her return. The baby dislikes being alone but can be comforted by the stranger.

Type B: Securely attached

The baby plays while the parent is present but shows visible distress when the parent leaves and play is reduced. The baby is easily comforted on the parent's return and carries on playing. The baby cries when alone because the parent is not there, but can by partly comforted by the stranger. Reactions towards the parent and stranger are markedly different.

Type C: Anxious-resistant

The baby is wary and explores less than Type A and Type B children. He or she becomes very distressed when the parent leaves and actively resists the stranger's attempts to comfort him or her. The baby wants immediate contact with the parent on return but is ambivalent, showing frustration and anger alongside clinginess, for example wanting to be held but then immediately struggling to get down.

Why are some children more securely attached than others?

Ainsworth came to the conclusion that the quality of attachment depends on the parenting that the baby receives. Where parents were able to sense and predict their baby's needs and frustrations, babies showed Type B behaviour (securely attached). This

meant that they were able to explore and play, knowing that their parent was a safe base.

What happens when babies and children are separated from their main attachments?

Most early years practitioners will notice that as children become older they find it easier to separate from their parents. This is because they have formed other attachments to staff and, as they get older, to other children. They have also learned that although their parent is absent, he or she will return later. Babies and toddlers, however, find it difficult to cope with the absence of their main attachments and will show distress.

Separation anxiety

Bowlby saw that there seemed to be a pattern to the way children reacted if they were separated from their main attachments. This pattern is often referred to as separation anxiety. There seem to be three distinct stages of separation anxiety, as described below.

Stages of separation anxiety

Stage	Features
Protest	Children may cry, struggle to escape, kick and show anger.
Despair	Children show calmer behaviour almost as though they have accepted the separation. They may be withdrawn and sad. Comfort behaviour, such as thumb sucking or rocking, may be shown.
Detachment	Children may appear to be 'over' the separation and start to join in activities. The child is actually coping by trying to 'forget' the relationship, hence the title detachment. The effects of detachment may be longer lasting as children may have learned not to trust the people they care for.

Separation anxiety is clearly seen in babies from around 7 months and seems to reach a peak around 12–15 months. Older children will show separation anxiety if they are separated for long periods, for example if a parent dies or goes away for a period of time.

Separating from carers

For most children, changing settings is a daunting experience and they have many fears. It is important for early years practitioners to understand these fears so they can reassure the child. Young children often have very specific fears, for example whether they will know where the toilet is or whether their parent will know where to find them. Older children are often concerned about whether they will make friends easily and whether the staff will be nice to them.

Age and separation

The age of children plays a crucial part in their reaction to being separated from their carers.

➔ Babies under 6 months are unlikely to show signs of distress, as they will not have formed a strong attachment with the primary carer.

➔ Children between the ages of 1 and 3 years are likely to show the most reaction to being separated. This means early years practitioners caring for children in this age range need to be particularly sensitive to children's needs.

➔ As children get older they are able to understand that being separated from their carer does not mean losing him or her.

➔ Children over 4 years are less likely to react to short periods of separation, although this will depend on their previous experiences of separation. Most children settle well, providing they know what the childcare arrangements are and that they like the setting they are in.

Experiences

Children's reactions to separation will be partly affected by their previous experiences. Children who, from an early age, have been cared for by someone other than their primary carer may be happier that those who have never been left before. Children whose previous experiences of being left were unhappy ones are likely to cling to their primary carer. This shows how important it is for the child's first experiences of separation to be good.

Children with older siblings may find it easier to separate from their primary carer as, quite often, they are already familiar with the setting and know some of the carers, for example a child starting the same school as her brother.

Quality of substitute care can make a difference

While Bowlby focused on what happened if the maternal bond was broken, two researchers – James and Joyce Robertson – looked in the late 1960s and early 1970s at the quality of substitute care and whether this might make a difference to the outcomes of children who had experienced temporary separation. Their work concluded that the effects of a temporary separation could be lessened if children were put in situations where they could talk about their feelings and were warmly cared for. This view has been supported by other researchers, such as Barbara Tizzard, who suggested that children could make and would benefit from substitute attachments.

Case study

Feeling guilty

Ruth has three children. Two are teenagers and the third child, Tom, is 2 years old. Ruth left her job when Tom was born, but two months ago she and her husband separated. Ruth has decided to return to work and has arranged for a nanny to care for Tom. She is not happy about this situation as she stayed at home when her other children were young. She feels that Tom will miss out by not having her there.

The nanny is fully qualified and experienced, but when Ruth comes home she always questions her or finds fault with what she has done with Tom. The nanny is beginning to consider finding another job because she feels that Ruth is 'nit-picking'.

1. Why might Ruth be reacting to the nanny in this way?

2. How can the nanny make Ruth feel more confident that Tom is fine?

Operant conditioning theory

The idea behind operant conditioning theory is that learning is based on the type of consequence or reinforcement that follows on from behaviour. While the theory is often used to manage children's and young people's behaviour it is actually a key theory of learning.

B.F. Skinner

B.F. Skinner (1904–90) is recognised as a key figure in developing the behaviourist approach to learning theory and, in particular, for developing the theory of operant conditioning. His work was at first based on E.L. Thorndike's law of effect.

Thorndike's law of effect

The original concept of operant conditioning was first pioneered by Edward Lee Thorndike (1874–1949), although he did not use the term operant conditioning. Thorndike (1898) showed through experiments with cats that the results of behaviour would affect subsequent behaviour. This he called the 'law of effect'.

In his experiments, hungry cats were put into a 'puzzle box' which had a lever that allowed the cats to escape. The cats could see from inside the box a piece of fish which they were able to eat every time they escaped. At first the cats took about 5 minutes to escape and did so the first time purely through trial and error. Subsequently they were able to reduce the time that it took them to escape until they were able to escape in less than 5 seconds. Thorndike suggested that the cats learned to operate the lever because their behaviour had been rewarded or 'stamped in' by being able to escape and, in particular, eat fish.

Skinner's model of operant conditioning

Skinner adopted and furthered the work of Thorndike into the now accepted model of 'operant conditioning'.

Skinner divided the consequences of actions into three groups:

1. Positive reinforcers
2. Negative reinforcers
3. Punishments

1. Positive reinforcers

Positive reinforcers are likely to make people repeat behaviour where they get something they desire, for example buying a new food product after having tried and liked a free sample. Skinner suggested that using positive reinforcement was the most effective way of encouraging new learning. Positive reinforcers for children include gaining praise, stickers, sweets and treats, but crucially adult attention. In the learning environment, positive reinforcers will be activities that the children have enjoyed doing and which have resulted in them feeling successful.

2. Negative reinforcers

These are likely to make us repeat behaviour in order to stop something unpleasant from happening to us. For example, you may continue to wear oven gloves to stop your hands being burned.

3. Punishers

Punishers are likely to stop people from repeating behaviour, for example you may learn to stay away from an electric fence after receiving a shock.

Skinner was clear that punishers and negative reinforcers may stop a particular behaviour in the short term; however, the behaviour is likely to reappear once the threat of punishment or negative reinforcement is removed. Thus positive reinforcers are the best way of dealing with children's behaviour.

Primary reinforcers

There are some reinforcers that give instant pleasure and satisfaction or meet a need. These are referred to as primary reinforcers – chocolate is a primary reinforcer because most people find that once they put it into their mouth, they enjoy the taste.

Unexpected positive reinforcers

Skinner found during his experiments that it was often hard to predict what would act as a primary reinforcer; it was sometimes only after the event that this became clear. An example of this is when children sometimes deliberately behave badly in order to attract their carer's attention. If they manage to attract attention, they are more likely to show the behaviour again although they might be told off. Gaining the carer's attention in this case is the positive reinforcer even if they are being told off (a negative response).

Secondary reinforcers

Secondary reinforcers are different because they in themselves do not give satisfaction; rather you learn that they symbolise getting primary reinforcement. A good example of secondary reinforcement in our daily lives is money. Coins and notes in themselves do not give reward but they can be used to buy something that will give primary reinforcement, for example expensive shoes or a meal in a restaurant.

Using star charts and other secondary reinforcers

Any model where children have to collect something such as points, tokens or stars before getting the actual reward is using secondary reinforcers. The advantage of a secondary reinforcing system is that it can help improve behaviour over the long-term; however, it is important to understand the pitfalls too.

The main pitfall when using star charts or other secondary reinforcers is to assume that the child will understand the rewarding mechanism. Young children tend to be more focused on immediate reinforcement, so for them secondary reinforcers may not be that effective. The other pitfall is to make star charts too difficult to achieve. Children and young people need to know the exact behaviours expected of them. Vague terms such as 'being good' are not as effective as 'keeping the sand in the tray' or 'tidying up when we remind you'. Children and young people will also be more motivated when they can see that with a little effort they will complete the chart and gain the reward. This may mean having a star chart that might just last a day.

Did you know?

Reward cards that supermarkets and other retailers use are secondary reinforcers – they act as star charts for adults!

Sensory and intrinsic reinforcements

As well as reinforcements and rewards that you might give children and young people, it is important not to overlook the fact that some actions and behaviours are self-reinforcing. For example, a child might tip up a box of toy cars and enjoy the feeling of power but also the sound that they make as they tumble out. The child is likely to repeat the action again later on because the feelings and sound have acted as an instant reinforcement. While this can explain some types of unwanted behaviour it is also the reason why children may also show wanted behaviour. For example, a child may sit and write with a marker pen because the marker pen feels good and the child is pleased with his or her efforts.

Frequency of reinforcement

Skinner looked at the effect that giving positive reinforcement at different intervals had on behaviour. For how long would behaviour continue without a positive reward before the behaviour stopped? Interestingly, he found that unpredictable reinforcement works better than continual reinforcement. This would seem to work because it teaches the learner not to expect a reward or reinforcement every time – hence they keep on showing the behaviour just in case reinforcement is given!

In practical terms, this means that children would not need to be praised for every single action they take, providing that you do notice and comment from time to time. But it also means that you need to think about how consistent you are when tackling unwanted behaviour. Consistency always sounds easy to achieve but most psychologists agree that adults are usually fairly inconsistent with children and young people as the case study below shows.

Case study

Earning pocket money

James is 14 years old. He has a mobile phone and likes going out with friends. His parents have a system whereby he has to earn his pocket money each week. This means keeping his bedroom tidy and walking the family dog each day. Some weeks his parents keep strictly to the system and do not give him his pocket money if he has not done the tasks or has failed to do them well. At other times his mother feels sorry for him and gives him his pocket money anyway even if he has not done anything. James now rarely 'earns' his pocket money.

1. What is the behaviour that James' parents are trying to encourage?

2. What reinforcement are they using?

3. Explain how their inconsistency will reinforce James' behaviour of not doing his tasks.

Applying the principles of operant condition to effective learning

→ *Success and praise are important.* Children and young people are more likely to study, concentrate or work hard in areas where they have gained a positive reinforcement. This will include praise but also the feeling of success.

Case study

Studying mathematics

Darren is 7 years old. He loves mathematics at school. He enjoys getting the answers right and seeing the ticks in his book. His parents are very proud of his ability and often comment on his mathematical ability to family and friends. Darren often practises puzzles and mathematical games at home.

1. What reinforcements does Darren get for mathematics?

2. How are they helping him to practise more?

3. Do you think that Darren would try as hard if nobody commented or his work was unmarked?

Applying the principles of operant conditioning to behaviour

There are many things that can be learned from this theory, and as it is widely used it is important to understand how it works.

→ *Adult attention is a powerful reinforcer.* This means that ignoring some unwanted behaviours may be a more effective strategy than intervening and thus giving attention. It also means that praising or acknowledging children and young people may be essential for wanted behaviour to be repeated.

→ *Distraction.* Distracting children is a useful technique – the distraction acts as an alternative reinforcement but encourages wanted behaviour.

→ *Reinforcements work better if they are positive and immediate.* It is also important for children and young people to know why they gained the reinforcement so they can repeat the wanted behaviour.

→ *Consistency is important.* Some unwanted behaviours are prolonged because adults are inconsistent. Realistic approaches are essential.

Current theorists

Many of the theories of development that you have looked at are the focus for ongoing research. In addition, there are currently many researchers and research projects looking at how children learn and the best environments for them to do so.

Margaret Donaldson

Margaret Donaldson reviewed Piaget's findings and challenged some aspects of his research. Her book *Children's Minds* was highly regarded when it was published in 1978. In the book, Donaldson argued that children found it hard to complete the tasks of 'conservation' and 'decentration' because they were not meaningful and contextual. She cited examples of other studies which had made the tasks more child-friendly and had produced different results. For example, a 'teddy' rather than an adult changing the position of the objects used in the conservation tests changed children's responses.

Margaret Donaldson's work has been influential. She has shown how important it is for activities to build on children's knowledge, experiences and interests.

The Effective Provision of Pre-school Education (EPPE) project

The EPPE project is an ongoing research project that is funded partly by the Department of Education and Skills, and has been undertaken by Kathy Sylva and colleagues Edward Melhuish, Pam Sammons, Iram Siraj-Blatchford and Brenda Taggart. The aim of the research is to look at how pre-school education might contribute to children's later achievement and what type of early years provision might be the most effective. As this is a longitudinal study, its findings so far are provisional. At the time of writing, it would appear that children who receive high quality pre-school education have advantages over children who had either none or of a low quality. You can read for yourself the current findings of this project by visiting the website (www.ioe.ac.uk/schools/ecpe/eppe/index.htm).

Cathy Nutbrown

Cathy Nutbrown is, at the time of writing, a lecturer at Sheffield University. She is known for her work on promoting children's rights and respecting children as 'capable learners'. She has written many books and articles on early childhood education including the influential book *Respectful Educators, Capable Learners* (1996). In this book she explores the importance of seeing children as being competent and capable and looks at ways in which adults can work with children to foster their individuality.

Getting ready for assessment

Choose two age groups from the following:

→ 0–3 years

→ 3–7 years

→ 7–12 years

→ 12–16 years

For each age group, describe how children develop in two of the following areas:

→ physical development

→ communication and language development

→ intellectual development and learning

→ social and emotional development.

Section 2

How to use a range of observation techniques appropriate to different stages of development and circumstances

In practice

A new boy has just started at Hippo's nursery.

Theo is 4 years old and has never been to nursery before. His key person wants to find out about his development, strengths and interests.

By the end of this section you will know what type of methods Theo's key person could use and the factors that might affect the observations.

The reasons for carrying out observations

Learning to watch and think about children and young people is part of being a professional. Noticing a child's reaction as she dips her hands into paint, being aware that a young person looks slightly uneasy as he walks into the room or spotting that a baby can pass a rattle from one hand to another soon becomes part and parcel of doing a good job. Experienced practitioners often use these informal 'snapshots' as a basis for further more formal observations that are recorded. Often their 'hunches' are actually insights and by observing further a child's needs can be met.

Why observe and record?

There are many reasons why early years practitioners observe and carry out assessments on children and young people. Observations and assessments should be thought of as tools that should help you to meet children's needs and learn about the effectiveness of your own provision.

Observing children helps us learn more about them and so should, in theory, help us to work more effectively. For example, you might spot a 4-year-old who is left handed and therefore remember to put out some left-handed scissors; by observing another toddler you might notice a movement that is made just before the toilet is needed! These are examples of small day-to day needs, but observing a child might also reveal that he or she is going to require more significant support such as speech and language therapy. Identifying children who require this type of support needs to happen as early as possible in a child's life since early intervention in some areas of children's development has been shown to result in positive outcomes. This is one reason, as you will see in Section 3, why those working with babies and toddlers carry out observations that are then looked at in comparison to milestones or 'expected development'. While a baby who is not crawling at 7 months will not give any rise for concern, the same would not be true if the baby was nearing 12 months.

As well as focusing on children, observations should also be used to focus on our practice with children. The term 'reflective practitioner' is often used in this context. It means thinking about the impact you have on children's enjoyment, learning and behaviour. By observing children's responses during sessions and activities, you can reflect upon how effective you are and from this reflection consider ways in which you might become more effective.

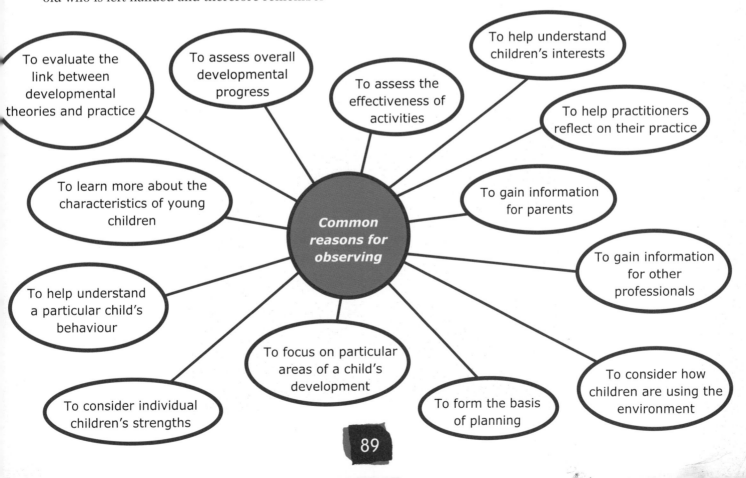

To help understand children's interests

To evaluate the link between developmental theories and practice

To assess overall developmental progress

To assess the effectiveness of activities

To help practitioners reflect on their practice

To learn more about the characteristics of young children

Common reasons for observing

To gain information for parents

To gain information for other professionals

To help understand a particular child's behaviour

To focus on particular areas of a child's development

To consider how children are using the environment

To consider individual children's strengths

To form the basis of planning

However, it is important not to fall into the trap of only observing children because there is a problem or concern. Observations should also be about children's strengths and interests, which will provide ideas for future planning. Observations should be something that you enjoy doing as they are another way of getting to know individual children and allow you to watch some of the child development theories 'in action'.

The spider diagram on the previous page shows some of the reasons why observations are helpful.

The range of techniques used and how to record observations

There are many different ways of collecting information about children and young people. Each technique will have advantages but also limitations and so it is useful if you can learn to use several. While there are different techniques, observing children is about collecting information. Knowing what you need to learn about the child is therefore important when choosing a technique.

In terms of the way in which techniques collect information there are two broad methods: closed data and open data.

Closed data methods

Closed data methods focus our attention very narrowly. A good example of a closed data method is a checklist. A checklist usually consists of groups of statements. The observer reads the statements and then considers whether or not this is what they are seeing while they observe the child.

Closed data methods are considered to be less subjective than open data methods. Their major drawback is that they can focus our attention so narrowly that some data might be missed, for example whether children smile as they skip. Closed data methods tend to be good for assessing children's skills and achievements.

Open data methods

Open data methods allow significantly more freedom as the observation format is not as narrow. The responsibility to decide what to focus on lies more with the observer, even when the situation is prescribed. This increases the likelihood of being subjective, but on the other hand more information about children might be gained.

A snapshot observation is one example of open data recording. In this type of observation, the observer jots down what he or she perceives as interesting when watching a child.

Written narrative/running record

This method is probably one of the most straightforward. It requires the observer to put into writing what is being seen. There is a surprising amount of skill required though, as it can be hard to find descriptive language quickly and to be able to write it down. This is a very subjective method of recording. The speed at which the observer must write and act means that only a small amount of information can be recorded and its selection is likely to be subjective. The language that is used to record can also be subjective. Observers will not have the time to consider carefully the vocabulary that is being used and will probably put down the first word that comes to them which they feel fits the situation, for example 'snatches' as opposed to 'takes quickly'. Most observers using this method find it helpful to take a pause from time to time so they can finish off a sentence. Afterwards, notes need to be written out so they are legible.

When to use this method

This is a versatile method and is often used as a starting point for future observations. You can choose to record any area of development or look at the child more holistically and note down things of interest as they occur. This method is often used to provide a 'snapshot' for parents.

How to use this method

You will need a reliable pen and notepad. You will also need to consider whether to be a participant or non-participant observer.

Begin by noting the start time of the observation as well as the context. Then, as you watch the child, write down what you are seeing. This method is sometimes referred to as 'running commentary' because the observer is providing a commentary. Most observers find that they need to stop after a few minutes as they are unable to write quickly enough to record down everything that a child is doing or saying. It is good practice to note the time of each 'stop' and 'start' so that anyone reading it later does not assume that it is continuous.

Advantages

- No preparation required
- Versatile
- Provides a 'portrait' of a child and so is popular with parents

Disadvantages

- Difficult to record for long periods
- Difficult to note everything that is happening

Date: 14/5/07

Child: Ayse, female, 1 year 10 months

Context: Ayse is trying to catch bubbles indoors

Ayse smiles as she sees the bubbles. Using her left hand she points to a bubble. She then stands up and uses her arm to reach it. The bubble falls to the ground and remains there. Ayse squats down and uses her index finger on her right hand to pop the bubble. She squeals and says 'more', 'more bubbles'. She stands up again and goes to the adult who blows some more bubbles. Ayse smiles and runs around in a circle. She is waving her arms in the air.

⇧ **Example of a written narrative/running record**

Find out!

1. Ask your placement supervisor if you can observe a child engaged in imaginative play. Use written narrative/running record as a technique. Your observation should include the start and end times. You should also make a note of the context and the age of the child in years and months.

2. Write a report that evaluates:

   a) your effectiveness in using this technique

   b) factors that might affect the objectivity of the observation

   c) your personal learning from using this technique.

Video and photographs

Using a camera either to photograph or film children and young people is becoming increasingly popular as an observation technique. Both techniques can help you to look and notice details that otherwise you might miss. Older children and young people can use this method to record their thoughts and be participative in the recording process.

When to use this method

This method can be used to film groups of children as well as individual children. If you wish to film children with sound, it is important to choose situations where there is not too much ambient noise. It is also important to be aware of any children who may wander into view whose parents have not given permission (this is a key disadvantage of this method).

How to use this method

This is a straightforward method as you need only to decide what to film and then to carry it out. It is worth practising first so that you can use the equipment easily. Remember to check that the camera has sufficient battery power. It is important to write down the time and date of the observation so that you do not forget. It is also important to get children used to this as otherwise they may be more interested in what you are doing rather than carrying on with their play or activity.

Advantages

- It is easy to review what children are doing and to notice detail.
- It is popular with parents as they can see what their children have been doing.
- Older children and young people can use this as a medium to show what is important in their lives.

Disadvantages

- Confidentiality can be an issue – children can only be filmed with parental consent and this includes children who are not the focus of the observation but who may stray into shot.
- Background noises can prevent you from hearing what the children are saying.

Target child observations

Target child observations note the actions and responses of a particular child over a continuous period of time. Target child observations require the observer to be very focused and to work intensively. The observer uses codes to ensure that they can record down what the child is doing minute by minute.

When to use this method

This method is often used to learn about individual children. While it can be used to provide a holistic observation, it is generally used to focus on children's social and language interaction.

How to use this method

This is an observation that needs to be planned ahead. It requires the observer to only focus on one child and so means that the observer is not able to work with other children at the time.

→ Begin by deciding which child is to be observed.
→ Consider whether this will be a participant or non-participant observation.
→ Prepare or photocopy a recording sheet (see example below).
→ Read through and check that you can remember the codes that are to be used.
→ Write the start time on the sheet and use a stopwatch or clock thereafter.
→ For each minute, record down what the child is doing. Use codes to ensure that you can keep up to date with the recording.

Advantages

- Provides detailed information about a child's activity over a continuous period
- Codes are used to enable the recorder to write more effectively

Disadvantages

- Observer needs to be familiar with the coding system and practice using it

---

Individual child-tracking observation

Name of child: Lee   Age of child: 3 years 2 months   Observer: Carrie

Date: 24/10/07   No. of adults present: 2   No. of children present: 6

Free play / Structured play / Directed activity

Time	Description of activity	Language	Grouping	Level of involvement
10.00am	TC scooping sand using left hand repeated movements	TC →	P	4
10.02	TC burying r. hand, scooping with other	→ TC ←	I	4
10.03	TC nods head. Other child copies TC. TC smiles	C → TC	P	3

Key:

Grouping	Language	Level of involvement
WG = whole group SG = small group P = Pair I = Individual	TC → A Balanced interaction between adult and child TC → C Balanced interaction target chld and another child A → C Adult interacts with more than one child C → TC Another child interacts with target child → TC ← Target child talks to himself/ herself TC → No interaction	1 = No activity 2 = Frequently distracted 3 = Fairly continuous activity 4 = Absorbed in activity

⇧ **Example of a target child observation**

Checklists and tick charts

Checklists and tick charts are a popular method of observing children. This is because they are easy to use and understand. They are used in many settings and form the basis of most systems of record keeping on children and young people.

When to use this method

This method can be used when you need to look at a child's or young person's skill or knowledge. A teaching assistant may, for example, use a tick chart in order to assess which letter sounds a 5-year-old knows. This is also a good method to see how much progress a child has made as the same tick chart can be used a few weeks later.

How to use this method

A sheet is prepared with a list of statements. You need to read carefully through the tasks or skills before beginning the observation. When you observe the child, you note whether he or she is able to do them; a tick or remark is recorded on the prepared sheet accordingly. This is an observation technique that can be done unobtrusively, by simply watching the child and hoping that he or she will show the skills to be recorded, or as a participant, by asking the child to carry out the required tasks.

Advantages

- Simple to use
- Easier to be objective

Disadvantages

- Does not show 'how' the child manages the skill as it is closed data recording

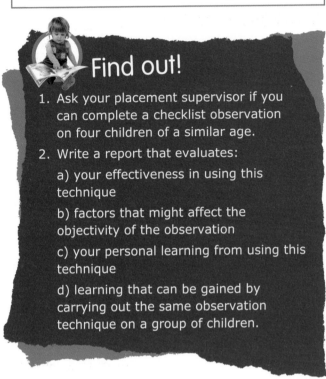

Find out!

1. Ask your placement supervisor if you can complete a checklist observation on four children of a similar age.
2. Write a report that evaluates:

   a) your effectiveness in using this technique

   b) factors that might affect the objectivity of the observation

   c) your personal learning from using this technique

   d) learning that can be gained by carrying out the same observation technique on a group of children.

Name of child: ....

Age of child: .... Observer: ....

Date of observation: .... Time: ....

Activity	Yes	No	Comments
Puts together three-piece puzzle			
Snips with scissors			
Paints in circular movements			
Holds crayons with fingers, not fists			
Can thread four large beads			
Turns pages in a book one by one			
Can put on and take off coat			

⇧ **Example of a checklist**

Graphs and charts

Strictly speaking, graphs and charts are not really 'observations' as they used to record information rather than to observe children. However, there are many situations in which graphs and charts might be used. These include tracking children's growth and providing information about a child's performance, for example the number of times a baby wakes in the night during one week. Graphs and charts can allow us to see quickly any trends that are developing such as a baby's weight gain slowing down. An example of a centile chart is shown on page 37.

Advantages
• Useful way of presenting information simply
• Easy to compare information

Disadvantages
• Does not explain the context, for example why a child has put on weight or how the baby is helped back to sleep

Time samples

Time samples are interesting and versatile. They provide information about a child's activity at regular intervals, for example what a child is doing during a session at 10-minute intervals. Time samples can be made structured and can be used with codes, but equally they can be freer with observers simply using a running commentary style when the sample is taken.

When to use this method

This is a useful method when looking at a child's activity over the whole or part of a session. It is less intensive than the target child observation or the written narrative/running records, and leaves the observer free to look at other children in between the samples. It is also a good method for looking at children's all-round development in a range of contexts, for example social interaction while the child is playing indoors with the sand, but also 20 minutes later when the child is playing outdoors on a tricycle.

How to use the method

The starting point for this method is to decide how structured the time sample needs to be. A structured recording will mean that a sheet will need to be drawn in advance and you will need to be familiar with codes. You will also need to decide how often you will 'sample' the child's activity. This may partly depend on the length of time you intend to observe, for example 5-minute intervals for observations that last for less than an hour, and 15-minute intervals for all-day observations. It is unlikely that sample times greater than 15 minutes will be very informative.

Once you have determined the range of the time sample, the next step is simply to record what you see when it is time to observe. While it can be helpful to observe the child in the interim, it is important only to record at the sample times.

⏱ **An unstructured time sample; recordings have been made at 15-minute intervals**

Time	Activity	Social group	Comments
11.00	Snack time	Whole group	Anna is sitting with her legs swinging on a chair. She is eating an apple. She is holding it in her left hand and she is smiling. She puts up her hand when a member of staff asks who wants a biscuit.
11.15	Outdoor play; climbing frame	Anna and Ben	Anna is on the top bar of the climbing frame. She is smiling at Ben. She calls 'Come up here!'
11.30	Taking coats off	Anna, Ben and Manjeet	Anna unzips her coat and pulls out one arm. She swings around and the coat swings with her. She laughs and looks at Manjeet.

Event sample

Event samples are sometimes referred to as 'frequency counts'. The aim of these observations is to find out how often a specific type of behaviour or response takes place and the context in which it occurs. They are often used when a child is showing unwanted behaviour, but can be used more broadly. They can help a practitioner to work out reasons behind certain responses, but also provide evidence to show whether the number of responses or incidents are increasing or decreasing. Event samples are not strictly observations as recording takes place after the 'event' or incident has occurred.

When to use this method

Event samples focus narrowly on a particular response of a child. For example, you might decide to investigate how often a child has a tantrum and the context in which this occurs, or you might look at how often a child interacts with other children.

Using this method

A sheet that directs the user to the type of information to be collected has to be drawn up. There are no 'standard' formats, as the recording columns should reflect the observer's requirements for information. Commonly collected information includes date and time as well as background context. The example below shows an event sample that is focusing on the number of times a child interacts with adults in a setting. In this situation, it will be important to see exactly who the child talks to and for how long. It will also be useful to find out whether the child initiates the contact or whether this is done by the adult.

Once the recording sheet is drawn up, it is only filled in when the specific behaviour or response is noted. In settings where several adults might work with a child, the person who was working with the child at the time might fill in the recording sheet.

Example of an event sample

Event	Time	Food eaten	Quality of food	Setting	Comments
1	8.04–8.09am	Squares of toast, drink of milk	Equivalent to half a slice of toast and half a beaker of milk	High chair, kitchen	Some squares of toast were dropped on the floor. Joachim sipped milk after eating toast and dropped beaker on the floor. Said 'No more, all gone' and raised arms to be taken out of chair.
2	9.45–9.47am	Biscuit	Most of biscuit	Lounge, standing up	Joachim went up to adult and pointed to her biscuit. Adult gave the biscuit.
3	10.15–10.20am	Biscuit	Half a biscuit	Kitchen, standing up	Joachim pointed to biscuit tin and said 'More, more!' Adult gave biscuit. Some biscuit eaten, rest dropped on floor.

Observing groups

It can be useful to observe groups of children together. This is not always easy to do, but can provide interesting information about how children interact with each other and use the environment.

Sociograms

Sociograms are a way of finding out about children's friendship preferences (see also pages 58–9). They are not a perfect tool especially with children under 4 years old as many children choose their playmates according to the play activity rather than a friendship loyalty. Neither are they strictly an observation method, as they rely on what children tell or show us rather than observing them directly.

When to use this method

This method suits children in the Reception class upwards or slightly younger children who are in full-time group care. The danger of asking children in sessional care situations is that they are likely to base their responses on who they have most recently played with. This means that a child who has been absent due to illness or a holiday might be 'forgotten'.

How to use this method

The simplest way of using this method is to ask individual children when they are alone, who they most enjoy playing with. You then need to write down their responses. You might also be interested in finding out what they like doing with this child, for example playing outdoors, as this can help you build up a picture of whether children are choosing playmates on the basis of shared play interests.

Once you have talked to each of the children in the group, a simple chart is drawn up such as the one shown below. Note that while you might find that some children are named more frequently than others, you cannot assume that children who are rarely or never named do not have friends. In schools, some children make friends with children who are in different classes. The next step from a sociogram is to observe individual children and see the quality of their social interactions.

⌂ **Example sociogram**

Name	Friend 1	Friend 2	Friend 3
Jo	Simon	Ian	Darren
Darren	Peter	Jo	Simon
George	Owen	Curran	Jo
Owen	George	Peter	Ahmed
Ahmed	Owen	Simon	Peter
Peter	Ian	Jo	Darren
Jose	Simon	Ahmed	Ravi
Simon	Darren	Curran	Ravi
Curran	Simon	Jo	George
Ian	Jo	Peter	George
Ravi	Becky	Marina	Simon
Sarah	Becky	Anne	Kirsty
Kirsty	Anne	Becky	George
Becky	Marina	Sarah	Ravi

Advantages

- Can identify children who may need support with social skills

Disadvantages

- There are many variables as children may not remember about friends who are absent or may give a name based on who they last played with

Mapping

Mapping is used to see how children move around the setting and how long individual children stay with particular activities.

When to use this method

Mapping can be used to assess how effective the provision is or when you have many children who do not appear to settle down to activities. Mapping can also provide insights into which materials and activities are the most attractive to children.

How to use this method

Begin by drawing a floor plan which shows the main activities and equipment that is available. The plan needs to be fairly accurate, although it does not have

to be to scale. You will also need an accurate watch, preferably digital, and a coloured crayon for each of the children whose movements you are mapping.

When you are ready to start the observation, note the children's movements and times as they move around during the session. Use a different coloured crayon for each child that you are observing.

Advantages

- Can provide information about popularity of equipment, especially if more than one child is being tracked at a time
- Can give an indication of a child's play preferences

Disadvantages

- A diagrammatic approach without any written information does not provide detailed information about what the child or young person was doing, so it can be difficult to draw conclusions about development
- Levels of concentration cannot be assessed from this as the observation only shows the movements of the child

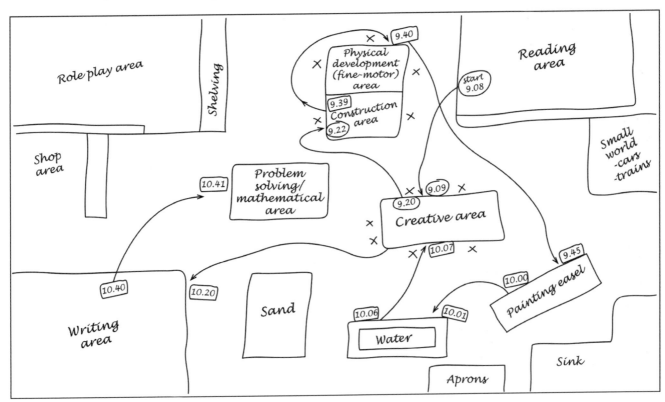

⇧ **An example of mapping**

How to practice the observation techniques in a range of practical contexts

It is important to practice carrying out observations so that you become more skilled at knowing what to look out for but also recording accurately. It is also important to try observing in a range of different situations so that you can 'see' children in a variety of contexts.

Getting ready to observe

As a learner, it is useful to plan observations carefully. You will need to think about the technique that you need to practise, the area of development or 'theory' that you want to look at and the context. You will also need to talk to your placement supervisor so that time is set aside when you can observe and so that you know you are observing with permission.

Asking permission

The starting point for any observation is to ask parents' permission or, in the case of learners on a placement, to ask their placement supervisor's permission. Most parents will happily give their permission as they are interested in their children's development and progress. It is usual for parents to sign to say that they give permission for observations and assessments to take place when their child first joins the setting. Observations should not be carried out without prior permission.

Good practice checklist

Preparing for an observation

✓ Talk to your placement supervisor about the type of observation that you wish to carry out.

✓ Find out when it will be convenient to carry out the observation.

✓ Make sure that you have everything you need to carry out the observation.

✓ Ask whether your placement supervisor would like to see your observation.

✓ Make sure that your observation is kept secure (read about confidentiality below).

What makes a good observation?

Many qualifications require that learners present observations and assessments of children. The reason behind this requirement is that it shows whether they have a good underpinning knowledge of child development. So, what makes a good observation?

→ *Clear aims and relevant method.* The more focused you are as an observer, the more accurate and detailed your observation record will be.

→ *Open methods of recording.* To show your skills, the best methods of recording tend to be open methods. This is because you can collect a wide pool of information about a child. Closed methods, for example, a checklist, provide less information about the hows and whys of a child's responses.

→ *Detail.* The more detailed your information, the easier it is to support your conclusions with evidence.

Practice observations linked to theories of development

Below are some suggestions for observations that you might like to try out. They are linked to some of the theories of development that were described earlier in this section.

The importance of confidentiality of information

All children, young people and their families have a right to confidentiality. Observations and assessments are useful tools that most parents are happy for early years practitioners to carry out. They are also potential sources of sensitive information. This means that you have to understand they are confidential.

Observations and assessments should be stored properly, which usually means in a secure place. It is therefore important that, as a learner, you do not discuss observations with anyone other than those people who are directly responsible for the care of the child. As the bounds of confidentiality can sometimes be difficult to establish, it is therefore always advisable to ask a supervisor first before disclosing any information about a child or young person.

As well as good practice in terms of confidentiality, you should be aware that there is legislation that looks at the way in which personal information can

Age group	Area of study	Method
0–1 years	Object permanence	• Begin by reading the theory of object permanence on page 68. • Ask permission from your placement supervisor. • Show the baby a toy. Make sure that the baby is looking at it as you 'hide' it close to the baby, e.g. under a box. • Observe to see whether the baby tries to find it.
2–3 years	Attachment	• Begin by reading the theory of attachment on page 80. • Ask permission from your placement supervisor. • Observe children's reactions as the parents pick them up at the end of a session. Look out for attachment behaviours.
3–7 years	Conservation	• Begin by reading about conservation on page 69. • Ask permission from your placement supervisor. • Show a child a ball of dough. Roll it out to make a long sausage. Ask the child whether there is now more dough. Record the child's response. • Repeat with an older child.
7–12 years	Self-image	• Begin by reading about the development of self-image on page 59. • Ask permission from your placement supervisor. • Ask two children of different ages to either write about themselves or to describe themselves to you.
12–16 years	Moral development	• Begin by reading about moral development on page 74. • Ask permission from your placement supervisor. • Ask a young person whether there are any circumstances in which it is morally acceptable to steal. • Tell a story about a poor mother whose family does not have enough to eat. The mother steals from a cruel shopkeeper who has already refused to give the family food. Ask the young person if this would be acceptable and to provide reasons for his or her thoughts.

be used. The Data Protection Act 1998 was passed to protect individuals' rights and to prevent breaches of information. The Act applies to all settings whether or not they keep computerised records (see also page 224).

Rights of access

It is good practice for parents to have access to observations and assessments and so the term 'open records' is often used in this respect. In early years settings, parents are positively encouraged to be part of the observation and assessment process. This is useful because it allows them to 'see' their children in a variety of different situations. In addition, in England, parents can request schools and other educational establishments to provide them with information they are keeping about their child under the Education (Pupil Information) (England) Regulations 2005. The only time that observations and records should not be made available is when the child's security and welfare may be endangered, for example where there is suspected child abuse, in which case the child protection procedures for the setting should be followed.

Learning the language of observations

It is always useful to think about how you write about a child or young person. It is worth remembering that one day, the parent, young person or child may read it. This means that you should be careful about what you write and think about whether you would like someone to write in this way about you or a close family member! In Section 3, you will look at ways to ensure that your assessments of children are accurate rather than simply negative (see pages 106–8).

The need for objectivity when observing children

You have a great responsibility towards children and young people when you observe and assess them. This may sound dramatic, but it is nevertheless true. This is because observations and assessments can lead to children and young people being labelled and thus stereotyped.

Adults' expectations have an important influence on children and young people's behaviour and achievement. This means that a child who is seen as being 'slow' may not be given the same challenges as another child and may thus unintentionally be held back. In addition, children and young people's development is not uniform and does not follow a neatly packaged journey; children develop at different rates and their own path of development can be irregular. Children and young people are also affected by factors outside of the setting. For example, the loss of a pet, the breakdown of a relationship or the excitement of a birthday are all factors that might easily influence the way in which a child or young person behaves or performs a task.

Aiming for objectivity

While observation and assessment of children and young people is not a perfect science, it is important that you take steps to make observations and assessments as objective as possible. The many ways in which you might attempt to do this are described below.

Building up pictures of development

Wherever possible, it is important to build up a picture of a child or young person rather than rely on a single observation or assessment strategy. This is important when you need to collect information about behaviour or an area of development as opposed to a skill such as whether a child can pour a glass of water.

Building up a picture means seeing the child or young person involved in different situations and, if possible, in different contexts. It may also mean talking to parents, other carers and even the child or young person. It is also helpful in building up a picture to use more than one observation or assessment tool. As you have seen, each method has its advantages as well as disadvantages so a mixture of open and closed data techniques is desirable.

It is also good practice to observe and assess children and young people over time. This can help you gain a better picture of development and behaviour. It also avoids situations where a child or young person is seen as being atypical, when in reality there was a 'blip' in their usual pattern of behaviour. Where a single observation or assessment is used, it is therefore essential to qualify it as such when writing a report or passing on information to parents or others or planning activities.

Trying to keep an open mind

Objectivity is about being open minded and suspending judgements. This is essential when observing and assessing, but it can be extremely difficult too. If you know the child, his or her family or have any prior knowledge, there is a danger that subconsciously you have already formed some expectations. It is therefore important to be aware that this is the case and try to see the child or young person with 'fresh' eyes. It is also important to avoid drawing premature conclusions as you look at a child during the observation.

In general terms, during the observation it is worth seeing yourself as a collector of information; working out what this means is a separate step (described in Section 3 of this unit). This is useful when observing and assessing all children, but particularly those that have already developed a 'label', whether a positive or negative one. There is a real danger otherwise that observations become tools to confirm rather than to learn by.

⚓ **When observing a child it is important try to keep an open mind**

Participant versus non-participant observations

When looking at objectivity, it is important to be aware that the way in which you have carried out observations and assessments can also have an impact. If you have been with the child or young person and have talked, played or watched him or her, you will have been a participant observer. The term non-participant observer is used when the observer is unobtrusive and does not interact.

Participant observations

The extent to which you engage with a child or young person during an observation or assessment can make a considerable difference to the outcome. A person who chats to a child while they complete a task influences the child. The child may, for example, try extra hard in order to please the adult or the adult's presence may make the child feel slightly nervous! The term 'participant observation' is used when the observer is involved in some way.

How well the child or young person knows the observer can also make a difference to the outcome. A child who likes being with you may be more relaxed but sometimes a young person, for example, may be embarrassed by being watched by someone they know.

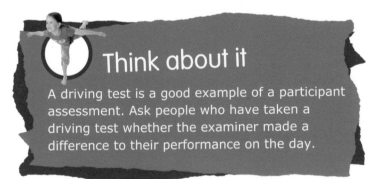

Think about it

A driving test is a good example of a participant assessment. Ask people who have taken a driving test whether the examiner made a difference to their performance on the day.

Observer bias

As well as children and young people responding differently when there is a participant observer, so too does the observer. First, the observer may 'miss' something as they are busy engaging with the child or young person. For example, you may not notice that a young person's body language is quite tense as your focus might be to listen out for their speech. A non-participant observer is literally at a distance and so can often 'see' more clearly what is happening.

As a participant observer you might want to encourage the child or young person and show in your body language or even comments that he or she is doing well. In the same way, you might be tempted to mark down that a child or young person has achieved something when in reality they need a little support! This is called observer bias and particularly comes into play when you know the child or young person, as the Case study on the next page shows.

Non-participant observations and assessments

Non-participant observations have some clear advantages when it comes to objectivity. Not being involved with the child or young person can make it easier to be more objective about what you are seeing or what the child is able to achieve. It can also be easier to actually record down what you are seeing if you are not 'part of the action'. Young children, for example, may want to talk to you or want you to play with them!

While there are advantages with non-participant observations and assessments, there are also disadvantages. As a non-participant you might not be able to hear or see the whole context in terms of what is happening. For example, a non-participant sitting behind a two-way mirror may not 'feel' the emotional climate that surrounds the child or young person.

A non-participant may also not be able to clarify with the child or young person what they are doing or what they mean. For example, a child may be talking about a 'dor-dor' but a non-participant observer will not be able to ask a follow-up question to find out what the child is referring to. In the same way, a young person solving a problem may have a clear rational for what they are trying to achieve, but the non-participant will not know this. This can be one reason why, for example, an exam or written test may sometimes throw up odd results: the marker of the maths paper will be a non-participant and therefore not necessarily able to know what is going through the mind of the young person who is sitting the exam.

Case study

Observer bias

Kylie is 4 years old. She is interested in writing her name and has been spending a lot of time sitting down at the mark-making table and having a go. Beth, her key worker, has noted Kylie's interest and has played games with her, focusing on her name. She has also been writing Kylie's name in front of her so that Kylie gets a feel of the shapes and how to form them.

Beth has been asked to assess whether Kylie can write her name. Beth asks Kylie if she would write her name on a piece of paper. Kylie writes her name but forgets one of the letters and reverses another letter. Beth is faced with a dilemma as the assessment sheet is a tick box. She must either tick a 'yes' or a 'no'. Beth thinks about the day before when Kylie almost perfectly wrote her name. She ticks the 'yes' box.

1. Explain the factors that may have influenced Beth's recording.

2. Would an adult who did not know Kylie have reached the same conclusion?

⇩ The advantages and disadvantages of being a participant and non-participant observer

	Participant observer	Non-participant observer
Advantages	✓ Is able to adapt tasks in response to the child's or young person's needs ✓ Can ask the child or young person to do something rather than wait for it to occur spontaneously ✓ Can ask the child or young person to explain why they are doing something or how they are feeling	✓ Is less likely to have observer bias ✓ Can be easier to notice and focus on body language ✓ May find it easier to record
Disadvantages	✗ Child or young person may feel under pressure and react differently ✗ Child or young person may focus more on pleasing the adult rather than the task ✗ Observer may be biased when recording	✗ May not see or 'feel' the context ✗ Is not able to ask for clarifications or explanations from the child or young person

Attitudes, values and beliefs

A person's attitudes, values and beliefs play a major part in their ability to perceive and select information. What you 'see' is significantly determined by what you expect to see. A good example of this is the way in which you might mis-read a word in a text such as 'the cat sat on the map and licked its whiskers'.

Research has shown that people have 'selective memory', which is linked to their expectations, stereotypes and beliefs. In terms of observing children, this can mean that early years practitioners focus on what they expect to see.

⇧ Have you worked out that there is an extra word here?

Counteracting the effects of attitudes, values and beliefs

A key step in striving for objectivity is to recognise that you hold attitudes, values and beliefs and to recognise them. You must also be ready to question how your thoughts might influence what you see. In practical terms, it is usually a good idea if more than one person observes the same child so that different viewpoints can be considered. It is also worth gaining information from adults who may see the child in a different light, for example parents, relatives or other professionals.

As the conclusions drawn from observations can heavily influence the way in which adults work with children, it is also important for you to observe 'positively'. This means looking out for the things that children can do and the times when they respond well. This is especially important when observing children because early years practitioners have concerns about their progress and development.

The limitations of observations in providing a complete picture of development and individual needs

Factors that might influence observations

As well as thinking about the techniques you use, it is helpful to be aware of the factors that might affect the observations. Children, young people and observers are not robots! This means that a number of factors can influence what you might see and record during an observation.

Environmental

The environment around you and the child can have significant effects. Children's responses might change during a thunderstorm or if they hear a doorbell ring. Your ability to observe might also be hampered if you are being interrupted or are distracted by other things around you.

Emotional

Children and adults are not machines. This means that your ability to observe can be influenced by what you are feeling and, in the same way, children's responses will be altered by their feelings. A child who has fallen out with a friend at break time might not respond in the same way as a child who is celebrating a birthday. Responses are particularly affected when children know they are being watched or feel under pressure.

Physical

Physical factors are another influence. Children who are tired or hungry may find it hard to concentrate while if adults are tired, the observation might not be as focused.

Other factors

There are many other factors that influence validity such as how interested the child is in the activity they are doing. The time that you have available to observe is also a key factor as sometimes you might miss a child doing something because you have left the room! In the same way, some children respond differently according to who they are with. Groups of friends might chat more and be distracted, while a child with unfamiliar children might seem quite quiet.

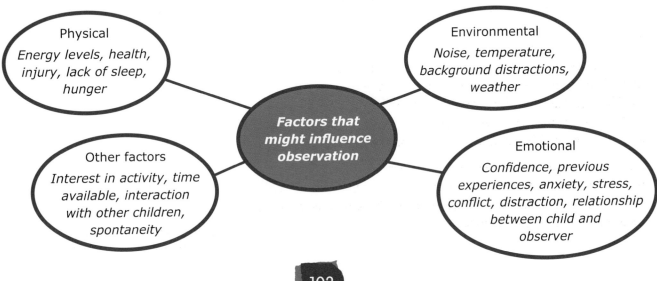

Case study

How being observed can affect children's responses

A physiotherapist is visiting a nursery to see how well a child is managing to cope with the steps. Today is a particularly hectic day as the children are getting ready for a party in the afternoon. The child who is to be observed has also been absent for a few days with a stomach upset and has not been eating as much as usual.

The physiotherapist is only able to spend half an hour in the setting and really needs to watch the child attempt the stairs to see what type of equipment or support is required, if necessary. She has not met the child before. After saying 'hello' and having a little chat, she asks the boy whether he would show her how he goes up the stairs. The child does so, but the key worker who is also watching notices that he is much slower and more deliberate in his steps than usual.

1. Is this an example of a participant or non-participant observation?

2. Consider the factors that might have affected this child's responses?

3. Why is it important to be aware of factors that can affect children's responses?

Good practice checklist

Recognising factors that might influence observations

✓ Have I used a range of different techniques?

✓ Have I used a mixture of open and closed data collection?

✓ Have I observed children in a variety of different situations?

✓ Am I aware of factors that might have influenced the child's responses, behaviour or achievement?

✓ Was I a participant observer and if so how might I have been influenced?

Getting ready for assessment

Choose an area of development from the list below:

➜ physical development

➜ communication and language development

➜ intellectual development and learning

➜ social and emotional development.

1. Carry out three observations on the same child using three different observation techniques, looking at this area of development.

2. Briefly outline how you have maintained the child's right to confidentiality.

How to assess the development of children and reflect upon the implications for practice

In practice

The key person at Hippo's nursery has now spoken to the new boy's parents and carried out several different observations. It is now time to look at the information that has been collected.

By the end of this section you will know how to evaluate information gained from observations and how to make the best use of the information.

Using observations to assess development

Collecting information by carrying out observations on children needs to be seen as the starting point rather than the end point. The next step is to evaluate the information although the way in which you might do this will vary. As a learner, you might evaluate observations as a learning tool for your own professional development and feedback your thoughts to your supervisor. As a practitioner, observations might be evaluated so that information can be passed on to parents and, more importantly, so that you can plan more effectively for the child's needs and interests.

Links to norms of development

Norms of development or milestones are often used as a starting point in order to interpret what you have seen. Looking at the normative development may help you realise that a child's development is completely typical of their age group. On the other hand, it may help you realise that the child might need further support.

Normative development is especially looked at in children's earliest years. This is because early identification of needs often makes a significant difference to later outcomes. One of the reasons why early identification is so important is that development is interlinked. For example, a child with atypical speech and language may find it harder to control behaviour and thus may not be invited into other children's play.

Visiting normative development can be especially important when looking at young children's behaviour. A child who is with a peer group whose behaviour is actually in advance of expected development may appear to be 'difficult and uncooperative', when in reality the behaviour is within the expected range for their age.

Looking at normative development can also help you to be aware of what the child needs to go on and do. This might help when planning equipment and activities and when checking that sufficient challenges are being provided.

Progress is also important

While looking at normative development is a good starting point, you also need to be aware that rate of progress is important. A child whose first words came at 20 months rather than the expected 14 months, but who is now making rapid progress, is probably not a cause for concern. It would be wise, however, to keep checking that the progress is ongoing.

Using curriculum guidance and profiles

Many practitioners will carry out observations on children as they have to assess them against curriculum objectives or profiles. Usually observations are planned with this in mind but there will also be occasions when a snapshot type of observation will be used to support records. It is important here to be aware that there are sometimes discrepancies between such profiles and the theories of child development/normative development. Knowing this can be helpful as sometimes a child may look as if they are not doing very well against a profile, when their development measured against normative development looks fine. The key is to understand the educational profiles have been drawn up with the agenda of improving standards.

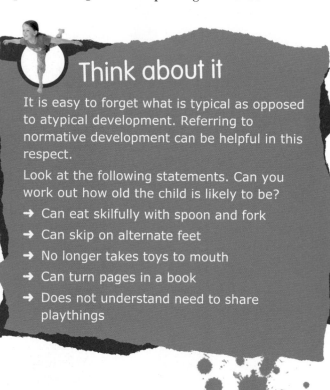

Think about it

It is easy to forget what is typical as opposed to atypical development. Referring to normative development can be helpful in this respect.

Look at the following statements. Can you work out how old the child is likely to be?

→ Can eat skilfully with spoon and fork
→ Can skip on alternate feet
→ No longer takes toys to mouth
→ Can turn pages in a book
→ Does not understand need to share playthings

How to use developmental theory to interpret observations

As well as looking at normative development, which is often linked to skills, you should also think about theories of development. Theories of development are often helpful in understanding the reasons behind the actions and thoughts of children and young people. This is very useful as it can help you to be more strategic in guiding behaviour and to 'see' what the child needs in terms of planning and further experiences.

In Section 1 of this unit you looked at some key theories of development (pages 66–87) and you are likely to be able to 'see these in action' when you watch children and young people. In addition, you should also be aware of theories that link to play which are covered in Unit 7.

More than one theory at work!

In most observations, you should find that there is more than one theory at work; the case study below is a good example of this. Children may be using language and symbols in their play. They may also be looking for adult support, attention or praise. In addition, the way that they are playing may be giving them particular cognitive benefits.

Case study

Linking to theories of development

Ayse is 18 months old. She has been given a washing-up bowl full of coloured dried rice. She has been dropping toy animals in the rice and covering them over. She has then taken great pleasure in uncovering them and showing them to her key person. She has spent fifteen minutes repeating this play.

1. Why does Ayse repeat these actions?
2. Is this behaviour typical of her age group?
3. Why does she keep showing them to her key person?
4. What is she learning and practising from hiding and finding?

The evaluation of individual needs through observation

It is important when evaluating observations to think about the meaning behind what you have watched or the information that you have collected. You have seen that one of the questions that you might ask yourself is whether the actions, skills or behaviour is typical of the age group (normative development). The next stage is to review theories of development and see if you can make a connection between these and the observation. Research and reading about children is therefore an important part of carrying out an observation. Part of the evaluation process can sometimes lead a practitioner to realise that they have not used the best technique to collect information or that they need to observe the child again. Finally, evaluation means thinking about how you can best support the child and this means observations have to link to planning.

A step-by-step guide to evaluating observations

1. Read about the age of child that you have observed.
2. Now read through your observations.
3. Underline or make a note of anything that links to what you have read about this age group or equally anything that you have seen that seemed surprising or interesting.
4. Each section that you have underlined can now form the basis of the points to write about.
5. Decide on a logical order for these points, remembering that this does not have to be in the chronological order in which it appeared in the observation. For example, you might write about the child's interactions with other children even though they were interspersed in the observation.
6. For each point, write about what you observed and then about the conclusions that you have drawn. For example, 'Meltem smiled several times while she was talking to Kylie. I think this means that she is fairly relaxed and has good social skills.'
7. To show that you have researched theories of development and have an understanding of normative development, you should then link your point to a theory of normative development by using a relevant quote either directly or indirectly (see page 22). Note that it is essential that the quote is relevant, otherwise you will look as if you don't really understand what you have seen!

8. After you have made your points, it is helpful if you can reflect on how you might work further with the child. This shows that you can link theory with practice and that you know how to plan.

9. Finally, you might write a conclusion which summarises your own learning about using the observation method and about the child. You might also include your ideas for future observations.

Using the planning cycle to meet individual needs of children and promote development

Observations not only need to be evaluated; feedback from the observations links into the planning process. The term planning cycle is often used to describe this process. It should be a continual process as children's development is not static and because their interests and needs will change over time. Continued observations also mean that early years practitioners are able to assess the effectiveness of their planning (see also page 373).

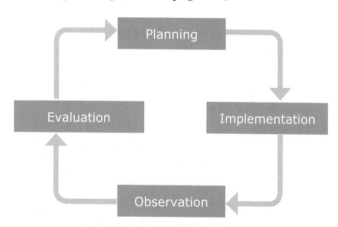

⬆ **The planning cycle – a term used to describe how planning, implementation, observation and evaluation work is an ongoing process**

How planning might be linked to observations

This can be at a number of different levels. One of the most important of these is to plan for individual children. The way in which this may be done will vary from setting to setting. Many settings looking after babies, toddlers and young children will produce individual plans for each child. Some settings will also have ways of showing how plans are to be adapted to meet individual children's needs and strengths.

Planning for individual children's interests and strengths

It is good practice for observations on individual children to be used in order to plan for their particular strengths or interests. This means that a child who is interested in toy cars or playing with water may have some activities planned to enhance their interest. This is particularly important when working with babies, toddlers and young children and is considered to be good practice.

Planning for individual children's interests means that they can learn more effectively as they are already interested in what they are doing. Older children and young people also need us to plan for their interests too, but this needs to be done in discussion with them. With older children this might be a case of noticing what they enjoy doing and talking through with them various options or asking them what they feel they need.

Planning for individual children's needs

The evaluation of observations may also help you to identify a child's individual needs. For example, you may notice that a child needs a little extra time or adult support, or that they might benefit by repeating an activity. Recognising needs is an important part of work with children and is sometime referred to as Personalised Learning. Observations may also help you realise that a child needs more support in a particular area of development such as speech and language. If these needs cannot be met by simply adapting equipment or activities, you may go on to create an Individual Education Plan (IEP) with the help of parents (see page 521).

Being aware of needs may also mean noticing activities where children need additional challenges or extensions. This is important as poor behaviour can sometimes be linked to a lack of stimulation.

Planning for groups of children

Evaluation of observations can help you plan your work for groups of children. You may use individual observations to realise that a group of children might have similar interests or be at a similar level of development. Planning for groups of children while taking into consideration individual needs is required when working with relatively large groups of children.

Case study

Using observations to review practice

Staff at Amershot Nursery looked at children's responses during story time and from this evaluated several individual children's speech and language. The observations proved useful in order to match stories to children's language levels. From this, they decided to change the way they organised story time to make sure that it met the children's language needs. Children were placed in smaller groups and the stories read were shorter and simpler. Staff found that children who previously found it hard to listen began to enjoy story time more.

1. What type of techniques could be used to observe story time and to assess individual children's speech and language?
2. Why is it important to use observations when planning activities that involve groups of children?
3. How might individual children benefit from the changes that have been made?

Planning changes to practice

Some observations may tell you about the setting's practice, for example the effectiveness of the layout or routine. Sometimes, children's behaviour may seem to follow a trend and the reason behind this behaviour may link back to what is being provided for them. Following the evaluation of the observations, you might therefore look at the planning of the room layout or the routine, as the case study below shows.

Case study

Changing practice

A member of staff at Greenfields Primary School decided to observe groups of children as they played outdoors at break time. Traditionally, this had been a time when there were often squabbles between children. He used several methods in order to look at what children were doing, where they were going and the type of play and interactions used. He did this for a week in order to build up a picture that could be used to evaluate.

After looking at the observations carefully, he came to several conclusions that he talked through with colleagues. First, he felt that break time may be too short as some groups of children settled down only to be told to line up. He also concluded that some children needed more adult support to get play going and that there needed to be a greater variety of equipment available. Afterwards, it was decided to make some changes and then to observe the children playing in order to assess the impact.

1. What observation techniques could have been used for this situation?
2. Why is it helpful to use observations to look at the setting's practice?
3. Why would it be important to carry on observing the children?

Using information from a range of relevant sources

There are many times when you may use information from others. For example, you might do this in order to find out whether your observations are reflective of a child's needs or you may need advice and ideas as how best to plan next for the child.

Parents

Parents spend a lot of time with their children. They tend to know their children well and have seen them grow and develop. Parents also see their children in a range of different situations and with a range of different people. This means that they are well placed to help early years practitioners make sense of what they have seen, but also contribute to the assessment of their children.

The way in which settings involve parents varies enormously, but in children's earliest years their involvement is seen as vital. Many settings therefore work with parents to look at their child's progress together. Parents may, for example, bring in photographs or videos clips, or take completed checklists home.

It is also good practice to show parents observations that you have done and to sound out with them whether the picture you are developing of their child seems to correlate with their knowledge of him or her. Working with parents closely also means that if ever there are concerns about development, they can be discussed immediately and further observations planned. This is better than parents being 'summoned' and told that there are concerns (see also Unit 12).

Parents are also able to help when planning for the child. Parents tend to know what their child has enjoyed before or their current interests at home. Parents can also let you know what has or hasn't worked before and they may also be able to give you ideas. This is especially important when working with children who have additional needs.

Note that as a learner you might not be able to work with parents in this way as it is normally the role of the child's key person, but you should remember that this is how it should work later.

Colleagues

Colleagues can be helpful in being objective and providing more information. They may have worked with the child previously and have come to different conclusions. Sometimes colleagues can be asked to look at an observation or to carry one out for you on the child you are interested in. A different pair of eyes can sometimes reach other conclusions and this can be helpful in terms of objectivity. When it comes to planning, colleagues may have more experience and a good knowledge of available resources.

Early Years advisory teams/additional support teams

In most areas, there are early years advisory teams and additional support teams that support children with special or additional needs. These can be good sources of support when trying to assess development, but can also give advice as to how to meet needs. It is worth noting here that you will need to find out the 'title' of the team in your area and the extent of their role. Some teams work only in schools while others will support all groups.

Voluntary organisations

Voluntary organisations can be extremely useful as sources of information, especially when you are trying to meet individual needs. An example of this might be a child who is left-handed and is finding writing a struggle; advice, information and lists of equipment are available from www.anythingleft-handed.co.uk. Voluntary organisations tend these days to have websites although some also have phone lines.

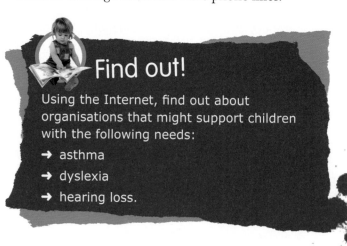

Find out!

Using the Internet, find out about organisations that might support children with the following needs:

→ asthma

→ dyslexia

→ hearing loss.

1. Ask your placement supervisor if you may observe one child.
2. Carry out three observations on the child using three different observation techniques.
3. For each observation, write:

   a) an analysis of the child's stage of development

   b) a description of the child's current needs.
4. Using these three observations, explain how you might support the child's further development.

Unit 3

Supporting children

In this unit you will learn:

1. The implications of relevant legislation on working practices with children

2. How to recognise strategies which are fair, just and inclusive and know how to promote them

3. Where to access the policies of the setting and how to follow the procedures for safeguarding children

4. How to empower children to develop self-confidence, self-esteem and self-reliance

5. How to support children to prepare for transfer or transition

6. The causes and effects of discrimination in society

The implications of relevant legislation on working practices with children

In practice

You are in the nursery when the phone rings. As there is nobody else near the phone, you decide it would be best to answer it. A prospective parent asks whether the nursery takes children who have learning disabilities. You are not sure about this and so take her name and number and say that someone else will call her back.

By the end of this section you will know about the legislation that is in place to protect children from discrimination.

Key legislation which relates to working with children

All children have the right to be in a safe and welcoming environment. In the UK there are many pieces of legislation that protect children and their families. The legislation is used to inform practice but is also embedded in the inspections of settings. Below are some examples of legislation that are currently in force in England. If you are working in other countries, you will need to check the legislation that is in place for your country. Scotland, for example, has its own legal system and while the legislation is at times similar, there will be differences.

The rights of children and their families

It is an accepted view in society and the early years sector that every child is special and should be given opportunities to fulfil his or her potential. This is the basis of anti-discriminatory practice in settings and the focus of many laws today. While some laws look at the rights of children, others focus on the rights of adults, which will include of course children's families. There are two significant pieces of legislation that protect children and their families:

→ Human Rights Act
→ United Nations Convention on the Rights of the Child.

Human Rights Act 2000

This came into force in October 2000 and has already had a huge impact on current legislation in the UK. It requires courts and tribunals to make judgements using certain articles of the European Convention on Human Rights as a starting point.

The Act was not designed specifically to protect children but they are accorded the same rights as adults. This means they have a right to dignity, respect and fairness in the way they are treated. Thus a setting is not able to use corporal punishment (smacking or caning) even if a parent consents to it, because it is seen as degrading and a violation of a child's rights. The Human Rights Act means that parents of children are also protected.

United Nations Convention on the Rights of the Child

In addition to the Human Rights Act, the UK is also a signatory to the UN Convention on the Rights of the Child (UNCRC). This was drawn up in 1989 and gives children and young people under the age of 18 years their own special rights. There are five main strands to the Convention:

1. Reinforces the importance of fundamental human dignity
2. Highlights and defends the family's role in children's lives
3. Seeks respect for children
4. Endorses the principle of non-discrimination
5. Establishes clear obligations for member countries to ensure that their legal framework is in line with the provisions of the Convention

The UNCRC is divided into articles. Below are some of the key articles that might affect your practice with children and young people.

→ Article 2: The right to be protected from all forms of discrimination
→ Article 3: The best interest of the child to be the primary consideration in all actions concerning children
→ Article 12: A child's rights to express his or her views freely; a child's view to be given due weight in keeping with the child's age or maturity
→ Article 13: A child's right to freedom of expression and exchange of information regardless of frontiers
→ Article 28: A child's right to education with a view to achieving this right progressively on the basis of equal opportunities

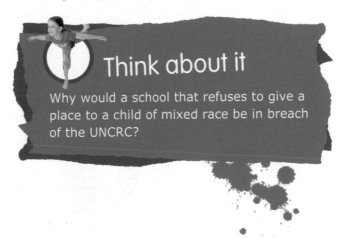

Think about it

Why would a school that refuses to give a place to a child of mixed race be in breach of the UNCRC?

Children Act 1989

As a result of adopting the UNCRC, new legislation was required. The 1989 Children Act, which came into affect in 1991 in England and Wales and in 1996 in Northern Ireland, attempted to bring together various pieces of legislation. It is wide ranging and covers child protection, parental responsibility and the inspection of settings. The 1989 Children Act is especially well known for its stance that children's welfare is of paramount importance. The 1989 Act also made it clear that children's and young people's views had to be taken into consideration when decisions about their future were being made.

Children Act 2004

There has been a subsequent Children Act which provided for a Children's Commissioner and also allowed the government to provide a legal framework for the Every Child Matters programme (see page 16). The Children Act 2004 is designed to ensure that difference services for children and young people work more effectively together.

Equality Act 2006

This Act is relatively new and comes into force from Autumn 2007. A key part of the Act is the establishment of the Commission for Equality and Human Rights. It will enforce equality legislation on age, disability and health, gender, race, religion or belief, sexual orientation or transgender status, and encourage compliance with the Human Rights Act 1998. The Commission for Equality and Human Rights will replace the following commissions: Disability Rights Commission, Equal Opportunities Commission and the Commission for Racial Equality.

Find out!

Find out more about the work of the Commission for Equality and Human Rights by visiting its website (www.cehr.org.uk).

Sex Discrimination Act 1975

The Sex Discrimination Act makes it illegal to discriminate on the grounds of gender. It covers pay as well as services and education. This means that it would be illegal for a setting to discriminate against boys or girls in the provision of play activities or during routines. This means that, in theory, an adult could not plan an activity for boys only and refuse to let girls take part.

Race Relations Act 1976 and Race Relations (amended) Act 2000

This Act made it illegal to discriminate against anyone on the basis of their ethnicity, skin, colour or race. The original Act also set up the Commission for Racial Equality (see above; note that this will soon be disbanded). The Race Relations Act applies to employment opportunities within a setting but also the way that a setting might treat a child or their parents. For example, it is illegal for a setting to discipline a child differently to other children or to humiliate a child or their parents because of skin colour.

Disability Discrimination Act 1995 and Disability Act 2000

The Disability Discrimination Act means that it would be illegal for a setting not to make reasonable adjustments to accommodate those with a disability, both children and their parents. The Act defines disability as 'a physical or mental impairment which has a substantial and long-term adverse effect on a person's ability to perform normal day-to-day activities'. This means that many children and adults are covered by it, for example children with asthma, diabetes, learning difficulties and problems with mobility.

The idea is that a disabled parent or a child is not treated less favourably than others. This would mean that a setting might provide wheelchair access to help a parent attend a parents' evening or produce documentation in a large font size so that a parent with a sight problem could read it. In the same way, a setting would need to make reasonable adjustments to meet the needs of a child so that he or she could participate alongside other children.

Special Educational Needs and Disability Act 2001

This Act applies to England and Wales. It is divided into two sections:

→ Part one strengthened the rights of access of parents and children to mainstream education. This reflects the idea of inclusive education in which children are not 'separated' from their peers because of a disability or particular need.

→ Part two expanded the Disability Discrimination Act 1995 to include education. This Act means that nurseries and schools would need to make reasonable adjustments to their premises to accommodate a child with special educational needs or a disability. Settings must also follow the SEN Code of Practice which outlines what they should do to support a child with special educational needs.

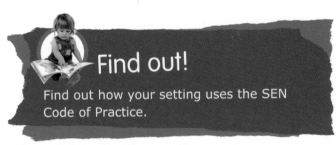

Find out!

Find out how your setting uses the SEN Code of Practice.

Child protection

There are many pieces of legislation that are designed to protect children from abuse and exploitation. The Children Act 1989 also looks at protecting children from abuse by requiring settings to be registered and for local authorities to provide services for children and families in need.

Protection of Children Act 1999

This Act set up a register of names of people who are unsuitable to work with children. It requires settings working with children to ensure they do not offer employment or volunteer work to anyone before they have been vetted by the Criminal Records Bureau.

Safeguarding Vulnerable Groups Act 2006

This Act comes into force from autumn 2008. It is designed to make sure that adults working with children and other vulnerable groups are vetted not just in childcare organisations but also in other organisations such as junior football clubs. This Act may make a difference to the way that settings use volunteers and also services, although the current standards make it clear that any adult who has not been checked with the Criminal Records Bureau must never be left unsupervised with children. This Act is also designed to cover adults who work with vulnerable adults such as those who may have learning difficulties.

Childcare Act 2006

This Act is due to come into effect in September 2008 and has significant implications for settings in England. The Act incorporates the welfare standards with which all settings registered to work with children under 8 years must comply, and also provides a learning framework for children aged 0–5 years called the Early Years Foundation Stage (EYFS). The welfare requirements affect much of the day-to-day practice within settings, for example the adult to child ratio in rooms, the qualification levels of staff and the types of snacks and drinks that are available for children.

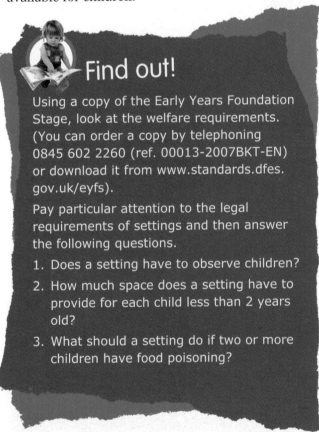

Find out!

Using a copy of the Early Years Foundation Stage, look at the welfare requirements. (You can order a copy by telephoning 0845 602 2260 (ref. 00013-2007BKT-EN) or download it from www.standards.dfes.gov.uk/eyfs).

Pay particular attention to the legal requirements of settings and then answer the following questions.

1. Does a setting have to observe children?
2. How much space does a setting have to provide for each child less than 2 years old?
3. What should a setting do if two or more children have food poisoning?

Health and safety

There are many specific pieces of legislation that affect practice in settings. They include the following:

→ Health and Safety at Work Act 1974
→ Control of Substances Hazardous to Health (COSHH) Regulations 2002
→ Reporting of Injuries, Diseases and Dangerous Occurrences Regulations (RIDDOR) 1995
→ National Standards for Child Care and Education Settings (Ofsted for England and Wales)
→ Motor Vehicles (Wearing of Seat Belts) (Amendment) Regulations 2006.

They are covered in Unit 4 so you will need to read pages 161–5 in order to complete this unit and its assessment.

The responsibility of the setting to have policies and procedures in place

All settings taking children under the age of 8 years in the UK have to be registered and are regularly inspected.

While each of the home countries has its own system of inspections, all of the inspectorates ask that settings should have policies and procedures in place. This means that your work placement or work setting will have many policies that will show how they intend to meet the legal requirements. Below is a spider diagram giving examples of policies that a nursery or pre-school will have.

The impact of legislation on working practices

You have seen that there is a significant amount of legislation in place to protect and safeguard children and their families. You will find that this legislation has an impact on the working practices in your setting as it will be reflected in the setting's policies and procedures. For example, a setting may have a policy on behaviour that states that no physical punishment can be used. This is because the Human Rights Act is clear that children and adults have the right to dignity.

Getting ready for assessment

Choose five pieces of legislation from those described above or in Unit 4 (pages 161–5). Explain how each one affects the practice in your placement or work setting.

Section 2

How to recognise strategies which are fair, just and inclusive and know how to promote them

In practice

Poppy is 4 years old. Her mother is looking around at different nurseries. She says how much she likes the atmosphere of the one where you work. She says that she felt welcome and she feels that Poppy would be very happy here. She asks you how this nursery manages to make parents and children feel so welcome. You have never really thought about it.

By the end of this section you will understand how policies and practices can create inclusive settings.

How to follow the policies and procedures in a range of settings

You have seen that settings have to abide by legislation and that policies in settings will reflect the latest legislation. While it is the employer's duty to make sure that staff know about the policies in the setting, it is your professional responsibility to make sure that you read and comply with them. Policies change over time in order to reflect any changes to legislation so should be regularly reviewed.

Most settings will keep a copy of each of their policies in the staff room or in the manager's office. New members of staff will be shown these policies when they first arrive and will often sign to say that they have read and understood them. It can be a good idea once you begin in a setting to ask if you can read them again as it can be hard to process information at the start of a new placement or job. It is also a good idea when reading a policy or procedure to see if you can work out what it means in practice.

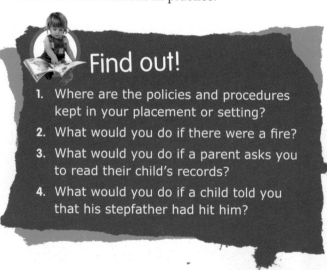

Find out!

1. Where are the policies and procedures kept in your placement or setting?
2. What would you do if there were a fire?
3. What would you do if a parent asks you to read their child's records?
4. What would you do if a child told you that his stepfather had hit him?

What are fair, just and inclusive strategies and what are their characteristics?

You have seen in the previous section that there is plenty of legislation designed to promote children's and their families' rights. This is important as children deserve to be treated fairly and should be given every opportunity to achieve their potential.

The term inclusion is often used to describe the concept of making sure that everyone feels welcome and part of a setting. This applies to parents as well as children. In order to achieve this, settings should constantly be looking at what they are doing and how they are doing it, and think about whether they are really meeting children's and their families' needs. Settings that are fair, just and inclusive recognise that anti-discriminatory practice means that individual needs are taken into account and that children and their families are not expected to all be 'the same'.

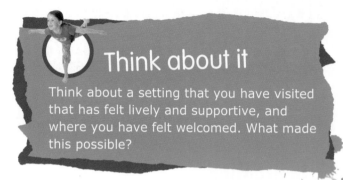

Think about it

Think about a setting that you have visited that has felt lively and supportive, and where you have felt welcomed. What made this possible?

How strategies can be successfully promoted

Settings that are proactive use many sources of information to reflect on their policies and activities. They may ask parents and children to provide feedback, suggestions and comments about a whole range of issues, for example what activities the children have enjoyed, session opening hours and requests for information. Settings also seek information from organisations locally and nationally who support children and families with particular needs.

Practical ways in which settings can be inclusive

Session times

Settings that are inclusive consider whether session times reflect the needs of parents and their children or whether they act as a barrier to some families.

Settling-in policies

Settings may have an individual approach to settling children in. For example, they recognise that some children need longer or more time to settle and talk to parents about how best to settle children.

Accessibility

Accessibility is an issue for many groups of people, including children with mobility needs. Many parents will have younger children in pushchairs; in addition, some parents will use devices to increase their own mobility. Settings that are inclusive will think about this as an issue and consult with local voluntary groups and parents in order to find solutions.

Financial assistance

The ability to pay fees or 'extras' can be an issue for many parents. While settings need to balance their books, they will also consider ways of making payments easier for parents and whether the 'extras' can be funded in different ways, for example by applying for grants in the local community or by carrying out fundraising activities. If financial assistance is available for some families, they will consider how it is offered and try to avoid situations in which children are labelled as being from a poor family.

Activities and curriculum planning

The Early Years Foundation Stage and the SEN Code of Practice make it clear that activities need to be planned in accordance with children's learning needs. This means that settings should look for activities that can be simplified, extended or adapted to allow each child to participate at his or her own level. Settings that are interested in inclusion will also make sure that children's interests are really being thought about and that children are involved in planning activities.

Partnership with parents

The way in which pre-schools work with parents can be an indicator of anti-discriminatory practice. A child whose parents are not valued and respected will come to believe that he or she is also not important. Reflecting on the way in which you communicate with parents is therefore essential. Settings that work well with parents consider whether some parents are 'favourites'. They might think about the way in which parents are addressed, in both speech or writing, and whether these communications contain assumptions about their lifestyle, culture and financial background.

Case study

Working with parents

Little Chicks Nursery prides itself on being open and friendly. It is at the centre of a village and so is part of village life.

When a new family arrived in the village, a member of the staff dropped in a leaflet about the nursery with a handwritten note inviting the family to visit. A few days later, the parent and her son, Jack, visited. The nursery manager showed the parent around and together they agreed on some session times. The parent was a little concerned that Jack would have difficulty settling in as he had been quite unsettled since the move and was adjusting to wearing a hearing aid for the first time. His speech was also delayed because of hearing loss. The manager reassured the parent and asked her about Jack's interests. Together they worked out a plan of how they would settle him in. The manager also said that the nursery would contact the local sensory impairment team so that they would be in a better position to support Jack once he had settled in. They decided that it would be best if a key worker visited Jack at home to begin with so that he became used to her before starting at the setting. The manager also photocopied some local information so that the family would know about what was happening in the local community.

While this conversation was going on, Jack had been busily playing with a toy car. When it was time to leave, Jack did not want to leave the toy car. Sensing that this was going to be difficult, the manager said to Jack that he could borrow the car for a few days. Jack's mum smiled.

1. How is this setting trying to meet this child's individual needs?

2. How did this setting try and make this family feel welcome?

3. Why might settings need to gain information from other sources in order to meet a child's or a family's needs?

Section 3

Where to access the policies of the setting and how to follow the procedures for safeguarding children

In practice

Paul is 7 years old. He always seems hungry and often looks tired. Today you have noticed that he has some burn marks on the back of one of his hands. You are unsure whether to say something to him about it.

By the end of this section you will know how to recognise possible signs of abuse and what to do if you have concerns.

Child protection

It is a sad fact that some children and young people are badly let down or treated by the adults around them. The statistics for abuse make for difficult reading and the consequences of abuse for many children and young people last a lifetime. It is therefore an important responsibility of all adults working with children to understand their role in relation to child protection. It is also important that everyone understands and follows the policies and procedures in place to protect children and young people. Over the past few years there have been some highly publicised cases where failure to report or follow up concerns has resulted in avoidable deaths of children (see also Every Child Matters, page 16).

The consequences of abuse

One of the main effects of being abused is emotional damage – children and young people can develop a low sense of self-esteem. They may feel neither that they are valued nor, more importantly, that they deserve to be valued. As you have seen in Unit 2, self-esteem is a major factor in achievement at school and in forming strong and healthy relationships. Children and young people who have been abused can sometimes find themselves drawn towards others who continue to mistreat them. They may also find themselves enacting the abuse they suffered. The long-term outlook for those who have been abused is thus quite bleak and is one reason there are currently strong campaigns, such as the one run by the NSPCC, to highlight the effects of abuse.

Who abuses children and young people?

There are many myths around child abuse which are not only misleading but can potentially mean that some abuse is not recognised.

✗ Strangers abuse children

Many people believe that child abuse is carried out by strangers. Surprisingly, this is not borne out by the statistics on child abuse: the majority of abusers are people known to the child. Abusers may be family members, friends or even adults working with children. Abuse can also be committed by young people on their siblings. Cases in which strangers abduct and abuse children do occur, but these represent only a small number of abuse cases.

✗ Abuse occurs in poor families

This stereotype is dangerous because it can mean that children from more affluent families are not thought to be at risk of abuse. While families on low incomes may be under greater stress, this in itself does not mean that abuse is inevitable. Plenty of low-income families provide loving and supportive environments for their children. Families on higher levels of income can still be under stress as they may, for example, have committed themselves to expenditure beyond their means. Sometimes children from 'wealthy' families who have been abused are not believed because of this myth.

✗ Abuse occurs in lone-parent families

Plenty of stereotypes abound about lone-parent families. Because child abuse occurs across the social and income spectrum, it is unfair to assume that children from lone-parent families will be abused. Focusing on single-parent families can mean that other children at risk of abuse are not identified.

✗ Only men abuse children

While statistically, more men sexually abuse children than women do, this does not mean that women do not sexually abuse children. Stereotypes about women as nurturing and 'safe' can mean that children who have been sexually abused by women are not believed. In addition, it is also important to recognise that older children and siblings can sexually abuse younger children. This tends to be a taboo subject as it is not in keeping with the image people have of children being 'innocent'. It is also important to remember that there are other types of abuse other than sexual abuse and that both men, women and other children can commit these types of abuse.

Forms of abuse

Abuse is generally classified into four categories:

→ neglect
→ physical abuse
→ sexual abuse
→ emotional abuse.

It is important to recognise that often children and young people will be subjected to more than one type of abuse. As psychological damage is a key issue in abuse, some people feel that emotional abuse is almost always present when a child or young person is subject to another type of abuse.

The following definitions of abuse have been adapted from the Department of Health's publication *Working Together to Safeguard our Children* (1999).

Neglect

Children and young people have some basic needs that have to be met in order for them to thrive. Neglect is the persistent failure to meet a child's basic physical and/or psychological needs. It is likely to result in the serious impairment of the child's health and development. It may involve a parent or carer failing to provide:

→ adequate food, shelter and clothing
→ protection from physical harm or danger
→ access to appropriate medical care or treatment
→ adequate responsiveness to a child's basic emotional needs.

Physical abuse

Physical abuse causes physical harm to a child. It may involve hitting, shaking, throwing, poisoning, burning, scalding, drowning or suffocating. Physical harm may also result when a parent or carer feigns the symptoms of or deliberately causes ill-health to a child.

Sexual abuse

Sexual abuse is forcing or enticing a child or young person to take part in sexual activities, whether or not that child is aware of what is happening. These activities may involve physical contact, including penetrative acts such as rape and buggery, and non-penetrative acts. Sexual abuse also includes non-contact activities, for example forcing children to watch or participate in the production of pornographic material, getting children to watch sexual activities or encouraging children to behave in sexually inappropriate ways.

Emotional abuse

For some years, emotional abuse was not seen as being as significant as some of the other types of abuse. Today it is recognised that children's and young people's emotional welfare is paramount in their overall development.

Emotional abuse is the persistent emotional ill-treatment of a child such as to cause severe and persistent adverse effects on that child's emotional development. It may involve conveying to a child that he or she is worthless, unloved or inadequate, or valued only in so far as he or she meets the needs of another person. It may feature age or developmentally inappropriate expectations being imposed on the child. Emotional abuse may cause a child frequently to feel frightened or in danger, or the exploitation or corruption of a child. Some level of emotional abuse is involved in all types of ill-treatment, though it may occur alone.

Recognising signs of abuse

It is essential that you are able to recognise possible signs and indicators of abuse. Sometimes you might notice physical signs that a child or young person is being abused, but in other cases you may become aware of behavioural indicators. It is important to be vigilant as many children and young people will not necessarily report that they are being abused. Babies and toddlers may, for example, not have the language skills required, while older children may not always recognise that what the adult has been doing is wrong. Children and young people can also be living in fear as their abuser is likely to have a great deal of control over them.

Physical abuse

Most children have falls and minor accidents that result in bruising, cuts and bumps. The difference between genuine accidents and deliberate injuries to the child is often the location of the injuries and the frequency with which they occur.

Physical signs

These might include:

→ unusual-shaped bruises
→ scalds and burns (sometimes from cigarettes)
→ bite marks
→ fractures.

A child who often has black eyes and bumps to the face may be clumsy or unlucky, but could well be a victim of abuse.

Behavioural indicators

Children who have been physically abused may show through their behaviour and play that they are being abused. Signs to look out for include the following:

→ aggressive towards other children
→ shows aggressive acts in role-play situations
→ withdrawn and quiet
→ seems stiff and sore, e.g. doesn't want to sit
→ seems reluctant to be with carer
→ carer seems to be aggressive with the child
→ child frequently brings in notes to excuse him or her from physical activity (the parent may not wish the child to undress and reveal injuries).

Asking children about their injuries

It is good practice to ask a child about an injury as most children who have had genuine accidents are happy to talk about what has happened to them. Children who have been physically abused might have been told by the abuser not to talk about what has happened and to say that they fell or bumped into something if they are asked about bruising or cuts. If a child seems upset or nervous when talking about an injury, you should always pass on this information to your supervisor. You may be asked to keep a note of the date and type of injury that you have seen, as well as a record of what the child said.

Sexual abuse

Sexual abuse can be hard to detect as the child may not outwardly seem injured. Some physical signs may be apparent but behavioural indicators can be a more obvious clue.

Physical signs

These will include:

→ bruises, scratches or other injuries unlikely to be accidental
→ difficulty in sitting or walking
→ frightened of passing urine or stools
→ difficulties in passing urine or stools
→ frequent urine and genital infections
→ frequent toileting accidents.

Behavioural indicators

Children who have been sexually abused might show the following behaviours:

→ babyish behaviour, including comfort habits such as thumb sucking and rocking
→ inappropriate behaviour such as undressing or exposing themselves
→ showing sexual behaviour in their play, such as trying to mate two dolls or cuddly animals
→ a knowledge of adult sexual behaviour that is unusual for their age
→ unwillingness to be with a particular carer.

ChildLine reports that sexual abuse often occurs while normal family activities are taking place, for example bathing, going to bed, play fights and cuddles. This means that some children may not know there is anything unusual in the treatment they are receiving from the abuser. Other children may have been told that the activity is a secret and are threatened with the idea that they will be taken away from the family if they tell.

The hidden nature of sexual abuse means that early years practitioners must listen carefully to children and consider whether the behaviour they are seeing might be a sign of abuse. If you suspect that abuse is taking place you should always make sure that you talk to your supervisor about your concerns; if you are working in a child's home, contact the NSPCC or local authority for advice.

Emotional abuse

There are few physical indicators of emotional abuse, although some older children may show self-destructive behaviour such as cutting themselves or drastic dieting. The main indicator of emotional abuse is the child's need for attention and low self-esteem.

Behavioural indicators

Signs of emotional abuse can include the following:
→ attention-seeking behaviours such as being deliberately disruptive
→ clinginess and 'hunger' for affection
→ telling lies (to gain sympathy or attention)
→ babyish behaviour, e.g. sucking thumbing, rocking, hair twiddling
→ tantrums beyond the age of 4 years
→ difficulty in socialising with peers.

Children who are being emotionally abused are very vulnerable because they are happy to receive attention from anyone. This means that some paedophiles can target them by offering the child love and affection. In the longer term, children with such low self-esteem are likely to underachieve at school and may form intense relationships at an early age. Teenage pregnancies are often a result of children feeling unloved.

Neglect

Parents who neglect their children may have significant personal and other problems of their own. The children might be loved but parents find it hard to provide the basic care that the children need.

Physical signs

These will include:
→ frequent accidental injuries (caused by lack of safety devices or supervision)
→ children being underweight and hungry
→ an untidy and dirty appearance
→ low-grade infections which appear untreated, such as frequent colds, coughs and earache
→ tiredness (seems to have no particular bedtimes).

Behavioural indicators

These might be signs of neglect:
→ children mention being unsupervised
→ older children seem to take significant responsibility for younger siblings, for example cooking meals
→ parents rarely appear in the setting, for example at open evenings or to collect children.

Children who are being neglected are at risk of having accidents through being left unsupervised, either at home or while out playing. They are also vulnerable to attack from strangers. If you suspect that a child is being neglected, you should talk to your supervisor.

Changes in behaviour patterns

Children who are being abused may show behaviour that is not part of their normal pattern or is out of character. This means that a child who has been sunny and outgoing may suddenly be more tearful or aggressive. The change in the pattern of behaviour may be short-lived and a reaction to something specific in their life, such as the death of a pet, but where behaviour seems to be more long term and there is no obvious cause the early years practitioner should consider the possibility of abuse. This means that the child will be observed more closely for other signs, and early years practitioners must always pass on their concerns about the child to their supervisor. If is likely that the supervisor will talk to the parents to see if there have been any difficulties at home.

The importance of recording and reporting signs of abuse and how to do this

It is important to read carefully and check your setting's policy about recording and reporting abuse. Make sure you know what to do if you suspect a child is being abused or a child confides in you. Your setting's policy should reflect the latest guidance from the Local Safeguarding Children Board in your area.

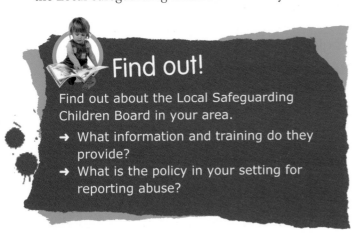

Find out!

Find out about the Local Safeguarding Children Board in your area.

→ What information and training do they provide?

→ What is the policy in your setting for reporting abuse?

Below are some general points that reflect good practice at the time of writing.

Suspected abuse

If you notice a mark or injury, ask the child or young person what happened. Consider whether they seem reluctant, defensive or unsure and whether the explanation seems plausible. With babies and toddlers where language is not sufficiently developed, you should query the mark with the parent. If as a result you still have concerns, these should be passed on to the person designated in your setting's policy. This is likely to be someone in a management position.

Confidentiality

It is essential that you do not talk to anyone other than those directly involved about either your concerns or what a child has told you. Maintaining confidentiality protects children and their families from gossip, but also prevents situations where an abuser mounts a legal defence based on the tampering of evidence.

Responding to a child's disclosure of abuse

Sometimes children will seek out the support of adults to prevent abuse from continuing. In other cases, children may unintentionally say something that is significant to you. The term 'disclosure' has been used to describe these types of event; however, this term is now used less frequently in court because the defendant's solicitors can then infer that adults have encouraged or led the child to make a claim. The latest guidance from the Department of Health warns adults working with children to be aware that the way in which they respond to a child who they suspect has been abused can affect the later outcomes.

What to do if a child tells you about abuse

There are some simple but essential rules to follow if a child tells you about abuse or says something that is of concern.

Do:

→ Reassure the child that you believe what he or she is saying.

→ Listen to the child carefully, but do not ask questions as this may jeopardise a police investigation.

→ Tell the child that you will do everything you can to protect him or her.

→ Tell the child that you will need to talk to other adults in order to help him or her.

→ Reassure the child that he or she is not in trouble and that he or she has acted properly.

→ Make notes in pen immediately after the conversation has finished and before talking to anyone else. Write down only what the child has told you. Do not speculate or add any comments. Include the date and time, and then sign the notes.

Do not:

→ Promise the child that you will be able to keep what he or she has said a secret. This is important because the child can feel let down later and will not trust other adults.

→ Question the child or pass any comment other than to reassure the child.

→ Make notes while you are with the child or after you have discussed what has been said with another adult.

→ Add additional information into the notes later.

→ Talk to other people about what has occurred, other than the designated person for dealing with child protection in the setting.

How to work with other professionals to support children

When child abuse is suspected, a multi-agency team comes together to investigate and take any necessary steps to protect the child and support the family. The team usually comprises child protection specialists from Social Services, the police and health professionals. You may be asked to attend this meeting.

Find out!

Find out more about the latest guidance on child protection, *Working Together to Safeguard Children*, by visiting the Every Child Matters website (www.everychildmatters.gov.uk workingtogether).

It is important when working with others that you remember that this work is confidential and the need to be accurate in the information you provide.

Whistle-blowing procedures

In situations where a member of staff is abusing or showing inappropriate behaviour, it can be hard for junior members of staff to report their colleague, as they may fear they will lose their job. The term 'whistle blowing' is used to describe someone within an organisation reporting the inappropriate actions of a colleague or line manager by alerting someone in a much more senior position. There have been some high profile cases in the past where 'whistle blowing' has helped bring institutional abuse to an end. In recognition of the difficulties that a junior member of staff may have in giving an alert, most organisations now have procedures in place so that 'whistle blowing' is easier. These should be set out in your setting's Child Protection policy.

Safe working practices that protect children and the adults who work with them

To prevent possible abuse from those working directly with children and young people, and to prevent allegations of abuse, it is important to adopt good working practices. These practices help young children to get a feel of what is appropriate and so may help them to respond if another adult behaves differently.

Registering visitors

All visitors need to be registered when they come into a setting and given some identification that shows they are not a member of staff. This is important especially in large settings. It is therefore important to show visitors straight to a reception point when they arrive and ask them to sign in and then to sign out when they leave. Maintaining an accurate register is also essential if the building has to be evacuated.

Accompanying visitors

Visitors should be accompanied around a building and should not be left alone with any children unless they have been specifically cleared to do so.

Volunteers and learners

Volunteers and learners who come to support settings need to sign in when they first arrive. In many settings they also wear identifying badges to help parents understand their role. As with visitors they should not be left alone with children; if they are regular helpers they should be checked with the Criminal Records Bureau (CRB). It is also good practice that they learn about child protection procedures in case a child or young person talks to them about abuse.

Staff

All staff should sign in when they arrive and leave. When they first join a setting they should undergo a CRB check. It is important that all staff read the child protection policies and procedures of the setting.

Working with children and young people

The basis of safe working practices is openness so that other adults in the setting can either see you or know what you are doing when you are with children. Note that as a learner you should never be left in a situation when you are alone with a child.

Being alone with a child or young person

Once you are qualified there may be situations when you are alone with a child or young person, for example taking a child to the toilet, nappy changing or talking to a young person away from others. When you are alone it is particularly important to remember the concept of openness. This may mean letting a colleague know where you are going, leaving the door of the room open or sitting where you remain in sight of others.

Privacy

All children and young people are entitled to privacy when they are dressing or going to the toilet. With very young children, one of your roles is to help them acquire this as a concept and to give them the skills they need so that they do not need an adult to help them. This means encouraging a 3-year-old to pull up their own pants, wash their hands or put on their own trousers. To maintain privacy of children and young people who have the basic skills, you might wait for them outside the toilet or only come and help them when asked. When dealing with dressing and toileting you should also adopt a 'business-like' attitude and encourage the child to do as much as he or she can. In these moments you should also ensure that another member of staff knows where you are. If you notice anything that concerns you about a child or young person while helping them, you should immediately pass on your concerns (see reporting above).

Physical contact

Physical contact needs to be appropriate for the age of the child or young person you are working with. All physical contact should be on the child's terms so that a toddler who wants to get off a lap must be allowed to do so. Recognising the body language of children and young people is therefore essential. For example, you may hold out your hands to an 8-year-old who is crying and needs reassurance so that the child can choose whether he or she wants this reassurance.

Children less than 3 years old

Babies and young children need physical contact and reassurance from adults in order to feel safe and develop a relationship with their carers. Hence it is perfectly acceptable to cuddle a baby or sit with a toddler on your lap as this is developmentally appropriate. Remember, though, that if the child shows that he or she has had enough and now wants to get down, you must immediately let go. Note that many 2-year-olds will alternate between this independence and clinginess so you may find that you do a lot of picking up and setting down!

Children aged 3–6 years

Most children in this age range still want some physical reassurance although this is likely to be hand holding or sitting next to you when sharing a story. You should be helping children in this age range get a feel of when and to whom it is appropriate to show physical contact. This means that should a 5-year-old want to sit on your lap at school, you settle the child next to you rather than allowing him or her to sit on your lap; in this way the child learns from this gesture that sitting on an adult's lap is not appropriate in this situation.

Children aged over 6 years

Most children and young people will have instinctively picked up that close physical contact does not feel right unless with parents or others who have a special relationship with them, for example siblings and aunts. This means that it is only in exceptional circumstances that physical contact will be necessary, such as when a child has had an accident or is very upset.

Good practice checklist

Working with children

✓ Never leave anyone who has not been given clearance the opportunity of working alone with a child out of the view of others.

✓ Make sure during nappy changes or intimate care routines that doors are kept slightly ajar.

✓ Always encourage children as much as possible to carry out their own personal hygiene.

✓ Do not play games involving blindfolding children.

✓ Do not play games involving secrets.

✓ Do not give children your home address, phone number or e-mail unless there is a particular reason to do so and parents and colleagues know about it.

Getting ready for assessment

Read your placement or work settings' policy on child protection. How does this policy and its procedures help to safeguard children?

How to carry out risk assessments

Risk assessments are a key component in maintaining the health and safety of children and young people. Interestingly, the aim of risk assessments is to identify and then minimise risks rather than to create totally risk-free environments. This means that you may identify that a climbing frame could create the risk of falling, however, the risk may be minimised by supervising children carefully and checking that they have the skill to be able to climb safely. The climbing frame will also be checked to see whether it is stable and strong enough to take children's weight.

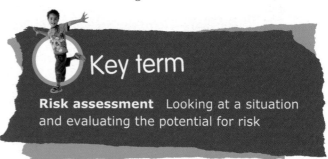

Key term

Risk assessment Looking at a situation and evaluating the potential for risk

Risk assessments are covered in detail in Unit 4 (pages 192–3). Every setting will have their own way of risk assessing and is likely to have their own documentation. Your setting should have a policy about health and safety and you are likely to find that within it are examples of risk assessment forms and instructions on how they are to be used.

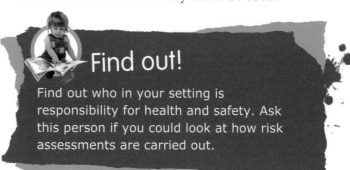

Find out!

Find out who in your setting is responsibility for health and safety. Ask this person if you could look at how risk assessments are carried out.

How to promote and maintain health and safety

As well as protecting children and young people from abuse, it is also important to be aware of their physical safety. Health and safety is a large area of study covering food hygiene, physical safety and risk assessment. It is an important area when working with children and as such forms an extensive part of Unit 4.

Procedures relevant to the setting

You will need to know about the health and safety policies and procedures for the setting in which you work or are in placement. These are covered in Unit 4 (pages 181–6), and you need to read this material in order to complete Unit 3.

It is worth noting that policies and procedures can vary enormously between settings so it is essential that you find out about how your setting evaluates and risk assesses. It is also important to note that you have a duty to follow procedures within a setting; if you are an employee this is a legal requirement.

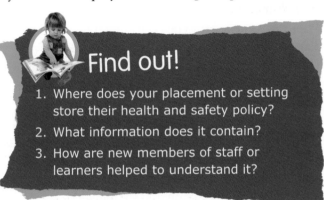

Find out!

1. Where does your placement or setting store their health and safety policy?
2. What information does it contain?
3. How are new members of staff or learners helped to understand it?

Planning outings

Outings are a source of great enjoyment and learning for children and young people. They can help children gain knowledge about new environments as well as gain independence. They do, however, need to be carefully planned to ensure that practical considerations and especially safety is maintained.

The spider diagram below look at issues that have to be considered when planning a trip.

Consent, emergency contacts and medical details

Once you have decided that an outing is to take place, you must obtain written consent from parents. This means that a form needs to go out and a signature and date must be obtained. It is worth keeping a list of forms as they are returned so that you can chase up any later on. Note that you must never take children away from a setting without this consent. It is also important to check that emergency contact details and medical details are up to date and that a copy of these are taken on the outing with you.

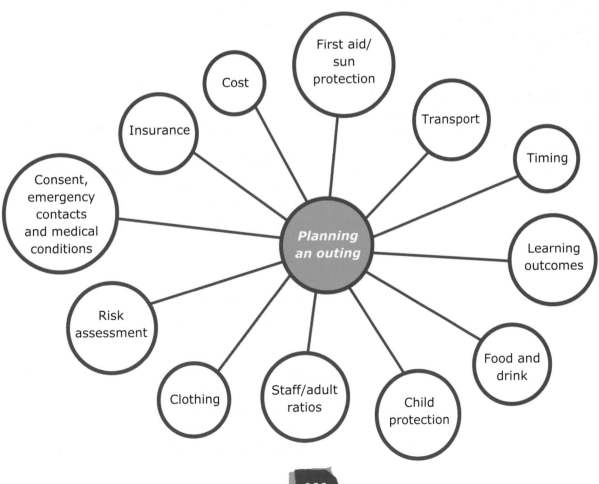

Insurance

Arranging or checking insurance is an important part of arranging a trip. Check what cover, if any, is already in place and whether you need to arrange additional cover.

Transport

If your outing requires transport you must cost it carefully and check that it is suitable for groups. Children being transported in coaches or minibuses have to be wearing seat belts. If private cars are used, insurance has to be in place to cover the drivers and children will need to be properly restrained to comply with the latest legislation. This covers all children under 4 feet 6 inches tall (1.37 metres) or 13 years of age. Where public transport is to be used, check beforehand with the operator that they can accommodate a group.

Staff and adults

It is important that sufficient staff and other adults go on outings. It is important that you find out what the staff to child ratio needs to be for the age group you are working with. Your supervisor should have up to date guidance on this from either a local education authority or, in England, Ofsted. You should also make sure that staff have suitable experience and knowledge for the type of outing that you are undertaking.

For staff and other adults to supervise children properly, it is important that they understand their role and responsibilities. You might therefore consider holding a meeting beforehand and give each person a pack containing the information they will need, such as a map of the venue, emergency numbers and a timetable for the day.

Timing

When planning a trip it is important to think about the timing. You need to find out how long the journey will take and how much time to allow at the venue. You will also need to build in sufficient times to physically group children together, for example getting them on and off a train or taking a register. It is also worth thinking about time to be allowed to visit gift shops and toilets and eat lunch. Unrealistic timings can result in a rushed outing which is stressful for adults and children.

Cost

Costing an outing accurately is essential, especially if you expect the trip to be self-funding. Remember to build in the costs of insurance, transport and extra adult places if these are not free. You may also need to consider how much is required to cover the cost of any children who cannot attend on the day because of illness, etc.

Some of the best outings for young children are not necessarily expensive ones, for example visiting a post office, supermarket or local park.

Learning outcomes

Trips that are meant to be educational need to be planned so that maximum learning can take place. Think about the learning outcomes of visits and how the visit will be used to extend what happens in the setting.

First aid/sun protection

A first aid kit and someone who has first aid training should be taken on an outing. It is also important to consider sun protection and to follow the latest guidelines from the Department of Health.

Risk assessment

In order to recognise any potential hazards you will need to go to the place that you wish to visit beforehand and carry out a risk assessment. You should consider the following:

→ how easily you will be able to supervise children
→ physical challenges such as steps
→ proximity to traffic or unfenced areas.

It is also worth noting where the toilets are, where you might eat and what you might do if the weather is not good.

Food and drink

When planning the outing you will need to think about whether the group will require food and drink and how and when you will organise these. If you are planning to provide food as part of the trip you must find out in advance whether any of the children or young people have food allergies. If parents are responsible for providing a packed meal it is also worth bringing some extra food along in case anyone forgets.

Clothing

Parents will need to know how to dress their children and what extra clothing needs to be provided. It is also useful to bring spare clothing with you.

Child protection

It is important to keep a close eye on children to avoid situations where they may get lost or abducted. As you have seen there are guidelines as to the staffing ratios for trips and this should allow for adults to be responsible for small groups and to regularly check that children are present. The risk assessment that is carried out before the outing should also have looked at whether children are likely to get lost or how protected an area is. With older children or young people who might be given more independence, it is important that they know what to do if they need help, although they should stay in small groups or pairs.

Did you know?

Traditionally, many younger children were given individual name badges. This practice has now been discontinued as it allows strangers to immediately use the child's name. This can fool a child into thinking that they 'know' the person and thus can make them vulnerable. For this reason, name badges are no longer used, but some identity such as wearing uniform or badges with the group's name is used instead.

Find out!

1. Look at the current advice for organising outings on the Health and Safety Executive's website (www.hse.gov.uk/schooltrips).

2. Read the latest advice from the DfES on organising educational visits, 'A handbook for group leaders', available on the following website: www.teachernet.gov.uk/wholeschool/healthandsafety/visits

Section 4

How to empower children to develop self-confidence, self-esteem and self-reliance

In practice

Yukari is 6 years old. She loves going to the breakfast club before school as she enjoys being with Janet. She always has a smile for her and is interested in what she is doing. She sometimes takes along her reading book to show her and reads it aloud before school. She says that she makes her feel special.

By the end of this section you will know how to empower children and how you might help them gain self-esteem.

The theories that underpin the empowerment of children

For many years children and young people had few rights and adults were often very authoritarian in their approach to them. Today it is recognised that outcomes for children and young people can be improved by working alongside them and giving them responsibility and choices. This approach empowers children and young people and helps them learn to take responsibility. It also seems to help develop a strong sense of self-efficacy, which in turn helps self-esteem. Positive self-esteem, as you saw in Unit 2 (pages 59–60), plays a significant factor in children's cognitive and social development.

Self-efficacy

The term 'self-efficacy' is used by Albert Bandura (see also Unit 2, page 71) to consider the extent to which we believe in ourselves. A child with a high sense of self-efficacy believes that they are capable and that they can have control over how well they do. This means that they may try out a new task because they feel that if they work and practice hard, they should be able to manage it. A child without a strong sense of self-efficacy may start from the assumption that a task might be too hard for them and they cannot do anything about it. Strong feelings of self-efficacy are more likely to be gained where children have sufficient support as well as a sense of control over events and activities in order to be successful.

Children, even babies and toddlers according to Bandura, need to be given tasks, activities and responsibilities that will allow them to feel independent, successful and competent. Too many experiences where an adult comes and takes over because a child is not doing well will result in the child developing a poor sense of self-efficacy. It also means that where children have not managed to achieve a task that you might help them to evaluate the reasons behind this.

Theory of emotional intelligence

For many years, intelligence was seen as having only a cognitive dimension. Today, many theories of intelligence explore the concept of multiple intelligences, including 'emotional intelligence'. A key theorist involved in this area is Howard Gardner, who originally proposed in *Shattered Mind* (1975) eight intelligences, one of which was 'interpersonal intelligence and intrapersonal intelligence'. The term 'emotional intelligence' has since been adopted after being used by Daniel Goleman (see below).

The exact nature of emotional intelligence is still a matter of speculation and even some disagreement. However, the following areas are included in research: perception of emotions, understanding emotions and managing emotions. It is thought that children and young people who are able to recognise emotions in themselves and others and find ways of relating to them will find it easier to socialise, communicate and relate to others.

Emotional intelligence is though to be an important tool in the empowerment of children. It means that they will be able to recognise their own emotions and feel more confident about themselves and their own abilities.

Think about it

The following five competencies have been outlined by Daniel Goleman (Goleman, 1995). How might they be considered useful in everyday situations?

1. The ability to identify and name one's emotional states and to understand the link between emotions, thought and action.
2. The capacity to manage one's emotional states – to control emotions or to shift undesirable emotional states to more adequate ones.
3. The ability to enter into emotional states (at will) associated with a drive to achieve and be successful.
4. The capacity to read, be sensitive to and influence other people's emotions.
5. The ability to enter and sustain satisfactory interpersonal relationships.

Strategies to develop self-confidence and self-reliance

There are many ways in which you might help children to gain confidence and feel self-reliant. The key is often to give children plenty of opportunities to make their own choices and to feel that they have some control. This should be reflected throughout your working practices and, of course, children's stage of development needs to be considered. Below are three examples of how choice might be built into working practices.

→ *Play* – Children should be given opportunities to initiate play, select resources and equipment. Free play or child-initiated play gives children plenty of opportunities to arrange their own play and materials. This allows them to gain a sense of ownership.

→ *Time* – Children might be able to choose when they do things, for example self-service snack time, flexibility as to when to do homework.

→ *Food* – Children might choose what to eat (assuming the food available is healthy) and be able to serve themselves. Older children and young people may help to decide what should be on the menu and may even be involved in cooking it.

How to develop relationships with children and adults

The quality of our relationships with children and young people will make a significant difference to their achievement, behaviour and overall well-being. This means that it is important to think about how you might develop relationships with different ages of children and young people.

The spider diagram below shows why relationships are so important.

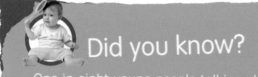

Did you know?

One in eight young people talking about their childhood say there was no one who made them feel special.

Coping with transitions
Children and young people who have stable and consistent relationships are more likely to cope with changes in their life

Child protection
Children who have good relationships with adults may find that they can talk to them about what is happening

Behaviour
Children and young people who have strong relationships in settings are more likely to show wanted and positive behaviour in settings

Why early years practitioners' relationships with children are important

Achievement of potential
Children and young people who feel that someone believes in them are more likely to try harder and thus achieve their potential

Self-esteem
Children and young people who feel valued are more likely to have higher self-esteem, which acts as a protective factor

Good relationships are based upon trust

The starting point when thinking about relationships is to understand that they are based on trust. Children and young people must feel that they can trust you. This means that you need to be consistent in your moods and behaviour so that your reactions are predictable. Young children are particularly wary of adults who one minute are aggressive and then another are loving. For young people, trust means knowing that someone believes in you and is also approachable. Communication skills are therefore particularly important for this age range.

Good relationships remain professional

It is important not to confuse being friendly with being friends – there is a distinction. Children and young people need you to act at all times as a professional and an adult in the relationship. They want you to be friendly, kind and even amusing, but they still need to feel that they can rely on you to keep them safe and to behave like an adult. Interestingly, children and young people are aware of the difference between friendly and friends, and tend to dislike or mistrust adults who blur the boundaries. Young people may even show this through their behaviour that might not be respectful.

Building relationships with babies and young children

In Unit 2 you looked at 'stranger danger' and the way that, from 8 months or so through until 3 years, most babies and children will be unsure about unfamiliar faces. This means that in the early days of meeting babies and toddlers it is important to develop a relationship at their speed rather than yours. Too much focus can send a toddler running behind his or her parent's legs. It can therefore be useful to begin by focusing on your relationship with the parent (see below) and 'gazing' at the child from time to time rather than intensely trying to make eye contact.

Many people also find it useful to have a puppet or similar distraction so that the young child has a different focus. Repetitive movements that the child can predict such as playing 'peepo' can also help the baby or child begin to trust you. Once you have gained the confidence of a baby or young child, it is still worth not rushing and allowing them time to work out that you can be trusted and are safe.

⇧ **A puppet can be used to help build relationships with young children**

When babies and young children are comfortable with you, it is important that you spend enough time supporting them. This is usually done through play, activities and by having some quiet moments with them, for example sharing a book or doing a jigsaw together.

Building relationships with parents

It is important to build relationships with parents alongside your relationships with children. There are many reasons for doing so, but in terms of building relationships with children it makes a significant difference. This is because babies and young children look at their parents' reactions in order to decide whether or not they should be fearful. This is sometimes referred to as social referencing and is an important part of early social development. Where babies and young children see positive interaction, smiles and even laughter, it helps children to settle in and to feel relaxed.

Building relationships with older children

While babies and younger children may find it hard at first to make a relationship with you, it can be easier for older children. This is because they have more language and also social skills. It is important here to recognise that this age range may be quite independent, especially if they are enjoying playing with other children; however, they will still need opportunities for individual time with the adults who look after them. It can be useful to think of ways to create opportunities for children to chat and be alongside you. Cooking activities are one example of a traditional way for children and adults to chat and thus form a relationship.

As you will see later on (page 139), it is important that you listen as well as talk and take time to find out about the interests of individual children. It is also important to recognise the 'on–off' pattern of children's interactions. One minute they may wish to chat, but a few minutes later they may want to go off and re-join a game with others.

Building relationships with young people

While young people are generally more independent, they also need to have strong relationships with the adults who work with them. Listening, being interested and not pronouncing judgements are skills to work on with this age group. You also need to be sensitive and to recognise times where you might ask questions such as 'Are you alright today?', but also times when you must wait for them to come forward. Young people particularly value adults who are good at listening, do not nag them and are ready to accept them.

How to value children and give them attention

You have seen that good relationships can make a significant difference to children and young people in many ways. Building relationships is done through spending time with someone and giving them attention. Giving children attention needs to be done on their terms rather than yours, so while there are some activities that are conducive to giving attention, you need to follow children's pace and pattern. Sometimes you can recognise when children and young people need attention because of their body language or because they have developed 'times' when they want it, such as just before having a nap or straight after school.

Activities that invite children to come alongside you

Simple and repetitive activities can encourage children to come alongside and have a chat. Seeing an adult sitting down and engaged with something that is not taking all of their concentration is very inviting for many children. When adults are slightly busy this can help children who are slightly shy from feeling that there will be too much focus on them. Below are some examples of activities that encourage all ages of children and young people to feel that they can sit and chat.

→ Shelling peas or peeling potatoes
→ Sorting out photos
→ Mending books
→ Peeling off stamps that have been soaked in water
→ Knitting, crotchet or embroidery
→ Doing a jigsaw (one at your level)

Taking photographs or films

Many children enjoy seeing themselves in photographs or films. Taking shots of children, assuming you have permission (see page 91), can help them feel that they are valued. It can be useful not to let the child see you take the photo so that it is more of a surprise. With young people it is important to involve them in taking photos. Some young people dislike being photographed or filmed and insisting on it will actually disrupt your relationship with them.

The importance of children's communication skills

In Unit 2 you looked at the way children learn language (pages 43–7), and it will be useful for you to re-visit these pages to remember the stages of language development.

In terms of empowering children, communication skills are critical. Being able to communicate helps children to express their needs and feelings and make friendships with other children. Interestingly, some children who experience difficulties in managing their behaviour are likely to have difficulties communicating. This means that helping children gain communication skills should be a major focus for your work with them.

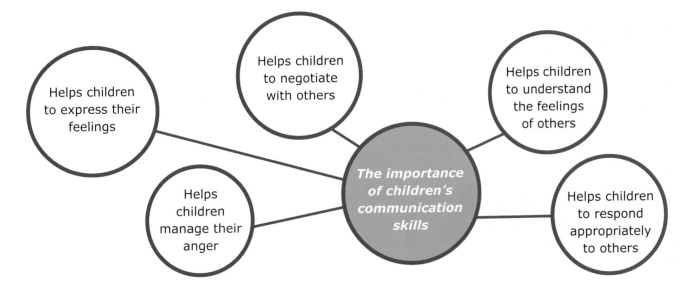

Helps children to express their feelings

Helps children to negotiate with others

Helps children to understand the feelings of others

The importance of children's communication skills

Helps children manage their anger

Helps children to respond appropriately to others

Ways of helping children to learn communication skills

Being a language partner with babies and young children

With babies and young children it is worth seeing yourself as a language partner. A language partner plays alongside children and follows their lead not only in play but also in communication. To be a good language partner you will need to respond immediately to babies' and children's attempts to communicate positively. For example, when a baby babbles you should make eye contact, smile and acknowledge what she has 'said'. In the same way, when a 4-year-old talks to you about what he is doing, you should get down to his level, smile and listen carefully to what he is saying (see also active listening below).

Physical contact

With babies and very young children, some communication accompanies physical contact, for example while holding a 6-month-old baby you might draw her attention to a mobile. Physical contact is a key element in good communication with this age range as it provides reassurance. A 2-year-old might want to sit down close beside you while you share a book and communication will take place in this situation.

For older children and young people it is important that physical contact is developmentally appropriate, i.e. it would not be appropriate for a 14-year-old boy to sit on your lap (see also page 129).

Time

Children and young people are not robots that can be turned on and off. Communication can take time and 'organised' activities for speaking and listening may not actually create meaningful communication opportunities. If you cannot take the time to listen and effectively communicate, you should make sure that the child or young person knows the reason why. You should also ensure that you do 'catch up' with them properly later. If children and young people are repeatedly left unable to communicate, they will quickly learn not to bother.

The importance of listening to children

Children and young people quickly recognise who really listens to them and who just goes through the motions. The type of listening that you need to practise is sometimes referred to as 'active listening'. Active listening is not just hearing but focusing on what the child or young person is trying to say and communicate. The term 'active' is an accurate description. Below is a list of things that you might do in order to be an active listener.

Eye contact

You need to show children and young people that you are interested in what they have to say. By looking (not staring) at a child or young person, you show them that they have your full attention. Sometimes, during a conversation, they may look away or down and this may be a sign that what they are about to say may be uncomfortable or difficult for them.

Body language

Adults who work with children tend to be busy! This unfortunately can send out signals that you have no time to listen. By coming down to a child's level or sitting with a young person, you can send out the signal that you are ready to listen. You must also be careful not to be distracted in this time and to look relaxed and settled.

⇧ **By coming down to a child's level and making eye contact, you show that you are ready to listen**

Summarising

It can sometimes be helpful to summarise what a child or young person is trying to say. This helps you check that you understand their meaning, for example 'So you wanted to play with Mark, but he wasn't at school.'

Reflecting

This is a useful technique that must be carefully used. The last few words are 'reflected' back which helps the child or young person to maintain communication.

Questioning

While children and young people do not want to be interrogated, asking odd questions that develop what they have said is sometimes useful. This might be through a mix of open and closed questions. For example, a closed question such as 'Are you enjoying this?' is quite safe as it allows a child simply to answer yes or no and they can add to it if they wish. Open questions such as 'Why do you like this one?' are good at encouraging children to talk a little more as they require a fuller answer. Using questions can show your interest and help you to explore some issues.

Strategies to show children you respect their individuality

You have seen that listening to children and young people is important in terms of building a relationship with them, but also giving them confidence. It is also important that you provide opportunities for children and young people to take on responsibility and to show their individuality. This is particularly important in group care situations where organisational needs and routines can create 'institutional' responses rather than individual ones.

Consultation

Today it is good practice for children and young people to be involved in making decisions, so they need to be given opportunities to be consulted and listened to. This means that there might be a forum for children and young people that meets regularly so they can feedback on the provision and be asked for their advice and ideas. In addition, children and young people need to be listened to at other times.

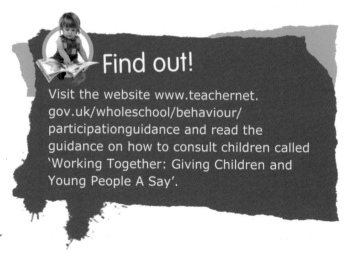

Find out!

Visit the website www.teachernet. gov.uk/wholeschool/behaviour/ participationguidance and read the guidance on how to consult children called 'Working Together: Giving Children and Young People A Say'.

Encouraging children to respect other people's views

In order to help children and young people respect others, it is important that you begin with yourself. Children and young people will learn a lot about your attitudes and values from the way in which you talk, listen to and think about others. They need to see that you listen to them and value their contributions, and that you are open minded.

The link between strong self-concept and respect

There is a strong link between self-esteem and the ability to respect others. Children and young people who are secure in their own identity and are confident will find it easier to be open minded and generous in spirit. It is important, too, that they 'perceive' themselves as being good at valuing others and that this becomes part of their identity. You need, for example, to acknowledge where children and young people are thoughtful about others.

Supporting children and young people

Learning to listen and respect other people's views is partly a modelled process, but it is also linked to skills and development. From Piaget's work it is known that young children find it hard to understand another's perspective (see pages 66–70), so your work here is more about modelling respect for others and praising children when they are able to listen without interrupting.

With older children and young people, modelling remains important but you also need to help them think through the importance of respecting other people's views. Exploring with young people the reasons why other people might feel strongly about an issue and have a different opinion to theirs can be helpful. Asking 'why' questions is therefore important, for example 'Why do you think he might feel this way?'

Have clear guidelines about comments and behaviour

It is essential that children and young people have clear guidance about how they can behave towards others. It is also important to intervene if you overhear discriminatory comments or behaviours that are unkind. This is important regardless of the age range you are with, although the way in which you might intervene will vary.

Circle time

Circle time is a useful technique to use with older children and young people. The aim is to give each person an opportunity to say what is on their mind, or their thoughts about an issue, and to ensure that their words are listened to. When circle time is well directed by adults it can be extremely empowering.

It can be used to change group dynamics, to discuss issues affecting the group or to share ideas.

Note that circle time is not always appropriate for young children as it is a sophisticated tool which requires that children are developmentally ready to sit still and listen without interrupting. These skills tend to be in place around 6 or 7 years of age.

Problem solving

Encouraging groups of children and young people to join together for an activity that requires problem solving or work on a project can be a practical way of finding out about other people's views. For example, a group may think about raising money for charity or, in the case of younger children, lay out an obstacle course.

Case study

Providing feedback on behaviour

Matthew is 4 years old. He attends a nursery five mornings a week. He disrupts other children's games by snatching toys or taking things away from them. His key worker, Shahida, has therefore decided to work on this behaviour. She begins by assessing Matthew's language and realises that Matthew rarely talks in the setting. She decides to spend some time each day talking and playing games with him and one other child, who also finds it hard to play cooperatively. They play games such as lotto but also do some activities together such as playing with the farm animals and playing in the role-play area. At other times, Shahida gives Matthew plenty of attention.

Over three weeks, Matthew's language improves and the extra attention helps him to modify his behaviour. He begins to find it easier to talk to the other children, and this shows in their responses. He also learns how to join other children in play.

1. Why is it important that Shahida considers Matthew's language?

2. How has Matthew benefited from the extra attention?

3. Why was it a good idea for Shahida to work with more than one child?

How to be fair and consistent in supporting children

Children and young people need to know what to expect when they are with us. This means that you need to be consistent and fairly predictable in your behaviour towards them and also other people. This creates a more emotionally secure environment for them. It is difficult for children and young people to trust someone who one day seems generous and on another is hard to please.

Fairness and consistency is especially important when it comes to managing unwanted behaviour. Children and young people tend to have a strong sense of fairness and they quickly lose respect for adults who jump to conclusions or who are inconsistent. This means that it is important to take time out to listen to both sides of any dispute or to ask a child whether there was a reason behind their actions. It is also important to be aware of the small things that matter enormously to children, for example that they were promised a turn on something. Remembering and keeping promises is therefore one thing that adults need to do. As with helping children and young people to respect other people's views, it is essential to remember that children are learning from you and the way in which you act.

Getting ready for assessment

1. Explain how your placement or work setting empowers children and helps them develop confidence.
2. Explain why emotional intelligence is seen as being important to children's development.

How to support children to prepare for transfer or transition

In practice

Darren is 4 years old and attends nursery. He is going to school in a couple of weeks' time. He is starting to be quite anxious about it and his mum says he has recently become quite clingy.

By the end of this section you will know how transition and changes can affect children and young people and ways in which you might help them to settle.

The transitions children will experience

Most children as they grow up will experience a range of transitions as part of the normal pattern of childhood. Most of these transitions will be planned, for example when a child moves from a pre-school to start their Reception year. The spider diagram below shows some of the changes that children may make during the first few years of their lives.

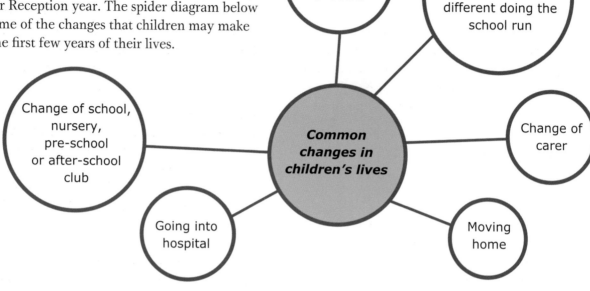

Change of group, class or room

Change of routine, e.g. someone different doing the school run

Change of school, nursery, pre-school or after-school club

Common changes in children's lives

Change of carer

Going into hospital

Moving home

How children feel when they transfer to a new setting

As an adult, it can be hard to think about what a child might be feeling as they change settings. Some children seem to cope with the transition fairly easily and appear quite confident, while other children may have fears and worries that to an adult might seem trivial.

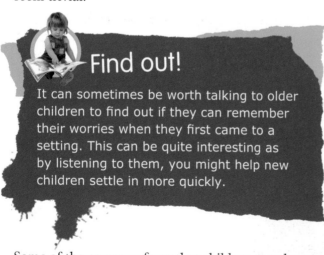

Find out!

It can sometimes be worth talking to older children to find out if they can remember their worries when they first came to a setting. This can be quite interesting as by listening to them, you might help new children settle in more quickly.

Some of the common fears that children may have on arrival into a setting include:

➔ Will I make friends?
➔ Will I know where the toilets are?

➔ Will they know that I am coming?
➔ Will the carers/teachers be nice?
➔ Will someone tell me what I have to do?
➔ Will I get lost or be left by myself?
➔ Will I get into trouble if I can't do something or don't understand?
➔ Will my mummy/carer know where to collect me?
➔ What will happen if I don't like the food?
➔ Will there be any food?

Children under 3 years

It is worth recognising that fairly small changes can have a significant impact on this age group and it is important not to underestimate this. A change to the routine because a member of staff is poorly may result in an unsettled child. It is also important to remember that children under 3 years have a limited understanding of time. This means that talking about changes too far in advance may actually confuse them rather than reassure them. Interestingly, many children of this age can cope with changes to their lives, providing they have strong relationships with the people who will be with them at the time. Thus moving home is likely to be fine, providing they move home with their family. On the other hand, a change of room in a nursery where the child will have a different key worker may be more problematic. The child's reaction will be bound up in their attachment to the existing key worker, so the way to prepare is to ensure that the child has already built up a relationship with their 'new' key worker before transition. (See also attachment theory, Unit 2 pages 80–2.)

Children aged 4–7 years

Children in this age range have more understanding about what is happening around them, although their concept of time is still developing. Again, this means that preparation for changes needs to be carefully timed so as not to unnecessarily alarm the child.

A good example of a transition that most children in this age group will go through is starting school or moving from infants to juniors. Talking intensely about the change too far ahead can make children feel unsettled and even fearful. Judging how far ahead to prepare children is thus a delicate skill and you may need to take into account individual children's needs. You also need to find out from parents about how well the child has coped before with any changes. Some children will have had good experiences of transition, while others may not have done and so will need sensitive support.

In this age range, children may also find it hard to imagine somewhere else or what it might be like, as this is a sophisticated skill. It is therefore useful to provide visual images, introduce key people such as new teachers or arrange a visit (see also page 148). As with the younger age group, children aged 4–7 years need to feel that they will be with people or other children they know, although the quality of their relationships with adults are likely to be more important to them.

Children aged 7–12 years

This age range will already have had experiences of transition and change in their lives. Their previous experiences will be ones they remember and on which any anxieties or expectations are based. Children in this age range are quite good at imagining things, both positive and negative. They may, for example, connect information they have seen on television or experiences they have heard from other children to base their thoughts on. This can lead to children having many fears or expectations that are not realistic.

Children aged 7–12 years have a good understanding of time so understand that a week is not that far away but a few months is. Children in this age range are often able to make transitions when they are given plenty of information and are able to ask questions. A key factor for them will be whether they will be with their friends or close adults. Interestingly, children of this age will also need repeated opportunities to discuss any transitions as they will often think of questions later on. It is also helpful to involve them as much as possible and give them some responsibility and opportunities to make decisions.

Young people aged 13–16 years

As you have read in Unit 2 (pages 33–4), young people aged 13–16 years are very much in a transition period in their own lives. This means they may 'hop' between the need for reassurance to seeming confident.

A key factor in coping with transitions for this age group is access to friends, as they now play a pivotal role in young people's lives. A good example of this

⇦ **Before starting school, it is helpful to arrange a visit for children to meet their new teacher**

is the way in which some young people will choose subjects to study based on what their friends are doing. Young people also need to be involved at the earliest and are likely to want to be part of the decision making process. This means that instead of telling a young person that he or she is to visit a setting, it will be better to ask whether this is something that will help. Taking control over some of the process will help the young person to gain in confidence.

Working with the child and family

Preparing children and young people for change

Preparing children and young people for eventual changes is an important way of helping them. In this process it is extremely important to involve parents, especially for young children as it can be confusing for a child if they receive mixed messages. The extent and way in which you might help children and young people will depend on their age.

Gathering information to support the child through a successful transition

In order to help the child or young person make a transition, you need to find out as much information as you can. You might do this via parents or directly with the new setting. This will depend on the type of transition that the child is about to experience. By finding out information you will be able to consider how best to prepare the child. This is important as sometimes adults can inadvertently raise expectations or mislead children in some way. This can actually make their first experiences within a setting more difficult.

As you have seen above, young people may need to be actively involved in finding out information about what is happening. They may, for example, want to visit a website or ask you to arrange a visit. Some of the ways in which you might gain information are described below.

Websites

Many organisations now have websites including schools. This can be a good way of getting some background information. It may also be possible to e-mail a specific enquiry as well.

Brochures and prospectus

Schools, clubs and care settings usually have some form of prospectus or brochure. These can be useful as they may contain photographs which will help older children visualise where they are going.

Leaflets

In some situations you may find that there are leaflets available that explain a procedure or event to a child, for example a hospital may have one designed for children.

Word of mouth

Sometimes you may know of another family or professional who can tell you more about the new setting or procedure. While word of mouth can be extremely useful, it is also important to be aware of accuracy. Things change over time and the experiences of one person may not be the same as those of another.

Letters and phone calls

Writing a letter to find out information or picking up a phone can help you find out information directly. Remember, though, that before contacting others you will need the permission of parents in some situations, for example a child going into hospital, otherwise the parents may feel that you are breaching confidentiality or simply meddling.

Strategies to support and prepare children for transfers and transitions

It is important to think about what the expectations of children and young people might be towards a transition. With younger-aged children, this requires you to use your previous experience and consider things from a child-centred point of view. It is often the 'trivia' that is the most important to get right, for example a young child going on a plane for the first time might not realise that there are toilets.

Strategies for identifying expectations according to the age of the child

With young children, talking alone may not be effective. Tools such as using a teddy or using drawing might be helpful, as described below. It can also be helpful to create a role play situation so that you can act out what will happen.

With older children and young people it is good to talk to them about the transition. Older children may talk about their fears and expectations as and when they surface in their mind, while you might ask young people directly about these. It is important to be flexible in the process of exploring transitions and arrangements. Children neither think nor talk to order! The spider diagram below gives example of fears or questions that children and young people may have.

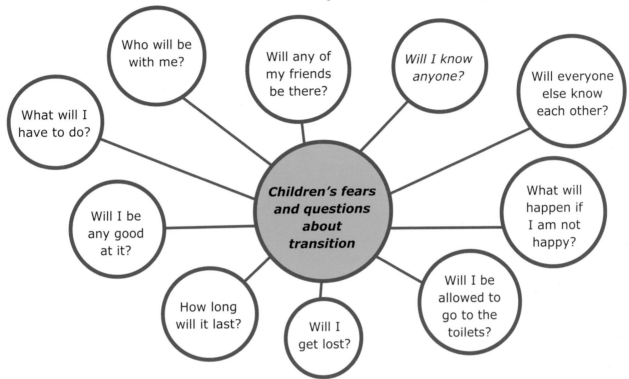

Who will be with me?

Will any of my friends be there?

Will I know anyone?

Will everyone else know each other?

What will I have to do?

Children's fears and questions about transition

Will I be any good at it?

What will happen if I am not happy?

How long will it last?

Will I get lost?

Will I be allowed to go to the toilets?

Identify how to provide children with further support

Some children will need more support than others in order to make a new transition. It will be important to recognise early on that a child may become distressed or is showing signs of anxiety. Signs that a child is not coping or is becoming anxious might include tearfulness, clinginess and some regressive behaviours such as bedwetting when previously the child was dry. It might be helpful in such cases to look at ways to make the transition more gradual and of establishing a strong relationship with the child's new key worker.

In some cases, the underlying difficulty with the transition may be linked to a child's previous trauma, in which case professional support will be needed to help the child. This might mean that the child is referred to the child mental health team in the local area, where specialist support can be provided. A child and sometimes the child's family might then receive counselling if this is appropriate or play therapy, so that the experience that is holding back the child can be explored in a safe environment.

Helping children to communicate their expectations and fears

Children often benefit from a visual route to help them sort out their thoughts. There are several ways of doing this, but role play and drawing are particularly effective.

Using a teddy

Bring a teddy into the setting. Tell the children that teddy is about to have a change in his life; the change is of course the same one as the children face. Ask the children if they think that teddy will have any questions. What do they think teddy is worried about or needs to know? The responses are generally things that children have been subconsciously thinking about.

Drawing

Put out some painting or drawing materials. Sit with children and ask them if they can imagine what the new situation will be like. If you have information about the new setting or procedure that is reassuring, you can help the child to draw this in, for example 'I think that there will be a special person who will be waiting for you and will be kind and smiley. Shall we draw her in as well?' As well as participating, it is essential to listen carefully.

Changes in activities

As well as hearing about children's expectations and fears, you might also need to prepare practically. Children may, for example, need to manage their own dinner money or get on a bus. Learning practical skills can give children and young people confidence although it is important that you have accurate information about the type of activities they will be doing.

Self-help skills

Self-help skills are important at all ages. Ideally, self-help skills are built into the way that you work with children from babyhood onwards. They include being able to dress, feed and use the toilet. For children about to enter school, self-help skills are essential as the staff to child ratio is different. As children get older they will need to learn some organisational skills. They may, for example, need to start taking responsibility for their own possessions such as coats and books, and may need gradually to learn to organise themselves. For older children and young people, they may need to learn skills such as coping with money and tickets and using transport.

How to promote communication between settings

Children benefit when everyone including parents work together. Communication between settings is therefore a vital element. This should ideally begin in plenty of time so that staff can get to know about each other's work and about the needs of the child or young person. In some situations, settings will regularly be working together, for example a pre-school may regularly be 'passing on' children to a nearby primary school. In these situations, it is good practice for 'exchange' visits to take place. For example, a teacher might visit the pre-school to talk

to staff and the leader might visit the primary school. Such visits can be extraordinarily helpful as adults then know how best to prepare children. It also means that together they can talk about the needs of individual children. (Note that parental permission is needed before records or discussions about children take place, to avoid a breach of confidentiality.)

Case study

Sharing information

Gemma works with the 4-year-olds at Little Foxes Nursery. Most of the children in her care will be attending the village primary school in the autumn. Preparation for the transition begins in February with the first of a series of visits and meetings. By the end of the summer term, Gemma has shared information about the group and their interests, and the children have also met their new teacher. They have also planned out ways in which they can make the transition easier by adopting similar routines and using similar books. For the two children who will not go to the village school, Gemma makes separate contact with their schools and talks to staff about how she can help prepare the children.

1. Why is it important to make contact with other settings?
2. Why is it useful that Gemma visits the primary school?
3. Explain how children benefit from this type of communication.

The importance of providing continuity of experiences for children

As a result of your contact with other settings, you should be able to ensure that you maintain some continuity. This is particularly important for babies and young children who can find transitions and changes difficult. Continuity of experiences might include ensuring that young children recognise a few familiar books, toys and songs. Continuity of experiences is also important in terms of physical care for young children, such as nappy changing, feeding and sleeping. Making sure that some elements of the new setting seem familiar can greatly assist children with settling in.

Did you know?

It is good practice for young children to be able to take familiar objects or comforters with them into a new setting. For some children this might be a piece of blanket, a teddy or a favourite toy. Having a physical object that is familiar can help the child feel more secure.

Case study

Identifying a child who needs extra support

Michael is 5 years old and due to start at a new school. With his mother, he has recently arrived at a local women's refuge after an incident in which his father threatened to kill him.

The teacher at the school has visited Michael and his mother and showed him photos of the school and his classroom. He has been into the classroom but will only stay there if his mother is close by. The teacher and his mother have tried gently to settle him in, but he seems very distressed by the idea that his mother must leave him. Together, they decide that Michael may need professional support in order to cope.

1. Why might Michael be showing signs of distress?

2. Why is it important that Michael is given professional support?

3. Explain why it is important to recognise promptly when a child needs extra support.

The promotion of citizenship and independence

It is recognised that children and young people need gradually to take on responsibility so that they can be prepared for independent living. This is one reason why it is important that from an early age you help children to develop self-help skills, for example encouraging a 3-year-old to tidy up or a 10-year-old to do some simple cooking.

It is also recognised that children and young people need some knowledge of how their country's political system works as well as life skills such as learning about finance. This means that citizenship is now taught in English schools from the age of 11 years. Citizenship and independence is also reflected in the personal, social and emotional area of learning and development in the Early Years Foundation Stage in England (a framework for children aged 0–5 years). It is expected that children will gradually learn how to cooperate in groups and learn skills such as tidying up and taking care of the environment. You can help children learn these skills by role modelling them (see also pages 71–2) and looking out for opportunities that link to their age and stage of development, for example encouraging a child to help prepare the group's snacks with you.

Think about it

1. Make a list of five things that you think all school leavers should know.

2. Visit the Department of Education's website (www.dfes.co.uk) and find out how citizenship is taught in schools.

Getting ready for assessment

1. Explain how a setting might help a child who is making a transition.

2. What issues would need to be considered?

Section 6

The causes and effects of discrimination in society

In practice

Matthew is keen to invite his best friend home for tea, but his mother has said that he can't do this. Matthew cannot understand this as he enjoys playing with his friend. His mother eventually tells him that having friends round costs extra money.

By the end of this section you will understand the nature of discrimination and the way that it can affect children and young people.

The characteristics of discrimination

Discrimination is principally about unfairness. Being discriminated against means not getting the same rights, services or opportunities as others do. Discrimination is complex, but certain groups of children, young people and their families are more likely to be discriminated against than others. The spider diagram shows the basis for much of the discrimination that is prevalent in our society.

Age
Example: Beth is 12 years old. The local shop has a notice that says that anyone under 18 years is not allowed inside unless accompanied by an adult. This is to prevent shoplifting, but Beth never steals.

Disability
Example: Alex is 14 years old and has epilepsy. He wants to join a local swimming club as he is a good swimmer. The club says he cannot be a member because of his epilepsy.

Gender
Example: Jason's friends all play football. He is interested in dancing. His friends keep teasing him so he has decided to give it up.

Income
Example: Ayse is 8 years old. She dreams of playing the piano like her best friend. Her mother does not have the money to pay for lessons.

Family structure
Example: Jasmine wants to take her two daughters on holiday. She has seen an advert for free child places. When she tries to book, she is told that this offer is for two-parent families and that she would need to pay full price for one of her daughters.

Common forms of discrimination

Religion
Example: Bekkir notices that other mothers talk to each other, but not to his mother. He is starting to wonder whether this has something to do with the way that she dresses.

Culture
Example: Jordan's family are Travellers. He is entitled to go to school, but his parents have been told that there are no spaces at the nearest school. When the Ethnic Minority Support teacher tries on their behalf, she is told that there are spaces but the school doesn't really like taking Traveller children.

Race
Example: Davie's ethnic background is black African. He loves reading and tries hard at school. He recently overheard a supply teacher saying that there was little point in setting and marking homework for children like him.

Types of discrimination

Discrimination can be categorised as either **direct** or **indirect**.

Key term

Direct discrimination This is active and deliberate, for example a sign saying 'No wheelchairs please'.

Indirect discrimination This is less obvious, for example steps at an entrance to a shop.

There is some legislation designed to prevent discrimination (see pages 116–7). In general this tends to be effective against direct discrimination but less so with indirect discrimination. Whatever the type of discrimination, it still has an effect on the child, young person or their family (see below).

The causes of discrimination and the effects on children

To understand the causes of discrimination, you have to begin by looking at attitudes and values.

How do children learn values and attitudes?

Young children develop their own attitudes and values by watching and learning from the behaviour and reactions of those around them. When presented with a new object or situation they are unsure of, babies will often look at their parent as a guide. This is often called social referencing. Children will learn attitudes and values in this way from several sources including:

→ family
→ early years practitioners and teachers
→ friends
→ peers.

Think about it

Indirect discrimination is often subtle and difficult to prove. The examples below show how indirect discrimination can affect individuals' lives.

→ Inderjeet has left school and is finding it difficult to get work. His friends with the same qualifications have had no problems. He is sure that his name and racial origin are stopping employers from interviewing him.

→ Katherine works for a large company. She has had some promotion but has noticed that some of the men who started at the same time as her have had more promotions, even though she is well qualified and her work is of the same standard.

→ Simon has a birthmark on his face which is visible. He wanted to work in sales and has had many interviews. He is sure that he isn't being offered the posts because of his appearance.

→ Zainab has a slight learning difficulty which means that she cannot always remember everything that she is told. She is fine if instructions are written down or if she is given them one at a time. She has learned to overcome this minor difficulty and in every other way she is perfectly capable. She was offered a promotion to another department and felt that she should mention this to her boss. A week later she was told that, unfortunately, the company has over-estimated its staffing requirements.

1. Why would it be difficult for the people in these situations to prove that they had been discriminated against?

2. How might this type of discrimination affect these people's lives?

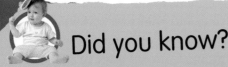

Did you know?

The family is probably the most powerful influence on children's attitudes and values. In their home, children learn about their own family's feelings about other people.

Stereotypes

Sometimes people's attitudes and values are not formed from their experiences but are based on **stereotypes**. Most people hold stereotypes of one form or another, and many of these will have been learned during childhood while others will have come from books, magazines and television. For example, a stereotype of people who are obese might be that they are lazy or greedy.

Key term

Stereotype A standardised or fixed image of a group of people

Think about it

1. Consider what the stereotype image is for each group listed below.

➜ Football supporters
➜ Teenage mothers
➜ Second-hand car dealers
➜ Scientists
➜ Nurses
➜ Librarians

2. Can you think of any other stereotypes?

Stereotypes can make a person think that they know what a group of people is like, and this may colour their attitude towards somebody who belongs to a stereotyped group. Once a person meets people from these groups, they often realise that their thoughts about them were not accurate. This is why it is important for early years practitioners to introduce activities and visits from many different people to show children the falsehood behind stereotypes.

Prejudice and discrimination

The stereotypes a person has about people can cause him or her to make judgements about them without knowing anything about them. This is called **prejudice**. In some situations you may pre-judge a person favourably, for example you might expect a minister of religion to be kind. But in other situations your thoughts about a person might be negative.

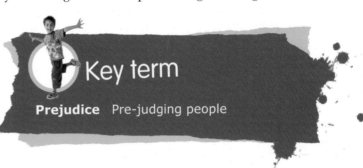

Key term

Prejudice Pre-judging people

People have all sorts of prejudices, but prejudice becomes more serious when people's actions are affected by negative stereotypes. In the news there are often examples of extreme behaviour caused by prejudice.

Allport (1954) studied prejudice and discrimination. He defined five stages of behaviour that could be shown by groups of people acting from prejudice, as follows:

1. *Verbal* – hostile talk, insults and jokes.
2. *Avoidance* – keeping a distance, avoiding, crossing the road.
3. *Discrimination* – exclusion from housing, rights, employment, etc.
4. *Physical attack* – violence against an individual from a group or against their property.
5. *Extermination* – violence against whole groups, e.g. massacres.

Effects of discrimination

Discrimination not only affects the individuals in our society who are not given the same life chances as others, it affects society itself.

→ The best people may not always be given jobs or positions of power.

→ The views and attitudes of groups of people may not be represented, for example there are not many black women judges or Asians in the police force.

→ Groups of people may turn against society because they feel that they have nothing to lose and are not part of any system.

Children and discrimination

During their early years, children are developing their sense of identity, self-worth and self-esteem. They are learning how others see them and treat them. They react to what they experience and see around them. By the age of 3 or 4 years, children have started to understand racial and gender differences.

Being a victim of discrimination can affect children's life chances in many ways.

→ It can damage their developing sense of self-worth and self-esteem.

→ They may grow up with a view of themselves as inferior.

→ They may not try out new activities for fear of failing.

→ They may achieve less at school.

→ They may develop serious emotional and social problems later in life, e.g. finding it hard to form relationships.

The adult's role in promoting diversity and inclusive practice

Taking positive action

It is recognised that some groups of people who have been traditionally discriminated against are under-represented in society. This means, for example, that there are very few black women Members of Parliament or disabled magistrates. Interviewers often select the interviewee who shares their attitudes and values.

To try to balance this situation, some organisations have a policy of positive action. This means that they may guarantee interviews for certain groups of people or ensure a quota of interview candidates from a certain group. Critics of positive action say it is very unfair, while others say that this is the best way of breaking the cycle of discrimination.

The advert below is an example of an organisation taking positive action in favour of disabled people.

Vacancies at Farningdon House

We are looking for Administrative Officers to work at Farningdon House.

Applicants should have 5 GCSEs, including English and Mathematics and/or worked in an office environment for a minimum of 1 year.

The position is full-time and working hours will by either 07.30–18.30 or 10.30–21.30. We would also consider a job share arrangement.

The salary is £13,000 per annum, pro rata.

Farningdon House is an Equal Opportunities Employer and we are keen to receive applications from all sections of the community. We are also a part of the Guaranteed Insurance Scheme (GIS) for disabled people. If you are registered disabled and do not have the minimum entrance criteria you will be offered a guaranteed interview which will include a test.

Please phone for an application pack.

Putting good practice into effect

To be able to challenge any form of discrimination, early years practitioners must be able to recognise that it is happening. Sometimes discrimination can be hidden and harder to detect, for example an early years setting that does not have any images of ethnic minorities on posters or in books – even though there are no negative images, it is still discrimination.

Direct discrimination – challenging remarks

Occasionally you will have to deal with children who behave inappropriately or make discriminatory remarks. For example, in a home corner a group of girls saying to a boy who wants to join in their play, 'We don't want you in here because boys can't play properly', or a child saying 'I don't like Charlene's hair.'

It is important that you do not ignore offensive remarks, even if children are just echoing what they may have heard elsewhere. Depending on how old the child is, you can do any of the following:

→ Ask the child what they meant and where they heard it.
→ Tell the child that what they have said is not appropriate.
→ Tell the child why their remarks are hurtful.
→ Correct any information that is untrue, for example 'Chinese people have slitty eyes.'
→ Support the other child or children and make sure that they know you care about them.
→ Mention the incident to the supervisor.
→ Consider whether the setting needs to look again at its policy on equal opportunities.

Direct discrimination – bullying

Children need to be encouraged from an early age to deal with bullying and discriminatory attitudes, although adults must always support and protect them. Bullying is never harmless fun and you must always act if you suspect that a child is being bullied, for example by talking to your supervisor about your concerns.

Children can also be taught techniques that empower them. Kidscape is a charity that produces several activity packs that teach children what to do if they are being bullied (see below).

Think about it

In pairs, choose one of the following scenarios and work out a role play to show other members of your group how you would handle the situation.

1. A parent comes to see you to say that her boy had been called stupid and fat by one of the other children.
2. You overhear a member of staff asking a child what her favourite food it. The child says that she likes chapattis and dahl. The member of staff says to the girl, 'I don't know how you eat that kind of funny food.'
3. A father asks if you can stop his 3-year-old son from playing with dolls and prams.

↥ An extract from *Stop Bullying!* by Kidscape

A child may indicate by signs or behaviour that he or she is being bullied. Adults should be aware that these are possible signs and that they should investigate if a child:

- is frightened of walking to or from school
- is unwilling to go to school
- begins to do poorly in school work
- becomes withdrawn; starts stammering
- regularly has books or clothes destroyed
- becomes distressed, stops eating
- cries easily
- becomes disruptive or aggressive
- has possessions 'go missing'
- has dinner or other monies continually 'lost'
- starts stealing money (to pay bully)
- is frightened to say what's wrong
- attempts suicide or runs away
- has nightmares.

These signs and behaviours could indicate other problems, but bullying should be considered a possibility and should be investigated.

Confronting and combating discrimination and discriminatory practices in settings

There may be times when early years practitioners recognise that discrimination is taking place in their early years setting. This may be intentional or unintentional, for example a setting may forget that some parents cannot afford to pay for their children to go on an outing. It is important for early years practitioners to be ready to challenge any discriminatory practice that they see. This does not necessarily have to be done in a confrontational way but it is essential that something is done or said. In some cases a simple reminder or comment may work well, but where discrimination appears to be more deep seated it may need reporting to the supervisor or manager in a more formal way. All settings should have an equal opportunities code or policy and this should include procedures for combating discrimination.

Why promoting a positive environment is important for all children

The UK today is a diverse multicultural society. In schools and nurseries there are children from many different races and cultures speaking many different languages. This is a rich cultural mix which has many positive effects for children.

→ Children learn that everyone is different and special.

→ Children are exposed to the wider world. They learn that there are different languages, different ways to pray and different ways to prepare food.

→ Children gain learning opportunities by tasting a range of foods, listening to a range of music, and hearing and seeing different art forms. This can help children to be more creative.

→ Children learn how to value each other through being in a positive environment.

Creating a positive environment – valuing children and parents

A positive environment is a caring and loving one. It accepts that all children are special and provides for children with special needs as well as being multicultural. To create a positive environment involves five main things:

⇧ **There are many positive benefits for children growing up in a multicultural society**

1. Valuing children
2. Valuing parents
3. Showing positive images of children
4. Being a good role model
5. Planning an anti-bias curriculum.

Valuing children

We know that children's self-esteem and confidence will affect their behaviour and emotional well-being, and in the long term their ability to fulfil their potential. This means that early years practitioners must be able to praise children and make them feel confident about their own identity.

Occasionally, some early years practitioners find it difficult to praise children freely because something in their own childhood is holding them back, for example they may not have been given much praise as children. This means that, as an early years practitioner, you must examine your own attitudes and experiences to make sure that they do not stop you from valuing children.

Positive attitudes towards families

Children will quickly pick up on the attitudes of staff. They will see whether a staff member seems to be interested and friendly with their parents. This means that early years practitioners need to understand that there are a variety of child-rearing practices which are equally valuable. There is no such thing as a 'standard' household and children come to settings with a wide range of experiences. Where parents have lifestyles that are different from yours, you will need to be sure that you do not make judgements based on your particular views of parenting – which may be very different.

You can show that you value parents by involving them. They may wish to help in the setting or be able to provide information, resources or books, for example families that have more than one language might be able to lend books and music tapes.

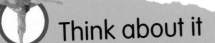

Think about it

Michael is 4 years old and goes to nursery. One day Michael's mother says to Michael's key worker that her partner, Chris, will be picking up Michael at the end of the session. At the end of the session, a woman comes and says that she is Chris and will be collecting Michael. At first the key worker says there is some mistake, before realising that this is the partner of Michael's mother. The key worker is embarrassed.

1. Why might the key worker's reaction make Michael feel different from other children?
2. Why is it important for early years practitioners to remember that children come from a variety of households?

Promoting positive images

Early years practitioners need to make sure that they show children positive images of others. In a setting, all equipment, pictures, books, activities and the way the nursery is organised should reflect all children in a positive light, for example books that show strong and capable characters who also happen to be black, disabled or female. This is particularly important when children are in settings or areas that are not multicultural or have no children with special needs. Positive images also help children who may in some way be in a minority in their setting, as children need to feel proud of who they are. For example, children who wear glasses need to see images of other children wearing glasses.

Find out!

Find out which are the four most popular books in your placement.

→ Why do they appeal to children?
→ Do they provide positive images?

Select the book that most encourages equality of opportunity, for example showing positive images of age, race, culture, gender, disability, etc.

Good role models

Children gain some of their attitudes and values from watching others (see pages 71–2), so early years practitioners need to be good role models.

→ Language must not be prejudiced, e.g. 'I thought you were a big strong boy.'
→ You must take care not to be dismissive of things that you are not familiar with, e.g. 'This strange looking fruit is called plantain' or 'I wouldn't like to wear one of those.'
→ You must ensure that children see you cooperating with and respecting everyone who comes into the setting. In this way they will learn that everyone must be treated well.
→ Children will also need to see you being open minded and genuinely interested in other people and their beliefs. You can do this by showing children objects from different countries, for example clothes, musical instruments and paintings.

Think about it

Many people understand the idea of equal opportunities but their everyday language lets them down. Look at the following sentences.

→ 'Boys will be boys.'

→ I like proper English food.'

→ 'I don't believe in celebrating all these funny festivals.'

→ 'She's such a pretty girl, yet she doesn't make the best of herself.'

1. In pairs, work out why each sentence contains an offensive or discriminatory message.

2. Can you think of some more of these types of sentences?

Planning an anti-bias curriculum

Louise Derman-Sparks (1989) talks about implementing an anti-bias curriculum. Anti-bias should permeate every aspect of a setting and is more than just celebrating the occasional festival. All nursery equipment should reflect the anti-bias and ensure that all children feel valued and at home in the setting regardless of their background.

→ To ensure cooperation and respect, discussions with children should stress similarities between people and races rather than emphasising the differences.

→ Children should be encouraged to look at other people's points of view, for example 'If someone said that unkind thing to you, how would you feel?'

→ Children need to be able to feel good and confident about themselves and be able to say 'That's not fair' or 'I don't like that.'

→ Children should feel that they can stand up for themselves and for others in unfair situations.

Anti-bias practice empowers children.

Good practice checklist

Anti-bias practice

✓ Have a comprehensive equal opportunities policy.

✓ Check and review the success of the policy.

✓ Plan the curriculum to ensure an anti-bias approach.

✓ Check books and equipment for negative images.

✓ Encourage positive interactions.

✓ Allow children to talk about their feelings.

✓ Value the community and home language used in the nursery.

✓ Encourage partnerships with parents.

✓ Tackle name calling, bullying and discrimination.

Getting ready for assessment

1. Discuss some of the causes and effects of discrimination on children.

2. Explain how your placement or work setting works to prevent discrimination.

Unit 4

Keeping children safe

In this unit you will learn:

1. How to identify and develop strategies to establish and maintain healthy, safe and secure environments

2. The procedures for dealing with accidents, illnesses and other emergencies

3. How to plan and provide an enabling physical environment for children

4. How to develop age-appropriate routines which encourage children to care for themselves

Section 1

How to identify and develop strategies to establish and maintain healthy, safe and secure environments

In practice

Little Trees Nursery has decided to offer out-of-school and holiday provision to the local community. The manager has asked all the staff to look at the health and safety arrangements in their area as part of a general review as well as preparing for the changes. Jane, who heads the nursery unit, decides she had better check the latest information to make sure she is up to speed on everything connected with keeping children safe.

By the end of this section you will understand how to identify and develop strategies to establish and maintain healthy, safe and secure environments.

Health and safety legislation

As an early years practitioner you have a key responsibility for the safety of the **children** in your care – parents and carers trust you to look after their children. There are often differences in the legal requirements in the different countries in the United Kingdom. Make sure that you find out if there are any differences in your country – especially in the National Care Standards. The new Statutory Framework for the Early Years Foundation Stage (EYFS), which takes effect from September 2008 for parts of the UK, now includes the legislation and standards for keeping children safe.

Key term

Children This covers the age groups 0–8 years, including boys, girls, disabled children and those with special educational needs.

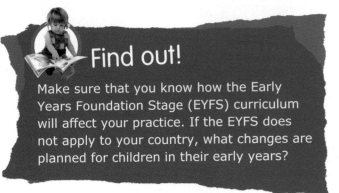

Find out!

Make sure that you know how the Early Years Foundation Stage (EYFS) curriculum will affect your practice. If the EYFS does not apply to your country, what changes are planned for children in their early years?

There are a number of legal and regulatory requirements that you need to know about to help to protect children and adults in any setting. These include:

→ the Health and Safety at Work Act 1974
→ Control of Substances Hazardous to Health (COSHH) Regulations 2002
→ Reporting of Injuries, Diseases and Dangerous Occurrences Regulations (RIDDOR) 1995
→ Motor Vehicles (Wearing of Seat Belts) (Amendment) Regulations 2006
→ Childcare Act 2006 – this sets out the statutory framework for assessment of settings, including health and safety in the Early Years Foundation

Stage (EYFS) in force from September 2008 (previously covered in the National Standards for Child Care and Education Settings (Ofsted)
→ the Food Safety Act 1990 and the Food Safety (General Food Hygiene) Regulations 1995 (see also Unit 12)
→ product safety marking
→ smoking ban in the UK in indoor public places, in force in Scotland from March 2006, in Wales and Northern Ireland from April 2007 and in England from July 2007. The EYFS includes a legal requirement to ensure children are always in a smoke-free environment.

Did you know?

Accidental injuries are the greatest single threat to life of children under 15 years in the UK – about 350 children die from these causes every year. They are also a major cause of disability and ill-health, with over 100,000 being admitted to hospital and over 2 million having to visit accident and emergency departments. In terms of the number of potentially healthy life-years lost, children's accidents outrank all other causes. (*Source:* Child Accident Prevention Trust 2003)

The Health and Safety at Work Act 1974

All employers have legal responsibilities under the Health and Safety at Work Act 1974. This means that employers must meet certain rules to make sure people are safe in their place of work. It also means that employees must be careful that there is no risk of injury to anyone. This means that everyone in a children's setting – including you – has responsibility for the health and safety of anyone who is there.

Regarding places where children are educated and cared for, the Health and Safety at Work Act states:

→ buildings should be in good condition and designed with the safety of users in mind
→ buildings and surroundings should be clean and safe
→ equipment must be safely used and stored

→ working practices must promote the health and safety of children.

In nurseries and schools, etc., everyone who works there (including learners) must know what the written statement about safety says and put it into practice.

Safeguarding employees

The Health and Safety at Work Act also makes sure that people who work in a setting (employees) are protected from harm.

→ The workplace should be safe and not pose a risk to workers' health.

→ There should be secure systems of working.

→ All articles and substances (e.g. cleaning materials) should be stored and used safely.

→ Welfare facilities for staff should be available.

→ Appropriate information, training and supervision should be made for the health and safety of employees.

→ Any protective clothing needed should be provided free of charge.

→ Certain injuries, diseases and occurrences should be reported to the Health and Safety Executive (HSE).

→ First aid facilities should be provided.

→ Each setting should have a safety representative who is asked about things affecting health and safety in the workplace.

Employees' responsibilities

Employees (including learners) must:

→ take care of their own health and safety and that of others affected by their actions

→ cooperate with their employer on health and safety issues.

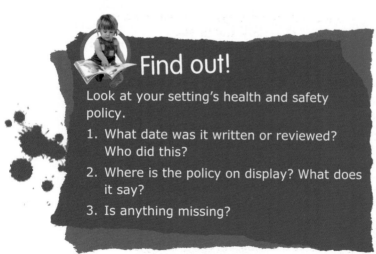

Find out!

Look at your setting's health and safety policy.

1. What date was it written or reviewed? Who did this?

2. Where is the policy on display? What does it say?

3. Is anything missing?

COSHH Regulations

The Control of Substances Hazardous to Health (COSHH) Regulations 2002 state that substances which can make people ill or injure them must be stored and used properly. Some examples of hazardous substances are:

→ cleaning liquids such as bleach

→ paints

→ chemicals.

Any potentially dangerous materials must have a label on them which shows that they are dangerous. They must be kept in special containers and stored in locked cupboards. Look out for the labels shown below.

Toxic – do not inhale, swallow or allow to come into contact with skin or eyes

Harmful – do not swallow or inhale

Corrosive – if comes into contact with skin or eyes or inhaled will cause burns

Flammable – will ignite in the presence of a naked flame

⇧ **The labelling of hazardous substances**

RIDDOR 1995

The Reporting of Injuries, Diseases and Dangerous Occurrences Regulations (RIDDOR) 1995 requires the reporting of work-related accidents, diseases and dangerous occurrences. It applies to all work activities but not to all incidents (see also page 165).

The Motor Vehicles (Wearing of Seat Belts) (Amendment) Regulations 2006

From September 2006 babies and children under 13 years old have to be properly restrained in cars and other vehicles. This will mean that if a setting wishes to go on an outing using parents' cars, they will need to make sure that the law is being followed.

Find out!

For information about car seats and the regulations visit the Think! Road Safety Website (www.thinkroadsafety.gov.uk).

Childcare Act 2006 – Statutory Framework for the Early Years Foundation Stage (EYFS)

Until September 2008, 14 National Standards apply to different kinds of childcare settings in England and Wales. The Office for Standards in Education (Ofsted) is responsible for registering nurseries, playgroups, childminders, crèches, after-school clubs and play schemes, and makes sure that all settings meet these standards.

From September 2008 the standards become part of the statutory framework of the Early Years Foundation Stage for England. The other countries of the UK are also reviewing early years provision and requirements. The framework covers the five outcomes for children, with safety aspects covering the staying safe outcome.

Section 3 of the statutory framework looks at welfare requirements under five main areas:

→ safeguarding and promoting children's welfare
→ suitable people
→ suitable, premises, environment and equipment
→ organisation
→ documentation.

Each area in the framework includes detail of the particular legislation that applies to the framework as well as statutory guidance that providers must be aware of and apply.

Product safety marking

Many items that are used every day have been tested for safety by the British Standards Institution (BSI).

Kitemarks

If a product, for example a toy, has a Kitemark, this means that the BSI has checked that it is safe to use. Manufacturers have to pay for this and their products are tested regularly. Products do not have to have a Kitemark, but many everyday items such as fridges, electrical plugs, toys and baby equipment do have them.

CE Mark

The CE Mark, together with the name and address of the supplier, should by law appear on all toys placed on the market in the European Union. The mark shows that the toys meet the essential safety requirements of the European Toy Safety Directive, but, it is not a quality mark.

Some products carry both a Kitemark and a CE Mark.

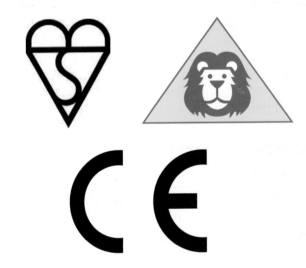

⇧ **Product safety markings; from left to right: Kitemark, Lion Mark and CE Mark**

Find out!

Get a copy of the new Early Years Foundation Stage (EYFS) framework and look at the statutory framework section.

1. Which of the framework requirements are about health and safety?

2. Design and make a poster for parents and carers that shows how your placement meets the new welfare requirements of the EYFS.

U4
1

Lion Mark

The Lion Mark is a symbol that only members of the British Toy and Hobby Association (BTHA) can put on toys. It is a symbol of toy safety and quality for the consumer, exactly what the CE Mark is not. The BTHA includes many major international and European companies and supplies around 95 per cent of all toys sold in the UK.

Find out!

1. Pick a room in your placement. How many items can you find that have the Kitemark? Write them down.
2. Pick five of the items you have found and discuss in a group why you think they need to meet safety standards.
3. Did you find anything that did not have a Kitemark that you thought should have?

Health and safety policy

Any person who runs a business where other people may visit must have a health and safety policy, and clearly any setting where children and young people spend time requires one. A policy makes it clear what everyone has to do to make sure that people are kept safe. It should explain what the law is in simple terms. Have a look at the following example.

How to establish and maintain healthy, safe and secure environments

First aid training

First Aid training is very important for anyone working with children. Children frequently have minor bumps and injuries, as well as those which are sometimes more serious. Make sure that you know what to do!

The welfare requirements of the Early Years Foundation Stage (EYFS) framework state that at least one person with a paediatric first aid certificate must be on the premises at all times, with at least one such person on outings.

Find out!

If your course does not include paediatric first aid, try your local St John Ambulance or Red Cross to see if they offer the course. It would certainly help you to get a job at the end of the course!

Health and safety policy

This policy makes sure that we meet all the requirements of European Community Law, the Health and Safety at Work Act 1974, and all other relevant statutory provisions.

All staff at the Nursery have a responsibility to provide a safe environment for your child and the Manager is responsible for health and safety matters concerning the nursery premises.

In the nursery we aim to:
- provide a safe and healthy environment for children and staff
- make all staff aware of potential hazards within the nursery and the surrounding environment
- involve and motivate nursery staff in all matters concerning health and safety
- provide all staff with first aid training
- protect children from hazards
- prevent accidents, injuries and ill-health
- record any accident or incident in the Accident Report Book and notify the child's parent/carer as soon as possible
- make sure all staff are aware of how infections can be transmitted
- follow hygiene rules relating to bodily fluids.

Recording mechanisms and reporting procedures

All settings must have recording **mechanisms** and reporting **procedures** for dealing with health and safety related incidents.

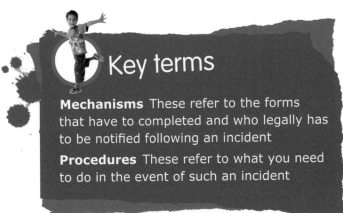

Key terms

Mechanisms These refer to the forms that have to completed and who legally has to be notified following an incident

Procedures These refer to what you need to do in the event of such an incident

For example, should a child in your setting fall from the climbing frame and receive a severe bump to his head, the procedure you would follow would include:

→ taking the child to a quiet corner away from the children and reassuring him and applying appropriate first aid
→ a colleague distracting the other children and calming them, perhaps starting a new activity
→ an ambulance being called if necessary
→ the child's parent or emergency contact being called
→ ensuring the incident is reported to the appropriate authorities.

The mechanisms that would support you in this procedure would include:

→ the setting's policy on accidents
→ the accident report book
→ the requirement to report the accident to Ofsted and local child protection agencies
→ the requirement for information to be held on a child's parents or emergency contact.

Recording accidents and incidents

The Reporting of Injuries, Diseases and Dangerous Occurrences Regulations (RIDDOR) 1995 (see below) requires that all accidents and incidents have to be reported in order to:

→ make sure there is an accurate record of the event
→ give detail of the reason for the accident or incident occurring
→ check whether it can be prevented from happening again.

There should be a separate accident report book for children and for employees of the setting.

Ofsted also requires that they and local child protection agencies should be notified of any serious accident or injury of a person while in the care of a setting. Failure to do this is an offence.

RIDDOR 1995

The Reporting of Injuries, Diseases and Dangerous Occurrences Regulations (RIDDOR) 1995 concerns the reporting of accidents and incidents that occur on an employer's premises, including early years and other settings. The following must be reported to the relevant health and safety person:

→ death or major injury to an employee or member of the public
→ an over-3-day injury, i.e. an injury which is not major but results in the injured person being away from work or unable to do their normal work for more than three days
→ certain work-related diseases
→ a dangerous occurrence − something which does not result in a reportable injury but which clearly could have done.

The responsible person (this may be the manager or another designated person) in a setting has a duty to record incidents and accidents. However, that person relies on staff reporting all accidents and incidents and following the procedures that are laid down for the setting.

Another important part of health and safety legislation is the need to carry out risk assessments (see also pages 192−3).

Find out!

Ask if you can see the accident book in your setting.

→ How should entries be made?
→ What happens after something has been reported?
→ What else has to be reported and to whom?

Security arrangements

Arrivals and departures

Parents and carers want to know that their child will be safe with you; for example that their child cannot escape on to the road and wander off. This is especially important for young children. Parents and carers also want to be sure that no one can get into the nursery, school or after-school club who should not be there. They expect to see good security arrangements in place. This means:

→ good locks and handles on doors and gates at the right height to stop small children opening them
→ an alarm system that operates whenever anyone comes into the building
→ information about who can collect a child; this should ensure that if someone else tries to collect the child who is not authorised by the parents or carers to do so, then they will not be allowed to take the child from the premises.

In the interests of
NURSERY SECURITY
VISITORS & DELIVERIES
Please ring the doorbell and wait for a member of staff to welcome you.
PARENTS
Please ensure that you do not let anyone who is not personally known to you into the nursery and also ensure that the door is firmly shut behind you at all times.
Thankyou

⇧ **Parents need to see that good security arrangements are in place**

It is very important (as well as polite) that a responsible member of staff greets the children on their arrival at the setting. This helps to make sure that important information about the children is passed on from the parents to the staff. The same applies when children leave for the day. Again, it is very important that the right person collects each child.

Recording authorised persons

Always check that adults coming into the setting are allowed to be there. All visitors should sign in and out, not just as a check on their identity but also in case of a fire or accident on the premises. If someone is allowed to be in the building or taking a child, they

will not mind waiting while you check them out – it is for the child's safety.

A key way to be sure about parents' wishes for their child is to have the correct details recorded on an easily accessible card. This will usually also have details about the child's diet, favourite toys, family doctor and any illnesses and allergies. There must also be contact numbers and information about who can and cannot collect the child from the setting. Emergency contact details are a requirement for the setting – the guidance from the EYFS says 'except where there is reasonable excuse, obtaining written permission from parents where children are to be picked up by another adult is essential'.

Think about it

Read the following news articles from the Internet then discuss in small groups how these incidents might have been prevented.

→ http://century.guardian.co.uk/1990-1999/Story/0,,112749,00.html
→ http://news.scotsman.com/topics.cfm?tid=774&id=895872006

Good practice checklist

Security and safety

✓ Always make sure that doors and gates are closed and locked as necessary.
✓ Every child and parent/carer must be welcomed each day.
✓ When the child arrives, ask how he/she is and what he/she has been doing.
✓ Tell the parent/carer at the end of the day what has gone on during the day.
✓ Never allow a child to leave with an unknown person.
✓ Make sure that no other children are near the doors or gates.
✓ Always ask for identification if you do not know someone coming into the setting.
✓ Always ask your supervisor if you are not sure!

Find out!

1. Does the policy for security at your setting cover:
   a) children arriving and leaving
   b) outings
   c) missing children
   d) unauthorised visitors
   e) other problems?

2. Go round your setting imagining it from the youngest mobile child's eye. Could you get out of the building or get hold of something that might injure you?

Identification of risks and hazards

To help protect children in your care from accidents and injury, you need to understand the **risks** they are exposed to. Risks are linked to the age of a child and their stage of development. If you know what a child of a certain age could be at risk from, you should then be able to identify the **hazards** for certain situations and certain groups of children. For example, young children under 2 years are at risk from falls but a child of 8 or 9 years is more at risk from a road traffic accident.

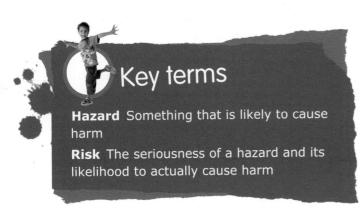

Key terms

Hazard Something that is likely to cause harm

Risk The seriousness of a hazard and its likelihood to actually cause harm

The more common types of accidents include:

→ choking
→ suffocation
→ burns and scalds
→ bumps, cuts and bruises
→ drowning
→ poisoning.

When you know what the risks and hazards are, you should then be able to put in place safety checks and procedures to make sure that a child is safe.

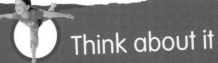

Think about it

Think about the various ways in which children at different stages of development can injure themselves. How could the children you care for be injured in the ways listed above?

Risks are linked to a child's stage of development

As someone who works with children you need to know what the associated risks are for each stage of development. Very often after an accident you hear parents or carers saying 'But I didn't know he could do that yet...', for example after a child has opened a cupboard to get at dangerous chemicals or fallen after climbing some stairs.

Case study

Dangers for Dan

Dan, aged 2½ years, is tall for his age. He is also extremely curious and has just discovered that he can now reach the door handles at home and feel the pattern on them. Dan goes to a childminder who lives in an old house with a cellar and a front door that opens on to a busy main road. When he is out and about Dan does not always like to have his hand held.

1. What are the hazards for Dan?
2. Why do you think these are hazards to Dan?
3. How can Dan be protected from these hazards?

Common accidents involving children and young people by age/stage of development

Age/stage: Birth to crawling (up to about 6 months)

Did you know?

In 2002, over 27,700 babies under 6 months were injured in accidents.
(*Source*: Child Accident Prevention Trust, 2003)

⇧ **Children up to 6 months old are very dependent and vulnerable but they can often move further and faster than you think!**

Common accidents	Reasons	Prevention
Falls from raised surfaces	Even small babies can move by wriggling; the risk of this type of accident increases as the baby grows.	Never leave babies unattended on a raised surface or put a bouncing chair on a raised surface.
Suffocation	Babies cannot push covers or other items away from their face.	Do not use duvets or pillows for babies under 1 year.
Choking	• Young babies cannot deal with a large volume of fluid or hard objects in their mouth. • Peanuts can irritate the airways of a young child.	• Never 'prop feed'. • Do not give babies solids and then leave them alone. • Keep small objects away from babies' grasp. • Watch that older children do not put anything in a baby's mouth. • Never allow a child under 6 years to eat peanuts as the oil in them can cause swelling of the bronchial tubes.
Strangulation	Ribbons, jewellery and wool can get caught in a cot or car seat, for example.	• Never put ribbons or jewellery around a baby's neck. • Check clothing is not too tight.
Burns and scalds	• Spilling a hot drink when holding a baby. • Not testing bath water. • Heating feeds in microwave. • Sunburn.	Avoid the risks: • no hot drinks near young children • test bath water carefully • no use of microwaves for feeds • keep babies well covered and protected from the sun.

Common accidents	Reasons	Prevention
Drowning	Leaving babies alone, even for a few seconds, or with other children in the bath.	Never leave a young baby in water without an adult present.

Age/stage: Crawling to walking (about 6–15 months)

Did you know?

In 2002, 38,300 babies under 1 year old were taken to hospital after a fall, and 17,000 were taken to hospital with burns and scalds.
(*Source*: Child Accident Prevention Trust, 2003)

⇪ **Stair guards will benefit younger children especially**

Common accidents	Reasons	Prevention
Falls (downstairs, from raised surface, high chairs, cots, etc.)	As babies start to become mobile they want to explore and have no understanding of danger.	• Always use a stair guard. • A suitable harness must always be used in a high chair • Never leave children on high surfaces.
Suffocation from bedding or plastic bags and choking on food or small objects.	• Babies at this age can still get trapped in bedding. • Exploration of plastic bags (seen as a toy). • Babies use their mouth to explore; therefore anything new will go in the mouth and may cause choking.	• No duvets for children under 1 year. • Keep plastic bags out of reach. • Always stay with a baby who is eating or drinking. • Keep small items out of reach. • Teach older children not to put anything in a baby's mouth.
Strangulation	• Still a risk from clothing. • Risk with mobile children of unexpected items causing problems (e.g. washing lines, window blind cords, belts).	• Never put anything around a child's neck. • Check clothing. • Keep blind cords, etc. short and out of reach and never position them next to a cot or bed.

Common accidents	Reasons	Prevention
Burns and scalds	• With their increased mobility children can now reach things placed on surfaces (drinks, radiators, ovens, etc.) and could pull on kettle flexes, pan handles, etc. • They are also more difficult to keep in the shade, to protect them from the sun. • They have no understanding of what 'hot' is and cannot learn from experience at this stage.	• As for young babies, plus use a coiled flex on kettles, a safety gate to bar access in the kitchen when cooking, etc. • Extra care with clothes, sun creams and hats in sun. Keep out of sun between 11am and 3pm. • Fit guards and keep all possible sources of burns and scalds out of reach.
Drowning	• Curiosity may lead children to peer into water containers. • They are likely to enjoy water play. • Being left alone in the bath.	• Supervise all water play very closely and empty water containers immediately when finished with. • Never leave children alone in the bath or with older children.
Bumps and cuts and bruises	• First mobile movements are often unsteady and poorly coordinated. • Curiosity may lead children to grab anything that takes their attention, even if it is big and heavy.	• Move dangerous and/or heavy items that are a risk. • Position furniture with hard or sharp edges so that there is less chance of injury.
Transport	• Failure to secure in a car seat. • Falling out of pram/pushchair. • Baby walkers are associated with a range of injuries, especially falls and burns.	• Always secure in correct car seat. • Use harnesses in prams, etc. • Do not use baby walkers.

Age/stage: Toddlers (about 1–3 years)

Did you know?

In 2002, over 212,000 children aged 1–3 attended hospital after a fall and 22,500 after a suspected poisoning.
(*Source*: Child Accident Prevention Trust, 2003)

⇦ **Children at this age are very inquisitive and full of energy. They have a short attention span and are absorbed in themselves. They are not old enough to understand the concept of danger and do not always learn from experience.**

Common accidents	Reasons	Prevention
Falls (e.g. downstairs, from windows)	New-found climbing skills and increased manual dexterity mean children can get up on to window sills, climb stairs and open catches.	• Use good safety gates and window locks that cannot be opened by toddlers. • Teach them to climb stairs but do not allow them to use stairs by themselves. • Avoid putting furniture underneath windows.
Suffocation and choking	• Plastic bags are still a danger. • Children may still be learning to chew and putting things in their mouth.	• Keep plastic bags out of reach, or preferably destroy them. • As for younger children, it is important to avoid peanuts.
Poisoning	Curiosity and increasing skills mean children can gain access to virtually anything, including medicines (despite child-resistant tops), chemicals and berries.	• Keep all medicines and chemicals locked away and out of reach. • Keep chemicals in original containers. • Do not keep medicines in handbags or by the bed. • Check gardens for poisonous plants.
Strangulation	• Children can get head into but not out of gaps. • Poor necklines on clothing, cords, etc.	• Supervise climbing games. • Check necklines.
Burns and scalds	• Curiosity is still an issue; so there is danger with pans and irons, for example. Children may start to imitate adults as well. • They will be more able to use matches if they find them. • Their skin is still fragile and easy to burn (in hot baths, etc.).	As for last stage but with extra vigilance.
Drowning	Increasing mobility, independence and curiosity means children are at danger, especially of garden ponds. Drowning is possible in very small amounts of water.	• Close supervision around any water. • Secure fencing of ponds. • Empty water containers when finished with. • Stay with toddlers when in the bath.
Bumps and cuts and bruises	• Trapped fingers in door jambs. • Cuts while trying to imitate adults using scissors, knives or razors. • Running into low glass in doors.	• Be aware of risk of doors when little fingers are around. • Keep scissors, etc. out of reach. • Use safety glass or board it up.
Car accidents	• Experimenting with car safety seat or buggy harnesses. • Being left alone in car. • Running off when out on the street.	• Use correct seat and harness and discourage messing with fastenings. • Never leave a child alone in a car. • Use a harness and reins when out on the road. • Start simple road safety training.

Age/stage: About 3–5 years

Did you know?

In 2002, over 4,400 children aged 3–5 years were injured in road crashes, and 527 were injured in fires, two of whom died.
(*Source*: Child Accident Prevention Trust, 2003)

⇦ **At this age children's coordination is improving and they have more understanding of action and consequence. They may well forget safety instructions when tired or distracted. They still enjoy testing their abilities and finding unusual ways to use toys and other objects.**

Common accidents	Reasons	Prevention
Falls (e.g. downstairs from windows, play equipment)	• Attraction of playing on the stairs and from windows, using their powerful imagination to be Superman, etc. • Testing own skills by climbing higher and so at risk of falling further.	• Do not allow stairs to be used for playing. • Fit window locks. • Tell children about the dangers. • Choose playgrounds with impact-absorbing surfaces. • Tell children how to use equipment properly.
Choking and suffocation	• Eating on the move. • Danger from ice cubes or some small sweets. • Peanuts still a risk.	• Encourage children to sit still while eating and not to run with sweets in their mouth. • Do not give peanuts to children under 6 years.
Poisoning	• There is still the risk of confusion between sweets, medicines and berries. • Children are better able to open locks and resistant caps.	• Keep medicines, etc. locked away. • Tell children not to eat anything they pick outside without checking with you first.
Burns and scalds	• Danger from hot foods, liquids, taps and candles. • Risks from children copying adults. • Children now understand concept of 'Hot! Do not touch!' but can easily forget, especially when practising increased manual skills of turning and switching.	• Keep dangerous items out of reach, especially matches, candles, etc. • Teach children what to do if a fire or smoke alarm goes off. • Use thermostatic valves on taps.

Common accidents	Reasons	Prevention
Drowning	• Any open water remains a threat, especially as children become more independent. • It is safe to leave a child in the bath from about 4 years, but still have an adult nearby.	• Ensure close supervision near water. • Fence off ponds. • Teach a child to swim.
Cuts	• Children can now be taught to use scissors and knives safely. • There are still risks with sharp objects if they are not used safely or are used in play.	• Keep out of reach. • Teach how to use safely.
Car accidents	• Children have little understanding or experience of dealing with traffic. • They may have started to ride a bicycle.	• Never allow a child less than 5 years on the road alone, whether on foot or bike. • Teach road safety but be aware of limits of remembering and understanding. • Always use a helmet when on a bike.
Falls, choking, poisoning, burns and scalds, drowning, cuts and bruises, car accidents	• Injuries at this age are often due to children being keen to help and copy adults but misjudging their abilities. • Boisterous play can result in accidents. • Friends and peers have more influence and a child can be persuaded to 'have a go'.	• As for last age stages, make sure dangerous items are not easy to reach. • Children should now be learning to take some responsibility for their own safety but the extent of this will vary. Being able to repeat a rule does not mean a child understands or will remember to follow it. • Safety awareness improves as the child gets older but outside influences can 'over-rule' this.

 Find out!

Think about the different hazards and risks for the children who go to your placement. Think about how these are different for children of different ages and stages of development.

1. Make a list of the safety features that are in place to prevent accidents.
2. What hazards are they intended to provide protection from?
3. Are there any hazards that are not well protected?
4. Ask your supervisor how hazards are identified in your placement.

Emergency procedures

As part of the Health and Safety at Work Act 1974 and other regulations, your setting must have a safety policy if it employs five or more staff. The policy will cover emergency procedures in the event of a fire, accident or other emergency. Fire and evacuation drills are also a requirement of the EYFS in England.

There are many different types of emergency and it is important to know what the different procedures are, especially for fires, security incidents or if a child goes missing.

Evacuation procedures

There are many reasons why a building may need to be evacuated, for example in the event of a fire, a gas leak or a bomb scare. All adults in the setting need to know what to do. In most settings, one member of staff is responsible for these procedures and will need to make sure that all staff are aware of them. Practices need to be held regularly and signs and notices must be kept in place. Drills and practices should always be taken seriously so that any difficulties can be reviewed; the EYFS also states that they should be recorded.

Find out!

What is the emergency procedure in your setting?

→ How is the alarm raised?
→ Who contacts the emergency services?
→ Who takes out the registers and checks them?
→ What are the safest exit points?
→ Where is the assembly point?
→ How often is there an emergency practice?
→ How are visitors to the setting made aware of evacuation procedures?
→ How are children reassured during evacuation practices?
→ Are there regulations and notices on view?

Good practice checklist

What to do in the event of fire

✓ Close doors and windows and try to get the children out of the premises by normal routes.

✓ Do not leave the children unattended.

✓ Do not stop to put out the fire (unless very small).

✓ Call the fire brigade by telephone as soon as possible, as follows:

- lift the receiver and dial '999'
- give the operator your telephone number and ask for 'Fire'
- when the brigade replies give the information clearly, for example: 'Fire at First Start Nursery, 126 Beach Drive, Blackpool AB2 6PY, situated between the clock tower and the promenade.' Do not replace the receiver until the address has been repeated by the fire operator.

Good practice checklist

Fire safety in the early years setting

✓ Have a fire drill every 3 months.

✓ If there are problems with the procedures, repeat the drill or seek advice from a fire officer.

✓ Reassure children during a practice by staying calm and explaining what is happening.

✓ Praise children and thank them for their help in carrying out the evacuation.

✓ After a drill, provide an absorbing activity such as reading a story or playing a game to help the children settle down quickly.

⇧ **Fire safety is of paramount importance**

Missing children

A child should never go missing from a care or education setting if all procedures are followed. A small child should not be able to open gates or doors, and any adult going through them should follow all precautions to make sure they are properly closed and locked. Strict procedures about the collection of children by parents or carers should be followed. On outings, making sure that the right ratio of adults to children is observed should be a safeguard. However, if a child does go missing, alarms should be raised immediately and the setting's procedures followed.

Notification of illness

Some illnesses must be reported to the local health authority. This gives the authority some idea of how many cases there are of an illness each year. It can also be a good sign of how effectively an immunisation plan is working. Family doctors know what these illnesses are and they are responsible for reporting them.

Notifiable diseases listed under the Public Health, Health (Infectious Diseases) Regulations 1988 are as follows:

- → Acute poliomyelitis
- → Anthrax
- → Cholera
- → Diphtheria
- → Dysentery
- → Food poisoning
- → Leprosy
- → Leptospirosis
- → Malaria
- → Measles
- → Meningitis
- → Meningococcal septicaemia (without meningitis)
- → Mumps
- → Ophthalmia neonatorum
- → Paratyphoid fever
- → Plague
- → Rabies
- → Relapsing fever
- → Rubella
- → Scabies
- → Scarlet fever
- → Smallpox
- → Tetanus
- → Tuberculosis
- → Typhoid fever
- → Typhus fever
- → Viral haemorrhagic fever
- → Viral hepatitis
- → Whooping cough
- → Yellow fever

A child with any of these illnesses should not be in an early years or education setting and parents should contact the child's GP.

Good practice checklist

What to do if a child goes missing

- ✓ Make sure all the other children are safe (i.e. with responsible adults).
- ✓ Make sure any external exits are secure.
- ✓ Inform the person in charge.
- ✓ Start a systematic search based on where the child was last seen and with whom, and make sure all areas are covered.
- ✓ Inform the child's parents.
- ✓ Inform the local police.

Find out!

In a group, divide the list of notifiable disease among you. Then find out the main signs and symptoms and the incubation period (how long it takes for the disease to show). Make a poster to display in a setting for parents' information.

Did you know?

With children travelling abroad on holiday and coming to live in the UK for the first time with their parents, even the more unusual diseases can occur in the UK. As they can easily pass from one person to another it is very important that the authorities are notified. Measures can then be taken to try to control their spread.

When is a child infectious?

In nearly all illnesses, children are most infectious before the symptoms appear. Many illnesses have a cold and/or fever as the first signs. It would not be practical to exclude all children with these symptoms from the setting as it would not have much effect on the spread of a disease. Different settings have different rules about excluding children with common illnesses, ranging from excluding children for a fixed amount of time to excluding them only while they feel unwell.

The Department of Health guidelines for infection control in childcare settings are described in Unit 11, pages 423–5.

Find out!

1. Find and read your setting's policy on infectious illnesses.
2. Compare your setting's policy with other examples from other settings. Are there any differences? If so, what are they and why do you think they are there?

Good practice checklist

Dealing with illnesses

✓ Make sure that you know the common signs of illness.

✓ Keep informed about outbreaks of infectious diseases currently in your local area. Make sure you know the signs and symptoms to look for and any special precautions to take.

✓ Keep up to date with your own immunisations, especially those for polio, rubella, mumps and meningitis – even early years practitioners can catch them, especially when working with young children.

Food hygiene and basic hygiene practices

The causes of infection

Infections are caused by tiny micro-organisms. Most of these are invisible to the human eye. There are four types:

→ *Bacteria*, for example streptococci, staphylococci, are single-cell organisms. They can cause infection if they enter the body in large numbers.

→ *Viruses*, for example influenza, colds and HIV, are much smaller than bacteria. Only a few viruses need to enter the body to cause illness.

→ *Fungi*, for example thrush and ringworm, are a type of plant which feeds off living or dead material. They include moulds, mildews and yeasts.

→ *Parasites*, for example head lice and tapeworm, are a plant or animal that lives on another organism (a host). They can get into the body via eggs laid on the skin or hair or on food.

Not all micro-organisms cause disease. For example, everyone has 'good' bacteria living in or on various parts of their body, including the surface of the skin and in the digestive tract. These bacteria help to keep the body healthy. Some fungi are useful to society, such as yeasts used in bread making and moulds used to make Stilton cheese.

Pathogens

Micro-organisms that cause disease are called pathogens. When these enter the body they can multiply in great numbers and cause illness. The person is then said to have an infection. Cross-infection is the passing on of infection from one person to another.

The immune system is usually very good at fighting any pathogens that enter the body. However, if the immune system is not working well, for example due to illness or old age, the body is less able to fight the infection and you are more likely to become ill.

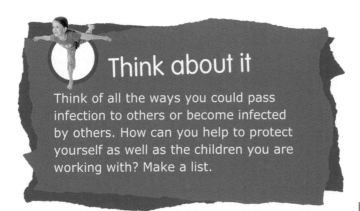

Think about it

Think of all the ways you could pass infection to others or become infected by others. How can you help to protect yourself as well as the children you are working with? Make a list.

Think about it

How many infections do you think you have had? Have some been more serious than others? How did you know?

How infection is passed on to others

If a person or object has come into contact with a pathogen, then he/she/it is said to be contaminated.

Handwashing and hygiene

Handwashing is one of the most important ways of making sure that infections are not passed between people. Even hands that look clean can have a mass of bacteria on them.

Everybody has bacteria in or on various parts of the body. These bacteria are useful in the right place, but some bacteria can cause serious illness if they get into the wrong place.

→ Picking your nose will transfer the bacteria *Staphylococcus aureus*, which lives in mucous, to your hands and then potentially to food, which could cause food poisoning.

→ *E. coli* bacteria help to keep the bowel healthy. However, if they get into the upper digestive tract via contaminated food, for example if hands are not washed after using the toilet and then food is touched, they can cause serious food poisoning. *E. coli* can also cause urinary tract and vaginal infections in girls. It is therefore very important to wipe a baby's bottom from front to back – from vagina to anus – to avoid contamination in this way. Little girls should also be taught to wipe from front to back when being toilet trained.

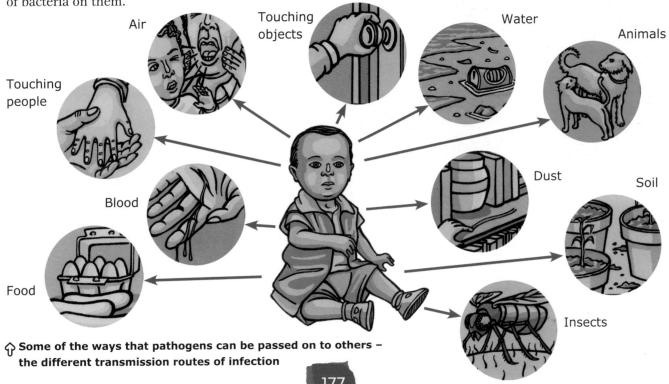

⇧ **Some of the ways that pathogens can be passed on to others – the different transmission routes of infection**

Trips to the toilet can transfer thousands of potentially harmful pathogens on to the hands, for example through wiping, touching handles and so on. A very quick swill under the tap without soap will leave most of these micro-organisms on the hands; if the hands subsequently go into a child's mouth, there is a serious risk of infection. Bacteria left on a doorknob by one person can be picked up by the next 14 people who touch it – and then passed on to everything they touch.

Think about it

Handwashing can be made into a game, with competitions for the cleanest hands. For older children, a science experiment in which bacteria from dirty and supposedly clean hands are cultured on plates can show them the results of poor hygiene.

Did you know?

In a survey by *Good Housekeeping* (August 2004), 1 in 3 men and 1 in 5 women admitted that they don't wash their hands after going to the toilet or before preparing food.

Food hygiene

If you are involved in preparing and serving food to children, you need to take a course in food hygiene to show that you are safe with food. There are thousands of cases of food poisoning every year, and in a group of young children one case can pass round the whole nursery or class very easily. Most cases of food poisoning are due to poor hygiene practices, for example not washing hands.

Step-by-step handwashing procedure

Remove rings, watch, braclet

Run the tap to warm temperature

Using soap, rub hands and fingers carefully covering all surfaces

Use nail brush

Rinse hands

Use paper towel to dry hands

Case study

Food poisoning outbreak

The nursery unit that Jed works in had a lovely party on Wednesday afternoon just before closing for the summer holidays. The kitchen staff had worked hard to produce food and some staff and parents had brought contributions. The nursery staff had arranged games and activities for the children.

By the end of his shift in the after-school club, Jed was feeling very sick and was ill all night with vomiting and diarrhoea. When he rang work the next day, he found out that almost half of the children and staff were feeling the same. Jed's manager rang the environmental health officer (EHO) to report the outbreak.

1. What do you think would happen next?
2. How could the food poisoning outbreak have been prevented?

Basic hygiene

Correct disposal of different types of waste

You will at some time in your career have to dispose of different types of body waste. It is essential that blood, vomit, urine and faeces are disposed of correctly. This is to avoid contamination of surfaces and materials that may be used to prepare food or which children may work on. You also need to protect yourself from possible infection from waste. But whatever the procedure is in your setting, *don't forget to wash your hands afterwards.*

Find out!

Make sure you know the procedures for the disposal of body waste in your setting.

Good practice checklist

Food hygiene

To prevent food from becoming contaminated and causing illness, you should always:

✓ avoid using raw eggs in foods such as mayonnaise and uncooked desserts

✓ cook foods thoroughly

✓ reheat food soon and thoroughly

✓ avoid reheating foods more than once

✓ keep foods at correct temperatures

✓ keep animals away from foods

✓ practise good personal hygiene (pay particular attention to handwashing before food preparation involving direct handling of foods)

✓ cover cuts with clean plasters

✓ avoid sneezing or coughing near food

✓ always keep cooked food covered

✓ keep cooked and raw foods separate, even in the fridge

✓ ensure all surfaces are cleaned at least once per day and are easy to clean

✓ ensure equipment such as can-openers, slicers and food processors are regularly cleaned and sterilised

✓ ensure all rubbish bins are kept well away from food and are regularly disinfected.

Good practice checklist

How to avoid infection

✓ Always carry out thorough handwashing after using the toilet, changing nappies and handling animals, and before any food handling.

✓ Follow your setting's procedures for the correct disposal of dirty nappies and other soiled items.

✓ Cough and sneeze into a tissue then correctly dispose of the tissues.

✓ Always cover up cuts or grazes and wear plastic gloves when dealing with children with cuts or grazes.

✓ Follow food hygiene precautions with vigilance – never use food or drink that is at risk of being contaminated.

✓ Take care when handing animals – make sure that children don't let them lick their face and that they always wash their hands afterwards.

✓ Check that gardens and sandpits are not contaminated by animal faeces.

Getting ready for assessment

→ Explain how to use legislation and policies to support work in establishing and maintaining healthy, safe and secure environments to protect children against the outbreak of an infectious disease.

→ Describe working practices which contribute to safe food and basic hygiene environments in early years settings.

Section 2

The procedures for dealing with accidents, illnesses and other emergencies

In practice

Samina has recently been promoted to manage the after-school club at the school where she works. There have been a number of minor accidents at the club and several of the children who attend have health issues such as asthma and epilepsy. Samina is keen that the children can all enjoy themselves and take part in lots of different activities. Although the health and safety procedures are good, Samina wants to be sure that she and everyone else is clear about how to respond to any accidents or illnesses.

By the end of this section you will understand the procedures for dealing with accidents, illnesses and other emergencies.

The procedures for dealing with accidents, emergencies and signs of illness

It is usually easy to tell when a child has had an accident. In a well-run setting, someone will have seen the accident or certainly heard the resulting cry. Further on in this section you will look at specific accidents.

How to recognise when children are ill

Babies and children can become very ill, very quickly. A child may arrive at nursery or school well and happy then, later in the day, have his carers seriously worried as a result of a life-threatening illness. If a child is unwell his or her parents should be contacted so they can take the child home and to the family doctor if needed. It is important to know when to call for help if a child is seriously ill.

Signs of serious illness may include:

➜ high temperature
➜ continual vomiting
➜ unusual drowsiness
➜ unexplained pain
➜ unusual crying in a baby.

When and how to call an ambulance

In a medical emergency you may need to call an ambulance. If a child is not breathing or is bleeding badly, call an ambulance straightaway – preferably while first aid is being given by someone else.

To call an ambulance:

➜ dial 999
➜ have details of the accident and injury, the age of the child and where the injured child is.

Common emergencies

Meningitis

Certain childhood illnesses require that medical help is sought immediately. One of the most common – and serious – of these is meningitis. There are several strains of meningitis and the immunisation programme in the UK currently offers protection from some of them. However, if you suspect a child may have meningitis do not wait and see – seek medical help immediately.

The signs and symptoms of meningitis are described on page 409.

Asthma attack or breathing difficulties

If a child is having an asthma attack or breathing difficulties while in your care, you should make them comfortable (let them sit in the position most comfortable for them) away from other children in a quiet area. Let them use their inhaler if they have one (usually this will be a blue reliever). (For further information and advice on dealing with asthma in a child, see also page 414.)

You should be shown how to help a child who uses an inhaler, and need to be confident that you know how to use the type of inhaler the child is using. Many settings will have slightly different policies on the storage and use of inhalers. A nurse from the local doctors' surgery that the child attends may be happy to come and talk to staff if needed.

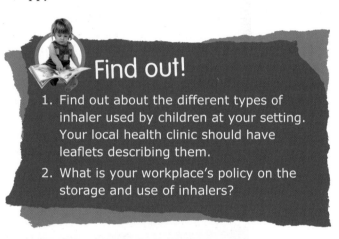

Find out!

1. Find out about the different types of inhaler used by children at your setting. Your local health clinic should have leaflets describing them.
2. What is your workplace's policy on the storage and use of inhalers?

Epilepsy

You may see a number of signs and symptoms in a child who has epilepsy. Some children may have 'absence' seizures or it may take the form of a typical tonic/clonic seizure involving shaking and rigidity followed by unconsciousness. Many children have some sort of warning that they are about to have a seizure, for example by hearing or smelling certain things (this is called an 'aura'). A child who is having a seizure needs to be kept safe from hurting themselves as they fall and will need lots of reassurance afterwards. Other children who are there need to be reassured that their friend will be alright. Sometimes a child does not recover immediately from a seizure and they continue to have them. If this happens you should ring for an ambulance immediately, as further treatment will be needed at the hospital.

Find out!

There are over 40 different types of seizure that may occur – have a look at www. epilepsyaction.org.uk for more information.

Sickle cell disease

Sickle cell disease is an inherited condition of the red blood cells. Children with the condition have a 'crisis' when the sickle-shaped red blood cells stick together in lumps in organs or joints and cause severe pain. If you have a child in your setting with sickle cell disease, make sure you know what the routine is in case of a crisis. The child's parents will tell you and the setting should have a supply of the child's painkillers in case of need. Keeping the child warm and reassured, as well as giving the painkillers, is all you can do until the parents and/or medical help arrives.

Diabetes

Diabetes is another condition that you should know about if a child in your placement has this condition. Diabetes is caused by the body not producing enough insulin to use the sugar and carbohydrates in a normal diet. Diabetic children usually need daily injections of insulin to 'use' the sugars properly. If they have been more active than usual, or are not well, they may have a hypoglycaemic attack. This is caused by a very low blood sugar level, similar to the way you might feel if you have not eaten all day and have been very busy. During a 'hypo', the child may look pale and be sweating, feeling faint and confused. The child needs sugar – fast! A glass of milk and some biscuits or a fizzy sugary drink and chocolate should be enough to restore the balance, providing the child is conscious. If not you may have further treatment and instructions from the parents; make sure you know what they are. If in doubt call for an ambulance and get help.

Common childhood illnesses and allergies

When a child is taken ill in your setting, the parents or guardians must be informed. While waiting for the child's parents to arrive, you should comfort him or her by sitting quietly with the child, perhaps reading a story.

After an illness, a child may need to take medicine while at nursery or school. Most settings have a policy that parents must give written consent for their child to have medicines administered by the nursery nurse or teacher. Early years practitioners are not allowed to give medicines to children without this written permission under any circumstances.

The signs of many of the common childhood illnesses, how long they take to develop (the incubation period) and how to support a child with the illness are described in Unit 11, pages 407–10 and 433–8.

Following appropriate procedures

The correct responses to accidents and injuries, and paediatric first aid

Young children have accidents. A child who has been injured will be very frightened and upset, as indeed will any other children who are in the area. Your main responsibility is to know what to do in an emergency and to carry out the required actions calmly and confidently, so that you meet one of the prime aims of first aid: to preserve life and to prevent the effects of the injury becoming worse than necessary.

The right actions after an accident can save life. For example, people have died unnecessarily as a result of a blocked airway that needed little skill to open. A valid paediatric first aid certificate is a requirement for many childcare jobs. Even if this does not presently apply to you, it is worth taking a recognised course, such as those run by St John Ambulance or the Red Cross, as this will give you the confidence to deal with incidents when they happen. These pages will then merely be a reminder to you about what to do. The most important rule is 'keep calm'.

First aid responses in emergency situations are described in Unit 11, pages 442–6.

Case study

Incident during outdoor play

You are in charge of a group of six children. During outdoor play, Ashok trips and falls heavily on his left leg. You see that his leg is swollen and it looks a strange shape.

1. What do you do immediately?
2. What, if anything, do you do with Ashok's leg?
3. What do you do with the other children?
4. Whom do you contact first and how?

Other actions to take in the event of an accident

When an accident occurs, in addition to helping the casualty, you or someone else needs to:

→ send for a qualified first aider if you are not qualified yourself
→ call for your supervisor
→ calm the other children
→ inform the child's parents
→ record the incident in the accident book.

Contacting the child's parents or carers

Whenever a child is involved in an accident, the person in charge must inform the child's parents or carers. The child will have a record card in the office giving emergency contact numbers. This may be the child's parents if they are at work, or the child's grandparents or aunt, for example – someone who is usually easy to contact and who in turn can contact the parents.

It is important that the person in charge gets in touch with the emergency contact as soon as possible and informs the relevant person of the incident and where the child is being taken. Obviously, someone the child knows well should go to the hospital with him or her until the parents or other carers arrive. This will help to reassure the child, and be a point of contact for the parents when they arrive.

Reporting accidents

Even with a minor accident that does not need hospital treatment, an entry should be made in the accident book (see also page 165).

Remember that Ofsted (in England) and the local child protection agency may need to be informed, particularly if the child is seriously injured. A full report should be made for the settings records in all cases. As the accident happened on an employers' premises, RIDDOR legislation (see page 165) may also require the accident to be reported to the Health and Safety Executive.

After an accident it is important that someone in charge looks at what happened to cause it. Then procedures, layouts, equipment, etc., can be changed if necessary to help prevent a repeat of the accident.

The appropriate contents of a first aid kit

All children's settings should have a well-equipped first aid kit that is easily accessible in the event of an accident. All staff should know where it is kept. Always make sure you know where the first aid box is found and what is in it.

A good first aid box should contain the following items:

→ a range of plasters in different sizes
→ medium and large sterile dressings
→ sterile eye pads
→ triangular bandages (slings)
→ safety pins
→ disposable gloves
→ crepe bandages
→ scissors
→ tweezers
→ cotton wool
→ non-alcoholic cleansing wipes.

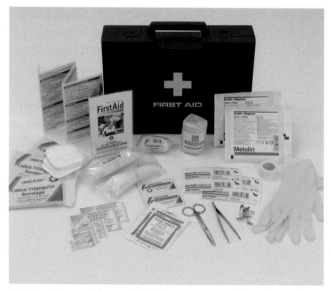

⇧ A well-equipped first aid kit

A named person should be responsible for checking the kit and replacing missing items, although anyone using an item from the kit has a responsibility to report this.

Find out!

1. Where is the first aid kit found in your setting? Is it easy to access?
2. Who is responsible for ensuring the kit is complete and in good condition?
3. Do the contents match the list above? Is anything missing? Are there any extra items, and if so what are they for?
4. What is the procedure following an accident involving a child in your setting?

Providing appropriate comfort and reassurance

When a child is ill or has had an accident, he or she is often frightened and wants lots of reassurance. Think about the following actions:

→ taking the child away from the rest of the children to a quiet area
→ making sure that you or someone else stays with the child all the time
→ sitting quietly with the child and reading a story
→ contacting the child's parent or carer
→ making sure that the other children are okay, especially if there has been an accident.

The procedures for preventing cross-infection

You have already read about the causes and spread of infection (pages 175–80). It is important that you know how to stop infection of any type being spread around.

Think about it

Think back to the earlier section on infection control. Working in pairs, list the different ways in which infection is spread and what to do to prevent cross-infection in each instance.

Good handwashing (see pages 177–8) is essential to infection control, as is following the correct procedures in your setting for cleaning and disposing of waste.

Good practice checklist

Disposing of waste

✓ Always wear disposable gloves and an apron when dealing with waste.
✓ Dispose of waste promptly and in the appropriate bin – do not leave it lying around.
✓ Always wipe surfaces that waste has been in contact with, using the correct cleaning fluids and cloths.
✓ If children's clothes are soiled with waste, put them in a plastic bag and wash separately from non-soiled clothes.
✓ Dispose of your gloves and apron and wash your hands thoroughly after dealing with waste.

How to establish and maintain healthy and safe routines

The best way to prevent accidents occurring in a childcare setting is to have clear and simple rules about basic behaviours that reduce the chances of them occurring. Likewise, good routines help to reduce the risk of infection spreading among children. Much of this is good common sense. If children are allowed to run around inside on slippery floors it is no surprise that they may slip and fall. If children cough and sneeze over each other they will pass on infection.

Establishing routines within your setting so that children and staff all follow safe ways of working can go a long way to reducing accidents and illnesses.

Think about it

1. List all the routines in your setting that help keep children safe and healthy.

2. Look at the good practice checklists below. Can you think of other ways to prevent injury and illness?

Good practice checklist

Preventing injury

✓ Routinely brief children about running inside.

✓ Teach children to use scissors safely.

✓ Brief children before outdoor play about safe play routines.

✓ Ensure routine checks of play equipment by staff.

✓ Establish clear routines and rules at mealtimes, for example sitting when eating.

Preventing cross-infection

✓ Regularly disinfect toilet areas.

✓ Establish routine hand washing by children after activities, using the toilet and before eating food.

✓ Set clear guidelines on the exclusion of children with infectious illnesses.

Getting ready for assessment

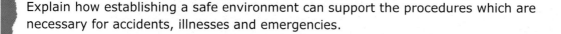

Explain how establishing a safe environment can support the procedures which are necessary for accidents, illnesses and emergencies.

Section 3

How to plan and provide an enabling physical environment for children

In practice

All of the staff at Jed's setting are excited about the new building they will soon move into. The school and nursery are to be built in a wooded area, with plenty of room for garden areas as well as outdoor activities. The school has a number of children with disabilities, some of whom use wheelchairs. Jed is already planning how he can help some of the children to become more confident and try out new things.

By the end of this section you will understand how to plan and provide an enabling physical environment for children.

Current national and international initiatives and philosophies around the indoor and outdoor environment

There is very little in child care and education that is new! Many of the so-called 'new initiatives' about outdoor and indoor education for young children have been around for years. For over a century, theories and ideas have been put forward and developed into different approaches to education. Many of them are based on the simple idea of encouraging children to explore their environment and for adult helpers to enable this learning without taking over. Over the next pages, you will read about some of these ideas from around the world as well as current initiatives in the UK.

International approaches

Reggio Emilia

Reggio Emilia is a town in Italy where parents developed an approach to pre-school education in the late 1940s. The Reggio approach is based on the idea of children as creative, competent learners who discover in collaboration with other children and adults, therefore social learning is central. Reggio pre-schools believe in the importance of discovery, stimulating learning environments (both indoor and outdoor), children reflecting on their own learning and documenting children's learning as part of this process. Adults are seen as the facilitators of children's learning; children are the initiators. The education of all children, including those with disabilities, is continually explored and developed by the staff, which always includes an artist, or *atelierista*.

The Reggio approach is based on

→ creative thinking
→ exploration and discovery
→ free play
→ following children's interests
→ valuing and encouraging all ways children express themselves
→ asking children to talk about their ideas
→ asking children to re-visit their ideas.

For more on the Reggio approach, see Unit 7 page 289.

Forest Schools

Forest Schools started in Denmark in 1950 and are based on the idea that children of all ages can benefit greatly from the learning opportunities presented by a woodland environment. Through regular weekly or fortnightly sessions in the same area of woodland with their teachers and a Forest School Leader, children are seen to develop:

→ personal confidence, self-esteem and social skills
→ a wider range of physical skills than are usually developed indoors
→ a greater understanding about their own natural and man-made environments
→ a greater understanding about wider environmental issues
→ motivation and a positive attitude to learning.

Did you know?

Many local areas in the UK have adopted the idea of woodland learning; see, for example the Forestry Commission website (www.forestry.gov.uk). As fewer children have the opportunity to learn outdoors, this offers them a way to learn and experience a full curriculum in a woodland environment.

For more on Forest Schools, see Unit 7 page 289.

Steiner education

Rudolf Steiner was active in the early 1900s but his ideas developed in the period 1960–90. Although Steiner schools in different countries vary, the basic principles are that learning should be designed to meet the changing needs of children as they develop physically, mentally and emotionally. Education should help a child to fulfill his or her potential but should not push children towards goals that adults, or society in general, believe are desirable.

Some of the key points of a Steiner education for children up to 8 years are:

→ up to the age of 7 years, encourage play, drawing, storytelling, being at home, nature study and natural things

- use activities like baking, gardening, modelling, painting and singing in a carefully controlled situation
- do not teach children younger than 7 years to read
- teach a child to write before you teach him or her to read
- do not keep changing a child's teacher; allow one teacher to carry on teaching the same class for seven years
- find links between art and science
- engage with children and make sure they are enthusiastic about the work they are doing.

For more on Steiner schools, see Unit 7 pages 281–2.

The outdoor environment

Educators as early as Maria Montessori (1870–1952) have recognised the benefits of learning through the world, and recent research on personalised learning and multiple intelligence theories has recently influenced a change in perspective. Research has shown clearly that the outdoors offers different learning experiences to children, encouraging them to use different learning styles, for example learning through using their senses.

 Did you know?

The government is recognising the benefits to children of the outdoor environment, both through supporting various schemes and by encouraging thoughtful design of school grounds. A guide, 'Schools for the Future: Designing School Grounds', encourages schools to consider how best to use their grounds for the educational, recreational and social needs of pupils.

Anyone who has worked outdoors with children knows how they benefit from their experiences of the living outdoor classroom – they respond with energy, enthusiasm and intelligence. However, in recent years the value of such learning has been overlooked – often seen as a pleasant end-of-term activity or something just for disaffected pupils.

Learning Outside the Classroom

In November 2006 the government in England launched the Learning Outside the Classroom (LOtC) Manifesto. The Manifesto is a joint undertaking by schools, outdoor organisations and others to make sure that all children and young people have a variety of high quality learning experiences outside the classroom.

 Find out!

Read about the Learning Outside the Classroom Manifesto on the following website:
www.teachernet.gov.uk/ learningoutsidetheclassroom

Learning Outside the Classroom links closely to Every Child Matters outcomes, in particular enjoying and achieving, staying safe and being healthy. It also supports personalised learning and the strategy for young people set out in Youth Matters.

Find out!

Use the Teachernet website (www. teachernet.gov.uk) to find out about some of the resources available on how to use the outdoors, including:

- *Growing Schools programme* – helps teachers and providers to understand how outdoor learning can be included in everyday teaching and learning.
- *The Countryside Foundation for Education (CFE)* – provides teaching materials and training about how to use the countryside in teaching.

The Growing Schools programme identifies the following benefits of Learning Outside the Classroom:

→ develop active citizens and stewards of the environment
→ nurture creativity
→ provide opportunities for informal learning through play
→ reduce behaviour problems and improve attendance
→ stimulate, inspire and improve motivation
→ develop the ability to deal with uncertainty
→ provide challenge and the opportunity to take acceptable levels of risk
→ improve young people's attitudes to learning
→ develop skills and independence in a widening range of environments
→ improve academic achievement.

Think about it

How do you think the benefits listed above might be achieved through outdoor learning? In a small group talk about each benefit and list other examples of outdoor activities that would be particularly good.

⇧ **There are many benefits of children learning outdoors. This 8-year-old boy is recording wind speed using a windsock he has made out of card and paper**

Case study

Growing Schools project

A Growing Schools project in a school and nursery on the edge of a large housing estate aimed to develop the school grounds which had very limited space and to create an 'outside classroom', which would enhance work going on in the 'inside classroom'. Plans included a small wood with bluebells, an orchard with daffodils, a vegetable growing area, a flower/salad area, a 'Bugs Hotel', a sensory and herb garden and an area for hens. A shed for storing tools and an incubator for keeping young chicks warm was provided. Help was given by people in the local community, and local landowner agreed to allow the schools to use more land so that the project could grow.

When asked what the benefits of the scheme are, the teacher in charge said 'We are learning to care for our environment and to celebrate what we are able to achieve. The delight on the children's faces when they eat our vegetable soup made from our vegetables and eat our apple pies is fantastic.' (*Source*: www.teachernet.gov.uk/growingschools/)

1. List as many benefits that you can think of for the children involved in this Growing Schools project.

2. How do you think the children are involved in the work?

3. List the ways that work the children do outdoors can be linked to indoor classroom learning.

The indoor environment

The way that children feel when they enter a building affects them considerably. If they feel relaxed, safe and comfortable, they can settle easily. This in turn means they are able to enjoy playing and learning and being with others, and can benefit from what the setting offers. This point is very important for children who spend many hours a day in a setting – it is vital that you get it right for them. Although the state of the building is important, it is still possible to provide a good environment in an old and maybe less than ideal building.

Failing to provide a good environment can result in children who are stressed and anxious. They will find it harder to learn, may show inappropriate behaviour and may not cope with separating from their family.

For children's families, the environment you create will affect how they feel about the setting. When leaving their children, parents and carers need to know that they are going to be happy and safe. It may make a difference to how often parents and carers come into the setting and how long they stay. As parents and professionals need to work closely together, it is essential that they, too, feel welcome and relaxed in the setting.

⬆ **The quality of the indoor environment will affect how children, parents and carers feel about the setting**

Your role in curriculum planning

The importance of the environment is recognised in one of the four key themes of the Early Years Foundation Stage (EYFS) curriculum. Enabling Environments recognises the key role the environment plays in supporting and extending children's development and learning. The environment is split into three aspects – emotional environment, indoors and outdoors; planning to support a child's development should recognise these three aspects. The table on the next page shows how the outdoors and indoors environments can be organised to provide for the EYFS areas of learning.

Think about it

1. If you are in an Early Years Foundation Stage setting, make a chart that gives examples of how the areas of development are planned for through the indoor and outdoor environments in your placement.

2. How important do you think each environment is in supporting each aspect of development in the EYFS?

Did you know?

As early as the late 1890s, Maria Montessori was developing her theory that children learn best by using their hands and through the everyday world. Her philosophy of providing didactic materials that encourage children to use their hands is demonstrated via the practical life area used in Montessori schools. Here familiar objects such as buttons, brushes and jugs are provided as it is thought that young children find tasks which an adult considers ordinary, such as washing dishes and polishing shoes, exciting. Although the practical life exercises may seem simple and common place, each task helps the child to develop fine and gross motor skills, hand–eye coordination, independence, social awareness, self-esteem, concentration and logical thinking. They also satisfy the child's need for order and indirectly prepare the child for reading, writing or mathematics, laying solid foundations on which to build for the future.

For more on Montessori's work, see Unit 7 pages 280–1.

EYFS area of learning	Outdoors environment	Indoors environment
Personal, social and emotional development	Allow children time to explore outdoors in order to develop their own interests	Provide opportunities for children to explore different cultural backgrounds, for example through role play or cooking activities
Communication, language and literacy	Help children share their thoughts and feelings about the outdoors environment, for example by describing different textures and colours	Ensure the environment is rich in opportunities for language development, for example books, posters, displays, songs, rhymes and pictures
Problem solving, reasoning and numeracy	Offer opportunities for children to discover about shape, spaces and measures, for example collecting and measuring rain water	Offer opportunities for learning about numbers, counting and calculating through practical situations, for example asking how many children want an apple for a snack
Knowledge and understanding of the world	Provide opportunity for first-hand contact with the weather, seasons and the outdoor world, for example observing the effect of the wind in the trees	Provide a range of tools, for example saws, hammers, rolling pins, sieves, for children to learn how to use them correctly and what they are called
Physical development	Provide opportunity to be physically active and exuberant outdoors, for example tricycles, climbing frames	Provide activities in which children prepare and then taste food
Creative development	Provide opportunities for children to use outdoor elements in their art, for example dried leaves, twigs, grass	Provide a range of creative materials, including paints, crayons, pencils, textiles, and encourage children to use them in different ways

The need for risk assessment in planning activities

Active learning will always involve risk, but while risk assessment is important it must not mean stopping children constantly from doing things. It is important to create an 'enabling environment' while thinking about safety issues.

Before you start to look at how you can provide this enabling environment, think about possible outcomes for yourself! An activity can be well planned with super outcomes for the children, but if a child is injured or has a near miss as a result of the activity, for example because it was not suitable for the children or there were risks in the area or equipment, then all your hard work is worthless. Worse than that, you could be held responsible for the accident.

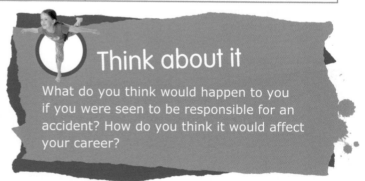

Think about it

What do you think would happen to you if you were seen to be responsible for an accident? How do you think it would affect your career?

Safe environment

Every environment is full of potential risks to a child's health and safety, and accidents do happen. However, with some care and planning, activities can and should be safe – allowing children to explore and develop their skills without unnecessary danger.

Everybody who works with children is responsible for their safety. It is important that the environment children are playing in is regularly checked, before and during activities. If you have checked an area and equipment for safety before children start playing there, and questioned whether the activity is suitable for the children, you will have carried out a 'risk assessment'.

How to undertake risk assessments

The following steps should be taken when assessing the risks in your setting:

1. Identify the hazards, for example gates that children may open, hard surfaces below equipment, ponds.
2. Decide who might be harmed and how.
3. Evaluate the risks and decide on precautions, for example locking gates, cushioning on the floor, fencing around a pond.
4. Record your findings and implement them.
5. Review your assessment and update if necessary.

When thinking about risk assessment, remember:
→ a *hazard* is anything that may cause harm, such as scissors, open gates, electricity
→ the *risk* is the chance, high or low, that somebody could be harmed by these and other hazards, together with an indication of how serious the harm could be.

The outdoor environment

It is important to check the outdoor play area as carefully as the indoor environment. When children are playing outdoors they are often more energetic than indoors, for example running around, so there can be more potential accidents waiting to happen. But as long as you have checked the area as suggested, the children will be free to enjoy themselves!

Did you know?

U4 3

In the UK in 1999, over 150,000 children were injured in school or nursery playgrounds. Climbing frames are most commonly involved, followed by swings. Falls account for at least 75 per cent of all playground accidents. Bumping into other children or stationary or moving equipment are common causes of injury.
(*Source:* Child Accident Prevention Trust, 2002)

Think about it

Can you think of other points to add to the checklists on pages 193–4?

Good practice checklist

Checking buildings and maintenance

✓ Young children must not be able to open doors that lead to the outside of the building.

✓ Emergency exits must be clear and easy to open from the inside.

✓ Floors should not have any loose rugs or pieces of carpet.

✓ Low-level glass must be safety glass or covered with a guard.

✓ Electrical sockets must be safely covered.

Safe storage and use of equipment

✓ Cupboards at 'child level' should not contain cleaning items, knives, tools or any other potentially dangerous items.

✓ Toys with very small parts should be kept well away from children under 3 years old.

✓ Heaters and radiators must be covered and not a risk to children.

Good practice checklist

Outdoor play

✓ Make sure that objects and equipment are regularly checked for wear and tear, such as fraying ropes and rusting joints.

✓ Check that equipment is clean and dry, especially slides and steps, etc.

✓ Make sure that each child has the space to move freely without bumping into other children or objects.

✓ Make sure that there are always enough adults to properly supervise the children. Never agree to be left on your own with children while you are a learner.

✓ Equipment such as outdoor slides and swings should be safe and have impact-absorbing matting underneath.

✓ Swings and rope ladders should be used by only one child at a time. Be careful that other children are not too near in case they are hurt by a swing or rope.

✓ Anyone supervising children should be able to see all the children.

✓ Check that outdoor areas are free from harmful waste such as dog faeces, broken equipment or litter.

✓ Gates should not be able to be opened by young children.

✓ Sandpits should be kept covered when not in use.

Safe activities

When you are supervising indoor and outdoor activities it is important that equipment is of the highest safety standard. Space must be allowed for children to run, hop, skip and throw, and so on. Space will obviously vary according to availability but no room should be overcrowded. This means that you need to think about the size of groups of children that are using an area.

Good practice checklist

Using equipment safely

✓ Before children use equipment, check all equipment and remove any broken or faulty items.

✓ Make sure you can see all the children who are using the equipment.

✓ Make sure that the equipment is used correctly – if necessary, show the children how to use it.

✓ Keep moving around so that you can see all activity.

✓ Check that the children do not become overexcited and so start acting in ways that may cause accidents.

✓ Encourage children to stop and rest for a few minutes if they seem tired.

Find out!

1. a) How many accidents have there been in your setting in the last year?
   b) What caused them?

2. How are children in your setting helped to use the outdoor play areas safely?

3. Spend some time observing how the children play outside. Look at how many are on equipment at any time. Do they run or walk, and how many adults are supervising them?

4. Could your placement reduce the number of accidents that happen? How?

Think about it

Look back at the different risks to children of different ages (see pages 168–73) to find out more examples of how children can be seriously injured and think carefully about your working practices – are they safe?

Encouraging children to take managed risks

Once you have carried out the appropriate risk assessments, you will be ready to plan activities to enable children to learn from their environment while taking managed risks. Children must have opportunities to explore their physical environment, both within and outside the setting. Many children do not have the chance to play in the woods, explore on the beach or even go to the park.

Think about it

Discuss the following quotation in small groups:

'Life is full of risk, so the best way to prepare children for life is to ensure that they [learn] how to judge risk for themselves.' (*Source*: Danks, F. & Schofield, J. (2005) *Nature's Playground*)

By helping children to manage risk, you are playing an important role in developing their independence. Think about:

→ talking to children about the potential risks in the environment
→ encouraging them to think of ways to manage those risks by:
  ● taking responsibility
  ● identifying and reporting hazards
→ encouraging older children to take care of younger ones where there are potential risks
→ agreeing appropriate behaviours.

Case study

Organising outdoor play

You are helping to support a group of eight energetic 5-year-olds – five girls and three boys. Sam is slower than the others in walking, due to a condition affecting his muscles. Prajat doesn't like rough games and is reluctant to join in groups. Lucy likes any game that is noisy and rough, but she broke her arm last week and has it in plaster. The weather was wet and windy all morning and now the sun has started to shine. The class teacher asks you to help the assistant take this group outside and organise some exercise for them in the grounds of the school for half an hour.

1. How do you think the half-hour could be planned to include all of the children?
2. What checks would need to be in place to make sure the environment was safe for all the children?
3. How could you help the children to manage risk in this situation?

Providing physical play experiences that support development and are age and stage appropriate

Play opportunities of any description should be appropriate to the age of the child. While children will find their own level of play, it is particularly important to provide relevant materials to support physical play.

Think about it

Remember that the outdoors offers play materials that are free – space to run around, trees to explore, etc!

⇩ **Materials to support the physical play experiences of children**

Age	Play needs of children	Indoor equipment	Outdoor equipment
0–2 years	Children are mobile and gaining gross motor and fine manipulative skills. They need plenty of opportunities to strengthen muscles and develop coordination.	• Push and pull toys • Toys that make music • Dolls • Trolleys • Building bricks • Posting toys • Bright simple books	• Paddling pool • Baby swings • Small slides
2–3 years	Children are starting to notice and play with other children. Language is increasing and much of their play is pretend play. Children are gaining confidence in physical movements and enjoy playing outside. Children of this age can be easily frustrated and have a short concentration span (less than 10 minutes) so they need opportunities to be independent in their play and range of activities. There should be plenty of equipment as children find it difficult to share.	• Dressing-up clothes • Home corner equipment, e.g. tea sets, prams, cooking utensils, pretend telephones • Building blocks • Toy cars and garages • Dolls and cuddly toys • Dough • Paint • Jigsaw puzzles • Musical instruments	• Paddling pool • Sand and water tray • Slides • Climbing frames • Swings • Sit and ride toys • Tricycles
3–4 years	Children are starting to cooperate with each other and enjoy playing together. Most of their play is pretend play, e.g. pieces of dough become cakes. Children enjoy physical activity and are gaining confidence in the use of large equipment, e.g. climbing frames. They are also developing fine manipulative skills and beginning to represent their world in picture form.	• 'Small world' play – e.g. dressing-up clothes • Home corner and equipment • Dough and other materials • Construction toys such as train tracks, building bricks • Jigsaw puzzles	• Climbing frames • Slides • Paddling pool • Tricycles • Balls and bean bags • Sand and water tray
4–6 years	Children are more interested in creating things, e.g. making a cake, drawing cards and planting seeds. Children enjoy being with other children although they may play in pairs. Children are beginning to express themselves through painting and drawing as well as through play. Children are enjoying using their physical skills in games and are confident when running and climbing.	• Materials for junk modelling • Cooking activities • Dough and other malleable materials • Jigsaws • Home corner • Construction toys • Small world play, e.g. Duplo people • Simple board games	• Mini gardening tools • Skipping ropes • Hoops • Climbing frame • Slides • Tricycles • Different-sized balls

Age	Play needs of children	Indoor equipment	Outdoor equipment
6–8 years	Children are confident and can play well with other children. Children are starting to have particular play friends and are able to share ideas about their play. Games that involve rules are played; rules are added and changed as necessary! Most children enjoy physical activity and play organised games. Sometimes children of this age can be very competitive. Children are also keen on making things, either of their own design or by following instructions.	• Creative materials – e.g. junk modelling, crayons, pieces of card and paper • Board games • Jigsaw puzzles • Complex construction toys • Books • Collections, e.g. stamps, stickers	• Balls • Hoops • Bicycles • Roller-skates • Skipping ropes • Climbing frames • Slides • Swings
8–12 years	• Ongoing development • Increasing independence	• Self-led displays • IT equipment • Resource areas • Quiet areas	• Large spaces • Formal games
13–16 years	• Ongoing development • Approaching independence	• Self-led displays • IT equipment • Resource areas • Quiet areas • Areas for meetings • Areas for socialising	• Large spaces • Formal games • Outdoor expeditions

⇧ **Children aged 6–8 years enjoy playing games with rules**

How to provide a stimulating physical environment

While children are very good at using their imagination to make even the most mundane setting exciting by turning it into something different, it is important to think of ways to make physical environments more stimulating. This does not take much – sometimes just changing the layout of a room or adding a new piece of equipment can make a positive difference.

Think about it

Think about the different children's settings you have seen, including those you have worked in and visited.

→ Does any setting stand out as being particularly vibrant and exciting for children?

→ Can you think why this environment was stimulating for children?

Outdoors

A good outdoor play area for children should be rich in opportunities for developing imagination and allowing the children to use plenty of energy. There should be enough resources and equipment that is challenge and interesting and can be used in different ways for different children. Outdoor play areas should be useable whatever the weather, so thought is needed about surfaces that will not be unusable when wet and suitable shade for sunny days. Ideally, especially for those in the EYFS, children should be able to move freely from the outside to the inside and vice versa.

Think about it

Look at the outdoor area in your setting. Are any of the following resources available?

→ Obstacle courses with opportunity to change the layout

→ Areas for children to hide in made of natural or man-made items

→ Areas where children can climb, balance, throw and just run around

→ Loose parts – attractive, flexible play materials which children can readily change, manipulate and control for themselves and use to feed their imagination

Did you know?

Loose part play was first introduced in 1971 by Simon Nicholson and is an example of how the environment can be organised to provide a range of opportunities for creative play. It is more than just touching or holding play materials, allowing for open-ended exploration in play (transformation, manipulation, creation and destruction).

An action research project called 'Play Pods in Primary Education' builds on the idea of loose part play. Play Pods are containers or 'pods' full of materials and equipment that facilitate and enhance children's play in the school playground. The loose parts are chosen by the children themselves from a list of recyclable or renewable resources.

Indoors

Displays

An important contribution to the atmosphere of a setting is the quality and effectiveness of the displays. These should be colourful, interesting and varied in their content.

Displays can be used to inform and raise awareness of issues for children, to help them learn about the world around them, for example different forms of transport, jobs, helping people, animals, etc. They can also be used as reminders for their learning, for example timetables or number squares in school. Above all, displays are the ideal way to allow a child to show off their work to parents and carers, which also boosts a child's self-esteem.

Displays can also range from being mounted on the wall to those which a child can look through at eye level, to low level displays full of different textures to encourage children to feel the display or even a whole section of a room. Of course, a display can also involve several senses and have sound included, and could also use ICT through a computer interactive display.

↓ **Displays which involve several senses are particularly stimulating for children**

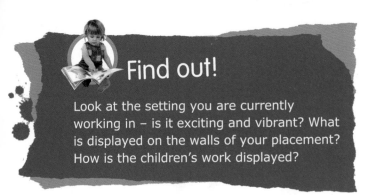

Find out!

Look at the setting you are currently working in – is it exciting and vibrant? What is displayed on the walls of your placement? How is the children's work displayed?

Whatever the type of material on display there are a number of important rules to consider:

→ The materials used should be in good condition – no tears or marks.

→ Is the display age appropriate to the setting?

→ Are appropriate formats such as language and symbols used?

→ Can the intended audience see it? For example, is information for parents near the entrance at the right height for small children?

→ Is the display inclusive – does it apply to a range of cultures and backgrounds? Does it avoid stereotypes?

→ The method of display should be considered, for example on walls, tables, folders, etc.

→ Consider safety when displaying, including safety when staff mount the display and then general safety once the display is mounted.

→ For what length of time will the material be displayed? (This will vary but should never be more than a few weeks.)

Involving children in the display of work is vital as it helps them to take responsibility and be part of the work of the setting. Even part of the background of a display can involve children, for example orange and brown handprints on a roll of backing paper for a display on autumn.

Interest tables

Interest tables usually have a theme, for example colours, toys, a country or holidays. It is possible to create a 'growing' table by planting bulbs, seeds or plants that can be observed in progress. Objects for interest tables can be collected on walks or outings from placement so that children feel a sense of ownership. Older children can also enjoy interest tables, perhaps based round a popular activity such as a recent film or skateboarding.

Once constructed, the interest table is a focus of attention and can be used to:

→ stimulate discussion about the objects, for example what they are, where they are from, what they are used for

→ stimulate creative activities, for example paintings, stories, model making

→ promote learning in areas of science, literacy and numeracy, and interest in the world at large.

Think about it

1. Working in pairs, list as many themes for an interest table as you can think of. The themes should appeal to children of different ages.

2. Ask if you can plan and prepare an interest table in placement. Write about your experience, including details of the items shown, the use made of the table and any problems encountered. If possible, include a photograph of the finished display.

Case study

Case study: Themed displays

Year 2 of Roshtown Primary School have been spending time on the theme of 'the jungle'. Miss Darzy, the class teacher, and Al, the nursery nurse, have spent a lot of time making the reading corner into a mini jungle. Children's paintings of jungles and animals line the wall. A line strung up around the area has dyed green sheets hanging with crepe paper leaves and creepers. Papier mache models of animals and birds done by the children are suspended. The book corner is full of books on the theme and Miss Darzy has a tape recording of croaking frogs and other jungle noises for occasional use.

1. Why do you think this theme corner display will be exciting for the children?

2. Suggest some ways children and staff can use this to its full potential.

Seeking out sensory experiences

Some settings have multi-sensory rooms that are full of opportunities for children to spend time in and experience different sounds, sights, textures and smells. Some of these are specialised for children with learning difficulties and/or disabilities to stimulate their development.

However, you do not need a multi-sensory room to encourage children to develop their senses. Activities within the setting can and should be planned to include several of the senses. There should be a huge range of different tactile materials in your setting, for example:

→ sand
→ water
→ fabric
→ floor surfaces
→ chairs

→ dough
→ paint
→ doors
→ different toys
→ paper.

Think about it

Consider another sense other than touch and list the many ways in which you can help a child explore this sense in your setting.

The importance and implications of providing risk and challenge in the environment

If a child never does anything which is slightly outside of his or her experience or skill, then he or she will not develop to the next stage of development. Think about how a baby starts to roll over – he or she is often trying to reach for something outside of his or her grasp. A child who is not allowed to take a risk will not enjoy the thrill of achievement, and more importantly will not try new challenges.

Opportunities to play in and experience different environments are important in allowing children to experience challenge. If children are helped to manage risk they can blossom and gain hugely in skills and confidence. Many outdoor activity centres specialise in giving children the chance to experience managed risks and challenges, for example by trying

out climbing walls or water activities. However, there are many other forms of challenges that children can try, from encounters with animals in a handling area at a zoo to simply experiencing a new environment.

⇧ **Children need to experience risk and challenge in order to develop**

Case study

Climbing frame

Lizzy, aged 6 years, has been watching the older children climb the big climbing frame in the park. She wishes she could have a go but her mum has always told her she is too young. Today, however, while her mum is called away by her little brother, Lizzy gets on to the frame. She loves the new challenge and nearly gets to the top. When Lizzy's mum returns she shouts to Lizzy that she should come down because it isn't safe. Lizzy suddenly looks down and becomes very nervous, and her mum has to climb up and help her down. Lizzy is very upset – she had been really enjoying herself until her mum came.

1. What do you think happened to Lizzy?
2. How could you have helped Lizzie and her mum manage the risks involved?

Did you know?

Short breaks to activity centres are a good experience for older children to experience challenge through activities such as climbing, water sports and caving. These are restricted by safety requirements and costs, but if you are in a placement that has such an activity, try to find out what is planned.

Dealing with the risks

Early years practitioners will sometimes not plan for outdoor learning with children because of the risks involved. As with any activity, the risks need careful consideration and managing. For outdoor activities, staff with particular training may be required, and a greater number of staff from the setting may be needed to ensure adequate supervision. It is also important to ensure that all children can participate, and special measures may be required to support those who need extra help.

As with any activity, the risks have to be balanced against the benefits. If the risks are minimised through effective risk assessment and management, the benefits of outdoor learning are well worth the extra effort and planning required. Some children may not have had the chance to explore the outdoors previously. Remember also, children need to be allowed to test themselves in a safe environment without being over-protected.

Providing for learning outdoors

Children need to be encouraged to explore and investigate. It helps them to understand and get involved in the world they live in. This is important for all ages but especially older children.

The attitude of adults is very important when providing for learning outdoors. Children will quickly pick up on the enthusiasm of staff and want to find out more. Children's interest in an outdoor excursion, such as an outing to a local wood, can also be stimulated through prior class discussion or research, watching a video or listening to a story.

Case study

A day in the woods

Neil has organised a day's outing for a group of 7–8-years-olds to a local beauty spot. The beauty spot is part of a deep wooded valley and has a stream with stepping stones across it. At the time of the excursion, a local group had also put up an outdoor exhibition of sculpture using natural materials.

On the day of the outing, Neil led the group on a walk through the wooded area, exploring the trees and environment. After time playing on the stepping stones and in the water, the group then looked at the sculptures. Finally, Neil encouraged the group to create their own artworks out of natural materials. He captured all the events on camera and used the photos along with writing by the group and 'treasure' they had brought back to mount a display of the day.

1. How has Neil provided for the children's learning outdoors?

2. What skills will the group have used and developed on the outing?

Find out!

Have a look at your local environment.

1. Is there a local park or open area?
2. Are there interesting places to go on a bus ride or a walk?
3. Are there trees that you could safely use for bark rubbings?

The need for age-appropriate activities

No two children are exactly alike, and an activity that is suitable for one 5-year-old may not be suitable for another. However, as the chart on pages 196–7 shows, there are some developmental guidelines you can follow. Good planning will ensure that there is sufficient flexibility, variety and choice of resources for play according to children's ages, need and abilities.

Depending on the age of the child, their attention span will be short relative to that of an adult. For example, an activity that absorbs a 3-year-old for 10 minutes will not maintain that same level of interest for 30 minutes. It is therefore essential that children have the opportunity to change their immediate environment and activity to keep them stimulated, even though they may come back to an earlier activity.

If a child has been ill or subject to some stress, be prepared to drop the age level of activities you are providing – often children seek out comfortable, familiar activities when they have been unwell or upset.

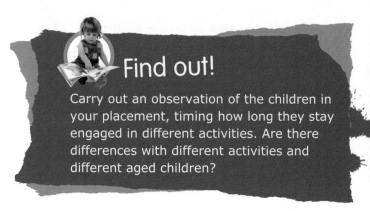

Find out!

Carry out an observation of the children in your placement, timing how long they stay engaged in different activities. Are there differences with different activities and different aged children?

Getting ready for assessment

Make a handout for a staff meeting in your setting that considers how practitioners can provide an enabling physical environment for children. Make sure you mention:

➔ issues that affect the planning of a suitable physical environment for children

➔ an evaluation of two examples that influence the provision of environments for children.

How to develop age-appropriate routines which encourage children to care for themselves

In practice

Lydia was impressed when she went to visit her friend who was working as nanny to a family of three small children, including a baby. Her friend seemed to be very well organised and able to provide for all three of the children's needs without too much trouble. The oldest child of 6 years was able to do a lot for himself and helped his younger sister. Her friend was very keen to support the children's parents in encouraging the children to be independent and to help themselves.

By the end of this section you will understand how to develop age-appropriate routines which encourage children to care for themselves.

The care needs of individuals from birth to 16 years

Children can relax and settle only when all of their needs have been met. This includes their physical needs. The extent to which you support children's personal care will depend partly on their age and partly on your role. Childminders or nannies may find that they need to care for children's hair and skin, while if you work in a pre-school you may find that your role involves providing food and drinks. This is an important part of caring for children and you will need to know how to ensure that children are eating a balanced and nutritional diet. (Providing food and drinks is covered in detail in Unit 12.)

Find out!

Compare a few children of roughly the same age. Observe what they can do for themselves in self-care. Think about:

→ dressing
→ washing
→ teeth cleaning
→ eating independently
→ preparing a simple meal.

Are there many differences between the children?

Think about it

Think about the amazing changes in a baby in the first three years of life. At birth the baby is totally dependent on his or her family for everything and needs protection by way of a routine being planned for him or her. By 1 year the baby can finger feed. By 3 years the child can take clothes off and put simple items back on. He or she can now use the toilet and may well be dry at night. With help the child can wash him or herself, but does need supervision especially in the bath.

Fast forward to a young person of 16 years and picture a fully independent person who can take charge of all his or her personal care needs. Even if that young person needs assistance due to a disability, most will be certain of how they want assistance and have very clear views about their personal needs.

Encouraging independence

Caring for young children involves helping them to become independent. This includes being responsible for their own eating, drinking, cleanliness and hygiene. (Encouraging independence is covered in more detail on pages 233–4.)

It is important to remember that some children with a physical disability or learning difficulty may require support with some of these activities. Also, if a child is seriously ill, his or her need for support may change.

Children's rights to privacy and how to meet them

Every child is entitled to privacy when having their cleanliness and hygiene needs met. It is essential that children are given as much privacy as possible, dependent on their age and needs. This means that, where possible, children should be able to close the toilet door; while adults might be on hand, they should be discreet. It is also important for children to take as much responsibility for their care needs as possible. For example, a 2-year-old may need help with fastenings on clothing but may be able to pull his or her pants up and down. Similarly, older children who have had an accident may be able to change most of their own clothing.

However, it is also very important that children are protected from abuse. There may be times when you have to care for children in potentially intimate situations, such as changing nappies, supervising them in the toilet or helping them if they have accidents. Only members of staff who have been vetted should have access to children during intimate care routines. It is important to take steps to protect children and yourself from allegations (see also Unit 3, pages 128–9).

How to assist daily living through practical activities

Caring for children's skin

Children's skin is particularly sensitive so needs to be well cared for. Skin products should not be used without checking with parents beforehand. When used, these should always be simple unperfumed products. Skin must always be dried thoroughly by being patted rather than rubbed, especially if children have eczema. This avoids sore areas and also can reduce the risk of infection. You need to pay especial attention to nappy area and skin folds in babies, i.e. underarms, groin and neck, as these areas can become very sore.

Handwashing

Washing hands frequently is a key way in which to prevent infection from spreading (see pages 177–8). Children generally handle objects but also often put their fingers and hands into their mouth. This means that bacteria, viruses and parasites can directly enter a child's body.

Hands need to be washed with warm water and soap and thoroughly dried. It is important to use mild soap and to check with parents that their children are able to use it; children with eczema may need special soap that is moisturised. Disposable towels are thought to be the most hygienic method of drying hands.

As early as possible, you need to encourage children to wash their own hands. It can be seen as an activity in its own right, although you do need to create a pleasant environment. As children become older, you may need occasionally to remind them to wash their hands, as it is not uncommon for them to 'skip' this. Explaining to them the importance of handwashing can help and you may wish to look at resources from your local health promotion team (which can usually be found by contacting your local NHS Trust).

⇧ **Handwashing is an important self-care skill that you should encourage in children**

Noticing changes

When caring for children, it is important to keep an eye out for rashes or changes to the skin, for example a child might have a fungal infection such as athlete's foot or dry skin. Concerns need to be reported to the child's parents and no treatment can be given until parental consent is obtained. It is also important to think about whether bruises or marks that you notice might be the result of abuse (see also Unit 3, pages 125–6).

Caring for skin in the sun

It is now recognised that skin cancers can be avoided if care is taken in the sun. Advice about how best to prevent skin cancer has changed over the past decade so it is important to keep up to date. The danger from UV (ultraviolet) rays is still not wholly understood and increasingly parents are warned that children must be kept covered up and out of direct sunlight. Children who have pale skin are particularly at risk, as it would now appear that being sunburned as a child can cause permanent skin damage.

Caring for children's hair

Childminders and nannies may have responsibility for looking after children's hair. Advice from parents needs to be taken regarding how often they wish their child's hair to be washed and how the hair should be groomed. This can depend on hair type as well as religious customs.

As early as possible, you should involve children in the care of their hair. They might hold a brush, choose a style or look in the mirror. As they become older, they should gradually take on responsibility for their hair.

Dealing with head lice

Anyone who works with children should keep a watch for head lice. These are very small parasites that live on the hair. Signs that a child has head lice include scratching, small red marks on the scalp (where the child has been bitten) and white egg cases (nits) on the hair. They do not move even after they have been brushed or combed. The lice themselves are small and translucent and so can be difficult to spot.

⇧ **It is important to check for head lice and nits in children's hair**

If you suspect that a child you are caring for has head lice, you must talk to the parents about the treatment they wish to use. Do not apply any lotions without their consent. It is also important to reassure children with head lice that they have done nothing wrong and are not dirty. Children can often sense from adults the revulsion associated with head lice. It is important, however, that the head lice are dealt with before the child has contact with other children.

Caring for children's teeth

Babies' first teeth usually arrive at around 6 months. From this point onwards, it is important that the teeth are regularly brushed. Teeth need looking after as soon as they start to appear. Plaque, a sticky substance that encourages bacterial growth, will attach to the tooth and start the process of decay. Despite the rise in the use of fluoride toothpaste, and the presence of fluoride in most water supplies, many young children are having their milk teeth removed due to decay.

Guidelines about how often brushing should take place have changed; currently, most dentists consider twice a day sufficient, but one brushing should certainly be after the last food and drink of the day. This means that the teeth can be 'food free' for a few hours. As with other aspects of children's physical care, it is important to talk to parents. Even when you are not directly involved with the brushing of teeth, you can help children's teeth to be kept healthy by thinking about the types of food and drink that children are given.

Good practice checklist

Promoting good dental health

- ✓ Encourage regular and thorough teeth brushing.
- ✓ Never give a baby fruit juice in a bottle or comforter (the acid will damage the teeth).
- ✓ Limit intake of pure fruit juices in all children (although they are nutritious, an excess can damage the enamel on teeth).
- ✓ Avoid giving sweetened drinks to children at any age.
- ✓ Encourage a child to drink plain water after meals.
- ✓ Eat sweets only after meals, followed by teeth brushing.
- ✓ Parents may be advised by health experts to give their child fluoride drops if fluoride is not added to the water supply.
- ✓ Encourage regular trips to the dentist as soon as teeth appear.
- ✓ Encourage a diet with plenty of calcium, fluoride, vitamins A, C and D, and foods that need chewing.

Did you know?

Young children usually produce all of their 20 first teeth by the age of 3 years. The 32 permanent teeth are present in the gums of young children, developing at the base of the primary teeth.

Think about it

→ Is dental care the responsibility of day or educational care for children? It could be argued that a child who cleans their teeth at home in the morning and at night does not need further cleaning at nursery or school.

→ Should children in day care settings clean their teeth after snacks and meals?

→ How does/could your setting provide and care for toothbrushes?

Ask your colleagues for their views. Perhaps your workplace has a view or policy on dental care. If so, what is it?

Nappy changing

When caring for babies and young children, you will need to know how to change a nappy. The best way to learn the mechanics of changing a nappy is to watch a competent person. You will also need to become familiar with the different types of nappy available.

Disposable nappies

Most parents use disposable nappies, which are convenient in that they do not require washing and can be bought relatively cheaply. They come in many different sizes and shapes with a range of special compounds to absorb wetness and various additional features for comfort and fit. However, they present society with the big problem of environmental waste.

Did you know?

Nearly 3 billion disposable nappies are thrown away in the UK each year. This is equivalent to roughly 8 million nappies going to landfill every day.

(Source: www.recyclesomerset.info)

Cloth nappies

In recent years, a move back to using cloth nappies has slowly been gaining ground. Cloth nappies also come in various sizes and shapes, but the two basic types are as follows:

→ Terry towelling squares are the cheapest form of cloth nappy but need to be folded to create the nappy shape and securing with a clip. The folding of terry towelling nappies is almost an art form and there are many ways to do it depending on the size and sex of the baby. While fiddly, this is one of their advantages as the nappy can be folded to be thickest at the position of urination. In addition, the same sized terry towelling nappy can serve a tiny newborn baby or a bouncing 2-year-old.

→ Fitted cloth nappies resemble disposable nappies in shape and are designed with extra thickness at the position of urination. Some types of fitted cloth nappy also include poppers or Velcro tabs for ease of fastening. Because the size and shape of the nappy is pre-determined, they are easier to put on than terry towelling squares. However, they need to be bought in different sizes to accommodate children at different ages, so are more expensive to use than terry towelling squares.

⇧ **Modern cloth nappies are shaped for ease of use**

Most types of cloth nappies also require:

➜ a thin paper lining, to make the disposal of faeces easier

➜ an outer waterproof pant, or wrap, to prevent wetness leaking through

➜ some form of fastening, for example safety pins.

Some 'all-in-one' cloth nappies are available with the nappy and waterproof cover stitched together.

Cloth nappies should be washed after soaking in solution at a temperature of at least 60°C and in non-biological powder. They should be rinsed thoroughly.

Find out!

Look at the range of nappies used by babies in your setting. Are they all disposable or do some parents using cloth nappies?

Procedure for changing a nappy

1. Wash your hands.
2. Collect all your equipment: nappy, water, soap, cotton wool or baby wipes, cream, changing mat, bucket or bag for the dirty nappy.
3. Always wear gloves and follow the policy of the setting.
4. After removing the nappy, clean the baby's bottom. If the nappy is a dirty one this will need greater care than if the nappy is wet. Cleaning can be carried out using clean water and cotton wool or baby wipes.
5. When cleaning female babies, always clean from the front to back to avoid introducing infection into the vagina. With boys, try to avoid soiling the foreskin area.
6. Apply a protective barrier cream if used. Be careful not to get cream on the adhesive fixings of a disposable nappy; if you do they will not stick.
7. Put the nappy on, being very careful with nappy pins if used, and dress the baby.
8. Dispose of the soiled nappy. Roll it up and put it into a nappy sack if disposable. If a cloth nappy, dispose of the paper liner and put the nappy into a bucket of sterilising solution.
9. Wash your hands.

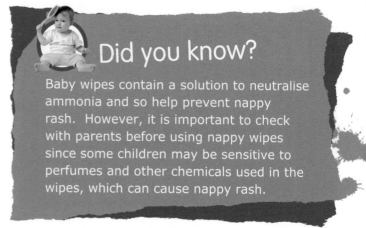

Did you know?

Baby wipes contain a solution to neutralise ammonia and so help prevent nappy rash. However, it is important to check with parents before using nappy wipes since some children may be sensitive to perfumes and other chemicals used in the wipes, which can cause nappy rash.

Nappy rash

Few babies will reach the age of 2 years without having had a nappy rash. Nappy rash appears as a red, sore area over the buttocks. In severe cases it can look like chafing. Sometimes a baby can develop thrush on the buttocks; this can be seen as small outbreaks of spot-type lesions away from the main red area. Medical advice is needed to deal with a nappy rash caused by thrush.

The best ways to prevent nappy rash are as follows:

➜ Ensure a baby doesn't spend too long in a wet nappy and change a soiled nappy as soon as possible.

➜ With parent's consent apply barrier cream to the nappy area (petroleum jelly is a good standby).

➜ Allow babies to spend some time each day without a nappy on, to help the skin dry out and 'breathe'. A warm room and a covered mat on the floor are a suitable place to let the child have time without a nappy.

How to plan care routines

For young children, care routines should be based around the child's needs and must be discussed with the child's parents. This means paying attention to existing home routines for personal care to encourage continuity for the child and to meet their individual needs. Most babies quickly develop a routine around feeding, nappy changing and sleeping, with increasing amounts of wakefulness and play developing. Parents prefer that most of the sleeping is done at night – for obvious reasons! However, young babies and toddlers need some sleep during the day as part of their rest needs. Research shows that young children must get enough sleep in order for their brain to develop and to prevent illness.

It is good practice to report any variations to the child's routine when the parents collect the child. You should also pay close attention to the child's specific needs, for example reminding the child or parent to take his or her comfort blanket home at the end of the day.

As a child grows their routine increasingly becomes dictated by the external demands of nursery and school.

Rest and quiet periods

The body needs time each day to recover from all the activity it has been doing. This is predominantly achieved through sleep and rest. Few children will spend all day running around actively playing. Most will enjoy some time to sit down and watch the world go by, or hear a story or watch television for a short time. These are all resting or quiet periods.

There are three levels of quiet period.

1. *Sleep times* are especially required by babies and toddlers, for example in a day nursery. Try to make sure that daytime naps are planned for the early afternoon so that the child will still sleep at night. Check with parents about home routines and try to follow them, for example reading a story or putting the child down just after a feed.
2. *Rest periods* are needed for toddlers and pre-schoolers.
3. *Quiet activities* are essential for all age groups as a break between other activities and a chance to recuperate. Quiet activities include story time, doing a quiet activity and listening to music, all of which should use material that is soothing and not stimulating. Older children may enjoy relaxation exercises and may watch a suitable television programme or video. Be careful with the TV though as it is advised that children under 3 years should not be exposed to television; it is thought that it might affect their brain development (see www.literacytrust.co.uk).

Most nurseries and Reception classes have a planned quiet time in their daily routine to allow children to recoup their energy. A skilled early years practitioner will build these times into the children's routine. When and for how long a setting has a rest or quiet period will depend on the ages of the children. Babies and toddlers will follow their own body clock, and you should discuss the child's routine with parents to find out the usual pattern. Older children

will usually fit within an overall plan of changing levels of activity.

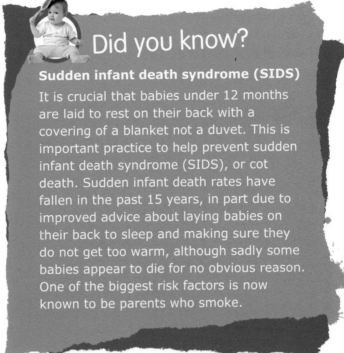

Did you know?

Sudden infant death syndrome (SIDS)

It is crucial that babies under 12 months are laid to rest on their back with a covering of a blanket not a duvet. This is important practice to help prevent sudden infant death syndrome (SIDS), or cot death. Sudden infant death rates have fallen in the past 15 years, in part due to improved advice about laying babies on their back to sleep and making sure they do not get too warm, although sadly some babies appear to die for no obvious reason. One of the biggest risk factors is now known to be parents who smoke.

Find out!

More information about sudden infant death syndrome can be found at the website of The Foundation for the Study of Infant Deaths (FSID) – www.sids.org.uk

Awareness of different cultural practices

It is important that not only are a child's care needs met, but that they fit with the wishes and customs of the parents. You should work closely with parents to ensure that individual children's needs are met. For example, a child may have an allergic reaction to certain skin products or parents may ask you to care for children in a way that meets their religious or cultural beliefs. It is important that information from parents is written down so that there is no confusion. This is particularly important where more than one person takes care of a child.

An important part of a child's identity is their home background. Children need to be able to talk to you about their home and what they enjoying doing. They may, for example, want to show you photographs or bring in things they have made or been given. Finding out about and valuing children's home lives helps them to feel more settled. It also shows parents that you are keen to work with them and avoid a 'them and us' atmosphere. This applies to everything a child does at the setting, including the way in which his or her care needs are met.

Think about it

Many cultural practices are very obvious if you too belong to that culture. However, other cultures may well have practices that are unfamiliar to you. Think about some of these examples:

→ families who are vegan cannot eat or use animal products.

→ children from some Muslim families must wash under running water, so will take a shower rather than a bath

→ some children from Afro-Caribbean families have plaited hair which needs particular care

→ children from families who are Jehovah's Witnesses do not celebrate festivals such as Christmas

→ some cultures have a different approach to encouraging independence, either expecting it earlier or later than you might expect.

It is very important not to make assumptions about any child's care needs. Every child and their family are unique, so the best way to find out how a parent wants their child to be cared for is to sit down with the parent, ask, and work out a plan of care that suits the child and their family.

Find out!

→ Do you know the particular cultural practices of the families of all the children in your setting?

→ Talk to some parents in your setting about their expectations of their children.

The role of the practitioner in encouraging independence

Raising children's awareness of their own body and how to look after it is an important part of growing up. Learning about the body and keeping it healthy should be fun and exciting for children. Eventually all children should be able to care for their body and take pride in doing so. The age at which this happens does vary (see also pages 344–6).

Activities to help children learn about their body

These include:

→ singing songs involving parts of the body (e.g. 'Heads, shoulders, knees and toes')

→ children drawing round their body on a large sheet of paper then drawing where organs such as the heart and lungs are

→ teaching about the importance of healthy eating through shopping at pretend shops in nursery

→ holding food-tasting events for new healthy foods

→ looking at the work of well-known chefs with older children

→ conducting quizzes about health for older children

→ looking at websites for children with information on health.

Find out!

Look at some of the books and games on the market aimed at helping children learn about the body. How could you use them to help children become more independent?

→ Think about children from cultures that you do not work with. Carry out research to find out if there are any care practices you would need to be aware of before you start to plan for their care.

Promoting children's independence and self-care

An important part of growing up is for children to learn to look after their own body. Your role is to know when children could be expected to do things for themselves and to plan care and activities to support this.

Think about it

How you could help a child with this list of daily actions?

➜ Having a wash
➜ Going to the toilet
➜ Washing hands
➜ Cleaning teeth
➜ Brushing hair
➜ Getting dressed
➜ Putting outdoor clothes on
➜ Eating independently

The first steps are to help children when they try to do things themselves and to encourage their independence. Be careful to allow the child to have a go before helping. As with other stages of development there is a 'best' time for them to try the next stage. Let them have a go and offer lots of praise for their effort.

For more on promoting and supporting children's independence and self-care see Unit 8, pages 344–6.

Sources of support for practitioners to help deal with own feelings

Sometimes when you work with people, including children, you may not always agree with their views and beliefs. Although there are similarities in the care of every child – they all need to eat, drink, sleep and be kept clean and warm – there are many ways of doing this, most of which are safe and satisfactory. It can be difficult if the practices of a family are opposite to yours. For example, you may be a vegan and not eat meat or animal products; if you are working in a setting where the meals include meat, you may

find this difficult. However, you cannot allow your own beliefs to intrude on the care of the children. In any case where you feel uncomfortable with what is happening or what you are being asked to do, the first thing to do is talk to your supervisor or tutor and discuss how you will deal with the situation.

Another possible issue you may have to learn how to deal with is if there is suspicion that a child is being abused. If you do not think this has been dealt with then you must report it, again to your supervisor, who will set the child protection policy in motion (see also Unit 3, pages 127–8). As a learner you must not talk to the parents about your suspicions or question the child – always refer to someone more senior than you.

Many adults who work with children fear that they are vulnerable to accusations of abuse. While such allegations are rare, it is a good idea to avoid putting yourself and the child in situations where such accusations might be made. As part of your child protection policy, you should have guidelines on how to work with children. This is especially important when you are supporting children with their physical care. It is also essential that volunteers, helpers and other parents in a setting also know and follow these guidelines. This can form part of an induction period, so that all adults in a setting understand the policies relating to child welfare, including those on confidentiality and behaviour, as well as child protection. (See also Unit 3, pages 128–30.)

It is also important that you keep up to date with changes in practice and current advice, guidance and legislation. As well as the wide range of books and journals that are available there are many websites that have a lot of information for parents and people who work with children.

Find out!

Look at some of the following websites and find out what sort of information and guidance you could get from them.

→ www.dh.gov.uk

→ www.direct.gov.uk

→ www.bbc.co.uk/parenting/

→ www.professionalchildcare.co.uk

→ www.surestart.gov.uk

→ www.nurseryworld.co.uk

→ www.nspcc.org.uk

→ www.ncb.org.uk

Getting ready for assessment

1. How would you plan the care for a full day for a baby and a toddler in their day care setting?

2. Explain how to meet the care needs of children in ways that maintain their security and privacy and respect their wishes.

3. How could you explain to parents how the setting encourages children to care for themselves?

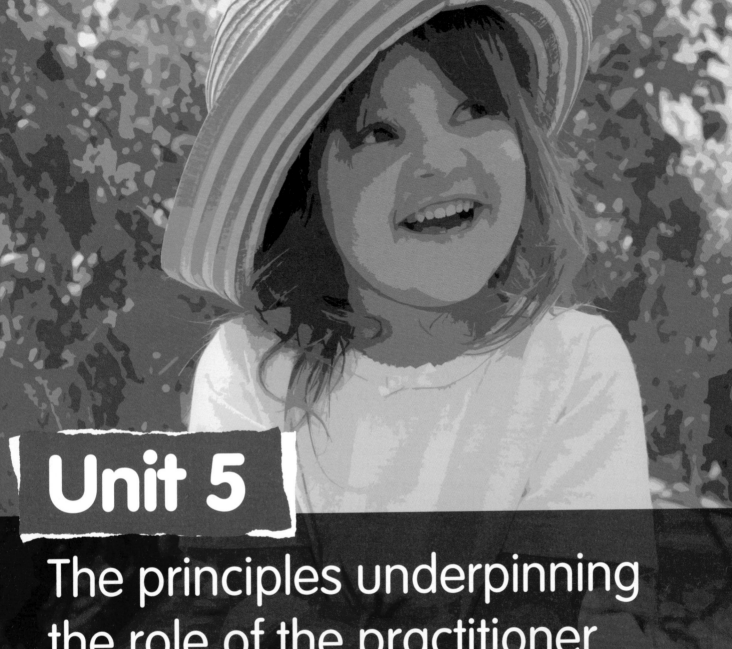

Unit 5

The principles underpinning the role of the practitioner working with children

In this unit you will learn:

1. How to maintain professional relationships with children and adults

2. The skills needed to become a reflective practitioner

3. The differing principles and practices that underpin working with different age children

4. Current national and local initiatives and issues relevant to the sector

Section 1

How to maintain professional relationships with children and adults

In practice

Lenka wants her child, Ike, to go to the nursery in the Lakeside Children's Centre three days a week. He is profoundly deaf and has never spent time apart from her. Lenka is concerned that the staff at the nursery might not understand Ike's needs or be able to communicate with him using British Sign Language, which she and her family have learned.

When Lenka visits the nursery she has a long talk with the therapist, who says they have a speech and language Special Educational Needs Coordinator who will support Ike, Lenka and the adults who will be working with him. He also promises that he will produce an individual learning plan for Ike so that the adults can support his needs and give him the same learning opportunities as his peers. Following this conversation, Lenka feels much more confident that Ike will be supported at the Centre.

By the end of this section you will understand the importance of working closely with parents and other professionals.

The range of professional relationships in multi-disciplinary teams

In your role as early years practitioner you will be expected to work with other professionals in some form. This may be in a Children's Centre, where services are more likely to be on the same site, or in a setting such as a private day nursery where you may work with other practitioners from the community as required. For example, if you work in a Children's Centre a speech and language therapist may work on the same site, but if you work in a small rural nursery the therapist may visit your setting regularly or when required.

The role of the professional in a multi-disciplinary team is to share his or her expertise for the sake of the child. Whatever the circumstances, you will only be able to respond fully to the needs of the children in your care by working with professionals with a range of expertise. This approach is central to the success of the government framework Every Child Matters: Change for Children (see page 16). Hopefully this will mean that none of the children you care for is excluded or disadvantaged because of ethnicity, culture or religion, home language, family background, special educational needs, disability or ability.

The range of professionals you may work with in your role as early years practitioner is shown in the spider diagram below.

There are a range of multi-disciplinary teams who work with children, including:

→ behaviour support teams
→ Sure Start teams
→ health awareness teams
→ family centres.

Children's Centres have multi-disciplinary teams that work together for children during their early years.

In order to be an effective part of any multi-disciplinary team working for children, you will need to:

→ feel valued as a member of the team
→ welcome and respect your colleagues' viewpoints
→ ensure members are welcome whatever their status, for example whether part-time or seconded from another service or agency
→ ensure that you attend regular team meetings as appropriate
→ be prepared to adapt your practice for the benefit of the child
→ attend training as needed.

Think about it

It is important to remember that not all multi-disciplinary teams are based in Children's Centres. Discuss the challenges that face multi-disciplinary teams when they do not operate on the same site.

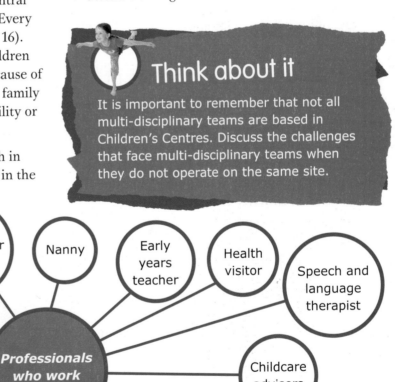

Professionals who work with children: Outreach workers, Nursery nurse, Childminder, Nanny, Early years teacher, Health visitor, Speech and language therapist, Childcare advisers, Social worker, Play worker, Portage workers, Occupational therapists, Dieticians, Specialist teachers

Case study

Promoting healthy eating at Redwood Children's Centre

Ravi is a health visitor at Redwood Children's Centre and is concerned about the level of childhood obesity among children attending the centre. At a team meeting he expresses this concern and a discussion takes place as to how the various adults at the centre could approach this issue. It is decided that the centre will have a healthy eating week. Pat, who leads the Children's Centre, agrees to incorporate a healthy eating focus into the nursery curriculum plan for that week. Ravi agrees to give an evening talk to parents, when they will also have a chance to sample healthy snacks from the Centre's catering department. The evening is to be open to parents whose children attend the centre and others in the local community. Ravi is aware that there are some ethnic groups who do not attend the Centre and hopes that this will encourage them to use the facility. William, who is an outreach worker attached to the Centre, agrees to invite parents of children he supports to come to the evening. Grace, who manages the Children's Information Centre on the site, agrees to publicise the event to ensure that there is wider access for the whole community.

1. How could other professionals working at Redwood Children's Centre be involved in the healthy eating week?

2. What sort of activities could Pat and her team plan for the children during the healthy eating week?

3. Are there any other activities that the multi-disciplinary team could plan for the healthy eating week that would benefit the community?

The roles and responsibilities of the practitioner in all professional relationships

Codes of practice

When working as an early years practitioner there will be **codes of practice** that underpin your practice. These state how you are expected to conduct yourself in your role as a professional adult. While a code of practice is not a law it often enables the employer and employee to comply with relevant legislation. Your employer will guide you through any relevant codes of practice, which should be available in your staff handbook. Codes of practice should be referred to and reflected upon frequently as a matter of good practice.

As an employee in childcare you will find codes of practice related to:

→ special needs
→ safeguarding children
→ children's learning
→ managing behaviour
→ working with parents
→ administering medicine to children
→ data protection
→ health and safety
→ confidentiality.

Find out!

Ask the setting you are currently working in if you can have a copy of their codes of practice to take to college. In your study group, discuss how these codes support the early years practitioner.

Key term

Codes of practice A set of rules that state the way you should operate in your job

Employees need to ensure that they comply with codes of practice that protect you as an employee. These could relate to:

→ storage of information (data protection)
→ smoking and the consumption of alcohol
→ recruitment procedures
→ professional development
→ workplace conditions such as hazards and temperature, etc.
→ risk assessment
→ equality of opportunity.

Key principles

When working with children there are ten principles that underpin most codes of practice, as follows:

1. The welfare of the child
2. Keeping children safe and maintaining a healthy and safe environment
3. Working in partnership with parents/families
4. Children's learning and development
5. Valuing diversity
6. Equality of opportunity
7. Anti-discrimination
8. Confidentiality
9. Working with other professionals
10. The reflective practitioner

These are influenced by the United Nation's Convention on the Rights of the Child (UNCRC; see also pages 6–7) and are designed to ensure that every child has the right to quality care and education. All countries in the UK have signed up to the Convention and must ensure that they comply with its articles.

Find out!

You can find out more about the UN Convention on the Rights of the Child by visiting the UNICEF website (www.unicef.org.uk/tz/rights).

When employers are drawing up codes of practice, they have to consider legislation such as the Health and Safety Act 1974 (see Unit 4 pages 161–2) and the Childcare Act 2006 (see Unit 4 page 163).

Responsibilities

You will have clear responsibilities in your role as an early years practitioner that should be outlined in your job description. Different settings will have their own job descriptions but the main responsibilities of every adult working with children are as follows:

→ Work as part of a team to provide a quality service for children and their parents.
→ Work with parents as partners, respecting them as having the main information about their child. Encourage parents' active involvement and participation.
→ Participate in providing an environment that is appropriate, warm, welcoming and stimulating.
→ Meet the learning needs of each individual child by providing a wide range of appropriate activities and experiences.
→ Work according to the principles of the sector and codes of confidentiality.

Each early years setting will have a management structure which should clarify practitioners' responsibilities and those of other adults working in the setting. Consider the example of an organisation structure given below.

TREETOPS BREAKFAST CLUB

Manager: Responsible for the development and running of the Breakfast Club. Must ensure that each adult has a job description and is aware of their responsibilities via informal discussion and appraisal.

Deputy Manager: Reports to the Manager and responsible for the day to day running of the Breakfast Club in his/her absence.

Qualified play worker: Reports to the Manager and Deputy Manager. Responsible for planning daily activities for children in accordance with the Breakfast Club's development plan. Oversees a key worker group of children and their parents. Responsible for liaising with parents. Mentors learners or trainees.

Assistant play workers: Unqualified or working towards a qualification. Reports to the Manager. Responsible for supporting activities with children and the daily routine of the Breakfast Club.

⇧ **Example of an organisation structure**

Policies in the setting

The policies in your setting will help you carry out your responsibilities as an early years practitioner. These will vary from setting to setting but will include the following:

→ *Health and safety policy* – this will give guidelines on how to keep children, parents and staff safe, for example guidelines on handing over children at the end of a session safely.
→ *Equal opportunities policy* – this will outline your responsibility to ensure that your practice is free from discrimination.
→ *Behaviour management policy* – this will guide you how to positively manage children's behaviour in accordance with good practice.
→ *Parents as partners* – this recognises the importance of working with parents and the responsibility you have in implementing this in your practice.
→ *Child protection policy* – this will emphasise your responsibility and line of communication when safeguarding children in your care.

Find out!

Ask if you can see the management structure for the setting where you work.

Establishing and maintaining relationships with parents

Working with parents is an essential part of your role as an early years practitioner. You will need to be able to listen to parents' advice and needs regarding their child and create a relationship of mutual trust and respect.

Respect for parents' role

In order that children of all ages receive effective care and education, parents must be acknowledged as their children's main carers and first educators. When working with parents it is therefore important to consider their wishes and to offer them high standards for their child. Remember that, as the main carers of their child, parents have a right to their own views about their child and to express concerns as appropriate.

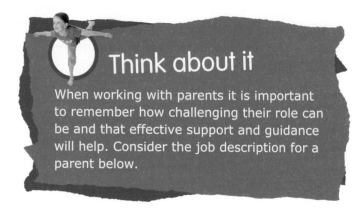

Think about it

When working with parents it is important to remember how challenging their role can be and that effective support and guidance will help. Consider the job description for a parent below.

Parent required

Responsible person, male or female, to undertake lifetime project.

Candidates should be totally committed, willing to work up to 24 hours daily, including weekends. Occasional holidays possible after five years service.

Knowledge of healthcare, nutrition, psychology, child development and the education system essential.

Necessary qualities: energy, tolerance, patience and a sense of humour.

No training or experience needed.

No salary, but very rewarding work for the right person.

(*Source*: National Stepfamily Association)

Building trust

One of the most important principles when working with parents is to build relationships based on trust. The chart below gives some suggestions for how to do this.

Area	How to build trust with parents
Communication	• Be honest • Be specific • Keep parents informed – give regular updates on their child's progress; pass on information and share records and observations as appropriate; involve parents in and inform them of planning • Ensure written communication is clear and well presented • Ensure parents' communication needs are met, for example provide translations of documents in home languages
Confidentiality	• Exchange information in appropriate areas • Ensure information about children is kept out of view from other children's parents • Pass on information only with permission from parents • Ensure parents give permission for photographs and documentation of their child
Environment	• Create confidential, welcoming areas for conversation • Have clear and attractive notice boards • Put up photos of children in the setting; create displays of children's work
Professionalism	• Avoid personal relationships • Respect parents' views • Remain objective
High standards of care	• Ensure parents understand the health and safety procedures and policies of the setting • Ensure that you share expectations with parents, e.g. with regards to behaviour

Communicating with parents

Talking with parents is not always easy and it may require a great deal of practice before you feel confident doing it. You should always seek guidance from your line manager if you are uncertain of how to manage a situation or if you have something sensitive to discuss.

⇧ **The ability to communicate effectively with parents is a skill you will develop with practice**

When talking with parents you need to think very carefully about what you say and the way in which you say it. It is also important to be sensitive to parents' needs – an insensitive comment can cause a worried parent unnecessary distress. In such a situation it is best to remain calm and be as reassuring as you possibly can.

Key worker system

The key worker system, by which children in early years settings are allocated one member of staff who is primarily responsible for their care, is an excellent way of working in partnership with parents. There are many benefits which include:

→ Ensuring a special relationship between the child's parents and the key worker.

→ That the key worker is able to keep the parents informed about their child's development and share essential information, such as observations, with them.

→ Helping to ensure that the care of the child meets with the parent wishes.

→ That the key worker can keep other team members better informed about the needs of the children, for example feeding information from parents into planning meetings.

→ Records can be made more accurate.

Did you know?

Elinor Goldschmied carried out research into the impact on children when parents had a specific member of staff to communicate with. From this research the key worker system was developed.

Find out!

Find out more about the research carried out by Elinor Goldschmied by reading articles, books and researching the Internet.

How to improve communication skills in your own professional practice

Effective communication with children, parents and colleagues is central to your work as an early years practitioner. To help children make choices, to build a relationship with parents and to work effectively with colleagues, you will need to be confident and overcome any barriers to communication.

Communication with children

To communicate effectively with children you need to be aware of their level of development (see Unit 2, pages 43–6). For example, if you wanted to talk to a 3-year-old about a painting she was doing at a table, you would sit or kneel next to her to make eye contact. To show interest in what she was saying about the painting you would listen and perhaps restate what she had said to show that you understand. But whatever the age of the child you should always do the following:

→ make good eye contact
→ check that you have the child's attention
→ show sincerity
→ avoid using phrases that they may misinterpret such as 'pull your socks up'
→ show real interest in what the child is saying.

You should also be careful to avoid the following:

→ interrupting children
→ dismissing children's ideas or laughing at what they say
→ changing the subject
→ allowing other children to interrupt
→ bombarding children with questions
→ hurrying children to finish what they are saying.

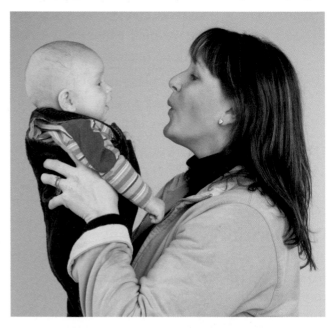

⇧ **It is important to respond to children's early attempts at communication**

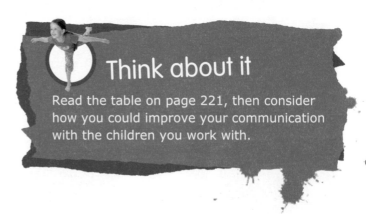

Think about it

Read the table on page 221, then consider how you could improve your communication with the children you work with.

Area of communication	Skills of adult required
Encourage children to ask questions, offer ideas and make suggestions	Be relaxed with children. Encourage opportunities for interaction such as asking them if they would like to help water the plants or choose a floor puzzle to play with. Try not to give commands but invite ideas and suggestions such as 'Where do you think we should put this picture?' If you cannot use a child's idea, give a clear reason why, for example 'I like that idea, but I think the picture may be ripped if we put it there.'
Listening and responding to children	All children liked to be listened to. From a young age, respond to children vocalising with a verbal reply or smile. Children will only learn to listen if the adult listens too!
Active listening	This involves really thinking about what a child is saying and giving the child all your attention. Although this can be hard when you are busy, a child will feel devalued if you only half concentrate on what they are saying, for example listening to them tell you about their weekend while setting up a table and giving instructions to other adults. For older children, you might need to find a quiet space and make time to listen actively to them without distractions.
Restating and extending language	Restating what children say is a good way of showing that you are listening to them. For younger children you may extend their statements; for example, a 2-year-old might say 'mummy gone' and you might reply 'Yes, mummy has gone to work and will come back when you have had some lunch.' In this way children will be encouraged to actively engage in conversation.
Adapting communication to meet children's individual needs	The children you work with may have communication needs, for example a language delay, English as an additional language, or a hearing or speech impairment. Children in theses situations need time and respect for their need, and you will need to gain as much information as possible from parents and relevant specialists. Remember that a child with a hearing loss may need to communicate in a space that is free from background noise so they are not distracted.

U5
1

Case study

Exciting news

Luke, aged 11 years, came home from school with exciting news about getting into the school football team. He rushed in through the front door and saw his Dad in the kitchen, doing some washing up. His Dad said 'Hello' and asked Luke if he had had a good day. Luke replied 'I don't think you really want to know as you haven't looked at me.' Luke's Dad immediately turned round, gave Luke a hug and sat down with him to listen to his news.

1. Why did Luke not want to tell his Dad that he had a place in the school football team?

2. What does this situation tell you about listening skills?

3. Can you think of a time when you didn't feel that you were being listened to? Can you recall how you felt?

Good practice checklist

Effective communication with children

✓ Show positive facial expressions.

✓ Restate what children say to you.

✓ Extend statements.

✓ Remain on the same level to make eye contact.

✓ Show interest.

✓ Ask questions.

✓ Try to sustain conversation.

Communication with parents

If you are friendly and make parents feel welcome, they should gradually develop confidence in you and the setting. However, it is important to bear in mind that parents have different needs – some may feel more comfortable talking to you than others. With experience you will be able to respond to parents' needs accordingly, for example encouraging parents who are shy to discuss less important matters before addressing their real concerns.

Active listening when communicating with parents remains a key skill. Through active listening you will show that you are interested in what parents say and this will help to build trust. You can show that you are actively listening by smiling and nodding as appropriate.

Many settings operate an 'open door policy' whereby parents are free to visit the setting at any time, for example to be with their child or talk to the child's key worker. This approach makes parents feel welcome and helps to build trust. Children also benefit from their main carers communicating in an informal way.

The spider diagram at the bottom of the page lists some of the key skills when communicating with parents.

Written communication

When exchanging information with parents you may need to use written communication. Written communication may take the form of:

→ letters
→ notices
→ permission slips
→ newsletters
→ labels
→ home books, observations or records
→ accident slips
→ notice boards.

If you need support with written communication, always get a colleague to check what you have written.

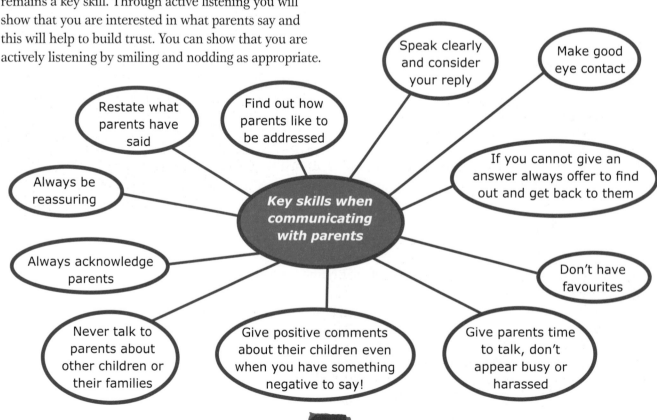

Key skills when communicating with parents: Restate what parents have said; Find out how parents like to be addressed; Speak clearly and consider your reply; Make good eye contact; Always be reassuring; If you cannot give an answer always offer to find out and get back to them; Always acknowledge parents; Don't have favourites; Never talk to parents about other children or their families; Give positive comments about their children even when you have something negative to say!; Give parents time to talk, don't appear busy or harassed

Good practice checklist

Written communication with parents

✓ Clearly address the note using correct names.

✓ Ensure punctuation and spelling are correct.

✓ Keep language clear and understandable; avoid using professional jargon.

✓ Ensure information is accurate.

✓ Date and keep a copy of your communication.

✓ If emailing, do not use overly familiar language.

✓ If parents are unable to understand written communication, perhaps because English is not their home language or they are unable to read, they will need sensitive support.

Communication with colleagues

The communication skills that you need to develop with children and parents are also required with colleagues. Do not assume that colleagues will always share the same opinion as you – you need to be able to show this in your communication. A very clear way to communicate with colleagues is to state what you know or believe by being clear, for example 'I am happy to organise the display about the trip to the duck pond' rather than 'If you want me to then I could do the display about the trip to the duck pond.' The first statement is much clearer and ensures that everyone knows what is to happen. Also, check other people's views and never assumes anything, for example check that a colleague is happy to cover for you when you have a meeting rather than assuming that he or she will. Often conflicts are the result of a miscommunication or a lack of confidence.

Think about it

Read the two styles of email below. Which is most appropriate for communicating with parents? Why?

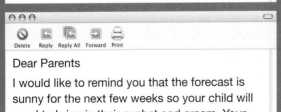

> Delete Reply Reply All Forward Print
>
> Hi
>
> Hope you are well and enjoying this fab weather! Don't forget that the children need a hat and cream to stop them burning.
>
> Cheers Molly

> Delete Reply Reply All Forward Print
>
> Dear Parents
>
> I would like to remind you that the forecast is sunny for the next few weeks so your child will need to bring in their sunhat and cream. Your key worker will ensure that your child is suitably protected.
>
> Best wishes,
>
> Molly Kahn
> Manager, Green House Children's Centre

Think about it

1. Reflect upon your answers to the following questions:

   a) Am I polite with colleagues?

   b) Do I show respect for other adults' ideas?

   c) Do I listen actively?

   d) Do I manage disagreements in a positive way?

   e) Do I clearly state what I mean?

   Try to back up your answers with examples.

2. In order to develop your communication skills, reflect upon your own practice in groups.

The need for reliability and accountability in professional practice

As an adult working with children, it is important that you are reliable and accountable for what you do. Reliability can range from arriving at work on time to following the time frame of the setting when leading an activity. Poor timekeeping can not only affect the running of the setting but can cause resentment amongst teams.

From the children's point of view, reliability equates to security. If an adult is inconsistent in their approach, for example sometimes patient and at other times very impatient, children will feel unsure and may react with negative behaviour. For example, a child who knows that an adult will always rub their back when they are going to sleep will feel reassured.

Being accountable for your actions means that you behave responsibly and take into account the needs of children, adults and colleagues in your setting. If you are able to clearly explain your actions then this will lay the foundations for honest and respectful relationships.

Employment rights and responsibilities

As an employee there are laws which protect you and ensure that you are treated fairly. However, you also have a responsibility to ensure that your practice is safe, reliable and trustworthy.

Laws to protect employees

The table below identifies the laws that are in place to protect you and ensure that the environment you work in is safe.

Law	Terms
Health and Safety at Work Act 1974	This Act outlines employers' duties to make sure that all employees and people using the work premises are protected from any risks to their health (see also pages 161–2).
Control of Substances Hazardous to Health Regulations (COSHH) 2002	The Regulations state that employers must ensure that employees know how to store hazardous substances such as adhesives and bleach and the procedures to follow when handling them (see also page 162).
Manual Handling Operations Regulations 1992 (amended 2002)	You may sometimes have to lift heavy and awkward objects (including lifting small children!). By law, you must receive appropriate training on how to do this.
Health and Safety (First Aid) Regulations 1981	The Regulations ensure that there are adequate and appropriate first aid supplies and a first aider at work who will be qualified to help anybody who becomes ill or is injured while at work (see also page 164).
Sex Discrimination Act 1975	This Act made it unlawful for employers to discriminate against employees because they are male or female.
Race Relations Act 1976 (amended 2000)	This Act made it unlawful for employers to discriminate against an employee because of his or her race, colour, nationality, ethnic or national origin or sexual orientation.
Disability Discrimination Act 1995	By the terms of this Act, employers must make reasonable adjustments to ensure the employment needs of disabled employees are met (see also page 116).
Data Protection Act 1998	This Act is concerned with the protection of personal information. Data stored on a person must not be given to anyone without that person's permission or kept for longer than necessary. Everybody has the right to see any records that are kept about them.
National Minimum Wage Act 1998	This Act ensures that there is a minimum wage that employees are paid for every hour they work.

Case study

Jumping in puddles

Adele was outside in the nursery garden with a group of 2-year-old children. It had been raining and she encouraged them to splash in the large puddle in the garden. They really enjoyed themselves but needed a change of trousers and tights when they came inside. Adele had taken photographs of the children to display outside her room. She explained to her manager that, while she knew it had caused a change of clothing, she felt that it was right to take the learning opportunity of splashing in the water. She also felt that it was not too cold and that none of the children were in any danger. Her manager asked her to explain to the parents when they collected their children. Adele did this and carefully put wet tights and trousers in bags for the parents.

1. How did Adele make herself accountable for the children getting wet tights and trousers?

2. How did Adele's manager encourage Adele to be accountable for her decision?

3. Adele was prepared to be accountable and tell the parents about the wet tights and trousers. How do you think she should talk to the parents about it?

4. How could Adele use the photographs in a positive way?

5. Do you think that Adele was professional in her approach to this situation?

Find out!

1. Check the current national minimum wage rate by visiting the website of the Department for Trade and Industry (www.dti.gov.uk).

2. There are further Acts of Parliament that ensure your employment conditions are fair. Some of the laws are very detailed. You can find out more about them by visiting the following website: www.acas.org.uk

Rights of employees

Some of the rights of employees are as follows:

→ Contract of employment – you are entitled to written terms and conditions of employment, for example a clear statement of your working hours, holiday entitlement and pay.

→ An itemised pay statement must be given to you.

→ You are entitled to time off work for antenatal care and public duty.

→ You are entitled to sick leave. This is time off paid at a statutory rate, though some employers pay more than this.

→ Maternity rights have recently been updated to allow employees to take one year off from their job to be with their baby. There are also paternity rights for fathers.

→ Termination of employment – both employer and employee are entitled to a minimum period of notice.

→ Terms of dismissal – guidelines are in place to ensure that employees are treated fairly.

→ Redundancy rights – if an employee has to stop work involuntarily then he/she has the right to payment after two or more years of continuous service.

Laws that affect adults working with children

These include:

→ Every Child Matters (see page 16)
→ Children Act 1989/2004 (see page 116)
→ Childcare Act 2006 (see page 117)
→ Care Standards Act 2000 (see page 250)

To ensure that you are familiar with these laws, you will need to turn to the pages listed above.

Find out!

You can also find out more about the laws that affect adults working with children by accessing the following websites:

→ www.surestart.gov.uk
→ www.ofsted.gov.uk
→ www.everychildmatters.gov.uk

Getting ready for assessment

1. Describe the responsibilities of practitioners in maintaining professional relationships.

2. List three issues that might affect professional relationships.

3. Explain why a multi-professional approach is taken when working with children.

Section 2

The skills needed to become a reflective practitioner

In practice

Rosie is a practitioner working with children under 3 years in a day care setting. She is key worker to Tom, who has been at the nursery full-time for two weeks but still becomes very distressed at times during the day.

At her team meeting, Rosie expressed her concern that she wasn't spending enough time with Tom. Other members of the team were also concerned that some children were taking time to settle. Together, the team discussed the key worker system that had been in place for some time. It was decided that all key workers should, where possible, carry out daily tasks with their children, for example nappy changing and feeds, in order to create a stronger bond. Where key workers were unable to do these tasks, they would pass on information about each child's preferences to the other team members. They agreed to review this practice regularly at team meetings.

By the end of this section you will understand the importance of reflecting on your practice individually and as a team.

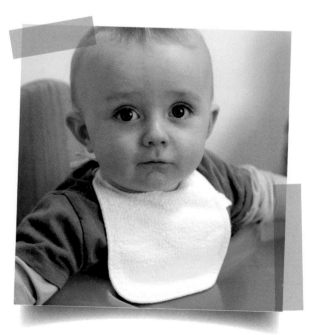

The reflective cycle and the skills of reflective practice

Reflection is an essential part of working with children in any setting. Think of it as a circular process whereby you think about what you have done and how well it went, get feedback from others and consider what you will do differently next time. As an early years practitioner, reflection gives you the ability to develop and improve your working practice.

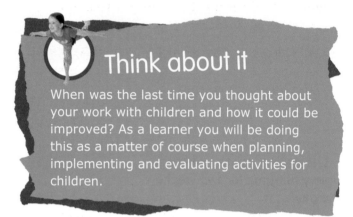

Think about it

When was the last time you thought about your work with children and how it could be improved? As a learner you will be doing this as a matter of course when planning, implementing and evaluating activities for children.

In 1998, Gibbs depicted reflective practice in a cycle. By relating this cycle to childcare the practitioner can review and improve their practice after thought and discussion. Consider the cycle below.

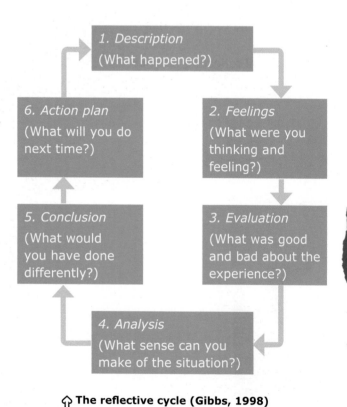

1. Description
(What happened?)

6. Action plan
(What will you do next time?)

2. Feelings
(What were you thinking and feeling?)

5. Conclusion
(What would you have done differently?)

3. Evaluation
(What was good and bad about the experience?)

4. Analysis
(What sense can you make of the situation?)

⇧ **The reflective cycle (Gibbs, 1998)**

The reflective cycle can be applied to any situation in your working practice, as the following example shows. This is a clear example of how thinking and discussing your practice can trigger changes for the better.

1. *Description* – Consider what happened, for example an emergency evacuation of your setting: who was there, what were you doing at the time, what was the context of the event, etc.
2. *Feelings* – Consider your thoughts and feelings at the time, for example you noticed that the gate the children go through to the evacuation point is too narrow when an adult is holding hands with two children.
3. *Evaluation* – What was good and bad about the experience? For example, the children remained calm during the evacuation but it took a long time to organise a roll call when outside.
4. *Analysis* – Making sense of what happened. For example, break the evacuation down into its separate stages and ask detailed questions about what should have happened at each stage and compare this with what actually happened.
5. *Conclusion* – What would you have done differently? With honest evaluation and proper analysis it should be easy to identify areas for improvement, for example the gate is not an appropriate exit; the roll call procedure needs to be clarified.
6. *Action plan* – What would you do if it happens again? This involves developing strategies for change, for example deciding to use another evacuation point (a wider gate a little further away); carrying out a practice evacuation using the new evacuation point; updating the emergency evacuation procedure as required.

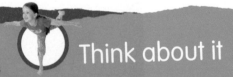

Think about it

Consider a problem that has arisen during your time in a setting, such as an activity that was not as successful as planned. Use the six parts of the reflective cycle to work out how the problem could be solved.

Problem solving in the workplace as a reflective practitioner

An important part of the reflective cycle is how you review your practice. It is important that the process of reflection is viewed as a positive process, rather than problems being seen as barriers to success. This approach is often called problem solving – a challenge has been set and the people concerned find ways to a solution. Problem solving can be achieved via discussion at team meetings, focus groups, delegation of responsibility and carrying out research. Consider the case study below.

Case study

Creating a peaceful outdoor space

The Foundation Stage team at Meadowbrook Infant School had observed that some of the children did not enjoy going outside at play time. It was decided that the children needed a peaceful outdoor area in which they could talk, read or perhaps draw. The problem the team initially encountered was how to fund the project, design the area and construct it. They decided to ask the Parents and Teachers Association for funding, which was granted. One of the team, Marilyn, went on a course about outdoor learning and enthusiastically returned with ideas about how the children could be involved in the design of the area. Marilyn managed this part of the project while Irena successfully gathered a team of friends and parents to construct the area. Within three months of raising concerns, the children had an attractive and peaceful outside area to spend time in.

1. How did the team view the problem positively?

2. What can you learn about the way the Meadowbrook Infant School team solved the problem of the outdoor area?

3. What do you think is the key to problem solving in a childcare setting?

How to improve and evaluate your own learning and performance

It is important to remember that you are not alone in wanting to improve your own learning and performance. Your line manager, for example, will be happy to give you feedback and discuss ways to improve practice at staff meetings.

Furthering your knowledge

Sources of information for improving your own learning and performance include the following:

→ Meeting other professionals, for example in focus groups, will enable you to share and discuss aspects of your practice.
→ Articles, books and magazines can give you ideas for practice and information about what is happening in the early years sector.
→ In-house and external training will extend your knowledge and give you the opportunity to meet and work with other practitioners.
→ Visiting other settings will allow you to find out how other people work in relation to managing children's behaviour, planning activities and planning the environment, etc.

Find out!

Children Now and *School's Out* can prove an invaluable source of ongoing professional development. Access some journals online via the following websites:
→ www.childrennow.co.uk
→ www.4Children.org.uk
→ www.nurseryworld.co.uk

Did you know?

There are a range of qualifications that you can study for as an early years professional. You can access training through your local Children and Family Services. Funding may be available through a variety of sources.

Further information about the qualifications can be found at www.cache.org.uk or www.cwdcouncil.org.uk

Peer observation

Peer observation (practitioners observing each other) is a very effective way of developing your practice with children and identifying training needs. It enables a colleague to focus on what is happening when you work with children and can help you improve your learning and performance. It also provides an opportunity to celebrate and recognise the things that you do well. Peer observations should be objective and detailed.

⇧ **Peer observation is an effective way of gaining feedback about your practice with children**

Personal development plan

A personal development plan will help you to achieve your own goals. It is far better that you create this plan than your manager does – after all, you are the one who has to follow it! However, it may be that you share parts of the plan with others as different viewpoints can help you to be objective and realistic. Such plans are widely used in business, and although one make take some time to create, it will help to shape your future practice.

Listed below is a suggestion for the steps you can take in creating your own personal development plan.

1. Think about your skills, strengths and weaknesses. Talk to others if this helps.
2. Focus on areas you will develop. You may discuss these at a meeting or appraisal with your manager.

3. Create the personal development plan in your own way. The plan should include the targets, or goals, you hope to achieve and the timescale for achieving them (see also page 231).
4. Share the plan with your manager or a colleague so they can provide feedback and encourage you along the way.
5. Implement the plan for as long as you have specified.
6. Review the plan; don't worry about having to change targets.
7. When the plan is complete, evaluate the targets you have reached and the overall effects on your performance.

How to evaluate your own performance and receive feedback

Ways of evaluating your own performance include:

→ self-reflection – thinking about what you have done in a thoughtful and objective way;
→ listening to others' comments and ideas so that you can look at your performance from different viewpoints;
→ considering the reasons and benefits to you and the children you work with for changing practice;
→ considering the impact of any changes to practice you have made by observing children and talking to them, your colleagues and parents about theses changes;
→ considering your training needs by talking to your mentor in an appraisal and then finding out what is available.

It may be helpful if you have a mentor to discuss any issues with, since evaluating your performance and identifying areas for improvement can be difficult. Remember, such conversations should be a positive experience and not undermine your confidence.

Receiving feedback

Feedback about your practice is an important part of reflective practice. This can be given in informal meetings or a more formal appraisal, which should be between you and your line manager.

An appraisal will include a review of your job description and a discussion of what you have achieved and targets for development. (This may link with your personal development plan.) It is usually signed by both you and your manager. The date for the next appraisal should be planned so you know what timescale you have to achieve your targets.

Any feedback should be given in a positive way. You will expect your manager to have planned what he or she wants to say and to start with the positive points. Any feedback, however brief, should be given in a comfortable area where you won't be interrupted.

If you listen carefully to feedback you may be able to gain information that will help you reflect upon your practice. It can be difficult not to be defensive and take feedback personally, but if you focus on improving your performance this will become easier with time.

How to use feedback to set SMART targets to improve practice

It is important to know what you want to achieve in your role as an early years practitioner. Once you have gained feedback from your mentor, together you should be able to compile a list of areas that you both think it is important for you to develop. This should take into consideration the time these will take and the support that you will need. These development goals will form the basis of your personal development plan.

There are no prescribed ways of creating a personal development plan from your feedback. However, it is important that any goals you set are SMART. This means:

→ *Specific* – Your plan should clearly focus on areas you want to develop such as IT skills.
→ *Measurable* – You need to consider how you will know when parts of the plan are achieved, for example gaining an IT qualification.
→ *Achievable* – You need to make sure that your targets can be achieved, for example that there is time in your lifestyle to study towards the IT qualification.
→ *Realistic* – Always allow yourself enough time to reach your goals, and don't give yourself too many targets to achieve.
→ *Timescale* – Consider how long realistically each part of the plan will take. You are more likely to succeed if you are realistic about the time you have available.

Getting ready for assessment

1. Explain how a setting might use reflective practice to improve its work with children.
2. Explain the importance of using reflective practice to improve your own performance.
3. Give two examples of how you might improve your own learning and performance.

The differing principles and practices that underpin working with different age children

In practice

Ruth and Penny are friends. They are both 11 years old and are really keen on football, playing in their local team. Whenever they can they go to the out-of-school club dressed in their football kit. They love spending time playing goal outside without socialising with the other children.

Beth, one of the adults at the setting, has suggested that the out-of-school club organises a football tournament. The children at the setting are involved in writing the fixtures on the board, arranging the teams and putting a notice up for the parents to see. The tournament is a great success and Kate and Penny become much more involved with the other children after the tournament.

By the end of this section you will understand the importance of encouraging activities based on children's interests.

The differing principles that underpin working with children

It is important to be aware of the principles and values that underpin the early years and education sector. These are discussed in Unit 1, Section 4. To complete your learning for this unit, you will therefore need to revisit pages 14–16.

Providing an environment for children that facilitates independence in learning

Independence is an important part of any child's development and adults have an important role to play in this as a guide and facilitator. In order to develop into an independent adult who feels confident to make their own choices, a child has to be able to be part of an environment that:

→ encourages them to make choices
→ enables them to follow their own interests
→ helps them develop self-help skills
→ gives them the opportunity to experiment and investigate on their own
→ respects their views.

Children of all ages can make choices but need to be provided with an environment that enables them to do so. If children are to investigate and experiment on their own they need a variety of areas that are well resourced to reflect their interests. Early years practitioners need to provide space for children to move freely between activities and recognise children's right to choose whom they play with. Activities and resources need to be accessible and support children in making choices, for example deciding what clothes to dress the doll in or whether to do drawing or sticking. If children are provided with a wide range of activities they will be able to lead their own learning.

Children should be encouraged to make choices and interests from a very young age, for example giving babies baskets of books to access so they can choose their own book to look at rather than rely on the choice of an adult. By observing younger children in the setting, you will soon come to recognise their views and preferences even though they may not be able to express these in their own words.

Good practice checklist

Providing an environment that encourages self-help skills

✓ Encourage children to wash their own hands, for example by providing basins at the right height.

✓ Provide snacks that children can access at any time and can help themselves to, such as raisins or breadsticks.

✓ Provide age-appropriate jugs to encourage children to pour their own drinks.

✓ Ensure that children are encouraged to set up and clear away activities.

✓ Ensure children can access their own resources, for example placing stationery on an accessible trolley that can be moved around the setting as the children need.

✓ Provide clear written or pictorial labels so that older children can access what they need.

U5
3

⇧ **The setting environment should encourage children to develop self-help skills, such as handwashing**

Case study

Encouraging independence in outdoor play

Colin was responsible for developing the outdoor space in the 3–5-year-old department of his day nursery. He was keen to develop the children's independence and researched ways that they could access safely their own resources to play with. He visited another setting and was impressed with the child-sized wooden storage sheds that children were able to access themselves.

Following the visit, Colin purchased two sheds. As Colin and his team were keen to ensure that the children could participate in indoor activities in the outside area, they decided to put chalks, crayons and other equipment in plastic boxes in the sheds. Wooden building blocks for the children to access for block play were placed in the other shed.

1. How would Colin know that the sheds were suitable for the children he was working with?

2. Which of the Early Learning Goals would the use of the sheds by the children promote?

3. Are there any other ways that Colin and his team could promote the children's independence in the outdoor area?

Did you know?

Both Montessori (see page 189) and Highscope settings encourage children to be independent.

• In a Montessori school, children choose their own activities and learn how to explore them after they have initially been guided by an adult. They are also provided with 'practical life exercises' such as sweeping, pouring and polishing, which are preparing them to be independent adults.

• In Highscope settings, children are encouraged to plan their own activities and thus become independent learners.

Did you know?

Adults supporting child-centred learning is evidenced in Reggio Emilia schools (see also page 188), where adults encourage each child to reflect, validate and document their own learning. Highscope also encourages children to be at the centre of their learning, with adults supporting children to plan, do and review.

The implications of child-centred versus adult-led practice

All practice with children needs to be centred upon the needs and interests of each child. You will need to ensure that children's interests are always reflected in what they do, that they participate in decisions about their learning and are able to develop to their full potential.

Early years practitioners should lead children's learning by interacting with children when appropriate. This may be to:

➔ extend their knowledge or thinking
➔ model ideas
➔ prompt questions
➔ nurture development
➔ support the acquisition of specific skills.

To ensure that practice is child-centred and that the adult leads the child as appropriate, it is important to acknowledge that learning is an internal process in each child which is seen when a child increases their skills, confidence or knowledge. It is then that the adult can be assured that they have kept the child at the centre of their learning and have led the child appropriately. If early years practitioners view their role as that of the nurturer and respond to each child individually, then their practice will be truly child-centred.

The role of the adult is therefore to:

➔ provide appropriate resources
➔ make resources accessible
➔ interact with the children
➔ observe, plan, review and reflect upon each child's learning.

Valuing children's interests and experiences

Babies and children will always concentrate and therefore learn more easily if they are doing something they are interested in and enjoying. This means that a key part of working with children is to be aware of their interests. Building on children's interests is thus considered to be good practice and is a major requirement of the Early Years Foundation Stage curriculum.

A main way in which you can find out about children's interests is through observation. By observing children you can see what they already enjoy doing and which activities help them to concentrate. From this starting point it is then possible to design further activities or interact with children in ways that will extend their learning. It is also important to talk to their parents and find out what the child enjoys doing at home.

Case study

Observing a child to find out what she enjoys

Kate is 3 years old and has recently joined the Grange Day Nursery. She is reluctant to join in any activities. After a team meeting it is agreed that Christina, Kate's key worker, will track Kate during a free-flow play session in the nursery and bring her findings to the next planning meeting.

When Christina observes Kate she notices that she spends a great deal of time painting and at the collage table but is reluctant to join in activities with other children. When Christina shares the observation with Kate's mum she confirms that Kate loves creative activities. Christina then shares the results with her team. It is decided that Christina will plan a group collage activity the next week where children are encouraged to make a large picture together.

1. How would the group collage activity help Kate?
2. What was important about Christina's observation of Kate?

3. In what ways did sharing the observation with Kate's mum prove helpful?
4. Consider other ways that Kate could be encouraged to integrate into the nursery.

How to recognise the needs of the child as an individual

Every child is unique and needs to have a sense of identity and belonging. You can support this in a variety of ways, such as providing drawers with each child's name on and pegs labelled with their own picture and name. Such items can make a child feel proud while also encouraging them to recognise their name and learn to organise their personal belongings.

The key worker system can play a very important part in ensuring that each child's individual needs are met. This can be done through:

→ talking to parents about their child's preferences, such as dietary requirements
→ having clear settling-in procedures, such as time to visit with parents
→ ensuring that as few adults as possible support the child in his or her care routines, for example changing nappies
→ ensuring that care routines such as nappy changing provide time for quality communication between key worker and child
→ ensuring that the child's preferences are considered when going to sleep, for example a child may need a favourite teddy or have his or her back rubbed
→ regularly observing the child
→ ensuring that children are able to, where possible, sleep, eat and snack when they are ready to rather than when it suits the setting.

 Find out!

Talk to your mentor in the setting where you work about how each child's needs are met in their care routines. Compare your findings with other learners in your study group.

You should be familiar with the importance of meeting each child's needs in your role as an early years practitioner – see, for example, Unit 1 pages 6–8 and Unit 3 pages 146–8. You will also have read how the five outcomes from Every Child Matters: Change for Children (see Unit 1, page 16) reflect the government framework that gives each child the right to have their individual needs met.

Think about it

Review the five outcomes of Every Child Matters (see page 16). How can you reflect these outcomes in your practice by meeting the needs of each child as an individual?

The benefits of a multi-professional, multi-agency approach in maximising children's experiences and learning

Much has been discussed about the optimum way to give children the best start in life. While early years practitioners aim to meet the individual needs of children, there may be times when they need the support of people with more expertise. Multi-professional, multi-agency working is about varied services, agencies and teams working together to meet the needs of children (see also pages 6–8). By making partnerships with outside agencies and services, the needs of children and their families are more likely to be met. Such partnerships can have an important role to play in ensuring that children's experiences and learning are maximised.

Ways in which you can recognise each child's needs are shown in the spider diagram below.

Listed below are examples of how partnerships with outside agencies and partnerships can benefit children.

→ Speech and language therapists can work with early years practitioners to ensure that children with a hearing or speech impairment can be effectively communicated with. This could be achieved through many ways including sign language. They might also provide support and advice about how to optimise the children's residual hearing.

→ Play therapists might work with a child who has suffered bereavement and guide early years practitioners in the type of activities to include in the curriculum, such as the use of a Persona Doll.

→ Educational psychologists could visit a setting to observe a child with behavioural needs and then work with early years practitioners to suggesting ways by which they can manage the child's behaviour positively.

→ A member of the sensory impairment team could visit a setting to suggest ways in which practitioners can work more effectively with, for example, a child with limited vision. They will also suggest how the environment and resources can be planned or adapted to enable the child to have varied and interesting learning opportunities.

→ A family worker or play assistant may encourage parents who are experiencing problems in relating to their child to play and interact with him or her. They will liaise with the setting to ensure that they too encourage the parents to be involved in their child's learning.

Did you know?

Steps are being taken by organisations such as Home Start to make families aware and encourage them to access early years services for their children, such as Children's Centres. There are some experts who believe that children will enter school at a disadvantage if they do not have access to nursery education.

Getting ready for assessment

1. List the principles that practitioners should put into practice when working with children.
2. For each principle, give an example of how it affects practice.
3. Describe why it is important to value children's interests and experiences.

Current national and local initiatives and issues relevant to the sector

In practice

Val is concerned that her son, Jake, will be leaving the Pioneer Children's Centre in a few months and going to school. Until now she has been able to access care for Jake while she works, sometimes until 6pm. Val is concerned that once Jake starts school he will have to be at home on his own while she is at work.

Sam, a practitioner in the nursery at the Children's Centre, advises Val that the local primary school offers extended care with a variety of activities that Jake could participate in. Val is also relieved to learn from Sam that she would be able to access care for Jake in a holiday club that the school runs.

By the end of this section you will be familiar with current national and local initiatives that aim to provide support to working parents and continuity of care for children beyond their pre-school years.

Government initiatives

Every Child Matters

The government framework which is currently being implemented through a variety of initiatives to ensure the well-being of children in England is Every Child Matters: Change for Children (see also Unit 1 page 16). Similar strategies are also taking place in Wales, Scotland and Northern Ireland.

Every Child Matters aims to consider children from birth to 19 years of age and involves everyone who works with children and young people. The programme's goal is that every child, whatever their background or circumstances, has the support they need to:

→ be healthy
→ stay safe
→ enjoy and achieve through learning
→ make a positive contribution to society
→ achieve economic well-being.

Children Act 2004

These five outcomes of Every Child Matters are at the centre of the 2004 Children Act. The Act made law the reforms that had long been discussed about improving and integrating children's services across the country. The main provisions that are being implemented are as follows:

→ a commissioner who represents all children and is an independent voice for their interests and all matters that effect them; this person should promote debate at the highest level about the importance of making positive changes for children
→ agencies to work together for children and young people
→ safeguarding of children and young people to include local safeguarding children boards
→ children and young people plans – these are created locally and are an important aspect of the Every Child Matters reform programme; they should encourage the integration of children's services
→ local directors of children's services and lead members, who will ensure that children are safeguarded and cared for according to their needs
→ frameworks for inspections and joint area reviews
→ new powers to intervene in failing local authorities

→ promotion of the educational achievement of looked after children
→ ensuring children's voices are heard in decision making.

Did you know?

'Looked after children' is the term used for children who are in local authority care because they cannot, for many different reasons, live at home with their parents.

Minister for Children

A Minister for Children is now in place to oversee the government initiatives to improve all services for children and young people.

The Childcare Commission

The Childcare Commission was set up in 2001 with the key objectives of:

→ reducing child poverty
→ supporting parenting
→ promoting employment
→ improving health
→ raising educational attainment
→ strengthening communities.

The Commission has shaped current government initiatives by finding out what is needed to fully support children and their families. It has made some major recommendations (see table below) and there is much debate at a local and national level as to how much progress has been made.

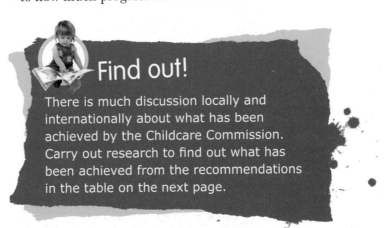

Find out!

There is much discussion locally and internationally about what has been achieved by the Childcare Commission. Carry out research to find out what has been achieved from the recommendations in the table on the next page.

⏳ **Recommendations made by the Childcare Commission**

Recommendations	What is involved
A Children's Centre in every community	• Integrated childcare • Nursery education • Playgroups • Out-of-school clubs • Childminder networks • Children's Information Services
Schools at centres of the community	To provide a variety of community facilities
Quality standards as a top priority in childcare expansion	• Revised Ofsted Standards to reflect the Every Child Matters outcomes. • A Common Assessment Framework to ensure that information about children's health, educational and social needs are gathered in a structured way, and that children of all ages get the right support as early as possible.
Additional support for children and families in rural areas	To ensure that children and their families have access to all facilities either through home-based sevices, mobile services or improved transport.
Major expansion and development of the childcare workforce	• Ensure quality leadership through new qualifications • Higher pay • Major recruitment campaigns • Special funding for local training and bursaries • Incentives for providers to raise salaries and support professional development
Develop support, advice and information available to parents	Through local sources: • Children's Information Services where parents can find out about a range of statutory and voluntary services for children in their area • Government publicity drives
Improve access to childcare services among children with disabilities and black and minority ethnic (BME) families	• Children's Centres and Sure Start programmes • Support groups

Children's Workforce Development Council (CWDC)

This has been set up by the government to improve the workforce as recommended by the Childcare Commission. Through financial provision called the Transformation Fund they are encouraging employers to recruit and retain people with the right qualifications without risking affordability for parents or the sustainability of business. Nurseries in the private sector, registered childminders and those offering sessional day care to children under 5 years can apply for:

→ training for Level 3 or higher qualifications, including an Early Years Foundation Degree
→ training to improve skills when working with children with special educational needs
→ reimbursement of eligible costs for new or existing staff to achieve their Early Years Professional Status (EYPS)

- money to spend on additional professional development if a graduate is employed
- a recruitment incentive if taking on a graduate for the first time.

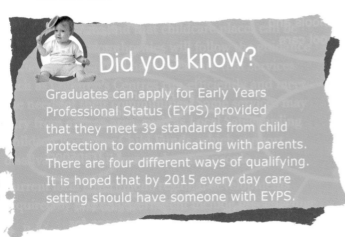

Parenting and family support

Government initiatives are trying to ensure that policies are more family friendly so that parents can stay at home for longer after having a baby. Parents also have a right to request flexible working and two weeks paternity leave. In the long term, it is the aim of the government to ensure that parents have the choice of affordable high quality childcare or support to stay at home.

Sure Start

Sure Start is a government initiative that encompasses health, education and social care. It aims to achieve better outcomes for children, their parents and local communities by increasing the availability of childcare through initiatives such as Children's Centres. It also encourages parents in effective parenting and returning to work by ensuring that affordable childcare is available and services such as parenting workshops are widely available. The health and emotional development of young children is developed through integrated services.

The policies and programmes of Sure Start apply to England, but Scotland, Wales and Northern Ireland have similar initiatives.

Find out!

You can find out more about the Sure Start programme by visiting its website (www.surestart.gov.uk).

The Children and Young People's Plan (CYPP)

The CYPP is an important element of the reforms underpinned by the Children Act 2004 and the Every Child Matters programme. It came into force in September 2005. By law, local authorities must work to achieve better integration of local children's services and their Children and Young People's plan is a way of showing the public how they intend to do this. Central to this is the recognition of the local needs of children, young people and their families, and the development of local partnership arrangements. The DfES guidelines advise that children, young people, their parents and carers are involved in local development plans to improve services for them; each local authority is inspected by Ofsted to check that this involvement has been effective in service planning and delivery.

Find out!

Look at your own local authority website and read about the Children and Young People's Plan they have created. Focus on what is being done to support children in their early years in your region.

Effective Provision of Pre-School Education (EPPE) project

Running over the period 1997–2003, this project was the first longitudinal study in the UK to focus on the effectiveness of early years provision. Among its findings it has shown the following:

→ If children have access to books in their home they will attain higher literacy skills at Key Stage 1. Consequently, Sure Start hand out free book boxes to pre-school children to encourage reading at home.
→ Attending high-quality nursery provision from 3 years can significantly improve children's educational attainment.

The results of the research emphasise the importance of adult-child interactions at a high level and creating a balance between adult-directed and child-initiated activities; an effective early years curriculum will have a balance of such activities.

Find out!

The full findings of the EPPE project are given on its website – www.ioe.ac.uk/schools/ecpe/eppe/index.htm

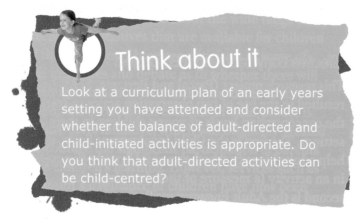

Think about it

Look at a curriculum plan of an early years setting you have attended and consider whether the balance of adult-directed and child-initiated activities is appropriate. Do you think that adult-directed activities can be child-centred?

The National Literacy Project (NLP)

Set up in 1996 in fifteen local education authorities, this research project aimed to improve standards in primary schools for literacy. As a result of the project's findings, the National Literacy Strategy was launched by the government in July 1997 and introduced into all English primary schools in the autumn of 1998. The Strategy provided a framework for teaching literacy at primary school which included a daily, structured Literacy Hour (this has now been replaced by the new Primary Literacy and Mathematics framework).

I CAN

I CAN is a charity that helps children communicate by encouraging the development of speech, language and communication skills in all children, with a special focus on those with a communication disability. Research by I CAN has revealed the importance of developing children's communication through health and education services working together. They have also found that early intervention will give a child with communication difficulties the best chance of success. As a result, I CAN formed a partnership with the DfES to create the I CAN Early Talk programme. This has been set up to meet the communication needs of all pre-school children and will be established in up to 200 Sure Start centres across England.

Find out!

You can find out more about I CAN and ts work by visiting its website (www.ican.org.uk).

Reggio Emilia

This school in Italy (see also Unit 7 page 289) places creativity at the centre of children's learning and emphasises the importance on observing children and encouraging them to observe. The centre has mounted a mobile exhibition of children's work that has influenced many practitioners in Europe. It also welcomes visitors from around the world.

Pen Green Centre

This is a Centre of Excellence and now a Children's Centre in Northamptonshire which carries out research and training on effective early years provision and working with parents. The centre has influenced current practice.

Find out!

To find out more about Pen Green visit their website: www.pengreen.org

Using professional literature and other sources

There are many books, journals, magazines and websites where you can review current research, as the list below shows. It would benefit your practice and research during your studies to collect as many articles as you can about current research and practice.

Journals and magazines

→ *4Children* (www.4children.org.uk)
→ *Children Now* (www.childrennow.co.uk)
→ *Montessori International* (www.montessorimagazine.com)
→ *Nursery World* (www.nurseryworld.com)
→ *Times Educational Supplement* (www.timeseducationalsupplement.com)

Useful websites

→ Sure Start (www.surestart.gov.uk)
→ Ofsted (www.ofsted.gov.uk)
→ Every Child Matters (www.everychildmatters.gov.uk)
→ Literacy Trust (www.literacytrust.org.uk)

Getting ready for assessment

1. Describe two recent initiatives that have affected practice in settings.
2. Describe two pieces of current research that have affected practice in settings.
3. Explain why it is important to be aware of the latest developments in the early years sector.

Getting ready for assessment

Short Answer Test for Units 3, 4 and 5

Read the following case study then answer the questions below.

Ramble Street Nursery is preparing to take some new children into the toddler room. The staff are preparing an information session for the parents of the new 2-year-olds. They will use this as an opportunity to talk to parents about settling in and how the outdoor area is used for play as well as policies and procedures that are used in the nursery. They have also planned some time for parents to informally talk to the staff about the children's care needs. This is the first time that the nursery is holding such an information session.

1. List two pieces of legislation that might have an effect on the nursery's policies and procedures.

2. Explain why this session might be helpful as part of the settling-in process.

3. Identify three pieces of information that parents might share about their child's care needs.

4. Evaluate how playing outdoors might contribute to the development of 2-year-olds.

5. Analyse the benefits of staff reflecting on the effectiveness of this first information session.

Unit 6

Promoting a healthy environment for children

In this unit you will learn:

1. The principles underpinning the rights of children to a healthy lifestyle and environment

2. The factors that affect the health of children

3. How to plan and implement routines and activities for children

Section 1

The principles underpinning the rights of children to a healthy lifestyle and environment

In practice

You are in placement in a school and are surprised to find that at snack time the children are offered a choice of fruit. The teacher explains that this is part of a health initiative.

By the end of this section you will understand some of the ways in which the health of children in the United Kingdom is being promoted.

Legislation that supports children's rights to a healthy lifestyle

There is significant amount of legislation that links to the health and well-being of children and their families. Legislation is important as it provides a framework for services to exist. Below are some examples of legislation that promote children's health and well-being.

National Health Service Act 1946 (Scotland 1947)

Today it is easy to take for granted that medical care is virtually free in this country. This has not always been the case: up until the launch of the National Health Service (NHS) in July 1948, most people needed to pay for medical treatment. This meant that many low-income families did not seek proper care when they were ill as they could not always afford it. The National Health Service was introduced after the Second World War (1939–45) along with other momentous social reforms. The aim was that healthcare should be provided based on need rather than ability to pay.

From the very start the NHS proved a complex and difficult organisation to manage and to fund. This remains the case today and is one reason why structures have changed frequently. In order to change the structure of the NHS, the government has to pass legislation through Parliament. The latest amendment to the law is the National Health Service Act 2006, which is supposed to simplify and update previous legislation. The main thrust of this Act is that healthcare should remain free, although there have been charges for prescriptions, glasses and dentures since 1951 and many other charges have since been introduced.

Find out!

For information about the health service in the UK, visit the following websites:
→ England – www.dh.gov.uk
→ Northern Ireland – www.n-i.nhs.uk
→ Scotland – www.show.scot.nhs.uk
→ Wales – www.wales.nhs.uk

The diagram below shows the current structure for the NHS in England.

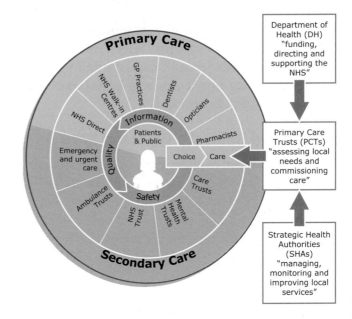

⇧ The current structure for the National Health Service in England (*Source*: www.nhs.uk/England)

The basic structure of the National Health Service

While the detail of the structure of the National Health Service may change, it is possible to understand its basic service and structures.

Primary care

Primary care services are made up of professionals who are visited mostly by children and their families. They often meet children's and families' day-to-day health needs and provide advice. The spider diagram shows some of the primary care professionals.

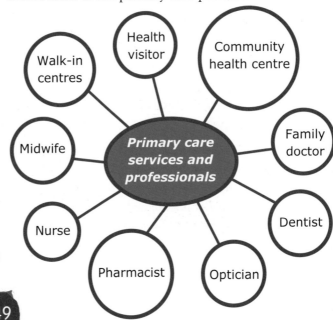

Secondary care

This is more specialist care and includes emergency treatment. Some specialist care is organised as a result of referral by a primary care professional, for example a health visitor may refer a child to the speech and language service while a doctor might refer a child to see a paediatrician if he has concerns about a child's development.

Health and Safety at Work Act 1974

This Act is designed to protect employees in England and Wales. In practice it also makes a difference to children's safety as many of its regulations help to keep them safe, for example guidelines on the storage of chemicals and the need for fire safety. This Act is described in greater detail in Unit 4, pages 161–2.

Care Standards Act 2000

This Act introduced national standards that settings have to meet if they are caring for children. Each of the home countries of the United Kingdom have a variance of this Act although the main focus is to ensure that children receive good quality of care and this of course includes health as well as physical safety. In England, Ofsted take on the role of inspecting settings against the standards. At the time of writing, the National Standards are being incorporated into a new inspection framework so that the new Early Years Foundation Stage and the five outcomes from the Every Child Matters programme can be brought together.

Education Act 2002

As part of this Act, local authorities and schools were required to 'safeguard and promote the welfare of children'. This includes health and safety practice and child protection as well as promoting the overall health and well-being of children.

Every Child Matters and the Children Act 2004 (England)

Every Child Matters is a programme in England that is designed to protect children and promote their welfare and well-being (see also Unit 1 page 16). The Children Act is designed to strengthen the programme and provides the legislation to do so.

There are five outcomes to Every Child Matters and the first two (Be healthy and Stay safe) concern the health and safety of children. The Every Child Matters programme is important because it ensures that health and educational professionals work together (see also Unit 5 page 239).

The concept of global rights in relation to children's health and well-being

The United Nations Convention on the Rights of the Child

Health is now seen as a right for all children in the world. The UN Convention on the Rights of the Child (UNCRC; see also Unit 3 page 115) sets out a list of rights that children should be entitled to. There are several that link directly to children's health, as can be seen in the table on the next page.

As the United Kingdom signed the Convention, the government has a duty to ensure that healthcare and protection is provided for children.

Find out!

Found out more about children's global rights by visiting www.unicef.org.uk

World Health Organisation (WHO)

As its name suggests, this organisation has a global remit for health. It was established in 1948 and is an agency of the United Nations. Its aim is to promote health and as part of its work it produces reports, information and actively engages in healthcare programmes.

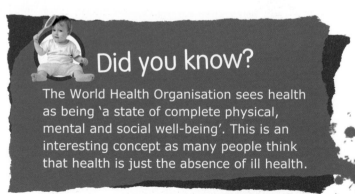

Did you know?

The World Health Organisation sees health as being 'a state of complete physical, mental and social well-being'. This is an interesting concept as many people think that health is just the absence of ill health.

👆 **Articles from the UNCRC that deal with children's health**
   (*Source*: The United Nations Convention on the Rights of the Child)

Article 6	1. States Parties recognise that every child has the inherent right to life.
	2. States Parties shall ensure to the maximum extent possible the survival and development of the child.
Article 19	1. States Parties shall take all appropriate legislative, administrative, social and educational measures to protect the child from all forms of physical or mental violence, injury or abuse, neglect or negligent treatment, maltreatment or exploitation, including sexual abuse, while in the care of parent(s), legal guardian(s) or any other person who has the care of the child.
	2. Such protective measures should, as appropriate, include effective procedures for the establishment of social programmes to provide necessary support for the child and for those who have the care of the child, as well as for other forms of prevention and for identification, reporting, referral, investigation, treatment and follow-up of instances of child maltreatment described heretofore, and, as appropriate, for judicial involvement.
Article 24	1. States Parties recognise the right of the child to the enjoyment of the highest attainable standard of health and to facilities for the treatment of illness and rehabilitation of health. States Parties shall strive to ensure that no child is deprived of his or her right of access to such healthcare services.
	2. States Parties shall pursue full implementation of this right and, in particular, shall take appropriate measures:
	(a) To diminish infant and child mortality;
	(b) To ensure the provision of necessary medical assistance and healthcare to all children with emphasis on the development of primary healthcare;
	(c) To combat disease and malnutrition, including within the framework of primary healthcare, through... the application of readily available technology and through the provision of adequate nutritious foods and clean drinking water, taking into consideration the dangers and risks of environmental pollution;
	(d) To ensure appropriate pre-natal and post-natal healthcare for mothers;
	(e) To ensure that all segments of society, in particular parents and children, are informed, have access to education and are supported in the use of basic knowledge of child health and nutrition, the advantages of breastfeeding, hygiene and environmental sanitation and the prevention of accidents;
	(f) To develop preventive healthcare, guidance for parents and family planning education and services.
	3. States Parties shall take all effective and appropriate measures with a view to abolishing traditional practices prejudicial to the health of children.
	4. States Parties undertake to promote and encourage international cooperation with a view to achieving progressively the full realisation of the right recognised in the present article. In this regard, particular account shall be taken of the needs of developing countries.

WHO is governed by representatives of the 193 countries that are members the United Nations. The representatives agree on a long-term programme of priorities for the organisation to focus on. The current ten-year programme began in 2006 and is called 'Engaging for Health'. Its seven points are listed below.

1. Investing in health to reduce poverty
2. Building individual and global health security
3. Promoting universal coverage, gender equality and health-related human rights
4. Tackling the determinants of health
5. Strengthening health systems and equitable access
6. Harnessing knowledge, science and technology
7. Strengthening governance, leadership and accountability

Find out!

Find out more about the work of the World Health Organisation by visiting their website at: www.who.int/en/

The centrality of the public health environment in modern life

The importance of providing advice and guidance to children and their parents so they are able to live a healthier lifestyle is now recognised. It is also recognised that early identification of potential problems is effective in combating ill health. This approach is reflected in current health policy.

National Service Framework for children, young people and maternity services

In 1998 the government began to devise National Service Frameworks (NSF), which were designed to set standards for specific areas of healthcare. In September 2004 the National Service Framework for children, young people and maternity services was launched. It is a ten-year programme and links closely to Every Child Matters, as it is recognised that health, education and social services are interlinked. There are five core standards (see list below) with additonal standards that look at children and their families who have particular needs.

→ Standard 1: Promoting health and well-being, identifying needs and intervening early
→ Standard 2: Supporting parents or carers
→ Standard 3: Child, young person and family-centred services
→ Standard 4: Growing up into adulthood
→ Standard 5: Safeguarding and promoting the welfare of children and young

There are many ways in which National Service Frameworks influence health initiatives. Currently there is greater emphasis on bringing the different professionals who care for children and young people together. It is also now recognised that it is better to work in partnership with parents rather than just to preach at them and this has meant that a more personalised approach is taken and that parents are given more responsibility. Below are some examples of how health promotion is currently working.

Child Health Promotion Programme

This is a multi-agency approach and replaces a health-only approach to child health. As part of this programme, health, education and other professionals work with parents to support their child's health. In practice this may mean that new parents may be given advice about fire safety by the fire prevention team as well as the more usual health checks and visits by health visitors.

The School Fruit and Vegetable Scheme

This is a government initiative for school children aged 4–6 years. It means that each day children are given one piece of fruit or vegetable. This strategy links to the 5 a day initiative (see also Unit 12, pages 481–2). The idea is that by introducing fruit and vegetables into children's diets at an early age, children will be more likely to eat them at home.

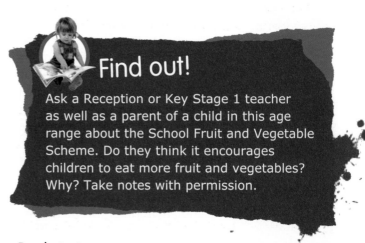

Find out!

Ask a Reception or Key Stage 1 teacher as well as a parent of a child in this age range about the School Fruit and Vegetable Scheme. Do they think it encourages children to eat more fruit and vegetables? Why? Take notes with permission.

Bookstart

This scheme encourages parents to share books with their babies and toddlers. Free books and leaflets explaining the importance of reading books and sharing books with children are given out to new parents. Traditionally, this would have been seen as an 'educational' activity but the Bookstart packs are currently given out by health visitors when children are babies, as well as by early years professionals once children are older.

Find out!

Find out more about the Bookstart scheme by visiting www.bookstart.co.uk. Visit the separate section on their website for early years professionals. How are early years professionals involved in supporting the Bookstart programme?

Find out!

Visit the Food Standards Agency website (www.food.gov.uk) and find out more about the following issues:

→ salt in children's diets
→ fruit and vegetables.

Food Standards Agency

The Food Standards Agency (FSA) is an independent government agency responsible for protecting the public's health and consumer interests in relation to food. It does this in a variety of ways but particularly by providing information and guidance about food and food safety. Its website and leaflets are useful ways of finding out more about the latest advice about healthy eating. The Food Standards Agency also launches public awareness campaigns. At the time of writing, it is encouraging the public to be aware of salt in foods.

Getting ready for assessment

If you complete the Find out! activities on pages 249, 250, 252 and 253 of this section, and take notes or print out information about what you have discovered, your findings may be used to form a basis for the portfolio for your research.

Section 2

The factors that affect the health of children

In practice

You are working in a Children's Centre in a deprived part of town. You are surprised when the manager tells you that one of their objectives is to improve the health of the children and their families. He goes on to tell you that where children live can play a major part in how healthy they may be.

By the end of this section you will understand some of the key factors that play a role in children's health and well-being.

Introduction

There are many factors that affect the health of children. These have been well documented and are central to current public health policies. When looking at factors that affect children it is always important to realise that they are based on statistics from large groups of children rather than individuals. This is essential to note as there is always a danger that individual children and their families may be stereotyped. Having said this, it is important that you understand the impact that some factors can have on children's health.

Influences of the wider environment that affect health

Working out the factors that affect children's health is complex. For example, children and adults may be genetically pre-disposed to some diseases such as asthma and diabetes, but the environment may also trigger the disease. This means that where children live and what happens to them in childhood may affect their health.

Sociological factors

The social position into which a child is born has the potential to impact on his or her health and development. One of the most important sociological factors is economic, with children born into low-income families being significantly more likely to be disadvantaged.

Poverty

Poverty is seen by many as a key factor in children's overall health and educational achievement.

There are many different ways of measuring poverty, which means that statistics about how many families are living in poverty will vary. The two main ways of measuring poverty are:

1. *Absolute poverty* – This means having not enough money to pay for food, water and shelter. This level of poverty is virtually unheard of in the UK but exists in some developing countries.
2. *Relative poverty* – This takes into account the standard of living of a country's population; a person whose income is much lower might be classified as living in poverty.

It is on the principle of *relative poverty* that most of the statistics used by organisations are based.

Causes of poverty

Although there are many reasons why families live in poverty there seems to be a strong link between employment and poverty. Where families do not have at least one member of the family working full-time, they are likely to be living in poverty. The link between employment and poverty is strong, although people can be working but still living in poverty if they are on low wages. Lone parents often live in poverty as they are unable to afford full-time childcare to allow them to work.

Who is most affected by poverty?

There are several groups of people in the UK who are more likely to be living in poverty. These groups are also more likely to be discriminated against in terms of finding employment and income.

→ Women often take part-time work, which tends to be less well paid, in order to care for their children.
→ Black and ethnic minority groups (BME) may be discriminated against when looking for work and rates of unemployment are far higher among this group than among the white population of the UK.
→ Disabled people many be discriminated against by employers or may be unable to work due to their disability.

How poverty can affect families

Poverty can affect families in many ways but essentially it removes choice from people's lives. They may not be able to choose where to live, where to send their children to school and where to shop. People living in poverty do not have the same choices about lifestyle as others do – choice revolves around what they can afford rather than what they want. The practical effects of living in poverty are described in the table on the next page.

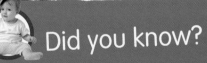

Did you know?

The Department of Health states that families living in poverty are less likely than other families to access health and other supportive services. In addition, their children have higher than average rates of obesity, tooth decay and unintentional injury.

Think about it

If you live on a low income, you may find that things are actually more expensive. In pairs, look at the examples below and see if you can think of other ways in which the poor pay more.

Housing:

→ Poor-quality housing means that heating is more expensive.

→ Poor heating systems mean that more money is spent on fuel.

→ House insurance may cost people more if they live in an area with poor housing as these areas are often hit by crime.

Food:

→ Lack of money means that families are unable to buy food in large quantities, which is often cheaper, or take advantage of offers such as 'buy two, get one free'.

Goods:

→ Lack of money to pay for goods outright means that poor families borrow money and have to pay interest.

Clothing and footwear:

→ Lack of money means that cheaper clothing and footwear is bought, which needs replacing more quickly.

The practical effects of living in poverty

Health	• Poor diet causes health problems • Poor housing contributes to diseases such as bronchitis and low-grade infections • Depression and despair can lead to addictions • Accidents are caused by lack of safety equipment or cheap goods
Poor housing	• Housing may be cramped and difficult to heat • Furniture may be unsafe • Choice of housing may be limited
Poor achievement in schools	• Parents may not have the resources to help children, e.g. books, space to do homework • Children may lack confidence as they feel 'different' from other children • Parents may not have the emotional strength to support their children or may have lost faith in the education system • Teachers may have low expectations of children living in poorer areas • Parents may not be able to pay for extras such as piano or swimming lessons or out-of-school activities
Depression and despair	• Constant worry about money can cause depression and tension in families • Parents can feel depressed because they cannot see how they are going to change their situation • Self-esteem and morale can be low because money is considered important in UK society • Parents can feel embarrassed because of claiming benefit or asking for help, e.g. not paying the full amount for school trips

Children and poverty

Children are often the real victims of poverty. They are five times more likely to have an accident, their overall life expectancy is likely to be shorter and their achievement in schools is likely to be lower. Poverty is in many ways an equal opportunities issue as children who are living in poverty will miss out. Their parents may not be able to afford to pay for them to attend dancing lessons, music lessons or even the school uniform to make them feel the same as other children.

It is gradually being understood that children living in poverty have lower expectations of what they wish to achieve in their own life, and this in turn leads to children leaving school early. They may also lack good role models, for example they may see older children committing petty crimes and come to the conclusion that this is normal behaviour.

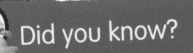

Did you know?

→ 3.8 million children live in poverty in the UK.

→ The proportion of children living in poverty grew from 1 in 10 in 1979 to 1 in 3 in 1998. Today, 30 per cent of children in the UK live in poverty.

→ The UK has one of the worst rates of child poverty in the industrialised world.

(*Source*: www.endchildpoverty.org.uk, June 2007)

Find out!

Find out more about child poverty by visiting the following websites:

→ www.cpag.org.uk

→ www.jrf.org.uk/child-poverty

Psychological factors

Traditionally, children's mental health has not been considered significant. Today, however, it is realised that children's health and happiness is critical to their development. It is thought that some children will be more susceptible than others to mental health problems and again poverty is cited here.

Did you know?

Research carried out by the Mental Health Foundation indicates that 22 per cent of pre-school children have mental health problems with 15 per cent having mild problems and a further 7 per cent having severe problems.

There is a range of factors that can affect children's mental health. Some factors are temporary and short-term while others have the potential to affect children in the longer term. The spider diagram below shows some common causes of stress in children.

Signs that children may be under stress

There are many signs that children may not be coping and how these are exhibited varies according to individual children and their age. The way that adults support children during times of stress can make a significant difference to their overall outcomes. Some children may also need professional counselling or support so it is important to recognise that a child needs help.

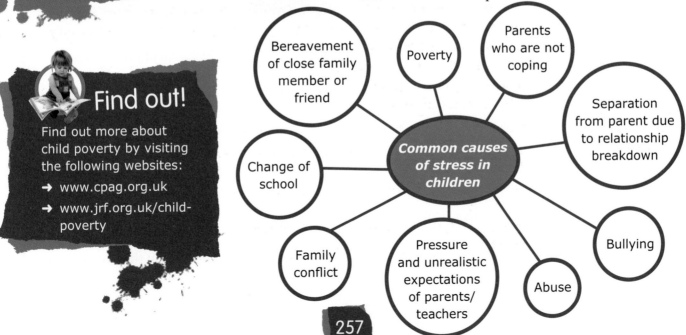

Signs that children may be under stress include:

→ loss of appetite or over-eating
→ bedwetting
→ regression, for example thumb sucking and rocking
→ withdrawn behaviour
→ aggressive behaviour and outbursts
→ headaches
→ nightmares and sleeping difficulties
→ unexplained aches and pains
→ difficulties with friendships and socialising
→ tearfulness and clinginess.

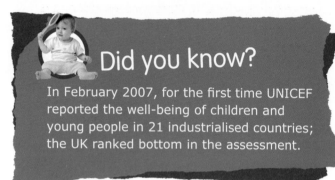

Did you know?

In February 2007, for the first time UNICEF reported the well-being of children and young people in 21 industrialised countries; the UK ranked bottom in the assessment.

Psychological health of immediate family members

At all stages of their development including infancy, children pick up on the psychological state of their parents, siblings and close family members. Depression and stress within the family unit will therefore affect a child's social and emotional development. Babies, for example, may smile less if their parents are not able to bond with them or do not interact with them warmly, while older children may become withdrawn in families where there is hostility between family members.

Physical factors

There is a range of physical factors that will impact on children's health and well-being. You have seen already that poverty may force families into poor housing and accommodation, which in turn may affect their health. Below are some examples of physical factors that may affect some children.

Pollution

This is an increasing problem in many cities and areas. Children who live close to a motorway or main road may breathe in higher levels of carbon monoxide and carbon dioxide. Pollution is often cited as a trigger for asthma.

Unsafe environments

Many children each year have accidents that are serious enough to affect their health permanently. Some accidents are caused by children playing in unsafe areas while others are a result of a lack of safety equipment. Children growing up in poverty are statistically more likely to have accidents as housing may not be designed with safety in mind and parents may not have sufficient money to buy the necessary safety equipment.

Housing

To prevent illness, houses have to be properly heated and ventilated. Housing that is poorly designed or maintained may be damp and this in turn can cause a variety of diseases, most notably asthma. Overcrowding can also be hazardous for health as diseases may be transmitted more easily between family members. As you have seen (page 256) there is a link between poor housing and poverty.

Find out!

Visit the Child Accident Prevention Trust website (www.capt.org.uk) to gain the latest child accident statistics. Which age group is involved in the highest number of accidents?

The range of factors that affect children at different times in their lives

Pre-conception and antenatal factors

Children's health can be affected by their parent's health and lifestyle. The health of women before conception (pre-conception) as well as during pregnancy has a significant impact on children's health. This is an area that is now being given quite a lot of attention as it is thought to be a key way in which outcomes for children can be improved. There is also a link between poverty and poor outcomes in pregnancy.

Low birth weight

The weight of a baby at birth seems to have the potential to have a long-term impact on development as well as making a difference in the survival of a newborn. There are two common causes of low birth weight babies: smoking and diet.

WARNING

CIGARETTES HURT BABIES

Tobacco use during pregnancy reduces the growth of babies during pregnancy. These smaller babies may not catch up in growth after birth and the risks of infant illness, disability and death are increased.

Health Canada

⇦ **Health Canada poster about the risks of smoking in pregnancy**

Smoking

There is very clear advice that women should stop smoking before they get pregnant and during pregnancy. Smoking increases the risk of miscarriage and later cot death. Smoking seems to considerably reduce the baby's supply of oxygen and this restricts growth. Cigarettes also contain more than 4,000 different chemicals.

Diet

In addition to eating an overall healthy diet, women in the earliest stages of pregnancy need to have sufficient folic acid as this seems to prevent babies from being born with a disability known as spina bifida. Spina bifida is caused when the neural tubes and spine do not close properly. This happens between the 25th and the 30th day of pregnancy when some women may not even know that they are pregnant. The advice is therefore that women planning on becoming pregnant should take a folic acid supplement of 400mcg each day until the 12th week of their pregnancy, although it is possible to get folic acid from dietary sources such as broccoli and spinach.

Drug and alcohol misuse in pregnancy

As well as smoking, drugs and alcohol can also affect the developing baby. Drugs both medical and recreational can damage the developing nervous system of the baby. Pregnant women should always check with their doctor or pharmacist before taking medication. The advice on recreational drugs is that they should be completely avoided.

In terms of alcohol, the overall advice is that women should avoid drinking as there seems to be no agreement on a safe level. Unborn babies whose mothers have drunk even relatively small quantities of alcohol can be born with Foetal Alcohol Syndrome. The effects of foetal alcohol syndndrome are permanent and include learning difficulties. Binge drinking where an expectant mother drinks several units of alcohol seems especially dangerous.

Lifestyle

Some children's development will be affected by their parents' difficulties. The Department of Health recognises that there is a higher incidence of mental health or behavioural problems in some children whose parents are more vulnerable. These include parents who:

→ are mentally ill
→ have learning disabilities
→ misuse drugs or alcohol
→ are unsupported by wider family
→ are the victim of domestic violence.

It is important to note that the above list is not about a lifestyle choice. Parents and their children are vulnerable because of difficult circumstances; here support will be needed in order to effect a change.

Families and community

Patterns of parenting and attitudes towards childhood vary enormously from family to family and across communities. Patterns have also changed over time. It is now known, for example, that fewer children walk to school than before and that how children spend their leisure time has changed in the past twenty years.

The health and development of children can therefore be linked to where they are growing up as well as families. A good example of this is the way in which families might spend their leisure time. A child growing up in one family may be introduced to sports and games early on while looking after pets might be a significant activity for another family.

The range of factors that may affect the health of children at different times in their lives

Diet and exercise

Diet and exercise play an important role in children's development. In Unit 12 you look at the importance of food on children's development. It will be helpful if you read the information about specific nutrient groups and energy requirements (pages 455–60) alongside this unit.

Breast milk

From very early on in a child's life, diet is critical to development. It is known, for example, that breast milk is associated with better cognitive development and lowers the risk of cardiovascular disease. In addition, there are many other advantages of breastfeeding (see Unit 12 pages 464–5). Breast milk also contains antibodies from the mother which means that babies are less susceptible to disease in the earliest months of life.

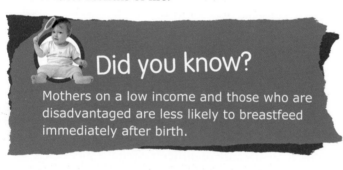

Did you know?

Mothers on a low income and those who are disadvantaged are less likely to breastfeed immediately after birth.

The importance of breast milk on children's development has meant more support and information about breastfeeding is given to pregnant women. While breastfeeding is usually the most common way of giving a baby breast milk, it is worth noting that it is also possible for mothers to produce or 'express' breast milk which is then used for bottle feeding. This is often how many working mothers manage to combine breastfeeding with working. It also allows the mother to have a break from night feeds.

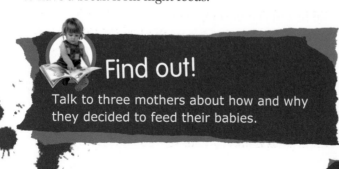

Find out!

Talk to three mothers about how and why they decided to feed their babies.

Effects of a poor diet

Children need a balanced diet that meets their energy requirements but does not exceed them. Food and drinks also need to be nutritious so that children receive nutrients such as vitamins and minerals as well as protein, carbohydrates and fats.

There are many effects of a poor diet on children, some of which are long-term. These effects include:

→ cardiovascular disease
→ cancer
→ tooth decay
→ low self-esteem and poor self-image
→ diabetes (Type II)
→ musculoskeletal problems
→ high risk of weight problems in adulthood.

It is recognised that today many children do not eat a balanced diet. This is shown by the significant increase in overweight and obese children. For most children their excess weight is caused by taking in more energy than their body requires. The excess energy is then converted into fat.

It is useful to note that many children who are overweight or obese may still not be getting sufficient nutrients, for example a child may be eating high levels of fat and carbohydrate but may be missing out on the vitamins found in fresh fruit and vegetables. This is an area where there are many initiatives at the moment.

The graphs below and on the next page show how the incidence of obesity in children in England has dramatically increased in the last decade.

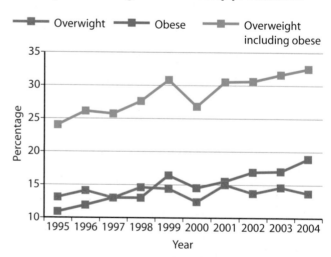

⬆ **Boys' overweight and obesity prevalence 1995–2004 (*Source:* Health Survey for England 2004)**

Girls' overweight and obesity prevalence

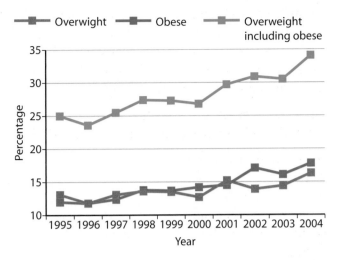

↑ **Girls' overweight and obesity prevalence 1995–2004 (*Source:* Health Survey for England 2004)**

The importance of exercise

Everybody needs exercise in order to develop and remain healthy. In terms of children, 'exercise' is really about play and physical activity. It should therefore be fun rather than something that is necessarily organised and arduous.

The spider diagram below shows the health and developmental benefits of exercise. It is also worth noting that children who are physically active and who have opportunities to play outdoors also learn to be self-reliant and develop practical as well as social skills.

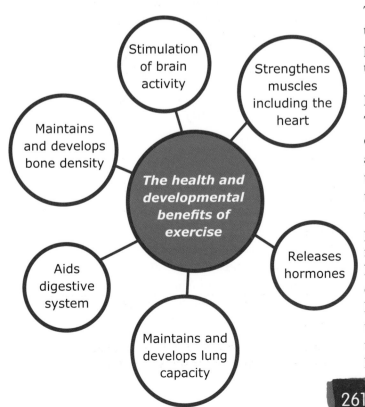

How much exercise do children need?

Children of all ages need physical activity. The British Heart Foundation suggests that children and young people need at least one hour of moderate activity a day. The hour does not need to be taken in one go but can be in small bursts over the day. Moderate activity includes brisk walking, cycling, dancing and active play. It is also recommended that some physical activity should also include elements of climbing and jumping as these promote agility and bone density.

Stop-start approach to exercise

It is important to recognise that young children need a stop–start pattern to their physical activity because their lung and heart capacity is still developing. This is why, for example, toddlers will run and then want to sit and ride in their pushchairs for ten or so minutes before wanting to get out again. The need for a stop–start approach to exercise continues until children are towards the end of primary school. When children are playing outdoors they tend to pace themselves naturally; this is why providing opportunities for outdoor play are so important. (See also Unit 4, pages 188–90.)

Current decline in physical activity

Today there is concern that children overall are not getting sufficient physical activity. Together with diets high in energy, this is thought to have contributed towards the increase in obese and overweight children. There are many reasons why it is thought that children today spend less time playing outdoors or engaging in physical activity than in previous generations; some of these are described below.

Fear of child abuse

Traditionally children used to spend time playing outdoors relatively unsupervised in the streets and in parks. Today there is greater awareness and therefore fear of child abuse. While statistics indicate that the majority of abuse is committed by people that children know rather than strangers, some high profile abductions and murders in recent years have meant that many parents do not feel comfortable letting children out of their sight. This has restricted considerably the amount of time that some children have been able to play outdoors. It has also restricted the amount of space that children have been able to access as even children who are lucky enough to have a garden may only have a small area available.

Fear of traffic

While fear of child abuse is one reason that many adults cite for not letting their children out to play, so too is a fear of traffic. This has resulted in fewer children playing in the streets and on bicycles but also in the number of children who walk alone to school.

Find out!

1. Find out about the following current initiatives that the government and local authorities have developed to encourage children to take more exercise:
   → www.walktoschool.org.uk
   → www.saferoutestoschools.org.uk
2. Ask your local school if they have a 'walking bus' service.

Lack of facilities

As well as adults' fears about the safety of children, in some areas there are fewer places for children to play safely. This may be because play areas have been vandalised or removed. Play areas may also have been re-designed with safety in mind but have proved not to be sufficiently challenging or interesting for children (see health and safety below). In addition, leisure centres and sports facilities can be difficult for some low-income families to access, both in terms of transport and cost.

Health and safety

While parents have grown increasingly anxious about child abductions, so organisations have become anxious about health and safety. Many local authorities, schools, pre-schools and nurseries are concerned that they might be taken to court by parents if any accidents occur on equipment or during physical activities. This has meant that many play areas have been re-designed or re-surfaced in order to reduce the risk of accidents. Adults working with children are also cautious and tend to stop some traditional play activities such as climbing or jumping. This in turn has meant that playing outdoors is not as fun for children because it is often less challenging. The push towards supervising children constantly has also meant that many adults restrict the amount of time for playing outdoors because they become bored and cold while supervising.

⇧ **Children today spend less time playing outside and more time watching television or using computers than previous generations**

Computer, media and television

In direct contrast to the reduced opportunities to play outdoors, children now have greater opportunities to play indoors. However, being indoors almost instantly reduces the possibility for more vigorous physical activity. Children are naturally told to walk rather than to run and to slow down as they move around. While play activities indoors can promote fine motor skills, it can be hard for children to engage in large-scale activity unless carefully organised. In addition, children at home have increasing access to television and computers. These make few physical demands on children apart from fine motor skills so can prevent them from getting into the habit of playing and finding stimulation for themselves.

Illness and disability

Both illness and disability have the potential to affect children's health and development, although the extent will depend on the nature and duration of the illness and/or disability. Individual responses towards illness and disability also vary so any effects can only be considered in very general terms. It is always important to bear this in mind to avoid making assumptions. It is also essential that adults work hard to create an inclusive environment which will incorporate children's needs (see also Unit 3, pages 120–1). Below are some possible effects of illness and disability on overall health.

Ability to take exercise

Some illnesses and physical disabilities may restrict the amount of physical activity that a child can undertake. For example, a child with a chest infection should avoid going swimming while a child with severe asthma may need to avoid some types of vigorous exercise (although it is known that some gentle exercise is essential to maintain lung capacity). Some disabilities may also make it harder to take part in physical activity, although quite often physiotherapists will be able to make suggestions as to how to adapt activities, resources or equipment in order to assist the child. Since exercise is fundamental for all children, it is therefore essential to seek further advice when working with children who are ill or who have a disability rather than to make assumptions about what they can or cannot do.

Growth and development

Some types of illness and disability affect children's growth patterns and overall development. This can in turn affect children's ability to participate with other children unless adults are sensitive and look for opportunities to adapt activities and ensure that the environment is inclusive. Some disabilities will also affect children's rate of physical development and this needs to be thought about when planning for children's needs.

Diet and feeding

Some illnesses and disabilities mean that children may require a diet or feeding pattern which differs from the setting's menu and general regime. A good example of this is diabetes: a diabetic child may need more frequent snacks and meals and the timing and food content of meals will need to be carefully monitored.

Case study

Supporting a child with a medical condition

Peter has epilepsy. He loves climbing and already attends a junior gymnastics club. His parents are determined that his epilepsy should not affect his enjoyment of activities or his childhood. The staff at Peter's pre-school have worked with his parents and a physiotherapist to ensure that Peter can participate in everything, although at times, such as on the climbing frame, Peter has to wear protective headgear. In order that Peter does not feel different, the setting has ordered several headgear and other children choose to wear them too.

1. Why is it important for Peter to take part in physical activity?

2. Why is it essential for settings not to make assumptions about children's needs or requirements?

3. How has this pre-school shown an inclusive approach?

U6

2

Getting ready for assessment

1. If you complete the Find out! activity on page 257 of this section, and take notes or print out information about what you have discovered, your findings may be used to form a basis for the portfolio for your research.

2. Use an Internet search to discover more information and statistics about factors that might affect children's health. Start by typing health+children+uk into a search engine. Check that the information is relevant and country appropriate. Take notes or print out information.

How to plan and implement routines and activities for children

In practice

You are hoping to work as a nanny at the end of your course. You have started to read some of the advertisements and are wondering how you would organise the day if you were caring for children of different ages in a family setting.

By the end of this section you will know why it is important to plan routines and activities and ways of doing this.

The reasons for and benefits of planning routines and activities to support a healthy lifestyle

You have seen that health is not just about keeping children free of illness but promoting their overall well-being. In terms of your work with children this means that, in addition to thinking about their care or education, you will also need to consider their overall needs. A good starting point is Maslow's hierarchy of needs.

Maslow's hierarchy of needs

Abraham Maslow (1908–70) argued that humans have a range of needs. He organised these needs into a priority order, with basics such as food, water and shelter coming before more sophisticated needs such as stimulation and curiosity. Maslow's hierarchy is usually represented using a pyramid with the basic needs at the base. While this was originally used to help business managers understand how to motivate their employees, it is now used more widely to show the importance of meeting the needs of different groups including children.

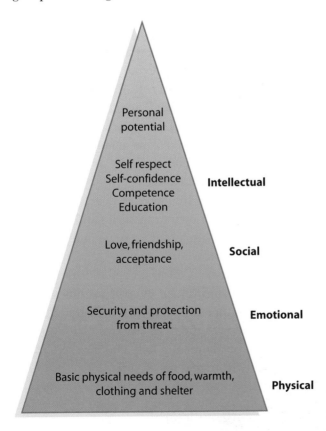

⇧ **Maslow's hierarchy of needs represented as a pyramid with the more primitive needs at the bottom**

Why planning is important?

It is important to actively plan to meet children's needs because there is otherwise a real danger that some children's needs might be overlooked. It is also important to regularly review any routines and activities to ensure that they continue to meet children's needs. This is because children's needs change according to their stage of development and individual circumstances and interests.

Signs that a routine is not working

Children often show through their responses that a routine is not working or that it is no longer suitable for them. It is therefore important to look at children's responses and consider whether or not the routine is appropriate. Below are three examples of common responses that might indicate that a routine needs to be reviewed.

Example 1

Khan is 2 years old. He normally has a nap in the afternoon and is woken up after an hour. Previously he used to wake up and be very bright and responsive. For the past few days he has woken up but been fairly groggy and irritable. He is also not finding it easy to settle to play and is clingy and tired. His mother says that his baby brother has been waking everyone in the night. Khan's key worker and mother have therefore decided to try giving him an earlier nap in the afternoon so that he can sleep for longer. This works well and Khan now sleeps for an hour and a half and wakes looking and feeling better. He is also more active in the afternoon and is eating better.

Example 2

Jemma is 6 years old and attends school. She is used to sitting next to her friend Katie in class. A new teacher has decided to mix up the seating arrangements in the room and Jemma is told that she can no longer sit with Katie in the morning. Jemma is very upset and over the next few weeks begins to wet the bed and complain of a tummy ache in the morning. Jemma's mother visits the teacher and explains that Jemma is not coping well with the new system. The teacher has also noticed that Jemma's work has regressed and that she is not as enthusiastic as before. The teacher decides to reorganise the seating arrangements.

Example 3

Jed is 3 years old. He has started to try to do many things for himself and becomes frustrated when his nanny takes over tasks such as putting on his coat. The nanny thinks about Jed's frustrated behaviour and realises that she needs to give him more time and opportunities to become independent. This new approach works quite well and Jed is showing less signs of frustration.

Case study

Reviewing the setting's play provision

Busy Bee Nursery has a large room and an outdoor area where children aged 3 to 5 years play. The staff have noticed that as the children become older some of them tend to play less actively – almost as if they have 'outgrown' the setting. They have also noticed that the older children tend to show more unwanted behaviour and have less respect for the toys and equipment. The staff decide to ask their early years adviser for ideas.

The early years adviser asks the staff how the routine and activities provided for the children have changed as they have become older. The staff begin to realise that aside from the occasional adult-directed activity, the type of equipment, layout and activities remains the same. The early years adviser asks them to think about what it must be like for a child to visit the same place each day for two years if there is little change to what is provided.

1. Why is it important that routines and activities are varied for different ages of children?

2. Discuss the signs that indicate to staff that a routine is not working for a child?

3. Suggest what the staff of Busy Bee Nursery might need to do next in order to meet children's needs.

The role of routines and activities in promoting and maintaining the health of children

A good routine should encompass a child's overall needs. It is important to recognise that if a routine is not meeting a child's needs this will impact on his or her health and behaviour. The following elements need to be built into a routine as they all contribute to children's overall well-being.

→ *Safety* – Routines need to be devised with children's safety in mind. Children's safety needs are linked closely to their age of development (see also Unit 4, pages 167–73).

→ *Diet* – Routines need to ensure that children have sufficient food and drink throughout the day or session. The quality of a child's diet has significant impact on their development (see also Unit 12, pages 473–4).

→ *Exercise* – Children need plenty of opportunity for physical activity. This includes opportunities to be outdoors where there is more potential for vigorous activity.

→ *Skin and toileting* – Routines must incorporate time for physical care routines such as washing hands and toileting.

→ *Sleep and rest* – Sleep and rest are vital for children's overall health. A routine should incorporate the sleep and rest needs of children.

→ *Stimulation* – Children of all ages must have opportunities to play, explore and be intellectually challenged. This means that a routine should incorporate plenty of varied play opportunities and activities.

→ *Independence* – Children need to develop confidence in their own capabilities and so need opportunities within a routine to be independent and to make choices.

→ *Love and affection* – Children need to feel that they are loved and valued. A good routine should give children time to spend with their parents or carers and with their key workers. A routine should also be planned to help children separate comfortably from parents or carers.

Think about it

Look at the morning routine of a nursery below. Think about how the children's overall needs are being met.

8am–8.30am	Parents come into the nursery and find their children's key workers. Parents can stay with the child and his/her key worker until they feel that their child is settled. The key worker and parents gradually devise a 'goodbye' routine for each child.
8.30–10.00am	Activities, toys and equipment are available indoors and outdoors for children to select. Key workers keep an eye out for their key children to check they are settled and engaged in play. Small group activities with adults are also available including small group stories.
10.00–10.30am	Key workers take it in turns to take their group of children over to the snack table. They make sure that children have opportunities to drink and eat a healthy snack. They note if any children are not hungry or thirsty at this point. They also use this time to interact with individual children and to check whether they are settled. This time is used with older children to talk about their plans for play afterwards and the key worker helps to assist them if required.
10.30am–12.15pm	Activities, toys and equipment are 'refreshed' or supplemented to ensure that they remain challenging and enjoyable. A range of activities planned by adults but based on children's observed interests are made available. Music and story sessions are also made available for children.

Throughout the morning:

→ children are able to go to the toilet independently, although adults keep a watchful eye so they can support individual children

→ children are able to play and choose equipment; adults have previously checked items for safety and supervise discreetly

→ children can go to quiet areas in the room if they want to rest or be in the company of an adult.

How to plan and implement activities in a range of settings that are appropriate for the age and stage of development of the child

Healthy diet

From the moment that babies are weaned it is important that you encourage children to eat a variety of foods that will keep them healthy. This begins early on in life as babies can learn to like most foods while their sense of taste is still developing. This is why a range of vegetables and fruit should be introduced early on and sugary foods avoided. As children get older they tend to develop strong taste preferences, but still new foods can be introduced if the child is involved in preparing them. This means that you should be preparing food with children from a young age. It is also important that children learn to serve themselves so they develop the skill of learning how much they can eat.

Home-based care

An advantage of home-based care is that it can be easier for the adult to help children be involved in the process of preparing and serving food. This means that even toddlers can be involved in helping to lay the table, wash fruit and vegetables and help in the preparation of snacks and drinks. The time spent preparing food and drink is important in children's learning about mathematics as well as healthy eating and can be seen as a planned activity.

Nurseries, pre-schools and day care

Preparing food and drink can be planned as a curriculum activity. Some settings may have limited facilities as the kitchen may not be a safe place for children to visit, though a range of cold cooking activities can still be carried out. These might include making salads, smoothies and yoghurt drinks as well as making simple dishes such as pizza or sandwiches.

Schools, after-school clubs and holiday clubs

As children get older they often become more interested and skilled at cooking. They can start to choose their own recipes and take on more responsibility. You may also use opportunities when preparing food to help children learn about eating a healthy and balanced diet. Children can also play 'taste-testing' games to try out new flavours.

Exercise

As you have seen (pages 261–2), children need exercise in order to remain healthy. Providing opportunities for physical exercise is therefore essential for all ages. This begins when children are babies, as babies need opportunities to crawl, move around and explore their environment. Once babies are walking they need plenty of space so they can develop their locomotive skills. Toddlers and older children need to have opportunities to walk, balance and run. Providing appropriate equipment, adult attention and encouragement is important in this.

Home-based care

In home-based care it is often possible to take children on outings such as to the park but also to incorporate exercise as part of the everyday routine by, for example, walking to school to collect an older child or going to the shops. In some home-based care settings, adults will have access to gardens.

Nurseries, pre-schools and day care

Most early years settings now have some form of outdoor area and the trend is to allow children to play freely outdoors. It is important that adults make sure they set a good example by being outdoors with the children and allowing children to have sufficient time to play. Equipment can be used to form obstacle courses, and role play and vigorous play can be integrated by, for example, children pretending to tricycle to the petrol station or shop. It is also possible to play some indoor games that will help children exercise, for example playing musical games such as musical bumps.

Schools, after-school clubs and holiday clubs

Children may enjoy taking part in competitive games such as football and netball but it is also essential that there are plenty of non-competitive activities such as dancing, playing hide and seek, chase and skipping. As children become older it is important that you think about providing activities that will suit children's skill levels and their own interests.

Getting ready for assessment

Collate the information that you have collected for this unit so far. Check what other information is required using the assignment task and assessment criteria given by CACHE. You should also have:

→ two examples of different routines that will promote a healthy lifestyle

→ information about a range of factors affecting children's health.

Consider whether you know enough to be able to:

1. Explain why the two examples of routines that you have would be helpful in promoting health.

2. Analyse the reasons for planning and implementing activities which promote health in children.

Unit 7

Play and learning in children's education

In this unit you will learn:

1. The relevant theoretical approaches in the field of play and education

2. How to use appropriate tools to assess the learning needs of individual children

3. How to plan and provide learning opportunities in consultation with others

4. How to record and evaluate the planning and assessment cycle

Section 1

The relevant theoretical approaches in the field of play and education

In practice

Hannah, aged 3 years, enjoys playing in the garden area of the nursery. With the wheelbarrow provided she transports bricks and pebbles. She also uses the wheelbarrow to transport some dolls and teddies around the nursery and give her friend Eric a ride.

Hannah's key worker, Sheema, notices that as the week progresses, Hannah begins to judge how much she can transport in the wheelbarrow without spilling the contents. She also notices that Hannah is fascinated by the pattern the wheels make on the grass and sand. Sheema makes some brief notes of these observations to share at the next team planning meeting.

By the end of this section you will understand why the pioneers you have studied placed so much importance on practitioners observing and analysing a child's play in order to plan the next step of his or her learning.

The relationship between play and learning

The importance of play

Play is central to the development of children, enabling them to make sense of their world as they learn through exploration and experimentation. Children develop through play, from first playing with their own fingers as a baby to creating complex games with rules.

While this unit focuses on learning through play in the early years, you will also look at the way young people engage in play and its importance in their development. Play opportunities can range from child-initiated activities to those led by adults. While play should always be an enjoyable experience, the energy and focus required of the child should not be underestimated.

Despite the different theories of the role of play in learning (see pages 279–89), there is general agreement about the opportunities that play should provide for children and young people. These are described in the spider diagram below.

The role of the adult in play

The adult plays an important role in providing children with the environment and resources to develop their skills through play. Even when play takes place within the structure of a curriculum, such as the Early Years Foundation Stage, the role of the practitioner is to provide challenging opportunities and guidance as appropriate.

Did you know?

Susan Isaacs, whose pioneering research in the 1920s and 1930s emphasised the importance of children as active learners (see also page 282), said 'Play is indeed the child's work and the means whereby he grows and develops' (Isaacs, 1929).

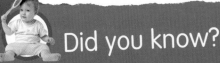

Did you know?

First-hand learning opportunities are vital to children's play experiences. Television is considered a second-hand learning experience as children are being provided with information and do not directly experience it. An example of this could be watching a programme about the seaside as opposed to visiting the seaside.

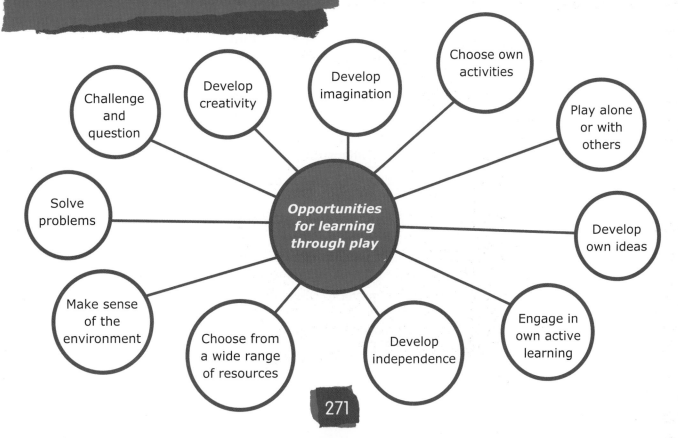

Opportunities for learning through play

- Challenge and question
- Develop creativity
- Develop imagination
- Choose own activities
- Play alone or with others
- Solve problems
- Develop own ideas
- Make sense of the environment
- Choose from a wide range of resources
- Develop independence
- Engage in own active learning

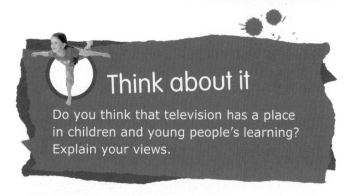

Think about it

Do you think that television has a place in children and young people's learning? Explain your views.

How children develop through play

Play enables children to progress in all areas of their development and should be considered when planning any experiences or activities. The table below outlines how play can support each area of development.

✋ **How play supports development**

Area of development	How play supports development
Physical development	• Develops gross motor and fine motor skills and coordination through use of appropriate equipment such as balls, bicycles, building blocks, pencils, etc. • Activities such as running, jumping, climbing and walking can promote balance and muscle tone. • Encourages individual and group exercise via games such as football, swimming, etc. for young people.
Social, emotional and behavioural development	• Enables children to relate to adults and children through both child-initiated and adult-led activities. • Children learn to share and take turns through the playing of games, etc. and to consider the needs and feelings of others. • Encourages young people to discuss and resolve for themselves any conflicts that may arise in play environments such as youth or sports clubs. • Helps children to explore their emotions through activities such as role play, book sharing and painting. • Provides opportunities for children to be reflective through the provision of quiet areas both indoors and outdoors. • Children may receive praise where appropriate, for example when a child helps to clear away play activities. • Can encourage independence, for example through activities young people are involved in planning, such as a camping weekend.
Intellectual development	• Through exploration and experimentation, children can develop problem-solving skills and understanding of concepts. This could range from the sorting of shells into different sizes to doing a puzzle or building a tower with blocks. • Young people can be provided with activities that encourage abstract thinking, planning and problem solving, such as organising a sports tournament.
Communication and language development	• Play experiences develop language via describing, labelling and commenting on the activity. • Communication and language can be developed through activities such as role play. • Adults can encourage communication skills by asking children to explain what they are doing in their play, to explain rules, to challenge and negotiate. • Young people who may prefer to spend time using the computer can be encouraged to maintain verbal communication through play activities that encourage social interaction.

Learning through water play

As part of the planning in a room for 3–5-year-olds at the Green Tree Day Nursery, Tom has set out a water play activity with water wheels and different sized containers. He has also put coloured ice cubes into the clear water. The children understand that only four children can play around the water tray at any one time.

1. Which areas of development will this water play activity encourage?

2. Consider which cognitive concepts the children could develop when playing with this activity.

3. Describe Tom's role in encouraging the children to explore these concepts.

Supporting children's play

To support a child's play effectively, it is important to recognise that the characteristics of his or her play will change as the child progresses through different stages of development. A child's environment or culture can impact upon how he or she progresses through these stages. For example, a child who is from a large family or is used to playing with other children may begin to play cooperatively earlier than a child who has little experience of being with other children. Children will play according to the needs of the time and their current situation. It is therefore important that you look broadly when observing and analysing a child's play.

Recognising children's needs

A range of specific needs may affect the type of play that a child engages in and how he or she plays. Strategies will have to be agreed to support any specific need that a child might have, so that no barrier is created to a child's sense of achievement or enjoyment. This could mean modifying equipment or providing additional resources. Resources may include another practitioner, for example someone who may be trained to support a child in their play using British Sign Language or the Picture Exchange Communication System (PECS). Such a person may play an important role in supporting children who

have communication needs or who find it difficult to form relationships with other children.

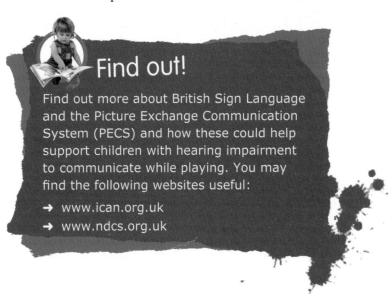

Find out!

Find out more about British Sign Language and the Picture Exchange Communication System (PECS) and how these could help support children with hearing impairment to communicate while playing. You may find the following websites useful:

→ www.ican.org.uk
→ www.ndcs.org.uk

The five stages of play

Stage	Age	Description
Solitary play	0–2 years	Children play alone with the reassurance of an adult close by. For example, exploring the contents of a treasure basket activity with an adult close by.
Spectator play	2–2½ years	Children like to watch other children around them but do not participate. This can often be seen when a younger child is happy to watch his or her older siblings play without joining in.
Parallel play	2–3 years	Children develop an awareness of each other and may play alongside each other without playing together. You can often see children of this age playing alongside each other in areas such as the home corner.

Stage	Age	Description
Associative play	3–4 years	Children begin to imitate each other and may cooperate in their play for a short time. They begin to have friendship preferences but will play with either gender.
Cooperative play	4 years plus	Children play together, talk and decide what they want to play. Their play becomes more complex. By school age they are often starting to play in single gender groups.

⇧ **Child aged 1 year engaged in solitary play**

⇧ **Children aged 4 years playing cooperatively in the home corner**

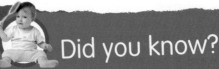

Did you know?

The terms 'heuristic play' and 'treasure basket play' are used to describe play with babies and toddlers. This is when children are given a collection of interesting and often natural objects to play with and explore alone, with an adult nearby. Elinor Goldschmied promoted this play and a DVD of her work is available from the National Children's Bureau.

Different types of play

Play can be planned for children and young people in a variety of ways. A quality setting will offer a wide range of opportunities in the curriculum that supports the development of the whole child and allows him or her to make informed choices.

Play is often categorised in several ways but is generally grouped into the following categories:

→ creative play
→ physical play
→ manipulative play
→ imaginative play.

Creative play

Creative play is an important means of encouraging children to experiment and explore the world around them. Through their senses they are able to explore the properties of different materials. If provided with a wide range of activities, children can develop in all areas and can gain a great deal of satisfaction from their creative play, increasing their confidence and self-esteem.

Supporting children's creativity

In creative play the end product should not be stressed and there should be no competition as a child's sense of self-worth can easily be destroyed if their creation is not praised or is questioned in some way. This will enable children to enjoy the process rather than the end product. If a group of children are painting a picture of a flower, for example, the role of the adult is to stimulate via discussion, observation and the provision of a range of exciting materials.

274

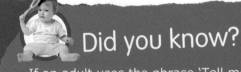
The importance of child-initiated activities

Tina Bruce (2004) refers to the importance of child-led activities in developing a child's creativity. She writes:

Adults play a critical part in whether or not children become creative people. ... Adults who tune in to what interests the child and who are informed participant observers are able to appreciate and value the beginnings of creativity in children without invading the child's creative idea or taking it over. (Bruce 2004: 74)

Physical play

This type of play encourages children to use their large muscles and exercise their whole body. They learn to control large and small muscles and develop coordination. As children become older they may begin to enjoy more organised physical activities such as football or athletics. Children may also engage in competitive sport.

Opportunities for physical play should take place both indoors and outdoors. Large apparatus or equipment that is provided should be challenging and appropriate for the age group of children involved.

Links to other areas of development

Physical play relates to other areas of development, as shown in the spider diagram below.

Components of coordinated movement

When children take part in physical play there are 10 components of coordinated movement that can be identified.

1. *Space and direction* – identifying position of body in relation to surroundings.
2. *Balance* – controlling the movement of the body by transfer of weight, moving backwards, forwards, sideways.
3. *Rhythm* – developing movement flows and coordination.
4. *Physical self-awareness* – understanding the way that the body moves and what each part can do.
5. *Fine muscle development* – physical coordination of fingers, toes and eyes.
6. *Large muscle movement* – particularly around the pelvic and floor girdles.
7. *Basic body movement* – moving skilfully and freely without thought.
8. *Symmetrical activity* – to develop both the left and right sides of the body.

U7
1

9. *Hand–eye coordination* – ensures the working together of hands, eyes and arms.

10. *Eye–foot coordination* – ensures the working together of eyes, legs and feet.

⇧ **How many of the 10 components of co-ordinated movement can you identify in this activity?**

Manipulative play

While the emphasis of physical play is upon the development of a child's large muscles, manipulative play concentrates upon how a child uses his or her hands. Hand–eye coordination is an important part of manipulative play, as are sight and touch. Children also need to be encouraged to concentrate upon what they are doing.

Did you know?

From a very early age babies can be observed trying to touch the mobile above their cot or pram. This developing sense of touch leads to an increased control of the finer muscles and fingers, development of perception and accurate hand–eye coordination.

Manipulative play is divided into gross and fine manipulative play.

→ *Gross manipulative play* encourages the use of the whole hand, arm or leg to grasp, push, hit, pick up or release, for example throwing a ball, climbing or kicking a ball.

→ *Fine manipulative play* encourages the use of the finer muscles of the fingers and thumb. In this type of play children learn to use their fingers independently, for example unscrewing a lid, cutting with scissors or using a pencil.

As an early years practitioner you have an important role in providing appropriate and stimulating materials for gross and fine manipulative play.

Case study

Learning through Duplo

Jude is the nanny for 2-year-old Luke. She decides to let Luke spend the afternoon playing with some Duplo that he has been given for his birthday. Jude lays the Duplo out on the carpet but decides to leave some in a box as he has been given a lot! Jude and Luke have a great time. He enjoys putting the bricks together and finding which colours and shapes he wants to use. Jude helps him when he has difficulty putting two bricks together. She also encourages Luke to talk about what he is doing.

1. Why did Jude lay the Duplo out on the carpet?

2. What do you think was Jude's role in the Duplo play activity?

3. Which manipulative skills would Luke have been using while trying to put the bricks together?

4. Using the development chart in Unit 2 page 41, list at least five manipulative play activities that would be suitable for Jude to provide for Luke.

Skills that could be developed by children and young people during a range of manipulative play activities include:

→ *Language and mathematical skills* – by describing activities, counting items and playing with shapes

→ *Perception* – by observing what happens during a manipulative play activity

→ *Cognitive skills* – by sorting and matching items

→ *Self-esteem* – through having control over activities and receiving praise from peers and adults

→ *Expression* – through a range of activities

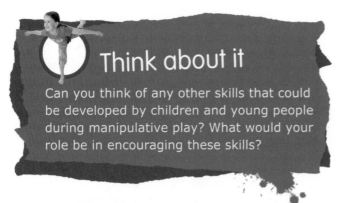

Think about it

Can you think of any other skills that could be developed by children and young people during manipulative play? What would your role be in encouraging these skills?

Imaginative play

During imaginative play, children take on the role of other people or situations. This often happens as they act out situations spontaneously. For example, children may turn the climbing frame into a tardis or pretend they are a dog and want to have their dinner in a bowl on the floor! Younger children playing in areas such as the home corner may benefit from being led by an older child so they can engage in a high level of imaginative play. The older child may be able to guide the younger children in their role or remind them of the plot of the story they are creating.

Sometimes imaginative play is instigated by the adult, so that children can explore familiar situations or fantasy worlds. Adults can support and provide a number of imaginative play activities to allow children to safely explore their own feelings and the world around them.

Key terms associated with imaginative play

There are four different terms that you may read in connection with imaginative play:

→ *Pretend or imaginative play* – this considers how children act out in a range of ways, such as going shopping or cooking a meal.
→ *Fantasy play* – when children use real life experiences to play imaginatively, perhaps turning a cardboard book into a bus that may go into space.
→ *Socio-dramatic play* – for older children who play together, agreeing and negotiating the roles they need. For example, a group of 7-year-olds may decide to act out a football game they have watched, taking on the roles of their favourite players, or perhaps act out a scene from Harry Potter.
→ *Symbolic play* – when children make one object stand for another. A common example of this is the child who offers you a cup of tea they have made for you in a flower pot!

The role of the adult in imaginative play

The role of the adult in imaginative play is important not only in supporting and creating opportunities but also in encouraging children to communicate through:

→ listening
→ developing body language
→ talking
→ symbolic and graphic representation (children's mark making leading to writing).

One of the most important aspects of the adult's role is to observe the child playing imaginatively in order to provide the appropriate resources. An environment that is rich with opportunities will enable children to express themselves freely and think independently.

⇦ **Adults can provide imaginative play activities, such as this doctor's set and dolls, to allow children to safely explore their own feelings and the world around them**

Supporting different types of play

The table below considers some of the resources you can provide and what you need to observe to support children's play.

Area of play	Materials and resources	What the adult can observe to support the child
Creative play	• Variety of paints and colours • Different textured and shaped paper • Variety of manipulative materials such as clay and dough • Rich choice of textiles, buttons, threads, bows, etc. • Variety of tools, such as different scissors, pencils, brushes, tape • Natural materials such as shells, pebbles and feathers • Inspiration via photos, objects, discussion, outings, etc.	• Children's interests and preferences • Stages of development, for example use of scissors, language, independence • Interaction of children and adults • The environment and layout of activities
Physical play	• Variety of small equipment, e.g. bean bags, balls, hoops, treasure basket contents • Space to move • Large equipment such as tunnels (man-made and natural), climbing structures, etc. • Specific activities such as PE, swimming, dance	• What children enjoy • Stages of development • The environment and layout of activities • How children participate in physical play
Manipulative play	• Variety of pencils, scissors, brushes, etc. • Opportunities to carry out self-help skills such as doing up buttons and zips • Opportunities to carry out activities which involve screwing and unscrewing • Small world play such as Lego • Natural materials such as shells and pebbles	• Children's interests and preferences • Stages of development, e.g. hand–eye coordination • Interaction of children and adults • The environment and layout of activities
Imaginative play	• Role-play areas such as home corner • Imaginative play opportunities such as space ships, builders' yards • Accessible resources for the children to use such as hats and bags • Empty boxes • Stimulation such as stories, rhymes, music • Space and time to play indoors and outdoors	• Children's interests and preferences • Stages of development, e.g. language • Interaction of children • The environment and provision of resources

The adult's role in supporting children's play

- ✓ Provide a range of play experiences.
- ✓ Provide a variety of resources and equipment.
- ✓ Provide opportunities that encourage children to play alone or in small or larger groups as appropriate.
- ✓ Provide a balance of adult-initiated and child-led activities.
- ✓ Use observation to inform planning of play experiences.
- ✓ Involve children in planning their play.
- ✓ Support play but encourage children to play independently.
- ✓ Extend and develop children's learning through play.
- ✓ Ensure that play takes place indoors and outdoors.
- ✓ Ensure that all areas of development and the appropriate curriculum are considered.
- ✓ Ensure that the children have fun.

↘ **Clockwise from left to right, Froebel, Montessori and Steiner – the pioneers of play**

Pioneers in play and the development of theoretical approaches to play and learning

For children and young people, play is now seen as an essential part of supporting their development, whether through the early years play-based curriculum or play-based activities that take place in a range of settings such as after-school clubs. Different approaches to play will vary according to the age and needs of the children involved.

Current theories of play are based upon the work of a number of pioneers. In the current context of the importance of learning through play, some of the work of the pioneers may not seem innovative. However, these pioneers started their work over 200 years ago in a climate when children led very formal lives, sometimes starting work at a young age. Their work has had an enormous influence on early years practitioners' practice today and still influences current approaches to children's learning.

Jean-Jacques Rousseau (1712–78)

Rousseau was a French philosopher whose thinking was ahead of his time. In a very formal educational climate he wrote a book called *Emile* (1762) which advocated that children under the age of 12 years explore through play. He wanted them to be able to discover their world for themselves without adult involvement. Although Rousseau's work met with disapproval (*Emile* was banned in France), it influenced pioneers such as Friedrich Froebel and Maria Montessori (see below).

Rousseau and early years practice today

Rousseau's approach to children's learning:

→ influenced the pioneers of play who followed him
→ helped to shape current thinking that young children should learn through a curriculum based on play.

Friedrich Froebel (1782–1852)

Froebel carried out pioneering work with children in Germany and in 1840 he founded the first kindergarten. Froebel's kindergartens were for children aged 3 to 7 years. The children played indoors and outdoors using the finger play and rhymes that he invented. Froebel stressed the importance of symbolic play where children make one thing stand for something else, for example a child using a yoghurt pot as a cup and offering the adult a drink.

Did you know?

Translated from German, 'kindergarten' literally means 'garden of children'.

Froebel also stressed the importance of imaginative play. He felt that through imaginative play children could learn at the highest level. He was also well known for block play, encouraging children to learn a variety of mathematical concepts and relationships through play with various wooden blocks.

Froebel and early years practice today

Frobel's legacy is the child-centred kindergartens which are still popular in Germany and other parts of Europe today. In England, the Froebel Institute in London trains early years practitioners in the Froebel method and is a centre of influential research for people such as Professor Tina Bruce and Chris Athey.

Froebel's pioneering work is now accepted as good practice:

→ the needs of the child are at the centre of the curriculum
→ children should be able to discover for themselves
→ songs should be used to teach children and finger rhymes are valuable learning experiences
→ block play can help children develop mathematical concepts through problem solving
→ the outdoor environment is vital to children's learning.

Maria Montessori (1870–1952)

Maria Montessori was a doctor. As the first woman to graduate from medical school in Italy, she was well placed to become a pioneer of her time. Her initial work was with children with specific learning needs. She then began working with young children of working families, setting up the famous 'Children's House' in San Lorenzo, the most deprived area of Rome. (This is why many Montessori settings are each called 'Children's House'.)

Montessori's work was innovative at a time when children learned by rote (by repetition of facts spoken aloud at the same time as others). She encouraged children to organise their own activities and absorb information from their environment. She believed in child-led education and learning through the senses, and developed constructive play materials. She believed in creativity in children's play, but felt that if children were encouraged to learn skills such as drawing then they would have the skills to develop their own ideas.

Montessori did not place a value on imaginative or socio-dramatic play but instead encouraged children to take place in real life activities such as sweeping and serving meals. Montessori schools have now adapted this philosophy through 'practical life activities' that provide children with child-sized versions of jugs and brushes, etc.

⇧ **Montessori encouraged children to learn through participation in 'real life' activities, such as sweeping leaves**

In a Montessori school, children are presented with pieces of especially designed equipment that are instructional and referred to as didactic materials. Montessori believed that the child will play with the equipment only if ready – that is, if it is the correct time in his or her development to do so.

Find out!

You can find out more about Montessori schools in the UK, including those in your local area, via the following website: www.montessoricentreinternational.co.uk

The sensitive period

Montessori believed that children were receptive at particular ages of their development and that the adult needed to guide them through these times. In the Montessori method, the early years are recognised as a time when the child has an absorbent mind and will learn through the sensory experiences provided. Above all, Montessori felt that children must have the opportunity to develop both morally and spiritually because a child's soul was like a mirror that could be affected by any influence.

Think about it

1. In small groups, discuss the idea of Montessori's 'practical life activities' and whether the children you have worked with have used this type of activity in their play.

2. Do you think practical life activities could be used in any area of the Early Years Foundation Stage curriculum? If so, how would you do this?

Montessori and early years practice today

Although Montessori valued structured activities rather than free play, her influence on play can be found in many settings through the following:

→ a holistic approach to development
→ a focus on the interaction of the child in their environment
→ encouraging the child to take responsibility
→ consideration of the child's stage of development when planning activities
→ emphasis on the spiritual development of the child so that he or she can become a confident learner.

Rudolph Steiner (1861–1925)

Steiner believed in community education and the importance of maintaining a bond between the child and the adult. Like Montessori and Froebel, he believed the self-esteem and emotional well-being of the child are central to the child's development. His approach to education was holistic, placing great importance on a healthy diet and general physical well-being. Like Montessori, Steiner also considered the environment to be central to a child's learning experience.

Steiner encouraged adults to assess the personality of each child and plan the curriculum around this. Children with special needs were included in play activities and children were encouraged to show empathy to each other.

Did you know?

Steiner believed that childhood was divided into three phases:

→ *the will* (0–7 years) – fusing of the body and the spirit
→ *the heart* (7–14 years) – the rhythm of the heartbeat meant that feelings are an important part of this stage of development
→ *the head* (14 years onwards) – a period of thinking.

There are still a number of schools in the UK and other parts of Europe that follow Steiner's philosophy.

Find out!

You can find out more about Steiner schools in the UK, including those in your local area, via the following website: www.steinerwaldorf.org.uk

Steiner and early years practice today

Steiner's influence can be traced in mainstream settings through the following:

→ Children with special needs are integrated into mainstream schools where possible. Children with special needs are considered when planning play and each setting has a SENCO to advise on their needs.
→ Circle time is widely used as a means of developing children's self-esteem and communication skills. This was originally developed by Steiner to enable all children of all abilities to join in and take turns.

Margaret McMillan (1860–1931)

Margaret McMillan was born in New York but educated in Scotland. She felt that a child could develop into a whole person by learning through play. She initially focused on developing the child's manual dexterity through exercises and developed the idea that social and emotional development are equally important. She also believed that children should have access to a wide variety of materials through free play. Like Steiner, McMillan placed great importance on a healthy diet and linked deprivation with a poor level of learning. McMillan also became a member of the Froebel Society, sharing Froebel's beliefs that first-hand experiences and active learning are important in children's learning.

With her sister Rachael, McMillan pioneered nursery schools that used the outdoors and worked in partnership with parents, offering classes to parents to help them develop the skills they needed to learn with their children. In 1914 she started the first open-air

nursery school in Peckham, south-east London. She pioneered healthy school meals and medical services for children. She also placed great importance on the training of people working with children.

McMillan and early years practice today

McMillan's legacy includes:

→ a child-centred curriculum based on play
→ working in partnership with parents and recognising them as the educators of their children
→ the current focus on healthy eating for children
→ professional development of adults working with children.

Susan Isaacs (1885–1948)

From 1924 to 1927, Susan Isaacs was Head of Malting House School, Cambridge, an experimental school which encouraged the individual development of children. She became the first Head of Child Development at the Institute of Education, University of London, in 1933. There she developed an in-depth course in child development for early years practitioners. She also trained and practised as a psychoanalyst.

Isaacs was influenced by the work of Froebel as well as two psychoanalysts, Anna Freud (Sigmund Freud's daughter) and Melanie Klein, who believed that a child's emotional life was revealed through the symbols and themes they explored in imaginary play. Isaacs therefore felt that play should be used to explore a child's feelings and that through play children would come to understand the world around them. She felt that children should have the space and freedom to move when playing and discouraged desk-based learning.

Isaacs felt that children should have a play-based education until the age of 7 years. She carried out research to show how children regressed if they started school at 5 years. Many early years professionals today share this view and are concerned with the current trend of children entering into compulsory schooling in the year of their fifth birthday.

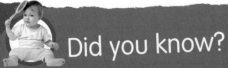

Did you know?

Many European countries such as Finland and Sweden do not believe in children going to school until they are 6 or 7 years old. Research has shown that children do well if there has been a focus on their emotional and social development before beginning formal education.

Isaacs and early years practice today

Susan Isaacs' influence on current play provision can be seen through:

→ emphasis on the importance of working with parents
→ the use of imaginary play as a way to explore feelings
→ freedom to move around the classroom
→ the current debate on whether children should have to enter school as early as 4 years of age.

Lady Allen of Hurtwood (1897–1976)

Lady Allen was a key figure in the development of play work in this country, which is primarily aimed at children over 8 years of age. She was an English landscape architect and campaigner for children, a member of the Nursery Schools Association of Great Britain and founder president of The World Organisation for Early Childhood. She wrote an illustrated book on children's playgrounds and campaigned for the first Children's Act of 1948. Inspired by the open space playgrounds developed by a Danish architect called C. T. Sorenson, she opened the first English 'junk' playground in Camberwell, London.

After visiting what she felt was a sterile play park in the United States in 1965, Lady Allen said: 'The successful playground is one in which children can move things and make new objects in their own way.' She went on to create imaginative playgrounds over old bombsites and founded the National Adventure Playgrounds Association (NAPA), now known as Kidsactive. She also campaigned for children living in high rise accommodation who needed space to play. In 1970 she opened the first adventure playground for disabled children.

Lady Allen and early years practice today

Lady Allen's campaign for exciting spaces for children and young people has influenced:

→ the child-centred open spaces that are widely available for young people today
→ the recognition of the importance of play spaces for children who may not have a garden of their own
→ the many adventure playgrounds that exist today for children and young people who are disabled.

⇧ **Lady Allen campaigned for the building of imaginative playgrounds for children**

Social constructivist theories of play in early learning

Jean Piaget (1896–1980)

Piaget is recognised for the way he influenced current understanding of how children learn. Although some aspects of his work have been disputed, his approach is fundamental to a play-based curriculum. Piaget felt that children should be actively involved in their own learning and that they pass through four stages of development from birth to adulthood (outlined in more detail in Unit 2, page 67).

Schemas

To Piaget, learning is an active process in which children draw conclusions through exploration. He called these conclusions 'schemas'. Piaget believed that through schemas, children develop and adapt their experiences.

Revisit the description of how children's schemas form and change from Unit 2, page 66. Then consider, in the following case study, how Ahmed adapts his schema.

Case study

Ahmed and the blue cup

Ahmed is 18 months old. He has always had his milk in a blue cup in the nursery. When the blue cups appear on the tray he knows his milk is coming. One day, Ahmed is given his milk in a red cup. He is upset and won't drink the milk. However, he soon realises that the red cup contains milk. Over time, Ahmed realises that milk can come in all sorts of cups and is happy to drink out of any cup provided.

1. What was the schema that Ahmed had constructed?

2. How did Ahmed experience disequilibrium?

3. How did Ahmed accommodate the idea that milk can be served in different coloured cups?

4. Can you think of any other schemas that 18-month-old Ahmed might develop in his play?

Developments of Piaget's theory

Despite general criticisms of Piaget's theory (for example, see Unit 2 page 67), his work on schemas has been developed, in particular by Chris Athey, who applied schemas while observing children's play. She describes the following different types of schemas:

→ *transporting*, when children move things from one place to another

→ *connecting*, when children enjoy putting things together and separating them

→ *trajectory*, when children want to see how things move

→ *rotation*, when children are interested to see how things move round

→ *enveloping*, when children are interested in containers and putting things inside each other.

Lev Vygotsky (1896–1934)

Vygotsky's work was unknown in the West until it was translated from Russian in 1962, and has since had great influence on play in the early years. Like Piaget, Vygotsky suggested that children were active in their learning, but he placed more emphasis on the role of the adult in supporting children to develop their ideas and thinking through their play. Vygotsky also believed that a child's potential rather than his or her ability should be assessed.

Vygotsky emphasised what children are capable of learning at various stages. He called this the zone of proximal development (ZPD), which is the distance between a child's actual development and his or her potential. This potential is only reached if the child and the environment are guided by the adult, helping the child to progress by **scaffolding**. (For more on Vygotsky's theory see Unit 2 page 70.)

Key term

Scaffolding The way in which adults help children to develop their knowledge and reasoning through guidance and support, the adult assisting the child through explanation, demonstration, questioning and correction.

Vygotsky and early years practice today

Vygotsky's influence today can be seen through a curriculum where the child is based at the centre. The role of the adult is to enable the child to reach his or her potential by planning activities in accordance with the child's stage of development. Even during adult-led activities the adult acts as the guide and is there to support, if necessary, in child-led play. In their planning, adults organise resources and experiences that will enable children to develop their own ideas.

⇧ **Vygotsky emphasised the role of the adult in supporting children's play**

Jerome Bruner (born 1915)

Like Piaget and Vygotsky, Bruner argued that children learn through choice and active involvement in their learning. He emphasised the following:

→ *Doing* (enactive mode of learning), whereby children need to have real first-hand experiences. In this way their thoughts and ideas are developed.

→ *Imaging* (the iconic mode of learning) – children need things such as books and interest tables to remind them of prior experiences.

→ *Making what they know* (the symbolic mode of learning) – codes are used such as language, drawings, paintings, dancing, making stories, music and maths.

Like Vygotsky, Bruner felt that 'scaffolding' can help children learn: adult support helps to develop confidence and control until it is withdrawn.

Psychodynamic theories of play in early learning

Psychodynamic theories were first pioneered by Sigmund Freud (1856–1939), who argued that people have a conscious and unconscious mind and that the unconscious mind guides a person in ways that he or she does not realise. Thus some of people's actions and speech, and aspects of their personality, are not always deliberate and conscious.

Freud's work led him to believe that childhood is crucial in the development of personality and behaviour. His findings had a huge impact both on attitudes to parenting and the treatment of people with emotional problems. Freud's theory was later developed by Erik Erickson (1902–94) in the 1950s and Donald Winnicott (1896–1971). (For more on Freud's theory see Unit 2 pages 74–6.)

The psychodynamic approach to play emphasises the importance of children being able to explore and act out their feelings. By exploring positive feelings it is thought that children can discover their deepest wishes, and by exploring their negative feelings they can confront their deepest fears. Children can also use play to face challenges in their lives, such as bereavement. Through play they might try things out as they are or as they want them to be; they can also gain a sense of what happens to them.

Did you know?

Play therapists use psychodynamic theories in their work to enable children to explore a variety of feelings and emotions.

Find out!

You can find out more about the work of the British Association for Play Therapists by visiting their website (www.bapt.info).

U7
1

Case study

Exploring feelings through play

Mika, Erik's nanny, realises that 4-year-old Erik is frightened of his mother going into hospital to have an operation on her arm. His grandmother died in hospital six months previously, so Erik associates hospitals with people being taken away from him.

Mika has a doll at home and decides to give the doll the same condition as Erik's mother and a suitcase ready to go to the hospital. Mika gradually introduces the doll to Erik and tells him about the doll's problems and fears. Gradually Erik begins to talk to the doll and, with Mika's help, is able to play at preparing the doll to go to hospital. In this way, Mika helps Erik to work through his own fears.

1. How does Erik's play illustrate the psychodynamic theory of learning?

2. How effectively do you think Mika supported Erik's play?

3. Outline another activity that Mika could have provided to support Erik's fear of going into hospital.

Other theories of play in early learning

Twelve features of play

Professor Tina Bruce is a current expert in early years education and sees play as vital to a child's development. Her definition of free-flow play has influenced the way children are offered a choice of activities in the early years curriculum. Through this type of play she argues that children are able to develop new skills at the highest level. Bruce feels that play provision should be of a high quality to enable this holistic approach. She believes that children actively incorporate a variety of learning experiences in what she refers to as the 'web of learning', which may include past experiences, relationships with other children and adults.

Bruce identifies 12 features of play to help recognise, monitor and cultivate free-flow play, as follows:

1. Using first-hand experiences
2. Making up rules
3. Making props
4. Choosing to play
5. Rehearsing the future
6. Pretending
7. Playing alone
8. Playing together
9. Having a personal agenda
10. Being deeply involved
11. Trying out recent learning
12. Coordinating ideas, feelings and relationships for the free-flow play

The spiral of learning

Janet Moyles focuses on play for children in the early years, arguing that free play without adults' input needs to be followed by play directed by the adult. Then, once the child has mastered the play, he or she can return to free play using the skills that the adult has helped them to learn. This is called the spiral of learning.

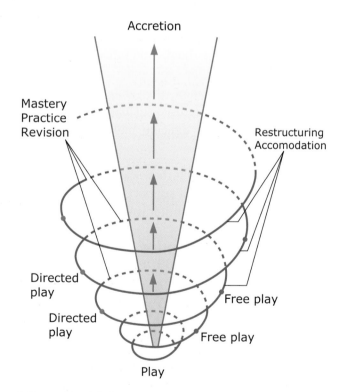

⬆ **Janet Moyle's 'Spiral of Learning'**

Current developments in the understanding of play

The work of the pioneers in children's play has ensured that early years practice continues to develop. Provision for children is currently high profile because policies that have been produced by central government impact on children's services.

Every Child Matters

Every Child Matters is a framework in England designed to ensure quality provision of children and young people's play and learning. It supports children from birth to 19 years and has an impact on all play-based provision. While the importance of the early years is recognised, the current legislation looks beyond traditional age boundaries.

As an adult working with children, you should be familiar with Every Child Matters (see also Unit 1, page 16). Whichever setting you work in, your planning will relate in some way to the five outcomes for children:

→ be healthy
→ stay safe
→ enjoy and achieve through learning
→ make a positive contribution to society
→ achieve economic well-being.

Ofsted inspections are also based around these five outcomes. The table below shows how the five outcomes of Every Child Matters can be used to support an environment where play is central to children's learning.

Find out!

You can find out more about Every Child Matters by visiting the government website www.everychildmatters.gov.uk.

Outcome	How it can be used to support the play environment
Be healthy	• Ensure that the learning environment is healthy. • Physical exercise should be part of any curriculum. • Learning about a healthy lifestyle should be encouraged. • Ensure that the curriculum considers the emotional and social well-being of each child.
Stay safe	• Ensure the setting is safe and that the children and young people are involved in creating a safe environment. • Implement policies and procedures to ensure safe play. • Ensure that the play environment, equipment and resources are regularly checked. • Adults need to have appropriate training.
Enjoy and achieve through learning	• Provide children with a wide range of structured and unstructured play-based activities in any curriculum. • Ensure that children have the freedom to choose when playing. • Provide an environment where children are free to experiment and explore. • Support differing learning styles and abilities.
Make a positive contribution to society	• Ensure children learn about their immediate and wider environment. • Encourage children to make choices and develop decision-making skills. • Help children explore their own culture and identity through play. • Help children explore new concepts. • Support children to gain confidence about their abilities and contributions.
Achieve economic well-being	• Ensure that children's play encourages them to develop into adults who can achieve a positive standard of living. • Ensure a curriculum full of rich learning opportunities to ensure each child reaches his or her full potential. • Ensure parents are supported and involved in their child's learning.

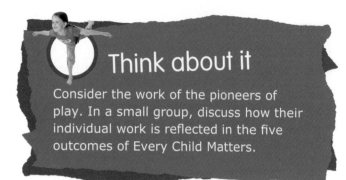

Think about it

Consider the work of the pioneers of play. In a small group, discuss how their individual work is reflected in the five outcomes of Every Child Matters.

The effects of Every Child Matters on curriculum provision

Every Child Matters has had far-reaching impact on curriculum provision for children and young people, as outlined below:

→ It brought about a review of the Children Act 1989, amendments of which can be found in the Children Act 2004.

→ The Children Act 2004 states that a new Early Years Foundation Stage (EYFS) will be mandatory from September 2008 for all providers offering education to children from birth to 5 years. This will absorb the existing Birth to Three Matters framework for children from birth to 3 years and the Foundation Stage curriculum for children aged 3 to 5 years.

→ It has led to the development in 2004 of a 10-year strategy which aims to ensure:
  - greater choice for parents to enable them to create a balance between work and family
  - flexible childcare for families with children up to the age of 14 years
  - quality provision that is professionally-led
  - affordable provision.

→ The Childcare Act 2006 is intended to reform the registration and inspection of childcare provision in England. One of its features is to develop a compulsory childcare register for settings offering provision for children aged 5 years and over. Those offering provision for children aged 8 years plus will be invited to join the register on a voluntary basis.

→ Children's Commissioners have been appointed in England, Scotland and Wales to ensure that children and their families benefit from the government commitment to children's services.

→ In 2005, Children's Trusts were created in each local authority to take on the responsibility of all children's services.

→ It is the role of the Children's Workforce Development Council (CWDC) to ensure that children's services can deliver the 10-year strategy. They are also making an official list of existing qualifications as a guide for people who want to work with children; progression routes will be clearly mapped.

Did you know?

An Early Years Professional Status Qualification (EYP) has been created to ensure that all Children's Centres and day care settings have at least one EYP in their centre with an appropriate degree-level qualification by 2015. There is a lot of debate among early years professionals about this development, which can be followed in periodicals such as *Nursery World*.

International perspectives of play and the impact on practice in a range of settings

To develop your practice you can learn from approaches to children and young people's learning in other countries. For example, it is worth considering that some countries in Europe do not implement formal education until children are 6 or 7 years of age but focus instead on the child's social and emotional development (see also page 283).

Find out!

While you may not be able to visit settings in other countries, you can use the Internet to research organisations that work together to share their practice and expertise. For example, the World Organisation for Early Childhood Education (OMEP) (www.omep-ong.net) promotes research and supports projects in early years education around the world.

Forest Schools

Forest Schools were developed in Denmark for pre-school children under 7 years. They encourage children to learn through play experiences in forests, with songs and stories forming an important part of their learning. Children are encouraged to learn about the outdoor environment through natural activities using adult tools such as hammers and saws, as well as develop social skills. Through encouragement and praise, children are given the confidence to continue their learning. (See also Unit 4, page 188.)

Did you know?

The work of the Forest Schools is influenced by many practitioners and pioneers, such as Froebel, Isaacs and McMillan, who share the belief in the importance of the outdoor environment to children's learning.

Find out!

You can find out more about Forest Schools in the UK by visiting the following website: www.forestschools.com

The Reggio approach

Reggio Emilia is a prosperous region of northern Italy which has become famous for its creative approach to early learning. The Reggio approach started as early as 1945, although it only gained worldwide attention more recently. The approach is founded on the work of the early pioneers of play and places importance on the quality of the experiences that children are given in their early years. It also highlights the importance of the involvement of the community and a democratic spirit. This approach was important to a community who was rebuilding itself after being torn apart by the impact of the Second World War.

Central to the Reggio approach are:

→ low adult to child ratios
→ teachers as learners and reflective practitioners
→ the important role of the environment
→ long-term projects that the children have time to explore and develop as part of curriculum strategy.

Learning is considered to be a journey for each child. Children's memories, thoughts and ideas are recorded in different ways, including:

→ samples of work at different stages
→ photos of work in progress
→ comments by adults working with the children
→ transcripts of children's discussions.

Adults can then begin to understand each child and plan learning experiences which he or she will enjoy and benefit from. A spacious environment is also important and is carefully designed to facilitate the range of creative activities that are available.

The 'Hundred Languages of Children'

Emphasis at Reggio Emilia is placed upon children's many 'symbolic languages'. These languages are made up of visual types of communication such as light and shade, texture, line, shape, colour and form. It is felt that by using these languages for exploration, children will begin to develop their own view of the world that they can share.

Find out!

You can find out more about the Reggio approach via the following website: www.reggioinspired.com

Section 2

How to use appropriate tools to assess the learning needs of individual children

In practice

The team at Sandford After-School Club want to plan an outside 'den' building activity for the 5–11-year-olds in their care. They have lots of their own ideas but agree to gather the views of the children, watch them in their play and consider their different needs and ideas before planning the activity in detail.

By the end of this section you will recognise the importance of assessing children's needs before planning activities and understand the different ways in which this can be done.

Introduction

The importance of understanding children and young people's stages of development

When planning any activities for children and young people it is important to understand their stage of development and how they learn. Assessing their progress is essential if they are to be offered activities that will challenge and extend them. Therefore the way a child is assessed is central to providing appropriate learning opportunities. Before assessing a child or young person's learning needs, the adult has to consider that children are individuals and that children of the same age vary in their development.

Read the child development guide in Unit 2, pages 28–34, to remind yourself of the suggested pattern of development of children and young people.

Think about it

Consider a group of 11-month-old children in the park with their parents. Two children are crawling, one is pulling himself up holding on to his dad's leg and one is making her first steps holding her mum's hands.

→ What advice would you give to the parents whose children are not yet making their first steps?

The chart below shows how you might observe children throughout their stages of development in order to plan activities for them.

Age	Type of play activities that may occur	Methods of observation
Birth to 6 months	• Holding a rattle • Action rhymes • Touching hanging objects • Responding to touch	• Narrative
6–12 months	• Simple games such as 'clap hands' • Treasure basket play • Rolling a ball • Playing with stacking beakers and bricks • Takes things out of containers • Banging saucepans	• Photographic
12–18 months	• Simple let's pretend • Pull-along and push-along toys • Picture books	• Target child • Checklist
18 months–2 years	• Repetitive games such as shape sorting • Screwing and unscrewing • Water play • Paints and crayons • Simple jigsaw puzzles • Action rhymes • Puppets	• Tracking • Narrative • Checklist

Age	Type of play activities that may occur	Methods of observation
2–3 years	• More sustained role play • Physical games • Construction toys • Musical games • Pretending one thing is another such as a yoghurt pot as a cup	• Tracking • Target child • Narrative
3–4 years	• Riding tricycles • Outdoor play • Active pretend play • Floor play with small world toys • Jigsaw puzzles • Model making	• Tracking • Checklist • Target child • Event sample • Time sample
4–7 years	• Acting out puppet shows • Elaborate role play, including role playing emotions • Team games • Craft activities • Fantasy play	• Sociogram • Target child • Checklist • Event sample • Time sample
7–8 years	• Complex cooperative play • Games with rules	• Sociograms • Target child • Checklist • Time sample • Event sample
8–12 years	• Competitive games • Physical exercise • Traditional board games • Craft activities • Construction kits	• Sociograms • Target child • Checklist • Time sample • Event sample

Think about it

Plan the following two activities for a group of 3–5-year-old children in the Early Years Foundation Stage of a nursery.

1. A matching table top game

2. A role-play activity

Look at the appropriate section of the table above and decide what observations may help you plan the activity appropriately.

When preparing a curriculum based on learning through play, it is important to consider the four areas of development of children and young people:

1. Physical development
2. Communication and language development
3. Intellectual development
4. Social, emotional and behavioural development

These will be taken into account whatever the curriculum framework you are planning for.

How to plan for play through observation and evaluation of children's activities

There are a number of different tasks that have to be carried out as a matter of good practice when planning activities for children. All adults working with children and young people should think about observation and assessment of children as an integral part of their practice.

The new Early Year Foundation Stage (EYFS) framework refers to observation and assessment as look, listen and note. This clearly describes your role and can be applied to children or young people of any age:

➔ *Look* – watching what children do in a variety of situations and environments
➔ *Listen* – listening to children; listening to a child's parents; listening to colleagues; listening to other professionals
➔ *Note* – recording observations, ranging from short notes to a more formal recording.

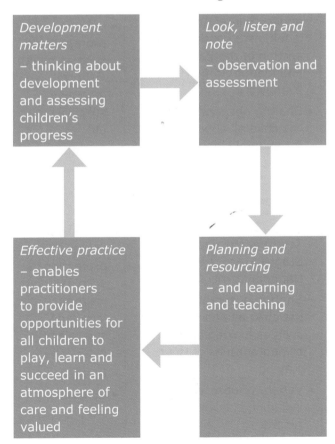

Development matters – thinking about development and assessing children's progress	*Look, listen and note* – observation and assessment
Effective practice – enables practitioners to provide opportunities for all children to play, learn and succeed in an atmosphere of care and feeling valued	*Planning and resourcing* – and learning and teaching

⇧ **The planning cycle as described in the EYFS consultation document, 2006**

Case study

Using observations to improve teatime provision

The Mayfield After-School Club decided to review its teatime provision as the children were noisy and behaviour often had to be challenged. Over a week the team decided to observe different aspects of the provision and divided an observation sheet into the following sections for note-taking: peer interaction; adult-child interaction; environment; serving of food. The team could add their comments to the sheet. The team noticed that the noise level was high, the tables were organised in rows, the food was on the tables as the children came in and the adults poured their drinks.

At a meeting the team decided that the children should sit in smaller groups at round tables in mixed age groups and should be encouraged to pour their own drinks. They also decided that the children could take it in turns to serve the food to each other on their table. It was also noted that rather than standing at the serving hatch, adults could be encouraged to sit with the children and engage them in conversation.

1. How do you think that observing the children enabled the team to review the teatime provision?

2. Which areas of development would the actions aim to improve as a result of the observation?

3. Can you identify other areas the team could have observed during this period?

The use of observations to assess and respond to individuals' learning needs

Planning any curriculum requires that you gather as much information as possible in the form of a variety of observations and assessments. This may take the form of:

➔ watching children
➔ talking to parents, colleagues and other professionals

- → researching children's individual stage of development
- → making formal assessments
- → reviewing the children's developmental records.

From these observations, information for children and young people's learning can be gathered about:

- → their routine needs
- → their play preferences
- → their cultural needs
- → their religious needs
- → material resources
- → human resources
- → the environment.

Settings will have systems in place to observe and assess children, ranging from the use of 'post-it' notes to formal assessment such as profiling.

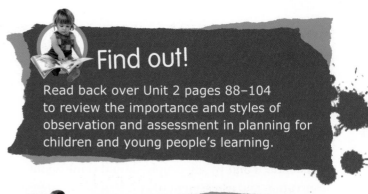

Find out!

Read back over Unit 2 pages 88–104 to review the importance and styles of observation and assessment in planning for children and young people's learning.

Think about it

Look at the table below and consider the different ways of collecting evidence of children's learning to inform your planning.

✍ **Ways of collecting evidence from observations and assessments to inform planning**

Age	Curriculum	Possible settings	Observation/assessment	Adults/ children involved
Birth to 5 years	Early Years Foundation Stage*	• Private home • Childminder's home • Day care setting • State nursery school • Children's centre • Crèche • Nurseries such as Montessori and Steiner • Foundation Stage of a primary school	• Observation of babies and young children using the 'Look, listen and note' section of the Early Years Foundation Stage (EYFS) framework • Sharing observations with the child as appropriate, for example looking at work or photographs of them playing • Foundation Stage Profile	• Practitioners • Other professionals such as health visitors, language specialists, etc. • Parents • Children
6 to 11 years	• Key Stages 1 and 2 of the National Curriculum • Play-based curriculum	• Schools • Before- and after-school clubs • Holiday clubs • Specialist clubs such as sport clubs • Youth clubs	• SATs (Special Attainment Tests) at the end of Key Stages 1 and 2 of the National Curriculum • Sharing observations with the child as appropriate, such as looking at work or photographs of them playing • Variety of observations including checklists and records	• Practitioners • Other professionals such as health visitors, language specialists, etc. • Parents • Children

Age	Curriculum	Possible settings	Observation/assessment	Adults/ children involved
11 to 16 years	• Key Stages 3 and 4 of the National Curriculum • Play-based curriculum	• Schools • Holiday clubs • Specialist clubs such as sport clubs • Youth clubs	• GCSEs (General Certificate in Secondary Education) • Variety of observations including checklists and records	• Practitioners • Other professionals such as health visitors, language specialists, etc. • Parents • Children and young people

(*The Birth to Three Matters and Foundation Stage curricula will continue until September 2008 when settings inspected by Ofsted will be expected to follow the Early Years Foundation Stage (EYFS) curriculum.)

In the Early Years Foundation Stage curriculum, guidance, observations and assessment are recognised as important under the heading 'Looking, listening and noting', as described on page 293. These are considered central because they help practitioners to:

→ 'get to know a child better and develop positive relationships with children and their parents
→ plan appropriate play and learning experiences based on the children's interests and needs, and identify any concerns about a child's development
→ further develop your understanding of a child's development
→ develop a systematic and routine approach to using observations
→ use assessment to plan the next steps in a child's developmental progress and regularly review this approach.'

(*Source*: Early Years Foundation Stage Practice Guidance, © Crown copyright 2007, page 11.)

Observation plays a valuable part in assessing children's learning and their needs. Not all observations are planned and spontaneous – they are often written in note form and added to the child's records as an individual piece of evidence or added to their profile. Any adult's observations of play will help to assess each child's progress.

Involving children in observations or assessments

Involving children in their observations or assessments can make them feel valued and generate a sense of belonging. If appropriate, it is a good way of encouraging children to think about their future learning or evaluate their environment. It can also help practitioners to find out more about the child's thinking and reasoning. Sharing observations with children and young people can be useful to discover more about an area observed. Photographs and samples of their work can stimulate discussion that might add value to the observation or assessment.

Observations can also be used to plan the environment for children and young people. These can be carried out by adults and take into account the views of children or young people.

Individual Learning Plans (ILPs) based on observations

Individual Learning Plans (ILPs) should be part of developing a profile for children.

An Individual Learning Plan is a way of tailoring the curriculum to meet a child's specific needs.

This is important because within any large group of children there will be a range of needs, strengths and interests. ILPs are therefore useful to ensure that each child's learning is catered for. As with other areas of planning, there is not a standard format for an ILP, although an example is given below.

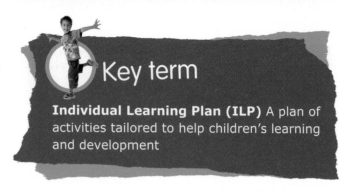

Key term

Individual Learning Plan (ILP) A plan of activities tailored to help children's learning and development

☟ **An Individual Learning Plan. These will vary according to each setting**

Name:	Liam
Age:	2 years/10 months
Key worker:	Joe

Observations/notes:

Liam has been in the setting for two weeks. He has made a close relationship with Joe but finds it difficult to leave his mum if Joe is not on duty. Joe has noticed that Liam likes to watch the other children and enjoys playing silently at the water tray and with the building blocks. At lunch time he likes to sit with Joe and is reluctant to socialise with the other children. His mum says that he enjoys eating snacks in the garden with his two friends when they come to play. The next day Joe encourages Liam to share his snack time with one of the other children. Joe initially joins in but then withdraws and notices that Liam chats happily with his friend for a few minutes before going to play with the building blocks together.

Next steps:

Activities/ experiences:	• Ensure that Liam begins to feel confident with other staff in the room and that they are aware of his settling-in routine. • Encourage Liam to socialise with other children through snack times, water play and building blocks. • Add different materials/equipment such as colouring, rubber insects, pebbles, different containers to the water tray to encourage Liam to explore, experiment and use language to increase his vocabulary. Encourage Liam to talk about his play.
Adult's role:	• Make other staff aware of Liam's needs. • Initiate Liam's communication through snacks and activities with other children and then withdraw as appropriate. • Introduce Liam to new experiences in water tray and encourage vocabulary and conversation. • Continue to observe Liam.
Resources:	New items for the water tray

Links with EYFS:

Personal, Social and Emotional Development	*Making relationships:* Learn social skills and enjoy being with and talking to adults and other children
Communication, Language and Literacy	*Language for communication:* Learn new words very rapidly and can use them in communicating about matters that interest them
Knowledge and Understanding of the World	*Exploration and investigation:* Describe and talk about what they see Communities: Begin to have their own friends

Case study

Turning the youth club sitting room into a chill-out zone

Mike held a regular meeting for the young people's committee of the Pound Lane Youth Club. He noticed that the young people were not using the sitting area for any length of time. When he discussed this with the young people's committee, they agreed with his observation but advised that he should gather the views of all the members before making any plans. They decided to put pictures of a dustbin and a heart on the wall. On the dustbin members could write things they didn't like about the sitting area, and on the heart they could write down what they wanted to improve. A week later the group discussed the views and observations of the members and as a result planned to turn the sitting area into a chill-out zone with subdued lighting, cushions and a sound system.

1. Do you think that Mike should have shared his observation with the committee?

2. What did you think about the 'dustbin' and 'heart' idea for the young people to share their observations?

3. What do you think the positive effects will be of the way Mike considered the views of the club members?

Individual Learning Plans should be written using children's profiles which in turn are based upon observations. ILPs provide suggestions for activities, equipment and support that will benefit the individual child. The idea is that children's progress is noted down and at the same time working goals linked to the curriculum are recorded. The best person to create an ILP is the key person with whom the child has the most contact and who has also observed the child. The child's key person will also be working in partnership with parents and thus be able to base the plans using their help. The key person can then use knowledge of the child to consider what the child enjoys doing and the best type of learning situations for the child.

How to access and use information from other services and professionals to assess learning needs

It is essential that a setting works closely with other professionals and services to ensure that each child or young person has the best possible opportunities in their learning. The spider diagram below shows professionals who might be involved in the assessment of a child or young person's learning needs.

The SENCO (Special Educational Needs Coordinator) in any setting will be responsible for accessing information about children's particular needs as part of his/her role. They will then share this information as appropriate with colleagues and parents. Parents may also have accessed appropriate information about their child's need and should be encouraged to share this with the setting.

Did you know?

CAF (Common Assessment Framework) is the term used for the new government framework that supports children and young people who have a low level of additional needs. It is in place to help professionals from relevant agencies to work together to assess the child or young person and therefore support their development and learning appropriately. Data from the CAF may be used to create an IEP.

Different learning styles and awareness of how to differentiate activities

Learning styles

In order to learn everyone has to process information. There are different ways in which this can be done and extensive research has been carried out to identify styles of learning. Even if a learning style can be identified, these will be used differently by each individual child or young person. Sometimes children display a mixture of learning styles or move from one to another. For example, a child may enjoy listening to stories while also enjoying books that have tactile parts to them.

You will be able to provide challenging activities that support and extend children if you find out about their learning style(s) and consider them in your planning. Observation and assessment will be an important way of discovering how children learn.

Think about it

In pairs, discuss your learning styles.

→ Do you have one leaning style or a combination of styles?

→ Is your learning style supported in your current course?

⇩ **Different learning styles**

Visual (sight)	• Watches people speak as well as listening to them
	• Looks for shapes and forms in both words and numbers
	• Enjoys pictures in books
	• Enjoys visual descriptions
Auditory (sound)	• Listens and talks – listeners retain and recall the spoken word; talkers have to hear a voice to process information
	• Prefers the spoken word
	• Enjoys different voices
	• Enjoys involved explanations
	• Enjoys communicating with others and themselves
	• Hears themselves speak the word when reading
Kinaesthetic (movement)	• Needs to sense relative position and movement
	• Likes to examine, touch and feel in order to learn
Sequential	• Needs to learn and remember things in order
	• Often organised in their learning
Holistic	• A combination of all styles

While children and young people learn in different ways, an active approach to learning ensures that all children can be given time to experiment, explore and make decisions. As with adults, children need to consolidate what they have learned and will then have the confidence to use the skills they have developed in other contexts.

Differentiation of activities

A curriculum that differentiates considers the needs of each child and ensures that leaning opportunities are provided to maximise each child's learning. Such a curriculum will account for children and young people's different styles of learning and give them time to engage in learning.

Differentiation takes place for a variety of reasons, as outlined below.

→ Children may have special learning or health needs, and may also have an **Individual Education Plan (IEP)** (see also Unit 14, page 509). For example, a young person on the autistic spectrum may require individual support.
→ Children with English as an additional language may need specific support, such as explanations with pictures or dual language as appropriate.
→ Children may be considered advanced in their learning and may need to be given extended opportunities.
→ Children may be at different stages of development. This may be because of a wide age range, for example an after-school club with children aged 11–16 years, or because children are naturally at different stages within a similar age range.
→ Children may have transient needs, for example a child may need additional support because his or her parents have recently separated or because he or she has broken an arm.

Early years practitioners have to consider a variety of issues when planning a differentiated curriculum. Adults providing a balanced curriculum for any age of child should consider:

→ the stages of learning that children and young people pass through
→ that activities are age and stage appropriate
→ the individual needs of children
→ adaptation of activities as appropriate
→ whether additional support is required and how to ensure its provision
→ differentiation in the planning process
→ that everyone involved in the planning process is aware of the needs of each child
→ how to work with parents to support the child
→ how to work with colleagues and other professionals as appropriate.

Consider the following example from a focus activity plan for a dough activity for a group of 3–5-year-olds. The aim of the activity is to make dough breads and pastries for a role-play baker's shop using cutters, rolling pins and different coloured paint. Differentiation of the activity includes:

→ Child X allergic to food colouring.
→ Child C has arm in plaster and may need support.
→ Some children may want to decorate with finer detail so provide appropriate brushes and tools.

Think about it

Consider an activity that you have recently been involved in planning. How could it have been adapted for a child with English as an additional language?

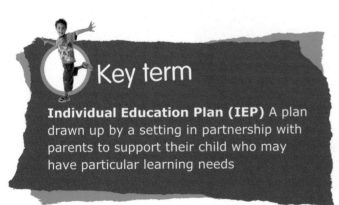

Key term

Individual Education Plan (IEP) A plan drawn up by a setting in partnership with parents to support their child who may have particular learning needs

Getting ready for assessment

Go to Unit 14 and find out which professionals may support practitioners when they are planning to meet the individual needs of children.

How to plan and provide learning opportunities in consultation with others

In practice

The team at Craycross Children's Centre were planning the curriculum for the next six months. They started the meeting by discussing observations they had made on children's participation in activities. Then they held a group brainstorming session before creating a plan. They considered the fact that it was Diwali during this period and that many of the children would be celebrating the festival with their families. They also asked Craig, the SENCO, to talk about the progress of children with an IEP. During the meeting they reviewed the effectiveness of recent planning in relation to the EYFS documentation.

By the end of this section you will understand why it is important to spend time planning the curriculum and to take into consideration the individual needs of each child.

Understanding of curriculum frameworks in own country and how these influence the provision of learning opportunities

The role of the early years practitioner is to ensure that all children are provided with a rich and varied **curriculum** with learning opportunities that will enable them to explore and gain understanding of the world around them. This section will consider the way in which a curriculum is planned and implemented.

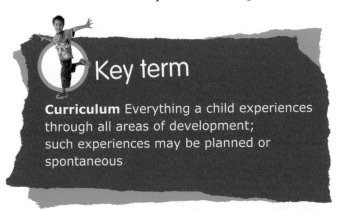

Key term

Curriculum Everything a child experiences through all areas of development; such experiences may be planned or spontaneous

What makes a good curriculum?

An effective curriculum will have a clear balance of activities that promote active learning. The spider diagram below describes what a good curriculum should contain in order to provide a range of activities that will encourage children to achieve from their learning and have fun in the process.

Curriculum provision in the UK

In all countries of the UK, the provision of quality learning experiences for children and young people is based around the Every Child Matters framework (see page 16), an initiative which aims to ensure that children receive the help and support they need in order to achieve their potential. Within the frameworks of all countries in the UK there is an increased understanding of the importance of early years provision and services for children during out-of-school hours. While England, Scotland, Wales and Northern Ireland have different curriculum requirements, learning through play is a common focus.

Curriculum provision in England

In England, at the time of writing, a change is underway to create one curriculum for children from birth to Year 1 onwards from the existing Birth to Three Matters framework and the Foundation Stage curriculum. By September 2008, all early years settings will be expected to implement the new Early Years Foundation Stage (EYFS) curriculum.

From 5 years onwards children are taught the National Curriculum in school settings.

In after-school clubs and holiday schemes the curriculum is very much based on different areas of play.

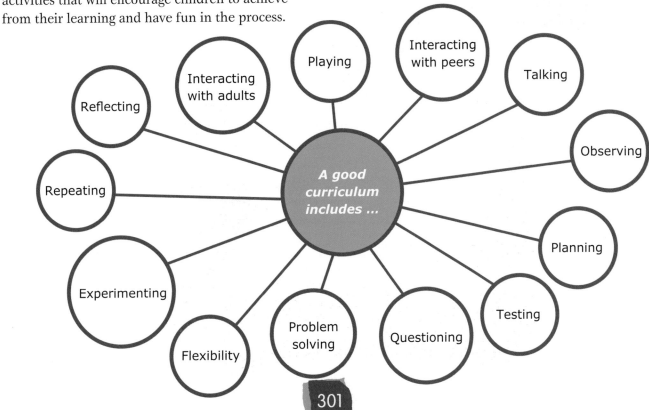

The Early Years Foundation Stage curriculum

The six areas of learning and development of the EYFS curriculum are:

→ Personal, social and emotional development
→ Communication, language and literacy
→ Problem solving, reasoning and numeracy
→ Knowledge and understanding of the world
→ Physical development
→ Creative development

Each area of learning is linked to the five outcomes of the Every Child Matters framework (see page 16) and key early learning goals (a statement of what most children should achieve in each area of learning by the end of the EYFS). The development stages outlined are broad and are intended to show the different ways children need to achieve the early learning goals. The framework is intended to be holistic and centred upon the needs of the child, to enable children to progress through the areas of learning and development.

Find out!

Obtain a copy of the Early Years Foundation Stage document and find out how the children's developmental stages are presented. (You can order a copy by telephoning 0845 602 2260 (ref. 00013-2007BKT-EN) or download it from www.standards.dfes.gov.uk/eyfs)

The Early Years Foundation Stage can take place in a variety of settings including:

→ children's centres
→ day nurseries
→ reception classes
→ day care settings
→ pre-schools
→ accredited childminders
→ approved childminding networks.

How children are assessed in the Early Years Foundation Stage is referred to in the next section of this unit.

The National Curriculum

Children in England follow the National Curriculum while at school (from 5–16 years). Children may also be following the curriculum while in hospital, where a team of specialist teachers support children and young people's continued learning.

Key Stage 1 (5–7 years, Years 1 and 2) and Key Stage 2 (7–11 years, Years 3 to 6) are defined by eleven subject areas, the first three of which are 'core subjects' (the remainder are 'non-core foundation subjects'):

→ English
→ Mathematics
→ Science
→ Design and technology
→ Information and communication technology
→ History
→ Geography
→ Art and design
→ Music
→ Physical education
→ Religious education

Did you know?

Great importance is placed upon the move from a play-based early years curriculum to more formal learning at Key Stage 1. This is called transition and during this time there remains an emphasis on learning through play.

Non-statutory provision

Children between 5 and 16 years of age can attend a variety of settings, including children's centres, out-of-school clubs, holiday play schemes, integrated extended schools activities, specialist clubs and youth clubs. The curriculum in some of these settings is based on different areas of play, usually defined as:

→ physical play
→ social play
→ creative play
→ imaginative play.

Activities in this type of provision are based around the children's preferences, so children are often involved in the planning and choice of activities. The emphasis in on the child's right to play in an environment that offers child-directed, freely chosen play opportunities.

Out-of-school care, such as holiday and after-school clubs, are inspected by Ofsted.

Curriculum provision in Wales

The Welsh Assembly has a ten-year strategy called 'The Learning Country'. A framework for children's learning includes a foundation stage for children and play is central to the early years curriculum. There is some funding for nursery provision and out-of-school activities. Children in school follow Key Stages but Welsh language is included, as the language of instruction can be Welsh or English.

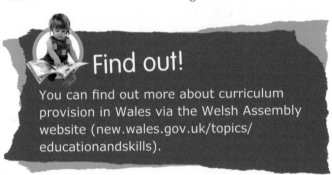

Find out!

You can find out more about curriculum provision in Wales via the Welsh Assembly website (new.wales.gov.uk/topics/educationandskills).

Curriculum provision in Scotland

In Scotland, the current curriculum brings the guidelines for children from 3 to 14 years together to ensure a smooth transition in children's learning. The emphasis is on purposeful and well-planned play, focusing on the importance of observation, equality of opportunity and supporting transition, home and family. Children up to 3 years are cared for in a variety of settings and learning through play is encouraged.

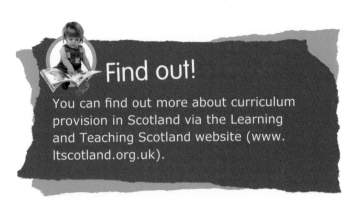

Find out!

You can find out more about curriculum provision in Scotland via the Learning and Teaching Scotland website (www.ltscotland.org.uk).

Curriculum provision in Northern Ireland

Education in Northern Ireland is complex as it had been devolved to the Northern Ireland Assembly but owing to political developments the Assembly had been suspended and reforms to the structure of the curriculum postponed. At the time of writing there is now devolved government in place and it is likely that changes to the curriculum will follow. If you work in Northern Ireland it will be important for you to keep track of what is happening.

The curriculum is the responsibility of the Northern Ireland Council for the Curriculum, Examinations and Assessment. For information about early years, it is worth contacting the Northern Ireland Pre-school Play Association (NIPPA), although at the time of writing there is not a specific framework for use in nurseries and pre-schools.

There are four key stages in the education system:

→ Key Stage 1: 4–8 years
→ Key Stage 2: 8–11 years
→ Key Stage 3: 11–14 years
→ Key Stage 4: 14–16 years

Inspectorates

Each country of the UK has a government department that is responsible for ensuring that curriculum provision for children meets the required standards, as the table below shows.

Country	Inspectorate	Website
England	Ofsted (Office for Standards in Education)	www.ofsted.gov.uk
Wales	Estyn	www.estyn.gov.uk
Scotland	HMIe (Her Majesty's Inspectorate of Education)	www.hmie.gov.uk
Northern Ireland	Department of Education	www.deni.gov.uk

Ofsted

Ofsted bases inspection upon the five outcomes of the Every Child Matters framework. Inspectors visit each setting and look carefully at the curriculum that is offered. It is accepted that curricula will vary (see page 163) are expected to be followed. Inspectors will want to see evidence that the registered person ensures that their team are familiar with the relevant curriculum and the Ofsted requirements. Settings are required to self-evaluate their provision and provide development plans that show evidence of team work and a shared understanding of best practice.

Settings offering an alternative curriculum

The following three settings are inspected by Ofsted and must show that they are able to meet National Standard requirements.

Montessori

There are a growing number of nurseries and schools based on Montessori philosophy. The curriculum is based on structured rather than imaginative play. Learning outcomes are met through a variety of practical life activities, such as sweeping and pouring, and activities with materials that are natural and used in sequence. A calm environment is encouraged. The manager of the setting will usually have a Montessori qualification and a clear understanding of the principles of Montessori. The team will be encouraged to support children's play and never to correct the child, thereby encouraging confident and independent thinking.

Highscope

This programme was designed in the United States in the 1960s. It has been adopted and adapted by a number of settings in the UK, incorporating the principles of Highscope into a more traditional curriculum. The environment is highly organised and adults are trained to encourage children to plan, do and review their own activities in a curriculum based upon play. Adults work with small groups of children to ensure the effectiveness of this curriculum.

Steiner

Steiner nurseries and schools are often part of a community that follows the principles of Rudolf Steiner. Steiner believed in a curriculum that fostered respect between adults and children. Children's temperaments are at the centre of the curriculum and children with special needs are integrated into the setting. The arts and sciences are balanced in children's activities, which are known as the Waldorf System. It is essential that the atmosphere is positive and that children have a healthy lifestyle, often helping to grow their own produce.

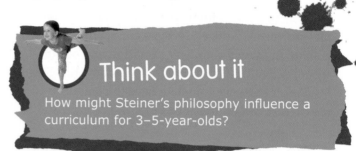

Think about it

How might Steiner's philosophy influence a curriculum for 3–5-year-olds?

How curriculum frameworks influence early years provision

Providing an appropriate environment

All children should be given access to an environment that encourages exploration and experimentation. Children need space in which to play and an environment that is safe. However, they also need to be able to take some ownership of their environment.

(The role of the adult in ensuring children's safety in the play environment is described in Unit 4, pages 192–5. You will need to read over this section to complete your learning for this unit.)

There are a number of ways that the environment can enhance the curriculum. The spider diagram in the next page describes the areas that should be a permanent feature in any environment and form a base to any curriculum planning.

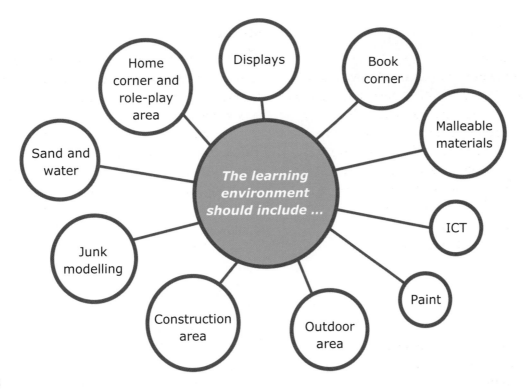

The learning environment should include ...

- Displays
- Home corner and role-play area
- Book corner
- Malleable materials
- Sand and water
- ICT
- Junk modelling
- Paint
- Construction area
- Outdoor area

Displays

Displays can be varied, involving children's work, posters and information for children or parents.

When displaying children's work the role of the adult is to enhance children's work and to ensure that it is respected. Sometimes early years practitioners make the mistake of talking about 'their' display and the results are often elaborate with borders and mounting making the work displayed secondary!

If you are nervous about displaying work it is often better to mount a simple display that engages the interest of both children and adults. By asking questions or by encouraging the recall of an event, children can be drawn to a display. The checklist below is useful for considering displays with children of any age.

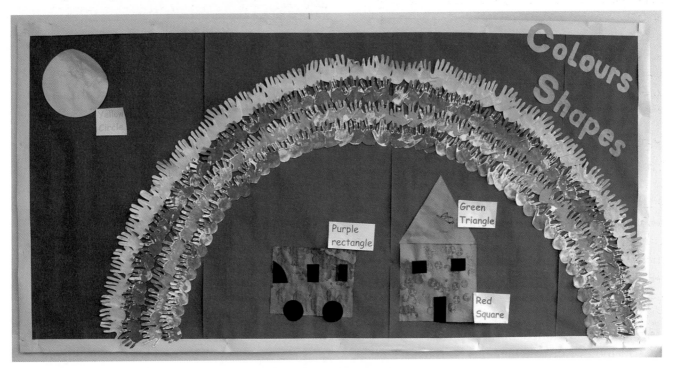

⇧ **It is important to involve children in displays as much as possible. Here, many children have made and then cut out hand prints to form a rainbow**

Good practice checklist

Displaying children's work

✓ If using children's artwork ensure that it is their own, however abstract the result.

✓ Display all work.

✓ Label clearly. If you write a description ensure that it is in the child's own words, e.g. 'This is me on the beach with my brothers.'

✓ Try to ensure that displays are interactive by adding items that children can remove and explore or by inviting them to look at things in the display. This can be done by printed comments such as 'How many different animals can you see in the paintings?'

✓ Use different print to encourage children to get used to different styles of print they will experience in their everyday environment. It also stimulates discussion.

✓ Ensure that displays are at the height of the children they are designed for so that they can gain full benefit from them.

✓ Involve children in displays as much as possible.

✓ Change displays regularly to maintain interest and relate to the curriculum.

✓ Consider giving interest to displays through the use of 3D, interest tables and hanging displays.

✓ Consider using photographic instructive displays such as photographic step-by-step instructions of handwashing or snack time.

Some further ideas for displays are:

➜ Consider each child having their own small display board on which they could put their own work or have displays that are moveable.

➜ Babies might enjoy a mat rolled out with different textures displayed that could be put away when they have finished with it.

➜ Older children might have a display board on which they can send kind messages to each other, for example 'Jo was kind and helped to clear the sand from the floor today.'

➜ Adults might have a display board for parents that shows photographs of activities that happened during the day.

You can read more about displays and interest tables in Unit 4, pages 198–9.

Book corner

Books are an important permanent fixture in any environment for children. Books should be accessible, stimulating and in good condition. Children of any age will need a quiet area that is comfortable with cushions and bean bags so they can sit comfortably and explore books alone or with other children and adults. A listening area with audio stories and headphones can enrich a book corner, enabling the children to access books in another way.

It is essential to provide a variety of fiction and non-fiction titles reflecting the diversity of society and children's varied interests and experiences. Children under 1 year can be provided with book baskets so they can access their own books safely; older children may help to choose and plan their own book corner. You can also provide homemade books illustrated with children's artworks or photographs of experiences the children have had.

Think about it

Consider how you could make a book with a group of 3–4-year-old children who had been on a local train journey to the river. To help you plan this activity you may find it useful to review this age group's stage of language development in Unit 2, page 45.

Home corner and role-play area

Children make sense of the world around them through role play. A home corner should reflect the children's homes so they can explore their own world and a variety of cultures. It is therefore important to consider the different ways that people live and to ask families for help and advice in providing the correct play materials. Suppliers will have a wide range of multi-cultural home corner resources and families may also be able to lend you some authentic resources.

The home corner and role-play area may change to reflect topics being explored or an activity that reflects the interests of the children. Such themes could be a garage, a travel agent or a shop, for example. If children are provided with a variety of equipment they will be able to explore these themes, extend their language, learn to cooperate, develop their physical skills and gain confidence. Sometimes adults may play alongside children in the role-play area to demonstrate vocabulary that can be used or take a role that the child invites them to play, such as a customer in a shop!

Case study

Providing a Chinese home corner

The team at Headstart Nursery were planning to celebrate Chinese New Year in a variety of ways in their setting. As part of this celebration they decided to create a Chinese restaurant in the role-play area. The practitioners only knew about China from books they had read and from visiting the local Chinese restaurant. It was decided they would ask Mrs Chung, Josie's grandmother, to advise them as to how they could make the restaurant more authentic. Mrs Chung, who had spent much of her life in Beijing, was delighted and told them about the many sorts of Chinese food from different areas of China. Mrs Chung offered to show the children how to make dim sum dumplings and offered advice as to how the restaurant could look authentic. She also lent the nursery some lanterns and mandarin jackets for the children to wear.

1. How did the team try to ensure that the role-play Chinese restaurant gave children a real taste of Chinese culture?
2. How do you think that Mrs Chung's input will enhance the children's play?
3. Which areas of the learning from the Early Years Foundation Stage curriculum will the children be able to explore?
4. How could the practitioners enhance and extend children's learning in the role-play area?
5. How could children aged 12 to 14 years in a play scheme benefit from Mrs Chung's cooking activity?

Sand and water

Water should be available all the time for children to play with in early years settings, both inside and outside. Water is something that all children are familiar with as part of their everyday lives and you can stimulate learning by providing activities and experiences that are appropriate for the age group of children you are working with. Water can also be provided in appropriate trays, bowls or added to other play activities.

Like water, sand can be enjoyed on its own as a sensory experience. Think of the times that you have sat on a beach and enjoyed the sand slipping through your fingers. Practitioners can develop this fascination by adding a variety of resources to sand that will encourage exploration and language. For example, sand can be presented in child-level trays or pits in the ground and can be added to small world play.

Sand and water can also be used together, enabling children to explore the change of state that occurs when they are combined. As with other areas of the environment, it is good practice to vary sand and water activities while also allowing for repetition if it is observed that children enjoy a particular experience.

U7
3

Did you know?

Ofsted inspectors will expect to see sand and water provided for children throughout the session in all early years settings, both indoors and outdoors.

Malleable materials

Dough, clay and cornflour 'gloop' are among the malleable materials that children should have access to. A variety of tools and resources can be provided to encourage children to investigate the material. Sometimes children will work towards an end product but often it is the process of manipulating the material that promotes development.

Children can learn from using clay whatever their age. Consider the spider diagram on page 308 which shows how a 4-year-old might meet some of the EYFS leaning goals for Knowledge and Understanding of the World through the use of clay.

Investigate objects and materials using all their senses as appropriate.

Children will do this by activities such as touching, rolling, cutting and making patterns in the clay.

Find out about and identify features of objects they observe.

Children can be encouraged to see what happens when they do things such as manipulate the clay, add water or try to recreate something they have observed such as a rabbit or person.

How a 4-year-old can work towards EYFS learning goals for Knowledge and Understanding of the World through the use of clay

Look closely at similarities, differences, patterns and change.

Children can see what happens when they make patterns in the clay with a tool or see what occurs when the clay is fired or baked.

Ask questions about how things happen and why they work.

Children can be encouraged to ask why, what and how questions about the clay, consider what they are making and where it comes from.

Select the tools and techniques they need to shape, assemble and join the materials they are working with.

Children can be given a variety of tools such as rolling pins and sieves to enable them to make different things. They can also use materials such as water to join parts of their designs.

Begin to know about own culture and beliefs and those of other people.

Children may be encouraged to make items that reflect other cultures such as eating vessels or animals. These can be discussed and researched before making.

Paint

Free painting is an important part of any learning environment for children. This can take the form of an easel or table-top activity. It can also take place indoors or outdoors. Children can use ready mixed paint or powder paint that can be mixed with water or other media such as PVA glue, to give a shinier finish. They can choose from available and varied paper and adults can change the paper as required. Brushes and paint pots should be non-spill to enable the children to focus on their painting. Children can also be encouraged to mix their own colours if using powder paint. If aprons, a bowl for washing hands and a drying frame are placed near the activity, the child can be truly independent, as appropriate, for self-expression.

Junk modelling

This activity is not always available daily in settings. However, it is a great way to use recycled materials and for children to work with materials they are familiar with, such as empty tissue boxes, kitchen roles or yoghurt pots. A varied range of materials should be provided and attractively presented so that children can make clear choices. Glue, sticky tape, scissors and, if age appropriate, staplers should be provided. This activity can be a good way of involving parents and the local community by asking them for resources such as paper off-cuts, empty containers, buttons, ribbons, scraps of material, etc. There are also a number of scrap stores available throughout the UK. Adults can visit these stores and collect a huge variety of recycled materials for a reasonable fee.

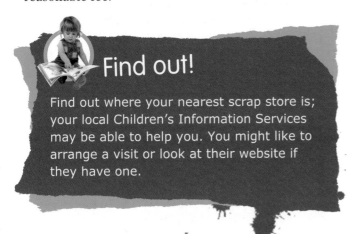

Find out!

Find out where your nearest scrap store is; your local Children's Information Services may be able to help you. You might like to arrange a visit or look at their website if they have one.

Through junk modelling, children can gain independence, develop physical skills, work in three-dimensional shapes, create their own designs, develop language, feel proud of their achievements and enjoy working with other children. If possible this is also an activity that children can revisit if the setting has space to store ongoing creations!

Construction area

Children can progress in all areas of their development when constructing. There is a huge variety of construction toys available that involve children fitting parts together to make a model, for example bricks, trains, puzzles, etc. Large and small equipment should be available both indoors and outdoors. The resources provided should take into account the varying manipulative stages of development of the children in the setting.

Children need space to construct, for example to lie down or construct a high tower that might fall down. Pictorial instructions can be provided to encourage children who are not yet able to read to create a wider range of models. If large wooden bricks are provided for 'block play' they could be placed in a small shed in the garden that is accessible to the children, encouraging their independence.

⇧ **Construction toys can be used to extend and develop children's schemas**

Think about it

Froebel developed block play with wooden blocks to encourage children to develop their schemas (see also page 280). Wooden sets of hollow blocks, often referred to as 'block play', are now an essential part of the early years curriculum.

Read Unit 2 pages 66–7 to remind yourself about schemas. Then, in small groups, discuss how the children could use wooden blocks to extend and develop their schemas.

ICT

Information and communication technology (ICT) now plays an important part in any learning environment for children. Programmable resources, interactive whiteboards, digital cameras and computers are used in a wide range of settings.

A computer should be a static part of every learning environment. One computer can be placed on an appropriate trolley or flat screens can be placed on a long shelf to encourage the children to interact or take part in an adult-led activity. Children can explore a variety of programmes with support. They can also learn to take turns by writing their name or mark on a whiteboard and can work together on the computer. Children can also take photographs and watch them on the computer in the form of a slideshow. Additions such as microscopes that link to a computer can enhance children's learning in many ways.

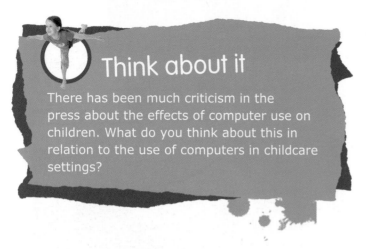

The outdoor environment

It has already been emphasised in this unit that most activities can take place outdoors as well as indoors. An ideal environment will allow children to move freely between the indoors and outdoors. This is not always possible but the outdoors should always add value to children's learning experiences. When planning an outdoor area, the focus should always be on the child. As children develop they can help to plan and develop the outdoor environment.

An outdoor area can include the following:

→ an area to ride bikes and trucks
→ a wooden construction to climb and explore
→ an area to sow and grow plants
→ a mud patch to dig
→ a quiet area with benches or seats and scented plants
→ sand and water play
→ a story circle made of logs for the children to use
→ natural tunnels and shelters made from wood or plants such as willow
→ long grass with wild flowers for children to run through
→ musical areas with chimes, etc.
→ animals
→ role-play areas
→ logs to climb on
→ child-sized sheds to take equipment out of
→ shaded areas for sunny weather
→ a painting area
→ mirrors
→ plants to attract birds and insects
→ a bird table.

The effectiveness of different approaches to planning

Any curriculum will have a number of different plans; these should allow for both structured and unstructured activities. The most effective planning will ensure that children's needs are met and that activities are appropriate to their stage of development. It should always be remembered that each child is unique and that their individual needs and interests should be at the centre of any planning process. Before any planning takes place, early years practitioners need to find out as much as they can about the children they are planning activities for.

Good practice checklist

Gathering information on children in order to inform the planning process

✓ Observe children.
✓ Spend time talking to and getting to know the children.
✓ Get to know the parents.
✓ Talk to other adults.
✓ Consider the diversity of the children, their families and the local community.
✓ Ensure you understand the expected stage of development of the children you are planning for.
✓ Review any relevant records on the children.
✓ Find out about the children's play preferences.
✓ Consider the children's routines.
✓ Consider children and their families' cultural and religious backgrounds.
✓ Take into account the environment you work in.
✓ Take into account the activities you are planning for.
✓ Take into account the resources you have, including other adults.
✓ Ensure that all adults are familiar with the curriculum framework relevant to the age group of the children.

Case study

Planning for Charlton School Reception Class

Jean, Kim and Faran were using an inset day to plan for the new September Reception class. Before they started to make any long-term curriculum plans they gathered as much information as they could about the children they were planning for. They had previously held a coffee morning for the children's families and had discovered that two of the children and their families moved to the neighbourhood from eastern Europe six months ago. English was an additional language for the children and their families. Another parent had chatted to one of the team about her interest in gardening and had said that she would be happy to help in the class. It was also noted that one child had recently suffered bereavement when her mother died.

1. How will the information Jean, Kim and Faran have gathered influence their planning?

2. As a result of the information gathered about the children with English as an additional language, do you think they will have to gather any more information before planning the curriculum?

3. What will the team have to consider for the child who has suffered a recent bereavement when planning the curriculum?

4. How could the parent who is interested in gardening be considered when planning the curriculum?

Observation has been discussed earlier as an important part of quality provision (see Unit 2 pages 89–90 and this unit page 293). It is important to remember that it is also part of the planning cycle (see page 293).

However formal the curriculum, all children need to play and therefore experience active learning. Whatever curriculum is being planned for, the five areas of play – creative, physical, imaginative, manipulative, social – should be integrated into curriculum planning.

Types of planning

A plan should be thought of as a framework that supports the learning opportunities provided by the setting. There are no formats for plans besides the principles of good planning already discussed, but different types of plan should allow for spontaneous learning and flexibility. Routines such as mealtimes should also be considered when planning.

Before considering how to plan activities it is important to consider the different sorts of planning, as outlined in the table page 312. The plans detailed are usually in the following stages:

1. Long-term plans
2. Medium-term plans; IEPs to be considered
3. Weekly/daily planners; IEPs to be integrated
4. Detailed/activity plans; IEPs to be integrated or planned separately as appropriate

⬇ Different types of planning

Plan	Timescale	Components
1. Long-term plan In schools these are referred to as schemes of work or a syllabus	Varies with each setting but may be a period of 3 months, 6 months or a year.	• An overview of the curriculum • Based on principles of good curriculum planning • Considers needs of children and how these will be met • Considers all areas of learning • Relates to School Improvement Plan (SIP) or Development Plan as required by OFSTED • Relates to policies and procedures of setting • Ensures advanced planning to consider specific activities such as celebrations • Ensures resources are available and used effectively • Meets the five outcomes of Every Child Matters
2. Medium-term plan Also known as curriculum plans or outline plans	Daily, weekly or monthly	• Based on observations of children • Considers relevant assessment such as Foundation Stage Profiles • May focus on an area of the long-term plan that may include a theme such as 'People who help us' • Considers differentiation • Should allow for spontaneous learning and flexibility • Will consider routines such as mealtimes as learning activities
3. Weekly/daily planners	Daily or each week	• States activities and experiences that are happening daily • May support curriculum plans • May support Individual Educational Plans • May show considered learning outcomes • Considers differentiation • Should allow for spontaneous learning and flexibility • Will consider routines such as mealtimes as learning activities
4. Detailed plan Also known as a short-term plan or an activity plan	Specific time the activity is planned to take. This may be as little as 20 minutes for a bubble painting activity or over a number of days, for example a planting and growing activity	• Gives details of how activity is to be carried out • Considers intended learning outcomes • Considers adult involvement • Describes resources • Considers differentiation • Allows for spontaneous learning and flexibility • Will consider routines such as mealtimes as learning activities
Individual Educational Plan (IEP)	Weekly, monthly	• Often the SENCO has responsibility for ensuring effective IEPs are created • Considers child's individual learning needs • Identifies intended learning outcomes

(Individual Education Plans are covered in more depth in Unit 14, pages 521–3.)

Creating plans

There are different ways of planning learning opportunities, as the spider diagram shows.

Ways of planning learning opportunities

- Structured activities
- Unstructured activities
- Adult-directed activities
- Adult-initiated activities
- Child-initiated activities
- Involving children
- Flexibility
- Anti-bias view
- Health and safety

Structured activities

These are activities that need adult guidance, such as making some sandwiches, finding out what happens if you add dye to the water of a cut flower, or showing children how to play a new game. The activity still has to be child-centred and meet the children's needs.

Unstructured activities

This type of activity is when children are able to choose materials and create their own play. It is often seen in the home corner or role-play area. Children can develop many skills in this type of activity such as self-esteem, independence, cooperation and creative thinking.

Adult-directed activities

The adult has a key role in these types of activity, for example reading a story, using a puppet and asking questions at the end of the session. However, children in their early years should only take part in such activities if they choose to do so as they will most likely lose interest quickly!

Adult-initiated activities

This is when the adult provides an activity for children, such as placing some sieves in the sand tray and watching them enjoy the new resources and, if appropriate, asking them questions about the sieving to extend their knowledge.

Child-initiated activities

Although started by the child this may result from an adult-initiated activity that the child has played previously. For example, the child might read a story to a group of friends using a puppet and asking them questions.

Involving children

This is important if the interests of the children are to be at the centre of any curriculum. Discussion can be invited and children can represent their ideas by words or pictures on paper.

Find out!

1. How does your current placement involve children in the planning of their curriculum?
2. Find out from a small group of children what they enjoy doing or would like to do again.

Flexibility

Early years practitioners should consider the fact that activities will vary according to the children involved. For example, one child may enjoy taking photographs of flowers on a walk while another child may be keen to draw pictures of the flowers on their return to the setting.

Flexibility when planning is also about accommodating unexpected occurrences. For example, a fall of snow should be seen as a great learning opportunity and may have to replace a planned experience. In this example, review of the curriculum would give practitioners a chance to discuss the learning opportunities covered during the snowfall experience and ensure that the abandoned activity has not left any learning intentions uncovered.

Anti-bias view

It is important to ensure that the curriculum represents the different cultures of children in the setting and promotes a world view. Practitioners must also ensure that there is no hidden discrimination such as the form of accessibility of activities and the language used. Images promoted should be positive and encourage children to think openly about their society. This can be done via resources such as posters and books that give positive images of people, but also by encouraging adults to reflect upon their attitudes and practice to continually ensure that their planning is promoting an anti-bias view of the world. (For more on anti-discriminatory practice see Unit 3, pages 156–8.)

Did you know?

It is possible to buy crayons that have a range of skin tones for children to draw with. They can also be purchased in a chunky shape for younger children. This is a positive way of ensuring that children can explore different cultures through a familiar medium.

Health and safety

Every adult working with children has a responsibility to ensure that the curriculum offered is both healthy and safe. The policies and procedures of the setting must be followed and the expected checks carried out. For example, resources should be regularly checked and recorded as appropriate. (For more on health and safety procedures see Unit 4, pages 161–80.)

Examples of planning

Earlier in this unit (pages 301–4) you read about the different curricula upon which the planning in early years settings is based. Some examples of planning are given on the following pages.

You will notice that all the plans have an aim or focus that will help to support the children you are planning for. They also present a broad and balanced curriculum, which is critical if you are going to consider each child holistically. The curriculum plans also refer to the areas discussed, including the role of the adult and the key learning intentions relating to the relevant curriculum.

Case study

Long- and medium-term planning

The staff at Greenbank Nursery met on a professional development day to discuss the long-term plan for the coming year. In pairs, they spent time looking at the guidance for the Early Years Foundation Stage and its links to the Five Outcomes of Every Child Matters. They then regrouped to reflect upon the previous long-term plan. They did this by reviewing the nursery development plan. Rosalind, the manager, encouraged staff to share any knowledge they had of the children they were going to plan for. It was agreed that the previous plan did not allow for enough flexibility and that more needed to be made of the outdoor area. After breaking into small groups and brainstorming ideas for the curriculum, they considered the following when formulating their plan:

→ the different range of interests that the children reflect in their play

→ ways of learning through experience and extending ideas, concepts and skills

→ the contexts for children's learning such as outdoors and indoors

→ the role of the practitioner in providing, extending and developing children's play

→ ways of developing observation as an integral part of curriculum planning

→ finding out how children play at home

→ valuing all types of play

→ ensuring children's welfare requirements are met

→ giving children mental and physical challenges so they can learn actively

→ empowering children to make their own decisions

→ ensuring that children can make connections between what they have learned at home, in the setting and the wider community

→ becoming more involved in children's thinking processes

→ all areas of learning and development.

As a result, the Greenbank Nursery team decided to focus on 'Our World'. The first medium-term plan, to last one month, was to focus on transport.

1. How did the staff team at Greenbank Nursery ensure that the long-term plan was centred on the needs of the children?
2. Why did the team decide that more flexibility should be considered in the long-term plan?
3. What are the areas of learning and development for the Early Years Foundation Stage?
4. What other topics could be used as part of the long-term plan based on the theme 'Our World'?
5. What will the difference be between the long-term plan and the medium-term plan of the Greenbank Nursery team?

Think about it

Having read the case study about Greenbank Nursery, consider the weekly plan for Transport below and the focus activity plan on pages 316–7.

⇩ **Weekly plan from Greenbank Nursery reflecting the medium-term theme 'Transport'**
(* = activities planned in response to interests of children; all other activities are designed to ensure a balanced curriculum)

	Monday	Tuesday	Wednesday	Thursday	Friday
Adult-initiated activities	Roller painting*	Tasting cress	Planting sunflowers	Drumming session*	Police car visit*
Social activities	Traffic light biscuits	Wheel painting*	Train station role play*	Transport matching game	Making smoothies
Continuous provision					
Malleable materials	Play dough, rollers and cutters	Jelly and boats	Cornflour gloop*	Soil, spades and pots	Clay and water
Sand	Tractors and diggers*	Wheels	Sand and washing-up liquid	Free choice*	Different sorts of containers
Water	Frozen coloured gloves	Boats and play people*	Jugs and funnels	Coloured water containers, shells and pebbles	Free choice*
Design and technology	Lego	Large building blocks	Floor train set	Cars and road play*	Farm play
Information technology	Alphabet soup	Car park	Digby the Mole*	Number Jacks	Paint*
Puzzles, games, toys	Car floor puzzle	Railway number game	Transport books and photos	Frog game	Animal snap*

	Monday	Tuesday	Wednesday	Thursday	Friday
Stories and group times	We're Going on a Bear Hunt by Helen Oxenbury*	The Little Yellow Digger by Betty Gilderdale*	Peace at Last by Jill Murphy*	The Gruffalo by Julia Donaldson*	Rosie's Walk by Pat Hutchins*
Snacks	Milk/water Raisins	Milk/water Breadsticks	Milk/water Apples	Milk/water Carrots	Milk/water Bananas
Outdoor activities	Large rollers, large brushes, buckets of water	Road safety play	Large building blocks	Wheel-barrows, brushes, rakes, spades	Role play garage

⇩ **Focus activity plan as part of Greenbank Nursery's weekly plan reflecting the medium-term theme 'Transport' (above)**

Date:	Tuesday 9 October 2007
Task:	Wheel painting
Children to be involved	All (groups of four at a time)
Areas of learning and development:	Personal, Social and Emotional Development Communication, Language and Literacy Problem Solving, Reasoning and Numeracy Knowledge and Understanding of the World Physical Development Creative Development
Objectives:	To choose colours and wheels To put on and take off apron To wash hands To become aware of pattern, shape and size To explore mark-making on paper To experience colour mixing
Vocabulary	Curve, straight Same, different Bumpy, smooth Print Around
Questions	Do you think the patterns are the same? How are the patterns different? How have you made the pattern on the paper? What happens when you mix the colours?

Resources:	Different coloured paint: red, yellow, blue
	Varied wheels
	Paper
	Aprons
Evaluation	• Children were fascinated by the patterns on the paper. A lot of discussion about the patterns and the 'big' and 'small' wheels.
	• AW, TB and SB found the small wheels difficult to hold and needed help to make the patterns.
	• EB and KT focused on mixing the colours and knew how to make orange, green and purple.
	• All areas of learning and development intended covered.

Implementing plans and activities

Before implementing any activity the environment must be carefully prepared and time allowed for this in the planning. The children may be part of the preparation process. When the activity has finished it is essential to ensure that everything is put away – it is very frustrating if a piece of the puzzle is missing or the red paint is empty!

The layout of activities must consider that children have space to play, areas to be quiet and enough variety to enable children to make informed choices. However, too many choices can cause chaos and confusion and make it difficult for children to focus – remember the problem of too many sweets in the shop!

There should be enough adult supervision to support the different types of activities planned and to meet the needs of the children. Adults should also take their role in encouraging and extending activities seriously.

Children younger than 3 years

For children less than 3 years of age, more adult support is needed, since the role of the adult is to guide children initially to develop their skills. Children will also use their senses to explore and experiment in their play. The interaction between the adult and child is important and babies will need physical contact and reassurance. Children of this age can learn through a curriculum that considers:

→ meal times
→ nappy changing/toileting routines
→ sleep time
→ rhymes and songs
→ sensory experiences
→ simple games
→ treasure basket play
→ heuristic play.

Good practice checklist

Implementing plans and activities

✓ Observe children so that activities build on their interests, knowledge and understanding.

✓ Help children make connections between what they are doing and what they have done before.

✓ Give children time to explore and experiment.

✓ Ask interesting and interested questions and stimulate thinking.

✓ Encourage children to repeat and revisit activities.

✓ Provide a range of sensory activities.

✓ Support appropriate play.

✓ Encourage children to mix play materials.

✓ Involve children in planning their own play.

✓ Consider the age and stage of development of each child.

✓ Guide children and allow them to experiment.

Case study

Planning a treasure basket activity

The following activity was planned for Bob, a baby of 8 months, to 'focus on and reach for and handle objects' (Knowledge and Understanding of the World, EYFS). In order to support this area of physical development a treasure basket activity was planned. It was filled by his key worker, Bahani, with natural objects such as sponges, wooden spoons and shells. She placed it on the carpeted area and arranged to sit nearby in case Bob needed support. She also watched Bob explore the objects in his mouth, particularly the sponge. When Bob picked up the wooden spoon he held it up to Bahani so she thanked him and then showed him how he could gently tap the shell with it.

Bahani's colleagues knew that she had planned this activity and ensured that other children were engaged in other activities. Bob concentrated on this activity for at least 10 minutes.

1. Do you think the treasure basket activity was successfully implemented? Why?

2. How else could Bahani have encouraged Bob to explore through his senses?

3. Do you think the activity encouraged other areas of development from the EYFS? If so, which ones?

Children aged 3 to 5 years

Adults will continue to plan activities within the EYFS framework for this age group.

Earlier in this unit the common play activities that should be in any early years environment were outlined (see pages 304–10). While planning may focus on a particular area of the curriculum, it should always be holistic. For example, an activity that encourages children to make a book of photographs they took of each other in the garden will be an adult-directed activity and will require adult input by:

→ looking at different sorts of books
→ encouraging the children to take photographs
→ working with the children to make the books
→ helping the children choose photos

→ writing the captions which children want for their photos
→ reading the finished book with the children.

In the implementation of the above activity, the practitioner will need to ensure that the children can make choices and work independently. The adult will also need to ensure that he or she interacts with, responds to and questions the children in order to extend their knowledge and give them further confidence.

Think about it

1. How could the above activity have been presented to the children?

2. Which areas of learning in the EYFS could this activity consider? You will need to read the EYFS document to help you with this.

3. Consider how the activity could be developed to extend the children's learning.

Children over 5 years

Practitioners implementing activities for children over 5 years might do so in a variety of settings. In Key Stage 1 it is essential that there is a smooth transition from the EYFS and that the key aspects of learning and cognition are considered. Literacy and Mathematics frameworks have been reviewed to provide guidance for transition from the EYFS to Year 6. The criteria for implementing activities are as for any age group, except that the adult should encourage the growing child to become as independent as possible in their learning.

For example, for a CDT (Craft, Design and Technology) activity that encourages a group of 7-year-olds to make a bed for their teddy, the adult's role in implementing the activity would be to:

→ clearly plan the activity according to National Curriculum criteria
→ encourage the children to design their own bed
→ encourage the children to considered proportion and size
→ encourage the children to make careful plans

→ encourage the children to choose appropriate materials through experimentation.

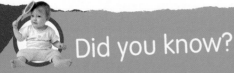

Did you know?

The National Strategy has key aspects of learning and cognition. They are as follows:

→ *Aspects of effective learning:* empathy, motivation, managing feelings, social skills, communication.

→ *Aspects of cognition:* reasoning, evaluation, creativity, enquiry, problem solving, information processing.

Group planning

Planning as part of a team is essential. Although an adult will most likely be responsible for coordinating the curriculum plans, the exchange of ideas and evaluation of ongoing plans will be more effective with a range of perspectives. If adults are involved and feel that their suggestions are valuable then they will be more likely to take some responsibility for parts of the planning. During initial curriculum planning, a team may brainstorm ideas and later evaluate and assess the opportunities planned and implemented.

Getting ready for assessment

U7
3

1. If you complete the Find out! activities on pages 273, 281, 282, 285, 287, 288, 289, 302 and 313 of this unit, and take notes or print out information about what you have discovered, your findings may be used to form a basis for the portfolio for your research.

2. Ask your placement supervisor if you can take a copy of their curriculum planning. Using the same format, see if you are able to construct your own plan. Ask your tutor or placement supervisor for feedback.

How to record and evaluate the planning and assessment cycle

In practice

Jo and his team at Mayford Nursery were considering how they needed to develop the outdoor environment. It was decided that they would carry out peer observations to explore the way practitioners interact with the children while outdoors. They received training and were supported in how they observed each other and shared feedback.

By the end of this section you will understand the importance of reflective practice and the part that peer observations can play in this.

The importance of sharing information with families and other professionals through the multi-agency approach

It is important to record activities so that their success can be evaluated. In this way changes can be made to continually improve the curriculum for each child. Observations and assessment play an important role in recording activities.

When recording the setting's planning, early years practitioners may be involved with a range of people, as shown in the spider diagram below.

A multi-agency approach is beneficial as the whole child is being considered. It may be that records are shared or that the records of the setting contribute to further assessments of a child.

People who may be involved in recording the setting's planning

Members of voluntary organisations · Ofsted · Co-workers · Health visitors/workers · Educational psychologists · Social workers · Parents · Play specialists · The children · Mentors · Advisers · Monitoring groups · Professionals from other settings

Did you know?

The government's Ten-year Childcare Strategy has invested in Children's Centres which have a multi-disciplinary approach to the care of the child. To find out more visit: www.surestart.gov.uk/surestartservices

Feedback from colleagues

There are many different ways to record planning with colleagues; most will include the aspects described below.

→ *Objectives* – These refer to the key issues to be covered in planning. Once a team has decided how to meet the objectives then the rest of the planning can take place.

→ *Actions* – These consider the action needed to draw up the curriculum plans. They should be very clear and specific.

→ *Roles and responsibilities* – Once everyone understands the action plan then people in the team can take on specific roles and responsibilities. One of the roles will be to monitor the success of the planning.

→ *Resources* – These will be recorded and may have to be part of a financial development plan. It is important to plan expenditure and share the search for the most reasonable prices. Resources may be borrowed from other settings or local museums and libraries, for example. Adults are also an essential resource and how people are going to be deployed should be shared and recorded.

→ *Timescale* – The timing of the curriculum should be realistic and clearly recorded. It is also important to ensure that the review/evaluation is planned as part of the process to ensure that it happens.

→ *Success criteria* – This should be recorded in a measured way in an action plan, outlining how objectives are to be measured.

→ *Feedback from children* – It is important to record children's feedback on the curriculum. This will be age appropriate and could include photographs, talking to the children, asking the children to do written or graphic evaluations as appropriate, and holding council meetings if the children are old enough.

Did you know?

It is good practice for schools and play schemes to have councils that are involved with the running of the provision as appropriate. At regular meetings they will minute their reaction to the curriculum. This is then fed back to the adults involved.

Record keeping

Keeping records on children is essential to inform planning. You can read more about this in Unit 14 page 523.

Case study

The manager of Binkfield Nursery, Chris, monitors the setting's long-term curriculum plan. She and her team have recently made a six-month plan for the Foundation Stage of the nursery. As the manager she creates the plan from the team meetings that have taken place and explains to her team that she will monitor the planning through reading the records and observations, encouraging peer observations, holding regular meetings, observing practice and talking to children and parents.

1. Which document will Chris have to ensure that her team are using in their planning?

2. What will Chris expect to see on individual activity plans?

3. What will Chris want to find out when she talks to the children in the setting?

Methods of involving families and other professionals in assessment and planning

It can be very helpful to involve families and other professionals in assessment and in subsequent planning. Parents, for example, will know what their children can do when they are with them at home and in some everyday situations such as at the shops. This means that involving them in the assessment can help to provide a better picture of a child's strengths and needs. Parents may also be able to suggest ideas for how you might further their child's development or build on their child's interests.

In the same way, some professionals such as speech and language therapists may be able to use their professional knowledge to assess a child more accurately or to give you ideas of what to consider when observing a child. They should also be able to suggest ways of working on specific areas of a child's development, such as how to encourage a child to make a certain speech sound or cope in a situation.

There are many ways of involving families and other professionals in assessment and planning and the methods used will vary according to the type of setting that a child is in as well as their needs. In some settings a child's key worker might meet parents to talk to them about their child's progress and draw up a plan, while in others, where parents cannot always attend, discussion might be written down using a home-setting book.

The way in which professionals will be involved will depend on their role and involvement with the child. It is important to remember, though, that parents should give their permission before another professional assesses a child. Some professionals will share their assessments and ideas that will feed into the planning at the time or in report form.

Making and recording valid assessment processes and methods

Assessments are a part of the planning cycle (see page 293). They ensure that children's achievements and needs are recorded and the information can be used to inform further planning.

Types of assessment

There are different types of assessments, as described in Unit 2 pages 90–7. They include:

→ written records
→ checklists and tick charts
→ event samples
→ target child observations.

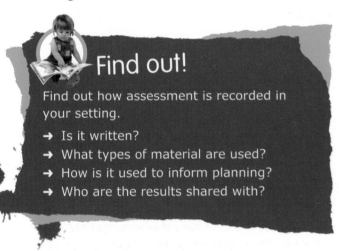

Find out!

Find out how assessment is recorded in your setting.

→ Is it written?
→ What types of material are used?
→ How is it used to inform planning?
→ Who are the results shared with?

Formative and summative assessments

All assessments can be categorised as being either formative or summative.

→ *Formative assessment* is a process of ongoing recording from which overall conclusions are not drawn. However, these assessments will make up the eventual assessment of the child's needs and behaviour and determine how the child can be supported in future summative assessment.
→ *Summative assessment* draws findings together and has an overall conclusion. Academic records, assessment and contributions from children, parents and other adults may contribute towards a summative assessment.

As result of assessments such as National Curriculum SATs (Standard Attainment Targets) in schools, children's progress can be recorded and the effectiveness of the curriculum and planning reviewed. It is important to audit assessments and track any significant issues that may cause the curriculum to change. Such audits may take place when reviewing the development plan of the setting. Recorded assessments should be shared with colleagues, parents and children in order for children to benefit and progress in their development.

Agreeing plans and setting targets for activities and for self-development

Agreeing plans and setting targets for activities

A range of evidence will be required to set learning goals for a child so that he or she understands what he/she is expected to attain in future activities. Some targets may be set individually while others may relate to a class or group of children. In order that targets are realistic it is important that the child is involved in the process.

In a primary school, before talking to the child, the teacher will need to find a range of evidence to establish the child's strengths and areas that need to be developed. This evidence could include:

→ Key Stage test scripts
→ samples of work
→ pupil profiles
→ previous targets that the child has been working towards.

It will also be important to consider the stages of children who may have English as an additional language and gather information from specialist practitioners who may be supporting them. The practitioner should always be sensitive to the needs of the child when setting targets for future activities such as numeracy.

Good practice checklist

Agreeing plans and setting targets with children

✓ Listen to the child.

✓ Be sensitive to the child's needs.

✓ Be positive.

✓ Clearly identify areas for development.

✓ Set realistic timescales.

✓ Discuss how the targets set will help the child.

✓ Agree to make a simple action plan.

✓ Record the action plan for the child and parent to share.

✓ Agree how to share, monitor and review progress.

Agreeing plans and setting targets for self-development

When setting and agreeing plans for self-development with children it is important to talk to each child individually to find out what they think their areas of strength may be. From this discussion and evidence, the practitioner can make a list of points to discuss with the child. It will be important that the child has strategies to achieve self-development targets. The practitioner will need to regularly observe the child and ensure their achievements are celebrated.

If a child sees that they are developing by achieving set targets, this can have a positive impact on their self-esteem and motivation. The child will also begin to take control of their own learning.

Getting ready for assessment

Collate the information and material that you have collected so far. Check what other information and materials are required using the assignment task and assessment criteria given by CACHE.

See also if you have:

→ two plans that show different approaches to planning the curriculum

→ information about the current influences in play.

Consider whether you know enough to be able to:

1. Analyse the importance of planning and providing learning opportunities to meet children's diverse needs.

2. Evaluate the current influences and theories on play and how these affect the planning and provision of learning opportunities.

Unit 8

Caring for children

In this unit you will learn:

1. The range of settings that provide care for children

2. The diverse care needs of children

3. How to work effectively in multi-professional teams to support the care of children

Section 1

The range of settings that provide care for children

In practice

You are starting placement in a Children's Centre. Your tutor has told that this placement will be interesting as the centre provides integrated services. You are not really sure what this means.

By the end of this section you will understand the range of settings that care for children.

Children, families and the outside world

Most children will have a significant amount of their care and education provided by their parents or primary carers. It is recognised that their role is crucial in children's overall development.

Why parents and primary carers are important

Parents and primary carers are the most important people in young children's lives. They will have more influence over children's development and identity than anyone else. Children learn about their family history and culture from them as well as the social skills that are needed for their cultural and religious background.

Think about it

Can you do any of the following things?

→ Play draughts
→ Make a bed
→ Iron a shirt
→ Make a phone call
→ Play cards
→ Wire a plug
→ Sew a button on a shirt
→ Use a washing machine

1. Do you remember where you learned to do these things?
2. Who taught you?
3. Can you work out five other skills that you have learned from your family?

Every family has its own rituals, jokes and ways of celebrating. This gives children a strong sense of identity and a feeling of belonging. Parents and primary carers are special for children; they are the people who know them best. This means that parents understand their children well and know what will make them happy as well as what is likely to cause them pain.

Parents are also their children's first educators (see also Unit 5 page 218). Children often learn many of the life skills they will need from their parents, such as being able to cook, read instructions and use tools. In this way you can often see that children learn about the interests and hobbies of their primary carers. Hence children whose parents are interested in pets will know how to feed and care for animals, while children who have a parent who is interested in computers may well be able to mend the classroom computer when it crashes!

Parenting styles

With a few exceptions, most parents love and care for their children. They also want the best for them, although the way in which parents bring up children can vary tremendously from family to family. For example, some parents have rigid bedtimes for children whereas other parents may not feel that this is necessary.

Researchers looking at the different ways in which parents discipline and bring up their children have concluded that there are three main styles of parenting, as follows.

1. *Authoritarian*
Authoritarian parents tend to have high expectations of their children and are likely to control and limit their behaviour. They may not spend time explaining the rules and can make statements such as, 'You must do it because I am telling you to do it.'

2. *Permissive*
Parents who are permissive may not take control of their children's behaviour but allow their children a lot of choices and responsibility. Permissive parents may say, 'He will learn from his mistakes.'

3. *Authoritative*
Most parents fit somewhere into this band of parenting. They spend some time explaining rules but will still enforce them. They also spend time listening to their children. It is generally thought that children benefit most from authoritative parenting because they know the boundaries set for them and so feel secure.

Children are strongly affected by the warmth and quality of communication with parents as well as parental expectations. Parents with high expectations of behaviour and independence are more likely to have children who have a higher self-esteem and are more independent. There are also cultural variations in styles of parenting. Some cultures place emphasis on authoritarian parenting but the children do well because of the consistent approach and warmth of communication.

'Good enough' parenting

Parents tend not to choose their parenting style. Most parents are influenced by the parenting they received as children and the stresses under which they find themselves. Most parents are not perfect but are generally 'good enough'. Increasingly, studies about parenting show that children do not need brilliant parents but just 'good enough' parents who are consistent in their care and love.

⬆ **Children need parents who take time to communicate with them and are consistent in their love and care**

Different family structures

In today's society, children live in a variety of family structures. The image of a 'normal' family as being children with two parents married to each other is no longer true. At the time of writing, it is estimated that around 40 per cent of marriages end in divorce, affecting some 140,000 children a year.

It is important that early years practitioners understand that there are many different types of family structure in which children grow up. Most family structures are able to provide the main ingredients for good parenting: love, consistency and physical care.

Nuclear families

This is the family structure that is often portrayed as 'normal' by the media. Parents and their own children live together, with parents having most of the responsibility for caring for their children. Some contact with grandparents and other relatives may take place, although many nuclear families live in a different town from their relatives.

Extended families

For centuries this was the traditional type of family structure in the UK; in other countries it is still common. Parents, children and other relatives may live together or nearby. Grandparents, aunts or other relatives may help care for the children. Children are seen as the responsibility of the whole family and often children living in extend families feel secure as they have built relationships with several family members.

Reconstituted families

A reconstituted family consists of one natural parent and one step-parent. Where the step-parent has children, the child will have step-brothers or step-sisters, and if the couple have further children the child will have half-brothers or half-sisters. This is becoming a common type of family structure as many parents divorce or separate then meet new parents.

Nomadic families

Some families may live by travelling from one place to another. There are two main types of travelling families: gypsies and new age travellers.

→ Gypsies are now recognised by European law as being an ethnic minority and as such are protected from discrimination. They have their own language and cultural identity, and generally travel as extended families.
→ New age travellers are often groups of younger people who wish to find an alternative way of living.

Both groups see themselves as separate from society.

Lone-parent families

Lone-parent families consist of one natural parent. There are many different categories of lone parent:

→ widowed parents who have lost a partner
→ separated or divorced lone parents

→ single women who have chosen motherhood

→ teenage mothers (statistically a small percentage of all lone parents).

It is important to understand that not all lone parents have the same needs. The image of lone parents needing financial support is not always accurate, for example some women choose to have children without a partner and are financially able to support them.

Homosexual/lesbian families

Some children live with one natural parent and a same-sex step-parent. Fears among the general public that this structure could influence a child's future sexual identity have not been proven.

Adoptive families

Some children live with adoptive families who may or may not also have 'natural' children. Some adoptive children will keep their birth family's surname whereas others will change their name to their adoptive family's surname. As part of the adoption process, most children will spend some time being fostered by their adoptive family before courts grant the adoption order.

Find out!

The website of NCH, the children's charity, has information on adopting a child. Make a list of people who are considered suitable to adopt a child. Go to www.nch.org.uk/getinvolved and click on the 'adoption' link.

Communal families

There are a few communes in the UK where several families who are unrelated live together and act as an extended family for the children. In Israel there have been many favourable studies which show that children brought up in communes, called kibbutzim, develop well.

Families and the outside world

While most families provide fantastic care and support for the children, sometimes families can come under pressure.

The way in which parents cope with stress depends on their life circumstances. When parents are under stress they may find it harder to respond to their children's needs or manage their behaviour. Some stresses that families find themselves under are short term, such as changing accommodation, while others are long term, for example long-term illness. These may affect the parents' ability to cope.

Think about it

The media often portray parenthood as being a consistently fulfilling and happy experience, although most parents find that there are times when they are exhausted and under pressure. The media also show traditional nuclear families, which tends to reinforce people's ideas that this family structure is the most common.

Look at the picture below.

1. What sort of image is portrayed?
2. How might this type of image make children from other family structures feel different?
3. Why might parents who are lacking in confidence feel threatened by this type of image?
4. Look through a package holiday brochure and consider the types of images that are presented. How many images portray 'happy families'?

Many parents are able to adapt to changes in their lives and will use their friends and families for support. Other parents may not have a strong network, for example they may have recently moved to a new area. Early years practitioners need to understand the pressures families can face as they may need to support such families, either by offering a friendly ear or by providing information about services.

Common factors affecting families are described below.

Financial difficulties

Some families may live on a low income. This might mean they cannot afford to clothe and feed their children as they would wish. Studies that have looked at families on low incomes have established a link between poverty, poor health and depression (see also pages 225–7). Living on a low income will also affect the type of housing that is available. Parents may find themselves living in cramped temporary accommodation which is unsuitable for children and makes it harder for them to cope.

Unemployment

When parents lose their job, they not only lose their income but can feel that they have failed in some way. Tensions between parents can be heightened as a result of one or more parents being unemployed.

Changing jobs

Starting a new job or changing job can put extra pressure on families, although these might be short-lived. Difficulties can occur when the parent who has previously cared for the children starts to work, as childcare needs to be arranged. Young children might not feel happy about separating from their parent, while the parent might feel guilty about returning to work. Older children can also resent being asked to do more for themselves, for example getting themselves ready for school.

Divorce and separation

Parents who are recently separated from their partner often find it difficult to manage on a lower income as well as cope with their own feelings. The situation is often made worse because children's behaviour alters as they react to the change in circumstances.

Caring for a family member

Sometimes a parent also has to care for another family member, for example another child with severe learning difficulties or an elderly relative. This puts a strain on the family as the parents can find themselves emotionally and physically drained.

Long-term illness

The long-term illness of a family member or the child can put enormous strains on a family. One parent may need to spend time caring for the family member who is ill. If the family member is in hospital, hospital visits have to be arranged and time to spend playing and meeting children's needs can be hard to find. In addition, when that person with the illness is a breadwinner, this can leave the family in financial difficulties.

Bereavement

Parents can be put under great emotional strain if they suffer the bereavement of a friend or close family member, particularly the death of a child or partner. They may find it harder to focus on the remaining children as they come to terms with their grief.

Social isolation

Most parents find that talking with other parents can help them cope. This is why there are many support networks for mothers and fathers, such as Parentline Plus, National Childbirth Trust and Families Need Fathers. However, there are many reasons why some parents are not able to do this. They may not be able to communicate with others, perhaps because they do not speak the language or because they are not accepted by other parents, for example a prostitute may be rejected by other parents. Other reasons for isolation include lack of transport, extreme shyness or lack of opportunity. When a family moves to a new area it can take time for them to settle in and make new friends and contacts.

The diverse groups that care for children

As you have seen, children and their families may need support at certain times. There are many organisations including self-help groups that provide this support. In addition, there are local facilities and services for children and their families. The chart on the next page gives some examples of support groups and organisations.

Organisation	Activity	Website address
National Childbirth Trust	Organisation which provides information and support for parents and would-be parents.	www.nct.org.uk
National Association of Toy and Leisure Libraries	Promotes play and learning through the provision of toys and equipment.	www.natll.org.uk
Child Poverty Action Group	Campaigns against child poverty but also provides advice for families on low incomes.	www.cpag.org.uk
Home Start	Home visiting service provided by volunteers to support parents with young children.	www.home-start.org.uk
Parentline plus	Confidential support and information for parents under stress. Also provides parenting classes.	www.parentlineplus.org.uk
Gingerbread	Support and information for single parents.	www.gingerbread.org.uk
Contact a family	A charity providing support and information for families with disabled children.	www.cafamily.org.uk

The differing roles of the statutory, private, voluntary and independent settings that care for children

There are many different settings where children may be cared for, as shown in the spider diagram.

In addition to a range of different settings, there are different types of organisations that provide care for children.

Statutory settings

These are services that by law have to be provided for children and families. The role of the government is either directly to provide statutory services or to supervise them through government departments. Each government department is headed by a Secretary of State who is responsible to Parliament. The Prime Minister chooses the Secretaries of State from the Members of Parliament (MPs); they are normally in his or her political party. Secretaries of State are responsible for making sure that the statutory services are provided. They often do this by supervising the work of local authorities, health authorities and other organisations. Parliament can ask a Secretary of State to explain if services are not provided, either by asking questions during parliamentary question time or by asking the Secretary of State to appear in front of a selected committee.

The main services that families use are health, education and social services. Services and support are provided either directly through central government, for example social security is directly under government control, or through local authorities.

Education is a good example of a statutory service. Schools have to be provided for all children, although their size and the age range that they cover is decided locally.

Find out!

Find out more about how government services are organised. Visit www.direct.gov. uk and click on 'Guide to govt'. Make a list of the current Secretaries of State who will have responsibility for the following areas: Health, Education and Social Services.

Voluntary settings

Voluntary organisations have become more complex to understand. Traditionally they were mostly charities who depended entirely on donations from the public in order to carry out their work and were staffed predominately by volunteers. Today the situation is more complex as many local authorities and other government-funded organisations will 'buy' voluntary organisations' services. A good example of this is the Pre-school Learning Alliance. The Pre-school Learning Alliance is a registered charity whose aim is to promote education, but as well as receiving funds from its members it also works for and receives funds from local authorities.

The key point about voluntary settings is that they are not profit-making and any surplus income is used to further their activities.

Private settings

Private settings aim to make a profit and therefore can be seen as a business. While some of the profits will be put back into the business, some of the income may be distributed to shareholders or to the individuals who own and control the business. Childminders provide a private service in this way as they are run as small businesses. As with voluntary settings, local

authorities may 'buy' their services or they may receive grants or funding from the government. Private settings that are being funded for education in some way by taxpayers will have to follow the National Curriculum and the Early Years Foundation Stage. They will also be inspected to ensure that the health and safety of children is maintained.

In addition to providing education, some private organisations also support social services. For example, many private companies recruit, train and monitor foster carers; such companies are paid for their work by local authorities.

Independent settings

Independent settings often have more freedom about the way they organise their provision as they may not rely on government funding. This means that an independent school who does not receive government funding may not follow the National Curriculum or in England the EYFS. Independent settings are still inspected to ensure that the welfare and safety of children is maintained.

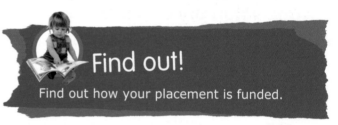

Find out!

Find out how your placement is funded.

Children's Centres

As you have seen there are many different types of settings where children are cared for. A recent trend has been to offer integrated services to parents. At the time of writing most local authorities in England are in the process of setting up Children's Centres. The idea behind Children's Centres is that they will improve the prospects for disadvantaged children and their families as a range of support will be on offer. Children's Centres will be expected to provide the following services to children under 5 years and their families:

➔ early education integrated with full day care, including early identification of and provision for children with special educational needs and disabilities
➔ parental outreach
➔ family support

- health services
- a base for childminders and a service hub within the community for parents and providers of childcare services
- effective links with Jobcentre Plus, local training providers and further and higher education institutions
- effective links with Children's Information Services, Neighbourhood Nurseries, Out-of-school Clubs and Extended Schools
- management and workforce training.

Find out!

Find out if you have a Children's Centre locally. What services does it offer?

Case study

Supporting a single parent

Aysel is a single parent. She has two children aged 2 and 3 years old. She has recently moved to the area and feels quite isolated. Her daughter has a rash so Aysel takes her to see the family doctor. The doctor's surgery is now part of the Children's Centre. Her doctor asks Aysel how she is getting on and tells her about the drop-in play sessions for parents at the centre in the mornings. She decides to go to one of the sessions and both she and the children enjoy their morning. After a few weeks, one of the staff tells Aysel about a computer course for parents and lets her know that the crèche will also be open. The short course is run by the local college and leads to a qualification. Aysel enjoys the course and begins to think that she might be able to get a part-time job. She gets advice from the Job Centre adviser who comes into the Children's Centre twice a week. She has practice interviews, is helped with application forms and childcare arrangements, and after a few weeks she finds a part-time job in an office.

1. Explain the importance of services being grouped together.
2. Discuss how Aysel has benefited from this service.
3. Consider how Aysel's children have also benefited from this service.

Helping parents to find out about services

It can be difficult for children, young people and their families to find out about the different services that might help them. To help families, the government in England under the 2006 Childcare Act has therefore made it compulsory for local authorities to provide an information service. At the time of writing, these are being set up, although previous legislation required local authorities to provide information about childcare in the area. These services are known as Children's Information Services.

In addition, it is also important for practitioners working with parents to provide them with information. This means that many settings provide information via notice boards, leaflets and word of mouth. This is a very effective way of helping parents to gain support and information.

Think about it

How easy would it be for a parent to find out about services in your local area?

The regulatory framework and its impact on the care given to children

In the United Kingdom, care for children is quite regulated. Each of the four countries has their own inspectorate and it will be important for you to find out about the regulations that your setting follows. Regulations are designed to keep children safe as well as to ensure in educational settings that their development and potential are being fulfilled.

U8
1

Early Years Foundation Stage framework

In England the latest regulatory framework is the Early Years Foundation Stage. If you work in England, you will need to read the statutory framework to find out about the standards that have to be met when caring for children. The examples in the table below show how some of the regulations would affect the care of children in practice.

☞ **How some of the Early Years Foundation Stage regulations would affect the care of children in practice**

Area	What the EYFS states	Example of what this means in practice
Staffing arrangements	'Providers must meet the requirements for adult : child ratios...'	The manager at Little Tots nursery has a member of staff off on sick leave. She has asked a part-time member of staff to do extra hours to make sure that the staff to child ratios are maintained. This is a legal requirement and is important as it ensures that children are properly supervised and that there are enough adults to interact with the children.
Children's behaviour	'Providers must have an effective behaviour management policy which is adhered to by all members of staff...'	A new member of staff is given the behaviour policy to read. The manager makes sure that the member of staff understands how the setting manages behaviour. The policy helps the new member of staff work in a positive way with children and encourages them to praise children's positive behaviour.
Food and drink	'Fresh drinking water must be available at all times...'	Each morning a member of staff at the Busy Bees pre-school puts out some small jugs of fresh water and some beakers. The children are encouraged during the morning to pour a drink if they wish. This will prevent them from becoming dehydrated.

Getting ready for assessment

1. Look at the spider diagram on page 331. What provision is available in your area? Find out about what each group or organisation aims to do and how they are funded. Keep notes that you can use as evidence for your portfolio.

2. If you complete the Find out! activities on pages 332 and 333 of this section, and take notes or print out information about what you have discovered; your findings may be used as evidence for your portfolio.

3. Find a copy of the regulatory framework for your country.

   a) Choose five regulations and consider how they may affect the day-to-day practice in a setting.

   b) Consider how the regulations promote children's welfare and safety.

Keep notes or print out any information gained from websites.

Section 2

The diverse care needs of children

In practice

You are hoping to find a job working as a nanny. You see an advert for a job working for a family with three children aged 2, 4 and 6 years. You are not sure if you should apply. You are worried that you will not know how to care for them.

By the end of this section you should be able to identify children's care needs and consider ways of meeting them.

How to use your knowledge of child development to recognise children's needs

While all children have the same basic physical and health needs, the way that these needs are met will depend on the age and stage of development of the child along with other factors such as the child's cultural needs. The diagram below outlines the basic physical and health needs of all children.

Fresh air, exercise and stimulation

Children need fresh air, exercise and stimulation in order to grow and develop (see also Unit 4). The amount of exercise and how it is taken will vary according to children's age and stage of development. Young children will find it difficult to maintain constant physical activity because their lung and heart capacity is still developing. This means that they will take exercise in 'bursts' by, for example, running and then wanting to sit for a few minutes before running off again.

Clean water and food

All children need to have sufficient water and food in order to remain healthy. At different ages, their nutritional requirements change. A good example of this is the way that very young children require smaller portions as their stomach capacity is more limited and so need a high-nutrient and energy-dense diet.

Suitable clothing and footwear

Children need to be suitably dressed. The clothing and footwear required will depend on a variety of factors including their size, stage of development, the weather and the activities they are engaged in. In addition, families will also have preferences as to what they feel is suitable, while children themselves will develop favourite items.

Clothing for babies

Babies will need layers of clothing that can be removed or added to easily. This is because babies find it harder to regulate their body temperature. It is essential to check that a baby does not become overheated as this is thought to contribute to an increased risk of cot death. Clothing also needs to be easily washed and easy to remove for nappy changing. In addition, clothes should be checked for safety, for example loose buttons, ties and tabs. In cool weather, babies may need a hat to prevent them losing heat, as well as mitts and bootees. In warm weather it is important that babies' skin is covered up as their skin is particularly sensitive and may burn. Cotton clothing is also preferable to avoid heat rash.

Clothing and footwear for toddlers

Clothing for toddlers needs to be easily washed and removed for nappy changing. They also need to be comfortable as toddlers spend much of their time bending down, sitting or on the floor. It is also useful if some items such as hats, socks and trousers allow them to dress themselves. By around 2 years, most toddlers have begun toilet training. Clothes during this period need to be easy to unfasten so that toileting accidents can be prevented.

Shoes are not normally advised until a toddler has been walking for a few weeks. Shoes need to fit well and support the ankle. As with babies, toddlers' skin is also sensitive. They need to be kept covered when it is sunny and will need a sunhat. Toddlers also enjoy going outside so will need protective clothing and footwear such as raincoats and Wellington boots.

Clothing for children aged 3 years onwards

It is important that clothes are chosen that will encourage children to dress themselves. This means thinking about the fastenings and the fit. Children from 3 years onwards will also start to have preferences. They need fewer clothes overall than babies and toddlers as generally they are less messy with their food and in their play. It is, however, important that protective aprons, etc., are available for painting and at meal times.

Children's skin is still vulnerable when it is sunny so care should be taken that their skin is covered up and/or they are protected with the use of sun cream. Children's feet continue to develop so they will need comfortable and well-fitting shoes.

Cleanliness

Meeting children's personal hygiene needs helps to prevent skin and other infections but also helps children to feel comfortable. The extent to which early years practitioners become involved with meeting children's personal hygiene needs will depend on the setting in which they work. Early years practitioners who care for toddlers and young children in their own home are likely to be more involved in this aspect of children's care.

Factors that might influence how children's care needs are met

It is essential that you find out from parents how you should care for children's hair, skin and teeth. Every family has its own personal hygiene routines and preferred products. These are sometimes influenced by religious practices and medical needs as well as social morals and cultural traditions. One family might, for example, boycott certain skincare products because they are unhappy about the manufacturer's policies, while another family might be trying to avoid certain products because they irritate a child's skin.

Caring for children's skin

Skin is actually considered to be an organ – the largest organ in the body. Skin has an important function since it acts as a barrier, protecting the internal organs and preventing infection from entering the body as well as providing protection from the harmful rays of the sun. Skin also helps to regulate the body's internal temperature by producing sweat. Sweat needs to be washed off the body regularly as otherwise it combines with dead skin cells and bacteria to cause sore areas and skin inflammation. Washing skin and, where necessary, moisturising it is therefore the main way in which early years practitioners care for children's skin.

Washing skin

There are two main methods that are used to wash skin all over – bathing and showering. Many families prefer to shower because they believe it is more hygienic. Some families may want their child to shower because this is a practice in their religion. It is therefore important to ask parents if they have any particular preferences.

Good practice checklist

Washing children

✓ Make sure that the water is not too hot – 63 degrees Celsius is a recommended temperature.

✓ Have everything to hand.

✓ Make sure that all the skin is washed and rubbed down.

✓ Encourage older children to wash themselves.

✓ Use soap products sparingly.

✓ Never leave a child unattended near water.

Skincare in the sun

It is now understood that exposure to the sun can cause skin cancer (melanoma) and premature ageing of the skin. Children have delicate skin that burns easily so particular care must be taken in the summer months when the sun is at its strongest.

Did you know?

Skin cancer is one of the most common cancers in the UK, with about 75,000 new cases diagnosed each year, although many cases are not reported so the real number is probably much higher. About 2,300 people in the UK die each year from skin cancer. (*Source*: Cancer Research UK, 2007)

The following advice from health professionals should be followed when there is strong sunlight:

➔ Keep babies under 6 months out of direct sun.
➔ Keep children out of direct sun between 11am and 3pm.
➔ Keep children covered up using T-shirts, sunhats, UV suits, etc.
➔ Use a high-factor sun cream – not less that SPF 15 – and reapply regularly.

Looking after children's hair

The way in which children's hair needs to be cared for will depend on their hair type and the parents' wishes. This means researching how best to care for the child you are looking after. It is, for example, common for black children to have oil rubbed into their hair which nourishes it, rather than washing it with shampoo, and for the hair to be braided.

⇧ **It is vital to take especial care to protect children's skin when they are playing in the sun**

Looking out for head lice

Head lice are parasites that live on the human scalp and they have made a dramatic reappearance in many settings. This means that hair should be checked for head lice and advice should be sought as to the best treatment. This may include special chemical lotions, electric combs or regular combing with a fine-toothed comb.

Signs that a child has head lice might include:

➔ itchy head
➔ small scabs caused by bites on the scalp
➔ tiny white or yellow eggs attached to the hair (nits)
➔ small, brown, quickly-moving creatures.

Choice of skin and hair care products

The choice of products may be influenced by any of the following:

➔ *Type of skin* – Some children may have skin that requires regular moisturisers or oils, such as cocoa butter.
➔ *Allergies or skin conditions* – Children with eczema, other skin conditions or allergies may use specific products that are particularly gentle on the skin.
➔ *Manufacturer* – Some parents may have a preference as to the manufacturer.
➔ *Type of hair* – Some children's hair does not benefit from being shampooed as this makes it dry and brittle or dull and lifeless. Hair oils might be used instead.

Find out!

Find out more about eczema by visiting the following website: www.eczema.org

Caring for children's feet

Feet support the weight of the body during standing and walking and while bending to help move forwards. Babies' and children's feet grow rapidly and it is important that any socks, shoes or other footwear do not restrict this growth. Blisters and corns can also be caused by footwear that is too small or badly-fitting. It is suggested that, whenever possible, children should be allowed to go barefoot and that babies are not put into shoes until they are walking steadily.

← Babies should not be put into shoes until they are walking steadily

Oral hygiene

Care of the teeth and mouth is important to prevent bacterial build-up. Some bacteria in the mouth are 'friendly' while other bacteria cause tooth decay. The most important way to prevent the build-up of bacteria is by regular brushing of the teeth, which literally removes the bacteria. This is best done after meals and before going to bed. Dentists also advise that sugary drinks and products containing sugar or acid, such as juice, are avoided between meals.

U8

2

👆 **Basic care needs of children**

Need	Reason	What early years practitioners should do
Changing nappies	This helps prevent soreness and infection.	Nappies should be changed at regular intervals and early years practitioners should always change a nappy when it is dirty or wet.
Helping with toileting	This helps prevent children from having accidents and losing confidence; wiping children's bottoms properly can also prevent infection.	As children get older they should be encouraged to take increased responsibility, with adults being on hand simply to offer support.
Handwashing	This is a major way of preventing the spread of bacteria and viruses.	Younger children will need to be shown how to wash their hands, while older children will need to be reminded and praised when they wash their hands thoroughly.
Keeping noses clean	This prevents children from developing ear infections and prevents cross-infection. This is one care need that is often overlooked although it can prevent the spread of colds.	Young children cannot blow their nose and so, when they have a cold, their nose may need to be wiped frequently. Older children may need to be reminded to wipe their nose and should be praised for doing so.
Feeding	Children need regular intake of fluids and food in order to remain healthy.	Early years practitioners may help children by cutting up food, helping them to feed themselves and by being observant and checking that children are not hungry or thirsty.
Washing and care of skin	This helps prevent spread of infection and diseases of the skin.	Early years practitioners may wash children's faces and, depending on where they work, may help children to take baths or showers.
Care of hair and teeth	This helps prevent cross-infection and tooth decay, and helps detect head lice in hair.	Early years practitioners in home settings often have a particular responsibility for the care of children's hair and teeth.

Bladder and bowel control

Leaving nappies is a significant step for children and their parents. It signals the first moves towards independence so is an important milestone in children's lives. The term 'toilet training' is often used to describe the process of moving out of nappies, although this suggests that children can somehow be taught to do this. This is not the case, as gaining bladder and bowel control is largely dependent on the maturity of the child's nervous system.

Recognising when children are ready to move out of nappies

Although there are different approaches to toilet training, it is generally considered advisable to wait until children are showing physical and other signs that they are ready. It is, however, important to work with parents and respect their wishes if they have other ideas or approaches that they wish to take.

Signs that children may be ready for toilet training include:

➜ they realise when their nappy needs changing
➜ their nappy is dry for long periods; this indicates that they are gaining some bladder control (this usually occurs between 18 months and 3 years of age)
➜ an interest in potties and toilets
➜ sufficient language or communication skills to indicate that they need to go to the toilet.

Did you know?

There are various children's books and stories about toilet training which can encourage children's interest; however, it is important to make sure that they do not put pressure on the child.

It is also a good idea to start by leaving a nappy off a child and showing them a potty when you know that their bladder is likely to be full. If a child seems fretful or resists sitting on a potty it is important not to become irritated and cross. This may indicate that the child is not fully ready to start the process and it is often best to simply put a nappy back on and try

again after a few days or even weeks. Keeping calm is essential as children must not feel under pressure to 'perform' – this tends to cause them to become overanxious and will result in their feeling too tense to allow the bladder to release the urine. The speed with which children master the process tends to vary, with most children having a few accidents at first.

Handling accidents

Accidents are inevitable, especially in the first few weeks of being out of nappies – children do not often understand the signals that their body is sending them until it is virtually too late. If they are engrossed in an interesting activity they will often not notice that they need to go. It can therefore be helpful to watch carefully and remind children from time to time.

If accidents occur it is important to be as matter as fact about them as possible so that the child does not become worried. This means that it is a good idea to take the child to a quiet place and help him or her get washed and changed into fresh underwear and clothes. You should also let the child take as much control of this process as possible so that he or she can remain feeling self-reliant. The wet or soiled clothes should be rinsed out and placed in a plastic bag ready for laundering; it is important to remember to wear disposable gloves at all times during this process. Parents should be kept informed of any accidents, but this should be done away from the child to prevent him or her losing confidence or, in the case of older children, becoming embarrassed.

Equipment for toilet training

There is equipment available that can make toilet training a little easier and attractive for children:

➜ clothes that unfasten easily
➜ inner toilet ring
➜ small step to help them reach the toilet if necessary
➜ attractive potties
➜ clean towels and interesting-shaped soap
➜ soft toilet paper.

Encouraging handwashing

As part of the toilet training process you need to get children into the habit of washing their hands afterwards. This is essential in preventing infections from spreading as bacteria are present in bowel motions (see also Unit 4 page 177). Children need to learn to wash their hands using hot water (63°C) and soap, and to dry them thoroughly afterwards. It is now suggested that paper towels are the most hygienic way of drying hands in group care settings.

Signs and symptoms that might be a cause for concern

When helping children to use the potty or toilet, you should look for any signs of illness or abnormality. For example, you might notice that children are in pain as they produce bowel motions; this could be a sign of constipation. It is also important to remember that problems in going to the toilet can sometimes be a sign of sexual abuse (see also Unit 3 page 125). Infections of the bowel and bladder can be painful for children so it is important to pass on promptly any concerns that you have to your supervisor or the child's parents or carers.

Concern	What it could indicate
Difficulty in passing bowel motion	This is often a symptom of constipation in children. It can cause the children pain which in turn puts them off from passing a motion – this becomes a vicious circle as the stools become harder and less easy to pass through.
Itchiness; white discharge	This can be a symptom of thrush (*candida albicans*); medical attention must be sought.
Itchiness around the anal area	This can be caused by a threadworm infection (see also page 418).
Diarrhoea	This will require medical advice.
Pain when passing urine and/or blood in the urine	Seek medical attention.
Strong-smelling urine	This can be caused by an infection or could be a sign of dehydration; seek medical attention.

Rest and sleep

Sleep and rest are important for all animals, and humans are no exception! Scientists do not completely understand the body's need for sleep but studies have shown that without sleep humans cannot function properly – concentration, mood and memory are affected and, if sleep deprivation is severe, the brain can suffer long-term damage. One theory about sleep is that the body needs time to rest and recover while the brain needs time to gather and sort information.

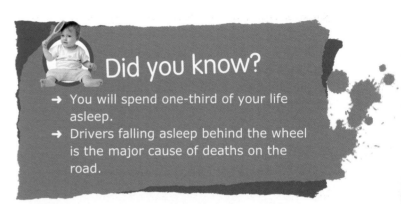

Did you know?

→ You will spend one-third of your life asleep.
→ Drivers falling asleep behind the wheel is the major cause of deaths on the road.

What happens to the body during sleep?

During sleep, the body's functions slow down. This means that breathing, heart rate and other body systems also slow down. However, during sleep the brain is active. There appear to be two types of sleep phase, with both being required in order to wake refreshed. Having enough sleep is particularly important for children because, during sleep, growth hormones are released from the pituitary gland.

Understanding children's sleep requirements

The amount of sleep that children and adults need is different. As you get older, you tend to need less sleep, with most adults requiring between seven and eight hours of sleep; most children under 5 years will need at last 12 hours of sleep a day, although this can vary from child to child. This does not necessarily mean that children will sleep for 12 hours at a stretch, as young children often have naps in the daytime as well as sleeping at night. It is important to find out from parents the sleep patterns of children and, wherever possible, make sure that a child's sleep routine is catered for. Keeping to a sleep routine helps children as their body will be ready to sleep at certain times. It also helps avoid the problem of parents being unable to get their children off to sleep because they are not tired in the evenings.

Helping children to sleep

Most young children under 4 years will need an opportunity to have a nap, or at least a rest, during the day. There are many ways of helping children to settle to sleep and individual children may have specific requirements such as having their comforter with them or being gently rocked. Children will also benefit from being with familiar adults when it is sleep time.

Most 'sleep clinics' that help parents and carers with children who are experiencing difficulties sleeping suggest that a 'wind down' period is planned before children are expected to sleep. This may mean reading a story or doing something that is calming for the children. A routine also helps children and this is why it is important to talk to parents about their child's sleep patterns and routines.

Find out!

Find out locally where parents and carers might gain advice about helping their children to sleep.

Waking children

Many children may feel groggy and disorientated when they first wake up. This means that plenty of reassurance must be given to children, especially if they are being woken up. Many key workers of younger children find it helpful to wake them simply by stroking the backs of their hands and quietly talking to them. After waking, children should be offered a drink as the body loses water during sleep. Most children will also need the toilet or to have their nappy changed. Many children will still need some time before they are ready to run around and may wish to rest for longer with their comforters.

Helping children to rest

Some children find it difficult to take a nap during a session. It is important not to force children to sleep, so when they are not sleepy you should encourage them to rest and have a 'quiet time'. This could mean reading a story to them or putting on a story or relaxation tape. The key to any rest activity is that it encourages children to be passive rather than active. A passive activity means that the brain and the body can slow down and so help the body to rest.

Building periods of rest into daily routines

As well as having opportunities for rest periods and naps, children will need time to relax and take it

Good practice checklist

Helping children to sleep

✓ Check that the room is well ventilated and not too hot or cold.

✓ Make sure that the mattress and bedding is dry, clean and comfortable.

✓ In group care settings, check that there is enough room between mattresses.

✓ Darken the room as this signals to the brain that it should be sleeping.

✓ Allow some time for children to relax and rest before going to sleep.

✓ Create a calm and peaceful atmosphere around the children.

✓ Make sure that the children are not hungry or thirsty.

✓ Check that children wearing nappies are clean and dry and that children out of nappies do not need the toilet.

✓ Make sure that children have their comforters if needed.

✓ Follow the sleep routine of the children – this may mean staying next to them until they have fallen asleep.

✓ Check children regularly when they are sleeping.

easy at different points in the day. This means that when planning a daily routine for young children you should make sure that there are opportunities for children to be able to play in a relaxed and restful way. You might, for example, have story time shortly after time spent running and playing outdoors, to allow children time to calm down and rest. Other activities that are restful include drawing, playing with small world toys such as farm animals and play people, and looking at books.

Signs and symptoms of potential concern when meeting children's basic needs

Early years practitioners need to be observant when caring for children. It is important to look for any early signs of infection, skins abrasions or injuries. In some cases you may suspect that a child is becoming unwell (see also Unit 11, pages 407–25) or, sadly, that they are being abused (see also Unit 3, pages 125–6).

The chart below shows some of the common skin and other conditions that you should look out for. If you notice that a child has a skin or other condition you should make a note of it and talk either to your supervisor or to the child's parents or carers.

Concern	Signs and symptoms
Athlete's foot	The skin between the toes is itchy and flaky; it is caused by a fungal infection.
Warts	These are caused by viruses and can be present on hands, knees and feet (verrucas).
Corns	These are hard areas of skin that are caused by the pressure of shoes or footwear. They are often a sign of ill-fitting shoes.
Eczema	This results in itchy skin and a red, prickly-looking rash.
Head lice	A small parasite living on the human scalp (see also page 338).
Nappy rash	A sore red rash around the genital area; it is often caused by ammonia in urine coming into contact with the skin (see also page 208).
Chapped skin	This is sore, cracked skin caused by inadequate drying of the area.

How to identify individual care needs

You have seen that the type of care that children need will depend on their age; in addition, some children will have individual needs that require meeting. The best way to find out about these needs is by talking to parents. Parents often know their children's likes and dislikes but also any medical conditions or additional needs. These may for example be dietary or cultural. In addition to work with parents it is also important to use observation. By observing children you may see that a child is tired at a certain time or that they are becoming warm. The three examples below show how three children of a similar age have different care needs.

→ Emily is 3 years old and is in nappies. She is currently in the process of being toilet trained. As she has a learning difficulty, her key worker, in discussion with her parents, has decided to use some visual signs to help Emily communicate her needs. Emily also needs extra support when she washes her hands as she tends to play with the water and soap rather than wash with it. Her key worker has found that if she offers her hands for Emily to wash, Emily's hands also get washed at the same time. Emily's parents now do the same at home.

→ Andreya is 3 years old. She has eczema that easily flares up. She has a non-dairy diet and her nursery has put up a sign to remind staff that soya milk and products are to be used in place of dairy products. Andreya has her own soap and moisturiser that must be used when she needs to wash her hands. Staff also think about Andreya's needs when they are planning activities; she cannot, for example, play with shaving foam or soap flakes.

→ Baran is 3 years old. His parents are Turkish and in their culture children are wrapped up more warmly when they go outdoors, even if it is sunny. They have asked the nursery to make sure that Baran does not go outside unless he is wearing a hat, scarf and gloves as well as a fastened-up coat. Baran is also used to his parents helping him to dress. Baran's key worker has explained to his parents that the nursery's policy is that children learn to do things for themselves. Together they have agreed that in nursery Baran will try and dress himself and that at home his parents may help him more.

Activities that support and maintain daily living for children

You have seen that children's care needs are important in maintaining their health and overall well-being. You have also seen that children will have individual needs alongside developmental needs. One of the skills in working with children is learning how to devise a daily routine that can meet these needs. Daily routines will vary enormously depending on where children are being cared for and their own needs. This means that a child who is at home with a nanny and a younger baby will have a different routine to a similar-aged child who is in group care.

It is good practice to work with parents in order that information about a child's needs can be used to devise a routine. Below are two examples of routines. Note how in each routine the child's need for stimulation, food and sleep as well as exercise have been balanced.

Think about it

Look at the routine of your setting. Evaluate how the activities contribute to the children's overall needs.

Promoting and supporting children's independence and self-care

You have seen in Unit 3 (pages 135–6) that children's self-image and self-esteem are crucial to their overall well-being. A key way of helping children to feel competent is through supporting them in gaining as much independence as possible when caring for themselves. This is a gradual process and will depend on children's stage of development as well as age. It is important that adults encourage independence as early as possible. The spider diagram opposite looks at some of the ways in which you might help children gain independence.

🕯 **Examples of different morning routines for 3-year-old children**

	Tom is 3 years old. He attends a day care nursery from 8.00am–6.00pm. He is with other 3-year-olds.	Bryony is 3 years old. She has an older brother who goes to school full-time. She goes to a pre-school three afternoons a week. She is looked after by a nanny.
Time	**Routine**	**Routine**
8.00	Breakfast and teeth cleaning	Washed and dressed
8.30	• Play indoors	In pushchair/walking to take brother to school
9.00	• Choice of activities including sand, water, dough and painting	• Plays in park on way home • Washes hands
9.30	• Adult-directed activities as well as child-initiated activities	• Plays indoors while nanny tidies away breakfast things • Helps to wash up
10.00	• Washes hands after messy activities and before snack time	• Goes into the garden to feed the birds and water the plants • Washes hands
10.30	Story and snack time	Snack and shares books
11.00	• Outdoor play including physical activities	Plays with selection of toys including Duplo, puzzles and small world toys
11.30	• Washes hands	• Drawing and painting • Washes hands
12.00	Lunch	Lunch
12.30	Quiet activities indoors, e.g. puzzles, story tapes	Nap
13.00	Nap	

Personal hygiene
- Actively cooperating, e.g. putting hands out to be washed
- Wiping face and drying hands
- Doing personal hygiene tasks with adult support
- Completing tasks with minimal adult support

Playing
- Choosing toys and equipment
- Tidying away toys and equipment
- Working out what things can do
- Following written instructions for games

Ways to help children gain independence

Meal times
- Feeding self
- Pouring own drinks
- Laying out plates
- Serving food
- Cooking

Dressing
- Actively cooperating, e.g. standing up or pushing arms into jumpers
- Simple undressing, e.g. gloves, hats, scarves
- Pulling up trousers, removing jackets
- Undoing large buttons, pulling up and down on zippers
- Putting on aprons
- Choosing clothes to wear

Ways in which adults can support children

Encouraging children to do things for themselves does take a little time and patience. Learning to manage tasks is a process and children will manage more easily when adults are relaxed and encouraging rather than in a rush. It is also important to think ahead and observe individual children so that you can be sure that the task is manageable. This is important because children thrive on success and are likely to become frustrated if a task is beyond their capability. The flow diagram opposite shows how learning to pour a drink and then drink from a cup is broken down into stages.

Motivating children

Children of all ages need to be motivated in order to develop self-care skills – this is where the role of the adult is so crucial. Adults need to be supportive and acknowledge children's efforts, however small, in trying to be independent. It is also important that the adult looks for situations in which children can help themselves successfully. Success is important as it gives children motivation to try again. Children who do not succeed are more likely to become frustrated and to lose motivation. Overleaf are some examples of ways in which adults have helped children to gain confidence and to build motivation.

1. Adult holds beaker with a lid and gently tips it
2. Child holds beaker and adult gently tips it
3. Child manages beaker with lid independently
4. Beaker without a lid is held by child but gently tipped by adult
5. Child manages this unaided
6. Beaker with no handles is provided
7. Small jug is provided so that child can pour own drink
8. Larger jug is provided so that child can pour own and others' drinks
9. Opportunities to make drinks such as milkshakes are provided

⇧ **Process of learning to pour a drink and then drink from a cup**

→ *Ayse aged 6 months*

Eileen encourages Ayse to get dressed by saying 'push' when she places Ayse's arms into her jacket. When Ayse pushes her arm in, Eileen smiles and says 'Well done'.

→ *Jordan aged 11 months*

Andy is feeding Jordan. He has given Jordan a spoon as well so that Jordan can feed himself. Andy smiles at Jordan and encourages him.

→ *Rahima aged 20 months*

Kerry asks Rahima if she needs her nappy changing. She gives Rahima the baby wipes to hold and Rahima lies down and puts her legs in the air. Kerry praises and talks to Rahima.

→ *Sam aged 26 months*

When it is time to come indoors, Kathryn lets Sam push the pushchair into the hallway. She always says 'Hats off!' and Sam takes his own hat off and puts it on the peg. Kathryn smiles and says 'Well done'. She undoes his coat buttons, but Sam then takes off his coat and goes to his peg.

→ *Emily aged 3 years*

The toys and equipment are arranged so that children can choose items and take them off to play. Emily wants to take a large tray of cars which is too heavy for her. Nick asks if she would like some help. He holds the tray but encourages Emily to help him by holding onto a corner. He asks her where she wants it to go.

⇧ **This child is learning that he is competent**

Case study

Encouraging toddlers to become more independent

Karen works in a busy day nursery. She is in the toddler room and does not give the toddlers many opportunities to do things for themselves. She finds it quicker to do things herself such as feeding and dressing because the toddlers are slow and often messy. Her manager has arranged for her to visit another setting. She is surprised at how much the toddlers are doing for themselves. She sees that most of them can feed themselves very well, help with the tidying up and do quite a lot of simple dressing and undressing. She also notices that the toddlers are much calmer and busier and that they have fewer tantrums.

1. Why might Karen's toddlers have more tantrums than those in the other setting?

2. Why is it important that children get opportunities to develop independence?

3. Suggest ways in which Karen might encourage her toddlers to become more independent.

How to work effectively in multi-professional teams to support the care of children

In practice

You are enjoying your placement in a Children's Centre. It is interesting to see how many different services work alongside and with each other. You have been asked to a large team meeting but are a little nervous. During the meeting several people talk about the Common Assessment Framework, but you are not sure what this means.

By the end of this section you will know how to work effectively alongside other professionals and as part of a team.

Introduction

Today, different professionals are working more closely together. In England this is a result of recent legislation such as the 2004 Children Act. In the other countries of the United Kingdom a similar approach is also been taken. The aim is that the needs of children are properly identified and that all the professionals working with children effectively communicate with each other. In order to make multi-disciplinary working more effective, local authorities in England are restructuring their services so they are more interwoven. In addition, a system of identifying children's and their families' needs, called the Common Assessment Framework, has been introduced. All services are meant to use this in order to build up a holistic picture of what support will be needed. The diagram below shows the holistic nature of the framework.

How to work with colleagues in multi-professional teams

Team work is a key way in which you can provide good quality care and education for children and support their families. There is a range of skills that you will need to consider in order to work effectively in a team.

Professionalism

The term 'professionalism' is used widely and you may have heard your tutors commenting on the importance of showing professionalism. In order to be a professional working with children you will need to develop several characteristics, as described below.

Self-awareness

It is important to get to know yourself and to be objective about your strengths and weaknesses, both in terms of your abilities and your personality. This means that if you know that you find speaking in public difficult you might then be able to ask for support or take more time to practise. Being self-aware is also important when it comes to working with children and other adults. You may, for example, recognise that when you are nervous you talk more or too quickly and so learn how to control this.

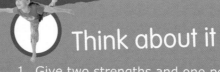

Think about it

1. Give two strengths and one personal weakness that you think that you have.

2. Explain how they might affect your ability to work with others in a team.

The holistic nature of the Common Assessment Framework (*Source*: Nottingham Integrated Children's Services)

Empathy

Empathy is about the ability to see something from another person's point of view – the phrase 'put yourself in their shoes' is therefore often used. Being empathetic is essential in the early years sector as you can therefore imagine what it might be like to be a nervous parent, a curious child or a busy colleague. By thinking about others in this way you will become more sensitive to others.

Interpersonal skills

Interpersonal skills are about the way in which you communicate and respond to others. Good interpersonal skills are essential in this sector as much of your work involves interaction with children, parents and colleagues. Many learners find at the start of their studies that communicating with adults is harder than communicating with children. This is often about confidence but also about practice. It is, however, essential that by the time you finish your studies you are able to talk to others in a way that makes them feel at ease.

Case study

Difficulties communicating

Joseph is in the first year of his course. He is enjoying being in placement because he is interested and enjoys being with the children. With other adults he is less confident and actively looks for ways to reduce contact with them because he is afraid that he will say something wrong or look silly. This means that in the morning he tends only to say 'hello' and if he is asked any questions tends only to reply with one-word answers without making eye contact. Unfortunately, this means that Joseph is developing a reputation in the setting for being stand-offish. Staff say that he is difficult to work with and that he makes them feel awkward.

1. Why might Joseph be unaware of how staff are feeling?

2. Why is it important to develop interpersonal skills?

3. Suggest three ways in which Joseph might be able to improve his interpersonal skills.

Reflectiveness

Professionals need to be able to reflect carefully as they work. This means thinking about how effective you have been in, for example, planning activities, communicating with parents or explaining a situation to a colleague. Through self-reflection it becomes possible to think about how to repeat something that has worked well or how to improve ready for next time. Through reflection it is also possible to improve your interpersonal skills. For example, you might think about how you responded or communicated in a situation and then be able to consider ways in which you might have been more effective.

Interest

People who work well with children are genuinely interested in their work. This means that they may attend training and read articles and books about their area of work. Interest in their work is often reflected in their day-to-day attitudes. For example, should a meeting run on into lunchtime, a person who was engrossed in the outcomes for the children and the setting being discussed at the meeting would not be concerned about having a shorter lunch hour.

Flexibility and openness

Change is a major feature of working in the early years sector. This requires a flexible approach and the ability to meet new ideas and initiatives with openness. The reason for changes in this sector link to new research about the way children learn, new government and funding initiatives as well as changes to the curriculum and arrangements for inspection. In addition, health and safety and other legislation may also create changes. Being able to adapt to changes is therefore essential. Flexibility is also required in terms of some everyday issues such as staff rotas, timetabling arrangements and changes to plans and activities.

Reliability

Being reliable should mean that parents, children and other professionals feel that they can count on you. This involves you being punctual and completing tasks and activities properly.

Emotional stability

Emotional stability is extremely important in terms of being a professional. It is about the way in which you can regulate your feelings and moods. This is particularly important as children need adults to be consistent and predictable. It is not fair on a child to find that one day an adult laughs and jokes with them but on the next day, for no reason, the same adult seems uninterested or bored. Parents, colleagues and other professionals also need you to show emotional stability so they can communicate effectively with and rely on you. While everyone will have their good and bad days, depending on home circumstances, health and general energy levels, a professional should still aim to deliver the same quality of care and energy so that nobody, other than close friends or a colleague, would know that anything is wrong.

Case study

Monday morning mood

Rhianna is working on placement. It is Monday morning and she is not feeling very lively. At the weekend she drank quite a lot and did not get much sleep. While she enjoyed the weekend she is now feeling very rough. This morning she finds the children very boisterous and noisy. She also does not feel like talking to them much. Last week the children enjoyed being with Rhianna because she played games with them and smiled. Two children today have already asked her to play with them, but she has told them to go away.

1. Discuss the effects of Rhianna's mood swings on the children.

2. Explain why emotional stability is important when working with children.

The importance of valuing and respecting families, colleagues and other professionals

In order to work effectively in the early years sector it is essential that you are able to show that you value and respect everyone that you work with. This includes children and parents as well as colleagues and other professionals.

There are many practical ways to show that you value and respect the people you work with. Below are some examples of how value and respect can be translated into practice.

Contribution to meetings

The way in which you contribute to meetings can send out both positive and negative messages. Listening and contributing shows that you value what others are trying to achieve. As a professional, you may attend meetings with parents as well as staff meetings and multi-agency meetings.

Punctuality

It is important to be on time at meetings. This shows that you are committed and therefore value others' contribution. If people have had to wait for you to arrive, this sends out a negative signal. Parents, particularly, may become frustrated if they have had to make special arrangements in order to attend.

Confidentiality

Understanding that some conversations and information are confidential is important. It shows that you are trustworthy (see also page 355).

In order to work ⇨ in the early years sector it is important to value everyone that you work with

Listening to others

By listening to others and trying to see things from their point of view rather than making assumptions, you show that you value what other people do and what they are trying to achieve.

Being interested

If you are interested in finding out about other people's work and their views, you showing to others that you respect them.

Managing disagreements

Interestingly, there are many points of view when it comes to how best to work with children. There are ways in which you can put forward a different point of view without it resulting in confrontation or a lack of respect. Below are some ways of showing respect towards someone while putting across an alternative view.

→ 'While I understand what you are trying to say, my view is different. I think that ...'

→ 'With all due respect, I see this in a different way. I think that ...'

→ 'I am not sure that I can agree with you because I feel that ...'

→ 'While your point is valid, I can see a different side to this. I think that ...'

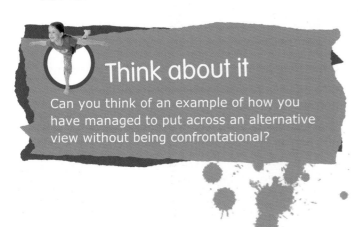

Think about it

Can you think of an example of how you have managed to put across an alternative view without being confrontational?

Case study

A confrontational style

A new approach to planning is being discussed in a team meeting. The manager is beginning to explain that the current way of planning does not demonstrate how children's individual needs are to be met. Joy-Ann, a member of staff, is concerned that this will create more work. She interrupts the manager and states flatly that she has no intention of changing her way of planning. This creates tension in the meeting.

1. How has Joy-Ann shown a lack of respect towards her colleague?

2. Why is it important to listen to others before putting forward a point of view?

3. Discuss ways in which Joy-Ann might have put her concerns across more positively.

Procedures and working methods

When teams work together it is important that everyone understands the procedures that are in place. In an organisation where several professionals with different roles work together this becomes increasingly important. Procedures and working methods are usually derived from the policies of a setting, for example behaviour policy or working with parents. It is essential that you are aware of the policies of your setting and that you follow them closely. Following the agreed procedures and working methods in a setting prevents situations where children or their parents are confused because they are given different messages (see the case study overleaf). It also prevents conflict in teams.

From time to time, procedures and working methods will need to be reviewed, for example they may be outdated because legislation has changed or there may be a change to the way in which the setting operates. This is when the flexibility and openness of staff becomes important so that changes can be made smoothly.

The importance of knowing procedures

Anne is a new member of staff at a Children's Centre which offers nursery provision as well as housing the speech and language team and health services. One morning, a parent approaches her and asks whether the speech and language team can see her son. Anne replies that the boy can be seen anytime and that all she has to do is bring him in. Later that week the parent takes a morning off work to bring her son into the centre. She is annoyed to find that an appointment was necessary and that she has wasted her time and money.

1. Why is it important that professionals working alongside each other know about procedures and working methods?

2. How could this situation have been prevented?

3. What might be the effects of this situation on the parent?

How to provide multi-disciplinary care of individuals

The aim of multi-disciplinary care is that professionals work together to meet children's differing needs. This might mean professionals with very different roles working alongside each other, such as a speech and language therapist working with a nursery. In addition, it is also common for children to move between different types of education and care provision over the course of a week, for example a child who goes part-time to nursery, spends time with a childminder and has respite care every other weekend. In such a situation, staff may not be working physically alongside each other but as they are all involved with the same child they need to communicate and work together.

In some settings, children will be involved with many professionals. The three examples below show how multi-disciplinary care might be provided.

→ Jay is 5 years old and attends school full-time. Jay has a learning disability and has a learning support assistant to help in class. Jay also attends the after-school club three days a week, which is held at a local community centre. She has a support worker who helps her there. Jay is also receiving speech and language therapy. She has exercises and activities to do and the speech and language therapist visits her in the school once a month. As Jay is on the special needs register in the school, she is also seen by the educational psychologist each year. The educational psychologist provides advice and suggestions.

→ Carl is 3 years old. He is in foster care awaiting adoption. He has a social worker who is responsible for his foster placement and for preparing him for adoption. Carl attends a Children's Centre every day. At the moment Carl needs support in managing his behaviour and has a member of staff who is dedicated to being with him while he makes the transition from foster care into being with his adoptive family.

→ Anneka is 2 years old. For two days a week she goes to a childminder who often takes her to drop-in sessions at the local Children's Centre. On three days a week, Anneka goes to the Children's Centre to be looked after in the day care section.

It has long been recognised that children need to develop a special relationship with at least one person within a setting. Where there is a range of people working with a child from different agencies, one person should take the lead and become a main point of contact for the child's family and other professionals. In some cases, the person who takes on this role will be the child's key person. This will mean that information can be coordinated and that important information is not 'lost'. In such a situation it will be important for you, as the child's key person, to find out who is involved with the child and who you should share information with. It is essential that everyone working with the child and their family work closely together so that the child and their family's needs can be met.

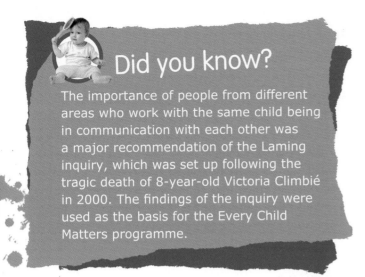

Did you know?

The importance of people from different areas who work with the same child being in communication with each other was a major recommendation of the Laming inquiry, which was set up following the tragic death of 8-year-old Victoria Climbié in 2000. The findings of the inquiry were used as the basis for the Every Child Matters programme.

Find out!

You can find out more about the circumstances of the Laming inquiry by visiting www.victoria-climbie-inquiry.org.uk

How communication and confidentiality are managed within the team

Communication

Where several professionals are involved in caring for a child, it becomes essential for everyone involved to communicate well. There are many ways in which teams will communicate. These include:

→ notice boards
→ diary boards
→ letters and e-mails
→ phone calls
→ team meetings.

Notice boards

Many organisations have a staff notice board in a communal area such as a staff room. This is a way of passing on information, although it can only be used for information that is not confidential or particularly urgent. It is important to remember that people other than team members may read the notice board and that a busy or absent member of

staff may not read notices there. It is essential that out of date notices are removed so that the board does not become cluttered.

Diary boards

Some organisations also have a diary board. This shows what is happening on each day of the week and may show when members of the team are absent, when visitors are expected or when special events are happening. As with notice boards, it is important that only general information that is not confidential is shown there.

W/C 25th June

Monday – P.T out. Anne McWilliams to see Hannah

Tuesday – Staff meeting 6pm prompt!!

Wednesday – A.T's tutor – 11.30am

Thursday – Blue room trip P.T covering

Friday – K.L & K.P out for training

Has anyone seen the gold paint? !! Ann

⇧ **A staff diary board**

Letters and e-mails

Written information is another important way of helping team members communicate with each other. As confidentiality is always an issue, it can be helpful to clearly indicate when something is confidential or personal. It is also important to remember that e-mails are not necessarily secure ways of passing information. Any written information needs to be legible, properly spelt and clear. You should also think about the tone and style of the information (see also Unit 5, pages 222–3).

Phone calls

Using the phone can be a useful way of gaining and passing on information. It is important, though, to remember to take notes of any calls that are particularly important so that afterwards you have a record of what has been agreed, who you spoke to and any decisions taken. Phone calls are not good ways of sharing and receiving sensitive information but are helpful as a way of keeping in touch.

Case study

Poor communication skills

Sharon is having a busy day in the nursery and is just about to take a quick coffee break when the phone rings. She talks to the speech therapist who is phoning her to let her know that she will not be able to come and see a child that she has arranged to assess later on in the week. She gives Sharon an alternative date and time and asks Sharon if she can let the child's parent know that the assessment has been moved. Sharon puts the phone down and then goes to have coffee. During the coffee break she is told that there is a parent waiting to see her in reception. She goes quickly down and meets with the parent.

A few days later the parent and child come into the centre expecting to meet with the speech therapist. She is told by a member of staff that the speech therapist has not arrived. She waits for fifteen minutes and then a member of staff calls the speech and language team who report that this meeting has been postponed.

1. What are the effects of Sharon's inefficiency on the parent?

2. How might this situation affect the trust between the speech therapist and the nursery?

3. Explain how this situation could have been avoided.

Team meetings

Team meetings can be an important way for teams to communicate and for different professionals working together to get an overview of each other's work. Team meetings may focus on the needs of individual children and be called specifically to look and plan for these, or they may be held to ensure the smooth running of the centre or service. It is now recognised that effective meetings should be properly structured so that time is not wasted and information not lost. The usual way to structure a meeting is to have a Chair and an agenda.

Chair

The Chair is the person who runs the meeting. The Chair will organise the meeting and produce an agenda (see below). A good Chair makes sure that the meeting runs to time and that everyone gets a chance to put forward their point of view. The Chair also prevents discussion from going off the point or becoming too personalised. Normally, if someone has a point to make, he or she will ask the Chair for permission to speak.

Some meetings are run without a Chair and an agenda but unless the group is very focused, there is a danger that the meeting will not resolve issues or be effective in terms of time. Some organisations have a 'rolling Chair'. The idea is that people take it in turns to take on the role of the Chair. This can work well as it spreads the workload.

Agenda

An agenda provides the structure for the meeting. It essentially defines the issues that are to be discussed and puts them in a logical order. Normally everyone is contacted before the meeting so that they can put any issues or 'items' on the agenda. The final agenda is circulated before the meeting so that everyone knows what will be discussed. This gives people time to prepare materials or do some research.

Preparing an agenda is a skill. If there are too many items there may not be time to discuss them all thoroughly and this can mean that the meeting overruns or will close without everything being discussed. This can be a source of dissatisfaction, especially if someone has attended the meeting only because there is an item on the agenda that is particularly of concern to them. It is usual for the Chair to draw up the agenda.

PONDLESHAM PLAYGROUP COMMITTEE AGM

Agenda

Meeting to be held in playgroup hall on 26th September at 6.00pm.

1. Apologies for absence (explanation in advance from absentees)

2. Minutes of last meeting (record of last meeting to be approved)

3. Matters arising (from minutes of last meeting)

4. Annual Report from Chairperson

5. Playgroup accounts and Treasurer's report

6. Activities for new year

7. Any other business (members given a chance to discuss items not on agenda)

8. Date of next meeting

⇧ **Example of an agenda for a meeting**

Minutes

The minutes of the meeting are a record that shows what has been discussed and any decisions that have been taken. It is usual that someone within the meeting agrees to take notes and to type up and distribute the minutes afterwards. This role is known as the Minutes Secretary. Again, some groups take turns at adopting this role.

It is important that the notes of the meeting are taken down accurately so that they can be written up properly. The skill of minute taking is to summarise what has been said or concluded. It can be useful if, after any complex discussions involving different points of view, the minute taker asks the Chair if it is possible to read back to the meeting the summary that they have written.

At the start of the next meeting, the minutes of the previous meeting are usually looked at and agreed by those present.

Attending a meeting

If you are asked to attend a meeting it is important to find out if there is an agenda and, if there is, to read it through carefully. You should make sure that you arrive in good time and are equipped with any documents and a diary along with paper and pen. If there is a Chair running the meeting it is important to respect their role and only contribute if you have been given permission to speak. It is normal to indicate that you wish to contribute by slightly raising your hand.

Most meetings that are productive will result in some action points for team members. It is important to make sure that if you volunteer or agree to do something that you are in a position to do so. Once the meeting is finished you should be sent or e-mailed a copy of the minutes. You should read them through and check that they are accurate. The minutes should also help you to remember what you have agreed to do.

At the end of a meeting it is usual to agree a time and date of the next meeting. It is therefore helpful to make sure that you have a diary with you.

Confidentiality within the team

You have seen that confidentiality is a major issue when working in the early years sector (see also Unit 3 page 127 and Unit 5 page 219). In this section you return to the importance of confidentiality in terms of working within a team.

In terms of confidentiality within the team, the key point remains that anything you learn about children, their families or others during the course of your work is likely to be confidential. When working with other professionals you are likely to hear comments and remarks that are not intended to be repeated outside of meetings or conversations. You may also see or be given documents that are a sensitive nature. This means that you should not disclose their contents and you must store them in a safe area. The case study below shows how a breach in professional confidentiality may cause difficulties in meeting a child's needs.

Case study

A breach in professional confidentiality

Louise is a nursery nurse. She works with a child who has significant learning difficulties. She attends a multi-disciplinary meeting and during the meeting the topic of respite care is mentioned. One of the other professionals mentions that the facility for respite care is due to be refurbished and that during the building works there is a possibility that non-urgent respite care will be unavailable there.

Later in the week, Louise meets the mother of the child she works with. She tells the mother that his respite care is likely to be cancelled. The mother is extremely distressed and tells other parents that she knows. They decide to organise a petition and write to the local newspaper. The head of service for respite care is furious because it was never their intention to close the respite care and plans were in place to increase capacity in another centre during the building work so that non-urgent respite care was still available.

1. Why was Louise wrong to repeat remarks that she had heard?

2. How might the trust between the respite service and parents be affected?

The roles and responsibilities of other professionals

It is important to understand the roles of the other professionals whom you work alongside. In Unit 14 you will look at the range of people who may support children and families with additional needs; it will be important to read pages 530–3 in order to understand the role that these professionals play as part of a multi-agency team. You will also need to talk to the people you work with to find out the exact nature of their work. By having good contacts and relationships with other professionals, you will be able to seek their advice and build on your own knowledge.

It is important to recognise that other professionals may see the needs of the child in a different way from you, as their background, knowledge base and training are different. This may mean that their priorities are different, as the case study below shows. Where professionals have different interests, it is essential that they are able to communicate in ways that show respect for each other's roles and that they are able to work together. This is important as professionals who work separately and without regard for each other's roles can create conflict and may also overlook children's best interests.

Case study

Different professionals, different priorities

Marlene is 6 years old. She attends a primary school that is part of a Children's Centre. She has some learning difficulties and is struggling to make friends in the playground. This is making her quite distressed. She is overweight and there have been some child protection concerns as she is showing some signs of neglect. A meeting is held and all those responsible for working with Marlene come together. This includes Marlene's teacher, a social worker, a dietician and other health professionals. Marlene's teacher is keen to focus on the need to provide her with support for her reading, while the health professionals are keen to assess Marlene's overall health. The social worker feels that the priority should be supporting the family.

1. Why will professionals have different viewpoints?

2. Why is it important that everyone has good communication skills?

3. Discuss why it will be important for everyone to agree on an action plan.

1. Ask three parents about the daily care needs of their children. Aim to choose parents who have children of different ages. Consider ways in which the care needs change according to the age of the children. Make sure that you keep notes.

2. Ask your placement supervisor about the key issues involved in working in teams. Ask if you can take notes that can be used in your portfolio.

3. Collate the information and material that you have collected so far. Check what other information and materials are required using the assignment task and assessment criteria given by CACHE.

See if you also have:

→ information to write up two activities which support and maintain a different aspect of the daily care of children

→ sufficient information to write up a summary of the main regulations that govern the care of children in different settings.

Consider whether you know enough to be able to:

→ analyse the ways in which legislation affects the way that settings provide care for children

→ evaluate the ways to work effectively in a multi-professional team.

U8

3

Getting ready for assessment

Research task (covering Units 1–9)

In order to gain the Diploma, you have to complete a research task that checks your knowledge of the mandatory units and your ability to analyse and evaluate. The task is externally marked. Below is a sample task that may help you practice this requirement.

Sample research task

'The first five years of a child's life may affect their later development and achievement.'

Evaluate how this statement is reflected in the delivery of child care and education both locally and nationally.

In order to complete this task you must:

1. Produce an action plan that shows how you intend to carry out the research and produce the evaluation.

2. Use a range of at least *four* different sources from the list below to help you research this topic.

   a) Interview with parents

   b) Interview with professionals

   c) Statistics from recognised organisations such as the Office of National Statistics

   d) Leaflets

   e) Books

   f) Internet

   g) Magazines

   h) Articles from professional journals

   i) Other media such as DVD

3. Produce an evaluation based on the information gained from researching this topic. You should demonstrate this through the use of references and bibliography, and where appropriate appendices.

4. Produce a reflective account that considers the validity of your sources and what you have learned from carrying out this assignment.

Unit 9

Development of professional skills within children's education

In this unit you will learn:

1. The professional standards expected of the practitioner
2. How to apply theoretical knowledge to the professional setting
3. How the planning cycle is used in various practical settings
4. How to meet the needs of individual and groups of children in a variety of settings
5. How professional practice is linked to legislation, policies and procedures

Section 1

The professional standards expected of the practitioner

In practice

It is your first day of a new placement. You are a little nervous and unsure about what exactly is required of you. You want to make a good first impression because you know how important it is to get off to a good start.

By the end of this section you will have learned some important skills and tips that should help you feel confident.

The professional standards expected of the practitoner

Timekeeping

It may seem very obvious but one of the most important things you must do on placement is to be there on time and ideally a few minutes early. This is an essential point to remember at all stages in your training, but also later in your career. Below are the reasons why good timekeeping matters.

Commitment

Punctuality shows people that you care about your work and that you are committed. Some placements get many requests to have learners and are therefore able to turn down those who do not seem interested.

Respect and politeness

Being on time is courteous and shows respect for other people. It also means that other people do not have to waste their time waiting for you to arrive. Keeping people waiting is therefore impolite.

Builds confidence

Being on time and having good timekeeping skills shows that you are not only committed but organised. As a learner this creates a good impression and helps others begin to feel that you can take on responsibility. Later on it helps inspire confidence in you from the people you work with, such as parents and other professionals.

Prevents disruption

One of the things that you might notice in the early years sector is the way in which people quickly count on you. Being late means that jobs might not get done and this will disrupt the smooth running of a session. Children, too, quickly get used to seeing you and start to count on you being there. They may become distressed if you are not there when you have said that you will be. Being on time is also important once you are qualified. A parent may not be able to leave for work until you arrive or a setting may not be able to open until the right ratio of staff is there.

Below are some very simple tips that can help you arrive on time. Remember, though, that good time keeping is a habit and you must be punctual every day.

Good practice checklist

Getting there on time

✓ Have an alarm clock that works – if you are a heavy sleeper set two!

✓ Buy a watch that you can read easily and try setting it 3 or 4 minutes early.

✓ Get as much done as you can the night before, e.g. pack bags, make lunch.

✓ Be realistic – many jobs do not take a 'couple of minutes'. Think through what you have to do before you can leave and build in enough time.

✓ Assume that there might be delays in your journey and allow yourself extra time.

✓ For an interview or for the first day, carry out a practice run so you know where to go and how long it will take to get there.

Case study

Getting to placement on time

Cassie lives a little way from her placement. She knows that she needs to take a bus to get there. When her college tutor asks if she has worked out her travel arrangements, she says 'yes', assuming that her friend will have a bus timetable. That night she asks her friend for the bus timetable but her friend doesn't have one. Cassie is still not too worried as she thinks that she can look it up online at home. She gets back late and finds that her computer is not working properly. She still isn't too worried and goes to bed.

The next morning, Cassie decides to walk down to the bus stop. She waits there for 10 minutes and a bus arrives. She asks if it goes to the stop near her placement and is told that no buses travel that way and she will need to go into the centre of town first. Now she is worried. She thinks about walking but realises that she has no map. She calls for a taxi on her mobile but finds that all the taxis are booked and doing school runs. She phones home but is too late as her mum has left for work. Another bus comes along and she takes it into town and changes there. She arrives at the placement nearly an hour late.

When she meets the manager, Cassie feels very uncomfortable. She says that she is sorry that she is late but the manager does not seem that interested in the reasons. The manager says that she cannot spend time with her now as she is expecting to meet some parents. Cassie feels quite miserable. After all, she says to herself, it's not her fault that there were no direct buses.

1. What impression has Cassie created by not arriving on time?

2. Why is her late arrival disruptive for the setting?

3. Explain how Cassie could have arrived at the placement on time.

Leaving placement at the end of the session

It is very important that you are not seen as a 'clock watcher' and someone who is always in a hurry to leave. This gives the impression of not being interested and lacking in commitment. You should therefore not leave placement early or ask if you can go earlier unless there is a genuine reason for this that has been agreed by your course tutor. For this reason it is a good idea to look around you at the end of the day. What are the other staff doing? Are there jobs that you could help them with? The end of the session is also time when staff are less busy and can properly talk to you. This is good opportunity to ask them about activities or observations that you need to carry out. It is also an excellent time to get to know staff so that you can feel more a part of the team.

Regular attendance

As well as being on time you need to demonstrate good attendance. The reasons for this are similar: good attendance shows people that you are committed, enthusiastic and reliable. It tells someone that you will not disrupt the organisation or, more importantly, upset the children. Children can get very anxious and distressed if they are let down by people who do not come when they say they will. In

terms of the quality of your placement, you will find that you are given more responsibility if you are seen as someone who will not let the team down.

Did you know?

Placement supervisors become reluctant to plan activities for learners to do with children if the learner has a track record of not turning up on the day. This is because an enormous amount of work goes into planning activities and an unreliable learner can disrupt the session.

What you should do if you cannot attend

It is important that you make every effort to attend your placement as not only are you letting the placement down and your tutor, you are also putting your qualification at risk. This is because you have to attend sufficient hours as part of the course.

If you cannot attend your placement you should always let them know at the start of the day. You should also let your course tutor know that you have been unable to attend. You may find that your course tutor asks you to provide some evidence such as a sick note from a doctor.

Did you know?

Being in placement is a practice for being in work, so in the same way that practitioners do not make appointments on work days, you should not do this either.

Appropriate dress code

It is important to dress appropriately for the work that you do and the setting that you do it in. Working with children is not high fashion and being practical about this is important. Clothes need to be easily washed as paint, sand or other marks can get onto them. If you are not sure about what you will need to wear before starting a placement, ask your tutor or another learner who has already completed a placement there. You could also phone in advance and ask for their advice, although note that people's ideas about terms such as 'comfortable' or 'smart' can vary. It is also important to understand that placement supervisors may not always feel that they can be totally honest with you about your appearance for fear of upsetting you. This means that you might not be told that your appearance is unsuitable until such time as your tutor visits you.

⇧ **It is important to dress appropriately for your work with children**

A good tip to ensure that you are getting it right is simply to observe the other staff – if you look around and see that they are wearing similar types of clothes, you are probably getting it right.

Jeans

Many placement settings, especially schools, do not allow staff and learners to wear jeans. If you are not sure about whether jeans will be acceptable, you might find it useful to wear another type of trouser instead. If jeans are allowed they should be 'smart' rather than scruffy.

Heels

High heels and young children do not go together! Firstly, you might step on a child, and secondly, you will not be able to move as fast. In the same way, heavy boots are often not worn. In some halls, pointed heels are banned as they damage the floors so you might even be asked to take off your shoes. Most practitioners wear low or flat heels. Trainers may not be accepted by all settings so do check first or observe what other staff are wearing.

Socks and tights

It is worth knowing that in some situations you might be asked to remove your shoes. This is common if you go into a baby room or into a hall. If you are easily embarrassed, you might like to check that your socks or tights do not have holes in them!

Jewellery

Discreet jewellery is usually fine, although dangly earrings are not a good idea with babies and young children as they may pull them and rip your ear. Rings can also be another problem if they are large or chunky as they can scratch children. They also make it hard to wash hands effectively. If you are involved in preparing food, snacks or drinks, you may be asked to remove them. Facial piercings such as tongue and eyebrow rings may also be problematic for settings and are best removed or concealed.

Aprons, tabards and uniforms

Some settings such as day care nurseries and pre-schools might provide you with a uniform, apron or tabard. It is important that you wear these and take care of them. At the end of your placement it is courteous to make sure they are returned in a clean state.

Appropriate logos and lettering

It is important to think about what is written on any T-shirts or other garments. Some garments have quite strong messages or comments which may not be to everyone's taste. Working with children and their families requires that you are sensitive to others' feelings. This means that any jokes, slogans or logos need to be appropriate.

Communication skills

Going to a placement for the first time can seem daunting. Quite often all the other adults are older and this in itself can feel strange. It is, however, important to develop good communication skills so you can meet other people confidently. This is important as your relationship with your placement supervisor, the team and the children will make a considerable difference to how much you can learn and enjoy the placement. In Unit 1 you looked at key aspects of communication and you will need to re-visit pages 12–13 as well as looking at the points below.

Basic presentation skills

Everyone knows that first impressions are powerful. This may not seem fair but it is important to recognise and work with this. As a learner you may feel a little daunted when you first arrive or are introduced to another adult, but being able to communicate well from the start will help you. Learning how to meet people is a skill you will need once you are qualified since you will need to make relationships with parents, show visitors around and work with other professionals.

Smile

Meeting another adult with a smile is a very good starting point. It is easy to forget to do this when you are in an unfamiliar environment and especially if you are feeling nervous.

Handshake

A handshake is a traditional greeting so be ready to shake someone's hand. It is thought that 'positive' handshakes send out good signals. They show that you are enthusiastic to meet someone and that you are confident.

⇧ **Making eye contact, smiling and showing interest are basic communication skills**

Eye contact

Looking at someone as you communicate is a basic requirement although some people forget to do this because they are nervous. Making eye contact and giving signs that you are listening, such as nodding your head or agreeing, tell the other person that you are interested in what they are saying.

Ways of showing interest

It is important that you show interest in the other person and any information that is being provided. Some learners also find it helpful to take a pad and paper with them so they can jot down any information that will be useful later. This is a good strategy especially if you know that you sometimes forget things because of nervousness, and when you start off in a new placement there is often a lot of information to take in.

You can also show interest by asking questions either about the setting or about the person. It is best to make questions general if you don't know someone well and focus on their role in the setting, for example 'Have you worked here for long?'

You may also be asked questions about yourself or your course. Again, another way of showing interest is by answering these questions fully. This helps the other person to learn more about you. One-word answers are often taken as a sign of reluctance or a lack of enthusiasm.

Meeting children

While communicating well with adults when meeting for the first time is a skill, so too is how you communicate when meeting children. It is important to remember about children's stage of development here as very young children are often unsure and even fearful of new adults.

Babies and toddlers

From 7 or 8 months up until the age of around 3 years, most babies and toddlers will appear timid, shy or even fearful if you approach them directly. Try instead talking to the adult they are with and from time to time meeting their gaze. Remember that smiling is important too. It can be useful to have a puppet or cuddly toy with you and to play with it so that the focus is not just on you. Gradually, babies and toddlers will come over to you.

Children aged 3–5 years

This age group are often less fearful but will find it easier if you are doing something of interest to them. This might mean taking out a pen and paper and doing a little drawing, bouncing a ball or using a puppet. Children can then come over and see what you are doing and start a conversation. Again, as with adults, making eye contact, smiling and being gently interested in them is essential.

⇧ **Babies and toddlers respond to adults smiling**

Children aged over 5 years

From around 5 years most children are comfortable talking with adults, although as with the younger age group it is important to take their lead as some children are shyer than others. It is essential to be interested and to listen carefully to what they want to talk about and show you.

Good practice checklist

Communicating with children and adults in the setting

✓ Show interest and enthusiasm when meeting adults.

✓ Make eye contact and show positive body language by, for example, smiling.

✓ Think about the age and stage of development of children when first meeting them.

✓ Avoid intense eye contact with babies and toddlers when they are showing signs of wariness.

✓ Think about using props such as puppets with young children.

Confidentiality

As a learner you will probably have access to information about children, their families and staff members. Any information that you gain while on placement has the potential to be confidential. Breaching confidentiality is a serious issue and may lead to you being refused a placement. This means that you need to be very careful when talking to your friends, family or classmates. You should think about whether the information is general and available to anyone. If this is the case, for example it is easy to find out the address of a placement or the name of the manager, then the information will not be confidential. On the other hand, any information that is linked to working at the placement may fall into a confidential category, for example the names of children, problems that families might be having and personal information about staff.

U9
1

If you are not sure about whether information needs to be treated as confidential, it is always worth asking. If this is not possible, err on the safe side. The case study below shows why confidentiality is so important.

Case study

The importance of confidentiality

Pauline is on placement at a local nursery. She is quite excited as she used to go there when she was little. Her mum is very interested in what she is doing there and asks her lots of questions. Pauline tells her about a child who keeps wetting herself and mentions the girl's name. Later in the week, Pauline's mum chats to a neighbour over the road whose daughter goes there. She asks the neighbour whether her daughter has problems with going the toilet as the name is the same. The neighbour later phones the nursery and is furious with the manager. She is angry because she thinks that her daughter's problems with toilet training are being 'broadcast around the area'. The manager realises that there has been a breach of confidentiality and begins to investigate.

1. How did Pauline breach confidentiality?
2. Why is the girl's mother so angry?
3. How might this breach of confidentiality affect the relationship between the staff team and Pauline?

Personal hygiene

It may seem obvious but personal hygiene is important when working with children as this is a key way in which infection can be avoided. Babies and young children are particularly vulnerable to infections, some of which can be spread via skin and clothing.

Clothing

Choose easily washable items of clothing and make sure that they are clean. Always use aprons whenever they are provided.

Hair

Hair needs to be clean, but long hair should be tied back. In many settings this is also in your own interest. Many early years settings and schools suffer from frequent bouts of head lice so check your own hair regularly for any white flecks that do not move when combed (these are usually the egg cases or 'nits') and be aware that a sign of having caught head lice is an itchy scalp (see also Unit 4 pages 205–6).

Hands and nails

Your hands need to be kept clean: you should wash your hands with soap before touching or eating food and after using the toilet. Good hand hygiene prevents cross-infection (see also Unit 4 pages 177–8). You should also keep your nails short. Long nails harbour germs but they can also scratch children.

Teeth

Children prefer to be with adults who smile. Clean teeth give you a better smile, but also prevent your breath from smelling. As working with children means coming into close contact with them, it is important that they are not 'put off' by someone with bad breath.

Good practice checklist

Personal hygiene
✓ Wear clothing that is washable and sensible.
✓ Check with your placement supervisor about the setting's dress code before attending placement for the first time.
✓ Look at what other members of staff are wearing for guidance.
✓ Tie long hair back and keep jewellery to a minimum.
✓ Check your hair regularly for head lice and use a nit comb.
✓ Keep nails short and do not wear nail varnish.
✓ Aim to look neat, clean and tidy.

Role models

There are some basic standards of behaviour, dress and hygiene that are expected of everyone who works with children. It is important to know about them so you can be sure that you are getting them right. Young children do not distinguish between the behaviour of qualified adults and learners so it matters that you get the standards right even when you are a learner.

In Unit 2 you looked at how children learn and saw that some children's learning is influenced by what they see (see pages 71–2). The term 'role model' is used to describe an adult that a child might copy. Even though you are a learner, you will still have a great influence on children. This means that you will need to remember that your actions will be noticed and copied by the children you work with. You will therefore need to think about your behaviour in front of children and make sure that you are acting as a good role model by, for example, being patient, listening to them and showing respect for them and other adults.

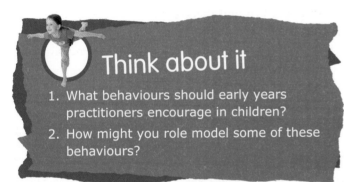

Think about it

1. What behaviours should early years practitioners encourage in children?
2. How might you role model some of these behaviours?

How to use placement diaries to reflect on experiences

Placement diaries are ways in which you can gain evidence as well as helping you to prepare and think about your practice. A placement diary shows first of all that you have been attending your placement regularly. This is important as it is a requirement of the course that you have direct experience of working with children.

Placement diaries can also help you to prepare, plan and reflect on your experiences, for example you may be asked to write down some notes about what you have done and what you have learned as a result. It is a good idea to think about what you have learned from your day in placement and from working with children.

→ Did you manage to observe children and think about child development theory?
→ What activities did you carry out? What did you learn from doing the activities that would help you in the future?
→ Were there any children who needed more support or for whom the activity was not appealing?

You can also reflect on the way that you work with other adults in the setting. Are you able to ask questions, use your initiative and contribute to the setting yet? Some tutors may ask you to write down a target as a result of this reflection.

The CACHE Statement of Values

CACHE's Statement of Values are reproduced below and reflect the early years sector's standards of conduct. They are important as they represent a professional way of working with children, young people and their families. It is important that you read through the standards and make sure that you adopt them in terms of your own practice. Throughout your course, placement and assignments these standards should be reflected as they represent good practice.

CACHE Statement of Values

The CACHE candidate will:

- Put the child first by:
  - ensuring the child's welfare and safety
  - showing compassion and sensitivity
  - respecting the child as an individual
  - upholding the child's rights and dignity
  - enabling the child to achieve their full learning potential.
- Never use physical punishment.
- Respect the parent, or those in a parenting role, as the primary carer and educator of the child.
- Respect the contribution and expertise of staff in the child care and education field and other professionals with whom they may be involved.
- Respect the customs, values and spiritual beliefs of the child and their family.
- Uphold CACHE's Diversity Statement.
- Honour the confidentiality of information relating to the child and their family, unless its disclosure is required by law or is in the best interest of the child.

(*Source:* CACHE 2007)

U9
1

Section 2

How to apply theoretical knowledge to the professional setting

In practice

It is your first day in placement and your supervisor shows you around. She takes you into a room where children are playing. You ask the supervisor about the age of the children and what they are doing. She looks surprised and says that she thought you would have been able to have worked this out by watching the children and the types of activities that they were doing. You feel a little embarrassed.

By the end of this section you will be able to make links between your knowledge of child development and what you see and do in practice.

Theories of development and learning and how to apply theory in practice

Most learners enjoy their placements because they are able to work with children. To be successful as a practitioner you need to find ways of linking what you have been taught with what you do. This means turning the theory into practice.

A good starting point is to observe children and reflect upon what you are seeing in terms of developmental theory. The table below gives some examples of ways in which you might see that theory links to practice.

Area of development	How theory might relate to practice
Physical development	Compare children's gross and fine motor skills. You might notice that a child can run easily but finds it hard to draw or cut neatly on a line.
Intellectual development	Look out for signs of egocentrism in children under 7 years; children assume that other people's world is the same as theirs, for example 'Is your mummy coming to get you?'
Communication and language development	Listen out for virtuous errors with nursery- and school-aged children, for example 'He has got five sheeps' or 'You wented swimming'. Children use grammatical rules they have absorbed but apply them to everything.
Social, emotional and behavioural development	• Look out for signs of attachment, for example parents who need to give their children a last kiss before they leave them or who remind them to wave goodbye. Children also show their attachment to their parents by running over to them at the end of the session. You might also hear children talking about what they do at home with their parents. • Look out for signs that children have developed some friendship preferences, including starting to play with same-sex friends. • Look out for children who copy other children's actions or expressions. This is role modelling. Notice also the ways in which children copy the actions or words of adults. • Notice how children enjoy gaining attention from adults, for example they may smile after they have been praised.

Range of observational techniques and how to make evaluations related to theories of development

As part of this course you are expected to carry out observations. In Unit 2 you looked at different techniques for observing children and how you might evaluate them and draw conclusions about children's development. In order to complete this unit you will need to read pages 88–104 carefully.

Why are learners asked to carry out observations and assessments?

Most childcare courses require learners to put together a portfolio of observations. Although learners will need to be able to carry out observations and assessments when they are employed, it is also an excellent way for learners to show that they have understood how the theories of child development relate to practice. It also shows that learners are able to assess and identify children's needs at different ages and stages of their development.

Unfortunately, carrying out observations and assessments is a skill that requires practice. This means that most learners need to produce many observations before they are truly competent. To help you learn the skill of observing children, a range of observation techniques that link to different areas of study are described in Unit 2 (see pages 88–104).

Presentation of work

There is a difference in the way settings and learners lay out observations. Learners use observations and assessments as a way of demonstrating their knowledge, so are required to write up and make comments about what they have seen. Most childcare courses ask that learners present their work using the sections described in the table below.

✏ **Writing up a presentation or observation**

Section	What section should include
Details of the observation, signature of workplace supervisor	Learners are asked to provide information about the observation they are submitting. Details help tutors to look particularly at the interpretation and consider whether the learner is coming to appropriate conclusions. Some courses provide front sheets to make sure that learners remember to include all the details.
Aim and rationale	This is a statement about why the observation or the assessment is being carried out and what the learner is hoping to observe.
Observation/assessment	This is a record of the observation and assessment, using one of the observation methods (see pages 89–102).
Evaluation (the heading 'interpretation' can also be used)	In this section, learners come to some conclusions about what they have observed. They should also look at the child's age and consider if the learning or development is typical for the age range. Where possible, learners should also write about how the actions of the child link to child development theories. Learners should also consider whether the observation method they used was effective.
Recommendations	This section identifies the child's immediate needs and considers ways of meeting them, for example a child who can steer a tricycle might now be ready to use a tricycle with pedals.
Personal learning	Learners write about what they have learned from carrying out the observation, either in terms of knowledge gained about the children, the setting or the method of recording they used. For example, 'From carrying out this observation I have found that Samantha can read some words. This has taught me that some 4-year-olds perhaps pick up words if they are familiar with a book.'
References and bibliography	At the end of the piece of work, books used for research are listed in alphabetical order by author.

Confidentiality and learners' observations and records

Observations and assessments on children are confidential (see also pages 98–9). Normally observations and assessments carried out by early years practitioners would be shown only to supervisors and parents. They would also be stored in a safe place. However, this is not the case with observations that learners carry out. This means that you have to protect the identity of children in the following ways:

→ Use only children's first names.
→ Change children's names if they are unusual or could lead to the child being identified.
→ Give the type of setting not the actual name, e.g. write 'nursery' not 'Tiny Tots Nursery'.
→ Write children's ages as years and months, e.g. 3 years 4 months. Do not write the child's date of birth.
→ Photographic records should not be used unless permission is gained from the child's parents and from the setting.
→ Make sure that your files contain either the college telephone number or your own, so that if necessary it can be returned safely.

Case study

Sharon is studying on a childcare course. She has carried out several observations and assessments. One day she tells her supervisor that she has left her file on the bus. The supervisor asks if she had anything in the file that could identify a particular child. Sharon nods her head and says that she had written up an observation but did not change the child's name. The supervisor is cross and explains that the child's family is living in a refuge because his father assaulted the mother and one of the other children. The supervisor feels that if the father finds out where the child is staying during the day, he would be able to work out where the whole family are staying.

Afterwards Sharon complains bitterly to her friends, saying that it wasn't her fault because nobody had told her about this child before and there was little chance that the father would get hold of the file anyway.

1. Why is Sharon wrong to believe that she should have been told about this child before?

2. Can you think of any other circumstances where a child's identity or location may need to be kept confidential?

The role of your workplace supervisor

Your supervisor will expect you to carry out observations and conduct activities with children, since this is a requirement of your childcare course. Most supervisors are keen to help you and should be able to give you their time and advice. To help them you need to be organised and sensitive to the demands on their time. Very few supervisors will be in a position where they can drop everything to read through your observations. This means that you need to find out when is a convenient time for you to carry out observations and make sure that, when they offer to help, you are appreciative. Some supervisors will be able to talk you through what you have recorded only 'after hours' or during your lunch break.

Once you have written up your observation you will need to ask for a signature. Most supervisors are interested in seeing what you have written, either in order to help you further or because they would like to find out more about the children you have been studying. In any case, supervisors have the right to look at learners' work because they are signing to say that it is a fair record of what took place.

Evaluating your observations and assessments

There is little point in carrying out observations or assessments unless you process the information in some way and draw conclusions. This next step is often called interpretation or evaluation. The aim is to look at the information and compare it to information you already have from other sources, such as books, and then draw some conclusions.

Linking your evaluations to normative development

You will need to show that you can compare children's behaviour and development to the normative development or milestones. 'Normative development' means development that is expected of children at certain ages. This means that if you have observed a 3-year-old girl turn-taking, you should look to see if this is considered normal behaviour. (It is!) This in turn allows you to come to a conclusion that the child you have observed is showing social skills that most children of her age group are demonstrating.

U9
2

Think about it

In pairs, read through the scenarios below. For each, is the child showing learning and behaviour that is typical for his or her age?

→ A 2-year-old hugs her parent's legs when she sees a stranger.

→ A 4-year-old pushes another child down the slide.

→ A child of 15 months has a vocabulary of 20 words.

→ A 3-year-old finds it difficult to use a pair of scissors.

→ A baby of 6 months is trying to feed himself.

Linking theories of child development to your observations

To show that you have understood the theories of child development, you should be able to link them to some aspects of children's behaviour. For example, you might see a baby of 9 months cry when his mother leaves the room. This is typical behaviour for this age of child, but it also shows that the child knows who his primary carer is. This behaviour fits in with Bowlby's theory on attachment (see page 80).

In this book many theories of behaviour and development are described (see Unit 2 pages 66–87). It is important to include references to theorists in your work. A correct link to theories of child development shows that you can link theory to practice. (Notes on how to include references in your work are found in Unit 1, page 21.)

The example below shows how a learner has linked normative behaviour and a theory of development in her evaluation.

> While carrying out this observation I noticed that the boys were quite imaginative in their play as they used a few pieces of Lego which were joined together as a gun. According to Davenport, Piaget's theory says that both boys should be in the pre-operations stage where symbolism is used: "By about 2 years of age a child can let one object stand for (or symbolise) something else" (1994).
>
> During this observation I noticed that both Sam and Jake were quite aggressive in their play - they spoke about making guns and shooting someone. According to Davenport (1994) the TV may have an effect on a child's level of aggression. Davenport outlines an experiment conducted by Stein and Friedrich in 1972 about children and TV violence.

Section 3

How the planning cycle is used in various practical settings

In practice

You have been asked by your placement supervisor to try an activity with a small group of children. You are not sure where to start.

By the end of this section you will know which factors need to be taken into consideration when planning.

The use of observations for planning activities that promote development and meet care, health and education needs

There are many ways in which observations can be used. Many settings use observations of individual children in order to work out how best to meet their interests and needs. They may, for example, make a note of a particular child's interests or development during the day then use these notes to inform their planning. As a learner you will need to find out about how your setting carries out observations.

It is important that you also learn to observe children as a tool for planning. You may, for example, have seen an idea of an activity in a magazine or another setting, but before trying it out you will need to consider whether it is suitable for the children you are working with. It may be that the activity is not right for the children's stage of development or that it does not build on their interests.

How to make assessments of development

There is a range of ways in which settings might assess children's development (see also Unit 2 pages 106–8).

Find out!

Ask your placement supervisor to show you how they assess development in the setting. Find out how the information is used and how parents are informed about children's progress.

It is also interesting to find out if there are any assessments that have to be completed at certain times of the year. In schools, for example, Reception teachers have to complete the Foundation Stage profiles by the end of the school year.

If you are given the task of helping to complete assessments, make sure that you understand exactly what you must do and how it needs to be recorded. It can be helpful to ask if you could watch someone carrying out the assessment on a child so that you can see how it is done. Note how much help children are given and what the adult says to encourage or support a child. This is important because assessments must be a fair reflection of the child's development. You may also need to find out what you should do if the child seems unhappy or is not interested in the task or activity.

Case study

Understanding the purpose of an assessment

Cassie is a learner on placement at a school. The teacher feels that she is doing well and has asked her to assess three children's acquisition of sounds. She passes some cards with letters on them to Cassie and a recording sheet. She tells Cassie to show the letters to each child and to note down whether they know the sound of the letter. Cassie is a little worried but does not like to say anything.

Cassie begins the assessment with one boy. He does not seem sure of his sounds and she decides to give him a few clues because she feels sorry for him. By the end he is able to say all of the sounds, so Cassie writes down that he knows them. The teacher seems a little surprised by the results; Cassie does not tell her that he needed quite a lot of help. Two weeks later the teacher realises that the boy is not confident and has to plan extra activities for him.

1. Why is it important to understand the purpose of assessments?

2. Why must assessment be accurate?

3. Explain how this situation could have been avoided.

374

Evaluations

Many settings will ask you to carry out tasks, activities or games with children. As with assessments it is important that you are clear about what you have to do and that you understand what learning intentions have been planned. A teacher may, for example, be hoping that children can do some independent writing or a nursery officer may be hoping that a toddler tries to use a spoon to eat with.

Once you have completed the task, activity or game, it is important that you provide some information about how it has gone. This information needs to be accurate, and where you have been working with groups of children you should be able to provide information about each child. Where children have needed support this needs to be noted as this information might inform future planning. Some settings provide written sheets onto which you must write an evaluation. Below is a list of questions that might help you evaluate effectively.

Good practice checklist

Questions to help you evaluate effectively

- ✓ Did most children appear to be engaged and interested in the activity?
- ✓ How much input from you was needed?
- ✓ Why was this input needed?
- ✓ What did the children learn from the activity?
- ✓ Was this learning planned or spontaneous?
- ✓ How could this learning be reinforced or built upon?
- ✓ What did individual children gain from the activity?
- ✓ What was your role in helping children to learn?
- ✓ What types of resources were used?
- ✓ Were there sufficient resources?
- ✓ Which resources attracted children's attention?
- ✓ What further resources could have been used?
- ✓ What were the limitations of this activity?
- ✓ How could these limitations be addressed?

How to plan activities to meet curriculum frameworks and learning needs within different settings

As part of your training you will need to learn how to plan activities in a range of settings (see also Unit 7 pages 300–19). To do this well you need to spend some time finding out which curriculum framework is used in the setting as well as the planning system and format that is used. This can vary immensely, even between settings working with the same age of children.

In some settings you may be invited to a planning meeting or asked if you would like to watch as planning is drawn up. In many settings this will often happen once the session has finished and after the normal time at which you could leave. It is important, however, to stay if invited as this will help you learn how to plan in a practical way. This can be different from how you might be expected to plan as a learner – activity planning as a learner is often used as a way of showing your knowledge.

During a planning meeting, look out for ways in which staff use curriculum documents, plan assessments and think about individual needs. Find out too how often planning meetings take place and the amount of time that a setting plans ahead for. Many settings will have long-term as well as short-term plans. You might also find that settings revisit plans they have used before in order to provide ideas for successful activities. Sitting in on a planning meeting will mean that when you qualify and have to plan, you will already have some of the necessary skills and knowledge in place.

How to plan for individual and group work

You will need to show as part of your course that you can plan and carry out activities with individual as well as groups of children. You should also be able to carry out a wide range of activities that cover different developmental areas.

As a learner you may find that your planning needs to be in more detail than that of the setting. This approach will help you to go through the process of thinking about the learning outcomes and prepare carefully for activities. Planning carefully for activities means they are more likely to be successful.

Below are some key points that you should consider when planning for groups and individuals.

Time

It is important to consider how much time you will need to prepare the activity. Some activities require the setting up or preparation of materials in advance. Wherever possible, much of this should be done with children as this is considered good practice.

It is also important to think about how long children might be interested in using or doing the activity. This is where observations are important. If you have observed an individual child or a group of children doing something similar, it may give you a feel of how much time is needed. This is important because it is frustrating for children to start something and enjoy it, only to be asked to stop or tidy up. In the same way, it is also frustrating for children to be made to stay at something that is no longer holding their interest.

Stage of development

Children's interests and skills do change with time; planning has to take into consideration their overall development. This is essential as otherwise children may find something too difficult or not sufficiently challenging. Children's stage of development may also affect your role in an activity; for example, babies and toddlers will need more support and supervision than older children. Again, observation beforehand is essential. If you have watched children playing and being involved with adults, it is easier to recognise and understand their stage of development and needs.

Interests

It is good practice to be aware of children's interests and to base learning upon them. Even babies develop favourite toys and books and have routines they like to follow. By spending time observing children before planning, you can begin to recognise what they will enjoy doing and how best they may learn.

Resources and equipment

Some activities require specific pieces of equipment and resources. It is important to identify exactly what is needed and to check upon its availability.

You will also need to be sure that you know how to use resources and equipment safely, including the potential pitfalls arising from their use. It is essential that any resources and equipment are stage appropriate as this can prevent accidents.

Learning intentions

For children to learn they need an environment that is stimulating for them. This includes opportunities for self-chosen play but also opportunities to interact and play with adults.

Planned activities should be fun and playful while also enhancing learning. As a professional you will need to learn how to enhance children's play and deliver the curriculum framework. This means that when you prepare a play environment or carry out a particular activity you should know how it helps children's development and how it links to the curriculum. Identifying learning intentions in activities as well as designing activities that provide learning intentions is therefore a skill.

Planning with individual settings

As part of your course you will need to show that you can plan for a variety of children's ages and in different settings. Each setting will have its own approach to planning, hence you might find that the paperwork that is used varies and how much detail is required. Settings will also have their own timescale. Some settings will plan in detail a month ahead while others will plan a week or so ahead.

In order that you can plan and carry out activities you will need to ask your placement supervisor about how and when you should plan activities. In order to do this you will probably need to have a good understanding of the curriculum they are using as most settings' plans link to curriculum outcomes. You may also find that staff use a different planning format to the one that you have to use as a learner; this may not show the level of detail that you are asked to provide. This is because as a learner you generally have to include more detail to show that you have the background knowledge.

Think about it

Below are five different activities. For each activity, describe the possible learning intentions. Think about the developmental benefits as well as how the activity will link to the curriculum framework.

Activity 1: Treasure basket play for babies

A range of natural materials is put out for the baby to choose, handle and explore. Objects have to be clean and checked for safety. Objects may include a leather purse, wooden spoon, metal scoop and some wine corks. There are plenty of objects available and they can be put directly onto the ground or better still into a basket. The adult stays near the baby to provide reassurance and to maintain safety, but leaves the exploration to the baby.

Activity 2: Sharing a book with a toddler (15 months)

The adult has the toddler's favourite books. The toddler and the adult sit closely together and share the books in a comfortable place. The adult encourages the toddler to turn the pages and to point to the pictures. The adult is ready to repeatedly look at the same book.

Activity 3: Imaginative play in the 'shop' with 3-year-olds

The imaginative play area has been converted into a shop. There is a counter, baskets, real money in the till and bags. There are tins, real fruit and vegetables as well as scales. The adult joins in the children's play by taking the role of the shopkeeper at the till. The adult counts out money as change and swipes 'credit' cards and asks the children to enter their PIN number.

Activity 4: Name Treasure hunt with children aged 4 years

Children's name cards have been hidden inside and outdoors. The adult works with two or three children at a time. The adult shows the children their names and asks if they would like to hunt for other copies of their name. The adult encourages the children and is ready to support them, but does not directly tell them where to look. When the names have been collected, the adult asks the children whether they would like to repeat the activity or to hide each other's names.

Activity 5: Den building with children aged 6 years

A selection of fabrics, large boxes, clips, string and other materials are put in the outdoor space. Children are shown what is available and are encouraged to make a den or house. They can choose what to use and the adult is on hand to support them and to provide any additional materials that the children want.

Section 4

How to meet the needs of the individual and groups of children in a variety of settings

In practice

You are working with a group of children and realise that one child needs more support. Your placement supervisor looks at your plan and suggests that next time you should show more differentiation. You are not sure what this means, but guess that it has to do with meeting individual children's needs.

By the end of this section you will understand the importance of adapting and differentiating activities and have clear ideas about ways in which to do this.

The practical application of knowledge gained through other units

You have already seen that you should be able to incorporate knowledge about child development into your ability to observe and think about children's needs. To be successful in placement you will need to be able to transfer the knowledge that you have acquired and demonstrate it in your practice. One way of helping yourself to do this is to read the units in this book that link to the age of children that you will be working with, as well as those that link to behaviour, planning and health and safety. It is also important that when learning new material you focus on the implications for your work with children.

How to apply differentiation in meeting the needs of children and encouraging development

Every child is unique and special; it is important that this is reflected through your planning and the way you work with children. The term **differentiation** is used in planning and when activities are implemented. This is an essential part of working when you are with groups of children. Below are some key reasons why differentiation is considered essential.

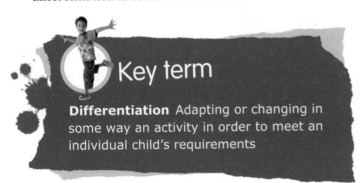

Key term

Differentiation Adapting or changing in some way an activity in order to meet an individual child's requirements

Avoiding frustration

Children whose needs are not met often show signs of frustration. They may 'give up' if they are finding an activity too difficult or may not participate. Differentiating an activity means that all children can join in at a level that is suitable for them.

Meeting the needs of children of different ages or stages of development

When working with groups of children, especially in mixed age range settings such as in a nursery, it is essential to differentiate. Unless you develop ways of adapting an activity you may find that some children find it too easy and not challenging while others may not benefit from doing it.

Ways of differentiating an activity

There are many ways in which you might differentiate an activity to meet the differing needs of children.

Level of support

You can differentiate by being aware of the different levels of support that children may need. One child might need you to hold a piece of card for them to cut, while another child might do it independently. Similarly, a child might need you to stay near for support and reassurance while playing outdoors, while another child may want to explore alone.

Equipment and resources

Sometimes providing a range of materials and resources can differentiate an activity. For example, you may provide a dice with numerals on it rather than dots for some children to use in a game, or get out a range of jigsaw puzzles including ones with larger or fewer pieces.

⇧ **Providing a range of resources is one way to differentiate an activity**

Group size

The size of group that children are in can be another way of differentiating. For example, story time might be split into two groups, with a smaller group for those children who need more adult time and support.

Case study

Differentiating activities

Sarah is working with 2- and 3-year-olds. She has organised a small world play area that children can come to when they want. She knows that the 3-year-olds often enjoy playing with more intricate pieces, while a couple of 2-year-olds prefer large and chunky items. When planning this area, Sarah therefore puts out several types of small world play. She puts some on the table and others on the floor, as she knows that some children prefer to play on the floor.

1. Explain how Sarah has differentiated this activity.

2. Discuss why this was necessary.

3. Consider any other ways in which this activity might be differentiated.

The importance of diversity and inclusive practice

A core value of the early years sector is to ensure that all children are given opportunities to fulfil their potential and that no child is discriminated against (see also Unit 3 pages 150–8). As every child is different, this means that within a setting, children will have a range of diverse needs, interests and backgrounds. To avoid discriminating against any particular child, it will be important to reflect their diverse needs in the routines and plans of the setting. Some children may also have additional needs that, if not met, will prevent them from benefiting from the care and education in the setting. This means thinking about ways of meeting their needs which are inclusive and does not mean that they have to play or learn separately from others.

You have seen that differentiation is an important part of working with children. It is also a way in which you can ensure children are not discriminated against. For example, a child who finds it hard to use a pair of scissors should be supported so they can still enjoy the activity alongside others. To fail to differentiate and provide the necessary support would therefore be discriminatory.

It is also a core value that you should find ways of helping children respect and value each other. This means that you must think about ways in which you help individual children develop positive respect towards others. You might, for example, help them talk about their feelings and encourage them to become empathetic towards others. You may also think about activities, resources and materials that will promote a positive view of others.

How to work with parents, carers and other professionals in a multi-agency approach

Working with parents and carers

A key way in which you can meet the needs of children is by working closely with their parents and carers. This is important across the early years sector and has been shown to make a significant difference to the outcomes of children.

As a learner you may have limited contact with parents and carers. This is because the child's key person will have responsibility for liaising with them. It is worth observing how the key person works with parents and carers and the type of information that is shared. It is also important to find out how parents and carers are encouraged to be involved in the setting.

Below are some examples of how working with parents and carers can help children.

Babies

Babies need adults to share information as they cannot tell us about their needs. Working well with parents and carers for this age range therefore means sharing information on a daily basis. You will need to know about babies' physical care needs (sleep, nappy changing and feeding) and pass back information on these to parents and carers. As well as physical care needs, parents will be able to tell you about their children's interests and the way in which their child needs to be comforted. When working with this age range, you will need to build on these interests and talk to parents about what their child has enjoyed doing with you.

Toddlers

While toddlers are beginning to use language you still need plenty of information from parents. They will help you understand their child's early communication style and this will help you to work with the child effectively. Parents also know what their toddler enjoys doing and what is likely to cause them to become frustrated.

Children aged 3–5 years

While children of this age are normally able to communicate, it remains essential to work well with parents. In this age range children are likely to make some transitions, for example into school or starting pre-school. You will need to know how settled children are and this can sometimes reveal itself in their behaviour at home. Research also shows that if parents and practitioners work together, children's early learning can be enhanced. This means that you need to find out about the child's interests as well as sharing with parents your plans for activities with their child.

Children aged 5–8 years

In this age range many children are in settings that work with large groups, so working closely with parents can help you to provide an individual touch. Parents can share with you their child's interests as well as tell you about changes to their child's life, for example the illness of a family member or the birth of a sibling. Where relationships are good between the setting and parents, children feel more settled. Parents are also likely to feel more involved with their child's education (see also Unit 14 page 518).

Working with other professionals

Today, many professionals can be involved in the lives of the child and their family (see Unit 5 pages 236–7). This means that working with other professionals is a feature of practice. A child may, for example, go to a childminder before school, attend school and then go to an after-school club. This would mean that the child and their family

(see also Unit 14 page 518)
(see Unit 5 pages 236–7)

Case study

A positive approach to working with parents

Naz is due to start pre-school next week. She is nearly 4 years old but has not attended a pre-school or nursery before. Her mother has visited the pre-school several times and staff have built a good relationship with her. Naz's key worker has asked her mother to suggest some activities that Naz is likely to enjoy and has learned about Naz's likes and dislikes.

Naz's mother is pleased that the staff are taking such care and interest in her daughter. This has helped her to feel more relaxed about Naz starting pre-school. She is also pleased that the pre-school has suggested that Naz can come in for half-sessions to start with, to help her settle.

1. Why is Naz likely to settle down quickly in the pre-school?
2. Why is it important for staff to build a good relationship with Naz's mother?
3. How does Naz benefit from the pre-school's approach to working with parents?

would be involved with at least three different professionals. Other children may be helped by health professionals such as speech and language therapists and physiotherapists.

Today it is recognised that children and their families benefit if professionals work together and make contact. By sharing information, experiences and ideas, you can often provide smooth transitions for children between different settings and meet their needs more effectively. As a learner you may not have direct contact with other professionals but it is important that you find out how the setting liaises with them.

U9
4

How to respond to behaviour positively

A key part of working with children is about supporting and developing positive behaviour. Learning how to do this effectively and appropriately makes a significant difference. There are three key principles that are important in behaviour management which should underpin the way in which you approach children:

1. Children show unwanted behaviour when their needs are not being met.
2. Some behaviour is linked to children's development.
3. Strong relationships with children are essential.

1. Children show unwanted behaviour when their needs are not being met

Children of all ages show you what they are feeling through their behaviour, even if they are unable to express this. The chart below describes the behaviour that arises when children's needs for stimulation, sleep, food, attention and friendship are not met.

2. Some behaviour is linked to children's development

Development plays a huge role in children's behaviour. Some behaviour is simply age/stage related so will pass in time. It is important to recognise such behaviour and to not overreact. Snatching, for example, is typical of most children under 3 years old as they do not yet have the skills required to wait or to ask for an object. Experienced practitioners will usually find ways of preventing incidents as they become good at predicting what acts as triggers. They may also use distraction techniques, especially with younger children.

Young children also need consistency as developmentally they find it hard to deal with changing rules for situations. This means that while a 7-year-old can appreciate that they are being allowed to stand on a table to play a special game, a 3-year-old will expect to be able to do this all of the time. The term 'consistency' is therefore used a lot in relation to managing children's behaviour.

🔖 **Behaviour arising from children's unmet needs**

Unmet need	Resultant behaviour
Stimulation	Babies, toddlers and children who are bored show this in a variety of ways. Babies might cry while toddlers might start throwing objects. Children often show that they are bored by fidgeting and lacking concentration. It is always worth thinking about the routines of a session and whether there are times when children do not have anything to do or play with. In addition, children tend to need times when they can play in their own way and set their own challenges.
Sleep	We all need sufficient sleep in order to cope. Children of all ages can become restless and irritable and find it hard to control their emotions when tired.
Food	As with sleep, food is a basic requirement for all people, and the behavioural signs that children are hungry are not dissimilar to tiredness. In addition, it has been shown that the quality of diet can make a difference to children: high levels of sugar, fat and additives commonly found in processed foods are linked to behaviour.
Attention	Children of all ages, including babies, need adults' attention. Some children will need more adult attention than others – there is no 'quota' so you may find significant differences between children. Children also need attention from their parents. When children do not get sufficient attention for their needs, for example when a parent is in hospital or after the arrival of a new baby in the family, this may show itself through attention-seeking behaviour. While it is not wise to respond immediately to this, it does, however, mean that at other times you need to spend more time with an individual child.
Friendships	From 3 years onwards, children start to need not just your attention but also that of other children. Children who are being rejected by others may show aggressive behaviours. Finding ways of supporting these children so they can develop social skills is therefore important.

⇧ **It is important to recognise and not punish behaviour that is age-related. For example, it is normal for a 2-year-old to have an occasional tantrum when becoming frustrated**

From around 3 years onwards, most children show fairly cooperative behaviour providing that their needs are met (see above). However, this may not be the case with children who have developmental delay or special needs, for example a child with atypical language development is more likely to show frustrated and aggressive behaviours. Where developmental needs are at the heart of the behaviour, it is important not just to deal with the behaviour but also to look for ways of supporting the child's development.

3. Strong relationships with children are essential

You have seen in Unit 3 (pages 136–8) that strong relationships with children are critical in terms of supporting their emotional development and well-being. They are also pivotal in terms of behaviour. Children who enjoy being with adults and get positive attention tend to show few incidences of unwanted behaviour. On the other hand, where adults have not developed good relationships, children may show unwanted behaviours in order to gain their attention. It is therefore essential that you are extremely positive with children; this will be shown through your comments, feedback and praise. It is also important that you spend time playing with children and following their interests rather than always expecting them to do as they are told. This balance is crucial to any relationship.

Think about it

Do you remember whether, as a child, you preferred to be with some adults rather than others? Why was this?

Case study

Unmet needs affect behaviour

Andrew keeps lashing out at other children. He is now 4 years old and other children are beginning to avoid him. He often snatches toys from others or goes up to other children who are playing and spoils their game. His language skills are similar to that of a 2-year-old. His parents and the staff at the setting are patient with Andrew and spend more time with him individually in order to boost his speech.

1. Describe Andrew's needs.

2. Explain the connection between his language development and his behaviour.

3. Consider why it is important that parents and staff work together to help Andrew.

Good practice checklist

Tips for dealing with unwanted behaviour

✓ Remain calm and think carefully about the triggers for the behaviour.

✓ Consider whether you can ignore or distract the child, especially if they are young.

✓ Avoid overreacting and giving too much attention to the behaviour so that children do not learn that by showing unwanted behaviour they can grab an adult's time.

✓ Give a child who has been showing unwanted behaviour more positive attention by, for example, doing a pair activity or sharing a book.

✓ Involve parents and agree a strategy for behaviours that look as if they are becoming a habit, e.g. biting.

Tips for preventing unwanted behaviour

✓ Remember that children's needs must be met first of all. Think about tiredness, hunger and boredom.

✓ Remind children what they need to do. Young children can forget or not apply a rule to a new situation.

✓ Make sure that there are plenty of varied play opportunities available for children.

✓ Give children plenty of time and warning if their play activity needs to come to an end.

✓ Think carefully about the children's routines – change them if needed so that children are not waiting around or bored.

✓ Make sure that you give children plenty of positive attention, e.g. encouragement, support and praise.

How to meet the needs of individuals and groups of children in a variety of settings

As a learner you should have the opportunity to work in a variety of different placements. This is important as you will then be able to see how settings catering for different age groups are able to meet children's needs. (See also Unit 14, pages 510–14.)

Meeting the needs of individuals

Some children will have needs that require specific planning and care. The range of additional needs is very wide and will include permanent needs as well as temporary ones. A few examples of some of the additional needs you might encounter when working with children are shown in the spider diagram below.

Supporting children

Most children at one time or another will have an additional need. For example, they may need a little temporary support while they adapt to being in the new setting or cope with changes to their family's structure. Recognising that children have additional needs is therefore important.

You will often learn that a child needs additional support through your relationships with the child's parents or carers. For example, parents may tell you about changes at home or to a child's health. At other times you may learn of a child's additional needs via other professionals who work with the child. Finally, you may notice that a child's behaviour is a little different and this may alert you to their needing more support.

Supporting children with additional needs is often about providing practical support. For example, you may have to ensure that a child with diabetes gets a snack on time or that a child with a broken arm is given support when putting on a dressing-up garment. Finding out exactly what you need to do is therefore essential, and to do this you might ask parents or, if appropriate, the child.

At other times the support you give may be more emotional. For example, children may need more of your time and encouragement, especially in situations where they need to express their feelings, fears or concerns. Learning to listen carefully to children is therefore an essential skill. You may also plan specific activities that will help children, for example a painting activity or an activity that will help the child relax.

Medical condition requiring support, e.g. asthma, eczema, cystic fibrosis

Physical care needs, e.g. special diet, skin care, toileting

Examples of additional needs

Emotional difficulties, e.g. separation of parents, bereavement, domestic violence, starting new setting, friendships, bullying

Developmental needs, e.g. speech and language, fine motor skills

As a learner on placement you may be asked to work with a child with additional needs. It is worth beginning by finding out as much as possible about the child's needs from the child's key person. You will also need to observe the child so that you can learn about his or her needs and interests. As with all areas of your practice, it is essential that you remember that any information you learn about the child must remain confidential.

Using individual observations to inform planning

You have seen in Unit 2 and above that observing children is an essential part of working professionally with them. Observations should help you to identify children who have additional needs and to reflect on how effective any strategies you are using might be. As a learner you should observe individual children and practice planning activities or play opportunities based upon your observations.

Two observation techniques are particularly useful when observing individual children. These are the target child method (see also page 92) and the event sample (see page 95). The case study below shows how these might be used to support an individual child.

Meeting the needs of groups of children

Working out how to meet the needs of children in groups is a skill. The starting point should always be to think about what children's basic needs are and then to devise a routine around them. The routine needs to be sufficiently flexible, though, to be able to cater for individuals within the group. As you have seen in Unit 8, children's care needs vary considerably. It is important that you use your different placement opportunities to learn about how a setting might organise children in group care. The questions below may help you to reflect on the practice that you are seeing.

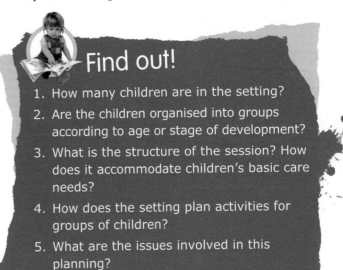

Find out!

1. How many children are in the setting?
2. Are the children organised into groups according to age or stage of development?
3. What is the structure of the session? How does it accommodate children's basic care needs?
4. How does the setting plan activities for groups of children?
5. What are the issues involved in this planning?

Case study

Using observations to inform planning

Harry is 4 years old and is about to join a Reception class. He has had some speech therapy, but his key worker, Ileana, is wondering how much Harry interacts with other children and adults apart from her. She thinks that it will be important for Harry to be able to do this in order to cope with the transition to the Reception class.

Ileana decides to carry out a couple of observations using the target child and event sample. She uses the target child technique to observe during child-initiated play and notices that during this time Harry tends to play in quite a solitary way, although very happily. The next day Ileana draws out an event sample and asks all the staff members if they can make a recording on to it, to show whether Harry talks to them or to a child

nearby. The event sample lasts for the day. At the end of the day Ileana notes that Harry has spoken to a member of staff on three occasions and spoken only four times to other children. With this information she decides to plan more adult-directed small group activities so that Harry will have more opportunity to interact with staff. She also talks to staff members so that they are aware of the importance of increasing their interaction with Harry and helping him to play and interact with others.

1. Why was it important to use more than one observation technique?
2. What was the advantage of using the event sample?
3. How did the observations help to inform planning?

Section 5

How professional practice is linked to legislation, policies and procedures

In practice

It is your first day in the setting. The doorbell rings and although you are the nearest, you are not sure whether to answer it. You also spot that one of the toys has a missing wheel which might be dangerous. You are wondering whether you should say anything when a girl comes up to you and pulls your hair.

By the end of this section you will know how to avoid being in this situation.

The policies used by settings

Every setting will have a range of policies that ensure children's welfare and safety. As a learner you must follow the procedures that are laid down in the policies so that children remain safe. While many settings will have the time to go through these policies, others may not and you might need to take responsibility for finding out about them. While you do not have to know about each policy in detail, you must know enough so that you can work effectively with children and keep them and yourself safe.

Find out!

Find out about the following three policies that are important in settings:

1. Behaviour
2. Health and safety
3. Safeguarding children (also known as child protection)

How do these affect your practice while you are on placement?

Safe working practices in a variety of settings

As well as policies you will also need to find out about safe working practices in your setting. This is because every setting will have its own policies and procedures which reflect the age of children, the location of the setting and the setting's aims.

As a learner you may not be able to undertake certain tasks or activities, for example intimate care or talking to parents. These limitations are designed to protect you as well as the setting and children. It is important that you find out about your role in the setting and what you can and cannot do. You should never, for example, be alone with a child or group of children until you are qualified.

Think about it

Opposite is a list of questions to help you explore how you should be working within your placement. See if you can answer the questions. If not, make sure that you find out the answers next time you are in placement.

Child protection

➔ Where should you sign in and sign out?
➔ Do you need to wear a badge while on placement?
➔ Are learners expected to answer the door or greet other adults?
➔ What should you do if a child says something that you are concerned about?
➔ What is the setting's policy about learners helping with toileting and personal care?

Behaviour

➔ What are the main rules in the setting or room in which you work?
➔ How does the setting deal with incidents of unwanted behaviour?
➔ Who should you talk to if you have problems with a child's behaviour?
➔ Does the setting have a reward system and how is it used?
➔ How can you act as a good role model?

Health and safety

➔ Who is the first aider for the setting?
➔ What should you do if there is an accident?
➔ Whom should you report to if you notice anything that might be dangerous?
➔ What should you do in the event of an evacuation or if you discover fire?
➔ What are the hygiene procedures for personal care and what resources are provided?

Meal and snack times

➔ What hygiene procedures must you follow if you serve or prepare food?
➔ Are there any children with specific dietary requirements and how are these met?

Working with children

➔ What checks should you carry out on equipment or outdoor areas?
➔ Are there any items of clothing that children should wear, for example aprons, coats?
➔ Do any children have additional needs that you should be aware of?

Parents

➔ How much involvement should you have with parents?

Case study

Safe working practices as a learner

Mark is on placement in the toddler room. He notices that one of the toddlers needs changing and that the staff members are very busy at the moment. He has a baby brother so knows how to change a nappy at home. He has also seen how the members of staff change nappies. Mark takes the toddler to the nappy changing room and begins to undress her. A member of staff comes in and immediately sends Mark out of the room. He is seen by the placement supervisor who tells him that his actions are inappropriate. Mark is disappointed as he was only trying to help. The placement supervisor asks Mark if he has read the child protection and health and safety policy yet. She shows him the sections for learners where it is clearly written that no learner should be left unattended with a child.

1. Why would the placement be concerned that Mark was not following the policies?

2. How has Mark put himself in a difficult position?

3. Why is it important to find out about your placement's policies and to follow them?

The importance of reflection to develop and improve your performance

In Unit 5 you looked at reflective practice. In order to complete this unit you should revisit pages 227–31.

Throughout your time on placement you should be thinking about ways to improve your practice. This is important because as the course progresses, placement supervisors and tutor will have higher expectations of you. It is assumed that as you gain experience you will increasingly become more capable. If you are able to reflect on your performance in placement you will probably find that you are able to make great strides in your practice.

Think about it

1. Think about what you have done well – how can you build on this?

2. What skills do you need to develop? How can you practice or acquire these skills?

3. Consider what you have learned about children – how can you use this knowledge?

Getting ready for assessment

In order to complete the assessment for Unit 9, you will need to make sure that all your Practice Evidence Records have been signed off and that your Professional Development Profiles have been completed. It is essential, therefore, that you are reliable on placement, work hard and make sure that you think about how to improve your performance. You must also make sure that at the start of your placement, your supervisor knows about the Practice Evidence Records and the Professional Development Profiles and their role in completing them.

Unit 11

Care of sick children

In this unit you will learn:

1 The principles of promotion and maintenance of health

2. The causes and prevention of ill health

3. The effects of ill health on children and families

4. The responses to childhood illness

5. The role of the adult in supporting children and their families suffering from childhood illnesses

The principles of promotion and maintenance of health

In practice

There have been several outbreaks of infection in Tiny Town Nursery. The deputy manager has therefore been asked to organise a Health Promotion Week to raise awareness of health issues among parents and staff. Each member of staff will have to plan an activity as part of the week. The deputy manager also looks at the policies for infection control and decides to get the staff involved in producing a large colourful poster of infection control during a staff meeting.

By the end of this section you will be able promote children's health and prevent infection in the setting.

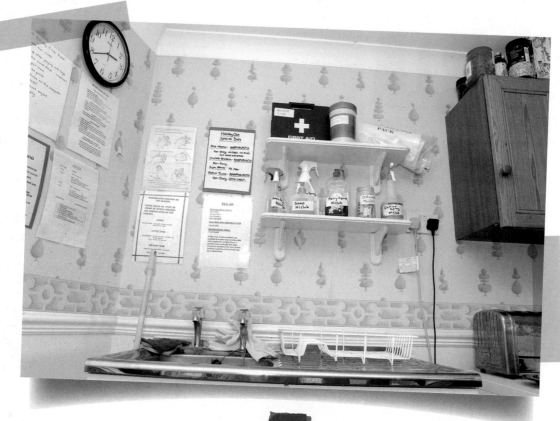

Introduction: definitions and rights to health

What is health?

To be healthy means very different things to different people, but it is generally associated with physical health rather than aspects of health such as mental or social health. While some people think that being healthy relates to the ability to resist infection and to cope with life's stresses and strains, others might feel that good health is a person's ability to cope physically, emotionally and mentally with day-to-day life. To some people, however, good health might mean the absence of any illness and simply 'feeling well'.

Find out!

What does health mean to you? Ask five people this question and compare answers. Do they mostly focus on physical health or do some people also consider other types of health important?

Types of health

Although the World Health Organisation's definition of health includes only physical, mental and social health, health is generally considered to also include emotional, spiritual and environmental/community/societal health – in other words, a more holistic approach to health.

Spiritual health
The ability to achieve peace within oneself; this is generally connected to people's religious beliefs

Physical health
The normal functioning of the body

Types of health

Social health
The ability to communicate effectively with others and to make and sustain relationships

Emotional health
The ability to acknowledge own emotions and deal with them appropriately, and to cope with stress

Mental health
The ability to think clearly and rationally

Environmental/community health
The ways in which the environment, politics and the health of the community affects people's health

Rights to health

The right to health is not a 'right to be healthy' but a right for each person to have access to health services. This requires the government to provide a range of services without discrimination, such as access to clean water, healthcare, sufficient food and sanitation. The public should also be able to participate in decisions made about public health.

U11
1

Think about it

Do you think everyone, including people who deliberately harm themselves by smoking, overeating or abusing drugs, has a 'right to health'?

The key factors in the promotion of community health and health education

The World Health Organisation defines health promotion as: 'the process of enabling people to increase their control over and improve their health'. This means that all people, including children, need the right information about their health and health issues so they can make informed choices about their lifestyle. This not only involves health education for individuals, but wider community issues such as healthy working conditions.

Health education

Health education aims at preventing illness. It emphasises being healthy and improving health and includes wider issues in society, such as anti-smoking campaigns. There are different types of health education programmes: primary, secondary and tertiary. The aims of each type of programme are described in the table below.

♻ **Aims of health education programmes**

Type of health education	Aims
Primary	To improve health by giving information and advice on staying healthy. Primary health education for children includes healthy eating, care of the teeth, hygiene and road safety.
Secondary	Early detection and treatment of conditions in order to prevent further complications or worsening of the condition. It can also involve educating people to change their behaviour in order to restore good health. This could include teaching obese children about their diet and encouraging exercise through sports schemes.
Tertiary	To limit the impact of a chronic illness or disability by teaching children how to reach their potential. This could involve teaching children to use specially adapted wheelchairs.

Different approaches to health education

Health educators will try to get their message across in a variety of ways in order to make an impact on the targeted group. These approaches include the following:

→ *The medical approach* – this aims to prevent illness through a series of public health measures, for example the health screening of all children.
→ *The educational approach* – this provides information and/or the necessary skills to enable the child or parent to make an informed choice.
→ *The behavioural change approach* – this aims to encourage people to change their behaviour, for example by giving up smoking.
→ *The empowerment approach* – this aims to help people develop the skills, confidence and self-esteem to make changes. It can be used on an individual basis or within the community and can include building up children's self-esteem through personal safety role plays.
→ *The fear creation approach* – this is where the health educator may try to change behaviour using frightening tactics, for example drink–drive campaigns which replay accidents or talk to victims of accidents.

Health educators will usually use a variety of approaches to educate. For example, when doing a topic on teeth, the children might be seen by the dentist to have their teeth checked (medical approach), have a talk by a dental nurse and do some worksheets (educational approach), be shown how to use a toothbrush and have a go at brushing some giant plastic teeth (behavioural change approach). Together, the different approaches will all help to empower the children to take some responsibility for the care of their teeth. They could also be shown some photographs of bad teeth which might frighten them into brushing their teeth (fear creation approach).

Health education within the family

Most first-time parents have little knowledge of parenting or caring for children. They need information on pregnancy, diet, breast- and bottle-feeding, immunisations, weaning, and many other less pleasant things like head lice! The health visitor is a useful source of this information. Early years practitioners may also be responsible for passing on information to parents.

Unfortunately, those in most need of health education are often the least likely to use the services provided or to attend clinics. This is sometimes due to fear or distrust of the services, lack of understanding about the importance of health issues or ignorance of the available services. Those who may be the most in need of health education and child surveillance might include:

→ single-parent families (if they lack support)
→ those living in poor housing or in overcrowded conditions
→ parents who have experienced neonatal death or Sudden Infant Death Syndrome in a child
→ people who are socially isolated, including those for whom English is their second language
→ people with a history of postnatal depression or mental health problems
→ families with a history of congenital defects in the family.

Health educators and health promoters

Everyone can be involved in promoting health. Early years practitioners and parents do this constantly through day-to-day routines such as handwashing and by being a good role model. Health education and promotion can be done both formally and informally to parents and their children.

→ Formal health education targets a specific group at a specific time, for example antenatal and postnatal classes run by community midwives and health visitors, and sex education in schools as part of the National Curriculum.
→ Informal health education is done on a one-to-one basis or through television, the media or magazines and provides information. Peer groups and the family also have a strong influence in promoting health at all ages.

Case study

At a staff meeting at Little Robins Nursery, the Manager was concerned over the amount of head lice among the children and that the children, despite reminders, weren't washing their hands correctly.

1. What approaches could be used with the children in order to improve the situation?
2. What approaches could be used with the children's parents and carers in order to change these issues?

The role of health educators and promoters

There are a number of organisations and professionals who promote health and provide health education. Examples are given in the table below.

Health promoters	How health is promoted
World Health Organisation (www.who.int/en/)	WHO sets global health targets, e.g. to reduce the incidence of skin cancer and to increase the uptake of immunisations. It researches ways of preventing infectious diseases and promotes improvement of nutrition, housing, sanitation and working conditions.
National Institute For Health And Clinical Excellence (NICE) (www.nice.org.uk/) (Fomerly the Health Development Agency)	NICE's role is to provide guidance on the promotion of health and the prevention and treatment of ill health in the UK. It focuses on three key areas: • promotion of the health of children and young people • accidental injury prevention • drug misuse.
National voluntary organisations and pressure groups	These either put pressure on the government to change policies, for example the Society for the Protection of Unborn Children, or give information about certain issues such as the National Asthma Campaign.
The media	Provides programmes on television and radio and articles in newspapers about health issues.

Health promoters	How health is promoted
Primary health team (see page 450)	The primary health team's role within the community is to provide health education and to promote health, to detect and treat illnesses and conditions and to provide a caring service. Health education is an increasing and essential part of the team's role. The health visitor, for example, works closely with parents giving advice and support on all parenting skills.
The school nurse	The school nurse's role is mainly concerned with screening but this role is extending into other areas such as promoting health education within the classroom.
The dentist	Teaching on dental hygiene and the prevention of tooth decay is one of the dentist's roles. The school dental service also visits children in schools.
Education services	Teaching on health issues is part of the PHSE (Personal, Social and Health Education) programme within schools and this area is being targeted in the National Healthy Schools Scheme.
Police	The police teach children to protect themselves and provide road safety training.
Fire brigade	The fire brigade teach fire awareness.

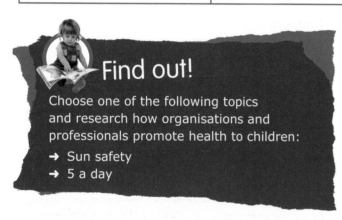

Find out!

Choose one of the following topics and research how organisations and professionals promote health to children:

➜ Sun safety
➜ 5 a day

The early years practitioner

Early years practitioners need to know and understand how to maintain their own personal health as well as that of the children in their care. This means they need to be a positive role model for children. It is also their role to help teach children about their body and how to care for it as part of the Early Years Foundation Stage (EYFS) Curriculum and the National Curriculum.

Healthy eating, for example, can be used as a focus in activities within 'Knowledge and understanding of the world' in the EYFS Curriculum and can be incorporated into the science curriculum in Key Stages 1 and 2. Examples of topics could include:

➜ healthy eating
➜ exercise

➜ care of the teeth
➜ sun awareness.

These topics could be done by:

➜ incorporating activities into the curriculum
➜ having 'health days' when outside professionals come to the setting and carry out health activities with the children
➜ talks to parents
➜ assemblies to include health issues
➜ displays and interest tables.

Further examples of health promotion topics and related activities are shown in the table opposite.

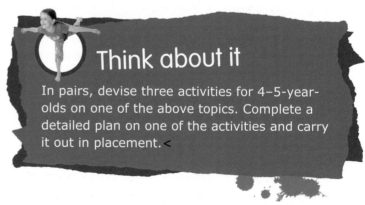

Think about it

In pairs, devise three activities for 4–5-year-olds on one of the above topics. Complete a detailed plan on one of the activities and carry it out in placement.<

Subject	Aim	Activities
Teeth	To help children understand: • the importance of brushing teeth • when and how to brush teeth.	• Games involving food that is good and bad for the teeth • Demonstration of correct tooth brushing with large set of teeth and brush – available from the health promotion unit (HPU) • Drawing pictures of their teeth • Visitor: dentist or dental nurse
Personal hygiene	To help children understand: • the reasons for and importance of washing • how to wash hands correctly • hair care.	• Handwashing games, e.g. painting the early years practitioner's hands and asking the children to guess how long it would take to get the hands clean • Videos from the HPU • Visitor: school nurse or health visitor
Diet	To teach children about: • healthy foods • the importance of healthy eating.	• Drawing healthy and unhealthy lunch boxes for fictional characters • Making posters of the different food groups • Visitor: dietitian, health visitor or school nurse

Methods to support education, public health, immunisation and screening programmes and the prevention of ill health

Causes of ill health are covered in Section 2 of this unit (see pages 403–25); you may wish to read through the material in Section 2 before reading about methods of preventing ill health.

Methods of preventing illness

There are a variety of ways to prevent illness and the early years practitioner needs to ensure that he or she is vigilant within the setting in order to prevent the spread of infections. These include the ways described below.

Environmental factors

The immediate environment within an early years setting needs to be kept clean in order to prevent illness. Adequate ventilation will decrease germs but the setting also needs to be warm; school classrooms should be kept at 18 degrees Celsius. Proper disposal of waste and good personal hygiene of staff and children will also prevent illness. In the child's wider environment, adequate housing and play areas, clean air and water and good sanitation are also necessary to prevent illness. A good cheap transport system will provide easy access to healthcare.

Nutrition

An adequate diet is essential in order for children to remain healthy; see Unit 12, pages 455–68, for details on a healthy diet and care routine.

Public health

Public health is the promotion of health to the whole population and includes many factors such as good transport, housing, the environment and governmental legislation. Public health measures relevant to childcare include training on food hygiene and health and safety for staff. Environmental Health Officers monitor housing conditions, manage pest control and deal with general public health-related matters. The Health Protection Agency monitors and responds to national outbreaks of notifiable infectious diseases; the law requires notification of some infectious diseases (see Unit 4, page 175). This will ensure that any outbreaks of infectious diseases are quickly picked up.

Education

Many infections can be avoided if children are taught how to wash their hands correctly and are regularly encouraged to do so. You also need to set a positive role model by washing your hands frequently and correctly. Regular health education on all subjects will help children to understand how to prevent illness and why it is important. This can be included as part of the curriculum and as part of PHSE: personal social and health education.

Immunisation

Immunisation is the use of vaccines to give immunity from a specific disease. They consist of a minute portion of the weakened bacteria, virus or of the toxins which they produce. These stimulate the immune system to produce antibodies against the disease. It is recommended that children have immunisations for the following reasons:

➜ they prevent a child from getting diseases and the associated side effects
➜ they protect children who haven't been immunised (this is known as herd immunity – these children are less likely to be exposed to the disease itself)

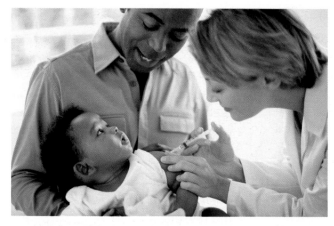

⇧ **Immunisation provides protection against many serious childhood diseases**

➜ it is cheaper to immunise than to care for the children who suffer from side effects of the illness; moreover, some diseases can lead to long-term problems and even death.

♨ **The immunisation schedule in the UK at the time of writing; for current information refer to www.immunisation.nhs.uk**

Age	Immunisation	How it is given
Newborn	BCG (only given if the baby is, or is likely to be in contact with, someone with tuberculosis (TB))	One injection
	Hepatitis B (only given if mother or close relative has hepatitis B)	One injection
2 months old	Diphtheria, tetanus, pertussis (whooping cough), polio and Haemophilus influenzae type b (Hib)	One injection
	Pneumococcal infection (PCV)	One injection
3 months old	Diphtheria, tetanus, pertussis, polio and Haemophilus influenzae type b (Hib)	One injection
	Meningitis C	One injection
4 months old	Diphtheria, tetanus, pertussis, polio and Haemophilus influenzae type b (Hib)	One injection
	Meningitis C	One injection
	Pneumococcal infection (PCV)	One injection
Around 12 months old	Haemophilus influenza type b (Hib) and Meningitis C	One injection
Around 13 months old	Measles, mumps and rubella (German measles) (MMR)	One injection
	Pneumococcal infection (PCV)	One injection
3 years and 4 months to 5 years old	Diphtheria, tetanus, pertussis (whooping cough) and polio	One injection
	Measles, mumps and rubella (MMR)	One injection
13 to 18 years old	Diphtheria, tetanus, polio	One injection

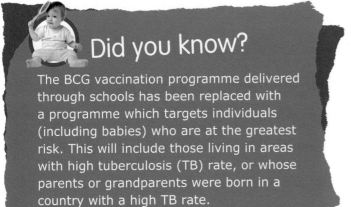
Care of a child following immunisation

Serious side effects to immunisations are rare, but some children may have a mild reaction, often within the first 48 hours. These include irritability, a mild fever or soreness, redness or a small lump around the injection site. It is often advised that infant paracetamol is given afterwards (with parental consent) if any of these symptoms appear. Serious symptoms such as high fever or convulsions need to be seen immediately by a doctor.

In a baby, the polio virus will be excreted in their faeces for up to six weeks, so handwashing is particularly important when changing nappies and babies shouldn't be taken swimming during this time.

Case study

Katie is a baby in the baby unit of Tweedlee Nursery. Her mother is very concerned about giving her daughter the MMR vaccination because her eldest son has been diagnosed as being autistic. She is concerned because someone told her about the research done on the links between autism and the MMR.

1. In groups, look at the advantages and disadvantages of vaccination.
2. Where would you advise this mum to go to find out the right information?

Child health surveillance

All children need to be checked at regular intervals to ensure that they are developing normally and that any condition is treated early and appropriate care given. For example, a child who has glue ear (see page 413) may have delayed language skills if this condition is not picked up and treated early.

At birth, parents are given a Personal Child Health Record Book in which healthcare professionals will record the results of all developmental checks, weight checks and any advice given by the health visitor.

Health and developmental checks

There are four main ways to check a child's development:

→ by asking questions of, and listening to, parents and/or carers
→ by measuring height, weight and head circumference
→ by physical examination
→ by observation of the child during structured or unstructured activities.

After the neonatal (at birth) checks, all subsequent checks are carried out by either the health visitor or the doctor. Each developmental area is checked to ensure the child is developing at the appropriate rate. The sooner a condition is detected, the sooner the appropriate treatment can be started or the appropriate care organised. If any problems are picked up on these tests, the child will be seen more regularly by the doctor or health visitor, or may be referred to a specialist.

Child Health Promotion Programme

The Child Health Promotion Programme has replaced the Child Health Surveillance Programme and includes:

→ childhood screening
→ immunisations
→ an assessment of the individual child's and family's needs
→ interventions and help to address these needs; for example, if the child is not growing correctly he or she will be referred to a paediatrician
→ providing health promotion.

CACHE Level 3 Child Care and Education Unit 11 Care of sick children

Check	Main reasons for check	Description of the condition
Weight and height	To ensure growth follows the norm for the child and to detect 'failure to thrive' (FTT)	FTT is when a child is not growing at the expected rate, e.g. through underfeeding, neglect or a serious physical disorder.
Head circumference	To detect: • hydrocephalus (water on the brain) • microcephaly (an abnormally small head).	• Hydrocephalus is associated with many congenital conditions. • Microcephaly is usually associated with mental retardation.
Heart	To detect congenital heart defect (common in Down's syndrome)	Any type of heart defect will usually need surgery. If undetected it could cause poor growth and chest infections.
Hips	To detect congenital dislocation of the hips – 'clicky hips'	The hip joint is dislocated; this often corrects itself but sometimes requires splints. If not detected early, traction or surgery may be required.
Testes	To ensure that both of the testes have descended into the scrotal sac	The testes usually descend naturally but surgery may be required. There is an increased risk of infertility.
Spine	To detect: • spina bifida • curvature of the spine	Spina bifida is a condition in which one or more bones in the back do not fuse properly. This causes a bit of spinal cord to be exposed. The associated effects can range from mild to very serious.
Reflexes	To ensure the reflexes are normal	Abnormal reflexes can indicate a problem with the nervous system.
Feet	To detect talipes (club foot)	Talipes is when the foot is twisted out of shape. It may be helped through physiotherapy or may require splinting or an operation.
Hearing	To ensure the hearing is normal	There are many different types of hearing loss, the most common of which is 'glue ear' (see page 413). The child may be referred to an audiologist.
Sight	To detect: • squint • cataract To ensure the child sees normally	A squint, where one eye is not aligned to the other, is initially treated with a patch over the affected eye, and later with glasses or surgery.
Guthrie 'heal prick' blood screening test	To detect: • phenylketonuria (all UK areas) • congenital hypothyroidism (all UK areas) • cystic fibrosis (most UK areas) • MCAD deficiency (fewer UK areas)	• Phenylketonuria is a condition which affects the child's ability to use a type protein in the body. • In congenital hypothyroidism there is a lack of the growth hormone thyroxine meaning that normal growth cannot occur. • Cystic fibrosis is an inherited condition that affects the lungs and digestive system. • MCAD is a condition in which fat metabolism is impaired. Modification of the diet can reduce symptoms.

Check	Main reasons for check	Description of the condition
Guthrie test (continued)	• sickle cell disease (fewer UK areas)	• Sickle cell disease affects the shape of red blood cells and reduces their ability to carry oxygen around the body.
Palate	To detect cleft palate	Cleft palate occurs when there is a gap in the roof of the mouth leading to difficulties in feeding and breathing.

Development checks and screening

At birth	
Physical examination:	Eyes, heart and hips, spine, testes, palate
Developmental check:	Weight, head circumference
Injections:	Administration of vitamin K (to prevent vitamin K deficiency)
Health promotion:	Breastfeeding, sleeping position, dangers of passive smoking and other advice to reduce sudden infant death
Within first week	
Hearing test:	Automated Otoacoustic Emissions (AOAE) test (within first 7 days). A small probe is placed in the ear canal which sends out a series of clicks; a microphone detects 'echoes' produced by hair cells in the cochlea within the inner ear. This is then recorded on a computer. It is quick, painless and best done when the baby is asleep.
Blood test:	The Guthrie 'heal prick' blood screening test (at 5–7 days).
Within 10–12 days	
New birth visit:	Home visit by a health visitor to assess the child and family's health needs
Health promotion:	Breastfeeding, advice on establishing a routine
At 6–8 weeks	
Physical examination:	Heart, hips, eyes and testes; spine, genitals and palate
Developmental check:	Weight, head circumference
Health promotion:	Immunisation; breastfeeding and other advice on feeding and weaning; sleeping position and other advice to reduce sudden infant death; dangers of passive smoking; dental health (sugar-free medicines and avoid sugary drinks); car safety and other injury prevention strategies
At 2, 3 and 4 months	
Developmental check:	Weight. Checks will be completed by the health visitor at the same time as the routine immunisations (see page 396)
At 1 year	
Developmental check:	The health visitor will have completed an assessment of the child's physical, emotional, social development and family needs by the time the child is 1 year old.

At 12–15 months	
Developmental check:	This will be completed by the health visitor at the same time as the routine immunisations (see page 396)
Health promotion:	Injury prevention: stair gates, fireguards, small toys
At 2–3 years	
Developmental check:	The health visitor will review the child's progress and ensure that health and developmental needs are being addressed.
Age 4–5 years	
Review at school entry:	Opportunity to provide children, parents and school staff with information about specific health issues, e.g. safety, dental hygiene, diet
Developmental check:	Height and weight. General development is also assessed by listening, talking and observation of the child's gross motor, fine motor, social and language development. Bladder and bowel control, sleep problems and behavioural difficulties will also be discussed and advice given if necessary.
Review of health:	Check that immunisations are up to date, that the child has seen a dentist, review of any previous physical, developmental or emotional problems.
Hearing test:	The Sweep test is a basic hearing test. Although children with profound hearing loss should have been diagnosed before this, this test can pick up glue ear or hearing which is progressively getting worse.
Vision test:	A vision test will be done to pick up any eye problems. A national programme for pre-school vision screening is due to be introduced, performed by an orthoptist (an eye specialist who diagnoses and treats problems with the eyes).
Age 5–18 years	
Ongoing support at primary and secondary schools	This is mainly coordinated and provided by the school nurse and includes the following: • access to a school nurse at drop-in sessions and clinics by parents, teachers or through self-referral • provision for referral to specialists for children causing concern, for example the dietician for children with suspected eating disorders • children and young people with medical needs and disabilities may receive nursing care or extra resources within school • immunisation when indicated (see page 396).
Vision test:	Some areas perform a vision check, and a colour vision test, in older children or teenagers.

The role of the early years practitioner in child health screening

Although health professionals carry out health screening, early years practitioners will be in daily contact with children so are in a good position to identify any problems. Hearing problems, particularly glue ear where there is intermittent (occasional) hearing loss, are a common condition which can be detected in this way. If there are concerns about a child's health or development, the child's parents should be informed.

The influences on health and access to healthcare

The main influences on a child's health will be the child's family, culture, environment and access to health services. The range of factors affecting the health of children is described in detail in Unit 6, pages 254–63; it is recommended that you read these pages before completing this section.

Did you know?

According to the National Service Framework for Children, Young People and Maternity Services, certain choices made by the child or their parents have the most impact on the child's subsequent health. These include:

→ breastfeeding (see page 464)
→ a healthy diet and exercise throughout childhood into adulthood (see pages 261 and 455–8)
→ social and emotional well-being
→ children being kept safe
→ the avoidance of smoking, drugs and excessive alcohol intake
→ the prevention of teenagers getting pregnant or acquiring sexually transmitted infections.

Access to health services

Families need to have easy access to their GP, health visitor and other health services in order to make full use of the service. If there is a poor bus service, for example, the family is less likely to attend developmental checks and immunisations.

The influence of attitudes and culture

The family's attitude to health and their culture will influence a child's attitude to their own health. For example, if members of the family distrust doctors, the child is less likely to be taken for routine check ups and immunisations. Consider the case study below.

Case study

Barriers to effective healthcare

Sarah is a single mother who lives in a block of flats which is seven miles from the local hospital. Her son, Shane, who is 3 years old, has recently been diagnosed as diabetic and is supposed to have regular appointments at the hospital with the diabetic nurse and the dietician. Shane is very overweight and doesn't like walking, and tends to have tantrums every time that Sarah tries to take him out. She has always tried to bribe Shane with sweets to go anywhere but the nurse has told her that Shane mustn't have sweets. Sarah's mother continues to give him sweets to control him, saying that her grandmother had diabetes and she ate what she wanted. Sarah has very little money and doesn't understand the diet sheet she has been given, and feels that the food she should be giving Shane is too expensive. Sarah keeps missing appointments at the hospital but manages to take him to the nursery.

1. What factors are affecting Sarah's attitude to her son's illness?
2. What is preventing Sarah taking Shane to the hospital?
3. How could the early years practitioner from the nursery support Sarah?

Think about it

How might access to health services be difficult in the following situations?
1. A parent who has four children under the age of 6 years
2. A parent who doesn't own a car and who lives down a country lane in a village
3. A parent who has a disabled child and a newborn baby
4. A parent who has an autistic son who reacts badly to any change in routine

The role of the adult and other professionals in supporting children and their families' health

It is important that all settings promote health; staff should ensure that they regularly plan activities that teach children to eat well and look after themselves. Early years practitioners should also aim to promote health for the whole family by, for example, inviting health professionals to the setting to give talks or sending leaflets home with the children.

Preventing ill health is an important role for all early years practitioners. By ensuring that staff are constantly aware of infection control and ways of preventing illness, illness can be prevented in the setting. (See also pages 395–7 at the beginning of this section and pages 176–9.)

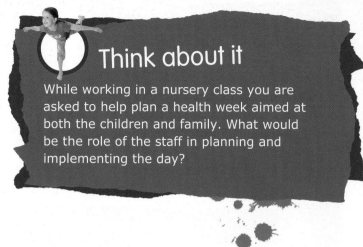

Think about it

While working in a nursery class you are asked to help plan a health week aimed at both the children and family. What would be the role of the staff in planning and implementing the day?

Section 2

The causes and prevention of ill health

In practice

You are working in a Sure Start crèche with many children who have a variety of chronic and life-limiting illnesses. You also support the parents and run regular workshops.

By the end of this section you will be able to identify causes of ill health in children and understand the ways in which illnesses can be prevented.

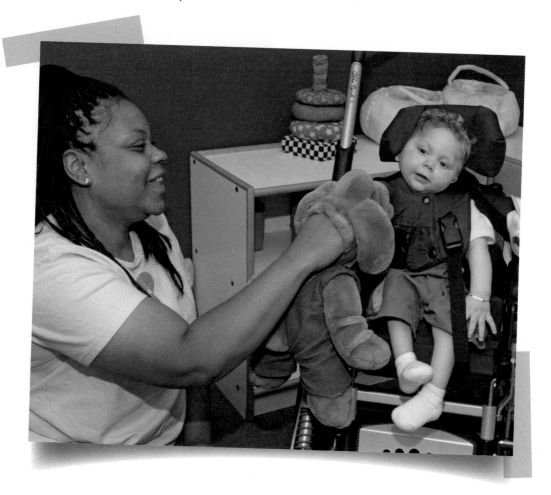

The causes of ill health

In order that you can understand how to help maintain and improve children's health, it is important to know what factors can influence a child's health. There are a wide variety of factors that can cause children to become unwell.

Lifestyle

Children's health can be affected by their parent's health and lifestyle. The health and lifestyle of the mother in particular can have an important impact on the future health of the child. These factors are described in Unit 6, pages 254–63.

Genetic causes

You cannot change your genetic make-up, and everyone will inherit factors from both parents that will affect their health. Some conditions, such as sickle cell disease (see page 421) and cystic fibrosis (see page 415), are passed on from one or both parents to the child. Sometimes there can be a chromosomal abnormality such as Down's syndrome, where there is an extra chromosome. Other disorders are familial; this means that there is a tendency within the family to have certain conditions, such as asthma, eczema and hay fever.

Socio-economic factors

Poverty

There is an inverse proportion between wealth and health – the poorer the family, the greater the health risks. Children from socially deprived families are less likely to attend screening and developmental checks or to have immunisations. Children who are born into poverty are more likely to:

→ eat a poor diet
→ live in poor housing conditions
→ die younger from accidents or illness
→ be ill and hospitalised
→ have decayed teeth
→ develop mental health problems
→ be born premature or have reduced birth weight
→ be bottle fed.

For more on the effects of poverty on health see Unit 6, pages 255–8.

Housing

Living in crowded, damp conditions increases the risk of accidents and respiratory infections. Children and young people are more likely to play in unsafe areas if they live in tower blocks or have no access to a garden; this can lead to an increase in accidents. Infections such as tuberculosis, bronchitis and gastroenteritis are more common where there is poor housing and overcrowding, and asthmatics are twice as likely to live in damp homes. Poor housing can also cause children to have sleep problems, and increases the risk of hyperactivity, bedwetting and aggression.

Did you know?

According to Shelter, the charity which fights homelessness in the UK, 11 per cent of childhood accidents are the result of badly designed housing and dangerous fittings.

⇧ **There are many negative health effects associated with poor living conditions**

Employment and unemployment

Some occupations are more at risk of accidents or from catching infectious diseases. For example, healthcare professionals are more likely to catch infections.

Unemployment can cause mental health problems and stress-related diseases. Due to a low income, families who are unemployed are more likely to have a poor diet and housing conditions (see also Unit 6, pages 255–8). For parents in low-income groups there can also be a shortage of affordable and appropriate childcare.

Social class

Research has shown that children who are born to parents who are unemployed or who are manual workers are far more likely to be hospitalised, become ill or die than children who are born to professional parents.

Did you know?

In 1998, Sir Donald Acheson produced a report which highlighted the fact that the gap was widening between the health of professional people and those who are unemployed or untrained manual workers; the government has since been trying to address this issue.

Age

The younger the child, the more vulnerable he or she is to infection and illness. At the other extreme, the elderly are also very susceptible to ill health. This is because their immunity is lower than that of healthy adults, particularly during times of stress.

Gender

Boys are more likely to die in childhood than girls, mostly because they are more prone to having accidents. Boys are also more likely to have a chronic (long-term) condition in childhood, although this trend changes in mid-adolescence. Girls, however, are less likely to participate in sport than boys.

Cultural factors

There is evidence of a north–south health divide in the UK, with children in the south generally having better health than those living in the north.

Some conditions are more common in different ethnic minorities. Sickle cell disease is more common in children of Afro-Caribbean parents and Tay-Sachs is more common in Jewish people.

Think about it

A new nursery has been established in a large housing estate where unemployment is high and many of the flats are overcrowded. There is a diverse mix of cultures, including some refugees who have apparently lived in great poverty.

Produce a report for the staff in the nursery describing the potential impact of socio-economic factors on the health of the children in the nursery.

Environmental factors

→ *Air* – high levels of air pollution can cause eye irritation, coughs and breathing difficulties in those who are sensitive; this may include some asthmatic children or children with chronic lung conditions such as cystic fibrosis.
→ *Water* – in the UK the water supply is regulated by DEFRA (the Department for Environment, Food and Rural Affairs) and there are few problems with water-borne diseases such as cholera. However, there have been some well-publicised incidences where the water supply has become contaminated and caused ill health.
→ *Sewage and waste control* – this is essential for community health; a poor water supply can spread infections such as polio and typhoid.

Find out!

Carry out research into the air quality in your local area via the following websites:

➜ www.defra.gov.uk/environment/airquality

➜ www.airquality.co.uk.

Compare the reports for your local area with those for two other areas. What differences do you notice and why might these differences occur?

Allergies

Allergens are the cause of allergic response in children. Some children can have an allergic reaction to anything, including some food substances, grass, animal hair or saliva and house dust mites. Children react to these allergens in a variety of ways including anaphylactic shock (see pages 422 and 445). There are various tests which are available to diagnose allergies and these are available from the GP.

Key term

Allergen Substance which causes an allergy

Infections

Micro-organisms can enter the body and cause illness; these are divided into four main groups: bacteria, viruses, fungi and parasites (which include protozoa). (See also Unit 4, pages 176–8.) Infection can be spread very quickly from one child to another through a variety of ways, as shown in the table (next column).

Did you know?

Protozoa are one-celled organisms such as toxoplasmosis, which is an infection that can be caught from cat litter trays.

Ways that infection can spread	Examples of infections
Droplet infection: speaking, sneezing, coughing and kissing	Colds, coughs and tuberculosis, rubella
Hands: contamination from airborne droplets, urine and faeces	Gastroenteritis, colds, tapeworm
Body fluids	Hepatitis, sexually transmitted diseases and HIV
Contaminated water	Polio
Contaminated food	Food poisoning
Animals	Rabies (from dogs), toxoplasmosis (from cats)
Insects such as flies	Food poisoning, malaria (from mosquitoes)
Dust	Diphtheria

Think about it

Children at Little Lambs Nursery are constantly catching colds and there has been an outbreak of gastroenteritis recently. The manager has asked you to investigate how these infections might be spreading and to make recommendations on how to improve infection control in the nursery.

The signs and symptoms of common childhood illnesses and action to be taken in both serious and non-serious situations to safeguard all children

When working with children it is important that you are able to recognise some of the common childhood illnesses and know when it may be necessary to contact the child's parents or call a doctor. Children sometimes do not have the experience to know that they are unwell or the vocabulary to tell someone how they are feeling. It is therefore important to observe children for changes to their behaviour or physical or emotional well-being in order to detect signs of illness. It is also important to be able to record and pass on information about a child's health to their parent or carer.

Signs that a child is unwell

Children's behaviour sometimes changes when they are becoming unwell before any specific signs and symptoms develop. Signs that a child might be unwell are shown in the spider diagram below. Specific terms associated with illnesses are shown in the Key terms box.

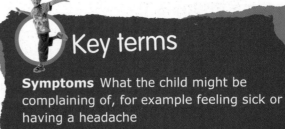

Key terms

Symptoms What the child might be complaining of, for example feeling sick or having a headache

Signs What you will notice about the child, for example a rash or a change in behaviour

Acute illness Illness which generally comes on suddenly, is short-lived and may well have a rapid onset of symptoms from one day to the next, i.e. may be severe

Chronic illness A prolonged illness with little change in symptoms from day to day; there is often, but not necessarily, a slow progressive deterioration; some chronic illnesses have acute episodes

Life-limiting illness or condition Where a child is unlikely to live to adulthood or a condition which causes progressive disability

U11
2

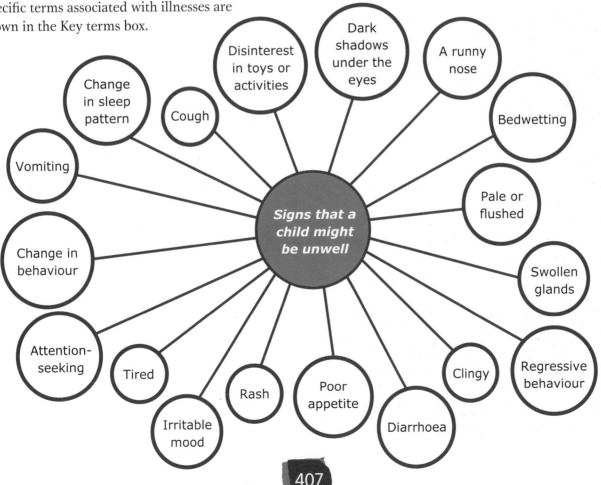

Signs that a child might be unwell

- Change in sleep pattern
- Cough
- Disinterest in toys or activities
- Dark shadows under the eyes
- A runny nose
- Bedwetting
- Vomiting
- Pale or flushed
- Swollen glands
- Change in behaviour
- Regressive behaviour
- Clingy
- Attention-seeking
- Tired
- Rash
- Poor appetite
- Diarrhoea
- Irritable mood

Infectious diseases

Particular care needs to be taken to limit the spread of infectious diseases among children. It is therefore important that you are familiar with the signs and symptoms of the infectious disease listed in the table below; you must also know the treatment and action required.

✥ **Signs, symptoms and treatment of childhood infectious diseases**

Illness, incubation time, immunisation, method of spread	Signs and symptoms	When to call doctor immediately	Specific treatment and complications
Chicken pox (*varicella*) • Common in children under 10 years • Can be uncomfortable and serious in very young babies, children who are HIV positive or are taking medications for childhood cancer (and adults, especially pregnant women) *Incubation time*: 11–21 days *Method of spread*: droplet infection	• Rash starts on head and behind the ears • Pink spots turn to blisters which dry and form scabs • Spots often come in crops – new batches appear over a few days • Slight fever and headache • Child may *feel* well • Intense itching	• Coughing • Seizures • Abnormal drowsiness • Unsteady when walking	*Treatment*: • sodium bicarbonate in a cool bath and calamine lotion to relieve itchiness • keep child cool as warmth makes the spots and itching worse • dress in loose cotton clothing • soft food if the mouth is affected. *Complications*: • scarring • secondary infection from scratching, especially impetigo • pneumonia • chest infection • encephalitis (inflammation of the brain).
Erythema infectiosum (also called 'fifth disease' or 'slapped cheek') • Caused by a virus called parvovirus B19 • Very common in children under 2 years • Not usually serious *Incubation time*: 4–20 days	• Rash resulting in bright red cheeks (as if child has been slapped) • Pale area around the mouth • Temperature *After 1–4 days*: • blotchy, lace-like rash may appear on arms and trunk, occasionally lasting 7–10 days on trunk • rash may get worse when warm • child may feel well.	Paracetamol to reduce temperature.	*Complications*: • can be serious if child has sickle cell disease (see page 421) or thalassaemia (hereditary blood disorder) • if a pregnant woman becomes infected during the first 20 weeks of pregnancy there is a small risk of miscarriage or stillbirth. Because the child is infectious before the rash appears, inform pregnant women who have had contact with the child to contact their GP or midwife

Illness, incubation time, immunisation, method of spread	Signs and symptoms	When to call doctor immediately	Specific treatment and complications
Measles Caused by a virus, is highly infectious and can be serious *Incubation time*: 10–14 days *Immunisation* available for children aged 12–15 months (see page 396) *Method of spread*: droplet infection	• Generally unwell initially • Koplik's spots (blueish white spots) appear in the mouth • Temperature, runny nose, red eyes and cough • A flat, blotchy red rash starts behind the ears and on the face and spreads to the rest of the body • Photophobia (dislike of bright light)	• Severe headache • Earache • Vomiting • Rapid breathing • Drowsiness • Seizures	*Treatment*: • nurse in a slightly darkened room. *Complications*: • conjunctivitis • otitis media • bronchitis • pneumonia • encephalitis.
Meningitis Infection of the brain and spinal cord – always very serious. *Incubation time*: 2–14 days *Immunisation*: Hib vaccination can prevent one type of viral meningitis in children under 4 years (see page 396); there is also a meningitis C vaccine available	Children can develop these signs and become seriously ill very quickly: • signs of cold/flu initially • drowsiness • loss of appetite • restlessness • temperature • nausea or vomiting • severe headache • photophobia (dislike of bright light) • stiff neck • joint pains. In the late stages there may also be a rash – flat purple or pink spots which do not fade if pressed. Babies may also: • arch their backs • have a shrill cry • have a bulging fontanelle.	As soon as meningitis is suspected The rash in meningitis is very distinctive and can be recognised by doing the glass test, as follows: • press a glass over the spots • if the rash is due to meningitis, the rash will not fade when pressed (whereas other rashes will).	*Treatment*: • antibiotics in bacterial meningitis • will be nursed in hospital • darkened room. *Complications*: • brain damage • deafness • epilepsy • loss of limbs • death.

Illness, incubation time, immunisation, method of spread	Signs and symptoms	When to call doctor immediately	Specific treatment and complications
Mumps Viral infection of salivary glands – not usually serious except in adolescent boys *Incubation time*: 14–24 days *Immunisation* available for children aged 12–15 months (see page 396) *Method of spread*: droplet infection	• Generally unwell initially • Fever *After 1–2 days*: • swelling and pain on one or both sides of the face under the jaw line – lasts for five days • dry mouth • loss of appetite. Confirm diagnosis with doctor – it is a notifiable disease (see Unit 4, page 175)	• Severe headaches and signs of meningitis • Abdominal pain	*Complications*: • orchitis (inflammation of the testes) in adolescent boys, which very rarely can cause infertility. *Rarely*: • meningitis • encephalitis • deafness in one or both ears.
Pertussis (whooping cough) Can be a very serious infection *Incubation time*: 7–10 days *Immunisation*: children can be immunised at 8, 12 and 16 weeks (see page 396) and again before school	• Starts like a cold • Bouts of short dry coughing • Long attacks of coughing followed by a whoop (deep intake of breath) • Vomiting • A cough may last for months	• Consult a doctor as soon as whooping cough is suspected • Poor colour (grey/bluish/pale) • Difficulty in breathing • Baby not feeding	*Treatment*: • antibiotics – need to be given early • soft non-crumbly food • plenty of fluids • sit child up during an attack • it is very frightening, so reassure child and stay close by, especially at night. *Complications*: • weight loss • dehydration • pneumonia • bronchitis • encephalitis.
Rubella (German measles) A viral infection which causes a mild illness which is not serious (except to pregnant women: it has serious effects on the unborn child) *Incubation period*: 14–21 days *Immunisation* available for children aged 12–15 months (see page 396) *Method of spread*: droplet infection	• Slight fever and generally slightly unwell • Swollen glands behind the ears and at the back of the neck • Rash of tiny flat pink spots which are not itchy and start on the face and spread to the body and limbs; these only last for a few days	• Joint pain • Any sign of meningitis (see below)	*Complications*: • encephalitis • can cause serious defects to the foetus if a woman contracts rubella in the first 12–16 weeks of pregnancy. Because the child can be infectious for 5–7 days before the rash develops, inform pregnant women who have had contact with the child to contact their GP or midwife

↑ Erythema infectiosum is characterised by a 'slapped cheek' rash

↑ The rash in meningitis is very distinctive and can be recognised by doing the glass test (see page 409)

↑ Mumps results in swollen salivary glands in the neck

Illnesses of the respiratory tract and ears

Respiratory infections are the most common of the childhood illnesses. There are over 200 viruses that cause cold symptoms, which is why children may seem to get one cold after another. Children are particularly prone to infections when they first start nursery or school because they are suddenly exposed to more pathogens.

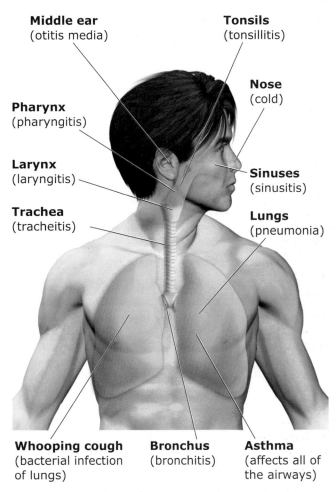

Middle ear (otitis media)

Tonsils (tonsillitis)

Nose (cold)

Pharynx (pharyngitis)

Sinuses (sinusitis)

Larynx (laryngitis)

Trachea (tracheitis)

Lungs (pneumonia)

Whooping cough (bacterial infection of lungs)

Bronchus (bronchitis)

Asthma (affects all of the airways)

↑ Respiratory tract and ears, showing areas affected by different illnesses

Colds

Children will, on average, have six to eight colds a year. They are caused by viruses and are spread by coughing, sneezing or by contact with secretions on toys and other surfaces. Colds often last five to nine days, but children can have a runny nose for one to two weeks after this.

⇩ **The signs, symptoms and treatment of a cold**

Signs and symptoms	Treatment and care	Refer to a doctor if...
• Runny nose • Sore throat • Sneezing • Cough • Slight temperature	There is no specific treatment available: plenty of fluids to drink. To reduce cross-infection: • teach child to blow nose and ensure regular handwashing • use tissues rather than hankies and throw them away straight after use • put cream on nose if sore • use a decongestant at night if the child is having difficulty in sleeping; a chemist can advise which is most suitable.	• Child complains of earache • Child becomes worse after 2 or 3 days • Baby is unable to breathe properly or drink due to being congested • The nasal discharge remains thick and yellow after the cold has finished

Sore throat and tonsillitis

The tonsils are fairly enlarged in a child because they are active in preventing infections. If there is a large invasion of germs, the tissues swell and become inflamed which usually causes pain. With tonsillitis, the throat initially becomes sore; the infection then spreads to the tonsils which become enlarged. Many childhood illnesses have a sore throat as one of the symptoms.

Coughs

Coughing in children is usually associated with an upper respiratory infection and can sometimes follow a cold. It is one of the body's defence mechanisms to get rid of irritants, chemicals or germs. Coughs can be caused by viruses or bacteria, dust, smoke, tuberculosis and asthma (a dry cough at night can sometimes be an early sign of asthma).

⇩ **The signs, symptoms and treatment of a sore throat and tonsillitis**

Signs and symptoms	Treatment and care	Refer to a doctor if...
• Sore throat • Swollen glands • Difficulty in eating • Refusing to eat • Snoring • Stomach ache • Able to see sore throat/enlarged tonsils when mouth is open	• Plenty of fluids to drink • Children's paracetamol if needed • Soft food • Antibiotics might be prescribed • If a child has repeated attacks a tonsillectomy (removal of the tonsils) may be carried out	• There is pus in the throat • There are white spots on the tonsils • Baby is refusing feeds • The child appears ill

⇩ **The signs, symptoms and treatment of a cough**

Signs and symptoms	Treatment and care	Refer to a doctor if...
• Cough • Raised temperature • Rapid breathing • Looks and feels unwell • Dry mouth	• Plenty of fluids to drink • Avoid smoky atmosphere • Breathing may be easier if top of bed is raised slightly • Seek advice from doctor or chemist if parents feel a cough syrup might help • A cough suppressant should not be used if the child is coughing up mucus, because this will actually be clearing the lungs	• The cough lasts more than 1–2 days in an infant • Coughing prevents feeding in babies • Child is constantly gagging • Child has high temperature • Ribs sink in when child is breathing • A whooping sound is made • Child looks very unwell

Earaches and middle ear infection (otitis media)

Middle ear infections are very common in children under 8 years and often follow respiratory infections. They are caused by a virus or bacteria and some children have frequent attacks, especially children who are bottle-fed, live in a smoky house and have frequent colds.

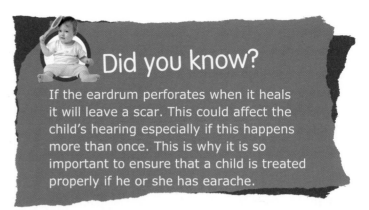

Did you know?

If the eardrum perforates when it heals it will leave a scar. This could affect the child's hearing especially if this happens more than once. This is why it is so important to ensure that a child is treated properly if he or she has earache.

⇩ The signs, symptoms and treatment of earaches and middle ear infections

Signs and symptoms	Treatment and care	Contact a doctor immediately if...
• Painful ears • Child clutches ear • Vomiting • Ears 'crackle' and 'pop', feel 'tight' or 'full' • Ringing or buzzing in ears • Raised temperature • Difficulty in hearing	• Child needs to see a doctor • Give children's paracetamol to relieve the pain and reduce fever • Getting child to yawn or swallow may help to relieve feeling of tightness • Place warmth against the ear but do not allow child to sleep with a heating pad or hot water bottle as it may cause burns • If warmth doesn't help, try wrapping an ice pack (or pack of frozen peas) in a towel and apply for 20 minutes every hour • Plenty of fluids to drink • Do not pack the ear with cotton wool if the ear discharges	• Child has a stiff neck • Child is unsteady on feet • Child has a head injury before the earache • Child has a high fever and appears very unwell • The ear discharges pus (the pain may fade) – this is caused by the eardrum perforating (tearing)

If a middle ear infection is not properly treated, the following complications may occur:

➜ inflammation of the outer ear (otitis externa)
➜ glue ear (chronic otitis media; see below)
➜ brain abscesses (very rare).

Glue ear

Glue ear is caused by a build-up of fluid in the middle ear and is usually associated with upper respiratory infections, such as colds, and ear infections. It usually occurs in both ears. Glue ear affects young children; they will usually 'grow out of it' by the age of 8 years.

⇩ The signs, symptoms and treatment of glue ear

Signs and symptoms	Treatment and care
• Partial and intermittent deafness • Behaviour changes • Lack of concentration • Speech may be affected • Poor school performance	• A doctor will monitor the child • A hearing test will ascertain the degree of deafness • Be understanding – it can be very confusing for a child to suffer intermittent hearing loss • Occasionally grommets (small tubes) may be inserted into the ear drum to allow the fluid which is trapped in the ear to escape

Asthma

Asthma is a fairly common condition affecting more than 1.1 million children in the UK – there is a person with asthma in every one in five households in the UK. It can occur at any age, and half of all children will grow out of it. There is often a family history of asthma, hay fever or eczema.

Causes of asthma

The airways in an asthmatic become oversensitive to certain conditions or triggers. These triggers cause the muscles around the airways to tighten, the lining of the airway to become inflamed and the airways themselves to fill with mucus. This in turn causes the airways to narrow, which causes the symptoms of asthma.

The 'triggers' which can cause the airways to become more sensitive include:

→ an allergy to one or more irritants such as pollen, house mite dust, cats, dogs or horses (the allergen is in the fur, saliva and urine)
→ chemical irritants such as tobacco smoke, exhaust fumes, perfumes and household cleaners
→ exercise
→ cold air
→ chest infections
→ emotional stress such as anxiety or excitement
→ food especially peanuts, seafood, eggs and some additives and food colourings
→ mould (especially in damp living conditions)
→ air pollution – although there is no evidence that this can cause asthma, it can be a trigger if the child has asthma.

There is also a higher incidence of asthma in children whose mother smoked in pregnancy and in those who were bottle-fed.

Signs and symptoms of asthma

The symptoms vary in each child, and can range from mild to very severe or life-threatening. Attacks may be very occasional or frequent and are a major cause of absence from school.

The first signs of an attack might be:

→ a persistent cough, especially in cold air, after exercise or at night
→ colds which go 'straight to the chest'
→ breathlessness and wheezing when the child exhales (breathes out).

During an attack there may also be:

→ difficulty in speaking
→ grey-blue colour, especially around the lips
→ a dry tickly cough.

The child will also be frightened and anxious.

Management of asthma

This consists of medication and controlling the triggers. Medication consists of two types:

→ 'Relievers' are used to treat the acute symptoms. They open up the air passages in the lungs and are given in syrup form, tablets or in an inhaler, which will always be blue.
→ 'Preventers' reduce inflammation in the airways and prevent attacks or reduce their severity. These are usually brown but sometimes in a maroon or orange inhaler, and they need to be taken regularly.

If a child is less than 5 years old or has difficulty using an inhaler, they might use a spacer device such as a Volumatic or Nebuhaler, where the child inhales the drug as a mist. For children under 2 years, there is a Babyhaler which has a soft mask.

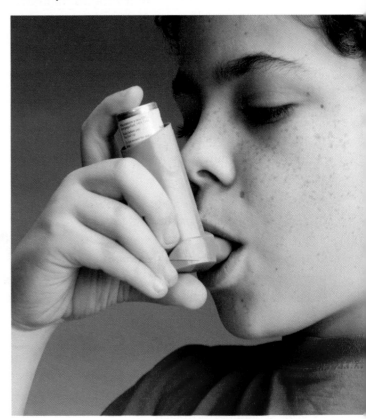

⇧ **When looking after children with asthma, you will need to be familiar with the type of inhaler the child uses**

Cystic fibrosis

Cystic fibrosis (CF) is an inherited condition which affects the respiratory and digestive systems. The mucus produced by the lungs is thick and sticky causing the airways to become infected or blocked and this causes difficulty in breathing. The ducts in the pancreas (see illustration opposite) also become clogged with mucus which prevents the digestive enzymes produced here from breaking down fats in the digestive tract. This results in poor weight gain because the body cannot gain energy from fats.

Disorders and infections of the digestive system

Pancreas
- Diabetes is a lack of insulin produced by the pancreas
- Cystic fibrosis causes the ducts of the pancreas to fill with mucus

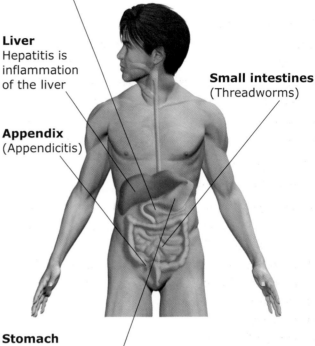

Liver
Hepatitis is inflammation of the liver

Small intestines
(Threadworms)

Appendix
(Appendicitis)

Stomach
- Pyloric stenosis is a narrowing of the pylorus, the lower part of the stomach through which food and other stomach contents pass to enter the small intestine
- Gastroenteritis is an irritation or inflammation of the stomach and intestines
- Travel sickness is caused by motion

⇧ **The digestive system, showing areas affected by different illnesses**

U11
2

Vomiting

Vomiting is a common symptom in children and can be associated with an infection anywhere. Some children will be sick every time they have a slight fever or if they are excited or frightened. However, there are many causes of vomiting and it is important to note the time of sickness, the colour, any pain or diarrhoea and whether the child appears unwell. Children should always be sent home from the setting if they vomit.

The different causes of vomiting in children are shown in the spider diagram overleaf.

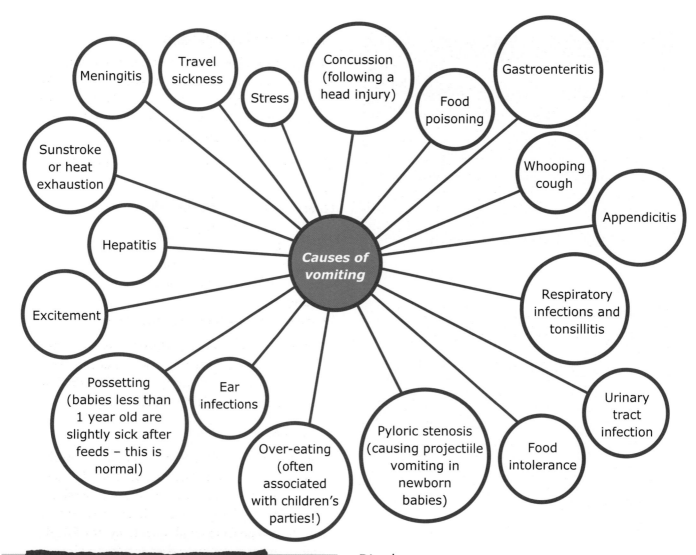

Meningitis

Travel sickness

Stress

Concussion (following a head injury)

Food poisoning

Gastroenteritis

Sunstroke or heat exhaustion

Whooping cough

Appendicitis

Hepatitis

Causes of vomiting

Respiratory infections and tonsillitis

Excitement

Urinary tract infection

Possetting (babies less than 1 year old are slightly sick after feeds – this is normal)

Ear infections

Over-eating (often associated with children's parties!)

Pyloric stenosis (causing projectiile vomiting in newborn babies)

Food intolerance

Good practice checklist

Care of a child who is vomiting

✓ Reassure and stay with the child.

✓ Ensure there is a bowl nearby and disinfect after use.

✓ Support the child's head when vomiting.

✓ Wash the child's hands and face after vomiting and encourage rinsing of the mouth with water.

✓ Allow the child to rest/lay their head on soft towels in case of accidents.

✓ Change clothes when necessary.

✓ Encourage sips of water to prevent dehydration (see page 417).

✓ Once the sickness has stopped, provide small portions of dry food, e.g. toast; this should be started gradually.

Diarrhoea

Diarrhoea (frequent runny stools) is fairly common in children and is often due to an infection. It can be distressing for a child and it may cause accidents in younger children when unable to get to the toilet in time. Diarrhoea is not an illness in itself but, like vomiting, is a symptom of many different conditions.

Causes of diarrhoea in children include:

➔ toddler diarrhoea (see below)
➔ a side effect of some medicines (especially antibiotics)
➔ food poisoning
➔ gastroenteritis (see page 417)
➔ food intolerance (see pages 422 and 484)
➔ excitement, nervousness or stress
➔ chronic constipation, which can cause an overflow of diarrhoea.

Good practice checklist

Care of a child with diarrhoea

✓ Reassure the child – diarrhoea can be very distressing.

✓ Give regular drinks of clear fluid to prevent dehydration.

✓ Keep a potty nearby, if possible, for a younger child.

✓ Keep spare pants handy!

✓ Avoid going out (except if toddler diarrhoea).

✓ If gastroenteritis is suspected, isolate the child from others and send them home.

✓ Good hygiene is important – ensure that the child washes their hands after using the toilet.

Prevention of dehydration

Children should be drinking between 1 and 1.5 litres of fluid a day. If a child has diarrhoea and/or vomiting, fluid can be lost very quickly. Therefore regular sips of clear water or an oral rehydration solution, such as Diarolyte, should be given.

The signs and symptoms of dehydration include:

➜ sunken eyes
➜ dry mouth/cracked lips
➜ pasty colour and dry skin
➜ dark urine
➜ sunken fontanelle (in a baby)
➜ increased pulse and breathing rates
➜ headache
➜ passing no urine for six hours in the day.

Children do not always feel thirsty when becoming dehydrated, so it is very important to encourage them to drink. If there are any signs of dehydration, the child should see a doctor straight away.

Gastroenteritis

Gastroenteritis is irritation or inflammation of the stomach and intestines and is contagious. Because the infection is in the bowel, proper handwashing is essential. It is fairly common in children and can easily be spread from child to child by unwashed hands touching food or equipment. It can also be caused by poor sterilisation of bottles or teats. Gastroenteritis can spread very quickly from one child to another in a nursery.

U11
2

⇩ **The signs, symptoms and treatment of gastroenteritis**

Signs and symptoms	Treatment and care	Contact doctor immediately if...
• Vomiting • Diarrhoea (6–10 times a day) • Loss of appetite • General abdominal pain • Fever	• Give clear fluids every 30 minutes • Give regular sips of a rehydrating solution, e.g. Diarolyte • Stop food and milk (except breast milk) for 24 hours • Avoid all food initially • When diarrhoea and vomiting have stopped, reintroduce half-strength milk then gradually introduce food	• Child is under 2 months • A baby has missed two feeds • There are signs of dehydration • Child cannot keep any drinks down • There is no improvement after 24 hours

Threadworms

Threadworms are tiny worms in the digestive tract which look like threads of white cotton when excreted. Children catch them by getting eggs on their hands from food, the sandpit, play dough, clothing and other equipment.

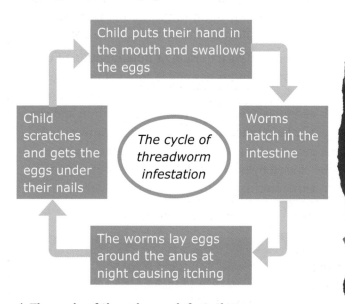

⇧ **The cycle of threadworm infestation**

Symptoms of threadworms include:

→ itching around the anus, especially at night
→ sore anus due to the scratching
→ occasionally white worms can be seen in the faeces.

The whole family will need to take medication prescribed by a doctor.

Threadworms can be prevented through:

→ good personal hygiene
→ the use of separate towels
→ keeping children's nails short
→ ensuring play dough is stored correctly in the fridge and toys and equipment are regularly washed.

Think about it

Several of the children at nursery have had threadworms recently and a few of the parents are concerned that their children might also catch it.

Either produce a fact sheet for the nursery to inform staff about the facts of threadworms and what can be done to prevent children being infected, or complete a leaflet for parents giving information about threadworms and how to prevent and treat them.

Skin conditions and infections

One of the main functions of the skin is protection against the environment – if the skin becomes broken then infection can easily enter the body. Skin conditions and infections are fairly common in children and often cause great discomfort and itchiness. It is important that children are kept away from the early years setting if their condition is infectious, because these infections spread very quickly among children through touch. Some of the most common skin conditions and infections are shown in the table opposite.

Condition and cause	How it is spread (transmission route)	Signs and symptoms	Treatment and care	Possible complications
Scabies; caused by an insect burrowing under the skin and laying eggs	• Direct contact • Indirect contact, for example, via clothing and towels	• Tiny grey swellings appear, particularly between the fingers or on the wrists, armpits or sides of feet • Intense itching, especially at night • Waking frequently at night	• See a doctor; all the family will need treatment with an insecticide lotion • Isolate the child	Scratching can cause impetigo (see below)
Impetigo; caused by bacteria – usually *streptococcus* or *staphylococcus*	• Direct contact with other children • Break in the skin caused by a cut, insect bite or eczema • Chapped lips	• Small blisters which crust and ooze; these often form around the mouth and nose • The infected area spreads rapidly	• Antibiotic cream which needs to be applied using gloves, or medicine • Child should be isolated • Discourage the child from touching the area • Separate towels and flannels should be used • Personal hygiene is very important	• If untreated it spreads rapidly • Can cause generalised infection and septicaemia (blood poisoning)
Cold sore; caused by *herpes simplex* virus. Triggers can be cold weather, the wind, sunlight or having a cold.	Direct contact	• Starts as tingling around the mouth. • Small blisters which form a crust appear after 1–2 days (these are smaller and more regular than impetigo). • Itching	• Often disappears on its own • Anti-viral cream may be used early on • After infection the virus lays dormant until a 'trigger' restarts the infection • Use lip salve in the winter and sunscreen in the summer	

Eczema

Eczema affects about one-fifth of all school-age children. It can start in children as early as 2 months old and 60–70 per cent of children grow out of it by adulthood. The characteristics of eczema include:

→ A dry, itchy rash appears which becomes red and starts to weep. In very young children the rash can affect the face, scalp, trunk and the outside of the arms and legs; in older children it can affect the bends of the elbows and knees, the feet and the hands. The skin can become broken and be raw and bleed.

→ The skin becomes itchy, especially at night.

U11
2

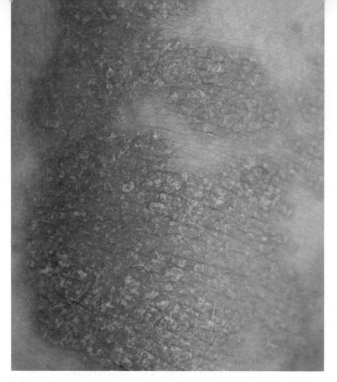

⇧ **Eczema appears as a dry, itchy rash which becomes red and starts to weep**

Caring for the child with eczema

Each child's eczema is very different and therefore it is important to discuss the child's treatment and care with the parents before coming to the setting. It is also important to keep updated on the child's condition. Some children are unable to touch paint, play dough, sand, clay or even water without causing the eczema to flare up, so it is important to find out from the parents what the child is unable to touch or use. This can potentially restrict the opportunities available for the child, and to ensure equality of opportunity the early years practitioner needs to be aware of the child's needs and ways of coping with these in the classroom. Strategies for supporting children with eczema are suggested in the table below.

⇩ **Strategies for supporting children with eczema**

Potential difficulty	Potential strategy
Contact with soap	Special emollients brought from home.
Contact with paint, salt, dough, clay, sand or water	Cotton gloves can be worn or plenty of cream applied first.
Swimming	Emollient cream can be applied beforehand. Remind the child to dry properly and then to reapply cream afterwards.
Pets	Some children will need to avoid the pet altogether.
Becoming hot which will worsen the itching	• Seating away from the radiator and windows. • Plastic seats may be covered if necessary.
Uniform	Children are better having cotton next to their skin and should avoid getting overheated.
Scratching	Distract the child as much as possible.
Lack of concentration due to itching	• Try to avoid telling them not to scratch because it can make them worse or build up resentment. • Further applications of cream may help.
Cooking	• Children should avoid contact with any food they are allergic to. • Use different ingredients for all of the children. • It is important to know if any of the children has a severe reaction to a food such as anaphylactic shock.
Worry over school work, friends or appearance can affect some children's eczema	Encourage the child to talk over any worries with the staff.

Disorders of the blood

Sickle cell disease

Sickle cell disease is an inherited blood disorder. Some children will be born with the disorder which will be inherited from both parents, while other children may be born with a 'sickle cell trait' which means they are carriers. Sickle cell trait cannot turn into the disorder and these children will usually be perfectly healthy.

In the UK, sickle cell disease is most common in people of African and Caribbean descent. Normal red blood cells are doughnut-shaped; in people with sickle cell disease, the red blood cells become hard, sticky and shaped like sickles or bananas. The sickle-shaped blood cells can clog the flow of blood to an area of the body, causing pain and **anaemia**. These episodes of anaemia and pain are called crises. In between these crises the child is usually quite well, although they are more prone to infections. Crises are more likely to happen following exercise, when the child is dehydrated and during illness, especially with a fever.

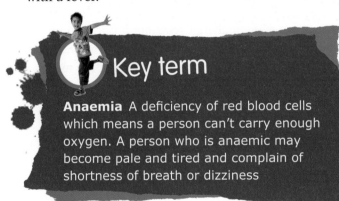

Key term

Anaemia A deficiency of red blood cells which means a person can't carry enough oxygen. A person who is anaemic may become pale and tired and complain of shortness of breath or dizziness

Children with sickle cell disease may be absent more frequently from settings because of crises or infections, which may require hospital treatment. Some young children will be on permanent antibiotics to prevent infection.

Good practice checklist

Care of children with sickle cell disease

✓ Allow the child to drink plenty of water – they may need to keep a water bottle with them. This will necessitate frequent visits to the toilet as their kidneys cannot retain water as well.

✓ Try and prevent the child from becoming over-heated or exposed to cold temperatures.

✓ Because of their anaemia, children with sickle cell disease may get tired before others and a rest period may be appropriate.

✓ Encourage gym and sports participation but allow the child to stop without undue attention.

✓ Medical attention should be sought if any of the following occur: fever, unusual headache, joint pains, chest pain, abdominal pain or swelling, numbness or weakness, shortness of breath or sudden vision change.

Hormonal disorders

The endocrine system of the body consists of glands and the hormones they release. Hormones are the body's chemical messengers. They are produced in glands and travel in the bloodstream to tissues or organs. They work slowly over time and affect growth and development, reproduction, the internal balance of body systems and metabolism (how your body gets energy from food). When there is an imbalance of one of the hormones, it can affect the whole body.

Diabetes mellitus

There are two types of diabetes mellitus: childhood diabetes and age-onset diabetes.

In childhood diabetes the body stops making the hormone insulin. Insulin allows the body to use and store glucose (sugar from food) for energy. Without insulin, the glucose cannot be used by the body's cells and remains in the blood before passing out of the body in the urine. In the past, before synthetic insulin was produced, most people with diabetes died because they could not gain energy from food and gradually wasted away. Today, all children with diabetes must have insulin injections for the rest of their lives.

The first signs of diabetes mellitus are generally:

→ frequency in passing urine
→ excessive thirst
→ tiredness and lack of energy
→ poor appetite
→ weight loss.

Management of diabetes

Once the family doctor suspects diabetes in a child, a blood and urine test will be done and the child will be admitted to hospital for a short time while insulin treatment is started. The parents and child – depending on the child's age – will be taught how to test the blood for glucose and how to give the injections.

The role of the early years practitioner

If you are working in a home setting you may need to do the following with the child:

→ test for glucose in a child's blood (a special machine is typically used to get a pinprick of blood for testing)
→ record the results
→ give injections of insulin
→ store and dispose of syringes
→ manage the child's diet – this should be a regular, balanced diet (the child's dietitian will give the parents information on this).

Hypoglycaemia

If, for any reason, the child does not eat the correct amount, takes extra exercise or is unwell, there may be danger of a hypoglycaemic attack. This occurs if the blood sugar level drops suddenly. It is essential that everyone involved in caring for the child – for example, teachers and early years practitioners – knows that the child is diabetic and what to do if the child has a hypoglycaemic attack. The child should always carry sugar or chocolate in case they become hypoglycaemic. (See also Unit 4, page 183.)

Allergic reactions

The immune system fights infection in the body by producing antibodies. Allergic reactions occur when a substance, which is not necessarily harmful in itself, enters the body and triggers an exaggerated immune response. This may result in symptoms ranging from sneezing and a runny nose to shortness of breath and anaphylactic shock.

Some children get severe allergic reactions (anaphylactic shock) when they either eat or come into contact with something to which they are allergic. The most common allergens are nuts, especially peanuts, and wasp and bee stings. The treatment is an adrenaline injection given by an EpiPen, which the child will be taught how to use when old enough. However, it is important that all staff who come into contact with the child are given training on the recognition of anaphylactic shock and know how to use an EpiPen (see also pages 445 and 484.)

Symptoms of anaphylactic shock include:

→ swelling and itching where the allergen has entered; food may cause swelling and itching of the mouth and throat while a wasp sting may cause intense itching and swelling at the sting site
→ an itchy rash may then spread over the whole body
→ the face and throat may swell and breathing becomes difficult
→ the child may become very agitated and experience tightening of the throat and chest
→ the child may then lose consciousness.

In order to prevent allergic reactions it is important that contact with the allergen is avoided. This means that care must be taken when cooking, but the most difficult time is at break and at lunchtime when other children may eat, for example, peanut butter sandwiches. Some children will react if they touch anything with the substance on, so all children must be encouraged to wash their hands after eating in order to prevent severe allergic reactions in other children.

Child and adolescent mental health problems

There is evidence to suggest that although children's physical health is improving, there are an increasing number of referrals to the Child and Adolescent Mental Health Services (CAMHS) with the following:

→ emotional disorders (including depression, anxiety and obsessions)
→ hyperactivity (involving lack of concentration and over-activity)
→ conduct disorders (involving aggressive and antisocial behaviour)
→ eating disorders, self-harm, panic attack and phobias (including school phobia).

There are some children and young people who are at greater risk of developing mental health or behavioural problems. They include children:

→ whose parents have learning disabilities or who are mentally ill
→ whose parents misuse drugs or alcohol
→ who have been abused or neglected
→ who have physical disabilities or learning difficulties or disabilities
→ who smoke, use illegal drugs or misuse alcohol
→ who are living in a household where there is domestic violence
→ who are looked after by a local authority.

These children will need more support by all professionals in order that they can achieve and reach their potential. If you have any concerns about a child you should discuss these with the parent and your manager or school nurse.

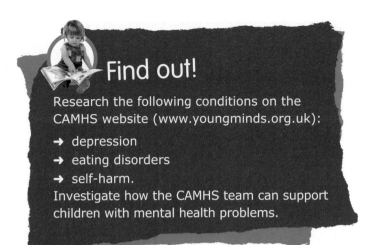

Find out!

Research the following conditions on the CAMHS website (www.youngminds.org.uk):

→ depression
→ eating disorders
→ self-harm.

Investigate how the CAMHS team can support children with mental health problems.

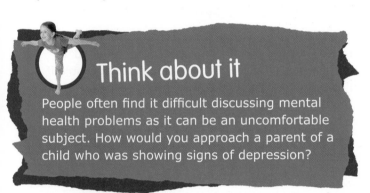

Think about it

People often find it difficult discussing mental health problems as it can be an uncomfortable subject. How would you approach a parent of a child who was showing signs of depression?

The policies and procedures for dealing with childhood illnesses for the protection of all children

The Health Protection Agency has produced guidelines for infection control in schools and other childcare settings (see chart below and on pages 424–5). These guidelines give advice on exclusion times from the setting when a child has an infectious condition. The child's GP will sometimes increase the exclusion time and the GP's recommendations should be followed.

☝ **Health Protection Agency guidelines for infection control in schools and other childcare settings (*Source*: Adapted from www.hpa.org.uk)**

Infectious illness	Recommended period to be kept away from childcare setting	Comments
Chicken pox	5 days from onset of rash	• Children with medical conditions resulting in reduced immunity (see page 425) will be particularly vulnerable if exposed to the virus; the child's parents/carers should be informed promptly and medical advice sought. • Pregnant women who have not previously had chicken pox and are exposed to the virus in the first 20 weeks of pregnancy or last 3 weeks should be referred to their GP or midwife.
Shingles	Exclude only if rash is weeping and cannot be covered	• Refer to comments on chicken pox for advice on vulnerable children and pregnant women.
Scabies	Child can return after first treatment	Two treatments 1 week apart. Contacts of the child should have one treatment at the same time as the child's second treatment. Treatment should include the entire household.

Infectious illness	Recommended period to be kept away from childcare setting	Comments
German measles (rubella)*	5 days from onset of rash	• This is the most infectious before the rash develops. • Children with medical conditions resulting in reduced immunity (see page 425) will be particularly vulnerable if exposed to the virus; the child's parents/carers should be informed promptly and medical advice sought. • Pregnant women exposed to the virus should be referred to their GP or midwife immediately for investigation. • All female staff under the age of 25 years should have evidence of two doses of MMR vaccine.
Slapped cheek / fifth disease / Parvovirus B19	None	• Exclusion is ineffective as nearly all transmission takes place before the child becomes unwell. • Pregnant women exposed to the virus in the first 20 weeks of pregnancy should be referred to their GP or midwife.
Hand, foot and mouth	None	This is very infectious mainly before symptoms develop (it is not related to foot and mouth disease).
Impetigo	Until lesions are crusted or healed	If lesions can be kept properly covered, exclusion may be shortened.
Measles*	5 days from onset of rash	• Children with medical conditions resulting in reduced immunity (see page 425) will be particularly vulnerable if exposed to the virus; the child's parents/carers should be informed promptly and medical advice sought. • Pregnant women exposed to the virus should be referred to their GP or midwife immediately for investigation. • All female staff under the age of 25 years should have evidence of two doses of MMR vaccine.
Scarlet fever*	5 days from commencing antibiotic treatment	Antibiotic treatment recommended for affected child.
Warts and verrucae	None	Verrucae must be covered in swimming pools, PE and dance lessons and in changing rooms.
Tuberculosis*	Always consult with local Health Protection Unit (HPU)	• Not usually spread from children • Requires prolonged, close contact for spread
Whooping cough* (Pertussis)	5 days from commencing antibiotic treatment	• Preventable by vaccination. • If child not given antibiotics they can be infectious for 21 days. • Non-infectious coughing may continue for many weeks after treatment.
Diarrhoea and/or vomiting	48 hours from last episode of diarrhoea or vomiting	Exclusion from swimming should be for 2 weeks following last episode of diarrhoea.
Mumps*	5 days from onset of swollen glands	• Preventable by vaccination (MMR x 2 doses) • The child is most infectious before the diagnosis is made.

Infectious illness	Recommended period to be kept away from childcare setting	Comments
Diphtheria*	Exclusion required; consult with local Health Protection Unit (HPU)	• Preventable by vaccination • HPU will organise any contact tracing necessary.
Hepatitis A*	Exclusion may be necessary – always consult with local Health Protection Unit (HPU)	• Good personal and environmental hygiene will minimise the danger of cross-infection. • It may not be necessary to exclude older children who are well and have good hygiene.
Hepatitis B* and C*	None	• Not infectious through casual contact • Good hygiene will minimise risk of cross-infection
Meningococcal meningitis* / septicaemia*	Exclusion until recovered	• Meningitis C is preventable by vaccination. • There is no reason to exclude siblings and other close contacts of a case from the setting. • The local Health Protection Unit (HPU) will give advice on action needed and identify contacts who need antibiotics.
Meningitis* due to other bacteria	Exclusion until recovered	• Hib meningitis and pneumococcal meningitis are preventable by vaccination. • There is no reason to exclude siblings and other close contacts of a case from the setting. • The local Health Protection Unit (HPU) will give advice on action needed and identify contacts who need antibiotics.
Meningitis viral*	None	• Milder illness. • There is no reason to exclude siblings and other close contacts of a case from the setting.

(* Denotes an infection which is 'notifiable'. Under the Public Health (Infectious Diseases) Regulations 1988, there are a number of infections which a doctor has to report to the Local Authority Proper Officers. These also include food poisoning.)

Vulnerable children

Some children have medical conditions that mean infections can be more frequent and more serious for them. This includes children being treated for leukaemia or other cancers and children on high doses of steroid medication. These children are particularly vulnerable to chicken pox or measles and every attempt should be made for these children to avoid contact with these infections.

Case study

A case of impetigo

Heidi's mother brought her to nursery this morning despite Heidi being sent home with impetigo the previous day. Heidi's mother says that she cannot take any more time off work and explains that the impetigo has healed. When you look at Heidi's face you notice that the impetigo has spread from the previous day and is weeping.

1. What would you say to Heidi's mother?
2. How long should Heidi stay away from the nursery?
3. What would be treatment for the impetigo?

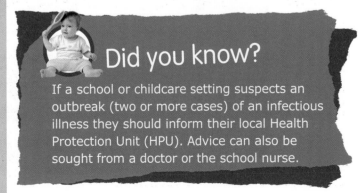

Did you know?

If a school or childcare setting suspects an outbreak (two or more cases) of an infectious illness they should inform their local Health Protection Unit (HPU). Advice can also be sought from a doctor or the school nurse.

The effects of ill health on children and families

In practice

In the Year 1 class in which you work there are two children who have chronic illnesses and are often away from school. There is also a child who is due to be admitted to hospital shortly.

By the end of this section you will understand how illnesses can effect the whole family and how to prepare a child for admission to hospital or a hospice.

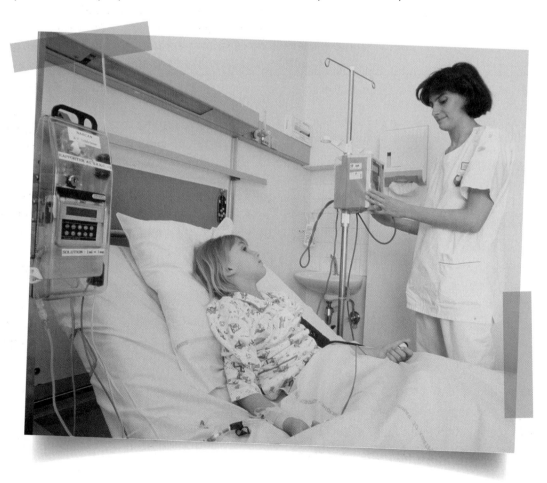

The possible effects of chronic and acute illnesses, hospital admission and care

All illness is stressful for the child and the family, especially if it is chronic or life-limiting. But even short-term illnesses can cause problems in the family. The effect of the illness on the child and family will depend on:

→ whether the child is at school or an early years setting
→ the child's age and stage of development
→ the parent(s) work, and whether they would need to take time off to care for the child
→ the illness itself – whether it is acute, chronic or life-limiting (see page 407)
→ the type of treatment
→ previous experiences of illness
→ how the family cope with the illness and the support they receive
→ how often the child is away from school or the early years setting – this may affect their development
→ whether the child needs hospitalisation.

Effects of acute illnesses

Even acute common childhood illnesses have an impact on the child or family. Coughs and colds in children are common but may cause sleepless nights for both child and parents! Even slight changes in routine can affect some children and cause them to feel anxious or distressed. However, these changes are short term and the child usually gets back to the normal routine quickly once they have recovered. Some acute illnesses, however, have more serious consequences: meningitis, for example, will require hospitalisation and can have long-term effects on the child, such as recurrent headaches.

Effects of chronic illnesses

A chronic illness can place restrictions on a child and limit his or her opportunities. Epilepsy, for example, can mean a child is not allowed to play on or use some equipment. The drugs used to treat epilepsy can cause a child to be drowsy, lethargic and clumsy, and can also dampen the child's curiosity, which will hinder development. Chronic illnesses can also mean

that a child has frequent absences from school and/or frequent hospital admissions, both of which can affect the child's development.

The spider diagram on the next page shows the effects of illness on a child's needs.

Effects of hospitalisation

When a child is admitted to hospital it is a stressful time for the whole family. This is particularly true if it is in an emergency because the child cannot be prepared beforehand. If it is known that a child is to be admitted to hospital, the child and family can be prepared appropriately. Children and young people up to the age of 16 years are usually admitted to the children's ward and these have facilities to allow parents or carers to stay, which can relieve some of the stress of admission.

The way a child copes with the admission will depend on a variety of factors, including:

→ the age and stage of the child's development
→ the personality of the child
→ the type of illness or operation
→ the length of stay in hospital
→ the anxiety of parents and carers
→ the atmosphere of the hospital and the support given by the hospital staff.

If a child is well prepared and the family is not unduly anxious, the child is more likely to cooperate with medical procedures and less likely to have behaviour problems afterwards or be stressed – which would delay recovery.

Some hospital procedures can cause more distress than others and this can make the children anxious, withdrawn and stressed. Children may also be fearful about the future and if they don't have the vocabulary to talk about their feelings, they can become angry or depressed. Some children may also develop phobias (fears). The play workers and nursery nurses on the ward try to reduce stress by preparing the child and using hospital equipment in play to reduce fears as much as possible.

U11

3

Children's physical needs

The child's physical needs will change during illness:

● appetite will often decrease and therefore nutritional needs change
● the child will often need more fluids to drink, especially in acute illnesses
● the need for sleep and rest will usually increase
● if the child has a temperature, clothing will need to be reduced
● the child may need more help with personal hygiene and have more washes instead of baths
● the need for warmth and fresh air may change, especially if the child has a temperature.

Children's social needs

● Children will not feel like interacting with their friends when they are feeling very unwell
● If children are away from school or nursery school for long periods they may become isolated and have difficulties maintaining friendships when they return to the setting.

The effects of illness on a child's needs

Children's cognitive needs

● Children often sleep for longer periods when unwell and they aren't interested in much, except perhaps being read to.
● During recovery, they may become bored and frustrated, and require activities which are short and simple, and which require little concentration.
● Children may start to get behind in their work if they miss school regularly through illness.

Children's emotional needs

Children who are unwell need more support than usual and will need to be cared for by someone they know and trust. Children in hospital cope far better if they have a parent or carer with them, and hospitals cater for this by providing beds and facilities for parents. Children often become:

● clingy – they want more attention from their carers
● frightened and need reassurance
● show signs of regression, i.e. behaviour typical of an earlier age group and refusal to do things that they previously did, e.g. talk, feed or dress themselves (see also page 430).

⇦ **Play workers and nursery nurses on hospital wards prepare children for their treatment using hospital equipment in play**

Preparing for an operation in hospital

Gemma, who is 5 years old, has had frequent bouts of tonsillitis and her doctor feels that she needs to have her tonsils out. Gemma's mother is extremely anxious about her daughter going into hospital due to a bad experience when she was younger. Gemma has a nanny who cares for her after school and one of the other children has recently been in hospital.

1. How can the school help prepare Gemma for hospital?
2. What games could the nanny play with Gemma to prepare her for hospital?
3. How could the nanny support Gemma's mother?
4. What might Gemma be frightened of and how can the nanny and the play worker in hospital help Gemma to overcome these fears?
5. Gemma's mother is frightened of hospitals. How could the hospital staff support her?

The impact of ill health on the development of the child

Acute illnesses are usually short-lived and therefore shouldn't have any long-term effects on children's development. Chronic conditions, however, can have a dramatic impact on a child's development, especially if there are frequent absences from nursery or school. These effects can be due to lack of independence, stimulation or play opportunities or the result of bullying. Medications can affect the concentration of children and have other side-effects which affect the child's learning. Even a condition such as glue ear can affect children's development; when a child has fluctuating hearing loss they will miss important information in class and among their friends, and behaviour problems can be common due to high levels of frustration. The table below shows the potential effects of illness on a child's development.

The impact of illness on children's communication and language development

Communication and language development can be affected by chronic illness due to lack of friendships. Some children, however, develop very good language skills from being in regular contact with a variety of adults.

↻ **The potential effects of illness on a child's development**

Area of development	Potential effects of illness
Physical development	• Poor or delayed growth • Developmental delay • Nutritional deficiencies • Delayed attainment of gross motor and fine motor skills
Social, emotional and behavioural development	• Lack of confidence in making and sustaining friendships • Delayed development of independent living skills (e.g. tying shoelaces) • Regression (see page 430) • Behaviour problems • Poor self-esteem • Poor attachments
Intellectual development	• Delayed literacy and numeracy skills • Delayed learning
Communication and language development	• Delayed communication skills

U11
3

The impact of illness on children's physical development

Physical development may be affected by chronic conditions; an acute illness rarely has long-term effects except when complications occur, for example a perforated ear drum causing ongoing hearing difficulties following an ear infection. The impact of chronic conditions could include:

→ *Poor or delayed growth.* Children who are unable to eat sufficiently may have poor growth or a 'failure to thrive'. This may be the result of congenital abnormalities (a defect in the baby which is present from birth) or from conditions where food is not absorbed properly.

→ *Developmental delay.* Where children are not able to move sufficiently they will not be developing their muscles. For example, if a baby has to have his feet in plaster for some time, his walking will be delayed.

→ *Nutritional deficiencies.* Some children don't absorb some types of food properly and this could lead to deficiencies if not treated early.

→ *Delayed attainment of gross motor and fine motor skills.* When a child is unwell for periods of time, they will be tired and will lack the energy to develop physical skills. It will therefore often take children longer to reach their developmental milestones.

The impact of illness on children's social, emotional and behavioural development

Development can be affected in the following ways:

→ *Friendships can suffer if a child has frequent or prolonged absences from nursery or school.* This can cause a lack of confidence in keeping friendships so it is very important that friends are encouraged to visit the child, if possible. Letter writing, emailing or sending pictures to each other can also help to maintain friendships.

→ *Delayed development of independent living skills.* Some children are more dependent on their parents and carers to help in their day-to-day care, for example when a child is confined to a wheelchair she may need help going to the toilet. It is important for children to gain as much independence as possible by allowing them to do what they are able, even if it takes longer for them to do it themselves.

→ *Behaviour problems.* These are sometimes the result of frustration, especially when a child cannot do what his or her friends are able to do. This can cause tantrums, aggressiveness or attention-seeking behaviour. Behaviour problems can also be due to regression (see below).

→ *Poor self-esteem.* Because children with health problems often miss school, they aren't always able to keep up with their peers or do everything that their friends are able to do. This can cause poor self-esteem and even depression in some children.

→ *Poor attachments.* When young babies are unwell and need frequent hospital visits, parents aren't always able to stay with the baby all the time, especially if there are other young children in the family. This can occasionally lead to poor attachments with the parents and rest of the family.

Regression

If emotional needs are not being met, the child may **regress**. This can happen with any illness and is normal for a short period, but over longer periods can affect development. It is important to recognise this and provide reassurance, routine and extra attention.

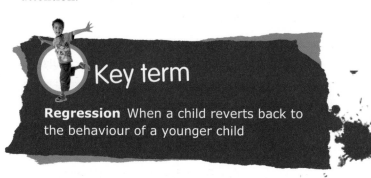

Key term

Regression When a child reverts back to the behaviour of a younger child

Signs of regressive behaviour include:

→ behaviour typical of an earlier age group and refusal to do things they previously did, for example refusal to talk, feed or dress
→ playing with toys from an earlier age group
→ excessive crying
→ lack of concentration
→ inability to learn
→ clinginess
→ aggressiveness
→ unusual behaviour such as head banging.

The impact of illness on children's intellectual development

Children who have to be absent from a learning environment for a period of time will lack the stimulation offered by the environment and will also be restricted from learning through observation and imitation of others. If this pattern of absence continues, the child can get further and further behind in all aspects of their learning. This includes delayed literacy and numeracy skills, since children require regular repetition to develop such skills. When children are unwell they also often don't have the energy to concentrate for any length of time, which can affect their ability to learn.

The impact on parents and other family members when children are ill

Even a short illness can cause disruption to family life and routine. If the parent works, alternative childcare may need to be arranged. Chronic, long-term and life-threatening illnesses may cause the family to make adaptations to many aspects of their lives to meet the needs of the child and other family members. A child's illness may therefore affect the family in the following ways:

→ *Physically*: It can be physically demanding and exhausting to care for an unwell child, especially if any lifting is required. Sleep can be more difficult during times of stress, and when it does occur often is not restful and this can lead to exhaustion. Some parents and carers get so worn out they cannot take care of other children. If the child is in hospital, the families' nutritional needs can suffer if they rely on fast food or vending machine snacks in order not to have to leave the child's bedside for long.

→ *Emotionally*: There is always a multitude of emotions, such as fear, uncertainty, anxiety, insecurity, guilt and depression, especially when there is a long-term illness or if hospitalisation is required. Parents may not have enough time to spend with their other children and this may also leave them feeling irritable or angry, or guilty for neglecting their family. If the child is in hospital, parents can feel helpless due to losing control of the child's care and frustrated at not being able to ease the child's fear or pain.

→ *Financially*: If a parent has to give up work either temporarily or permanently this can have huge financial implications for the family. If a child is in hospital this can cause further expense.

→ *Isolation*: It is often not possible for the parent to have the same contact with friends or work colleagues when a child is ill, and this can cause the parent to feel isolated, especially if the care is very demanding.

The effect on the child's siblings

When a child is unwell it can upset the routine of other children and can cause a variety of different emotions to surface, especially if the child is seriously unwell. Siblings often have ambivalent (opposing) feelings towards each other – they are the best of friends one minute and mortal enemies the next; illness can cause them to feel guilty if they think unkind thoughts about their sibling and they might also feel that they have caused the illness in some way. Other children might feel jealous of the attention the ill child is getting or feel confused. Siblings may become attention-seeking or develop behaviour problems and they therefore need quality time spent alone with their parents and carers.

Older siblings may be expected to help more and behave more responsibly; as one child explained: 'Just for once, I wish I wasn't the one that my parents say they can always rely on.' If the child is seriously ill, siblings can worry that their brother or sister may die or that they may also catch the illness.

> ## Case study
>
> **Dealing with sickle cell disease**
>
> Jacob has sickle cell disease and has frequent absences from school due to crises. He is often admitted to hospital. Jacob's brother is in the Reception class and also has sickle cell disease but very rarely has problems.
>
> 1. Describe how Jacob's condition and his frequent absences from school may affect his development, learning and behaviour.
> 2. Describe the potential effects of Jacob's condition on his family.

In practice

You have just got a job as a nanny looking after two children. You are worried about looking after them in case they become ill.

By the end of this section you will have gained an understanding of how to care for children who are unwell in a variety of settings.

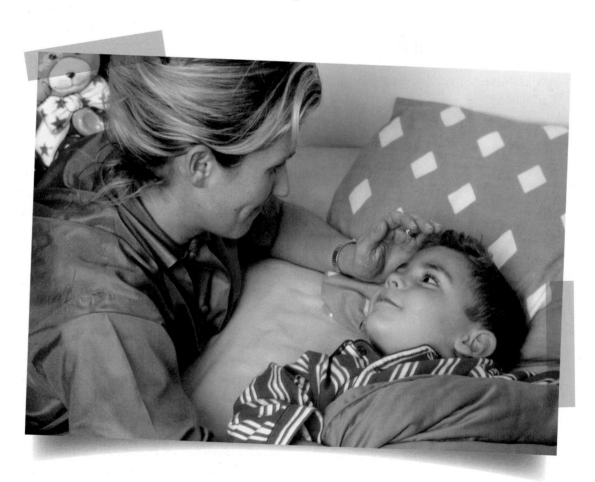

Different responses which are age and stage appropriate, including strategies for dealing with distress

Responding to a child's needs in a childcare setting

When a child has an acute illness they should usually be sent home in order to prevent other children catching the infection. However, children will still be in the setting if they have colds and coughs.

If a child has a chronic condition, such as asthma, the setting needs to find out as much as possible about the condition in order to ensure they can support the child. This may involve the staff going on staff training or attending a first aid course.

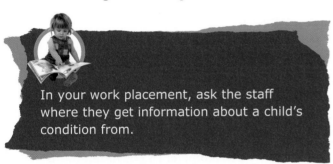

In your work placement, ask the staff where they get information about a child's condition from.

Caring for a child's physical needs

Children will need to be kept in a warm but well-ventilated room; if infectious, the child will need to be isolated from other children. Some settings have a medical room which means that the child can be supervised and kept comfortable while remaining isolated from other children. Where there is no medical room, it is important that the child is kept away from others until their parent or carer collects them. Children need to be encouraged to wash their hands frequently to avoid passing the infection on.

Responding to the child's physical needs in a home setting

Routine

Children need the security of a routine when they are unwell. Drinks, meals and rest times should, where possible, continue at the usual times. If the child cannot be cared for by the parent then a familiar adult needs to be around, as well as any comfort objects.

Warmth

Children will need to be kept in a warm but well-ventilated room. In a home setting, children will often prefer to be cared for in the sitting room on the sofa rather than in their own bedroom.

Food and drink

Children are often not very hungry when unwell but it is not generally a problem if they are drinking plenty of fluids. Food doesn't always taste the same as usual so it is important that the food is nutritious and presented in small appetising portions. However, it is far better to allow the child to have a favourite food than eating nothing at all! Food such as ice cream, fromage frais, toast and marmite, puréed fruit, eggs and ice lollies (made with fruit juice) will all provide the child with energy and some vital nutrients. It is often better to offer regular snacks when a child is unwell.

It is very important that the child drinks frequently while unwell to prevent dehydration. It is better to offer a child their favourite drink, but drinks which are high in vitamin C, such as diluted orange juice or squashes, are ideal and will help the child fight infection. To encourage a child to drink, use a special cup with a straw or make ice lollies or flavoured ice cubes from fruit juice and water; these should be offered at least every hour.

Rest and sleep

Most children require more sleep when they are unwell, giving the body time to recover. Children should therefore be encouraged to rest wherever they feel comfortable and be given quiet and simple activities to do.

Personal hygiene

It is important that the child's normal hygiene routine continues although washes may be more acceptable than a bath; hair brushing and teeth brushing should continue as normal although this may also be done after a child has been sick. The child will need to wash their hands frequently especially if they have an infectious illness.

Care of a child with a temperature

When a child has an infection the body temperature is raised in order to fight the infection. The normal body temperature of a child is 36.5–37.0°C and will vary throughout the day, often being higher in the evening, after exercise and bathing, and in hot weather. Babies, who have a very immature temperature-regulating mechanism, can show large fluctuations in temperature and can develop high temperatures very quickly. The temperature is usually taken under the armpit (axilla) or by using a fever strip on the forehead in young children and babies; the reading will be 0.5°C lower than if taken by mouth (orally).

A high temperature can cause **febrile** convulsions (see below) in children under the age of 5 years; therefore the child should be cooled if the temperature exceeds 37.5°C.

Key term

Febrile Relating to a fever

Good practice checklist

Caring for a child with a temperature

✓ Maintain room temperature at 15°C (60°F) and remove clothing down to the underwear.

✓ Offer sips of cool drink regularly.

✓ With parent's permission, paracetamol syrup can be given to children over 3 months old (see page 440).

✓ Fan the child.

✓ If the temperature is over 38.5°C, tepid sponging can be done: dip a sponge into lukewarm water and sponge over the child's skin but do not dry. Repeat until the temperature falls below 38.5°C. The temperature should not fall too quickly because this can cause shock. *Never* use cold water.

Febrile convulsions

Febrile convulsions can occur in children aged 6 months to 5 years and are caused by a rise in temperature. The convulsions begin with the child losing consciousness and shortly afterwards the body, legs and arms go stiff. They often throw their head backwards and their legs and arms begin to shake. The child's skin goes pale and they may even turn blue briefly. The convulsion should end after a few minutes and the shaking stops. The child then goes limp and will regain consciousness, although they will be very sleepy.

Children who have had a convulsion have an increased risk of further convulsions. It can be frightening dealing with convulsions and it is important to know whether the child has a history of them. (See page 445 on how to deal with febrile convulsions.)

Taking a child's temperature

There are four different types of thermometer which can be used:

→ A digital thermometer is unbreakable, easy to read, accurate and fairly quick to use.

→ A mercury thermometer can be hazardous if made of glass because it contains mercury, which emits fumes if the glass is broken. It is accurate and cheap but is difficult to read and should never be placed in a child's mouth. There are plastic ones available.

→ A fever strip is not as accurate as other methods but is cheap and very easy to use by placing the strip onto the child's forehead. The strip changes colour and shows the temperature of the child.

→ An infra-red thermal scanning thermometer is very accurate and it only takes a few seconds when placed in the ear to take a reading. It is expensive but very easy to use on children.

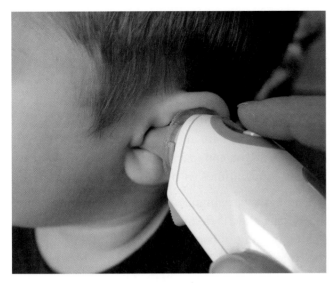

⇧ **You will need to be familiar with the different types of thermometer available and how to use them when taking a child's temperature**

Older children can have the thermometer placed under their tongue, which gives a more accurate reading. However, it is important that the thermometer is disinfected before and after use.

Dealing with children's pain

Children express and deal with pain in very different ways. Young children won't have the vocabulary to describe pain which can make your role very difficult. Hospitals use pictures to help children describe how much pain they are in; older children can describe their pain on the scale of 0–10, with 0 being pain free and 10 being the worst imaginable pain. This can help the carer to know when pain is easing or getting worse.

There are various ways of helping a child to deal with minor pain, such as giving extra cuddles, distraction with a book, puppets or a game, heat or cold. Deep breathing, slowly counting four breaths in and four breaths out, or blowing bubbles can also reduce pain. Children's paracetamol or ibuprofen can be given with parent's permission (see page 440 on medicines).

U11
4

0 No pain	2 Hurts a little bit	4 Hurts a little more	6 Hurts even more	8 Hurts worse	10 The worst possible pain

⇧ **A visual pain scale like this can help children describe the level of pain they are feeling**

Children sometimes have to have tests that are going to hurt. Fear increases pain and therefore children need to know what to expect and to be given choices and some control. They will feel less upset if they are told honestly when something is going to hurt, why they are having something painful done to them and that it is meant to help them and not to punish them.

When children have chronic pain they can become very irritable, tired and demonstrate poor behaviour. The GP may refer the child to a pain specialist if painkillers are not managing the pain properly.

Responding to children's social, emotional and behavioural needs

In order to minimise the effects of illness on a child's social, emotional and behavioural development, it is important for the practitioner to support the child and family. Children who are unwell need more support than usual and will need to be cared for by someone they know and trust. Children cope far better in hospital if they have a parent or carer with them, and hospitals cater for this by providing beds and facilities for parents.

In the home environment, sick children need the security of their normal routine to continue as much as possible. Mealtimes and bedtimes should, where possible, continue as normal. It can be very worrying for a child to be ill and young children may not have the right vocabulary to express how they are feeling. Allow children to express their fears and be careful to validate their feelings. There is nothing worse than feeling scared and confused and not being able to talk about it. Some children will become clingier when unwell and behaviour changes might be noticed in others. They need to be reassured that they are going to get better and that they are still loved. It is often advisable to make up a bed on a sofa in the sitting room so that the child knows that the carer isn't far away.

In a nursery and school setting, all staff should have an understanding of chronic conditions and ensure that they give activities which are achievable and help raise the child's self-esteem. However, it is also important that a child with a chronic condition is not overprotected. Children want their parents or carers around them when they are unwell and may therefore become more distressed in school or nursery. The practitioner needs to reassure the child

and take them somewhere quiet until their parents arrive.

If a child is seriously ill, it is usually better to be honest with the child about their condition and explain what is to happen in a clear and simple way. Part of growing up is learning how to deal with frustration, pain and loss. As an early years practitioner, you can teach children effective ways of handling tough times with honesty and love.

Play remains very important for a child even when ill. When a child is first unwell they often need to sleep more, but in between periods of sleep and rest the child can quickly become bored and frustrated. In hospitals, play workers help children to work through their fears and worries using play. They can also explain what may be involved in their treatment through play.

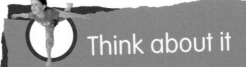

Think about it

You are caring for Michael and Paul who are 3-year-old twins in a home setting. Michael is recovering from chicken pox and Paul has just started to feel unwell.

Plan a routine including activities for both children for a day, bearing in mind the different needs of the children.

Responding to children's intellectual needs

Children often sleep for longer periods when unwell and they aren't interested in much, except perhaps being read to. During recovery, however, they may become bored and frustrated and require activities which are short and simple, and which require little concentration. Children often play with toys and read books which are suitable for a younger age group when unwell, and the carer needs to play appropriate activities throughout the day. School children can be sent work from school if they are away for a length of time. (See also pages 448−9 for play activities for sick children.)

How to report and record illness and seek help

Reporting illness

Generally, it is not advisable to have children who are unwell at any setting. The following people may be contacted when a child is unwell:

→ *The school nurse.* Where a school has a nurse on the premises, the child will usually be sent to the health room to see the nurse, who will then contact the necessary parties as required. In settings where there isn't a nurse, this will be done by the key worker, first aider, nursery manger or head teacher.

→ *The parent/guardian.* The parent should be informed if the child becomes unwell, has an accident or if their condition changes while in your care. If the parent is unavailable, the emergency contact should be phoned.

→ *The general practitioner (GP).* Occasionally it may be necessary to contact the child's GP if the practitioner is unable to contact the parent and is concerned about the child's condition. The GP will need to know the signs and symptoms of the child, any care or treatment given and the progress of the condition since you first became aware of the illness.

→ *The emergency services.* In an emergency, call 999 (or 112) for an ambulance and be ready to answer some questions about the child and the signs and symptoms. The parent would need to be informed and the child's key worker, first aider, school nurse or head teacher may accompany the child. Anyone under 16 years must be accompanied to the hospital.

Emergency situations

A practitioner should always call for help if they are concerned about a child. The spider diagram below describes some of the situations which should be treated as an emergency.

Recording child illness

If you are caring for a child in their own home, it is good practice to ensure that you record any change in a child's health and any medication which you have been requested to give. In all other settings, it is important to keep accurate records of the following:

→ the name, age and address of the child
→ contact numbers of parent(s) or guardian's, both at home and at work
→ two further contact names and their telephone numbers
→ the GP's name, address and telephone number
→ long-term illnesses, allergies, conditions or operations

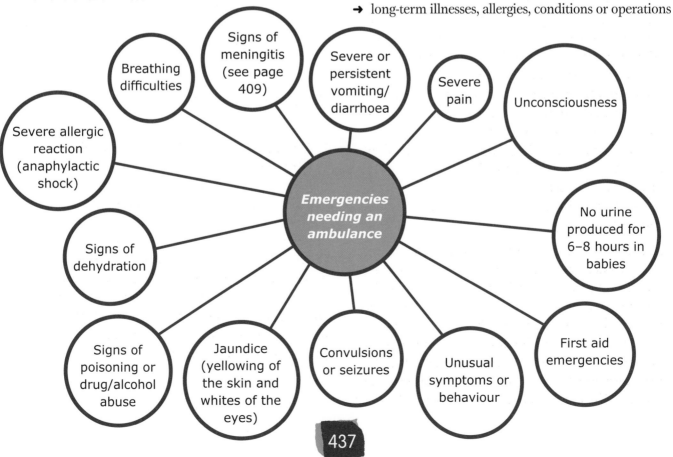

437

- → medication
- → special dietary requirements
- → difficulties with hearing, speech or vision and whether glasses are worn
- → immunisations given.

These records of a child's health are confidential and should only be seen by those who really need to know. Parents might not want some information to be disclosed in case the child is treated differently. It is also very important that the practitioner does not discuss the contents of the record sheet with anyone else. Records should be kept in a locked cupboard and be updated regularly, usually manually.

It is important to remember the Data Protection Act (see page 224) and the policies of the setting when dealing with children's illnesses and their records.

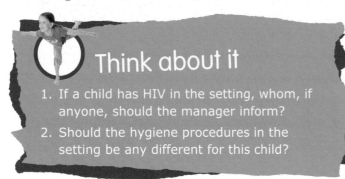

Think about it

1. If a child has HIV in the setting, whom, if anyone, should the manager inform?
2. Should the hygiene procedures in the setting be any different for this child?

How to record and monitor children's health

When caring for a child at home, the practitioner needs to make records of the child's illness in order to show the parents, or doctor, if necessary. These need to contain details of:

- → the child's temperature
- → the date and time of any medication given
- → any changes in the child's condition, for example if the child develops an earache or a rash.

If the practitioner becomes concerned about a child's condition they should always contact the child's parents and/or seek medical assistance.

When a child has a chronic condition in other early years settings, it is important that information between the parents and setting is shared regularly. This is often done as a 'home–school' book which goes between the different settings with the child. This enables up-to-date information and changes in the child's condition to be shared quickly and easily.

Basic hygiene routines in caring for children who are sick

Infections can spread very quickly within an early years setting as children are vulnerable to infection but often don't have very good hygiene habits (such as throwing tissues away after use). A number of procedures which can help prevent the spread of infection are described below.

Personal hygiene

It is not only important to have good personal hygiene to protect yourself and others from infection but also to provide a good role model to children. In any childcare setting, infection is spread by the hands more than anything else. You will need to refer back to Unit 4, pages 176–9, and Unit 9, page 366, for tips on good hygiene practice.

Keeping the setting clean

It is important that the setting be kept free from pathogenic micro-organisms (see page 176) as much as possible in order to avoid cross-infection. The following should therefore be done:

- → If the child has an accident, use gloves and cover the area with a bleach solution (consult the setting's policies). Wipe over the area with disposable towels which should be disposed of according to the setting's policy and then wash the area with soapy water.
- → Use tissues instead of hankies and dispose of them into a bag.
- → Ensure that the room is warm but well ventilated in order to disperse germs.
- → Toys should be washed thoroughly and sand should be sieved and washed.
- → Ensure that all children wash their hands after going to the toilet, before and after eating or handling food, after messy activities, handling pets and being outside.
- → Ensure that all surfaces are regularly cleaned.
- → Toilets should be regularly cleaned.
- → Parents should be encouraged to keep their children at home if they are unwell in order to prevent spread of infections.

In a home setting the following should also be done:

- → If a child has sickness or diarrhoea, cover their bed sheet/sofa with soft towels because these are easy to wash on a high heat (60 degrees Celsius).

→ Children are more likely to wet the bed when unwell so you may need to use a mattress protector. The child's bedding should be washed on a high heat to destroy germs.

→ The child may need their own towel, especially if they have an infectious skin condition.

Disposal of waste

Every setting will have a policy on the disposal of waste which may contain infectious material (such as urine, blood, vomit or faeces). In order to prevent infection being spread, it is important to follow the policy of the setting when disposing of all waste which contains body fluids. Gloves should always be worn and hands washed with liquid soap. Nappies, dressings, gloves and anything else which might have been in contact with body fluids should be placed in a sealed bag and then placed in the correct colour bin bag (usually a yellow bag with black stripes) in a foot-operated pedal bin with a lid.

Case study

Poor hygiene practices

On her first day at her new work placement, Jenny is very nervous. Although she has put up her hair and removed her rings and earrings, the first thing that she notices is that the manager has long flowing hair and is wearing an engagement ring and loop earrings. Jenny finds the setting very hot but the manager said that they couldn't open any windows because they had been painted and were stuck shut.

Because it was her first day, Jenny was asked to observe one of the staff who was working with a group of children who were playing with water. She noticed that several children had colds and kept wiping their noses on their sleeves or their hands. One child kept drinking the water and another kept spilling water on the floor. Another child brought a 'cup' made of play dough to fill it with water – the play dough disintegrated into the water. The children went straight to have drinks and fruit from this activity and those who went to the toilet weren't supervised.

Later on that day a child was sick on the floor. Jenny was asked to wipe it up with a kitchen towel and sit the child in a corner with a bucket.

1. Identify how infection could be passed on in this setting.

2. How should Jenny deal with this situation? Should she talk to someone, and if so to whom?

3. Produce a poster to show the staff how they could prevent the spread of infection in the setting.

Find out!

At your work placement, find out about the policy for dealing with spillages and disposing of waste.

Health and safety policies and procedures for dealing with children

There are many health and safety policies and procedures which settings have developed from health and safety legislation, as shown in the spider diagram below. You will need to refer to Unit 4, pages 161–5, for more detail on health and safety legislation.

- Infectious diseases
- Infection control
- School trips
- Administration and storage of medicines
- First aid
- Reporting accidents
- Moving and handling
- Asthma policy

Relevant health and safety policies and procedures

439

Each setting will have their own policy on medicine, covering administration of, recording, written parental consent and storage, and it is important that the practitioner follows these guidelines.

Procedures and regulations for administering medicines

Each country within the UK has different legislation regarding medicines. For example, in England, the Statutory Framework for Early Years Foundation Stage provides settings with specific legal requirements regarding medicines. These are as follows (*Source:* The Statutory Framework for Early Years Foundation Stage, 2007):

→ Early years settings must have an effective policy on administering medicines which should include ways to manage and support children with specific medical needs.

→ Written parental consent needs to be obtained before giving any medicines.

→ Written records should be kept of all prescribed medicines given to children and parents should be informed when medicines are given.

There is also some statutory guidance which should be followed:

→ Settings should have appropriate information about the medical conditions of children with long-term medical needs. This means that the setting should ask all parents and carers to complete a medical form on admission and the setting should regularly check to see if there are any changes to these.

→ Parents should provide details of the child's medication and information about any changes to the child's prescription or to the support their child may need.

→ Some medicines can be administered only with medical or technical knowledge, in which case training should be given by a qualified health professional. This training would be specific to the medicine and the child, for example giving insulin injections to a diabetic child.

→ Medicines should only be given if they are essential and have been prescribed by a doctor, dentist, nurse or pharmacist. This would mean that settings could give a child's antibiotics but couldn't give a child cough medicine unless it had been prescribed.

→ The setting has to arrange for a member of staff to give the medicines.

→ Prescribed medicines have to be kept in a locked, unmoveable container unless the medicine has to be kept in a fridge. Only named staff should have access to the medicines and records should be kept.

Although this legislation is for the Early Years Foundation Stage only, primary schools would have to develop their own policy to include the above. All practitioners will therefore need to follow the policies of the setting.

Giving medicines to children

Children often need medicine when unwell, but medicines are potentially dangerous and therefore great care should be taken in their giving and storage; it is best to avoid giving medicines if at all possible but if this is part of your role, ensure that you have been adequately trained. In most settings the first aider gives medicine.

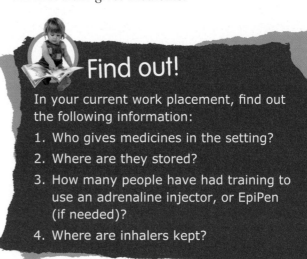

Find out!

In your current work placement, find out the following information:

1. Who gives medicines in the setting?
2. Where are they stored?
3. How many people have had training to use an adrenaline injector, or EpiPen (if needed)?
4. Where are inhalers kept?

Children under the age of 12 years are usually supplied with medicines in syrup form which are flavoured and generally sugar-free. They usually are supplied with a 5ml spoon or a syringe (for babies and young children). Most children are happy to take their medicine but some are not so eager! Try offering young children their favourite drink afterwards, making it into a game. If the taste is a problem, the child's parent could talk to the doctor about changing the flavour.

Good practice checklist

Giving medicines to children

✓ Before giving medicine ensure you know the reason for the medicine, the dosage, storage (some medication needs to be stored in the fridge), side effects and whether it should be given before or after food.

✓ Read the label on the medicine to ensure that it is the correct one. Check the dose and the time that the medicine should be given. Check the expiry date.

✓ If you are giving a medicine from the pharmacist, such as paracetamol, check that the dose you have been asked to give matches the instructions provided.

✓ Wash hands.

✓ Shake the bottle if necessary.

✓ Explain to the child about the medicine and sit the child down, preferably on your knee.

✓ Always use the measure that is provided with the medicine (teaspoons are not equivalent to 5ml measure).

✓ Pour medicines from the bottle with the label facing upwards, to prevent drips ruining the label.

✓ If using a syringe, point this towards the inside of the cheek and give slowly to prevent choking. For a baby, sterilise the syringe.

✓ Ensure the child takes the full dose – medicine should never be added to drinks because the full dose might not be given.

✓ Give the child a drink after taking the medicine.

✓ Store the medicine correctly according to instructions.

✓ Record the date and time that you gave the medicine.

✓ If a child develops a side effect, such as a rash or diarrhoea, the GP needs to be informed before the next dose is given.

✓ It is important, when taking antibiotics, that the course is finished even if the child appears to get better, otherwise infection might reappear.

✓ A pharmacist should dispose of any unused medicines.

Records of medicines

Each early years setting will have a policy on recording medicines. This will require the parent to complete a form before any medicine can be given in the setting. If you are caring for a child at home, the parent should record all instructions for medicines and you must get permission from the parent before giving medicine.

The details needed on a child's medicine record should be completed by the child's parent or carer and include:

→ the name and address of the child
→ the child's date of birth
→ the child's medical condition or illness
→ the name of the medication to be given
→ the required dosage of the medication
→ the time and date that the medication is to be given
→ the method of administering the medication
→ the possible side effects of the medication
→ the length of time the child is to be on the medication
→ the date the medication was dispensed and date of expiry
→ emergency procedures
→ the parents'/carers' and emergency contact details.

⇩ **Example of a form to record details of medication given to a child**

Date	Name	Time	Name of medication	Dose given	Any reactions	Signed	Print Name
20/10/05	Robert Jackson	12.15	Epilim	5mls	None	A.L.	A. Lee
20/10/05	Sophie Eldridge	13.00	Amoxycillin	5mls	None	A.L.	A. Lee

Storage of medicines

Medicines may be dangerous to anyone for whom they are not prescribed. The Control of Substances Hazardous to Health (COSHH) Regulations 2002 (see also Unit 4, page 162) requires that the setting protects others from this risk. Medicines must therefore be kept in a locked cupboard out of the reach of children in an early years setting. Inhalers (which need to be easily accessible) and medicines which need to be in a locked fridge are the exception to this rule.

It is important in a home setting that medicines are kept out of reach of children. Children can very quickly find an open medication, including those with a childproof lid – these only delay a child for a few seconds. Care must be taken never to keep any medicines in a handbag because children find these very quickly.

Appropriate responses in emergency situations

Because babies and children are prone to accidents, it is recommended that all early years practitioners complete a first aid course and keep up to date with first aid procedures. This section will give a summary of some first aid procedures, but it is meant for revision only and not as a substitute for a course.

Responding to an emergency

In a work setting, always call the first aider for any accident or incident. In a home setting, you will need to be able to deal with any incident until an ambulance arrives (see page 437 on calling emergency aid).

Find out!

In your work placement, find out:

1. Who are the first aiders and where are they in the building?
2. Where are the first aid boxes kept?
3. What is the policy on first aid for trips?

Case study

Giving medicine to a child

You are looking after a 2-year-old girl called Sophie, who has an ear infection. Her mother has asked you to give Sophie the next dose of her antibiotic after lunch at 1pm and some children's paracetamol if she has pain.

1. What do you need to find out from Sophie's mother?
2. What would you need to check before giving any medication?
3. When you try and give the medicine, Sophie is very reluctant to take it. How could you encourage her to take it?
4. How would you record what has been given?
5. What would you do if Sophie refused the medicine?
6. How could you tell if Sophie needed the children's paracetamol?
7. Where would you store the medicine?

Good practice checklist

What to do in an emergency situation

✓ Stay calm.
✓ Assess the situation – is the casualty, you or any other children in danger?
✓ Think of safety – remove any danger.
✓ Make a quick assessment of what is wrong with the child and call for help if necessary.
✓ Treat serious injuries first.
✓ Get help.
✓ Deal with the emergency and reassure the child until help arrives.

Dealing with minor injuries

It is far more common to deal with minor injuries, such as cuts and bruises, than life-threatening situations. The table opposite shows common minor injuries and their treatment.

Injury	First aid treatment
Graze	Rinse with clean water.
Nosebleed	Tip head forward and pinch nose just below bridge. Seek medical advice if bleeding continues for 30 minutes.
Foreign object in the ear or nose	Do not try to remove it. Take the child to hospital.
Bruises and sprains	Apply cotton wool dipped in cold water. For a sprain, rest the limb, apply an ice pack and apply a bandage. Raise the limb.

Responding to unconsciousness in a child

If a child is breathing but not responding to your voice or to being shaken by the shoulders, the child will need to be placed in the recovery position. The procedure for this is described below.

1. Remove glasses and bulky objects from the child's pockets.
2. Bend the arm nearest to you so that it makes a right angle and lay it on the ground with palm facing upwards.

3. Bring the other arm across the chest and hold the back of the child's hand against their opposite cheek – and keep holding it.
4. Use your other hand to firmly grasp the thigh opposite you and carefully pull the knee up to bend the leg.

5. Pull on the thigh of the bent leg to roll the child towards you and on to their side. Use your body to stop the child from rolling over too far.

6. Bend the top leg to prevent the child from rolling over.

7. Tilt the child's head up to open the airway. Make sure the upper arm is supporting the head.

8. Call an ambulance.
9. Check the child's breathing and circulation until help arrives.

U11

4

For a baby less than 1 year old, a modified recovery position must be used. Cradle the infant in your arms, with the head tilted downwards to prevent choking on the tongue or inhaling vomit.

A child who has been unconscious, even for a short time, must be seen by a doctor or go to hospital.

Modified recovery position for a baby under 1 year old ⇨

Treatment of injuries

Injury/ incident	Symptoms	Treatment
Bleeding	Signs of bleeding; if severe, there may be signs of shock: the child will be pale, feel cool but have clammy skin	• Check for objects in the wound but do not remove them. • Apply direct pressure to the wound with a pad. • Raise the injured limb above the level of the heart. • Apply an extra pad if necessary but do not remove the old pad. • Lie the child down with the legs raised to prevent shock. • Call for help.
Breaks (fractures)	Pain, loss of movement, swelling and bruising; possible deformity of limb	• Do not move the child unless he or she is in danger, e.g. from falling equipment. • Help the child to support the injured limb above and below the injury and support with pads. • Call an ambulance.
Burns	Mild burns will include a pinkish area on the skin which could become blistered. There will also be pain in the area.	• Place affected area under a running tap of cold water or dip into a bowl of water (or any cold liquid) for 10 minutes. Chemical burns need 20 minutes of cold water. • Remove watches and rings from the site. • Cover with a clean, non-fluffy cloth. • Call 999 for a severe or chemical burn. • Do not apply cream or butter to the area.
Choking	Difficulty in breathing and speaking; flushed face; may clutch throat or chest	• Remove any obvious obstruction from the mouth. • Give up to five back blows. • Check the mouth and remove any obvious obstruction. • If this fails, give up to five abdominal thrusts (chest thrusts in a baby under 1 year – it is vital that you never do abdominal thrusts on a baby). • Check the mouth and remove any obvious obstruction. • Continue with three cycles of back blows and abdominal thrusts (or chest thrusts). • If this fails, dial 999 (or 112) for an ambulance. • Continue until help arrives.

Injury/ incident	Symptoms	Treatment
Head injury (all head injuries are potentially serious)	Lump on the head and headache. Signs of concussion or a serious injury may also include vomiting, dizziness, unusual drowsiness or unconsciousness, or a clear fluid or watery blood leaking from the ear	• Apply a cold compress to the head. • Ensure the child sits down and rests. • Watch for signs of concussion or a serious head injury (see opposite). • Go to the hospital if the child was unconscious, even if only for a short time.
Hypoglycaemia (low blood sugar) in a diabetic child	Weakness, faintness or hunger; aggression or confusion; sweating and cold, clammy skin; pulse may be rapid and strong	• Help the child to sit or lie down. • Give the child a sugary drink or chocolate. • If the child responds quickly, give more food and drink and allow to rest until feeling better. • If the child doesn't respond quickly, call an ambulance. • If the child becomes unconscious, place in the recovery position (see pages 443–4).
Seizure and febrile convulsion	Sudden rigidity of the body; twitching and jerking of the limbs; the back may arch, eyes may roll upwards; breath-holding; possible incontinence; loss of or altered consciousness	• If possible, remove anything which could cause injury and protect the child's head by putting something underneath it. • Do not restrain the child. • When the seizure finishes, place the child in the recovery position (see pages 443–4) and reassure the child on regaining consciousness. • Call for an ambulance unless the first aider knows that the child has occasional seizures. • If the seizure is due to a febrile convulsion (see page 434) the child will need to be cooled. • The child should never be left alone.
Severe allergic reaction	Anxiety; difficulty breathing; swelling and puffiness of face, neck and eyes; red, blotchy skin; itchiness	• Call an ambulance. • Help the child to use their adrenaline injector (EpiPen) (if they have one) or give it yourself *if trained to do so*. • Help the child to sit in a position that most relieves any breathing difficulty. • If the child becomes unconscious, place him or her into the recovery position.
Swallowed poisons	Symptoms will depend on the poison but could include vomiting, impaired consciousness and pain or burning sensation	• Dial 999 (or 112) for an ambulance. • Ensure you have the bottle of tablets or medicine to take to hospital – it is essential that you record how much you think the child has ingested. • Do not make the child sick, but if he or she vomits, check the vomit for tablets and take a sample with you to the hospital. • Reassure the child. • If the child is unconscious, place in the recovery position (see pages 443–4). • Record any changes in the child.

(For advice on dealing with asthma in a child, see pages 414–5.)

U11
4

Informing parents

Parents need informing about *all* accidents that occur. When there has been a serious injury, the parents need informing immediately. All settings will inform parents of minor injuries when the child is collected, either by a written note or verbally. It is very important that parents are aware of all head injuries because signs of concussion can occur many hours later; many settings have a sticker which the children wear if they've bumped their head, which is used in addition to the note.

Recording accidents

Under the Reporting of Injuries, Diseases and Dangerous Occurrences Regulations (RIDDOR) 1995, *all* accidents involving children, staff and visitors need to be recorded in an accident book. The following information needs to be included:

→ the name of the injured person and the first aider
→ what happened and where
→ the date and time of the accident
→ the treatment given.

(See also Unit 4, page 165.)

Think about it

In groups, discuss what you would do in the following situation:

You are called to an incident in the playground following a fence collapsing. Rohini is screaming and has a bad nosebleed and a graze on her arm; Joshua is sitting quietly on the ground but has a bump on his head; Adrianne has fallen and has a graze on her elbow and a deep cut on one of her arms which is bleeding profusely. Brittany is lying on the ground and is not moving.

1. What are your priorities?

2. Decide what you would do in this situation.

3. Who would need to be informed and what would you record?

The role of the adult in supporting children and their families suffering from childhood illnesses

In practice

You're working as a Nursery Nurse in Children's Outpatients at a local hospital. Your role is to play with the children and support parents and carers.

By the end of this section you will have identified ways in which you can support children who are unwell and their families.

The identification of, and support for, the range of responses from children and their families when children are unwell

Children and their families need support throughout a child's illness, especially if the child has a chronic condition which requires frequent hospital appointments and visits. This support may be provided by a variety of different professionals and services but also by the child's nursery or school and from friends and family.

This support needs to include:

→ support provided by peers, both among children and young people and between families with similar problems (see support groups on pages 451–2)

→ provision of information on support groups and voluntary organisations

→ help with childcare arrangements for siblings

→ help with transport and travel to the hospital or other centres

→ advice on available financial support including, for example, for families whose child is in hospital at a distance from home

→ advice on respite care

→ spiritual support provided by religious leaders or the chaplaincy service in a hospital

→ specialised support such as that provided by a counsellor, mental health professional or social worker for those with emotional and psychological difficulties

→ facilities within the hospital to enable a parent to stay.

In addition, the family will need to be given time to express their concerns and to be given honest answers to their questions. Siblings need time with parents and carers to be able to express their feelings and have the details about their sibling's illness explained in a simple way. They should be included in family discussions and know in advance whether there will be any change to their routine, for example who might pick them up from school. It is very important that good communication exists between home and settings in order that the early years practitioner can support the child and the siblings appropriately.

It is important that the support needed is identified early on in order that the family can be fully assisted. Support is given by a variety of health professionals and support groups as well as the education service; these are discussed on pages 450–2.

The role of play and specific activities in meeting the individual needs of children who are ill

Play will continue to be important when a child is ill because young children often don't have the vocabulary to explain their symptoms and fears. Play can therefore:

→ help the child to communicate how they are feeling

→ allow the child to act out any fears

→ provide some sort of normality for the child

→ provide a distraction from their illness

→ help the child gain new information about their condition or treatment.

In hospital, specialist play workers are trained to use play to help children to adjust to being in hospital. Play can also help children to cope with procedures and operations and to recover quicker.

Play activities for sick children

When children are first ill they often need to sleep for long periods and may not be interested in doing much, except perhaps having a simple book read to them. When they start to recover, they still need plenty of rest but will tend to become bored and frustrated. They therefore need activities which are short and simple and do not require too much concentration; some appropriate activities are described in the table opposite.

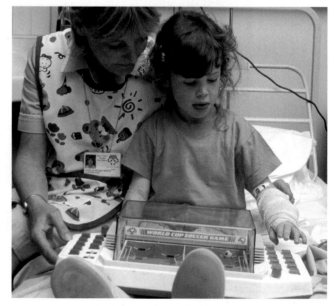

⇧ **Children who are ill need activities which are short and simple and do not require too much concentration**

Books	Young children often have favourite stories which they like to have read to them over and over again. The local library or the child's school may be able to provide school-age children with further reading. Books which are easy to read and have some illustration make reading easier when the child is unwell.
Story tapes or CDs	These can be obtained from the local children's library and enable the child to listen to the best bits over and over again. They are useful if the child has a headache which makes reading too painful.
Treasure box	This is a collection of toys, books and games which is kept aside and used only occasionally to provide something different for the child to play with.
Puzzles	These can be done on a tray and need to be fairly simple to prevent the child from becoming frustrated.
Games	Board games and simple card games can provide good quality time that an early years practitioner, sibling or family member can spend with the child. These can be borrowed from the local toy library, if you have one near you. Older children can also do simple word puzzles, crosswords and word searches.
Family photographs	If a child has a very poor concentration span, then photos of familiar people, pets or places can relieve boredom and provide a good talking point.
Play dough or plasticine	These activities can help a child to express some of their feelings and frustrations and need not be too messy if done on a tray.
Drawing, colouring or sticking	This is a good activity for all ages.
School work	If school-age children are to be away from school for an extended period, the school can provide them with some appropriate work to help prevent them getting too far behind.
Visits from family and friends	Providing the child is not infectious, visits from friends and family can prevent the child from becoming isolated. They will also help to maintain friendships.
Videos and DVDs	Videos and DVDs can help the child relax and distract them from their symptoms. They should not, however, be relied on too heavily, especially in chronic illnesses, because children can become too dependent on the television to provide them with entertainment.
Storyboard and fuzzy felt	These can help the child work through any worries or concerns they may have about their illness.

When children have a chronic condition which keeps them away from school for long periods they will lack the stimulation offered by a learning environment and therefore won't be learning through observing and imitating others. The child will need to be provided with school work and other activities which can stimulate them. Home tutors can be provided by the Local Education Service if the child is off school for an extended period.

Think about it

You are caring for 4-year-old Isobel at home who has tonsillitis. Plan a skeleton routine for her to include activities for when she is unwell and for when she is recovering.

U11

5

The role of other professionals in the support of children who are ill and their families

Children are mostly cared for at home by a parent or carer when they are unwell. However, there are a large variety of professionals who could help to care for a child. This care is initially provided by the primary healthcare team which is based in the GP's surgery. If specialist care is required, the GP will refer the child to a specialist children's service based in the community, or a hospital.

The Education Service

It is important that the child's school develops policies which ensure that the child's needs are met within the school environment, for example an asthma policy will ensure that all staff are aware of the child's triggers and know the treatment for each child.

The child's teacher should liaise with the parents to provide work if necessary and with the school nurse, who can give the staff advice and training as required.

The Primary Health Care Team (PHCT)

The PHCT is based at a GPs' surgery and their role is to prevent, diagnose and treat ill health. This responsibility includes provision of the following services:

→ immunisation clinics
→ antenatal clinics
→ child health clinics
→ family planning clinics
→ specialist clinics such as those for asthma or weight control.

The PHCT is made up of a variety of professionals including the following:

→ The GP is usually the first health professional that a child is taken to when they are unwell. Their role is to diagnose (find out what is wrong) and give the appropriate treatment to the child. They may refer the child to other health professionals if necessary.
→ The Practice Nurse helps the GP and runs some of the clinics in the surgery such as immunisation and asthma clinics.
→ The Community Nurse visits patients in their own home.

→ The Community Midwife carries out antenatal clinics, classes and postnatal visits with the mother and baby, and deals with normal pregnancy, the birth and the postnatal period.
→ The Health Visitor visits the mother and baby after the midwife finishes visiting. They work mainly with families with children under 5 years old and promote health and prevent ill health. They are involved in child developmental checks, hearing tests and advise on childcare.

Other professionals may be involved but this will vary from practice to practice.

Health and social care professionals in the community

NHS Direct	This is a 24-hour telephone helpline service via which parents can seek advice about a child with a fever or other symptoms of acute illness, or if they need support or reassurance in caring for a child with a minor illness. A website is also provided (www.nhsdirect.nhs.uk).
School Nurse	School Nurses provide health and sex education within schools and carry out developmental screening, undertake health interviews and administer the immunisation programme. They can give school staff training on various conditions and can support a child's health needs.
Community Paediatric Nurse	Some areas have these nurses who visit sick children and provide support to the family in their home when the child has been discharged from hospital or if the child has long-term health problems.
Social Worker	Social Workers are usually based in the community and can offer advice to the family on financial issues including benefits, respite care and transport to and from the hospital.

Child and Adolescent Mental Health Services (CAMHS)	CAMHS provide help and treatment to children and young people who are experiencing emotional or behavioural difficulties or mental health problems, disorders and illnesses. They often visit schools or are based in the community or GP/health clinics.

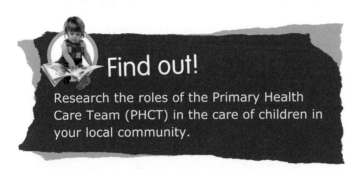

Find out!

Research the roles of the Primary Health Care Team (PHCT) in the care of children in your local community.

Hospital-based professionals

If a child attends outpatients or is admitted to hospital, there are a wide variety of professionals they may encounter during their stay in hospital. These may include the following:

→ *Paediatrician* – a doctor who specialises in the care of sick children

→ *Paediatric nurse* – a nurse who specialises in the care of sick children

→ *Play specialist* – a nursery nurse with specific training who encourages the child, through play, to come to terms with being in hospital, with their condition and with any procedures, for example surgery, which they may need

→ *Nursery nurse* – will support the nurses and play specialists on the ward to ensure that the child settles into the ward and isn't frightened

→ *Play therapist* – will work with children who have had traumatic experiences

→ *Speech and language therapist* – works with children who have problems with communication and provides help with speech development and speech defects, such as a stammer

→ *Occupational therapist* – helps children who have been disabled to relearn muscular control in order to do everyday tasks

→ *Radiographer* – diagnostic radiographers perform X-rays and scans and therapeutic radiographers use radiation to treat cancer and tissue defects (radiotherapy)

→ *Dentist* – specialises in prevention and treatment of tooth decay and gum disease

→ *Orthodontist* – gives specific advice and treatment to correct teeth and jaw problems

→ *Anaesthetist* – will give an anaesthetic to a child if they require an operation

→ *Physiotherapist* – specialises in treating physical problems affecting the musculo-skeletal system but is also involved in the care of children with respiratory conditions such as cystic fibrosis

→ *Audiologist* – measures hearing problems

→ *Dietician* – works with children to promote good eating habits and to give specific advice to children who require special diets, such as diabetics or those with food intolerances.

Multi-agency working and the sharing of information

It is important that all professionals who are working with a child cooperate with each other to provide the best service possible for the child and their family. Members of the primary health care team (PHCT) meet together regularly but it is the child's GP who will coordinate the services required for the child and the hospital will keep the GP informed of all treatment done at the hospital. It is important that the child's school is fully aware of the child's condition and the support needed, a role usually undertaken by the school nurse.

The support for parents and families who are looking after children who are ill

Local support groups

When a child has a chronic or life-limiting condition, great support can be found through other families with similar problems. Local organisations and support groups run for a variety of conditions and are usually led by a parent. They usually have regular meetings and can provide valuable support to the child and the family. Knowing how other families have coped with some of the practical aspects of the child's condition can help other parents pick up good tips and provide very valuable support. The child's social worker, health visitor or GP should be able to provide information about local support groups.

Find out!

Investigate the local support organisations in your area.

In addition, there are a variety of national organisations that can provide detailed information about children's medical conditions as well as advice and support. Such organisations include:

→ *NCH, the children's charity* (www.nch.org.uk). NCH's work includes providing family support services to support GP practices and child and adolescent mental health services that work to prevent mental health problems, as well as working with children with significant and severe mental health issues. They also run projects in some areas working with children with terminal illness or chronic conditions, supporting the child and their family.
→ *Action for Sick Children* (www.actionforsick children.org). This is an advice service providing information and support to parents and families of sick children who have concerns about their health and care.

There are also many national organisations which can provide advice and support about specific conditions, including:

→ Association for Spina Bifida and Hydrocephalus (ASBAH) (www.asbah.org)
→ Asthma UK (www.asthma.org.uk)
→ Diabetes UK (www.diabetes.org.uk)
→ National Eczema Society (www.eczema.org)
→ National Society for Epilepsy (www.epilepsynse. org.uk)
→ Sickle Cell Society (www.sicklecellsociety.org).

Find out!

In pairs, pick one chronic condition and carry out research into the role of the national support organisation associated with that condition.

Getting ready for assessment

Below are some questions that you can use to check your understanding and recall of this unit.

1. Outline three factors in the promotion of community health and health education.
2. Describe four causes of ill health in children.
3. Explain three ways in which ill health can be prevented.
4. Evaluate the role of the practitioner in supporting children who are ill.
5. Describe the roles of three professionals who may support children who are ill and their families.

Unit 12

Nutrition and healthy food for children

In this unit you will learn:

1. The essential food groups and a balanced diet for children

2. Nutrition and the growing child

3. Influences on food and diet

4. Disorders requiring special diets

5. Safe food preparation

Section 1

The essential food groups and a balanced diet for children

In practice

Lisa, aged 3 years, was really worrying her parents. All she ate was cereal and milk or cheese and crackers, with an occasional banana or apple and a glass of fruit juice. After they kept a food diary for two weeks they shared it with Lisa's key worker at the nursery she attends before going to see the dietician. The early years practitoner was able to reassure them to some extent that Lisa seemed to be having a reasonable balance of nutrients.

When you have worked through this section you will understand about the different food groups and what children need to eat a balanced diet.

The principles of nutrition for children

The basic needs of the body

The human body is entirely dependent on regular fuel to grow and develop. No single food contains all the essential nutrients the body needs to be healthy and function efficiently. The nutritional value of a person's diet depends on the overall mixture, or balance, of foods that is eaten over time, as well as the needs of the individual. That is why a balanced diet is one that is likely to include a large number or variety of foods, so adequate intakes of all the nutrients are achieved (see below).

Think about it

'You are what you eat' is a view held by many. What do you think?

Different food groups

The five main food groups, the nutrients they provide and their role in the body are described in the table below and on the next page.

Food group	Main nutrients provided	How they are used in the body
1. Bread, other cereals and potatoes	Carbohydrate (starch), some calcium and iron, B vitamins and dietary fibre	• Carbohydrate is needed to provide energy. Starchy carbohydrates are broken down and converted to glucose which is either stored as glycogen in the liver and muscles or is circulated in the bloodstream where it can enter cells and be used as energy. • Dietary fibre is not absorbed but passes through the gastrointestinal tract, helping to keep it healthy before being excreted. • Calcium has a role in the development and maintenance of teeth and bones. • Iron is needed for the formation of haemoglobin in the blood. It is also a component of many enzymes. • B vitamins are principally involved in energy metabolism.
2. Fruit and vegetables	Vitamin C, carotenes, folates, carbohydrate and dietary fibre	• Vitamin C helps in the structure of connective tissue and bones. It is needed for wound healing and helps the absorption of iron from non-meat sources. It may help to prevent the risk of chronic diseases such as heart disease and cancer. • Carotenes contribute towards the development of vitamin A. • Folates are needed for the formation of blood cells.
3. Milk and dairy foods	Calcium, protein, vitamin B12, vitamin A and vitamin D	• Calcium is used in the development and maintenance of teeth and bones. Protein is essential for the growth and repair of the body, with any excess used to provide energy. • Vitamin B12 is needed for the formation of blood cells and nerve fibres. • Vitamin A is needed for the maintenance and repair of tissues necessary for growth and development. It is also essential for the immune system to function and to help night vision. • Vitamin D helps with calcium and phosphate absorption from food and is essential for healthy teeth and bones.

U12
1

Food group	Main nutrients provided	How they are used in the body
4. Meat, fish and alternatives	Iron, protein, B vitamins (especially vitamin B12), zinc and magnesium	• Iron is needed for the formation of blood. It is also part of many enzymes. • Protein is essential for growth and repair of the body, with any excess used to provide energy. • B vitamins are important for energy metabolism. • Vitamin B12 is needed for the formation of blood cells and nerve fibres. • Zinc is needed for growth of tissues, immune function and wound healing. • Magnesium is needed for bone development and nerve and muscle function. It also helps in the function of some enzymes involved in energy use.
5. Foods containing fat and foods containing sugar	Fat and carbohydrate (sugar); some also provide other nutrients, e.g. fat-soluble vitamins (A, D, E and K), and some contain salt	• Vitamin A is needed for healthy mucous membranes and helps with vision. • Vitamin D is essential for the body to be able to use calcium to strengthen bones and teeth. • Vitamin E helps the development of strong muscles and is also important in healthy skin. • Vitamin K is important in the blood clotting process.

The British Nutrition Foundation developed the Balance of Good Health as a simple pictorial guide to the essentials for a healthy diet, based on the UK government's Eight Tips for Eating Well (see page 482). The guide shows that all foods can be part of a healthy diet and is designed to be displayed and used in schools, workplaces, health centres and supermarkets to promote a consistent message to the public. Foods from the largest groups should be eaten most often and foods from the smallest group should be eaten least often. The guide is shaped like a dinner plate which has been designed to make the principles of healthy eating guidelines simpler to understand.

⇧ **The proportion and types of foods required to make up a healthy diet**

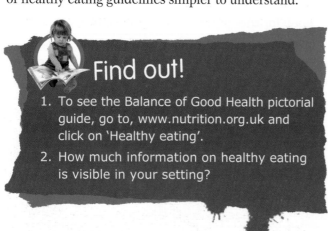

Find out!

1. To see the Balance of Good Health pictorial guide, go to, www.nutrition.org.uk and click on 'Healthy eating'.

2. How much information on healthy eating is visible in your setting?

Grouping foods by nutrients

You might also see foods grouped into six key nutrient groups, as follows:

→ *Carbohydrates* – found in bread, cereals and potatoes
→ *Fats* – found in cheese, butter, margarine and cream
→ *Protein* – found in meat, fish and alternatives such as pulses and soya
→ *Fibre* – found in cereals, peas and beans, wholemeal bread, green leafy vegetables, brown rice and pasta
→ *Minerals* – found in calcium, phosphorus, magnesium, sodium, potassium, iron
→ *Vitamins* – these are vitamins A, B group, C, D, E and K.

The balanced nutritional needs of young children and appropriate daily portion intake

Children need a balanced diet to grow and thrive. Eating only one type of food to the exclusion of others will cause ill health – the balance between carbohydrate, fat and protein must be right for a person to remain healthy. Too little protein can interfere with growth and other body functions; too much fat can lead to obesity and heart disease. Adequate intakes of vitamins, minerals and dietary fibre are vital to health and there is growing evidence that a number of bioactive plant substances (also termed phytochemicals) found in fruit and vegetables play an important role in promoting good health.

The best diet for children

Children need to be encouraged to eat a healthy, balanced diet which is varied and rich in fruit, vegetables and starchy foods. Wherever possible, foods should be freshly prepared rather than processed foods, and the following foods should be included:

→ Milk, cheese, yoghurt, soya beans, tofu and nuts are rich in calcium and support healthy bones and teeth.
→ Fortified breakfast cereals, margarine and oily fish are good sources of vitamin D; this helps to ensure a good supply of calcium in the blood

and therefore healthy bones. The main source of vitamin D is from the action of sunlight on skin, but great care is needed to protect children's skins from strong sun (see Unit 8, page 337).

→ Red meat, liver and fish are rich sources of iron. Pulses (beans and lentils), green vegetables and fortified cereals are also good sources. Iron is needed for healthy blood.
→ At least two portions of fish a week provides a good source of protein, vitamins and minerals that is low in saturated fat. Oily fish, such as mackerel, salmon and sardines, also contain omega 3 fatty acids.
→ Vitamin C is provided by citrus fruit (oranges and lemons), tomatoes and potatoes. Vitamin C may help the absorption of iron, so having fruit juice with an iron-rich meal will increase iron absorption.
→ Milk, margarine, butter, green vegetables, carrots and apricots are all good sources of vitamin A which is important for good vision and healthy skin.
→ Water is important to keep the body healthy – children should drink throughout the day, particularly plain water, milk or diluted fruit juice.

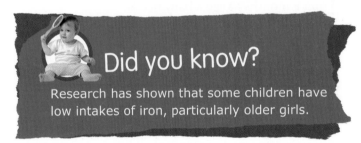

Did you know?

Research has shown that some children have low intakes of iron, particularly older girls.

Changing dietary needs

Throughout life, a person's food requirements will change according to their age, size, activity levels and gender. As you work with children at different ages it is important to understand their dietary needs. The added complication is that, apart from age, lots of other factors affect a child's diet.

U12
1

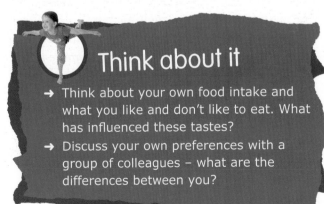

Think about it

→ Think about your own food intake and what you like and don't like to eat. What has influenced these tastes?
→ Discuss your own preferences with a group of colleagues – what are the differences between you?

Babies up to 1 year old

During pregnancy the developing child obtains nutrients from its mother via the placenta. Once the baby is born, energy and nutrients are supplied by breast milk or formula milk for the first six months of life.

Did you know?

It is recommended that babies should not be given anything other than milk until they are 6 months old – if solids are given before this time then anything with gluten in should be avoided. Gluten is part of wheat and can cause a severe reaction in some babies' guts, leading to a condition known as Coeliac disease (see page 486). This causes severe diarrhoea and prevents food being absorbed.

From 6 months of age a baby needs:

→ other foods in addition to breast milk or formula milk
→ a first solid food that is sloppy and smooth – baby rice is the most common first weaning food used in the UK
→ food that has been softened by cooking and then puréed, mashed or chopped
→ changing food textures so that the child learns to chew
→ the slow introduction of new foods including vegetables, meat, fish, dairy products and fruit
→ iron in a form that can be easily absorbed, such as minced meat or green vegetables
→ vitamin supplements containing vitamins A and D are recommended from 6 months for babies receiving breast milk as their main milk drink. Babies fed an infant milk or follow-on milk do not need vitamin supplements if they take more than 500ml per day, but if their intake is less than this they will need to have vitamin drops.

A baby under 1 year should not be given:

→ cows' milk as a drink (it can be used in cooking after 6 months)
→ added salt to food
→ sugar, unless it is essential, for example with sour fruits.

Pre-school children (1–5 years)

Care is needed when following healthy eating guidelines with pre-school children (aged 1–5 years). A diet which is low in fat and high in fibre may not supply enough energy for a young child. However, a healthy family lifestyle will encourage a child to eat more healthily, as food preference will first be established during this stage of life.

Pre-school children:

● are growing quickly and becoming more active
● are developing teeth and bones
● have high energy requirements for their size
● have small stomachs.

So they need:

● foods which are high in energy and rich in nutrients
● small and frequent meals
● protein, calcium, iron and vitamins A and D
● full-fat cows' milk – a rich source of several nutrients.

School-age children (5–16 years)

School children are growing quickly and becoming more active and they have a high energy requirement for their size. They therefore need:

→ foods which are high in energy and rich in nutrients
→ small and frequent meals for younger children (e.g. 5–6-year-olds)
→ a good supply of protein, calcium, iron and vitamins A, C and D.

It is thought that between 5 and 15 per cent of school-aged children are overweight. However, they should not be expected to lose large amounts of weight but encouraged to remain at a constant weight or to increase their weight slowly while their height increases, so that they grow to be an acceptable weight for their height. Developing a healthy family diet and lifestyle is important in the weight management of children.

Did you know?

→ Most fast foods have an extremely high energy density – this means they contain a lot of fat or sugar so have huge amounts of calories in them. Studies have shown that people struggle to recognise foods with a high energy density and to appropriately reduce the amount of fast foods they eat. (*Source*: Prentice, A.M. and Jebb, S.A. (2003) *Fast Foods, Energy Density and Obesity: a possible mechanistic link*)

→ A king-size chocolate bar can provide around one-fifth of the daily calorie needs of a 10-year-old. (*Source*: Chief Medical Officer, Annual Report 2002)

→ School children in the UK spend more than £1.3 billion a year on food. Almost one-third of their pocket money goes on snacks eaten while travelling to and from school. (*Source*: Survey by catering company Sodexho, 2002)

Think about it

The *National Diet and Nutrition Survey: young people aged 4–18 years* (2000) found that:

→ Children eat less than half the recommended five portions of fruit and vegetables a day. In an average week, one in five 4–18-year-olds ate no fruit at all.

→ Over 80 per cent of the group surveyed ate white bread, savoury snacks, potato chips, biscuits, boiled, mashed and jacket potatoes, and chocolate confectionery.

→ Chicken and turkey were the most popular types of meat with over 70 per cent of the sample eating these foods.

→ Under half the boys and just over half the girls ate raw and salad vegetables (excluding tomatoes and carrots) during the seven-day study period, while 40 per cent ate cooked leafy green vegetables and 60 per cent consumed other types of cooked vegetables.

→ Four per cent of the sample did not consume any vegetables during the seven-day survey period.

→ The most commonly eaten fruits, consumed by over half of the sample, were apples and pears followed by bananas.

→ Carbonated soft drinks were the most popular drink, with three-quarters of the group consuming standard versions and less than half drinking low-calorie versions.

→ Generally, the quantities of foods eaten increased with age with the exception of whole milk and vegetables, which both decreased with age.

1. What do you think are the positive points from the survey?

2. What are the negative points? Why?

3. Do the findings match your eating habits?

4. Discuss your reactions in small groups. What do you think could be done to improve the situation?

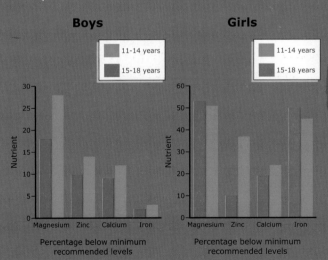

⇧ **Percentage of 11–18-year-olds with intakes of selected nutrients below minimum recommended levels**

U12

1

Daily portion intake

The amount of food each child needs to eat on a daily basis will vary from child to child and throughout different ages and stages of life. It is very difficult to give a guide for the amount of food a child should be offered. However, there are some general guidelines that are worth considering.

→ Children up to about the age of 6 years have relatively small stomachs and so need more frequent smaller meals and healthy snacks.

→ The energy requirements of children increase rapidly as they are growing quickly and becoming more active – they have a proportionally higher energy requirement for their size and so need regular 'top ups'.

→ Without adult pressure, children will eat what they need and will not overeat or undereat. Parents often give children too much food and then make them eat it all. They can also offer food as a comfort when a child is upset.

As with adults, children's appetites vary. Some children seem to eat huge amounts of food while others may seem to eat hardly enough to survive. If you are concerned about a child eating enough, ask yourself the following questions:

→ Is the child healthy?
→ Do they have a lot of energy?
→ Do they sleep well?
→ Does their diet seem to meet a healthy balance?

Did you know?

A study from the Peninsula Medical School in Plymouth in 2006 revealed that:

→ three-quarters of parents fail to recognise when their child is overweight
→ 45 per cent of parents consider their child's weight to be 'about right' when the child is actually obese
→ 10 per cent of parents express concern about their child being underweight when the child is a normal, healthy weight.

(*Source*: www.weightlossresources.co.uk/children/childhood_obesity.htm)

Childhood obesity

There has been a huge amount of research into the problems of childhood obesity. It is understood that this is caused by a combination of:

→ eating too much, especially too many fatty and sugary foods
→ frequent, poor quality snacking between meals
→ not doing enough exercise.

It has been proven beyond doubt that diet and physical activity in a child's early years can affect their health in later life. Childhood eating habits tend to determine adult food tastes and the body's metabolic rate. Overweight adults who were overweight children find it more difficult to lose weight than those who were a healthy weight as children.

Did you know?

In England between 1995 and 2005, the proportion of boys aged 2–15 years who were categorised as obese increased from 10.9 to 18.0 per cent; the proportional increase in obesity in girls aged 2–15 years was from 12.0 to 18.1 per cent. (*Source*: Statistics on Obesity, Physical Activity and Diet: England, 2006; available from www.ic.nhs.uk)

Think about it

Monitor the nutritional intake of a small group of children in your setting. You could produce a table measured against the recommended daily intake for that age group.

How to provide healthy snacks

As you read on page 460, children need snacks to keep their energy levels high. It is important, though, to count these snacks as part of a child's daily food intake.

It can be too easy to let a child eat fatty or sugary snacks that have little or no nutritional value and are filled with empty calories. Snack foods such as cakes, biscuits, crisps, chocolate and sweets are generally high in sugar and saturated fat and low in certain vitamins and minerals. Eating sweet and sticky foods frequently between meals also causes dental decay. It may be impossible to exclude these foods altogether from a child's diet but think about the following 'rules' for them:

→ make sure children eat fatty or sugary snacks only occasionally or in small amounts and so make up a relatively small part of their overall diet

→ help and encourage children to clean their teeth at least twice a day

→ encourage a weekly sweet day.

Healthy snacks include:

→ dried fruit and nuts (though no nuts for children under 5 years)

→ canned fruit in juice

→ sticks of raw carrot, celery, cucumber and pepper

→ segments of orange, satsumas and slices of pineapple

→ a pot of chopped fruit salad

→ fruit loaf

→ fruit buns or scones

→ malt loaf

→ cereal bars – although some of these, especially those with a sugary coating, can be high in fats and sugar

→ mini-sandwiches (such as cream cheese and cucumber)

→ breadsticks

→ plain popcorn

→ breakfast cereal with a sliced banana

→ flavoured milk

→ cartons of yoghurt or rice pudding

→ cubes of cheese.

U12
1

Good practice checklist

Providing healthy snacks for children

✓ Make snacks part of a child's balanced diet.

✓ Try to provide healthy food for most snacks.

✓ Allow treats as part of snacks.

✓ Don't give food between meals and planned snacks except in very special circumstances.

Think about it

1. How do you make sure that children understand about healthy food and make choices?

2. How are children in your setting involved in the planning and preparation of food?

Section 2

Nutrition and the growing child

In practice

James is looking forward to starting his new job as nanny to a family of four children – a baby of 6 months, a 3-year-old, an 8-year-old and a teenager of 14 years. The parents are keen that the children eat a good diet and grow up with a healthy approach to food. This is one of James' real interests – he has a passion to try to help children not to become fat and unhealthy.

When you have worked through this section you will understand about the nutritional needs of the children in James' care and how to encourage them to eat healthily.

Baby and infant feeding

Breastfeeding and bottle feeding

The debate about whether breastfeeding or bottle feeding is best has continued for many years. Today, national guidelines relating to the feeding of babies clearly state that breastfeeding alone is best for babies until they are 6 months old.

The advantages of breastfeeding

The main advantages of breastfeeding are:

→ breast milk contains the right amounts of nutrients at the right temperature, and is always available without risk of contamination
→ breast milk contains antibodies to boost immunity – these give resistance against different infections, for example chicken pox
→ it is less likely to result in an overweight baby
→ it helps delay or avoids eczema
→ there is no additional cost
→ it helps in the bonding process.

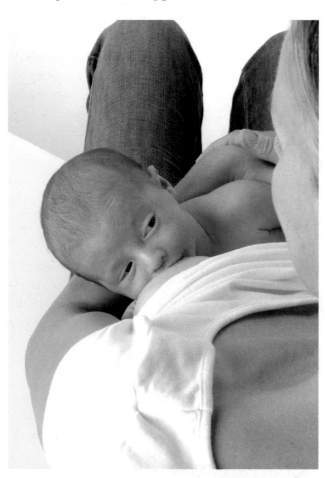

⇧ **There are many recognised advantages to the baby of breastfeeding**

Find out!

Find out more about the benefits of breastfeeding by visiting the following websites:

→ www.breastfeeding.nhs.uk
→ www.nct.org.uk/breastfeeding
→ www.babyfriendly.org.uk
→ www.laleche.org.uk

The facts about formula milks

Modern infant formula milks are scientifically modified to make them as near to human milk as possible, and there are a number of milks available. Current formula infant feeds are almost a replica of breast milk as they are manufactured to match the protein and salts in breast milk. In one important respect, however, formula feeds cannot match breast milk: the antibodies that are passed on from mother to baby in breast milk cannot be replaced in formula milk.

→ Cows' milk infant formulas should be the alternative to breast milk unless there is a medical reason to use another type of milk, for example an allergy to cows' milk.
→ Formula milk should be used until a baby is 1 year old; follow-on milks are not necessary.
→ Hydrolysed protein infant formulas are available on prescription if a baby has an allergy to cows' milk.
→ Soya-based infant formulas should only be used on medical advice – babies who are allergic to cows' milk may also be allergic to soya.
→ Goats' milk infant formulas and follow-on formulas based on goats' milk protein are not suitable for babies and are not approved for use in Europe.

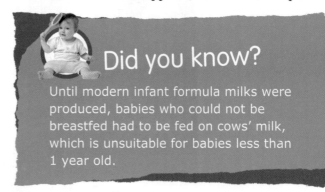

Did you know?

Until modern infant formula milks were produced, babies who could not be breastfed had to be fed on cows' milk, which is unsuitable for babies less than 1 year old.

Supporting parents' choice

An early years professional's role in the choice between breast and bottle feeding is only to give impartial information if asked and then to support the parents in their choice. The choice about how to feed a baby is a personal one for the parents of the baby, made with support from midwives, health visitors and doctors.

Although breastfeeding is considered the ideal way of infant feeding, not all mothers enjoy it or may prefer bottle feeding. Some mothers may supplement breastfeeding with formula feeds, for example if they are unable to produce enough breast milk to feed a hungry baby or are returning to work. However, reducing the amount of breastfeeding reduces the supply of milk, and this can ultimately bring breastfeeding to an early end. Other reasons for stopping or reducing breastfeeding include:

→ in the very early days the baby has difficulties latching on (attaching to the nipple) and does not feed properly from the breast
→ a breast infection (mastitis) or sore and cracked nipples can make breastfeeding extremely painful for the mother
→ the mother finds breastfeeding too tiring (it takes a lot of energy for the body to produce enough milk for a growing baby)
→ if the mother takes certain prescription medication
→ embarrassment of the mother or others at breastfeeding in public
→ partners' jealousy of the baby breastfeeding.

Some mothers express their breast milk using an electronic or hand-held pump to enable the baby to be bottle-fed. Some of the advantages associated with bottle feeding are:

→ it is obvious how much milk the baby is taking so this reduces any concerns about underfeeding
→ it reduces any embarrassment about breastfeeding in public
→ other people can feed the baby, such as the father or an early years practitioner
→ it can be helpful for mothers returning to work.

Although increasing numbers of mothers are starting to breastfeed in the UK, there remains a rapid decline in breastfeeding rates in the first few weeks after birth. In the UK as a whole, one-fifth (21 per cent) of breastfeeding mothers stop within the first two weeks of their child's birth and over one-third (36 per cent) stop within the first six weeks.

Did you know?

Around three-quarters of women breastfeed their babies at birth in the UK. But there are huge variations in breastfeeding rates according to social class, age and area of the country. For example, 84 per cent of mothers aged 30 years or over start breastfeeding compared to 50 per cent aged 20 years or younger. (*Source*: Infant Feeding Survey 2005)

With all types of bottle feeding, whether formula feeds or expressed breast milk, care must be taken to ensure proper cleaning and preparation. Poor hygiene and preparation can lead to potentially fatal gastroenteritis (stomach upset). 'Prop' feeding – wedging a baby in a pram or chair with a pillow so the feeding bottle can be left with the baby – can result in choking. It is also important to use feeding as an opportunity to improve the bond between carer and baby.

Weaning

Weaning is the term used to describe the process of changing a child's feeding from being dependent on milk to eating solid foods. A newborn baby does not have the digestive system to cope with solids, but a baby of 1 year has a more mature system which is able to cope with different foods. The process of learning to enjoy a wide range of foods can be an easy one or it can be difficult for carers and the baby alike.

When to wean?

The UK and Irish Department of Health guidelines of August 2005 recommend that a baby should have nothing but breast or formula milk for the first six months of life. The guidelines recognise that all babies develop at a different rate but advise that it is not a good idea to introduce solid foods before a child is 20 weeks (5 months) old because the digestive system and kidneys are too immature to cope. This means that you should never give a very young baby anything other than breast or formula milk.

A baby could thrive very well on milk alone until the age of 12 months, but at this age the iron stores from birth will be diminishing (getting low) and the baby will be at risk of becoming **anaemic**. Leaving the start of weaning as late as 12 months could also make it difficult for a baby to make the change from breast or bottle to eating from a spoon.

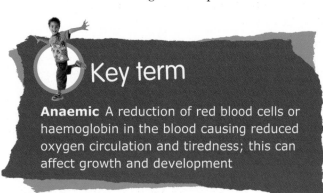

Key term

Anaemic A reduction of red blood cells or haemoglobin in the blood causing reduced oxygen circulation and tiredness; this can affect growth and development

Within the guidelines, the best judge of when to wean a baby is the baby him or herself. You will find that some babies are ready earlier than others. Look out for babies who:

→ are still hungry after feeds
→ can sit up
→ show interest in solid food
→ pick up food and put it in their mouth
→ want to chew.

Sucking the fists is not a sign of being ready for weaning – this is a normal part of development as the baby has discovered how interesting their hands are.

Find out!

There are many fashions related to weaning. Ask your parents and grandparents when they weaned their children and what foods they used, and you will probably receive several different answers. Parents in the UK may say they started their child on baby rice, while parents in Israel may have used avocado pear as a first weaning food.

Developing a range of tastes

The important thing to remember about weaning is the purpose of it, which is to safely introduce children into the normal eating patterns of their family by familiarising them with a wide range of new tastes. Trying to rush the process can at best overwhelm a child's taste buds and at worst cause health problems through the use of inappropriate foods.

Think about it

It can be easy for carers of children to pass on their own food dislikes to them during mealtimes. How difficult would it be to feed a baby with something you dislike? Think about your body language and facial expressions.

Stages of weaning

There are several stages involved in weaning, as shown in the table opposite.

⇧ **Mashed avocado is a good first stage weaning food**

Weaning stage	Suggested foods
First stage (ideally from 6 months) – sloppy foods, slightly thicker than milk foods	• Thickened milk – baby rice • Puréed or stewed apple, banana, avocado • Bland tastes
Second stage – thickness increasing but no lumps; increase variety and strength of taste	• First stage commercial foods • Home-made puréed vegetables with gravy, e.g. carrots, yam, sweet potato • Fruit and custard
Third stage – food less puréed; coping with thicker texture and some lumpiness; starting to finger feed	• Home-made food mashed with fork: potatoes, vegetables, fish, fruits • Rusks, bread crusts, peeled pieces of apple, mango or banana, cubes of cheese
Fourth stage (by 12 months) – eating most family foods; avoiding tough or stringy textures	• Most foods can be offered, except those listed at the bottom of page 468.

Home-cooked and commercial baby foods

Nutritionally there is little difference between commercial baby foods in jars or packets and home-produced weaning food. Commercial foods can be expensive and the consistency is often unlike ordinary food. Home-produced weaning foods are nearer in texture and taste to the child's eventual diet, but can take time and effort to prepare. Some parents prefer to feed their baby home-produced food, but this can be difficult if the family is out for the day or the rest of the family are having a meal that is spicy or otherwise unsuitable. A sensible mix of commercial and home-produced foods is a good compromise.

Find out!

Investigate all the different commercial weaning foods available in supermarkets and other shops. How many of the products that you looked at were suitable for vegetarians? How easy do you think it would be to provide similar foods at home?

Good practice checklist

Weaning

✓ Offer the first spoonfuls of a bland, very liquid mix part way through a milk feed or near the end, when the first pangs of hunger have been satisfied.

✓ Introduce new tastes gradually. Offer only one new taste a day in the first months of weaning and if a new food is rejected one day, try it again later; it may then be accepted with pleasure.

✓ Gradually thicken food, eventually mashing it with a fork.

✓ As the amounts of solid foods increase, the amount of milk feeds offered should be reduced. By the time a baby is eating three substantial meals of solids a day, milk feeds should be reduced to morning and evening only, with water or diluted fresh juice between meals and at mealtimes.

✓ As soon as the baby starts trying, let him or her join in feeding, even though everything will fall off the spoon and it will go anywhere but in the mouth. A vital piece of equipment at this stage is a sheet of plastic to protect the floor if it is not washable.

✓ Offer finger foods as much as possible, for example lumps of cheese, apple pieces, small sandwiches. (It is no coincidence that a baby is ready to start self-feeding when his or her gross and fine motor skills have reached the stage of sitting up and a pincer grip.)

U12

2

⇦ **Self-feeding can be a messy business at first, but one the baby will find enjoyable**

Menus for babies at different stages of weaning

A suggested day's menu as a baby progresses towards a normal family diet could be like the one shown below.

⇩ **Suggested day's menu for baby aged 6–12 months**

Time of day	Daily diet 6–9 months	Daily diet 9–12 months	Daily diet 12 months plus
On waking	Breast or bottle feed	Breast or bottle feed	Drink of milk
Breakfast	Baby breakfast cereal with puréed fruit	Porridge made with 90 ml infant/follow-on milk	1 slice of toast; wheat cereal with milk; well-diluted orange juice
Mid-morning	4 satsuma segments	2 breadsticks and cheese cubes	Carrot sticks and chickpea purée (hummus)
Lunch	3 tablespoons of broccoli and potato with cheesy sauce; 90 ml infant/follow-on milk; chopped melon pieces	1 hard boiled egg with soldiers; 1 fromage frais; 90 ml water or well-diluted orange juice	Scrambled egg on toast; banana and custard; 90 ml water or well-diluted orange juice
Mid-afternoon	Half a small mashed banana or mango; water as a drink	Toast fingers; water as a drink	90 ml fruit smoothie; 1 pitta bread or bread with cheese or ham
Tea	Tomato sauce with mince and pasta shapes; 90 ml follow-on milk; 1 small yogurt	Shepherds pie with meat or lentils, broccoli and carrots; 1 banana, water or juice	Fish pie and vegetables; seedless grapes or stewed fruit; water or juice
Evening	Breast or bottle feed	Breast or bottle feed	Breastfeed or milk

Good practice checklist

The rules of weaning

✓ Do not give cows' milk as a drink until the baby is 1 year old.

✓ Never give nuts to a child until the age of 5 years as there is a strong risk of allergy and choking.

✓ Avoid products containing wheat until at least 6 months of age; some babies are allergic to the gluten in wheat, resulting in coeliac disease.

✓ Eggs should be well cooked and only offered after 6 months.

✓ Citrus food and shell fish should not be given before 6 months.

✓ Never add extra salt and avoid salty products until 12 months.

✓ Avoid honey and soft and blue cheese until 12 months.

The social and educational role of food

Food is a central part of many family occasions, whether daily or weekly communal meals, special occasions such as Christmas or Eid, or family events such as weddings. Eating together as a family is seen by many as a central socialising activity. Concern is often voiced today that many families rarely if ever eat together; this is sometimes blamed on busy lifestyles, fast foods and takeaways, and meals being eaten in front of the television. There is also concern that families not eating together result in antisocial behaviour in children.

⇧ **Mealtimes play an important role in developing children's social skills**

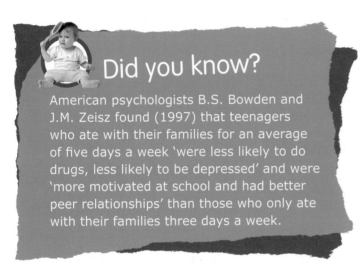

Did you know?

American psychologists B.S. Bowden and J.M. Zeisz found (1997) that teenagers who ate with their families for an average of five days a week 'were less likely to do drugs, less likely to be depressed' and were 'more motivated at school and had better peer relationships' than those who only ate with their families three days a week.

Mealtimes provide opportunity for family members to talk to each other, to observe table manners and to eat a balanced meal. Even if the whole family does not eat together, one parent will usually sit with young children while they eat – giving the opportunity for conversation. Food and eating meals can and should be enjoyable for parents and children.

Think about it

How often does your family eat together? Do you agree that families not eating together could cause antisocial behaviour in children?

The educational role of food

Food can be a good starting point for discussions on a range of topics, for example:

→ texture
→ tastes
→ colours
→ shapes
→ numeracy
→ origins of food
→ food preparation.

Think about it

Can you think of other topics of discussion for which food is a good starting point?

Food and mealtimes can also be used to encourage many aspects of development, for example:

→ *Language* – talking about different foods, textures, size, shape colours
→ *Numeracy* – counting, shape and size
→ *World around us* – where food comes from, different cultures
→ *Science* – changes in texture and form
→ *Social skills* – learning to eat in a group; conversations during meals
→ *Food buying and preparation* – involving children in the planning, buying and preparation of food.

U12
2

Good practice checklist

Involvement in mealtimes with children and young people

✓ Make time to sit down with them.

✓ Try to create a relaxed social atmosphere.

✓ Never rush mealtimes.

✓ Talk to the children during the meal.

✓ Use the different foods to initiate conversation at the appropriate level.

The presentation and preparation of food with children and the role of mealtimes

Encouraging children to cook

From a very young age, children enjoy preparing food – and eating the results! There are many good cookery books for children that can help with ideas. In addition, consider the following:

→ cold cooking for very young children

→ simple recipes they can quickly see the results with

→ letting children cook food they like

→ encouraging children to prepare parts of the meal, for example vegetables, fruit

→ safety aspects, for example the age-appropriate use of knives and hot implements

→ hygiene – handwashing and tidying up afterwards

→ working with parents to encourage home cooking.

Learning to cook is an important social skill – read any article about a famous chef's family and there will often be a section talking about how they either started cooking with parents or grandparents, or how their children take part in cooking at home.

Presentation of food

The presentation of food at mealtimes is important – would you rather have a pile of food dumped on your plate or an attractively arranged meal? Children feel the same, and often enjoy a bit of imaginative arrangement of food into faces or pictures. Some

foods can be bought in shapes, but care is needed as these can be reconstituted foods loaded with chemicals to help in the shape formation. It is easy to make shapes from potatoes using a pastry cutter or other template, or to shape home-made burgers or fishcakes into an interesting shape, for example.

How to prevent food dislikes and minor eating problems

If most children have a varied range of suitable foods offered at mealtimes, are introduced gradually to new foods and there is no pressure to eat, they will eat as much or as little as they need, develop a varied range of tastes and maintain a healthy weight. So why do so many children appear to have eating problems?

Food can be the source of conflict between parents and children from as early as the first year of life. Many people see a thriving child as the sign of 'good' parenting. A child who does not eat well could be regarded as not being cared for properly. Parents can become upset about what their child is or is not eating and many parents come under pressure from grandparents. Despite being aware of the latest healthy diet issues, they may find it hard not to follow their own parents' suggestions.

Dealing with problems

It is rare for a child to make the transition to everyday family meals without a few tears and tantrums on the way. Many children are seen to have a problem with their eating habits at some time. The approach that early years practitioners take is an important part of dealing with this.

Refusing food at a mealtime is not a problem. Any child who has food offered in a relaxed, thoughtful manner will eat as much as he or she needs if opportunities are provided. This continues throughout childhood; eating and not eating only become a problem if the child's carers see it as a problem. Babies have every right not to eat if they do not feel hungry or to refuse a particular food, in the same way as you have.

Think about it

What situations in your life affect your appetite? Now think about the different factors that may affect a child's desire for food:

➔ excitement at a forthcoming event such as an outing or holiday

➔ engaging activities such as a new toy, other children playing outside or a newly learned skill such as walking

➔ tiredness

➔ stressful events can result in 'comfort eating', typically of less healthy foods, or reduce the appetite

➔ illness may initially reduce the appetite but once the child is well and active again the appetite may increase significantly for a while.

Introducing new tastes

A child's tastes are very unadventurous in their early years − for up to 6 months all they have experience of is milk. Breastfed babies have a wider experience of different tastes as the taste of breast milk reflects the mother's diet.

Babies have very sensitive taste buds that need gradual introduction to new flavours. The transition from a pure milk diet to eating the full range of food is crucial. New tastes need introducing one at a time, and if they are rejected at first they should be reintroduced later without fuss. Some foods do genuinely taste unpleasant to some people or have strong associations with a place or person.

Did you know?

Studies have shown that some people are 'super tasters' and have an unusually large number of taste buds. The bitter tastes of many green vegetables, such as sprouts, are much more intense for super tasters, so they eat less of them.

Good practice checklist

Preventing food dislikes in children

✓ Introduce new foods gradually.

✓ Give children the opportunity to try different tastes and textures.

✓ If a food is rejected by a child, don't make a fuss about it – try it again a few days later.

✓ Disguise disliked foods in dishes, for example try cheese in mashed potato or vegetables in a casserole.

✓ Do not tell a child you don't like a food as you are helping them to eat it!

Case study

A cause for concern?

Amir is 3 years old. He was born prematurely and was in hospital until he was 3 months old. His mum struggled to breastfeed him and has always worried that he does not eat enough. At mealtimes Amir soon gets bored with his food and wants to go back to playing with his toys. His mum follows him around with his food trying to get him to eat. Whenever he wants food between meals, something is provided for him. Every time Amir's grandparents see him they comment how thin he is. Amir has lots of energy, sleeps well at night and is within the average weight range for his age and height.

1. Why do you think Amir's mum is worried?

2. Should she be worried?

3. How can Amir's mum be helped to relax about her son's eating?

U12

2

The role of the adult in promoting healthy eating

The importance of setting a good example

Children learn from those around them. If a child sees the adults in his or her life enjoying their food and eating a healthy diet with plenty of fruit and vegetables, this will be understood as normal behaviour. Conversely, seeing adults eating unhealthy food and generally showing poor eating habits will be seen as normal.

Children easily pick up subconscious messages from adults' body language and behaviour. It is therefore easy to communicate your attitudes to food regarding:

→ different tastes
→ types of food
→ use of junk food
→ attitudes to healthy eating
→ how much to eat
→ when to eat
→ where to eat.

A relaxed attitude to food together with the firm belief that a child will eat what they need, provided

⇧ **It is important to be aware of the example you set children with regard to what constitutes normal eating habits**

that small amounts of a range of foods are offered at intervals, is the best way to promote a healthy attitude to food.

The role of the early years practitioner

The diet that a child follows will influence their future health, and as an early years practitioner you play a key role in children's care and education. It is therefore important that you actively promote a healthy diet both to the children you work with and their parents. Although children are greatly influenced by the meals they have at home and their family's approach to eating, you can make a difference by showing or reinforcing healthy eating principles. If your work involves out-of-school activities or work with parents it may be possible to have an even bigger impact.

Working with children under 3 years of age

The key to encouraging healthy eating practice in children under 3 years is to let them be involved in their food as soon as they show interest. Children in this age group are also most responsive to experimenting and are not totally set in their ways.

It is important to encourage an interest in how food is made, a range of different foods and healthy eating from a young age. Cookery classes are no longer part of the curriculum in schools and many children do not have the opportunity to cook with their parents or family at home, so activities based around food will be a valuable source of learning for young children.

Working with children over 5 years of age

Children over 5 years start to take responsibility for their own food intake so it is important that they understand the need for a healthy diet. However, their eating habits will have been influenced by the family earlier in life and it is difficult to change these once established. It is therefore important that parents are also involved in education about a healthy diet and lifestyle.

Working with older children

Older children enjoy greater involvement in choosing menus, helping with meal planning, shopping and making meals. At the same time they can develop vital numeracy and literacy skills and science concepts by identifying items, deciding how much is needed and seeing the changes in food as it is prepared.

Good practice checklist

Supporting children's interest in healthy eating

✓ Eating habits are developed in early childhood, so children should be encouraged to try different types of food before the age of 2 years.

✓ Encourage children to eat by themselves with finger foods such as cooked chicken strips or cheese cubes.

✓ Let them experiment with self-feeding using a spoon and/or fork.

✓ Choose foods that are naturally brightly coloured to make meals more appealing.

✓ Let a child help to prepare meals – simple activities like stirring jelly or arranging things on a plate can help them learn about food.

✓ Eat as a group as much as possible; it will encourage children to enjoy mealtimes.

Supporting parents in feeding their children

Early years practitioners may need to offer support to parents in encouraging healthy eating in their children. Good practice includes:

→ discussions with parents about their child's diet (content and timings)

→ consulting with parents on the settings' meals; always having the menu on view

→ providing a listening ear if parents are concerned about their child's diet and offering support and suggestions for advice such as visiting their health visitor

→ encouraging parents to join in theme days on healthy eating

→ displaying informative posters and leaflets for parents.

However, it is important to remember that parents are responsible for their child's diet and that (as far as possible) early years settings should follow the wishes of parents in all aspects of care unless there are health and safety issues at stake. This applies particularly to food. Parents are the most

informed about their children's needs so requesting that they do not give their children certain foods is inappropriate. It is also important to remember to:

→ respect cultural variations when designing menus for young children

→ avoid offering 'forbidden' foods, such as pork to Muslims or meat to vegetarians

→ follow instructions about children's allergies to certain foods as failing to do so could cause a child to die. Remember, the allergen could be hidden in a seemingly innocent food so you must always read food labels!

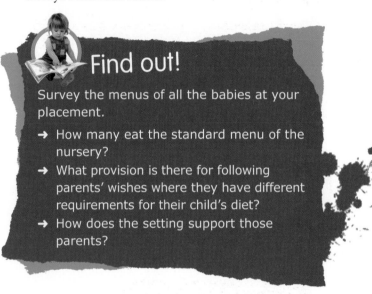

Find out!

Survey the menus of all the babies at your placement.

→ How many eat the standard menu of the nursery?

→ What provision is there for following parents' wishes where they have different requirements for their child's diet?

→ How does the setting support those parents?

The effects of poor eating on the overall health of the child

A good diet is essential from the very start of life. Nutritional deficiencies (a lack of nutrients) can prevent a child from reaching his or her full potential.

This entire unit is focused on encouraging children to eat healthily. However, many children do not eat well and it is important to be aware of the possible impact of this. Effects can be short-term, for example poor concentration through not having breakfast, to longer-term health impacts such as obesity and heart disease. Remember, a poor diet in childhood leads to health problems in adulthood because eating habits are developed as a child.

Signs of **malnutrition** and **undernutrition** in children may include:

→ tiredness, lack of energy, lack of mental alertness
→ failure to gain in height and weight
→ lowered resistance to infection, e.g. frequent colds, sore throats
→ bleeding gums
→ poor skin and hair condition.

Key terms

Malnutrition When one or more nutrients are lacking from a diet

Undernutrition When insufficient quantities of food are eaten

Did you know?

Iron deficiency anaemia can be a problem in some groups of young children, such as those who have had poor iron intake from solid foods or were given cows' milk (as a main drink) before 12 months of age. Anaemia can result in frequent infections, poor weight gain and delay in development.

Children who are poorly nourished will suffer from a number of serious health effects. These include:

→ weight loss and stunted growth
→ excessive weight gain and obesity, which can lead to a number of serious medical complaints including diabetes, high blood pressure and heart problems
→ poor physical development
→ poor intellectual development
→ diets that have too much fat and salt can lead to heart problems in later life (children as young as 7 years have been found to have fatty deposits in their arteries)

→ not eating enough fibre and eating too much fat and red meat can contribute to cancers
→ research has demonstrated that a diet high in artificial additives can have negative effects on behaviour, for example hyperactivity.

Did you know?

A recent survey among young people in the UK found that:

→ 25 per cent say they try to eat as little as possible
→ 42 per cent regularly skip breakfast
→ nearly 50 per cent have fizzy drinks every day
→ 10 per cent eat fast food at least once a day
→ 83 per cent aren't eating the recommended five portions of fruit and vegetables a day
→ 33 per cent argue with their parents over what they eat.

(*Source*: National Diet and Nutrition Survey: young people aged 4 to 18 years.)

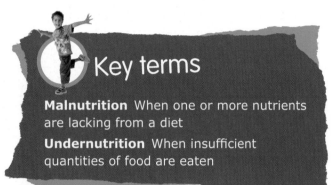

Think about it

1. How might you encourage a child with poor eating habits to eat more healthily?
2. What could you say to the child's parents?

In practice

Samina works in a Children's Centre in a town with significant social and economic deprivation. Many of the families who use the centre are on a low income. The centre has an active programme supporting families to eat well. Samina has been responsible for informing the rest of the staff and the families about the importance of eating a healthy diet.

When you have worked through this section you will understand the different influences on food and diet, including the ways in which children and their families are encouraged to eat a particular diet.

The effects of the food industry, media and healthy eating campaigns

People's attitudes to food are influenced by their parents and their own experiences, and develop from a very early age. There are many food advertisements and varying advice on which foods to eat, as well as many different types of food available. Together, this can create confusion as to what the healthiest options are.

The power of the food industry

Think about it

Where is the majority of your food purchased? Who makes the majority of the foods that you eat?

In the UK today, most people shop for food at one of the large supermarkets, which are supplied with foods made by a fairly small number of food manufacturers. (The majority of well-known food labels are owned by a very small handful of manufacturers.) In recent times there has been a lot of publicity about the use of additives and the salt and fat content of processed foods. Consequently many manufacturers have changed the make-up of their products. However, until consumers force changes, food manufacturers have a lot of power about the food people eat.

Find out!

Have a look at the tins and packets of food in your cupboards at home or on your next visit to the supermarket. Note down the brand name of the different items and then look on the back of the label to see which manufacturer that label is part of. How many manufacturers are there, compared to the number of names on the labels?

Think about it

It is interesting to watch how food manufacturers use government campaigns to launch new products or promote existing ones. For example, think about how cholesterol-lowering foods and drinks are advertised on TV.

The influence of media advertising

Almost every magazine or commercial television programme has adverts for food and drink. Many of the food adverts on children's TV are for popular fast foods that can be a harmful part of a diet.

Studies have shown that the primary means of advertising to children is television. Children are regularly bombarded with adverts and TV programmes about food. Many people think this is a negative influence linked to poor eating habits, and calls have been made to stop adverts for junk food during children's viewing times. Ofcom, the independent regulator for the Communications industry, has been looking at how to tighten the rules on advertising food and drink to children.

Did you know?

In July 2004, Ofcom published wide-ranging research which showed that television advertising of food and drink products only has a modest direct effect on children's food preferences. The research showed that indirect effects are likely to be larger but there is insufficient evidence to determine the size of these effects. However, the research also concluded that the influence of advertising is small when compared with other factors potentially linked to childhood obesity such as exercise, trends in family eating habits, school policy, public understanding of nutrition and food labelling. (*Source*: www.ofcom.org.uk)

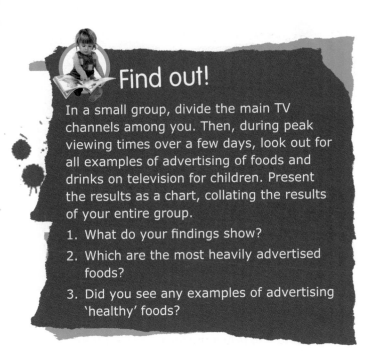
Healthy eating campaigns

There have been various healthy eating campaigns promoted primarily by the government through the Food Standards Agency (see www.eatwell.gov.uk) over the past few years. Other agencies such as the BBC and various public figures have further developed the campaigns, which have focused on issues such as reducing heart disease by lowering fat and salt intake, lowering cholesterol levels and improving the quality of school meals. (For more about different healthy eating campaigns in the UK, see pages 481–2.)

Do healthy eating campaigns work?

Successfully promoting healthy eating through advertising and campaigns is not easy. Research by Social Issues Research Centre (SIRC) in Oxford has shown that shock tactics in health promotion campaigns have backfired. SIRC has monitored media coverage of health issues and public responses over the past three years and identified three types of negative reaction to the high 'doses' of health scares and warnings received by the British public:

1. *'Warning-fatigue'* – the most common effect, in which people become used to and desensitised to health promotion campaigns. Eventually people pay no attention at all. Constant reminders on healthy eating and exercise, for example, have had little effect on obesity, which continues to rise.

2. *'Hyper-sensitivity'* to health warnings occurs in some people and they become increasingly scared and anxious about the hazards and 'risk factors' in their diet, lifestyle and environment.

3. *'Riskfactorphobics'* tend to be enthusiastic readers of health pages and health magazines, often over-reacting to each new scare and attempting to follow contradictory advice.

The role of poverty and economy on food choices

Poverty is a major issue affecting children's health and development. People in the UK who are poor and living on benefits may have little money for food, clothes and heating. Children living in poverty may have limited life choices and limited chances to develop their full potential. (See also Unit 6, pages 255–7.)

Poverty and children's diets

There is a strong link between a family's income and its diet. Children whose families are on high incomes tend to have a healthier diet than those living on state benefits. There are many reasons why families find it difficult to give children the right types of foods if they are on a limited income:

→ Buying food is not easy if the only local shop is very expensive and has limited choice of poor quality food.
→ Going to a supermarket for cheaper, better quality food is not easy if it involves an expensive bus journey.
→ Poverty may mean that a family does not have adequate cooking facilities, for example families living in bed and breakfast accommodation.
→ There may not be enough money to buy all the ingredients for a healthy meal.
→ To avoid spending money on gas or electricity, families may buy takeaways.
→ Some families may lack the skills or knowledge to prepare healthy food.
→ Processed foods, such as tinned soup, pies and crisps, are filling and cheap. Parents may worry that if they spend money on fresh fruit and vegetables their children will not eat them.

U12

3

Find out!

Compare the range of goods available in food shops and supermarkets in different areas, for example a town centre supermarket compared with shops on a large run-down estate near a Sure Start centre.

→ What are the differences in the range and quality of foodstuffs?

→ How do prices compare?

→ Are healthy food options available at a reasonable price in both cases?

Find out!

1. What types of different dietary needs are there among the children in your setting?

2. Are you aware of all the particular needs of those diets? If not, where could you find the necessary information?

3. How could you make sure that all the children eat a diet that meets all their needs?

Different religious and cultural requirements

Many people have specific dietary patterns that are part of their culture or religion. It is important when working with children that you know what their dietary needs are and that these are met within your setting. Different dietary needs are a great way to extend children's understanding of diversity and the need to respect and understand difference.

Vegetarian diets

A vegetarian diet is healthy for young children provided a good supply of all the nutrients needed for growth and development are in the diet. Children on a vegetarian diet need:

→ a good intake of energy and nutrient-heavy foods such as milk, cheese, margarine, pulses and nut butters, such as peanut butter

→ at least 1 pint (500ml) of cows' milk or its equivalent in yogurt or 'vegetarian' cheese (nearly all cheese is now produced using synthetic rennet) or a fortified soya milk daily

→ adequate amounts of calcium, vitamin B12, vitamin D and riboflavin by supplements or fortified foods in a **vegan** diet.

☟ **The dietary requirements of different religions**

Religion	Dietary requirements
Buddhism	Many Buddhists are vegetarian as they respect all life and avoid killing animals.
Hinduism	Eating of meat is forbidden, especially beef as the cow is a sacred animal. Many Hindus will not eat fish or eggs.
Islam	Muslims will not eat pork or pig products and all animals must be killed according to Islamic regulations (*halal* meat). Halal food must be cooked with separate utensils and should not be stored or cooked with non-halal food.
Judaism	Food acceptable to the Jewish religion is known as *kosher*. Jews may not eat fish without fins or scales, shellfish, pigs, birds of prey and rabbits. Meat and milk may not be eaten together and the same utensils may not be used for each of these.
Rastafarians	Rastafarians tend to prefer to eat natural foods and many avoid pork; many are vegetarian. Fruit and vegetables are important and are called *ital*.
Sikhism	Beef is forbidden and dairy products are important as many Sikhs are vegetarian.

Did you know?

According to the Department of Health's report on weaning, breastfed children born to vegan mothers in the UK and weaned on to a vegan diet grow and develop normally (Department of Health 1994). However, great care is needed to ensure that energy needs are met and that the diet provides sufficient fat and **amino acids**. Malnutrition and poor growth have been reported among infants and children fed very restricted **macrobiotic diets** and these diets are not recommended.

Gaining protein from a vegetarian diet

Most plant food proteins (with the exception of soya) have a low content of one or more of the amino acids needed by the body. Also, different amino acids are missing in different plant foods. Plant foods therefore need to be combined to provide high quality protein. Good combinations include:

→ pulses and rice, for example bean casserole and rice; dhal and rice
→ pulses and cereal, for example baked beans on toast
→ nuts and cereal, for example peanut butter sandwich, nut roast.

If the proteins from different plant sources are eaten together or over the course of a day, the diet should contain enough of the right sorts of protein. The main food nutrients that are usually supplied by meat or dairy products can be provided by plant sources, as the chart below and overleaf shows.

Key terms

Vegan Person who does not eat any food sourced from an animal, fish or bird including meat, eggs and dairy produce

Amino acids The main building blocks of protein; needed for growth and repair

Macrobiotic diet A diet based on whole, unprocessed, living foods. These include a variety of vegetables, whole grains such as brown rice, barley, quinoa, oat groats and corn on the cob, dried beans including lentils, chickpeas and aduki beans, fruits, seeds, nuts and naturally fermented foods such as tofu (soya bean curd)

Animal and plant sources of the main food nutrients

Nutrient	Animal sources	Plant sources
Protein	Meat, poultry, fish, eggs, milk, cheese, yogurt	Soya, pulses (including lentils, chickpeas and baked beans), bread, grains, seeds, potatoes, nuts
Calcium	Milk, cheese, yogurt, tinned sardines and salmon including the bones (the soft bones should not be discarded)	Fortified soya milk and tofu, seeds (e.g. sesame seeds), green leafy vegetables (e.g. spring greens), nuts (e.g. almonds), bread (especially white bread), dried fruit (e.g. apricots)
Iron	Liver, red meat, chicken, fish (haem iron), eggs (non-haem iron)	Fortified breakfast cereals (the label should be checked to see if iron has been added), bread, pulses (e.g. soya beans), green vegetables, dried fruits (e.g. apricots), nuts, plain chocolate

U12

3

Nutrient	Animal sources	Plant sources
Vitamin A	Liver, butter, whole milk, cheese	Yellow/orange vegetables (e.g. carrots) and dark leafy ones (e.g. parsley, watercress), yellow/orange fruit (e.g. mangoes, and apricots, fresh or dried), fortified margarines and spreads, sweet potato
Vitamin B12	Liver, meat, poultry, fish, milk and milk products, eggs	Fortified products only (check on the label)
Vitamin D	Oily fish, meat, whole milk and its products, fortified milk products such as skimmed milk powder, eggs	Fortified margarine and spreads, fortified breakfast cereals (the label should be checked to see if vitamin D has been added)

Case study

Summer party time

Jess's early years setting is having a summer party for all the children and their parents, and Jess is in charge of the food. There are 30 children aged 2 to 5 years and at least one if not two members of family for each child. Among the families and their children are several Muslim, Hindu and vegetarian families. Jess is a bit daunted by the prospect of planning the food and seeks the help of the nursery cook.

1. What sort of food do you think the cook might suggest?

2. What sort of foods might not be suitable for some or all of the party?

3. What type of party foods would Jess need to avoid giving this age range of children?

The role of school meals in promoting the health of children

Most children eat their lunch at school. This meal will be provided by the school or taken in as a packed lunch. School meals can make an important contribution to the energy and nutrient intake of children. They are thought to be the best option when compared with food brought from other sources such as cafés and takeaways, although there is considerable variation in the nutritional quality of school meals.

Until 1980 the government set basic nutritional standards for school meals. However, in 1980 they removed the basic nutritional standard with the result that school lunch provision in many schools was far from satisfactory. In April 2001 the government reintroduced regulations in England and Wales on national minimum nutritional standards for schools that opt to provide lunches. This was aimed at recognising the importance of the contribution that school lunches can make to the health of children. Separate school lunch standards have been developed in Scotland.

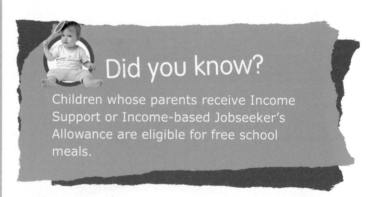

Did you know?

Children whose parents receive Income Support or Income-based Jobseeker's Allowance are eligible for free school meals.

⇧ **School meals are an important source of nutrition for many children**

Some schools offer parents guidance on the content of packed lunches. This is often as part of a whole school approach to healthy eating through which the food eaten at school is part of the principles of healthy eating taught in the classroom.

Did you know?

The Nursery Milk Scheme is operated by the Department of Health and ensures that children attending nursery sessions of two hours or more are eligible to receive one-third of a pint of free milk on each day they attend. Children under 5 years whose parents receive Income Support or Income-based Jobseeker's Allowance are currently eligible to receive a free pint of milk daily under the Welfare Food Scheme.

Find out!

→ If you work in a school investigate the menus available for school meals. What sort of advice is given to parents about the content of packed lunches?

→ If you work in a nursery do children receive free milk each day?

Government initiatives to promote healthy eating

The government receives a wealth of independent advice on what constitutes healthy eating, including the nutrient content of individual foods, diet and the nutritional status of people. This advice comes from organisations including:

→ the Food Standards Agency, an independent government department set up by an Act of Parliament in 2000
→ the Scientific Advisory Committee on Nutrition (SACN), an group of independent experts who advise various government agencies and departments.

Find out!

Carry out research into the role of the Food Standards Agency (www.foodstandards.gov.uk) and the Scientific Advisory Committee on Nutrition (www.sacn.gov.uk).

Healthy Start

Healthy Start helps families from low-income and poor households in England, Scotland, Wales and Northern Ireland by giving vouchers for free milk and fresh fruit and vegetables to children and pregnant women. The scheme also encourages earlier and closer contact with health professionals who can give advice on pregnancy, breastfeeding and healthy eating.

At the time of writing, vouchers were worth £2.80 each. Pregnant women and children over 1 year and under 4 years get one voucher every week, and children under 1 year get two vouchers a week. Vouchers can be spent in small shops, chemists and supermarkets or given to milkmen.

Find out!

Find out more about the Healthy Start scheme by visiting its website (www.healthystart.nhs.uk). Where can vouchers be spent in your local area?

5 a day

The 5 a day programme promotes the benefits of eating at least five pieces of fruit or vegetables each day. This is done in a number of ways including:

→ raising awareness of the health benefits
→ improving access to fruit and vegetables
→ a national School Fruit and Vegetable Scheme – this entitles all 4–6-year-old children in LEA-maintained infant, primary and special schools to a free piece of fruit or vegetable each school day

→ local initiatives, for example joint work between health workers and schools

→ work with industry and food producers and retailers – many supermarkets have local promotions to encourage the purchase of fruit and vegetables, with special offers and links to recipes and ideas for childrens meals.

Find out!

Carry out research into one of the government health campaigns listed on pages 481–2. What are the benefits of the scheme? Can you identify any problems with it?

Find out!

Find out more about the 5 a day campaign, including the School Fruit and Vegetable Scheme, by visiting www.5aday.nhs.uk.

Have a look in your local supermarket to see if there are any promotions linked to 5 a day. Has your placement run any activities with the local health authority?

Eight Tips for Eating Well

This government also issues general advice on diet. The current recommendations are given in its Eight Tips for Eating Well (see also www.eatwell.gov.uk/healthydiet/eighttipssection):

1. Base your meals on starchy foods.
2. Eat lots of fruit and vegetables.
3. Eat more fish.
4. Cut down on saturated fat and sugar.
5. Try to eat less salt – no more than 6g a day.
6. Get active and try to be a healthy weight.
7. Drink plenty of water.
8. Don't skip breakfast.

In practice

Leanne has found working in a school that has a number of children with special dietary needs a challenge. After one child who is allergic to peanuts had a severe reaction she made sure that she knew everything about the special dietary requirements of all the children in the setting.

When you have worked through this section you will understand about disorders requiring special diets and how to support children with special dietary needs.

Food allergies and intolerances

Children can be allergic to any food but the commonest causes of food allergy or intolerance in the young include:

➜ milk and milk products
➜ wheat and gluten (in wheat products)
➜ eggs
➜ food colourings
➜ nuts.

Food allergy and food intolerance are both types of food sensitivity but there are key differences:

➜ when a person has a food allergy, their immune system reacts to a particular food as if it isn't safe (see also Unit 11, page 422)
➜ food intolerance doesn't involve the immune system and is generally not life-threatening. However, if a person eats a food they are intolerant to, this could make them feel ill or affect their long-term health.

Did you know?

Any substance that causes an allergic reaction is called an allergen. Allergens in food are normally proteins and there is usually more than one kind of allergen in each food.

If a child appears to have a food allergy or intolerance, it is important for the child's parents or carers to get a proper diagnosis. Food groups should not be removed from a child's diet without medical advice as there is the danger of missing out on important nutrients.

Symptoms of allergic reaction

Allergic reactions to food vary from mild irritation and skin rashes through to eczema, vomiting and diarrhoea to malabsorption (failure to gain nutrients from food, which can limit growth and development). If someone has a food allergy they can react to just a tiny amount of the food they are sensitive to. The symptoms of an allergic reaction can vary and the reactions can be more or less severe on different occasions. The most common symptoms of severe allergic reaction are shown below. Symptoms can appear within minutes or up to several hours after someone has eaten the food they are allergic to.

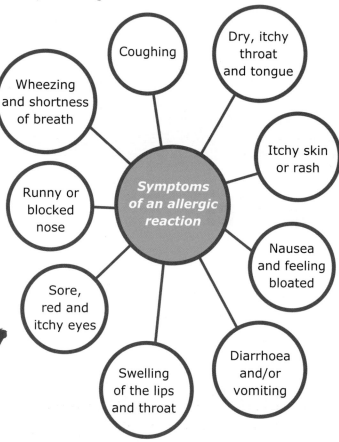

Symptoms of an allergic reaction

- Coughing
- Dry, itchy throat and tongue
- Wheezing and shortness of breath
- Itchy skin or rash
- Runny or blocked nose
- Nausea and feeling bloated
- Sore, red and itchy eyes
- Diarrhoea and/or vomiting
- Swelling of the lips and throat

Anaphylactic shock

People with severe allergies can have a reaction called anaphylactic shock (anaphylaxis) which can be fatal; see also Unit 11 page 445. People at risk from anaphylaxis usually carry an adrenaline injector (EpiPen); it is extremely important for someone with a severe allergy to take their medication with them wherever they go.

Anaphylaxis can also be caused by bee and wasp stings and drug allergy, but food allergy is one of the most common causes. In the UK and Europe, peanuts, milk, eggs and fish are the most common foods to cause anaphylaxis.

Food additives

Most reactions to foods are caused by natural food ingredients, but some can be caused by additives. Reports also suggest that certain food additives may cause behavioural changes in some children.

The recording and reporting of allergies and intolerances in a range of settings

If children eat or drink while at your setting, it is important that any reactions to food are noted and reported to the child's parents. Likewise, it is important that parents tell the child's setting or school of any allergies.

If there is suspicion a child has food intolerance or allergy, parents should be encouraged to see the child's GP, who can then arrange for tests. Once a diagnosis has been made the food or foods the child is sensitive to should be avoided. This information should be clearly recorded on a child's file and clearly displayed in food preparation and serving areas. People with severe food allergy should also wear a bracelet or necklace giving details of their allergy, so medical staff will know about it in an emergency.

In the case of a child who has been diagnosed with a food allergy, it is important that everybody who looks after them (including teachers and the parents of friends) knows how to avoid the foods they are sensitive to and what to do if they have an allergic reaction, including how to use their adrenaline injector if used. This is vital to avoid tragic accidents in which children die as a result of staff not being aware of children's food allergies – around 20 children die each year in the UK from anaphylaxis.

Supporting children and their families who have special diets

Children who need to follow a special diet require thought and support. It can be difficult for a young child to understand why they cannot eat the same food as their friends. It is also easy for them to eat something they should not have and it not be known until they are reacting badly to the food. There are many ways that early years practitioners can support such children and their families, as shown in the good practice checklist below.

Good practice checklist

Supporting children with special diets

✓ Ask parents for guidance about the foods their child can eat and ones they enjoy.

✓ Always think about special dietary needs when planning meals and events.

✓ Look for ways of using special ingredients in 'normal' recipes.

✓ Make effort to ensure that special foods are tempting and exciting.

✓ Do not put allergy-causing foods out if there is a sensitive child present.

✓ Be aware of general allergens such as nuts in basic foods.

✓ Put up a notice in a prominent place to advise other parents not to leave food containing nuts with their children – they may give a friend with an allergy something that is harmful for them.

U12
4

The coeliac condition

Coeliac disease means that the body is unable to absorb food properly. It affects the small intestine and is caused by sensitivity to gluten – a protein found in wheat. Similar proteins are found in rye, barley and, to a much smaller extent, oats. Symptoms can occur at any age and may include weight loss, vomiting and diarrhoea. A baby with coeliac disease will start to show symptoms after the introduction of gluten-containing solids. These include pale, bulky and offensive-smelling stools; the child will be miserable, lethargic and generally fail to thrive.

Coeliac disease is diagnosed by examining the intestine, which will be inflamed due to the reaction to gluten in the diet. There is now a reasonably accurate blood test available for screening.

Coeliac disease is treated with a gluten-free diet, which allows the mucosal lining of the intestine to heal and return towards normal. It is thought that coeliac disease in the general population may be as high as 1 in 100, but many cases often go undiagnosed so the number of diagnosed cases is 1 in 1,000.

Find out!

Find out about the types of foods available to children with coeliac disease.

Cystic fibrosis

Cystic fibrosis is a condition in which the mucous glands in the body produce abnormally thick, sticky mucus and the sweat glands produce excess salt. The lungs and the pancreas (part of the digestive system) are the main organs affected by this condition.

In children with cystic fibrosis the lungs are normal at birth but become affected as the thick mucus collects in the lungs, blocking some airways and resulting in bacterial infection and damage. Much of this damage can be prevented through treatment of infections.

In the pancreas, the small channels through which enzymes produced in the pancreas flow to reach the intestines become blocked with mucus. This results in cysts being formed which damage the pancreas, causing a reduction in the production of vital enzymes. The enzymes produced by the pancreas are vital to normal digestion. Fortunately, digestive enzyme preparations can replace most of the digestive enzymes produced by the pancreas.

Find out!

Carry out research into the restrictions placed on a child with cystic fibrosis. A good place to start with is the website of the Cystic Fibrosis Trust (www.cftrust.org.uk)

Insulin dependency in children

Diabetes mellitus (see also Unit 11, pages 421–2) is a condition in which the amount of glucose (sugar) in the blood is too high because the body cannot use it properly. Glucose comes from the digestion of starchy foods such as bread, rice, potatoes, chapatis, yams and plantain, from sugar and other sweet foods, and from the liver which makes glucose. Insulin (a hormone produced by the pancreas) is essential for the body to use glucose. It helps the glucose to enter the cells where it is used as fuel by the body.

→ Type 1 diabetes (childhood diabetes) is the most common type of diabetes in children and develops if the body is unable to produce any insulin. It is treated by insulin injections and diet.

→ Type 2 diabetes (age-onset diabetes) develops when the body can make some insulin but not enough, or when the insulin that is produced does not work properly (known as insulin resistance). This type of diabetes usually appears in people over the age of 40 years and is treated by diet alone or by diet and tablets or, sometimes, by diet and insulin injections. However, an increasing number of children are developing Type 2 diabetes. This is thought to be due to children becoming less active and more overweight.

The main aim of treatment of both types of diabetes is to achieve near-normal blood glucose and blood pressure levels. This, together with a healthy lifestyle, will help to improve well-being and protect against long-term damage to the eyes, kidneys, nerves, heart and major arteries.

Ways to deal with emergencies

Every setting should have plans to deal with emergency situations (see also Unit 4, pages 173–4, and Unit 11, pages 442–6). A severe food allergy (anaphylactic shock) is an emergency situation, as is a child choking on food or hypoglycaemia (low blood sugar) in a diabetic child.

Did you know?

Hospital admissions from allergies have increased sevenfold over the last decade. In 2006, 47,000 adrenaline injectors were issued to children under the age of 7 years, compared with just 7,500 in 1996. (*Source*: *The Observer*, April 2006)

Think about it

Revisit Unit 11 pages 442–6.

1. What would you do if a child in your care chokes on food?

2. How should you help a child with diabetes who is having a hypoglycaemic attack?

Find out!

Find and read your setting's policy on dealing with emergency situations related to food.

The issues of overweight children and obesity

Being overweight has significant health problems including:

→ age-onset diabetes
→ heart problems
→ strokes
→ mobility problems
→ some cancers.

Being overweight or obese is due to two factors – eating too much and not exercising enough.

It is thought that between 5 and 15 per cent of school-aged children are overweight. However, children should not be expected to lose large amounts of weight but encouraged to remain at a constant weight or to increase their weight slowly while their height increases, so that they grow to be an acceptable weight for their height. Developing a healthy family diet and lifestyle is important in the weight management of children. (For more on childhood obesity see also pages 460–1).

Did you know?

Most overweight children go on to become overweight or obese adults. Adults who were overweight as children find it far more difficult to lose weight.

U12
4

Section 5

Safe food preparation

In practice

The owner and staff of a nursery and after-school club were delighted to pass their visit from the environmental health inspector. After a number of cases of food poisoning in the area, the owner had worried about the setting's hygiene standards. However, after the visit they were told that the standards were the best the inspector had seen and that all staff were very well informed about how to safely prepare and serve food.

When you have worked through this section you will understand about the safe preparation of food in early years settings and how to avoid contamination of food.

Basic food hygiene

If you are involved in preparing or serving food to children it will be necessary for you to take a course in food hygiene. This is a legal requirement and will show to employers that you know how to be safe with food. There are thousands of cases of food poisoning each year in the UK, and in some cases deaths occur, simply from poor food hygiene practices.

The causes of food poisoning

A few types of micro-organisms are harmful in food. These fall into two types:

→ *Spoilage bacteria.* Certain types of bacteria cause food to rot and decay but do not necessarily make people ill. They hasten deterioration of food and produce changes in the food which may be seen as smell, taste, colour and texture. These effects are usually sufficient to alert people to the fact that the food is no longer fit to eat.

→ *Pathogens.* A few types of bacteria in food are responsible for causing illness and are referred to as pathogens. They may be present in food in large numbers but are not visible and may not cause obvious changes to the food so that it still looks tastes and smells perfectly wholesome. One example is salmonella, which is found in some chickens and eggs.

→ *Viruses.* Some food poisoning can be caused by viruses that are passed on through poor hygiene from food handlers who have a viral infection. If the food is cooked these viruses are destroyed, but contaminated ready-to-eat foods or undercooked foods can cause illness. Some viruses, for example the Norwalk virus, can also be passed on through contact with other infected people.

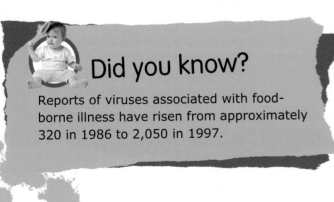

Did you know?

Reports of viruses associated with food-borne illness have risen from approximately 320 in 1986 to 2,050 in 1997.

Preventing food poisoning

How to prevent food poisoning is described in Unit 4, pages 176–9; you will need to revisit these pages to complete your reading for this unit.

Legal requirements for safe food preparation in a range of settings

Laws are in place in the UK to protect the public from the risk of food poisoning; these apply to child care and education settings and the people who work there. They are summed up in the Food Safety Act 1990 and the Food Safety (General Food Hygiene) Regulations 1995. These laws concern all parts of the food chain, from the growing of crops and rearing of animals to the serving of food itself.

The Food Safety Act 1990

Under the Act:

→ ministers can make regulations for all parts of the food industry, to ensure that food does not harm the people who eat it

→ it is an offence to cause illness by preventable contamination of food

→ deliberately or knowingly contaminating food is a criminal offence

→ premises may be closed, and for those found guilty of breaking the Act there may be large fines and possible imprisonment

→ all managers and staff have responsibilities, with anyone who handles or serves food being required to be qualified with a basic food hygiene certificate as a minimum qualification.

Food Safety (General Food Hygiene) Regulations 1995

The Regulations aim to ensure common food hygiene rules and apply to any person who handles food or whose actions could affect its safety. This includes people who provide food to others and those who clean equipment which comes into contact with food. The Regulations set out basic hygiene principles, with a focus on how to identify and control food safety risks at each stage of the process of preparing and providing food.

U12
5

Find out!

How does your setting comply with the Food Safety Act and Food Safety Regulations?

Health and safety policies and procedures

All settings are required to have health and safety policies relating to a range of issues, including food and drink. It is essential that you are aware of the policies of your setting and that you follow them closely (see also Unit 4, pages 161–2 and Unit 8, page 351).

Think about it

Have a look at the policies on food and drink from two different settings below.

1. What are the differences between the two policies?
2. Which policy do you prefer? Why?
3. Is there anything that these policies do not cover?
4. How do these compare to the policy in your setting?

Sample health and safety policy relating to food and drink A

- Staff who prepare and handle food must first receive appropriate training and understand and comply with food safety and hygiene regulations.
- All food and drink is to be stored appropriately.
- Adults must not carry hot drinks through the play area(s) and should not place hot drinks within reach of children.
- Snack and meal times must be appropriately supervised and children are not to walk about with food and drinks.
- Fresh drinking water should be made available to children at all times.
- The setting operates systems to ensure that children do not have access to food and drinks to which they are allergic.

Sample health and safety policy relating to food and drink B

- All staff must be familiar with the policy concerning the safe handling and storage of food.
- Staff should wash their hands in one of the handwashing basins before handling any food.
- All foods and drinks prepared should be consumed immediately or stored appropriately.
- The kitchen will be kept clean and tidy, with surfaces being hygienically cleaned before and after food preparation.
- When windows in the kitchen are open to supplement ventilation, they must be screened if there is a risk of food becoming contaminated by insects or dust.
- All food and drinks that are prepared must be covered with a clean cloth or stored appropriately.
- The fridge temperature should be 5°C. There is a thermometer in the kitchen and temperatures are recorded daily.
- Any chilled foods bought are transported in a cool bag and placed in the fridge as soon as possible. Any food brought in from children must also be stored in the fridge.
- The temperature of all foods will be checked carefully before serving them to the children.
- Staff must ensure that individual dietary requirements are carefully detailed and strictly adhered to.
- High chairs must be wiped down hygienically after every use and stored away. The safety harnesses are used at all times and also wiped down after every use.
- Food for toddlers must be cut into bite-size pieces.

Below are some questions that you can use to check your understanding and recall of this unit.

1. Describe the key principles in planning a balanced diet for children.

2. Explain some of the issues that you may encounter that can affect a child's diet throughout childhood.

3. Outline some of the key influences on a child's diet. How might these affect the food a child eats?

4. How would you help a child to eat the correct diet who has diabetes, coeliac disease or an allergy to nuts?

5. How can you make sure that the food you prepare is safe?

6. Explain and discuss the responsibilities of practitioners who are involved in the provision of suitable food and nutrition for children.

Unit 14

Working with children with special needs

1. The concept of special needs and current attitudes and values

2. The range of factors affecting children's ability to learn

3. The provision for children with special educational needs

4. The roles and responsibilities of professionals working with children with special educational needs

The concept of special needs and current attitudes and values

In practice

You are talking to a parent about her son. During the conversation she mentions that her son has special needs. You are not sure what this means, but don't feel that you can ask. She says that she gets upset because some people focus only on his special needs rather than on him as a child.

By the end of this section you will know what the term 'special needs' might mean and will understand why the mother in this scenario is upset about other people's attitudes towards her son.

The common theories, definitions and models of 'special needs'

The term special needs arose from an influential report in 1980 known as the Warnock Report. At the time of the report, the term 'special needs' was seen as being helpful and it was a move away from the medical terminology; however, since then the term has become more controversial. Some people feel that it continues to act as a label and argue that truly inclusive settings see all children as special and having their own needs. It is also argued that finding ways to classify children is in itself discriminatory. These arguments mean that you will probably find a variety of terms and expressions used, as at the time of writing a consensus has not really been reached. Some documents may, for example, use the term 'additional needs' or 'support needs'. In addition, you may also see the term 'special educational needs' or SEN, which is used to describe children who need additional support in their education.

Definitions used in legislation

The following definitions are used in current legislation.

Education Act 1996

By the terms of this Act, children are said to have special educational needs if they have a learning difficulty which calls for special educational provision to be made for them. Children have a learning difficulty if they meet any one of the following categories:

→ children with a significantly greater difficulty in learning than the majority of children of the same age
→ children with a disability which prevents or hinders them from making use of educational facilities of a kind generally provided for children of the same age in schools within the area of the local education authority
→ children under compulsory school age who fall within the two definitions above or would do so if special educational provision was not made for them.

Disability Discrimination Act 1995, Section 1 (1)

For the purposes of this Act, a person has a disability if they have a physical or mental impairment which has substantial and long-term adverse effect on their ability to carry out normal day-to-day activities.

Children Act 1989, Section 17 (11)

This states that a child is disabled if they are blind, deaf or dumb or suffer from a mental disorder of any kind or is substantially and permanently handicapped by illness, injury or congenital deformity or such other disability as may be prescribed.

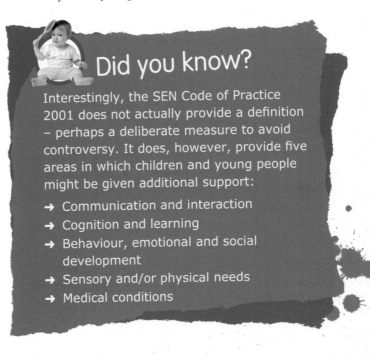

Models of special needs

Everyone who works with children knows that each child is unique and individual. While this sounds obvious, it remains a key source of tension for those working in education and care. How children's needs can be described and met without losing sight of their individuality is a key question for policy makers and those directly working with children.

U14
1

Medical model

For many years, children who had a disability were taken to a doctor; 'What is wrong with them?' could in some ways describe this approach. The medical approach stresses the importance of curing and nowadays preventing disability – as though disability is in some ways a tragedy. This has resulted in screening in pregnancy which is quite controversial in itself. In previous generations, children for whom no 'cure' was found were sent away to institutions or kept out of sight. Later, children were sent to specialist schools rather than to mainstream schools. It is now recognised that for many children this meant they had a limited education, as expectations were low. The medical model is therefore criticised for stigmatising disability.

Deficit model

The deficit model is similar to the medical model in it focuses on the difficulties the children have and how to provide support for them. Critics of this approach argue that this model continues to see children with needs as 'problems' that need to be fixed. In this sense they view some current practice, such as providing statements of special needs and individual plans, as focusing on the 'deficits' of the child.

Inclusion/social model

This model assumes that all individuals have needs but also strengths, skills and preferences. The approach taken is to provide inclusive environments as a starting point for all children. It considers that the environment, attitudes towards disability, curricula and resources may be the 'problem' that requires fixing rather than the child. This approach has resulted in many children who would previously have been educated separately in specialist provision being educated in mainstream schools.

The inclusion/social model has recently come in for some criticism by parents as being too idealistic and failing to meet the needs of children. Many parents have thus campaigned to keep open specialist provision. Advocates of the inclusion model say that any failing is a result of a lack of funding and society's attitudes towards disability.

Future directions

It will be very important to keep up to date, as this area is one that is undergoing change. In Scotland, for example, policy makers are talking about a 'Rights model' for all children in order to refocus practitioners and step away from the current conflict between opposing views. Legislation and practice is to be driven by the United Nations Convention on the Rights of the Child (see pages 6–7), with children's and young people's rights and wishes being seen as paramount. This may result in children having the right to both mainstream provision and specialist provision depending on what they and their families feel is best for them.

Case study

Inclusive practice

Darren is 4 years old. He attends a nursery and has made several friends. Darren's mother is determined that he should have the same rights as any little boy, but is concerned that, because he has Down's syndrome, the primary school will not accept him. She understands that he needs support but argues that he should also have the right to be with his friends. She also feels that Darren will be labelled if he attends a special school and that he will miss out on being a normal boy. She is surprised when the head teacher of the primary school reassures her that there will be a place for Darren at the school and is hugely relieved.

1. Why does Darren's mother want him to attend the primary school?
2. Explain why traditionally this might not have been possible.
3. What are the benefits for Darren of attending the primary school?

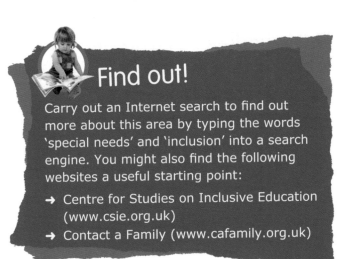

Society's attitudes towards disability are undoubtedly complex. Medical advances mean that most pregnant women are offered tests that will indicate whether the foetus is likely to have a medical condition such as spina bifida or chromosomal disorders such as Down's syndrome. Women are then offered the option of terminating the pregnancy. Opponents of such screening argue that the philosophy underpinning screening is the medical model that views all disability as a tragedy. As medical technology becomes ever more sophisticated, this is increasingly becoming a hot topic.

Attitudes, perceptions and beliefs and their effect on the care and education of children

Changing attitudes

There was a time when disability was not understood and was actually feared. This resulted in children being isolated from communities and even their family sometimes felt ashamed of them. Today, attitudes have moved on but many disability campaigners would argue that the attitudes in the UK remain restrictive (see also page 515). Interestingly, statistics bear this out: a high proportion of children who are excluded from school have special educational needs, which perhaps indicates that their needs are not being understood or met.

Perceptions and beliefs

There has been a perception and belief that disabled children would not necessarily be able to lead independent lives. The focus tended to be on their disability rather than their ability. This led to a culture of low expectation and was one of the reasons why it was seen as important that many children with special needs are educated alongside their peers. Today, this situation is improving although many children and their families report that they have to fight to get equal access to education.

Avoiding stereotyping

In order to be an effective practitioner working with children, it is essential to see them as individuals. All children have their special interests, needs and little ways. Getting to know children and their families is the best way of working effectively.

The Origin of the Universe
Stephen Hawking

⇧ **Do you see the ability or the disability?**

U14
1

Sadly, in the area of special needs there are many stereotypes and expectations. These need to be avoided because they can prevent you from focusing on the individual child. Some of the common stereotypes are listed below.

"Victims"

A common stereotype that reflects the medical approach to disability is to view children and their families as being victims. The media in particular is guilty of this. Children and young people are often portrayed as helpless, needy and weak. This focus means that their strengths, abilities and personalities are often overlooked.

"Patient and brave"

A traditional stereotype is that children and/or their families are always brave, patient and heroic; 'I don't know how he copes' or 'she never makes a fuss' is the type of expression you might hear. This is very hard to live up to, and in reality children and adults will have their moments of frustration as well as patience. This stereotype forgets that children and their families are real people!

"Grateful"

A common expectation is that children and their families should be grateful for support, for example a child who needs a computer to assist them with their schoolwork should be pleased and say 'thank you' to the person who provided it. This expectation assumes that children are not entitled to the same provision as others as a right. It also assumes that facilities and adaptations to the environment are 'extras' rather than a necessity.

The importance of avoiding labelling and the use of appropriate and sensitive language and terminology

As well as stereotypes, there is a danger that children can quickly become labelled. This means that people talk about their condition and make assumptions about it rather than getting to know the child. For example, a child with a hearing **impairment** may always be referred to as 'the deaf boy' by staff rather than using his name. The danger of labelling children means that adults may not look beyond the child's **disability** or **handicap** at the child's interests, strengths and personality.

Key terms

Impairment The loss or abnormality of development of growth, for example a hearing impairment means that a person has a loss of hearing

Disability The restrictions that impairment causes

Handicap The disadvantage that the person has compared to others. Note: the term handicapped was frequently used to describe the person but this is now considered offensive

Find out!

Look at several newspapers. Can you see any evidence of traditional stereotypes being used in connection with disability?

Think about it

Would you like to be known by one characteristic, for example 'the glasses one' or 'the ginger one'?

Find out!

Listen for the way that labels are used when people talk about disability.

Use of appropriate and sensitive language and terminology

Language is a powerful tool as it demonstrates attitudes and beliefs. You have seen that the term 'special needs' was once well received but may well have become dated. This should act as a warning that you need to keep up to date with your use of language. Terms such as 'mentally retarded', which were once commonplace, are now considered offensive.

If you are unsure how to write about a child's needs, it is worth taking the time to learn more. This may mean talking to a support group that specialises in the disability, condition or need, finding out from colleagues or even talking directly to parents or, with older children, the child.

Below are some examples of terms that are no longer considered appropriate and can in some cases cause offence. Many of these terms reflect the medical model of disability. Appropriate alternative terms are listed in the right column of the table.

Term considered inappropriate	Appropriate alternative term
Handicapped person	Disabled person
Wheelchair bound or confined	Wheelchair user
Sufferer, victim, crippled with	Person living with or person who has
Spastic	Cerebral palsy
Mental	Learning difficulties
Idiot, imbecile	Learning difficulties
Mongol, mongoloid	A child with Down's syndrome
Congenital	Genetically impaired
Invalid	Disabled person

Section 2

The range of factors affecting children's ability to learn

In practice

You are working with a group of children in a school. You are told that one child in the group needs additional support as he has dyslexia and epilepsy. You are not sure what this means exactly or why some children may have more difficulties than others in learning.

By the end of this section you will understand the many factors that might affect children's ability to learn.

Factors before, during or after birth leading to delayed development, physical or sensory impairment or learning difficulties

There are many reasons why children may need additional support with their learning. For many parents, understanding why their children are not learning in the same way as others of the same age can be extremely important for them.

Genetic factors

Some children's genetic make-up will cause them learning or sensory difficulties. A child's genetic make-up is decided at conception when the egg and sperm fuse. While some conditions are inherited, such as Fragile X that causes difficulties in behaviour and concentration, others such as Angelman's syndrome are 'one offs' and the result of a chromosomal fault.

Pregnancy

It is now recognised that what happens to the mother during pregnancy can impact on the later development of the child. The general health of the mother is important and this is monitored during pregnancy.

→ Some medical conditions that are pregnancy-related, such as pre-eclampsia, can cause premature birth, while infections such as rubella (German measles) can cause blindness and deafness in the developing foetus.

→ Diet seems to play a crucial role, especially in the earliest weeks. Green vegetables that contain folic acid help prevent spina bifida while eating fish seems to be helpful for brain development.

→ Drugs, both medical and recreational including alcohol, also have the potential to affect the developing child as they are absorbed into the bloodstream and taken into the baby's body. This is why pregnant women are advised to restrict or avoid alcohol and why there are warning signs on the packets of many drugs and tablets. Smoking restricts the uptake of oxygen into the developing foetus and so can limit development, which is why pregnant women are urged to stop smoking (see also Unit 6 page 259).

Find out!

Find out more about pre-conceptual care and having a healthy pregnancy by visiting the website of Tommy's, the Baby Charity (www.tommys.org).

Pre-maturity

The usual gestation period for babies is 40 weeks. Babies who are born before 36 weeks are considered to be premature. The incidence of learning difficulties among premature babies, especially those born before 30 weeks, is higher than those born at full term. This is because premature babies' lungs are not always mature enough to allow them to breathe unassisted and a lack of oxygen can cause damage to the brain. Also, the final weeks in a pregnancy are linked to brain growth so being born early can be disadvantageous.

While health professionals tend to look at how a baby is doing in relation to their due date if they were full term, this is not often the case in educational settings, although prematurity may have a significant impact.

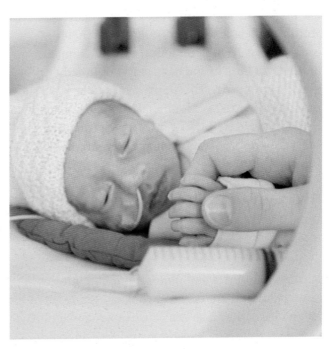

⇧ Medical advances mean that babies born prematurely in the UK are more likely to survive, but very premature babies run a higher risk of brain damage and disability

U14
2

Did you know?

Birth

Birth itself can be extremely hazardous. Some learning difficulties are a result of the baby not getting sufficient oxygen during the birth, for example because the umbilical cord is wrapped around the neck or the baby does not breathe quickly after birth. This is one reason why babies are monitored during labour. In addition, occasionally babies receive birthing injuries which can affect the brain as a result of emergency interventions such as forceps delivery.

Accidents and illness

While some learning difficulties and sensory impairments are directly related to factors before and during birth, some can be caused through accidental injuries and illness. Common injuries in young children are falls and choking. While these can be fatal, they also can cause brain damage. This is why in children's earliest years it is essential to be aware of safety (see Unit 4, pages 168–73). In addition, some illnesses such as whooping cough, mumps and measles can have long-term effects on young children. This is why vaccination is recommended for most babies and children.

The characteristics of common conditions and impairments in children

It is useful to have some understanding of the needs that children may have, as a starting point for working with them and their families. It is vital, however, that you do not assume that you 'know' the child or young person just because you have some knowledge of impairments, learning difficulties or medical conditions. The most important person is always the child or young person, and to work well with them means getting to know the individual. It is important also to recognise that many medical conditions such as diabetes, asthma or a visual impairment will not necessarily create any difficulties in terms of the child's ability to learn.

Asthma

Asthma is a common medical condition that affects breathing (see also Unit 11, pages 414–5). Children with asthma are usually prescribed two inhalers: one that will manage the condition and acts as a preventive medicine, and another that is used if the child is having difficulty breathing. Children with asthma complaining of a shortness of breath or who are coughing must be given access to their inhalers as the condition has the potential to be fatal. Note that asthma is a medical condition which if managed should not result in a child having learning difficulties.

Attention deficit/hyperactivity disorder (AD/HD)

This disorder creates difficulties in concentrating, sitting still and controlling behaviour, which in turn makes it harder for the child to learn. Treatment for this disorder is variable and some children are given drugs while others are supported using behavioural modification techniques.

Autistic spectrum disorder

This disorder affects children's ability to communicate and make social relationships. The extent to which children can be affected is wide. The term 'spectrum' is now used to reflect this and Aspberger's syndrome is considered part of the spectrum.

Cerebral palsy

This is a general term used to describe disorders that prevent the brain controlling the muscles and movements in the body. There are three types of cerebal palsy, with some children having more than one type. The extent to which a child might be affected will vary enormously. Many children with cerebral palsy have no learning difficulties although they need support in order to learn.

Diabetes mellitus

Diabetes is a medical condition in which the body is unable to regulate the amount of sugar in the blood stream (see also Unit 11, page 421). The condition is controlled either with insulin injections and/or diet. It is a serious condition if it is not being managed properly. Note that diabetes is a medical condition which if managed should not result in a child having learning difficulties.

Dyslexia

Dyslexia is a specific learning disorder that causes difficulties in processing information. This results in difficulties in reading, writing and spelling, although speech is usually not affected. The condition is often recognised once children begin to find reading and writing difficult. (See also Unit 16, page 549.)

Dyspraxia

This is a developmental disorder that affects motor movement, coordination, speech and thought. Some children with dyspraxia will also have dyslexia. It is usually recognised in children's early years as they may not reach the physical developmental milestones.

Fragile X

Fragile X is a genetic condition that affects boys more severely than girls. It is the most common form of inherited learning disability. It creates difficulties in behaviour, concentration, speech and physical development. Once suspected a chromosomal test will confirm the diagnosis.

Hearing impairment

There are two types of hearing impairment: sensor-neural and conductive. Sensor-neural hearing loss is likely to be picked up early on in a child's life and is usually permanent. Hearing loss if undetected can affect children's speech and ability to communicate and this in turn can affect their behaviour (see also page 524). Note that hearing impairment will not necessarily mean that a child will have learning difficulties.

Visual impairment

There are many different degrees of visual impairment so the extent of children's difficulty will vary. Some children with sight loss are not picked up until they have difficulties in learning to read, while sight loss in others is detected earlier because children might have difficulty with their fine or gross motor skills and may be seen as 'clumsy'. Note that children with visual impairment will not necessarily have learning difficulties.

Find out!

Find out more about the conditions and impairments listed on pages 502–3 by visiting the following websites:

➔ Asthma UK (www.asthma.org.uk)
➔ ADDISS, The National Attention Deficit Disorder Information and Support Service (www.addiss.co.uk)
➔ The National Autistic Society (www.nas.org.uk)
➔ Scope, disability organisation in England and Wales whose focus is people with cerebral palsy (www.scope.org.uk)
➔ Diabetes UK (www.diabetes.org.uk)
➔ The British Dyslexia Association (www.bdadyslexia.org.uk)
➔ Dyspraxia Foundation (www.dyspraxiafoundation.org.uk)
➔ The Fragile X Society (www.fragilex.org.uk)
➔ The National Deaf Children's Society (www.ndcs.org.uk)
➔ National Blind Children's Society (www.nbcs.org.uk)

Factors affecting children's ability to learn

There are many factors that can affect children's learning. Sometimes these are temporary and their effects might be short-lived if the child is given support.

Loss and separation

In Unit 2 you saw the importance of attachment to children's emotional development (pages 53–4). Children who have experienced bereavement or separation in any form from a loved one are likely to find it harder to learn. Coping with loss and separation is a process and it will take time to adjust. Children may be distracted, find it hard to enjoy learning and may show behaviours linked to emotional upheaval, including withdrawal, aggression and uncooperativeness.

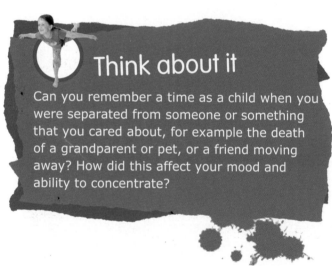

Think about it

Can you remember a time as a child when you were separated from someone or something that you cared about, for example the death of a grandparent or pet, or a friend moving away? How did this affect your mood and ability to concentrate?

Stress

Children are not immune from stress and this can impact on their learning. Arguments in a family, moving home and financial pressures are all examples of stresses that some families might undergo. Children and young people are often sensitive to moods within their family and while they may not always know the underlying causes behind the tension, they may still react to it. While stress in families can affect children and young people, it is also important to remember that settings themselves can create stress. A good example of this might be children taking tests or being under pressure to perform in a play. While this type of stress is usually temporary, it can affect children so should be reflected upon.

Abuse and deprivation

In Unit 3 you looked at child abuse and saw that it has many effects on children and young people (see pages 124–6). Coping with what is happening or has happened to them tends to preoccupy children so will affect their ability to learn, for example they may find it hard to focus and concentrate. For young people, the learning itself may not seem relevant to their life and they may not be especially motivated.

Children who have been abused are likely to have also been deprived of the emotional security that is necessary for them to trust others and make friends. Some children who have been abused are therefore more likely to show difficulties in managing their behaviour, trusting adults and socialising with other children. Where children have been neglected, they may also not have had access to stimulation such as toys, conversation and outings. This has the potential to affect their cognitive development.

Drugs

Some medication can have significant effects on children's learning so it is important to find out about any medication that is being taken; parents should be able to advise you on their effects. Some drugs may, for example, cause drowsiness or affect concentration and memory. By understanding the effects of drugs you can then tailor the timing of sessions, the way in which you present information and the material to support children.

Absence

Some medical conditions may result in children being absent from settings, whether for regular appointments or more prolonged treatment. This can be disruptive for children's learning. They may, for example, return to find that a new topic has been introduced or that other children have developed new skills or knowledge. It is therefore important to find ways of reassuring children and practically helping them to continue their learning at their own pace.

The emotional and social impact of illness on children's ability to learn

Feeling successful and having strong peer relationships are important factors in children's learning. There are many ways in which having a medical condition, disability or any difficulty in learning affects children emotionally and socially.

Self-esteem

Self-esteem plays an important part in children's sense of well-being. Feeling good about yourself and believing yourself to be capable and competent is linked to a range of positive outcomes including academic achievement, strong relationships and the ability to persevere. Many children have low self-esteem, perhaps because they have noticed they are different in some way from other children. Adults, too, may have drawn their attention to these differences through actions and comments. In addition, children may have experienced situations when they have tried hard to achieve a task but in spite of their efforts have not succeeded. This can prevent children from gaining a sense of self-efficacy. Adults can also play a part by inadvertently disempowering children. They may, for example, take over tasks rather than encouraging children to have a go or even answer for them.

Friendships

Friendships play an important role in children's lives, especially after the age of 3 years. Some children may miss out socially for a range of reasons.

→ Some children may have periods of absence which can mean that other children 'forget' them, or as they get older they may lose out on the intensity of the friendship.

→ Some children do not experience 'equal' relationships. These are important for friendships. For example, other children may be supportive but take on a 'parenting' role and not see them as friends.

→ Finally, in a society where inclusion is in its infancy, bullying remains a problem in some educational settings. Difference can be seen as weakness and is used by other children as a reason for name calling, teasing or simply rejecting others.

Access to opportunities

Children can miss out socially as they may not be able to take part in the same activities as others. This can affect friendship in the early years, as friendships are partly based on mutual play preferences. Thus a child who cannot physically get into the role-play corner will be unable to access this opportunity and may miss out. Difficulty in accessing opportunities does not just apply to educational settings. Many children and young people also take part in outside activities such as swimming classes, football and dancing.

The provision for children with special educational needs

In practice

While on placement, you notice that ramps, an accessible toilet and a stair lift are being added to the setting. You wonder why these are necessary as there is no child in the setting that has difficulties with mobility. Your placement supervisor says that while currently no child has mobility needs, the setting would be required to make these adjustments if needed in the future and that this is part of the law.

By the end of this section you will know more about the legislation in place to support children with special needs and the ways in which settings must work with children.

The legal requirements for working with children with special needs in a range of settings

Changes in legislation

Legislation is a powerful tool which, like language, reflects the thinking of society. Today's legislation needs to be understood in the context of the previous legislation on which it was built.

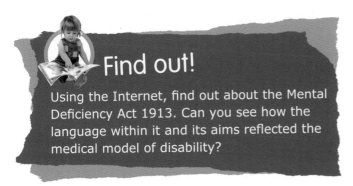

Find out!

Using the Internet, find out about the Mental Deficiency Act 1913. Can you see how the language within it and its aims reflected the medical model of disability?

Providing education

Up until 1976, children who had special educational needs or a disability were the responsibility of the health service. This approach reflects the medical model of the time. In 1976 the Education Act (Handicapped children) was passed; this passed responsibility for the education of children to local education authorities. They now had a duty to provide full-time education and many complied with this legislation by building special schools.

Introduction of the term 'special educational need'

This term was introduced by a committee whose purpose was to look at the educational provision for children and young people. The report is known as the Warnock Report, after its chair Mary Warnock. The report suggested a title of 'special education need' (SEN) which would include any child who needed some form of extra support. The report suggested three types of support:

→ special means of access to the curriculum
→ changes to the curriculum
→ changes to the environment, including the provision of emotional or social support.

The term 'special educational need' was an all-encompassing one and included children who had slight difficulties with their reading and writing as well as children who had major care needs. It also included children who had short-term needs that were causing them difficulties in fulfilling their potential alongside children who had long-term needs. In this way it focused professionals on the idea of how to meet the needs that children might have, rather than on the condition or cause of them. This was a major breakthrough and one that the Warnock Report was noted for.

The beginning of statementing – the Education Act 1981

Most of the Warnock Report's recommendations were adopted and included in the 1981 Education Act. This was an important Act as it gave parents more powers than before, but crucially it also introduced a process that is now known as statementing and is still used. By this process, children are assessed by a team of professionals alongside the parents and a statement is drawn up of how the child's needs are to be supported. The statement of special educational needs is a legally binding one and commits the local authority to providing for the child.

Currently, as a result of the latest Code of Practice, the number of statements being issued has decreased. This is another source of controversy as many parents feel that unless they are given a statement their child's needs might not be properly met. The argument in favour of reducing the number of statements is that it takes a lot of time and thus funding out of the system.

Introduction of children's rights

In 1989, the United Nations Convention on the Rights of the Child was drawn up and the UK became a signatory (see also Unit 3, page 115). Among many rights, two in particular went on to change practice and legislation: the right to an education and the right to be free from discrimination. These rights brought into question the way in which children were often automatically and sometimes against parents' wishes sent to special schools.

Recognising children in need – the Children Act 1989

Being a signatory to the United Nations Convention on the Rights of the Child meant that legislation had to be changed. This culminated in the 1989 Children Act and the government used this in England to bring together many pieces of legislation concerning children and their families. The Act was wide ranging and looked at many elements of work with children and their families (see also Unit 3, page 116). As part of this Act, local authorities had to draw up a list of children and their families who needed additional support and provide for them.

Supporting children under 5 years, extending parents' rights and publishing Codes of Practice – the Education Act 1993

This Act made health services work more closely with local education authorities, voluntary organisations and parents where children under 5 years were involved. In addition, local education authorities had to work more closely with parents, and parents were for the first time given rights to appeal where there was a disagreement with the local education authority. Parents could also ask for an assessment for a child under 2 years; this allowed for statements and therefore funding to be given.

The 1993 Education Act also provided for the use of codes of practice. Codes of practice are legally binding but have the advantage of being able to be changed without further legislation being passed. This Act has since been superseded.

Meeting the needs of carers – the Carers and Disabled Children Act 2000

Many parents who cared for a disabled child often felt that their needs and those of the family were overlooked. This legislation came into force in April 2001. It is designed to help the people who care for children to get their needs met alongside those of their children. The idea behind this law is to help carers manage more effectively. They may be given respite vouchers as well as being offered services directly from Social Services.

Inclusion – the Special Education Needs and Disability Act 2001

This is the Act currently in force in England. It is divided into two parts:

1. Part 1 reforms the framework of special educational needs to strengthen the rights of parents and children to access mainstream education.
2. Part 2 extends the Disability Discrimination Act 1995 to education, extending the civil rights of disabled children and adults in schools, colleges and universities.

Key features of the Act include:

→ the right of children with special educational needs to be educated in mainstream schools (where this is what parents want and where it is appropriate for the child)
→ the requirement of local education authorities to provide parents of children with special educational needs with advice and information and a means of resolving disputes with schools and local education authorities
→ the requirement for local educational authorities to comply with orders of the special educational needs tribunal
→ the requirement of education settings to tell parents where they are making special educational provision for their child and allow schools to request a statutory assessment of a pupil's special educational needs
→ the introduction of disability discrimination rights in the provision of education in schools, further education, higher education, adult education and the youth service
→ the requirement not to treat disabled students less favourably, without justification, than non-disabled students.

The identification and assessment process and the principles of inclusion

Understanding how the SEN Code of Practice works

It is important to understand how the key features of the Special Education Needs and Disability Act 2001 work in practice. First of all it is important to note that children are not seen as having special educational needs unless they need support that is additional in order to learn. For example, a child who has asthma may not have special educational needs as this is a medical condition which does not usually create any learning difficulties.

Each setting including schools has to have a special education needs policy and a person who coordinates and implement the policy. This person is known as a SENCO (Special Educational Needs Coordinator). SENCOs play an important role because they liaise with other professionals and parents and support members of staff.

The SEN Code of Practice sets out a process which settings including schools must follow; the term 'graduated response' is used in the Code to describe this process. The aim is that most children's needs can be met through early identification and action.

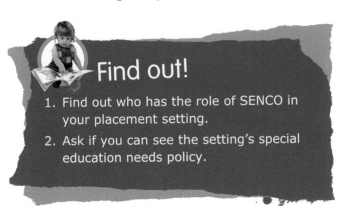

Find out!

1. Find out who has the role of SENCO in your placement setting.
2. Ask if you can see the setting's special education needs policy.

Early Years Action/School Action

Where a parent or member of staff believes that a child needs additional support, they will seek support from the SENCO of the setting. The Code of Practice is clear that early identification and assessment is important. A meeting is then held involving the parents, child's key worker and the SENCO. The aim of the meeting is to talk about how the child's needs can be met. Talking to parents at the earliest is essential, as permission is needed before other professionals can be involved unless there are exceptional circumstances.

As a result of this meeting, an action plan for working with the child is drawn up, known as an **Individual Education Plan** (IEP). (You will look at how these are used and how to draw these up on page 521.) As part of this process, a review date is set. At the time of the review, or earlier if needed,

the SENCO, parent and key worker look and consider whether the IEP is effective or whether outside professionals need to be involved.

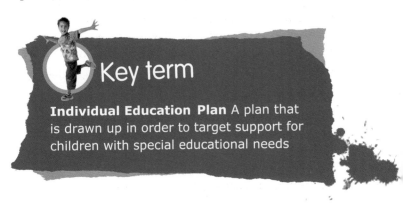

Key term

Individual Education Plan A plan that is drawn up in order to target support for children with special educational needs

Early Years Action Plus/School Action Plus

Where it is agreed that the child needs further assistance, other professionals become involved. In schools this is likely to be a referral to the educational psychologist. Other professionals are likely to look at the work that parents and the setting have already done via the Individual Education Plans. There is likely to be a multi-disciplinary meeting and, again, parents should play an important role in discussing how the child's needs can be met. Individual Education Plans are drawn up again and are reviewed regularly.

Find out!

Find out which professionals support children in your setting who are on Early Years Action Plus.

Assessment and statementing

Where additional support is required beyond that of the Early Years Action Plus or School Action Plus, settings, external agencies or the parents may request a statutory statement from the local education authority. As part of this process, the child's needs are assessed and if it is thought that additional support and funding is required, a statement will be drawn up. This is legally binding on the local education authority.

Since the introduction of the SEN Code of Practice, there has been a marked reduction in the numbers of children and young people gaining statements.

Principles of inclusion

We have seen in Section 1 that children were often excluded from mainstream schools and classrooms in previous years. Today it is recognised that wherever possible, children need to be educated alongside their peers. This is seen as being positive for everyone involved.

The term '**inclusion**' is used to describe the way in which all children need to be given the same opportunities to access the curriculum. It is a wide-ranging concept which covers children who may traditionally have been discriminated against on account of their culture, race or family background.

Key term

Inclusion A concept that looks at ways of making sure that all children have the same rights and are not excluded because of a disability

Inclusion means more than just adapting the environment. At its heart is the requirement that attitudes and therefore practices change. Instead of expecting a child to 'fit in' to the usual teaching methods or routines, it means looking at what you are doing and checking that it fits with their needs. This is a different approach as it turns the situation around. You may, for example, notice that a child finds it hard to sit still at story time. Instead of removing the child from this activity, you might instead think about why the child finds story time difficult and then look for ways to make it easier for them.

The range of provision available to children and families

There is a variety of provision that is provided for children, including statutory as well as voluntary and private organisations. There is an increasing trend for provision to be holistically organised rather than splitting it into health and education, which is a move towards interdisciplinary working. It also means that children and their parents

are not constantly travelling or making separate appointments. For example, a speech therapist might be based in the same centre where a child attends nursery or a social worker might make an appointment to talk to parents at one of the new Children's Centres.

Provision is variable

At the time of writing, the type of provision available for children is hugely variable – even within the same region or city, children may receive different types of services. The trend, however, remains towards multi-disciplinary working and integration of services between health, education and social services.

The spider diagram below shows examples of provision for children.

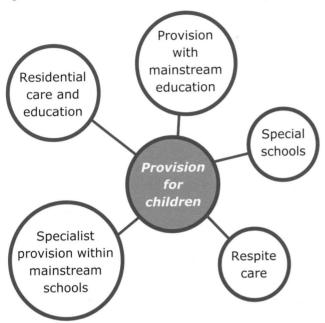

Provision within mainstream classes and settings

This is the favoured option wherever possible for children and young people. The Code of Practice states that mainstream provision should meet the needs of the 'vast majority' of children. The advantages of receiving education alongside other children are that expectations tend to be higher and children with special needs are not stereotyped.

Support can vary according to the needs of the child. Some children have permanent one-to-one help, often a special needs or learning support assistant who only works alongside them and changes classes or group in early years settings with them at the end of the year. Other children might have a support teacher who works regularly with them while other children might be given extra attention by the classroom teacher.

Specialist provision within mainstream schools

In some areas where special schools have been closed, local education authorities have provided units within mainstream schools. The units allow children to have access to specialised equipment and low staff ratios. Children may visit the unit for certain periods during the day or they may spend most of the day there.

Residential care and education

Despite the move towards inclusive and integrated education, there is still a need for some children to be cared for in residential centres, although a very small minority of children need this type of help. Many of these specialised centres are run by voluntary and private organisations but are funded by local authorities, although some of them are privately run. These centres tend to help children with complex needs where the family would have difficulty in caring for them at home, or where children need short-term respite care.

There are also private schools that specialise in educating children with specific learning disabilities such as dyslexia. Ofsted are responsible for inspecting and checking that these centres provide good care, education and protection for the children. Interestingly, there has been an increase in the numbers of children attending private provision. Many of these children have their fees paid for by local authorities as a result of parents arguing in court that their children's needs are otherwise not being supported.

Respite care

Respite care is usually provided by the local authority as part of their duty towards children and families in need. The way that respite care is organised varies according to the needs of the child and family. This means that some children may stay with foster families overnight or for short periods, while others will go to residential care. The amount of respite care is negotiated with the family and may range from a few hours a week through to fortnightly breaks.

Special schools

There are still many special schools to help children whose needs cannot be met within mainstream provision. These include children with complex needs.

Special schools have many advantages for these children including:

→ specialist equipment such as multi-sensory rooms and hydrotherapy pools
→ specialist staff trained and experienced in working with children with special needs

→ special schools often take children from 2 to 19 years of age which means that children do not have to move site and readjust to new staff
→ on-site speech and language therapists and occupational therapists
→ active parent support groups
→ a small, homely atmosphere with 40 to 60 pupils.

⇧ **Special schools are able to provide children with specialist equipment, such as multi-sensory rooms**

Find out!

Find out what provision is available in your local area for children with additional needs.

The adaptation of curricula and techniques for supporting learning in a range of settings

Good practitioners always look at individual children and consider how to meet their needs. This is the basis of successful working with all children, not just those with 'special educational needs'. One of the ways in which you can help all children fulfil their potential is by being flexible in your approach to work and adapting as needed. Parents, other professionals and the children themselves are key sources of information about how best to do this. It is also important not to make assumptions about children's needs as every child is unique.

Adapting and reflecting on your practice

While some physical adaptations to activities, the environment and resources may be necessary (see below), perhaps the most important skill when working with children is to consider the way in which you work, the routines that are established and whether they are effective for individuals. This is a major way in which you can make inclusion a reality rather than just a word. Altering how you work rather than expecting individual children to cope is thus essential. This can be difficult especially when balancing other pressures such as curriculum demands, expectations from colleagues and managing groups of children. It is nonetheless essential.

Case study

Adapting routines

Staff at Little Gems Nursery have noticed that three children seem to be quite disruptive at lunchtime. A new SENCO has organised a staff meeting to talk about these children. She suggests that instead of focusing on the children's unwanted behaviour, they might instead think about the children's needs and how the current lunchtime routine is meeting these needs. The staff begin by thinking about situations when these children seem happy and settled. They begin to realise that the current lunchtime arrangements are making children wait for too long and that these children are probably getting bored. The team then go on to think about the different options. Eventually, they decide to stagger lunchtimes so that children can continue playing until the food is literally on the table. This works well and lunchtime becomes a more enjoyable experience for everyone including the staff.

1. Why is it important to begin by focusing on children's needs?
2. Explain why traditional routines might sometimes need to be reviewed.
3. How has this setting put the principles of inclusion into practice?

Adapting activities

All children need to experience success in order to maintain motivation and promote a positive self-esteem. This means that it is important to think about planned activities and consider their suitability for individuals. The next step is to consider how best to adapt the activity in order for the child to have opportunities to learn and feel successful. This may mean changing the format to making it more or less challenging or using a different approach or media (see also sensory activities on page 514).

⇧ **It is important to adapt activities in order to provide children with opportunities to learn and feel successful**

Adapting the environment

In some situations it is not the activity that needs adapting but the physical environment in which the activity is taking place. You may, for example, have two tables facing the wall in order that children who need peace and calm to concentrate can use them. In the same way, resources might be moved from one area to another so that children with mobility needs are still able to access them.

Case study

Adapting the environment

Max is 5 years old. He finds it difficult to concentrate and is easily distracted in large spaces. His teacher and the learning assistant have looked closely at the environment and how it is meeting his needs. They decide to watch closely during the session times and think about how the layout of the room is working. At the end of the first session, they realise that they need to find a way of making the room seem calmer. They also think about how they might create some smaller spaces.

Over the next few days, Max's teacher and the learning assistant change one or two features of the layout and observe how this affects Max and the other children. After a week, they feel confident that the layout is working better as Max is less distracted and overall the room feels calmer. A couple of parents also comment how much their children are enjoying the new-style layout; consequently the teacher and assistant realise that the previous layout might have created difficulties for other children too.

1. Why is it important to begin by thinking about children's individual needs?

2. Explain how the teacher and the learning assistant used observation in order to assess needs.

3. Why is it useful to assess any changes to practice or the environment?

Adapting equipment and resources

Sometimes equipment and resources need to be modified in order that children can successfully use them. Again, this is an area where advice may need to be sought in order to provide equipment that works for individual children. In some cases, though, it is possible to make simple adaptations. For example, buttons on dressing-up clothes might be substituted for Velcro, while a non-slip mat might be provided to prevent a puzzle from falling off a table.

U14

3

Case study

Adapting equipment

Sophie loves doing jigsaw puzzles. Her favourite jigsaw puzzles have around 50 pieces. Many jigsaw puzzles of this size are too 'babyish' in content for Sophie, who is 7 years old. Her key worker has seen a catalogue where photographs can be transferred on to jigsaw puzzles. The key worker asks Sophie's mother if she thinks that Sophie might enjoy doing some puzzles with photographs of her family and her dog on them. Sophie's mother is delighted with the idea and together they choose some photographs to send away. A few days later, Sophie is excited to find a jigsaw puzzle which has a photograph of her dog on it.

1. Why was it important for the key worker to think about Sophie's needs and interests?

2. How has Sophie benefited from having a jigsaw that meets her needs and interests?

3. How did Sophie benefit from the key worker involving Sophie's mother?

The use of a sensory curriculum for profound needs

Sensory activities are used to stimulate and help children learn who have profound needs. Specialist equipment and rooms are often used to provide light, texture and sounds so that different parts of the brain and body can be stimulated. Some children with profound needs will also benefit from swimming and from outside activities such as riding or touching horses and other animals. This means that for children with profound needs, a curriculum needs to be developed around sensory experiences.

Sensory activities

Sensory activities are great tools to assist learning for all children and it is worth remembering this when creating environments and planning activities. Sensory activities help children to learn as they engage all the senses and this stimulation can make it easier for information to be processed and stored by the brain. This means that children may have a greater recall afterwards. Using a sensory medium is therefore one way in which you might assist children's learning, for example children might practise spelling a word by writing it out in a small sand tray or relax by floating in a sensory pool.

Before using sensory media with children, it is important to talk to the children or find out from their parents if they have any sensory preferences or more importantly dislikes. This is essential as some children can feel distressed by some sensory materials, for example hand painting may feel wonderful for some but awful for others. Some medical conditions can also be exacerbated by certain materials or conditions, so working out what to use is important. Some examples of sensory activities are given in the spider diagram below.

Water

Water is a particularly popular medium. Some settings have sensory pools that encourage physical movements as well as relaxation. Sensory pools incorporate light and sound and so stimulate many areas of the brain.

For some children, water can be used as a way of learning about size, shape, volume and density. Simple games can be played such as finding matching shapes in a water tray or fishing for magnetic numbers.

Cultural and social influences on the care and education of children with special educational needs

You have seen that the way in which children are educated often reflects society's attitudes towards disability. Today the concept of inclusion has meant that how early years practitioners work with children has changed significantly. A good example of this is the way that children with complex needs might be taken to a riding school and given opportunity to interact with horses, or the way in which children with severe learning difficulties might be taken to a local supermarket to buy ingredients for making a sandwich.

While it is generally recognised that inclusion is important for children's and society's well-being, it is also vital to realise that there remain many people who are not comfortable with this approach. They may be from a previous generation where attitudes towards children with special needs was different or from a different culture where disability is still feared or something to be ashamed of. It is important to realise, therefore, that there is still much work to be done on changing attitudes.

Case study

Attitudes to additional needs

Lutfi is worried about his daughter. He knows that she should be speaking by now and feels that this will reflect badly on him and his family. He is also worried that someone might take his daughter away and that he might not be able to see her. The staff at the nursery have tried to talk to Lutfi and his wife about his daughter, but he kept insisting that she is fine. They have explained that she can be referred to speech therapy and that this will help her, but Lutfi has refused to let her be referred. He is starting to think about keeping her at home instead of sending her to nursery.

1. Why might Lutfi be feeling this way?

2. Explain how staff might need to work with Lutfi in order to reassure him.

3. Why is it important for early years practitioners to promote a positive view of inclusion?

Section 4

The roles and responsibilities of professionals working with children with special educational needs

In practice

You are working in an organisation that runs drop-in sessions for disabled children and their families. You are worried that you will not know how to work with children with learning difficulties and are concerned that you might not have the skills.

By the end of this section you will know how you might support children who have additional needs and understand the importance of establishing good relationships with children and their parents.

Development of personal relationships between children and staff

All children thrive on good relationships with adults. Good relationships are at the heart of effective practice as they mean that you are able to get to know children well and understand their interests and strengths as well as needs. Where relationships with children are strong, many adults will say that the disability, medical condition or special educational need fades into the background as they see the 'person' rather than the diagnosis. Relationships are based on trust, good communication skills and respect.

Getting to know children, enjoying their company and learning about who they are is therefore the starting point. This can take a little time and you may need the help of parents, who will know their child in depth. Parents may, for example, tell you that their child is a fan of a football team or particularly enjoys a certain nursery rhyme. As you get to know a child better you will come to recognise his or her needs more clearly, for example when he or she is becoming frustrated or bored or needs more time. You may also be able to plan more effectively and interpret your observations more effectively.

The importance of a sensitive, non-judgemental approach in dealing with children with special educational needs

You read at the start of this unit (pages 497–8) that there are many stereotypes surrounding disabilities. It is important that you are aware of these as you must monitor your own assumptions. You may, for example, have experience of working with another child who had similar needs. While this experience might be helpful in some respects, it is also important to realise that no two children are the same; each will have their own personality and interests and this requires that you are sensitive and reflective. Observing children and thinking about their responses is therefore useful, especially where a child's communication skills are limited.

Strategies to develop and encourage independence and promote self-esteem

There is a potential emotional and social impact on children who need additional support (see also page 523). A key way in which this impact can be eliminated or at least reduced is by empowering children – independence is linked to self-esteem. The more that children can do for themselves, the more in control they will feel (see also Unit 3, pages 134–42).

Adults can sometimes feel that they need to protect children and may in their way of working take over rather than provide opportunities for independence. They may also reward children for being passive, for example saying 'he's no trouble'. Passivity rather than independence can lead to **learned helplessness**. This is where children have stopped looking for ways of challenging themselves and allow others to do everything for them. This lowers self-esteem and children may even stop 'trying'. This is why it is essential to find ways of helping children to be independent.

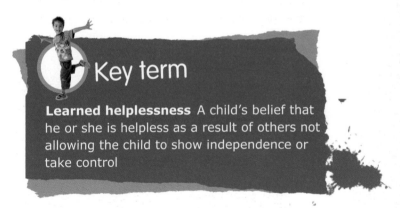

Key term

Learned helplessness A child's belief that he or she is helpless as a result of others not allowing the child to show independence or take control

Independence is about many things. It includes physical and practical skills such as dressing, washing or feeding. These self-care skills are valuable and wherever possible you should encourage children to do as much as they can to help themselves (see also Unit 8, pages 344–6). Independence is also about other skills, such as being able to make choices. Some children may not be able to dress themselves but can choose what they would like to wear, eat or play with. Finding ways of helping children to make decisions and choices may take a little longer than deciding for them, but it provides genuine opportunities for independence. It also important to see that children's behaviour reflects their need for independence.

U14
4

In some instances, uncooperativeness may be a child's only way of establishing their identity and gaining some power over their life. If you identify this reaction in the children you work with, it might be necessary to reflect on practices within the setting and consider whether children are being empowered.

Case study

The importance of promoting independence

Michael uses a wheelchair as an aid for mobility. He is 8 years old. His key worker is absent today and a learner is working with him. The learner has wheeled Michael into the school corridor but has gone off to talk with a friend. Michael is bored and angry. He can hear other children outside in the playground and wants to join them. He cannot move the wheelchair by himself. He calls over to the learner but is told to be quiet. He starts to pull pictures off a wall and then his actions are noticed.

1. How might the learner's actions have affected Michael's self-esteem?

2. How has Michael's frustration affected his behaviour?

3. Explain why this learner does not understand the principle of inclusion.

The practitioner's responsibilities in caring for bodily needs

Some children may have physical care needs that need attending to. It is therefore important to find out from parents how these needs might be best met. The focus should be on attending to these needs in ways that maintains privacy and respect. As with the care of younger children, one of the keys is to be organised so that pads, underwear and toiletries are ready. It is also important for any changes to be carried out in a place that affords some privacy. You have seen that self-esteem is linked to independence; this means that even in tiny ways it is important to help the child do as much as they can. There are also child protection issues involved here and it is important that you carry out any changes of clothing, pads or toileting in line with the procedures of your setting.

How to establish partnerships with parents and carers

It is now recognised that parents form an important role in children's lives. They are often the true 'experts' on their offspring – they know what their child responds well to and they also know their child's past history. The role of parents and carers has been increasingly strengthened through legislation (see page 508) and this means that you should be working in partnership with them. Some parents and carers, however, can feel overawed by professionals; they may not realise that they have rights and that they can contribute.

The SEN Code of Practice 2001 which is used in England (see pages 508–9) outlines seven key principles for practitioners working with parents and carers (see below). These principles can be applied to working with parents and carers in any situation.

Principles of working with parents and carers

1. *Acknowledge and draw on parental knowledge and expertise in relation to their child*
   This principle reminds practitioners that parents and carers will usually be able to share some valuable advice, thoughts and strategies with them.
2. *Focus on the children's strengths as well as areas of additional need*
   This principle is about remembering that children are 'whole people' and not problems that need curing or sorting out. Think about the language you use and how your words might sound if said to you.
3. *Recognise the personal and emotional investment of parents and carers and be aware of their feelings*
   Parents love their children unconditionally and see them as valuable. If you focus only on the child's areas of needs, parents and carers will feel that you do not really know their child.
4. *Ensure that parents and carers understand procedures, are aware of how to access support in preparing their contribution and are given documents to be discussed well before the meeting*
   Since meeting with parents/carers and working through individual learning plans is an essential part of supporting children, this principle is about making parents and carers feel at ease. It is

also about ensuring that parents and carers can properly contribute.

5. *Respect the validity of differing perspectives and seek constructive ways of reconciling different viewpoints*
This principle is about understanding that parents and carers will have and are entitled to their own opinions about what is best for their child.

6. *Respect the differing needs that parents and carers themselves may have, such as a disability or communication and linguistic barriers*
Some parents and carers may have particular needs which may prevent them from contributing. Inclusion means thinking about parents' and carers' needs and looking for ways of meeting them. This might mean translating documents, encouraging parents and carers to bring along a friend or putting up a travel cot so that a baby can be brought along!

7. *Recognise the need for flexibility in the timing and structure of meetings*
This principle reminds practitioners that parents and carers may have jobs, difficulty in transport or other commitments. Partnership with parents and carers means that you look for times which everyone finds convenient, not just you!

Cultures, beliefs and expectations

As well as the principles above, for good partnership working there needs to be respect for the fact that parents and carers may have different ideas from you about what is best for their child. There are many reasons why this may be the case, but sometimes culture can play a part. Parents' and carers' own experiences may also be an influence, for example deaf parents may have strong feelings about whether their child who is also deaf should learn sign language. Parents' and carers' expectations can also be different to those of professionals. For example, a carer's main goal for her child might be toilet training while a teacher may focus on the child being able to enjoy a book.

The needs and rights of individuals, parents, carers and families

There are significant effects on families who have children with special needs. Understanding their needs can help you to build a relationship with them and to support them. Interestingly, few parents and carers want pity or to be cast in the role of hero. Most find that even when under stress they can make time to enjoy and cherish their child. This is an essential point to remember, especially if parents need to have a 'moan'.

It is important when working with parents, carers and families to understand that they may have very individual needs, feelings and attitudes. This means that while you can be aware of some of the major issues that commonly affect parents and carers, you must remember that every family will be different.

Understanding the needs of parents and carers

⇧ **The families of children with special needs will have their own special needs**

Stress on family

The families of children with special needs often have their own special needs. Couples can find that their own relationship is put under enormous stress at times, and it is not uncommon for couples to split up soon or shortly after a child is found to have special needs, especially if they are complex or severe. Many parents of children with special needs find that so much of their time and energy is used in caring for the child that it is hard to find the extra time for each other or for themselves, especially where there are other children in the family.

Social need

Some parents and carers find that having a child with special needs, particularly learning difficulties or emotional and behavioural difficulties, is isolating. Public places can be nightmares to negotiate and finding friends who can cope with the behaviour of the child can be difficult. Most parents and carers find that local support groups give them opportunities to make friends.

Information

Parents and carers can also find it difficult to access information, although this situation is now improving. Legislation means that professionals have to involve parents in decision making (see page 508). Also, the Internet has opened up more opportunities as parents can 'talk' to other parents and search the web for information that is available both in this country and internationally. Parents and carers also need to have information about what will happen 'next' to their child. The future can seem daunting, but it is easier when parents and carers are involved and informed about services and future provision.

Financial issues

Money is another source of worry for most families as in many cases one parent has to give up work in order to care for the child. Places with childminders or in day nurseries for children with special needs are rare, especially if the child has complex needs that require experience or specialised training. This means that the family income is often hit and many families, especially lone parents, find themselves reliant on state benefits.

Effects on siblings

Siblings in some families can also be affected. While there are sometimes some negative effects such as not being able to have as much attention from their parents or not having as many opportunities to socialise or play, there are also some positive effects too. Some siblings are given responsibility, which helps their self-confidence. They may also develop positive and caring relationships.

The rights of parents and carers

You have seen that legislation has strengthened parents' and carers' rights in respect of their involvement in decision making. It is important

that these rights are respected and that parents are informed of their rights. As one parent commented, 'I always felt as if I should feel grateful in some way. It never occurred to me that it was actually my right.'

Settings should also adhere to the spirit of the rights rather than just 'go through the motions'. Below is a list of some of the main rights that parents should have:

→ involvement in Individual Education Plans and settling-in procedures
→ choosing the setting
→ right of appeal
→ assessment of their needs
→ access to provision.

The role of observation and assessment in producing Individual Education Plans in a variety of settings

You have seen that the SEN Code of Practice in England required practitioners to observe children and then, if necessary, draw up an Individual Education Plan, or IEP. This is in essence an action plan.

It is worth noting here, that in some areas, the term Individual Learning Plan or Programme is used instead of Individual Education Plan.

Deciding whether a child needs an IEP

To help decide whether a child needs an IEP, a range of observation techniques can be used. However, the techniques are usually chosen so that information about a specific area of development or behaviour can be gained. It is important that parents are aware that observations and assessments are taking place so that they can become involved.

The following questions can be used to help you think more closely about a child who might need an IEP:

→ In what situations does the child need further support?
→ How does the child respond in these situations?
→ Does the child have any particular interests?
→ What are the child's strengths?
→ Are there any strategies or situations that appear to be helpful?

Creating an IEP

If an IEP is considered necessary, a meeting is organised in which parents and practitioners discuss how best to help the child. Discussion about the child's needs should take place followed by consideration of those targets that might be recorded as a focus for further work with the child (see below).

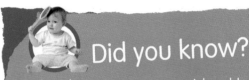

Did you know?

As a learner, you may not be able to see an IEP or be involved in drawing one up because some settings see them as confidential. You might, though, be able to see a sample plan which will give you an idea of how your setting uses them.

People involved in writing the IEP

Once the observations have been carried out, it is important to talk through with the child's parents and carers what has been learned. This is a key feature of drawing up a successful IEP. It is also important that the child's key worker or a practitioner with responsibility for the child is involved. The idea is that these people should be able to tailor the plan of action to best suit the child. The person who should coordinate the creation of the IEP is the Special Educational Needs Coordinator (SENCO), although he or she may not necessarily write it.

⇩ **Example of an Individual Education Plan**

Name Shona
Action
Date of Birth 14/4/00
Area/s of concern Fine motor control
Interests of the child Shona enjoys helping adults
Review Date 15/3/04
Practitioner responsible for implementation Margery Dobbs

Targets to be achieved	Achievement criteria	Possible resources/ techniques	Possible strategies	Ideas for support	Outcome
1 To grasp a small object between finger and thumb	1 To pick up 10 small beads using finger and thumb	1 Sorting activities including rice, buttons and threading beads	1 Make sure items are appealing. Make sure that she gains success	Demonstrate movements. Plenty of praise	
2 To strengthen palmar grasp	2 To squeeze dry a small wet sponge	2 Wringing actions, squeezing sponges	2 Put out sensory materials such as dough, sponges and water in trays	Demonstrate movements and make sure that Shona is praised. Look out for opportunities to practise these movements in the routine e.g. wiping tables	

Parents' contribution Encourage Shona to be more independent at home, e.g. pouring own drinks out of a small jug, serving herself with spoons and helping out with household tasks such as wiping tables.

Parent's signature	Date
Practitioner's signature	Date

Information to be recorded

There is no standard format for IEPs but the following information is usually recorded:

→ the child's name and date of birth
→ the date of the IEP
→ the date and level of support, for example Early Years Action/Plus (see page 509)
→ a brief summary of the child's area of need
→ the child's strengths and interests
→ the targets the plan is to cover
→ how the targets are to be measured
→ the teaching methods and strategies to be adopted
→ the staff who are to be responsible for the implementation of the plan; this might be more than one named person
→ the date the IEP will be reviewed
→ signatures of parents and staff.

Writing the IEP

The IEP should not be a lengthy document. It is important to remember that it is a short-term action plan and is not designed to provide a long-term overview. However, it does help to focus practitioners, parents and carers on short-term targets and priorities that will help the child. Many settings have developed a format so that the information can be fitted onto an A4 sheet of paper. There are also software packages that can be used to write IEPs on computers; however, these need to be carefully evaluated as they may not have been written with very young children in mind. The first pieces of information that are recorded on an IEP, such as the child's name, are straightforward. Other pieces of information require more thought, as detailed below.

Areas of need

This section should simply outline the child's current difficulties. It should be quite short and focused on why the child needs additional or different support. For those children who have many needs, it is important to identify which aspect the IEP will be working on.

Setting targets

As part of the creation of the IEP, some targets are set. These targets allow practitioners and parents to focus their work on developing particular skills in the child. It is important here to note that the targets are not for the child but for the adults working with the child!

Ideally, targets should be small and very achievable. This allows everyone, including the child, to feel a success. Targets are like small stepping stones that will help the child on his or her journey. Each IEP builds on the last; the aim is thus for the child to complete his or her journey little by little. The acronym SMART is used in relation to setting these targets (see also Unit 5, page 231). It is helpful because targets must be:

S – specific
M – measurable
A – achievable
R – relevant
T – timebound

Case study

Individual Education Plans

Shona is 4 years old. She was a premature baby and her physical development is giving her parents and her key worker cause for concern. She sometimes shows signs of frustration during activities and finds it difficult to concentrate. The Special Educational Needs Coordinator and Shona's parents have decided to draw up an IEP that will focus on Shona's fine motor skills. This is because they believe these skills to be the underlying reason for Shona's frustrated behaviour and poor concentration. Shona's parents are keen to play a part at home.

1. Explain why Shona's frustrated behaviour may be linked to her physical development.
2. Why will it be important to choose targets that are manageable?
3. Explain why it is essential that Shona's parents are involved.

Specific	Targets are small steps – break down anything you would like the child to achieve into small skills. For example, if it is felt that it would be helpful for the child to use a pair of scissors, a first target might be to focus on the child being able to hold the scissors correctly. The SEN Code of Practice suggests that IEPs might have three or four targets.
Measurable	To help monitor the effectiveness of the IEP, targets should be measurable. If they are not, it is hard to check that the child has made progress and is ready for the next target. This means that targets have to be specific and also there needs to be a way of observing progress.
Achievable	Targets must be achievable otherwise all involved – the parents, the child and the practitioners – can become despondent and lose motivation. Choosing targets that are relevant is therefore important.
Relevant	Ideally, the targets should concentrate on helping the child rather than the setting. Sometimes parents may have different views about what is relevant, for example they may want their child to achieve a skill that will help the child at home and this is why it is important to work alongside parents.
Timebound	IEPs are short-term action plans. This creates a sense of urgency which means they are less likely to be forgotten. The IEP should state when it will be reviewed. Most early years settings will draw up IEPs every six or eight weeks.

The principles of recording, reporting and record keeping

Recording and record keeping

It is important that observations are ongoing so that any progress or changes to a child's interests can be immediately picked up. This is central to ensuring that Individual Education Plans remain effective. It is also essential in day-to-day planning. Parents should also be involved in record keeping as they see their children in various situations and will interact with them in different ways.

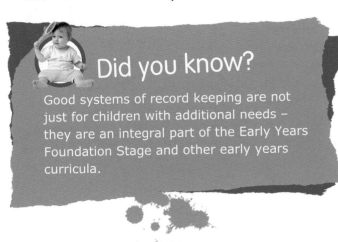

Did you know?

Good systems of record keeping are not just for children with additional needs – they are an integral part of the Early Years Foundation Stage and other early years curricula.

Reporting

As a result of ongoing observations there will be times when information needs to be passed on. It is good practice for parents to be kept informed of their children's progress so staff will usually talk to parents frequently. In addition, you may also report to other professionals who are involved with the child. This might be a speech and language therapist, physiotherapist or educational psychologist. By sharing information with other professionals they may provide you with more support or advice, or if they actively work with the child adapt their programmes. Reporting may take the form of a multi-disciplinary meeting, a written report or, if urgent, a phone call.

The promotion of appropriate behaviour of children with special educational needs

Being able to socialise, feel part of a community and understand how to behave appropriately are important skills for children. Children whose behaviour and social and emotional development are atypical are often 'excluded' by both adults and other children. They may be told by other children

U14
4

that they cannot join in the game or may be made to sit on a different table during an activity by an adult. Sadly, excluding children in this way only creates further difficulties.

Behaviour is often linked to a child's needs

One way of looking at unwanted behaviour is to see it as a reflection of a child's unmet needs. Children who show attention-seeking behaviours are telling you that they need more attention. Children who bite and are aggressive to other children are telling you that they do not have the skills or understanding to play with them. Seeing behaviour in this way is useful: it can indicate what you need to do in order to help the child.

Frustration

Many behaviours especially aggressive acts are signs of frustration. A child might bite another because he cannot tell the other child that he wants that toy too. In the same way, a child may deliberately throw all the pieces of a puzzle on to the floor because she knows she cannot do it. Frustrated behaviours can be helped by looking for ways of helping the child to be as independent as possible and by planning activities that will suit the child.

Boredom

Some children's behaviour is linked to their levels of engagement with an activity. A child who is not enjoying a situation may look for ways of changing it! In the same way, a child who cannot see anything they want to do may go and disrupt another child's game. Good observation of children can provide you with early warning that a child is becoming bored. Look out for signs of restlessness, anxiousness or fidgeting.

Understanding the boundaries

Some children find it hard to remember the boundaries and may not be able to apply a rule from one situation to another. This can be frustrating for staff but it is essential that you are patient and look for ways of reminding children. In the same way, the level of some children's cognitive skills may mean that they do not understand the need to wait or share or do not have an understanding about possessions. It is worth thinking

about ways in which you might remind children to remember the boundaries or, if necessary, create the physical environment that prevents children from being tempted if they find it hard to control their impulses. For example, a child who cuts his and other children's hair might need you to put the scissors out of sight until they are needed.

Attention seeking

Some children crave adult attention. Unfortunately they can learn to get it by showing inappropriate behaviours. It is worth observing children carefully and considering if this is the root cause of their behaviour.

Difficulty in concentrating

Some children may find it difficult to remain at one activity for any length of time; they may require constant stimulation and higher levels of attention, being easily distracted and finding it hard to settle. Observing a child in a situation where they are showing higher levels of concentration can help you to work out how to plan activities that will assist them.

Avoiding using punishment

Punishing children whose behaviour is challenging is rarely helpful. It does not do anything to support the child and if often used can simply create more fixed behaviours. More often than not the behaviours that children show are spontaneous reactions to situations. Much behaviour is linked to a child's difficulty in reasoning or controlling their emotions.

The spider diagram below lists key reasons why children should not be punished.

Strategies that can be useful

There are no definite answers or 'cures' when it comes to working with any child. Good practitioners are able to observe the child, plan ahead and consider what is working. The following general strategies are usually found to be effective.

Think carefully before reacting to unwanted behaviour

Some children learn how to get adults' immediate attention and eye contact for inappropriate behaviours. Sometimes it can be best to ignore inappropriate behaviour especially if you believe that the child is doing something only to gain your attention.

Praise and acknowledgement

This is perhaps the most important strategy to develop. Children who are given frequent positive feedback on their behaviour find it easier to maintain it. Praising children or in some cases giving them something tangible such as a sticker is effective. It is worth working hard to praise and acknowledge children's wanted behaviour while they are showing it. This helps children to learn how to gain adult attention appropriately.

Plan and be pro-active

It is important not to be constantly reacting to children. Plan ahead so that children are busy and have sufficient adult attention, so that they do not need to show inappropriate behaviour.

Think about group size

Some children are able to show appropriate behaviour if they are in small groups or with one other child. Match the group size according to the child's ability to cope.

Think about activities

Children need activities that engage them and are sufficiently challenging. Consider whether the activity is actually causing frustration and is matched to the child's abilities and needs. Look out for multi-sensory activities or those where the child is active.

Routines

Some children need a definite routine in order to cope in a setting; disruptions, however minor, can cause them anxiety and distress. Work with parents and carers beforehand to consider how best to help the child cope with any planned changes.

Observations

Observing children can help you to think about situations in which they are able to show appropriate behaviour. For example, you might think about the circumstances giving rise to the behaviour and opportunities to repeat them. In the same way, it can be helpful to think about triggers for unwanted behaviour. Are there any particular times, situations or groupings that seem to be present?

The skills needed for working with children with language, hearing or visual difficulties or limited attention span

Supporting children's communication and interaction

Some children may have difficulties with communication and interaction. This may include difficulties in communicating their needs or not being able to understand what is happening, which can cause children to feel frustrated and isolated.

Being a language partner

Some children need additional time with an adult in order to boost and develop their language and communication skills. If you are working with children in this way, think of yourself as a language partner. Children learn best when they are enjoying themselves and have a warm relationship with the adult. You may work with one child at a time or have a small group with whom you play games. It is essential that this type of work is fun for the child.

U14

4

Good practice checklist

How to be a good language partner

✓ Avoid taking the child away from what they are doing – consider whether you can be a language partner and play alongside the child.

✓ Make good eye contact with the child.

✓ Choose times when the child is relaxed and not overtired.

✓ Plan activities that are enjoyable and are play-based.

✓ Acknowledge positively children's communication.

✓ Do not correct children's speech – respond by slipping the same words or sentence back into your own speech.

✓ Speak clearly and adjust your language to suit the child.

✓ Be ready to stop before the child's concentration slips.

✓ Use puppets and props to help the child communicate.

⇧ **Being a good language partner can involve using puppets to help the child communicate**

Helping children who are not hearing fully

Many young children have temporary hearing loss (known as conductive hearing loss), especially in the winter months. This is usually caused by a build-up of fluid within the ear and can affect children's speech, especially if they have long bouts of loss. Some children will be given grommets if it is thought that their hearing is being seriously affected. These act as a drainage system within the Eustacian tube and will prevent fluid from building up.

Other children will have been identified with a hearing loss early on in their life and may use a hearing aid. For children using a hearing aid, it is important to find out from the parents about how best to help the child and to learn a little about how the hearing device works. It can also be useful to talk to the sensory impairment team within your area. It is particularly important to check that a child's hearing aid is working and that they are wearing it correctly.

Good practice checklist

Supporting children with hearing impairment

✓ Check that you have the child's attention before talking.

✓ Maintain good eye contact with the child.

✓ Identify the topic of conversation early on, for example point at what you are talking about.

✓ Speak normally but clearly.

✓ Be expressive with your speech and body language.

✓ Make sure that you face into the light so that children who are lip reading can clearly see your face.

✓ Use props, pictures and visual aids to support your speech.

✓ Do not speak extra loudly or put your hand over your face.

✓ Make sure that you know how to check and if necessary change the battery of a hearing device.

Stammering (dysfluency)

Stammering affects the fluency in children's speech and is also known as dysfluency. While many children between the ages of 2 and 3 years will stammer, this is usually temporary. It is often a result of the child knowing what to say and finding it hard to get the words out as quickly as their thinking. For some children, however, stammering becomes more permanent and affects their confidence.

The best way to help children who stammer is to reduce the amount of tension and pressure on them – relaxing will help the child to speak more fluently. Situations which cause the child to feel nervous, excited or tense are therefore likely to cause stammering.

Good practice checklist

Supporting children who stammer

✓ Avoid situations when the focus is on the child, for example circle time.

✓ Do not finish off the child's sentences to 'help' or let other children interrupt him or her.

✓ Reduce the speed at which you talk – this can help the child to relax and speak more slowly.

✓ Make sure that the child feels that you have plenty of time for him or her; sit down and make good eye contact.

✓ Avoid asking direct questions as they can put the child under pressure.

Early speech therapy can be effective for children. This means that adults who notice that stammering in young children is becoming more frequent should follow their setting's procedures in sharing this information with parents.

Alternative and augmentative methods of communication

To help communication and interaction there are both alternative and augmentative communication methods:

→ Alternative methods are ways of communicating without using speech. The best known of these is probably British Sign Language.

→ Augmentative methods are ones that are used alongside speech, often to help the child make sense of what is being said.

The decision to use alternative and augmentative methods of communication is often taken by speech therapists and other specialists alongside parents. Over the past few years the range of methods has increased and technology is increasingly being used. Voice simulation has, for example, meant that children can press a picture or type and have 'their voice' heard. In the same way, for children who find it hard to write, voice recognition can put their words into writing.

Visual systems

Some children will need visual cues in order to make sense of language. If the child you are working with uses a system of visual communication, it is important that you spend time learning how to use it quickly and fluently.

Picture representations

Some children benefit from using pictures to supplement communication. You may show a child a picture of an apron and at the same time say the word so that the child knows that he needs to get his apron. Many settings use visual timetables as a way of helping children understand what is happening and what is going to happen.

U14

4

⇧ **Picture representations can be used to help children with communication difficulties**

Picture Exchange Communication System (PECS)

This system is based on pictures – the child takes and receives pictures and in this way learns about interaction. The PECS system therefore helps children to understand the meaning of words as well as the way in which communication is a shared, two-way process.

Did you know?

PECS was originally developed to help young children with autism learn how to initiate requests and communicate their needs.

PECS is an augmentative method as speech is still used. It is important that this system is not used instead of language and that children are encouraged to vocalise alongside it.

Find out!

You can find out more about the Picture Exchange Communication System by visiting the following website: www.pecs. org.uk

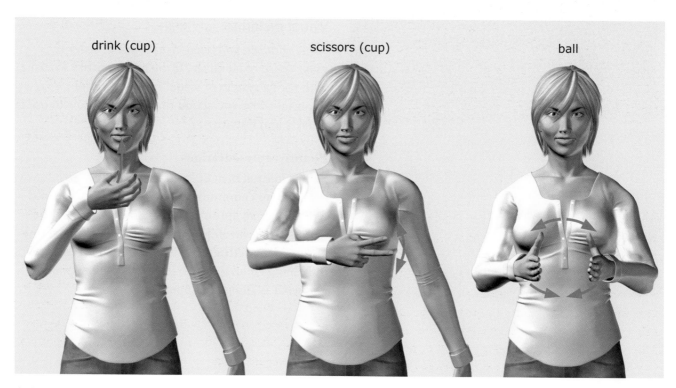

drink (cup)   scissors (cup)   ball

⇧ **Some common Makaton signs**

Sign representations

Some children's cognitive development is the reason why they find it hard to talk and communicate.

Babies at first learn about language by seeing the object you are talking about at the same time as hearing the word, for example pointing to a cat and saying 'cat'. The child then remembers the word and so eventually does not need the cat to be around to know what the word means. For some children, sounds alone are not enough and they need to have their language supported by signs. A common sign system is Makaton (see opposite). Makaton helps children link the word to an action or object so is easier for them to understand. Makaton is not a language in itself, but a tool to help language. (It is important not to confuse Makaton with British Sign Language which is not used for the same purpose.)

British Sign Language

British Sign Language is an alternative form of communication. It is a complete language and is used instead of speech. It is important to realise that users of sign language do not have learning difficulties. Most users have significant hearing loss and so need a different way of talking.

Find out!

To learn about British Sign Language visit the following interactive website: www.british-sign.co.uk

Supporting children's cognition and learning

How and why some children learn more easily than others is still not fully understood, because the way in which the brain takes in and handles information is quite complex. Some children may be good at some types of learning and thinking and have weaknesses in others. In other cases, children's difficulty in learning is also linked to their language development, because language and thought are closely connected (see also Unit 2, pages 43–7).

Helping children to concentrate

Some children have difficulties in concentrating and this will mean that you have to adapt the way in which you work to meet their needs.

Good practice checklist

Helping children to concentrate

✓ Base learning on activities that already appeal to the child.

✓ Be ready to change activities before the child's attention wanes.

✓ Look for activities that keep children active.

✓ Avoid activities where children are expected to wait or sit for periods of time.

✓ Give simple and clear instructions, one at a time.

✓ Observe the child and notice what holds his or her attention.

✓ Use props and visual aids.

Using a multi-sensory approach

The brain takes in information through the five senses. Many children who have difficulties in learning will therefore be helped if you present information in a more sensory way. Counting by squashing down sandcastles and drawing letter shapes in shaving foam are examples of activities that involve the child in doing, touching and seeing while also learning.

Consolidation

Children may need to repeat an activity several times before they are completely confident. They may also benefit from the same idea being presented in a variety of ways. This is called consolidation. You may, for example, play the same game several times but change one feature each time. It is important not to get frustrated if a child can do something on one day but finds it hard on another day – this is often a pattern of learning.

U14
4

Timing

Some children are able to respond better at certain times of the day or even in the week. This information can be gained by talking to parents or by observing the child. It is also important to take note of the length of activities and whether the child's concentration is waning. Look out for signs such as a child yawning, fidgeting or becoming slower to respond. Some behaviour will show you that you need to end the activity; it is important to recognise that this means that the child has had enough.

Success

Enjoyment is a key to learning, so it is important to make sure that children feel some success or satisfaction. Children who remember doing well and having a pleasurable time are more likely to want to return to the activity another day. Sometimes it is worth ending an activity when the child is enjoying it and is feeling successful – carrying on beyond this point may mean that the child begins to lose their focus (see timing above). Some children may also need a reminder of their success. You might, for example, take a photograph to remind them of how well they did or write a note in their home book so that their parents can comment. You could also give children a reward, such as a sticker, for their success, but wherever possible you should aim to make the activity itself the reward.

⇧ **Sensory activities, laughter and fun help children remember activities**

Helping children remember

To learn something effectively means having a good memory of it. One way in which you can help children learn is to look for ways of making activities memorable. This might involve using a puppet or looking for activities that are new or surprising. It can also help children if they see a photograph of themselves later on.

Sensory activities are a good way of making activities memorable. Try looking for a tactile or physical approach when presenting new information. It is also important to realise that laughter and fun help children remember.

The role of specialist professionals and how to work in a team with other professionals

Most families and children with special needs will gain support from some of the many different agencies and professionals available. Before 1994 many parents became frustrated as there seemed to be little communication between the various professionals and agencies. This meant that time was wasted in giving children the support they needed. The SEN Code of Practice 1994 improved this aspect of supporting families as it stressed the importance of inter-team collaboration. The Every Child Matters programme and the current SEN Code of Practice (2001) both continue to stress the importance of collaborative approaches. Increasingly, teams of professionals involved in delivering services to children and their families work out of the same centre. This might mean, for example, that a child will go to a nursery where there is also a speech and language therapist, physiotherapist and educational psychologist on site.

An outline of the roles of different professionals and agencies is given below.

SENCO (Special Educational Needs Coordinator)

The role of the SENCO is now well established within settings. This is person is responsible for coordinating the policies and liaising with other professionals (see also pages 508–9).

Key worker

It is increasingly understood that one person needs to develop a strong and individual relationship with a child and their parents. The key worker will spend time with the child and will be the person who in practice works alongside the child and gets to know their strengths and interests (see also Unit 18, page 595). Individual education plans will be implemented by the child's key worker. In many schools, the child's key worker will also be the teacher or classroom assistant.

Educational psychologists

Educational psychologists consider how children learn so are used to help identify learning difficulties in children. They visit schools and settings regularly and work alongside parents and professionals in the setting. They draw up individual educational programmes and give guidance to staff as to how they can be implemented. Where a child needs a statement or has a statement, educational psychologists are involved in the assessments and drawing up of the statements.

Physiotherapists

A physiotherapist helps to identify a child's main physical problems while working alongside other professionals and parents. They often devise a programme of exercises or treatments which either they administer themselves or teach parents and others how to administer.

Find out!

Find out more about the Portage service, and whether there is a Portage service in your local area, by visiting the following website: www.portage.org.uk

Speech and language therapists

Speech and language therapists work with children who have some difficulties with their language. They identify the causes of the problems as well as devise speech and language programmes. These may include exercises, advice for parents, early years teachers and other professionals. The range of children they work with can be quite wide and includes children with cleft palate, lisp and children who are autistic.

Community paediatricians

Paediatricians are mainly based in hospitals and clinics. They have specialised training in children's medicine and children are referred to them via their family doctor for diagnosis. They make regular assessments of children's progress and medical needs. They are able to refer children to other health services such as speech and language therapy and dieticians.

Community nurses

In some areas, community nurses visit schools and settings to help provide advice and support. They may undertake general health promotion work with parents or they may work with particular children and their families. Integrating health and education is a major focus of the Every Child Matters programme so some early years centres will have a community nurse based at the centre.

Family doctor (general practitioner)

The family doctor, or GP, has general training in medicine. GPs form part of the community health team and act as a base for a child's ongoing medical treatment and notes. The family doctor is often the person who referred the child to a paediatrician when impairment was suspected.

Case study

Building skills

Oliver is 3 years old. His mother and the Portage worker, a trained volunteer who visits the home each week to help his mother develop Oliver's skills, have decided to work on Oliver's feeding skills. The aim for this week is to get Oliver to put his fingers round a spoon. Three times a day his mother will enclose his fingers round a spoon at meal times. She will praise him during this process.

1. Why will Oliver benefit from breaking the task of feeding into small steps?
2. Explain why it is helpful that Oliver's mother is involved in the programme.

U14
4

Child psychologists, psychiatrists and psychotherapists

There are a range of professionals who support children who may show emotional and behavioural difficulties.

→ *Child psychiatrist.* Children who are showing depression or emotional difficulties may be referred to a child psychiatrist. A child psychiatrist has been trained as a doctor specialising in mental health and is able to prescribe medication as well as being able to consider the underlying issues behind a child's emotional state.

→ *Child psychologist.* A child psychologist looks at a child's development and learning in a similar way to an educational psychologist. The main difference between their roles is that a child psychologist may support children in a range of different settings rather than just in an educational context.

→ *Child psychotherapist.* A child psychotherapist will work with children who are showing emotional distress by talking through their experiences with them and helping the child to explore these.

→ *Play therapist.* A play therapist helps children to explore trauma or experiences through the medium of play. This can be particularly effective for young children who may not have the language to express their feelings and thoughts as well as for children who may subconsciously be repressing trauma.

Educational welfare officer/educational social worker

The main function of these professionals is to liaise between home and families in cases where school attendance is infrequent. (It is an offence for children not to be in some sort of full-time educational provision.) Their role is particularly helpful in cases where children are refusing to attend school (known as 'school refusal'). They are often able to work alongside parents, the child and other professionals to make sure that children's needs are being met.

Special needs support teacher

These teachers travel between schools or visit children in their homes or in pre-school settings. They are able to help a wide range of children and are often seen as useful sources of support and guidance. Special needs support teachers tend to build up a good relationship with the child and may even work with children when they are admitted to hospital.

Classroom assistant/learning support assistant

There are many variations on the title used for classroom assistants. Their main purpose is to support an individual child or group of children within a classroom under the direction of the classroom teacher. They may also be responsible for carrying out the activities listed in the individual education plan as well as recording the child's progress. Most classroom teachers, SENCOs and special needs assistants work closely together and draw up the individual education plan.

Social worker

The majority of social workers are employed by the local authority, although some are employed by voluntary organisations. They are generally deployed in teams according to specialist areas, for example social workers may be involved in caring for older clients, adoption or fostering work. Children with special needs often have an assigned social worker as they are seen as potentially vulnerable. Social workers can provide guidance and advice as well as practical support for families and as such can be welcome visitors. Many social workers also have a liaison role and will, for example, organise respite care.

Respite carers

Respite carers look after children for short periods of time so that their parents can have some time out. Respite care may be for a few hours, a weekend or for a week. Respite carers may look after the child in their own home or may work in a residential centre.

Working in a team with other professionals

You have seen that a variety of professionals provide support for children and their families. Working well with other professionals in order to meet the needs of the children in your care is a requirement of law but also has practical implications. When professionals work together, share information and have contact, a better service can be provided. It prevents situations where parents have to repeat the same information to many different people or where provision is duplicated or missed out. This means that you need to find out who else supports the child that you are working with.

In some cases, other professionals will give you advice about how best to work with children and it will be important to implement programmes and provide feedback.

Good practice checklist

Working with other professionals

✓ Find out which professionals are involved in supporting the child and their family.

✓ Find out the ways in which they support the child and their family.

✓ Keep in regular contact if this is appropriate.

✓ Share information where permission has been granted by parents.

✓ Attend and be well prepared for multi-disciplinary meetings.

The emotional needs of staff

Being with children is known to be a hard and demanding job. It is also a rewarding one, especially when you feel you are making a difference. Sometimes meeting the needs of children can be emotionally draining, especially in situations when a child's behaviour needs to be managed.

It is important to recognise if you or someone else working with a child is finding it stressful. This is important as all children have the right to be treated professionally and appropriately regardless of their behaviour or needs. In some situations, all that is needed is a five-minute break away from the child; this will provide a useful opportunity to reflect. In other situations, advice and guidance should be sought from the line manager or a senior member of staff.

The support available for practitioners

Working with children who have a range of difficulties can be tiring and in some cases emotionally draining, especially where children have life-threatening or life-limiting conditions. It is therefore important to be aware that you may need support in order to cope well. The type of support available tends to depend on the setting that you are in and the provision in your local area. If you feel that you are not coping or that there is an issue you are finding hard to deal with, you should talk to your line manager who should have a knowledge of what is available locally.

Getting ready for assessment

Below are some questions that you can use to check your understanding and recall of this unit.

1. Contrast two models of disability and explain how each may affect practice.

2. Analyse a range of factors that might affect the development of children and their ability to learn.

3. Give three examples of how legislation affects the delivery of services to children with additional needs and their families.

4. Describe the role of an Individual Education Plan in supporting children with additional needs.

5. Explain the roles of three different professionals who may work alongside practitioners to support children.

Unit 16

Developing children's (3–8 years) communication, language and literacy skills

In this unit you will learn:

1. The stages of development of children's communication, language and literacy aged from 3 to 8 years

2. How to help children develop their communication, language and literacy skills

3. The role of the adult in supporting communication, language and literacy

The stages of development of children's communication, language and literacy aged from 3 to 8 years

In practice

Georgina is 4 years old. She loves being in the Reception class. Her mother gets the impression that she plays all the time. She is a little disappointed because she thought that Georgina would be reading and writing fairly well by now. Instead she seems to produce a lot of 'scribble' which her teacher calls mark making.

By the end of this section you will know about the stages of language and literacy development and the teaching methods, techniques and resources that are used to support children as well as the government's Primary Framework for literacy in England.

The areas of language and literacy

It is useful to understand the skills required in language and literacy (see table below). To an extent these skills are fairly interlinked and while it is possible for children to develop one without another, this is fairly unusual. This means that most children who are talking are also able to listen and that a child who is able to write is likely to be able to read.

Non-verbal communication

Non-verbal communication is about the signals that your body gives out to others, either consciously or unconsciously. Good levels of non-verbal communication are essential for interpersonal situations, for example listening to a friend or making a good impression at interview. Effective communicators are able to understand others' non-verbal communication and are able to adapt, control or reflect on their own. Note that non-verbal communication can also refer to signing, which some children will use as a language (see also Unit 14, page 529).

Speaking

Learning to speak means using words to communicate with others. To do this, children need to put words in the right order, use grammar and know what words mean. Good speakers can also judge the effect of their words on others and can adapt their speaking to suit a situation, for example explaining how to make a snowball is different from chatting to a friend.

Listening

Listening is an active skill – it is more than just hearing. Listening requires concentration and the cognitive skills of memory. Good listeners are able to concentrate and think about what they are listening to and how it links to what they already know. Good listeners are also able to analyse what is being said and why as well as any emotions that are present.

⇩ **Language and literacy skills for children to master**

Area of language and literacy	Skills required
Non-verbal communication	• Recognise others' feelings from their facial expressions, posture and gestures • Understand the impact on others of facial expressions, posture and gestures • Adapt non-verbal communication to suit social situation
Speaking	• Use talk to help organise personal thinking, e.g. talking to yourself • Use grammar correctly and have a wide vocabulary • Recognise the effect of words on other people • Be able to tailor speech according to the situation and group size
Listening	• Being able to listen to others • Recognise emotions in others' tone of voice • Make connections between new information and existing knowledge • Think about what has been said and its intended meaning • Remember spoken information
Reading	• Decode words fluently and quickly • Understand what the print means once it has been decoded • Analyse and reflect on the writer's purpose
Writing	• Tailor writing to suit the audience or the purpose, e.g. shopping lists, reports • Use language and vocabulary to express ideas and feelings • Structure texts so they are logical and well presented • Be able to use handwriting, typing and ICT • Use punctuation and spelling so that others can understand the writing

Reading

Learning to read requires that children can decode words and sentences, but also that they can understand their meaning. Good readers also know about how to use a book or website well, for example the index and content page. They are also able to judge which texts will be the most useful or pleasurable for them.

Writing

Writing requires that children first have reasonable spoken language as they need to be able to 'hear' words and sentences. They also need to know how to sequence and organise what they want to communicate. As text needs to appear on either screen or paper, children have to master the tools of writing, which are handwriting, typing or dictation. If they use handwriting or typing as tools, they also need to learn the conventions of writing so that their words will be understandable to others.

The principle characteristics of the stages of development of communication, language and literacy

It is useful to gain an understanding of the way in which most children learn to speak and listen and later to read and write.

Speaking and listening

The process of learning to speak and listen begins almost before birth as the unborn baby is able to hear music and the sound of the mother's voice. In Unit 2 you looked at the sequence and stages of language (see pages 44–6) and saw that language development has two distinct stages: a pre-linguistic and a linguistic stage.

➜ The pre-linguistic stage is marked by the way in which the baby learns about communication, the meaning of some words and the exploration of sounds, patterns and tones. This stage seems to be fundamental in later language learning, even though the baby will not be 'talking'.

➜ The arrival of speech takes the child into the linguistic stage. In this stage, children will gradually become fluent users of language.

Some of the expected milestones in the development of speaking and listening skills are described below. It is important to have an awareness of these milestones, as if a child is not reaching them it may indicate that he or she requires extra support.

Further development of speaking and listening

While you have seen that children by 3 years are fairly fluent users of language, further development is still important. Cognitive as well as social and emotional development is closely linked to the level of language use. The acquisition of higher level language skills tends to be a more individual journey and so one in which it is hard to link developmental milestones with age. Interestingly, in terms of building vocabulary there is a strong link to the amount of reading that a child does. As well as vocabulary, children also need to learn to use their language to assist in their thinking. They need to be able to explain their thoughts and use language to help reason and problem solve. The spider diagram below shows some ways in which speaking and listening skills continue to develop.

Development of vocabulary, e.g. for concepts, technical words, description

Using language to explain thinking and actions

Listening to others to gain information

Further development of speaking and listening skills

Using language for self-direction and organisation

Using language to persuade and negotiate

Using language in different social situations e.g. pairs, groups

Listening to understand others' actions, feelings and thoughts

Reading and writing

In Section 2 of this unit you will look at the stages of development of reading and writing skills (see pages 545–53).

As with speech it is interesting that there is a period in which children do not read or write but are learning some of the background skills. This is known as pre-reading and pre-writing and these stages are similar in nature to the pre-linguistic stage. Supporting children in these stages is important until they are ready for more formal learning at 4 to 5 years of age. As speech is linked to reading and writing it should be a major focus in pre-reading and pre-writing. Note that in most other countries these stages are more extended as formal reading and writing begins when children are 6 or 7 years old (see also Unit 7, page 283). The table below shows some of the skills that young children acquire in these stages.

Skills acquired by children during the pre-reading and pre-writing stages

Pre-reading skills	Pre-writing skills
• Spoken language including rhymes	• Spoken language including rhymes
• Handling books	• Wide range of mark making and drawing with a variety of materials
• Noticing print	• Using marks for communication
• Retelling stories	• Gross motor arm movements
• Using and recognising shapes and patterns	• Fine motor movements
• Recognising whole words that have a particular meaning, e.g. names	• Hand–eye coordination
	• Pencil grip

The stages of development of reading and writing skills

From the pre-reading and writing stages, children go on to learn how to read and write (see also Section 2, pages 545–53). A feature of both of these stages is that they are fairly long. Most children will not be fluently reading until at least 7 years old while fluent writing, which is usually dependent on reading, will take a further few years.

The speed at which children gain fluency is dependent on their level of spoken language. Spoken language is important as once a child has decoded a word when reading it has meaning for them. In writing, children need to hear the words in their head first so they can then write them down.

As well as spoken language levels, children also have to be motivated and confident in their abilities. This means that they are more likely to read and write for pleasure rather than just when directed.

Find out!

It has been argued that the increase in media games and television programmes for children has led to a decline in reading. Others believe that the Literacy hour is to blame. Read more about this debate by visiting the website of the National Literacy Trust: www.literacytrust.org.uk

National and local frameworks and policies for communication, language and literacy

Language and literacy are important life skills – children need to acquire these in order to gain qualifications and manage in many everyday aspects of life. In addition, language levels are linked to children's behaviour, as you saw in Unit 14 (page 503). This means that language and literacy is of major interest to education policy in England. This has resulted in the development of a Literacy strategy.

The National Literacy Strategy in England

The original strategy introduced a Literacy hour into primary classrooms but did not include speaking and listening. In the autumn of 2006 a new strategy was developed which includes and emphasises the role of speaking and listening. It also encourages teachers to be more flexible with the way in which they might incorporate language and literacy across the curriculum.

It is important that you use the National Literacy Strategy if you are working with children in English schools from Reception to Year 6. The primary strategy incorporates outcomes from the Early Years Foundation Stage.

Structure of the Literacy framework

The literacy framework divides speaking, listening, reading and writing into 12 different strands. Objectives for each year group are then provided for each of the strands. The headings for each of the strands are shown below.

Speaking and listening:

1. Speaking
2. Listening and responding
3. Group discussion and interaction
4. Drama

Reading and writing

5. Word recognition
6. Word structure and spelling
7. Understanding and interpreting texts
8. Engaging and responding to texts
9. Creating and shaping texts
10. Text structure and organisation
11. Sentence structure and punctuation
12. Presentation

In order to help teachers plan for their year group, the Department of Education and Skills has produced resources. These are available on DVD and via their website (www.standards.dfes.gov.uk/primaryframeworks/literacy). The suggestion is that planning is divided into blocks of time and according to three major themes: Narrative, Non-fiction and Poetry. If you work in a school it will be important to find out how the teacher is planning and whether they are using the materials that are provided. Note that teachers are free to devise their own systems and ways of planning for literacy.

Early Years Foundation Stage

While the primary framework for literacy incorporates the final year of the Foundation Stage (Reception year), it is important to understand the structure of the EYFS in relation to language and literacy.

The EYFS covers children from birth through to the end of the Reception year. It is divided into six areas of learning (see also Unit 7, page 301). One of these areas is Communication, Language and Literacy; you may sometimes see this written as CLL in settings' planning. Communication, Language and Literacy is subdivided into six aspects of learning. For each of the six aspects, there are early learning goals. Most children are expected to reach these goals by the end of the Reception year. The early learning goals are included in the table opposite.

Local frameworks for language and literacy

While most schools in England will follow the primary framework for literacy, some nurseries and pre-schools may use guidance given by local early years advisers. In some areas these have been devised with the support of speech and language teams and they are often tailored to help settings support children's spoken language. This means you might find that alongside the framework or the EYFS, additional materials or ways of planning are used.

Policies and procedures within a variety of settings which support the development of communication, language and literacy skills

In order to show how they intend to implement the Early Years Foundation Stage curriculum and the National Curriculum, schools in England must develop policies on language and literacy. Normally, a teacher within the school will have responsibility for developing the language and literacy policy for the school. Policies usually contain the outline of the aims of language and literacy teaching for within the school and consider the resources, methods and training that will be used to support each year group; an example of part of a literacy policy from a school is shown overleaf. In addition, schools may also have procedures for record keeping, lending resources for parents and for identifying children who will need additional support. If you are working with a school setting, you may therefore need to look at the language and literacy policy that has been developed.

Aspect of learning	Early learning goals
Language for communication	• Sustain attentive listening, responding to what they have heard with relevant comments, questions or actions • Listen with enjoyment, and respond to stories, songs and other music, rhymes and poems and make up their own stories, songs, rhymes and poems • Extend vocabulary, exploring the meanings and sounds of new words • Speak clearly and audibly with confidence and control and show awareness of the listener
Language for thinking	• Use language to imagine and recreate roles and experiences • Use talk to organise, sequence and clarify thinking, ideas, feelings and events
Linking sounds and letters	• Hear and say sounds in words in the order in which they occur • Link sound to letters, naming and sounding the letters of the alphabet • Use their phonic knowledge to write simple regular words and make phonetic attempts at more complex words
Reading	• Explore and experiment with sounds, words and texts • Retell narratives in the correct sequence, drawing on language patterns of stories • Read a range of familiar and common words and simple sentences independently • Know that print carries meaning and, in English, is read from left to right and top to bottom • Show an understanding of the elements of stories, such as main character, sequence of events and openings, and how information can be found in non-fiction texts to answer questions about where, who, why and how
Writing	• Use their phonic knowledge to write simple regular words and make phonetically plausible attempts at more complex words • Attempt writing for different purposes, using features of different forms such as lists, stories and instructions • Write their own name and other things such as labels and captions, and begin to form simple sentences, sometimes using punctuation
Handwriting	• Use a pencil and hold it effectively to form recognisable letters, most of which are correctly formed

The need for policies and procedures within the pre-school and nursery settings is much less, so most pre-schools and nurseries address this curriculum area within their long-term planning and the prospectus that is given to parents.

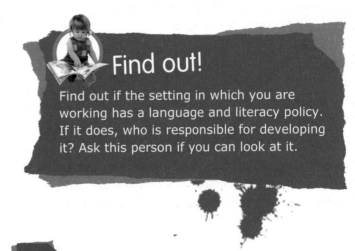

Find out!

Find out if the setting in which you are working has a language and literacy policy. If it does, who is responsible for developing it? Ask this person if you can look at it.

U16

1

BEECH HILL PRIMARY SCHOOL

Communication and literacy policy (May 2007)

Introduction

The skills of communication and literacy are essential for all children to develop in order that they can achieve both academically and socially. They are skills for life and our aim is that we will provide both the teaching and the opportunities for children to acquire them to the highest possible level.

Aims and objectives

- To ensure that each child in the school is given sufficient support in order to read, write, speak and listen fluently
- To provide a learning environment and curriculum that provides opportunities for children to practise their communication and literacy skills
- To assess all children's progress in communication and literacy and to provide appropriate support for children who may require additional help
- To work in partnership with parents in recognition of their contribution to their children's communication and literacy skills

Teaching and learning

The following strategies will be used to develop children's communication and literacy:
- Role modelling of all skills
- Focused teaching of individuals, pairs and groups
- Opportunities for children to apply their skills to 'real' tasks as appropriate, e.g. production of a newsletter, reporting to school council
- Regular and sensitive feedback to children about their work
- Opportunities for children to use communication and literacy skills outside of lessons e.g. paper and writing tools available at break times, play walkie-talkies
- Regular opportunities for reading to teachers, peers and parents and other adults
- Regular story times and circle times

⇧ **Part of a literacy policy from a school**

How to obtain information about individual children's progress and plan appropriate activities in a variety of settings

Every setting will have a system of recording children's individual progress in language and literacy. Children in the Early Years Foundation Stage will be making progress towards the early learning goals and records will be kept by staff as to their progress. Children in Key Stages 1 and 2 will also be individually assessed. Some assessment will be ongoing with teachers making notes, but reading and writing tests are also used.

Finding out about a child's progress is important if you are planning activities, although detailed information may not be available if you are a learner. This is because children and their parents have a right to confidentiality and while this information is available for staff, it might not be considered appropriate to give to a learner. This means that you might have to rely on observing the child before you plan for them. The table opposite lists some points that you might like to consider when observing individual children.

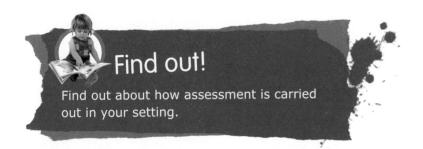

Find out about how assessment is carried out in your setting.

Considerations when observing individual children's progress in communication, language and literacy

Speaking	• How does this child's speech compare to others of a similar age? • How clear is the child's speech? • Is speech grammatically correct and fluent? • Are there any sounds that the child has difficulty with? • Is the child a confident speaker? • How much encouragement does the child need to talk? • Is the child using talk to organise and self-direct? • Can the child use talk to explain their thoughts and reasoning? • Is the child able to use talk to negotiate and play with other children?
Listening	• Does the child make eye contact with you in conversation? • Does the child find it easy to follow simple instructions? • How easy does the child find it to sit and listen to a simple story for five minutes? • Does the child talk aloud during group or story times? (Common in children under 6 years) • How easy does the child find it to listen to other children? (Difficult for children under 5 years) • How well does the child recall information later?
Reading	• How much does the child appear to enjoy reading? • Does the child enjoy looking at books alone? • Is the child able to use the pictures to assist them in decoding? • Can the child recognise some words? • Does the child use initial sounds to attempt words? • Does the child break words down in order to decode them? • Is the child putting expression into reading? • Can the child read 'internally' rather than have to read aloud?
Writing	• Does the child look relaxed when writing or mark making? • Is the child trying to use mark making in order to write rather than draw? • Are any letters legible? • Which letters are correctly formed? • How easy does the child find the physical task of writing? • How effective is the child's pencil grip? • Can the child write any recognisable words? • Does the child use their knowledge of sounds to attempt words? • Is the child starting to use punctuation? • How much of what the child wants to say can he or she write down?

U16

1

Section 2

How to help children develop their communication, language and literacy skills

In practice

You have been asked by the manager in your setting to think of some activities that will support the children with their emergent writing. From observing the children you have seen that many of them can make writing-like marks on the page, but you do not know what 'emergent writing' means nor how to help the children with this.

By the end of this section you will understand what emergent writing is and how to support children through different activities to develop their communication, language and literacy skills.

The stages of development of reading and writing skills

The development of reading

The development of reading can be linked to the method used (see pages 558–60), but some broad stages can be identified.

Knowledge about books

The starting point is for children to know about books. This can begin during the first year of life. Many babies are able to point to pictures in books and toddlers can often turn pages and 'tell' a story. It is essential that children have experience of handling books and have opportunities to enjoy them.

Print carries meaning

Once children know how to handle books they then learn that print runs from left to right in English and that each block of letters is a word. Children can learn this if adults point to words as they read them and if they develop some favourite texts. Children also start to recognise some key words such as their name, a supermarket or a favourite character. They learn these as whole words.

Symbols and sounds

Children also need to learn about shapes of letters and about how they make sounds individually as in 'a' and when put together 'ea'. Some children seem to understand this relationship easily and barely need teaching, while for others this is much harder to grasp.

Reading for meaning

When children can do a little decoding they need to learn to read for meaning. Once they start to do this they can read much more quickly as they will sometimes be able to predict the next word. This comes with practice and is why children at first need books with good illustrations – the illustrations help them to understand what is happening.

Fluency

Most children start to sound fluent in their reading by 7 or 8 years of age. They will, however, need more practice to become fast readers. A turning point is when children are able to read in their head and no longer need to read aloud. To reach this point children need to be motivated and have confidence. It is also important that they are given or choose books that are within their reading capabilities; books that are too difficult or long can dishearten children.

The development of writing

Learning to write is a complex task and is linked to children's reading and speech.

Mark making

The starting point for writing is mark making. Mark making helps children to learn to control a pencil and link the idea that thoughts, feelings and ideas can be recorded. Early mark making can be very experimental, with young children trying out rotational marks and vertical marks. Early mark making is also linked to drawing and painting. Mark making can take place using a range of materials, with sensory materials such as water, paint and sand being especially popular. Some adults dismiss early mark making as just scribble but this is not so. Children are learning some fundamental attitudes towards recording and this needs to be encouraged.

Emergent writing

The term emergent writing is used to describe children's attempts to make marks that have meaning. Most children will be doing some emergent writing from 3 years of age and this will continue until the end of the Reception year. As with mark making, this is an extremely important stage in the development of writing. With encouragement, children's emergent writing becomes more sophisticated and, little by little, their early shapes start to transform into letters and then words. By the end of the Reception year, most children can write their name and a few key words that are of interest to them, and are trying when writing to think about the initial sounds. It is important that adults support rather than intervene during this stage of writing. Retaining children's confidence is key as otherwise they start to produce less and less.

⇧ **Example of emergent writing**

First words

The first word that most children write is their name. This is because their name is one of the first words that children can recognise or read. Most children are able to write their name at around 4 years if they have had good experiences of mark making and opportunities for emergent writing. (They will, of course, also need to be familiar with their name.)

Once children have written their first words they continue to use emergent writing for some time afterwards. This is because writing and reading are interconnected. Once children have gone beyond the mark making stage, they start by reading and once reading is established they make good progress in writing.

⇧ **Writing own name**

Initial letters

Once children begin to associate letters with sounds and are familiar with them, they begin to use them in their writing. At first children put down the first or initial sound in the word as they attempt to write and then put down others that they know or enjoy writing. The letters in a child's own name figure quite a lot at this point!

Whole words

From initial sounds, children start to write short words that they can spell out easily such as 'c-u-p' and words that are used frequently such as 'like' and 'the'. This is a delicate stage in children's writing as too much pressure can cause them to lose confidence. As they learn to read, they also become aware that their spelling is not always correct as they can see the difference. This can again cause some children to lose confidence, resulting in them limiting the amount of writing or only writing down words they are sure they can spell. This can have the result of reducing the quality or quantity of what they want to 'say' in writing.

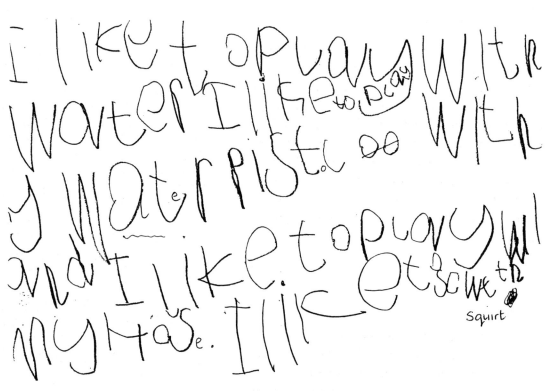

⇧ **Writing simple words**

Learning the conventions of writing

Once children start to write more fluently, they can begin the process of learning about punctuation and other conventions in writing such as capital letters and speech marks. It is helpful if children have had plenty of experience of telling stories so they can 'hear' the rise and fall of intonation that usually marks things such as questions or the end of a sentence.

While learning the conventions of writing is important, it is essential to remember that writing is far more than this. Good writers have something to say and enjoy words. At this point in the development of writing there may be some children who find spelling, punctuation and the physical process of writing difficult. For these children it can be helpful to find ways of scribing for them, for example voice-activated writing programmes or allowing them to dictate so they can still put their words into print.

Handwriting

Handwriting is a tool for writing. It is important to make this distinction because a child can have lovely handwriting but may not be good at actually writing. There are other tools that can be used for writing including typing, texting and dictation. Handwriting has been the traditional tool that children learn to use first of all, but as they become older they are likely to use a computer.

Handwriting requires good hand–eye coordination, a firm but relaxed hand and a tripod pencil grasp. All of these will develop over time and it is not until most children reach 6 or 7 years of age that they will find the physical process of writing easy. This is one of the reasons why other countries do not start formal writing until children reach this age. To help with later handwriting, children need plenty of activities which build fine motor control such as building with blocks, threading and everyday activities such as pouring out drinks.

How to use constructive feedback to support children

One of the main ways in which you can encourage children's reading and writing is by being positive with them. Learning to read and write is partly about confidence and motivation so it is important that you consider this first when providing feedback to children. Constructive feedback needs to be personalised as every child will be at a slightly different stage and will have different needs. Below are some of the points that you will need to think about when giving feedback.

Consider the confidence level of the child

It is important to think about the level of confidence that a child has when providing feedback. Children need confidence in order to succeed so reflecting on how confident a child is will be extremely important. With some children who are lacking in confidence it is often sensible just to praise rather than to point out anything that needs correction. Where a child is confident you will be able to make a point directly (but still sensitively) about their reading or writing. It is often a good idea to let them know that other children and maybe even adults also make similar mistakes.

Think about it

Look at the two conversations below. Which one do you feel will be more effective in maintaining the child's confidence and supporting their learning? Why?

Conversation A:
Child: I have finished now.
Adult: Right, let me see it.
Adult (underlining words with a pen): No, that's not how you spell that. You need another 't' in there.
Child: Oh.
Adult: And this one too. You must not put an 'e' in there. Make sure that you remember that. You need to copy this out now. Okay?
Child: Yes.

Conversation B:
Child: I have finished now.
Adult: Wow, well done. You have worked hard! Can I see it?
Child: Yes.
Adult: You've done very well. I like what you said about the butter.
Child: Yes, my mum read me a story once which had that in it.
Adult: Can I tell you one thing that might be helpful another time?
Child: Yes.

Adult: Well, it's an interesting word but it's a bit of a sneaky one too. It actually has two 't's in it, like 'letter'. I bet you didn't know that. Lots of children get caught out by it, but you won't from now on. Do you want to sneak up and slip the extra 't' in it if I give you my pen?

Child: Yes – and I wasn't sure about this word.

Adult: Yes, that's another tricky one too. Well done for realising that it doesn't look right. It needs an 'e' just there.

Feedback needs to be meaningful

For feedback to be effective, children need to remember it, otherwise you will have wasted your and their time! It is therefore important to think about how you will help the child understand and remember the feedback. This means being clear in the way that you communicate and looking for ways to involve a child. It is often helpful if a child can quickly use the new information that has been given. For example, you might point out that 'tion' says 'shun' and ask a child to point out other words that end in 'tion' for a mixed list such as *potion*, *ration*, *steeple* and *station*. By actively using the new knowledge immediately, the child is more likely to remember that 'tion' says 'shun'.

Feedback needs to be relevant

It is important that feedback is relevant to a child's stage of development. For example, there is no point in commenting on spellings that are beyond the child's current level of capability. If a child cannot spell c-a-t, it is unlikely that he is ready to learn to spell a more complex word such as 'f-r-i-e-n-d'. It is always therefore better to focus on one or two points at a time.

Feedback needs to be positive

Children need adults to be positive about their efforts and to be enthusiastic. This means that you must always check that your comments are particularly positive and encouraging. Some adults make the mistake of focusing first on what the child needs to learn rather than on what they have managed to achieve. This can seem very negative to children and

can prevent them in the future from putting in so much work. It is also important to remember that children often link praise for their work to being liked by the adult – being corrected or told about mistakes can in the child's mind seem like a reprimand.

Children also recognise when they are struggling and they need adults to reassure them that while they might be finding a task difficult this will not always be the case. It is important not to dismiss children's fears and worries about learning to read and write as from around the age of 6 years, most children compare themselves to others in their class (see also Unit 2, page 60). This means that they know how they are doing and need your reassurance that they will be able to manage.

Think about it

Look at the conversation below between an adult and a child who is finding reading difficult.

Child (*points to a word in the book that she is reading aloud to the adult*): I don't know that word. I can't read that one.

Adult: Don't worry. See if you can just get the first sound and then we will sort it out together.

Child: It's a 'Sh'.

Adult: Great! In fact it says 'Shake'. If you keep up with your reading, in a few weeks' time, this word will become easy like some of the other words that you can read now. It does take time and you have to do a little practice. How about seeing if you can find another 'shake' on this page?

1. Why is it important that the adult acknowledges that the child is finding reading difficult?

2. Explain why the adult reminded the child of her progress in learning to read.

3. How does the adult help the child to regain some confidence in her ability to read the difficult word?

The barriers to learning how to read and write

Some children find it easier to learn to read and write than others do. As you have seen, learning to read is far more difficult than it might at first appear. Below are some of the barriers that might affect a child's ability to learn to read and write.

Lack of motivation

Motivation is extremely important in learning to do anything. Learning to read and write is a long process that requires patience and practice. It is known that children who have had plenty of pleasant experiences of being read to and mark making will find learning to read and write easier. Children are also more motivated to learn when they see adults reading and writing, especially people they particularly admire such as their parents and teachers. The spider diagram below shows some of the ways in which you can motivate children to want to learn how to read and write.

Language use

Before reading and writing can really take off, children need to be fluent in the language that is being used. You have seen that reading is more than just decoding; for reading to be pleasurable it also has to have meaning. Children who have limited language find it harder to enjoy the process of reading. This is particularly true once children reach a stage in their reading when books do not provide illustrations and the reader has to turn the words into visual images in their head.

Good language use is also essential in learning how to write. Children need to have words so they have something to write about. Writing is, after all, a matter of putting the words that you hear in your head on to paper or screen. Children also have to be familiar with the sounds of the language they are learning to write in so they can spell. This means that children who have a language delay or are learning a second language may need extra support.

Dyslexia

The term dyslexia is used to describe a range of specific learning difficulties that might prevent a child from learning to read or spell effectively. Children who have dyslexia are often motivated to learn and have good language use. They seem, however, to have difficulties in recognising symbols and linking them to sounds. The disparity between dyslexic children's verbal skills and their ability to break into literacy is not fully understood; there are several explanations and research remains ongoing.

Find out!

Find out more about dyslexia and its causes by carrying out a general search on the Internet.

Factors which impact on a child's ability to communicate effectively

There is a range of factors that might impact on a child's communication skills. While most children do learn to communicate effectively, some will need support to do so.

Learning difficulty

The ability to communicate using words comes easily to most children but is actually quite a sophisticated cognitive skill. It requires understanding that sounds are being used to mean or stand for something else, for example that c-a-t refers to an animal that has four legs, a tail and says 'miaow'. Some children with learning difficulties find this quite difficult and may therefore have limited speech, as the case study below illustrates. Children may also have difficulties in understanding abstract concepts, such as the future or jealousy, which are not 'concrete' (cannot be seen or touched).

Case study

Learning difficulties can affect the acquisition of language skills

Ruth is 5 years old. She is a happy child who enjoys playing with others. She has a learning difficulty which is affecting her language skills. She can understand some words if they are nouns and if her key worker points to the object as the word is said. Ruth does not say many words and instead relies on pointing to get her needs met. If she wants to go out, Ruth goes over to the door and points at or collects her coat. If she wants to play a game she takes her key worker over to the play area. Ruth's key worker uses photographs and pictures to help Ruth understand what is about to happen and to communicate about things that are not within sight.

1. Why might Ruth find it easier to understand words that relate directly to familiar objects rather than words that relate to concepts?

2. Why is it important that Ruth's key worker has found a way to communicate with her?

Speech dysfluency

Some children are able to understand and use language effectively but have difficulties in saying words fluently and may stammer or stutter. This is extremely frustrating for them as they know what they would like to say. Stuttering and stammering is fairly common in children between the ages of 2 and 3 years, but for some children it becomes a longer-lasting problem that requires professional support. One of the problems with speech dysfluency is that a vicious cycle can develop whereby children become increasingly stressed and frustrated, which in turn prevents them from relaxing and allowing the words to be released. It is important to be extremely sensitive when working with such children; you should never, for example, force a child to stand up and speak in front of others. (See also Unit 14, page 527.)

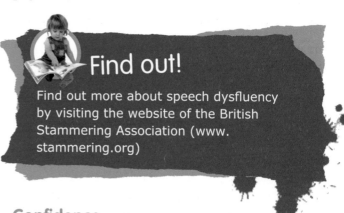

Find out!

Find out more about speech dysfluency by visiting the website of the British Stammering Association (www.stammering.org)

Confidence

For some children the main barrier to communication is confidence. Good communication requires that children believe that others will be interested in what they have to say and will give them time to listen. Children therefore need plenty of opportunities to talk with adults and gain communication skills and confidence. This is why it is important to have a key person system with young children and why it is imperative to find time to simply 'chat' with children.

As children get older, some find it hard to contribute in small or large group situations. You will therefore need to think about how these situations are managed. Sometimes adults unwittingly set up quite competitive situations where children who are able to think and speak quickly benefit but others learn to feel inadequate, for example by asking 'Who can be the first to tell me...?'

How to work with children with English as a second language

An increasing number of children in the UK speak more than one language. The ability to speak and communicate in more than one language is a fantastic asset for children which can enhance cognitive development. Being able to access your family's language also helps children's emotional development as language is linked to identity.

In England, children's education and assessment and therefore ability to gain qualifications is conducted in English. It is therefore essential that children are given the support they need to become proficient in the English language; supporting children in this way is also linked to inclusive practice (see also Unit 3, pages 120–1, and Unit 9, page 380). You will therefore need to know how to help such children with their communication, literacy and language.

Assessing the level of language use

A good starting point is to find out about each child's language use, as the level of fluency and exposure to English and other languages will vary from child to child. Key questions to be asked include:

→ Which languages are being used at home?

→ Who is speaking these languages?

→ How are they used?

→ How much time does the child spend speaking and listening to each language?

You should also find out whether there is any other language exposure, for example to languages that the child may become aware of but is not currently addressed in.

Think about it

Each of the children in the examples below are 4 years old and have additional language use.

Example 1:
Rahima's parents speak to her in Bengali. She also spends time with other adults who speak Bengali and plays with Bengali-speaking children. At home, books, films and most programmes are in Bengali. She recently started nursery and has just begun the process of learning English.

Example 2:
George's parents speak to him in Greek but talk to each other in Italian. He can now understand some Italian but doesn't speak it. His parents have a business and George hears a lot of English being spoken. The family watch a mixture of Greek and English films and programmes and have mostly English books. George has two older sisters whom he speaks to in English.

Example 3:
Kristen's mother speaks to her in Danish but she is the only person who does so. Her father, friends and neighbours speak to her in English. Kristen has been going to a childminder's since she was 6 months old for four days a week. The childminder speaks to her in English.

1. Explain why these children will have different levels of English?

2. Why is it important for practitioners to find out about home language use?

U16

2

How fluent is the child with these languages?

It is important not to assume that a child is fluent in the languages used at home. Find out how clearly they speak as well as their level of fluency. Sometimes children can have a speech delay that is not picked up as it is attributed to learning more than one language while in reality it might be caused by a hearing impairment or learning difficulty.

Did you know?

Fluency in a home language is important where a child is then introduced at a later age to another language. Children who have already cracked one language code find it easier to break into a second one.

Is the child learning to read or write in these languages?

It is useful to know whether children are learning to read and write in their home language. Children generally can make the switch from reading and writing from one language to another fairly well. Knowing how print runs in a language and how a pen is held in order to write is useful background knowledge. Learning to read and write in a home language is beneficial for children as this can improve their overall linguistic ability.

Supporting children who are new to a setting

Children who come into a setting without English need plenty of support. The starting point is to provide them with emotional support. This should be given by a key person who takes responsibility for settling the child in and developing a strong relationship with him or her. Children will need to feel secure in order that they can begin to relax and learn English.

Having a key person also has other practical benefits in terms of language learning. A key person provides constancy in terms of intonation and accent. This means that the child will find it easier to 'tune in' and recognise key words. The key person will also become familiar with the child's body language and

facial expressions and be able to work out what the child needs or is feeling. With older children it can be helpful to appoint another child to become the new child's 'key person'. This will help them make friends; lonely, scared and sad children will always take longer to learn a new language.

It is usual for a child new to a language to be fairly quiet at first and to literally 'absorb' the sounds and the routines of the setting. It is extremely helpful to use pictures and to physically show objects to a child. This will allow the child some understanding of what is happening. Children usually start by understanding words (receptive language) before actually using them (expressive language). This time delay is normal and it is better that children are not pressurised into repeating words or saying things until they are ready to do so. Once children begin to speak, they fairly quickly begin to use more and more words before eventually putting them into sentences.

Sustained conversations with adults

While other children can be good at supporting a child's language, it is unfair to expect them to be responsible for a child's language learning. Children while playing are normally effective at adapting their language to suit the needs of their playmates, but they may not necessarily explain the meaning of words or try and deepen a child's vocabulary. This is why adults must spend time playing, doing activities and chatting with children. Chatting is quite important as children need to hear grammatically correct sentences rather than an overload of questions.

Gaps in children's language

Most early language is learnt in context. This means that a child will learn words associated with nurseries, pre-schools and schools in English but may not know these same words in their home language. Equally, a child may have only heard the word for 'duvet' in their home language and may not know its equivalent in English. This means that even when children are able to speak fluently they can have 'gaps' in fairly common vocabulary. This can affect their understanding and enjoyment of stories or their ability to follow instructions or write about what they have been doing at home. It is therefore important to work on the breadth of children's vocabularies by, for example, using role play, showing children objects and taking time to explain unfamiliar words.

Case study

Supporting a child with gaps in her language

Janine is 4 years old. Her parents speak Farsi at home. Janine's English is fluent and it is easy for staff to forget that she has another home language. Today, Janine is playing in the home corner. A member of staff hears her pop a Farsi word into a sentence as she is playing. The team start to listen out and hear that she substitutes Farsi words if she does not know the English equivalent. They start to plan activities that will help Janine become aware of some the basic home words. As she enjoys playing in the role-play area, staff join her and take a role too.

1. Why is it important to find out where a child may have gaps in their vocabulary?

2. Why is it important to base activities on children's existing interests?

3. Suggest another activity that will help a child learn about 'home' words in English.

Good practice checklist

Tips to support children who are learning more than one language

✓ Assess language use and understanding.

✓ Remember that while children may be grammatically fluent they may have gaps in their vocabulary.

✓ Introduce and explain words in context. Consider the use of pictures.

✓ Always check that children have understood words.

U16

2

The role of the adult in supporting communication, language and literacy

In practice

You have been asked by the Reception teacher if you can plan some language activities and hear some of the children read. She says that you may need to help children to sound the words out. You are a little daunted by this.

By the end of this section you will understand how to support children's reading and the importance of reporting back to teachers. You will also know how you might support children's language skills.

Working with colleagues, parents and families

The role of parents in developing children's literacy

Parents have an enormous impact on the development of children's literacy. Learning to read and write does not begin and end in the nursery or school – research consistently shows that children whose parents read with them and share a bedtime story with them tend to pick up reading more quickly. This means that it is essential to work in partnership with families because children need as much one-to-one support as possible in the earliest years of reading and writing. This means you will need to share information with parents about their child's progress as well as the ways in which they can build on any work you are doing with them at home. It is also a good idea to share ideas and resources with parents: many settings will encourage parents to come into the setting and choose books to take home and read with their children. It is also useful for parents, if they wish to contribute, to become involved in record keeping and assessment. They may, for example, notice that their child has difficulties with certain words or is now able to read a text fluently.

⇧ **Children whose parents read with them tend to learn to read more quickly**

Family literacy

Some settings have sessions that encourage the whole family to do activities together that will support literacy. For example, a library may have a family session, while a pre-school may organise for parents and grandparents to make and use story sacks with their children.

Working with colleagues

You have seen consistently throughout this book that working effectively with colleagues benefits children in many ways. In terms of helping children's language and literacy it is essential that you are able to share information and adopt similar strategies. This prevents situations when children and their parents become confused about what is expected. Below are some practical examples of how colleagues need to work together.

Styles of handwriting

Since handwriting is the first tool that children use to allow them to write, it is important that the staff team agree on an approach to handwriting. In some schools, for example, cursive writing (joined-up writing with loops) is used in the Reception class. If this style is being used, all the adults working with children need to know this and model it in front of children. It is also important that schools talk to nurseries, pre-schools and childminders so they can model the type of handwriting that children will be expected to do.

Good practice checklist

Ways to work with parents to support children's literacy

✓ Provide parents with resources such as flashcards, books and literacy games.

✓ Send home the words of rhymes and songs that are being used.

✓ Organise a parent information session so that parents can learn how to support their child at home.

✓ Provide resources such as videos and booklets from organisations (see suggested resources on page 566).

✓ Value parents' contributions at home.

Pencil grip

Guidance from the National Primary Strategy is that children should hold the pencil in an 'effective' way. It does not necessarily state that this has to be the classic tripod grip, although this is usually the most effective. Again, for consistency and to avoid confusing children, it is helpful if colleagues agree on how they will help children gain their pencil grip.

Reading

It is important that children's progress is monitored and shared between colleagues and parents. Everyone needs to know if a child is losing confidence, needs extra support or even which sounds or blends he or she is learning. Colleagues also have to agree on the approach that is being taken. There are many different reading schemes and methods of learning phonics; again, consistency is essential so that children do not 'miss out' on learning.

Meeting the individual needs of children to promote their communication skills

You have seen that learning to speak, read and write is easier for some children than for others. This means that you need to find ways of recognising children's needs and supporting them. Whatever approach is taken to supporting individual children, building confidence and motivation is always central.

Reading

How to listen to a child read

When children first learn how to decode, they need plenty of adult time and support. They also need individual practice with an adult supporting them. Hearing children read is therefore an important part of supporting reading. By working individually with children it is possible to draw their attention to particular words or sounds. Most children enjoy reading to an adult, provided they have reading materials that are at the right level and feel confident.

Making reading fun

As with many areas of child development, children will do well if they are feeling confident and have a good relationship with you. This means that you may need to spend a little time with a child that you do not know well, having a little chat first. This will help them to relax and to feel more confident. It is also important that the adult gives out signals that they are looking forward to spending a few moments with the child.

Helping reluctant readers

The term 'reluctant reader' is often used to describe children who dislike the process of reading. Some children are aware that they are not reading as well as their classmates. This can mean they avoid reading and develop a fear or dislike of reading to an adult. With a reluctant reader it is important to begin with the relationship. It can also be helpful to choose a book which is slightly below their reading level at first. This can make a child feel more confident. Remember, reading is at first quite hard work and requires high levels of concentration. Reluctant readers often benefit from having little breaks where the adult does some reading. This is particularly useful if the speed of reading has been slow and the plot of the story is being missed because of the pace. It can also be useful to re-read what the child has decoded so they can hear the same sentences with a little more intonation.

Good practice checklist

Promoting children's reading skills

✓ Choose a good time for the child, for example not when a child is happily playing with others.

✓ Find somewhere comfortable.

✓ Encourage the child to explore and talk about the book.

✓ Let the child look at the pictures and make comments.

✓ Do not rush the child.

✓ Listen carefully and be interested in the book.

✓ Repeat with expression what the child has decoded or paraphrase.

✓ Provide plenty of encouragement and praise.

Writing

Reluctant writers

In the same way that there are some children who find reading difficult, the same is true of writing. As reading and writing are closely interlinked in the primary stage, the chances are that a child who does not enjoy reading will also find writing hard. Other children may be fairly competent readers but may lack confidence to actually write.

Supporting individual children

It is important to recognise why a child is not enjoying writing, for example a child who is afraid may prefer to write in a group or to take turns with you in writing. For some other children the key is to make the writing feel like a game. You may, for example, use unusual writing materials such as large board markers or invisible ink.

Supporting spelling

Many children will ask for help with spelling. It is important to find a balance between simply giving a child a spelling and insisting that they should tackle the spelling alone. If you always just provide a spelling, the danger is that children become over reliant on the adult, but insisting that they should manage alone can mean that they choose an 'easier' word to spell instead. It is possible to ask children to 'have a go' on a separate piece of paper or to encourage them to help you as you write it for them. Many children can get the initial sound. Writing an unfamiliar word out in different coloured pen can also be useful. This will draw the child's attention to particular blends or sounds in a word. This in turn may help a child to remember the word more easily.

Planning appropriate activities to develop and extend language and literacy

The starting point for planning activities is to consider the needs and developmental stage of the children that you are working with. It is also essential to consider the interests of children as this will make a significant difference in terms of their motivation and ability to remember the activity. The following examples of simple activities can be used to develop language and literacy with different ages of children.

Activity for speaking and listening

This simple activity helps children to learn conceptual vocabulary and to frame questions. As children become more skilled in speaking and listening, you should find that they begin to use language for thinking and reasoning.

What's in my bag?

Place a couple of objects within a cloth bag. With individual or pairs of children, encourage them to feel from the outside the shapes of the objects. See if they can work out what they are feeling by using questions. When a child makes a guess, see if they can provide a reason for their thinking, for example 'What made you think that it might be a teddy bear?' Try also to ask children to put a couple of things in the bag so that you are the one guessing. This helps them to see how you are using language.

Activity for reading

This simple activity draws children's attention to letter shapes or whole words. It is possible to do this activity even with older children. It can be differentiated by hiding words that can be put together to make a message.

Word or letter treasure hunt

Outdoors or indoors hide letter sounds or whole words. At first make it fairly straightforward for children to find them. If working with a group of children, you might like to ration the number of 'finds' they can have to avoid situations where some children discover a lot and others are left with nothing. You can also put children into teams so they work together to find what has been hidden. Listen to the children as they work. Afterwards, follow this up with other games such as word or sound lotto, to see if children have remembered the words or sounds.

Activity for writing

Children generally write best when they have a real and motivating purpose to write. Letter writing when children know that they are going to get a reply can work well with all ages of children.

Letter writing

Tell children that if they write a letter (or for older children an e-mail) they will get a reply. Once the child has written a letter or e-mail, try as quickly as you can to reply. Use vocabulary or words that you know will be helpful for the child. With very young writers who might not be reading yet, keep replies short and simple so they can remember what has been written. With older children, write the odd question in the reply so the child has something to continue writing about.

Preparation of resources

It is important that the resources you use with children are clean, attractive and enjoyable for children. In terms of speaking and listening, the most important resource is you! This means that you need to look for opportunities where children can come and talk to you easily.

Reading

Most settings have a reading area or quiet corner where children can go and choose a book. This area needs to be attractive and comfortable. It is important that books in this area are attractive and that any books which have become tatty are removed and replaced. It is also important that children are enticed to read. This is easier if you draw their attention to certain books by placing them so the covers can be seen.

Writing

Children need to enjoy the process of writing. In many settings a writing area is created, although it is actually possible to incorporate writing into many different play activities.

Good practice checklist

Creating an attractive reading area

- ✓ Make sure that books are attractive and appropriate for the children's age range.
- ✓ Lay out books so they can be easily seen.
- ✓ Remove damaged books.
- ✓ Place objects that link to stories near to books.
- ✓ Create a book display.

Good practice checklist

Creating an attractive writing area

- ✓ Make sure that writing materials are interesting for children – try markers and felt tips as well as pencils.
- ✓ Look out for opportunities to make writing a little more interesting by, for example, using coloured paper, envelopes and seals.
- ✓ Provide examples of print and text so that children needing a little more confidence can use them as prompts.

Methods of teaching reading

Finding the best approach to helping children to read is an area of ongoing controversy. Over the past fifty years there have been fashions in teaching children to read although there are in effect simply three ways: phonics, word recognition and real books. At the moment, the government through the Literacy strategy is backing phonics. This is a significant change of direction from the previous strategy where a mixed approach was suggested. However, there are some areas of agreement. Everyone recognises that a child needs a good level of spoken language and that all children learn best when they are having fun and making progress. Another area of agreement is the influence of parents – as you saw on page 555, parents who are interested in helping their children to read make a significant difference in terms of literacy.

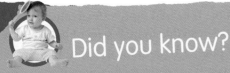
Phonics

Phonics is the method that teaches children to know the sounds that individual and groups of letters make. There are two types of phonics teaching that can be used: analytical and synthetic. The current method of teaching recommended by the Literacy strategy focuses on synthetic phonics. It is therefore likely that your setting will be using phonics with children.

There are many terms that are used when talking about phonics and it is helpful for you to be familiar with them (see the Key terms box below).

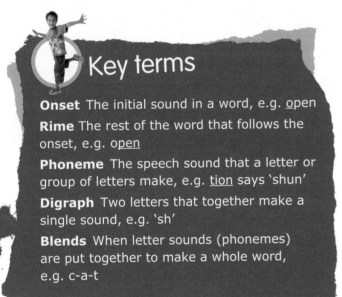

Key terms

Onset The initial sound in a word, e.g. <u>o</u>pen

Rime The rest of the word that follows the onset, e.g. o<u>pen</u>

Phoneme The speech sound that a letter or group of letters make, e.g. <u>tion</u> says 'shun'

Digraph Two letters that together make a single sound, e.g. 'sh'

Blends When letter sounds (phonemes) are put together to make a whole word, e.g. c-a-t

The difference between synthetic and analytical phonics

The difference between synthetic and analytical phonics is to do with early teaching.

→ Synthetic phonics in its purest form teaches children to learn the sounds of the letters and how to blend letters together without necessarily putting them into context. The aim is that children start to build up words themselves before being exposed to reading. Critics of synthetic phonics argue that the method is sterile and does not help children to enjoy books. Those in favour of this method suggest that this structured approach is more efficient.

→ Analytical phonics takes a different approach as children are encouraged to relate the sounds they are learning to whole words, for example 'a is for apple'. In this way, children break words down into sounds rather than building them up.

Difficulties with phonics

The main disadvantage with phonics is that many words in the English language do not blend together phonetically. Even the word English is not phonetic as it would need to be spelt 'Inglish' for it to be correct!

Another problem for learning to read in this way is that there are several ways of making the same sound, for example the 'f' sound can be made using 'f' or 'gh' (as in cough) or 'ph' (as in physical).

Word recognition

Word recognition is also referred to as whole word or 'look and say'. This method was particularly fashionable at one point and was the basis for the Peter and Jane reading scheme. Word recognition relies on children looking at a whole word and remembering its shape. This can help children quickly read simple books and learn some of the common or 'high frequency' words that occur in many English sentences, most of which are not phonic. Word recognition is often taught by giving children books that are repetitive so the child sees over and over again the same word. Flashcards are also used so that children can quickly recognise words.

Difficulties with word recognition

While many children make speedy progress with whole word recognition there are some significant disadvantages. First of all, children can reach a point where they have absorbed and cannot remember any more words. Second, and most importantly, children who only rely on this method have difficulties when faced with unfamiliar words. They may also struggle to spell as they may not associate letters with sounds.

Real books

In the 1980s there was a feeling that reading schemes were actually putting children off reading. Reading schemes, it was argued, were boring and predictable and did not give children a wide range of reading skills, such as the ability to choose a book. It was thought that if children had access to good quality children's books rather than reading schemes, they would learn through practice and enjoyment. It was a revolutionary approach that actually brought many publishers close to bankruptcy.

No particular reading approach was suggested although teachers were encouraged to hear children read and to tailor their teaching according to the child. Before this time, children were often only heard to read for a page at a time and it could take a few weeks before a child was able to finish a book. Parents, too, were often not involved and the real books approach was to encourage parents and children to share books together.

For some children this approach worked quite well, especially where children had effective support at home and good levels of spoken language. These children often worked out for themselves the links between sounds and letters. For other children, this approach was not so successful and bit-by-bit the more structured teaching of reading has returned along with revamped reading schemes. Interestingly, though, the importance of making reading enjoyable and the need to use 'real books' with children has been maintained.

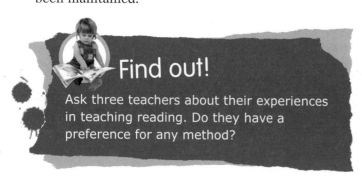

Find out!

Ask three teachers about their experiences in teaching reading. Do they have a preference for any method?

Resources for reading

You have seen that there are several approaches to helping children learn to read. In support of these approaches are many commercial schemes available for children. It is helpful if you are familiar with some of the popular ones; it will mean that if a child moves from a setting that uses a different scheme you will

be able to support the child more effectively. Some schemes are also available in high street bookstores so parents can purchase them for use at home. Bear in mind, however, that reading scheme materials are expensive, so knowing what is available can be useful in cases where you might be asked for your opinion.

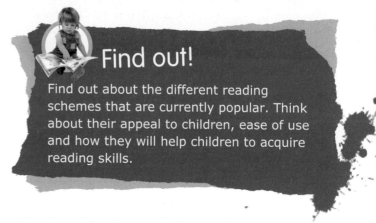

Find out!

Find out about the different reading schemes that are currently popular. Think about their appeal to children, ease of use and how they will help children to acquire reading skills.

Methods of teaching writing

As you have seen, reading and writing are interlinked. As children learn to recognise letter shapes and whole words, so these begin to appear in their attempts at writing. Children also begin to use their understanding of letter sounds and blends in order to put down words that they wish to write. This is a gradual process with most children being able to write a few sentences comfortably by the end of Year 1. It is important that children do not feel constrained only to write the words that they know. This can lead to safe but very repetitive writing such as 'I like to ... And I like to... and I like to...'!

Mark making

The starting point for writing is for children to enjoy expressing themselves using a variety of materials. These can be paint, pens or chalks as well as sensory materials such as sand, rice and shaving foam. The aim is for children to get used to holding implements and simply enjoy making marks. From this starting point children usually go on to produce letter shapes and eventually whole words.

Group writing

This works very well with children who are not confident in writing. By sharing and working together alongside an adult, children can help each other and watch as the adult writes. This type of writing is usually done in small groups. The group will decide what needs writing, which words will be useful and an adult may put them on to a white board or interactive board.

Scribing

At the start of the writing journey, many children benefit by having an adult act as a scribe for them. The child will tell the adult what they would like to write and the adult will write it for them. The starting point may be a picture that the child has drawn or a story they have told. Watching the adult write will be helpful for the child. Afterwards the child is likely to be able to read some of the words the adult has written.

Modelling

A major influence in children's writing is how often they see adults around them write. Modelling writing is an effective way of drawing children's attention to particular spellings and letter formation. Interestingly, over the past few years the amount of writing that children are likely to see in everyday life has declined. Seeing adults writing often provides children with the motivation to write.

Handwriting

Approaches to teaching children to use handwriting vary across schools. Some schools prefer that children begin with cursive writing (joined-up writing often with loops) from the very start, while others teach children to print in the first two years and encourage them to join up later on. There are advantages and disadvantages of both approaches (see table below).

Did you know?

Many European countries begin with cursive writing, although it needs to be remembered that children are older, have developed additional fine motor skills and that reading scheme materials are often also in cursive.

Think about it

How good is your handwriting? Do you join your letters up?

Find out!

What method of teaching handwriting is used in your setting?

🖐 **The advantages and disadvantages of different approaches to teaching handwriting**

	Advantages	Disadvantages
Cursive writing	• Can result in fluent writing by the end of Year 1 • Means that children do not have to 'unlearn' letter formation later on • Helps children to develop a flow of writing	• Some children's fine motor skills may not be sufficiently developed for cursive writing • Children may see more print rather than cursive writing, for example in books • Parents may not be sure how to model writing
Print	• Is easier for children to manage when they first start to write • Writing in the real world and in books tends to be in print	• Many children find it hard to change to joined-up writing later on

For adults working in nurseries and pre-schools, it is essential to find out what type of writing children will be doing in Reception. Children who will be going on to do cursive writing in Reception may actually be disadvantaged if they have learned to write too many words using print.

The methods and techniques used to support children with speaking and listening

Most children are born wanting to communicate. This means that if you provide the right environment, stimulus and support, most children will learn to speak and listen fairly easily.

Encouraging children's speech

Adults working with children have to be good at listening as children need to practise speech. Children need opportunities to talk and be listened to. It is important that you consider when working with children whether you are doing too much of the talking! A good listener acknowledges what has been said by commenting, asking a further question or through body language; they do not try to change the subject, interrupt or take over. They also let children lead the pace of the conversation so children do not feel hurried. Listening is thus a real skill, but one that can be developed and has huge benefits for children. Children who are lucky enough to have adults who listen to them and allow them to do the talking tend to become more articulate and fluent in their speech.

Think about it

Check how much of the talking you do while working with children by recording yourself as you work with a child or small group. Listen back to the recording and think about who said the most!

It is also important to remember that children are not robots who can turn speech on and off. Children tend to talk when they need to or feel that they have someone who will listen to them. This means that very structured activities rarely work, for example sitting all the children down and expecting them to take turns to talk to the group for 1 or 2 minutes.

Good practice checklist

Supporting children's speech

✓ Remember that young children may need time to formulate their thoughts.

✓ Try to increase the number of opportunities for one-to-one conversations.

✓ Sit rather than stand when listening to children.

✓ Avoid too many direct questions.

✓ Listen to yourself – are you directing children or allowing them to take control of the conversation?

Encouraging children's listening

Like adults, children find it easier to listen when there is something worth listening to! Encouraging children's listening means you need to start by thinking about their needs as well as their language level. It is hard to listen if you do not understand all of what is being said so it is essential that story times and other organised language activities take account of individual children's language levels. It is also important to think about children's interests: children who are enjoying a subject and can cope with the language level are likely to listen well. A good example of this is the way in which an adult telling a lively story with props can keep quite young children in rapture for fifteen minutes, but another adult who is talking in a monotone voice about something that the children do not understand can lose their interest within the first couple of minutes.

⇧ **Children who are enjoying a subject and can cope with the language level are likely to listen well**

Signs that children are listening

It is worth thinking about the signs that children are listening. A good sign is if they are interested and comment or ask questions. Children are also likely to be listening if they draw connections to what has been said and themselves, for example 'I've got a jumper like that at home too!' With children under 6 years old these connections are likely to be spontaneous and result in immediate speech. This must not be interpreted as a child misbehaving or interrupting – it is merely a sign that a child is listening but is not yet developmentally able to hold in their thoughts. The need for children under around 6 years to make connections and articulate them is one reason why story times and opportunities for language activities need to be kept in as small a group size as possible.

Interestingly, some adults believe that children who are sitting quietly and looking at them will be listening. This is not always the case as many children are able to listen while looking away and some children actually listen best when they have something to fiddle with in their hands.

Combining listening with visual information

Many children will find it easier to listen if there are visual stimuli such as puppets, props or gestures.

Combining words with visual stimuli helps children to process information more easily and so aids memory. Wherever possible, it is also a good idea to physically involve children as well.

The use of story and rhyme in supporting communication, language and listening

Children need to experience a language-rich environment in order to break into literacy because reading and writing are about words. Good readers and writers have a feeling for words – they enjoy the sounds of them and are confident about their use. You can help children develop this love of words in many ways.

Storytelling

A traditional way to help children develop a love of words is through storytelling. Storytelling helps children learn about the structure of most texts, which usually have a clear beginning, middle and conclusion. It is also a powerful medium. It allows you to make eye contact with children and to respond immediately to their reactions. Children can also be participative during the storytelling process. You can ask children questions, use props and incorporate their ideas into the story. Using storytelling as a starting point, you can then write out the story so that children learn the purpose of print. In this way children learn that recording things down is useful – it allows them to remember things and for others to see their thoughts even when they are not there.

Story time in groups

It is important that story times are pleasant and enjoyable for all children. You have seen already that children will find it easier to listen if they can understand what is being said. This means that stories have to be carefully matched to the language level of children. For story time to be pleasurable it also has to be physically comfortable. This means providing cushions, a carpeted area and encouraging children to find ways of sitting comfortably. Story time also tends to be more enjoyable when numbers are small and children can be actively involved. They may, for example, wish to look at the pictures in the book, turn the pages or join in any repeated phrases.

Group story times also need to be planned. Books need to be chosen that will appeal to all of the children. This is why it can sometimes be difficult if a child selects the story; while it might be fine for the individual, this might not work for a large group.

Story time with individuals

It used to be common for all children to be read a bedtime story by their parents. This is not necessarily the case today so many children miss the opportunity to have a one-to-one story. Ideally, you need to help parents realise how important these moments in a child's life are – not only do they help develop a positive attitude towards literacy, they also help children get to sleep.

Wherever possible it is essential to find ways of providing stories for individual and pairs of children. This offers a much richer experience of literacy than group stories as children can comment, point to pictures and help with turning pages. They can also watch as the adult runs their finger from left to right along the page. Finding the time to share a story also means that you can assess children's developing knowledge of literacy and encourage them to develop 'favourite' books. This is important as when children read the same book over again they become more confident and start to take a greater interest in the text.

Nursery rhymes

Nursery rhymes, especially some of the traditional ones, have wonderful meters, strong sounds and great examples of alliteration (where the initial sound of a word is repeated). This is one of the reasons why rhymes such as 'Diddle diddle dumpling, my son John' have survived for so long. Knowledge of nursery rhymes seems to help children develop a sense of individual sounds within words. This is sometimes referred to as phonemic awareness. It is useful if nursery rhymes can be inserted into long-term planning so that you can be sure that children learn several.

The use of technology to support language and literacy

There are many ways that you can use technology to support language and literacy. However, the effectiveness of technology is linked to the way in which it is used and, in relation to computers, the quality of the software.

Recording devices

Tape recorders and MP3 players can be good tools to record and then assess children's speech. They are also enjoyed by children who tell a story or read a story aloud.

Story and rhyme tapes

While nothing beats a 'real person' telling a story or singing rhymes, children can gain from listening to story and rhyme tapes. Wherever possible it is helpful with story tapes to also have the book alongside. This can be useful for children who have started to read but are not yet fluent; they can turn the pages of the book and run their fingers along the text. Story tapes can mean that when a child returns to the book alone, they are afterwards able to 'read' the text.

Computer

Writing

Some children who dislike writing often enjoy writing using word processing software. This may help them gain in confidence as it gets around the problem of handwriting, spelling and punctuation. Good writing using computers can be achieved by sitting alongside children so they can talk and be supported.

Reading

There are some useful computer programs that help children to recognise words and link sounds to letters. It is important, though, to be careful that programs are stimulating and are not worksheets in disguise! It is also essential to work alongside children to ensure that they understand what they are learning.

Speaking and listening

While there is some feeling that computer use may be contributing towards a decline in children's communication and literacy skills, there are computer programs that can help children work together. These programs usually have a problem-solving component and help children to negotiate in groups.

How to work with children whose progress may be causing concern

It is important that children who are not progressing as expected are supported. Language and literacy are essential life skills and children who do not develop alongside their peers can lose confidence as well as show frustrated behaviours. It is good practice that parents are involved when additional support is sought; this is a requirement of the SEN Code of Practice (see also Unit 14, pages 508–9).

Speech and language

Many settings now have good links with their local speech and language team. This means that referrals can be made more easily, although remember that parents must be involved in this process. Speech and language therapists will often provide suggestions as well as programmes for individual children.

Hearing and visual impairment

A good starting point for any child who is struggling with literacy is to consider whether they may have a hearing or visual impairment; these are common reasons why children do not break into reading. (Indicators for hearing and visual impairment are described in Unit 18, pages 587–8.) It is important to note that even a slight impairment can cause difficulties, despite children making good progress in other areas. To check for hearing and vision impairment, parents can visit their family doctor who will then make appropriate referrals.

Dyslexia

In the previous section you looked at children who might have difficulties in learning to read and write. Dyslexia is not usually diagnosed until children reach 7 years as some children take their time to pick up reading. It is important, however, that some investigation begins to take place if a child is not linking sounds to letters at around 6 years of age. The longer that children remain without support, the less inclined they may become to attempt reading and related tasks. Where dyslexia or a learning difficulty is suspected, children are usually referred to an educational psychologist.

How to monitor progress and keep appropriate records

There are many different record systems available and you will need to find out about the record keeping system in your setting.

Speaking and listening

It can be useful to record children's speech in order to assess progress, though many settings use a checklist to compile children's records. It is important, especially in the early years, to consider whether children's speech is developing in line with the expected milestones.

Reading records

When children are learning to read it is common for adults to hear them read. It is important to keep a record of what the child has read and how they have managed. Any difficulties with individual words or letter sounds should also be noted alongside skills that the child has mastered. Reading records should be shared with parents, and if they are hearing a child read at home it is good practice for them to contribute.

Pre-reading

In children's early years it is important to assess children's pre-reading skills. This might include whether a child is able to independently look at a book, turn pages and understand that print runs from left to right. Pre-reading skills also include whether a child is able to recognise their name, retell a story in sequence and can hear sounds in words. Many early years settings will keep records of pre-reading skills by using a checklist.

Collecting mark making and writing samples

A good way of assessing children's progress in writing is by collecting samples of their writing. It is important to make a note of the date and how they were produced. This is important as a piece of work that has been achieved with significant adult support may make a later piece of unaided work look as if a child has regressed. It is also useful to make some notes as to what is significant about the writing. In the case of mark making, it is useful to write down what children said as they were writing.

How to provide and prepare resources to support learning and development

Suggested resources

→ *Basic Skills Agency* (www.basic-skills.co.uk) – has a range of videos and booklets that provide guidance and tips for parents who wish to support their child's literacy.

→ *The British Association for Early Childhood Education* (www.early-education.org.uk) – has a series of 'Learning together' leaflets that are free.

Getting ready for assessment

Below are some questions that you can use to check your understanding and recall of this unit.

1. Outline each of the areas of language and literacy.

2. Describe the stages of development in children's writing.

3. Identify two barriers to learning how to read and write.

4. Give three examples of activities that might support children's literacy.

5. Explain how the practitioner can support children with speaking and listening.

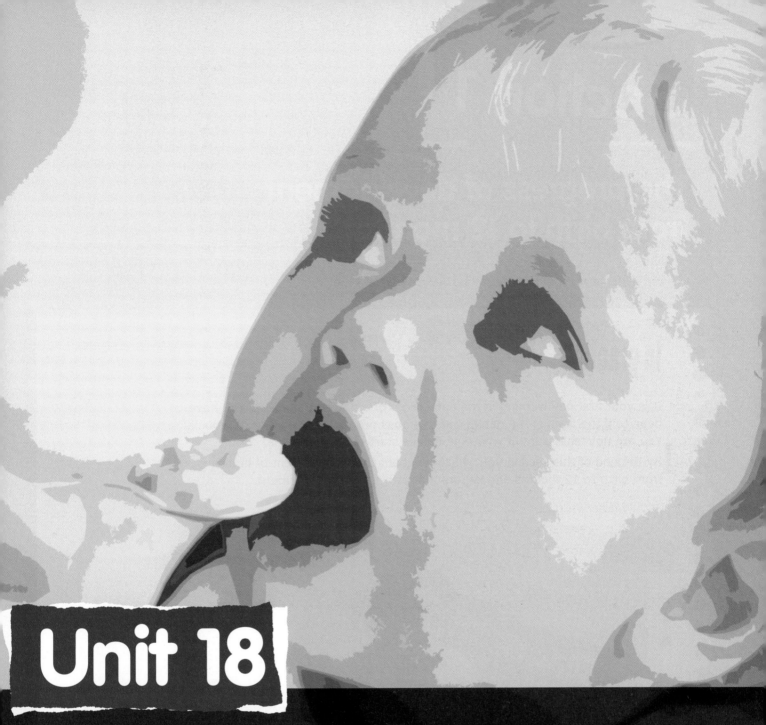

Unit 18

Working with babies from birth to 12 months

In this unit you will learn:

1. The progress of development from birth to 12 months

2. The role of the professional in promoting development

3. The roles and responsibilities of professionals working with babies

Section 1

The progress of development from birth to 12 months

In practice

It is your first day working in the baby room of a day care nursery. You have been told the ages of the babies but this does not really mean a lot to you. You are not really sure at what age babies start to crawl or walk.

By the end of this section you will know about the development of babies from birth to 12 months and factors that affect their development.

The patterns and sequence of development of babies from birth to 12 months

It is helpful to have an understanding of expected development for babies in their first year of life. In order to complete this unit you will therefore need to revisit pages 28–34 in Unit 2, which describes development of children including babies.

It is essential that adults working with babies have a good understanding of the normal pattern of development. This will help you to meet babies' needs, particularly for toys, equipment and safety. It will also ensure that any developmental delay is investigated and the child's needs met. Early identification is important because delay or difficulties in one area of development can impact on other areas.

Sequence of physical development

One of the most striking things about babies in their first year of life is the way in which they grow and learn to coordinate their body. By the end of their first year, nearly all babies are mobile and some babies can stand and even walk. Their physical coordination is so developed that they can feed themselves and pick up objects that interest them. This is amazing progress given that when babies are born they rely completely on instinctive reflexes for survival.

The chart below and on the next page looks at babies' physical development as this is one area which features huge changes during the first year. While babies learn the skills of physical development at different rates, it is striking that all babies follow a sequence or pattern in their development. As we saw in Unit 2 page 39, this means that babies do not suddenly stand up and walk but first need to be able to lift their head.

Sequence of physical development in babies from birth to 12 months

Age	Developmental pattern
Newborn  ⇧ **The grasp reflex**	A newborn baby has many developmental reflexes that are designed to help him or her survive, for example being able to cry and suck. These gradually disappear as the baby gains voluntary control of his or her body. • *Rooting reflex* – Baby will move mouth if face is touched to look for food. • *Startle reflex* – Baby throws out hands and legs as if trying to catch something if he or she hears a sudden sound. • *Grasp reflex* – Baby's fingers automatically tighten round anything put in the palm of the hand. The grasp is so tight that the baby can be lifted up, though this is usually only done by medical professionals. • *Crawling reflex* – When placed on his or her front, the baby's knees are tucked up underneath. This is because of being curled up in the womb.
6 weeks  ⇧ **Making eye contact with carer**	• Starting to have more periods of alertness • Looks at carer; stares at bright lights • Is soothed by carer's voice • Follows objects and faces at close range • Arm and leg movements are jerky

Age	Developmental pattern
3 months  **↑ Bringing fingers to mouth**	• Smiles and coos • Kicks legs strongly and moves arms • Movements are less jerky, although still not coordinated • Can find hands and bring them to mouth • Looks at and plays with fingers • Is alert and looks around • Can lift and turn head from side to side when lying on front • Can hold a rattle for a short time, although cannot coordinate arms to bring it to mouth
6 months **↑ Grasping an object while pushing head, neck and chest off floor when on front**	• Smiles, laughs and makes sounds • Follows adults' movements • Grasps objects • Beginning to roll over • Pulls up legs with hands when on back; may put foot in mouth • Sits up with support, although some babies are starting to sit up for short periods without support • Pushes head, neck and chest off floor when on front
9 months **↑ Sitting up without support and reaching for objects**	• Sits up well without support • Can reach out for toys from sitting • May be crawling or shuffling on bottom • Uses fingers and thumb to pick up objects • Can bang objects together • Babbles and starts to understand words such as 'bye-bye' and 'no'
12 months **↑ Walking with support**	• Most babies are mobile – either crawling, rolling or bottom shuffling • Starts to walk by holding on to furniture; this is often called cruising • May stand alone for a few seconds. • Points to objects using index fingers to show adults • Understands name and simple instructions • Drinks from cup; tries to feed using spoon and fingers

Understanding that normative development is only a guide

In Unit 2 the terms 'normative' and 'milestones' were explored (see page 106). When looking at babies' development, you must remind yourself that the speed with which a baby reaches milestones is variable: some babies learn to walk as early as 8 months old while others take double that time.

Factors which can influence the health of the newborn, before, during and immediately after birth

There are many factors that will influence the health of a newborn baby, although the majority of babies are born perfectly healthy.

Conception

At the moment of conception when a sperm and egg fuse, a transfer of genetic information takes place. The fertilised egg will have 23 chromosomes from the father and 23 chromosomes from the mother which determine the child's development. This mixing of genetic information is often described as nature's lottery as it can result in medical conditions and disabilities, such as sickle cell disease and Down's syndrome (see also Unit 11, page 404).

Pregnancy

The health of the mother as well as her lifestyle choices can impact on the health and development of the unborn baby. Stress, diet and alcohol are examples of factors that can affect development (see also Unit 6 pages 258–9). It is now recognised that the first 12 weeks of pregnancy is when the foetus is at its most vulnerable, as this is when the organs are formed.

Diet

The developing baby requires nutrients so the diet of the mother plays an important role throughout pregnancy – a malnourished mother is likely to give birth to a low weight or premature baby.

Diet is particularly important in the first 12 weeks of pregnancy when lack of a mineral called folic acid, found in green leafy vegetables, can cause spina bifida. Women who are considering a pregnancy are therefore urged to take a supplement of 400mcg of folic acid daily until the twelfth week of their pregnancy. Pregnant women can also become deficient in iron so are encouraged to eat foods high in iron such as red meat, green vegetables, dried apricots and fortified breakfast cereals.

Overall, women do not need a 'special' diet when they are pregnant although they do need to eat a balanced diet. They should also be careful to avoid certain foods which could cause illness, for example:

→ Soft cheeses, such as Camembert and Brie, and blue cheeses can contain the bacteria Listeria, which can cause miscarriage, premature delivery or severe illness in a newborn baby. Listeria is also found in old cuts of meat, pâtés and smoked fish, or ready meals which have been pre-cooked and then chilled for some time before consumption.
→ Raw or partially cooked eggs should be avoided during pregnancy since these can cause salmonella food poisoning.
→ Raw and undercooked meat and raw shellfish can also be a source of food poisoning so should be avoided during pregnancy.

Find out!

You can find out more about what to eat and what not to eat during pregnancy on the following website: www.eatwell.gov.uk/agesandstages/pregnancy/whenyrpregnant

Drugs

The use of recreational and prescribed drugs can affect the developing foetus. Drugs enter the mother's bloodstream and then cross via the placenta into the baby. The effect of drugs can be devastating especially in the first 12 weeks when the foetus is developing. Pregnant women are therefore advised not to take any drugs during pregnancy unless advised to do so by a doctor.

Alcohol

In the same way that drugs cross the placenta and enter the foetal bloodstream, so too does alcohol. Alcohol can have a serious impact on the developing child, especially in the first few weeks of a pregnancy (often a time when the mother does not know that she is pregnant). Alcohol consumption during pregnancy can cause a range of Foetal Alcohol Spectrum Disorders, the most severe of which is the condition known as Foetal Alcohol Syndrome (FAS). This refers to various physical and mental birth defects including low birth weight, a small head, facial deformity, learning difficulties and attention problems. Alcohol-related disorders which affect learning and social function may be caused by drinking only moderate amounts of alcohol (6 or more drinks a week) during pregnancy so doctors now advise that women should preferably refrain from drinking alcohol during pregnancy.

Did you know?

In the UK, it is thought that 1 in every 500 babies is born with Foetal Alcohol Syndrome and 1 in every 50 babies is born with an alcohol-related disorder. Both conditions are 100 per cent preventable. (*Source*: www.fasaware.co.uk)

Smoking

Smoking restricts the amount of oxygen the baby receives in the womb and this affects growth and development. Babies born to mothers who smoke are therefore more likely to have a low birth weight. They are also at greater risk of prematurity (birth before 38 weeks' gestation). Other related effects on health include a higher incidence of cot death and a greater predisposition to asthma. (See also Unit 6, page 259.)

Did you know?

Smoking increases the risk of miscarriage by up to 50 per cent. (*Source*: Tommy's the Baby Charity)

Infections

Some infections that a mother may pick up during a pregnancy can affect the development of the foetus. While a common cold is harmless, food poisoning, rubella (German measles) or sexually transmitted diseases such as genital herpes can put the foetus at risk. (See also Unit 11, pages 423–5.)

Pregnancy-related conditions

While most women have a healthy pregnancy, some women can develop complications during pregnancy including gestational diabetes and pre-eclampsia. If left untreated, these conditions can affect the health of both mother and child. This is why pregnant women are offered regular antenatal check-ups.

Find out!

You can find out more about pregnancy-related conditions on the following website: www.tommys.org/pregnancy-information/problems-in-pregnancy.htm

Birth

Birth can present various dangers to both mother and child, which is why mothers are monitored before and during birth. The main danger for babies during the birthing process is a lack of oxygen (anoxia). During labour, the oxygen supply to the baby might be interrupted for several reasons, including the umbilical cord becoming entangled or the baby being slow to breathe at birth. In extreme cases anoxia can be fatal or leave the baby with permanent brain damage. It is important to emphasise, however, that this is relatively rare and most babies are born safely.

Most women give birth vaginally but sometimes a Caesarean section is given. This is when an incision of approximately 20cm is made across the lower abdomen and the baby is delivered through this opening; the mother is given an anaesthetic beforehand. A Caesarean may be planned in advance (elective Caesarean), for example when a woman is carrying triplets, or be carried out at short notice (emergency Caesarean) if there are difficulties when giving birth.

Immediately after birth

Immediately after birth, checks that the child is breathing and healthy are made using an assessment scale known as the Apgar score.

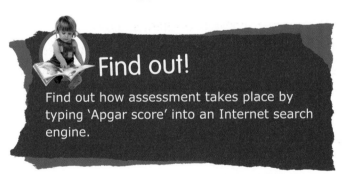

Find out!

Find out how assessment takes place by typing 'Apgar score' into an Internet search engine.

While most babies breathe immediately after birth, some need help to do so. They may, for example, need gently patting or a tube inserted to clear out any mucus in their mouth. Failure to get oxygen may mean that a baby will sustain some brain damage so midwives and doctors make this a priority in caring for a newborn.

As well as breathing, newborns need to settle into a feeding routine and midwives will check that babies are feeding well. Some newborns develop jaundice which is linked to the immaturity of the liver; this is recognised by the skin colour becoming yellow.

Usually jaundice disappears quickly but babies with severe jaundice will be given light treatment known as phototherapy.

Premature and multiple births

Birth before the full term of pregnancy can impact upon a baby's development. Full term is considered to be between 38 and 42 weeks, so babies born before 38 weeks' gestation are considered premature. This accounts for around 10 per cent of all births.

Some premature births are the result of medical intervention, for example when the health of the mother is considered at risk or it is recognised that the baby or babies (in the case of multiple births) are not thriving. Women may also go spontaneously into labour well before their due date.

The extent to which a child's development is affected by prematurity varies considerably and is linked to how early a baby is born. The last few weeks in the womb are vital as they allow the baby's organs and nervous system to mature as well as the baby to gain weight. This weight gain can help control body temperature and makes the baby less vulnerable to infection. Babies born between 35 and 38 weeks are usually mature enough to feed and breathe independently so development in the longer term is not usually affected. Babies who are born much earlier, for example at 25 weeks, will need significant medical support in order to survive; they are usually placed in an incubator that is designed to keep the baby warm and free from infection. While there have been medical advances in providing womb-like conditions, very premature babies are at a higher risk of developing hearing and sight problems as well as learning difficulties than those born later.

Measuring growth and development

Where babies are born prematurely it is important to take this into account when measuring their growth and development. On a percentile chart (used to measure growth) it is possible to plot a baby's height or weight in accordance with the week in which they were born, for example 28 weeks. In terms of looking at development it is usual to also consider how old the baby would be, had he or she been born at full term. Thus a baby now aged 4 months old, but born one month prematurely, would have his development looked at as if he was 3 months old.

Did you know?

In 2001/2002 around 7 per cent of all babies born in the UK were born prematurely. This is roughly equivalent to 125 babies born too soon each day in the UK. Although survival rates for premature babies have increased over the past few years as a result of technology and advances in medical understanding, the number of premature babies born each year has not significantly decreased since the 1960s. (*Source*: Tommy's the Baby Charity)

Multiple births

The number of multiple pregnancies has increased in the past few years as a result of women having pregnancies later in life and the use of fertility treatments. Women who have a multiple pregnancy are carefully monitored before and during birth. Multiple pregnancies can result in babies being born prematurely and/or being a low birth weight. As you have seen this may result in some longer term impact on a baby's health and development.

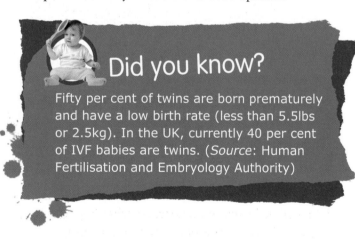

Did you know?

Fifty per cent of twins are born prematurely and have a low birth rate (less than 5.5lbs or 2.5kg). In the UK, currently 40 per cent of IVF babies are twins. (*Source*: Human Fertilisation and Embryology Authority)

Factors influencing development in the first year of a child's life

There are many factors that can influence a baby's development within the first year of life, as shown in the spider diagram opposite.

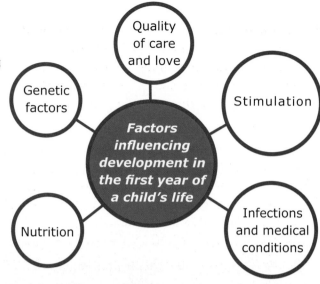

Quality of care and love

The way in which a baby is cared for plays a significant part in terms of development. In this section you will consider the bond formed between babies and their parents as well as their primary carers. The nature of these relationships seems to make a difference to the quality of care that adults provide. Good quality care means physical care but also interaction, love and reassurance. Where the quality of emotional care is lacking, babies' progress can be slower in many areas including growth and meeting the expected milestones.

Stimulation

Babies need opportunities to move and explore but also to be played with and talked to. These activities come under the umbrella term 'stimulation'. Babies who lack stimulation will show signs of developmental delay particularly in the areas of physical, language and cognitive development.

Nutrition

The first year of life is characterised by an amazing growth rate and the development of physical skills. These can only be achieved if the baby receives nutrients in sufficient quality and quantity. It is recognised that breast milk offers huge advantages for babies in the first few months of life (see also Unit 12, page 464). This is because breast milk is easily absorbed and meets the nutritional needs of babies exactly; it also provides protection against some diseases. Where breast milk is not available, babies are given formula milk. This is manufactured and processed to be similar to breast milk, although it cannot be an exact match.

In order to thrive, babies need to be given sufficient milk for the first six months of life and then weaned on to a diet containing adequate energy, minerals and protein. Babies who are underfed may lack energy and this will affect their physical development.

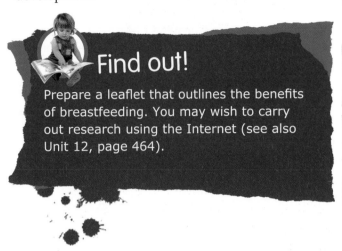

Find out!

Prepare a leaflet that outlines the benefits of breastfeeding. You may wish to carry out research using the Internet (see also Unit 12, page 464).

Infections and medical conditions

Repeated and/or severe illnesses can affect a baby's appetite and this in turn can limit the child's growth and physical development. Babies are more vulnerable to infections and medical conditions such as eczema as their immune system is immature. Some childhood illnesses can therefore be serious in babies, such as whooping cough. Vaccination is recommended for babies (see Unit 11, page 396) and hygiene must be a priority when working with them. The extent to which a medical condition may affect a baby's development will be dependent on the condition. Eczema, for example, may prevent a baby from sleeping and feeding well and this in turn may affect his or her physical development slightly, while a cleft palate may affect feeding and speech.

Genetic factors

While babies' development is linked to how they are cared for, fed and stimulated, it is also affected by genetics. Some babies will crawl earlier than others while some will be more interested in speech. The impact of genetics is an area that is still being researched and will undoubtedly become more important to understanding babies' development in the future.

Case study

A good start in life

Kerry is 8 months old. She is a happy baby and is sleeping and feeding well. She has started to crawl and is keen to babble. Her parents are delighted to have a baby following three earlier miscarriages. Kerry's mum has changed her working pattern so that she can spend three days at home with her. During this time she interacts and plays with her and enjoys taking her out and going to baby massage and yoga classes. Kerry's mum is keen for her daughter to have a good start in life so is breastfeeding and prepares home-cooked food for Kerry. Kerry has so far been in good health and has had all her vaccinations. This has been a priority for her parents as they know a friend whose baby soon developed whooping cough and was very poorly. Kerry has recently had some eczema and Kerry's mother is wondering if this might be genetic as her sister also has eczema.

1. Explain how Kerry might be benefiting from attention and care of her parents.
2. Discuss the advantages of breastfeeding.
3. Evaluate how important Kerry's parents are in supporting her early development.

Theoretical perspectives on development

When it comes to a baby's development, the nature versus nurture debate is of particular interest. Some aspects of a baby's development are clearly linked to instinct and biological aspects while others might well be linked to nurture, i.e. what happens to a baby. There are therefore many interesting perspectives you can look at in relation to babies. In Unit 2, pages 66–87, you looked at many theories that linked to development; it will be useful to revisit this material in order to complete this unit, although a summary of some key theories is given in the table on the next page.

Bowlby's theory of attachment	John Bowbly felt that babies had an instinctive need to form an attachment or bond with their mother. He suggested that babies who did not form this bond might otherwise find it difficult to form relationships in later life. (See also Unit 2, page 80.)
Robertson's theory of quality of substitute care	James and Joyce Robertson also looked at attachment. They considered what might happen if good substitute care was provided when a mother was temporarily unavailable to a child after an attachment had been made. They concluded that long-term emotional effects to the child could be avoided providing the substitute care was sensitive and met the child's emotional needs. (See also Unit 2, page 83.)
Chomsky's theory of language acquisition	Noam Chomsky looked at how babies and children learn language. He came to the conclusion that there was an instinct to learn language but that babies would need stimulation to do so. (See also Unit 2, page 72.)
Piaget's theory of cognitive development	Jean Piaget suggested that babies learn schemas to control their body in the first year of life. He argued that babies try to make sense of their world and reach conclusions about the objects and people around them. (See also Unit 2, pages 66–70.)
Elinor Goldschmied	While not a theorist, Goldschmied had clear ideas about how best to meet the needs of babies and toddlers. She was clear that personalised care (see below) is necessary in order that babies and toddlers can cope in a group care environment; from her work the key worker system evolved. In addition, she promoted the use of treasure basket play with babies (see also page 583) in order that they could explore using their senses. Treasure basket play involves the use of natural materials and is seen as having a key role in promoting babies' development.

The importance of attachment between infant and parent/carer

One of the most important aspects of caring for babies is to understand the impact of the bond that parents and their babies' develop. This special relationship is sometimes known as an 'attachment'. It is clear from research that babies and parents need to form attachments towards each other. The outcomes for babies where there are poor attachments are fairly negative.

In Unit 2, pages 53–4, you looked at the stages of primary attachment and saw that babies need to make strong attachments in the first year of life. You also saw that babies can make more than one attachment and that a substitute attachment is important for babies who are being cared for; you will explore this further later in this unit (see page 595).

Signs of attachment

In Unit 2 you learned that attachment was a process, and from an early stage it is possible to identify signs that babies are beginning to make attachments. They may, for example, stop crying when they hear their mother's or father's voice.

There are four broad indicators that babies begin to show once they are attached:

1. Actively seeking to be near the other person
2. Crying or showing visible distress when that person leaves or, for babies, is no longer visible
3. Showing joy or relief when that person appears
4. Acute awareness of that person's presence, for example looking up at them from time to time, responding to their voice, following their movements.

The reciprocal nature of attachments

Attachment is not a one-way process; parents and carers quickly become attached to their baby. The strength and speed with which these attachments are made can vary – some mothers report that they feel strongly about their baby soon after giving birth, while others may take a few days to 'bond'. For parents to develop an attachment or bond, time spent physically holding a baby seems to be important. This is why new mothers and especially fathers are encouraged to touch and hold their babies as soon after birth as possible. Where a baby is premature or too sick to be held, parents are encouraged to be as involved as possible in their child's care as it is recognised that some parents in the past have had difficulties in attaching to their babies.

Did you know?

Baby massage has become popular as a way of relaxing both baby and parent and thereby improving the bond between them.

⇧ **Holding and caring for a baby will improve the bond between parent and child**

Once strong attachments develop, it is interesting to observe that many of the indicators which babies show can also be seen in their parents! For example, parents will often report enjoying seeing their baby first thing in the morning and not being able to relax properly if someone else is caring for him or her. The strong nature of attachment means that few parents 'forget' where they have left their baby!

Case study

Prematurity and development

Frankie was born eight weeks premature and spent the first two weeks in an incubator. His mother was very anxious about him as he developed an infection. She stayed next to his incubator for several hours a day and supplied breast milk so that he could be fed. She was able to stroke his chest gently and this contact made her feel better. Her partner found it hard to come to the special care baby unit. He disliked seeing Frankie with tubes and felt anxious. He was also nervous about touching Frankie and stayed away from the hospital.

After four weeks, Frankie was discharged from hospital. While Frankie and his mother grew ever closer, his father remained more distant. This changed a few months later when Frankie's mother had to go into hospital for a routine operation for three days. Frankie's father was left in charge. During this time, he fed, changed and played with Frankie. He started to enjoy being with Frankie more. Frankie's mother was amazed at the difference when she returned home.

1. How might Frankie's prematurity have affected the attachment process?

2. Explain why Frankie's father now feels more strongly towards Frankie.

3. Discuss the importance of fathers taking an active role early on in a baby's life.

Did you know?

Research by Mary Ainsworth and her colleagues (1979) looked at the quality of babies' early attachments. It would seem that where babies and children are 'securely' attached they are able to explore and develop their independence. Babies and children whose attachment is less secure seem to show either indifference or clingy types of behaviour. (See also Unit 2, pages 81–2.)

Find out!

1. Observe a baby who is over 9 months old. How does the baby react when someone comes into the room with whom the baby is not familiar? Does the baby turn to look at the key worker or parent? Does he or she show any signs of distress if the person tries to pick him up?
2. Repeat this observation with a baby who is under 6 months old.
3. Can you see a difference in the babies' reactions?

The impact of the baby's temperament on parental/carer behaviour as a two-way process

Recent research findings

It is now recognised that babies show different characteristics from very early on in life. In the 1980s, Thomas and Chess studied the reactions of babies in the first few weeks after birth and were able to see clear differences between some children.

According to the observable features such as how easily babies were soothed, how often they cried and how much motor activity they showed, Thomas and Chess classified babies into three different temperament groups:

1. Easy
2. Slow to warm up
3. Difficult.

Measurements of the frequency of crying, activity level and interest in others as well as how easily babies were soothed or became irritable revealed that babies' temperaments do vary. A summary of their findings is shown in the table below.

⇩ **Summary of the three temperament groups identified by Thomas and Chess**

Easy	The majority of babies seem to fall into this category. Babies feed and sleep well, cry less and are easily soothed. They adapt well and show that they are happy.
Slow to warm up	These babies are more passive, reluctant and do not show their emotions. They take time to adapt to new foods, people or routines but then are happy.
Difficult	The minority of babies fall into this category. Such babies cry more, are hard to settle and have irregular feeding and sleep patterns. They are more unpredictable and are harder to please and keep happy.

Subsequent follow-up work found that the characteristics which babies showed early on in life tended to still be present later. Thus, easy babies often became easy toddlers and so forth. This was not universal, however, as some babies who had been characterised early on as difficult seemed to show improvements in their responses. This was attributed to sensitive and skilful parenting.

The impact of temperament

At first glance the work on temperament would suggest that parents' responses might also be altered by the characteristics that their baby shows. A baby who smiles easily, sleeps and feeds well is likely to elicit more relaxed and positive responses from parents and carers than a difficult baby who may be physically tiring and demanding. While this might seem straightforward, the reality is more complex as there are many other factors that can influence the behaviours and responses of parents. These include the parents' own emotional well-being, the support they receive in their role as parent and, crucially, their own experience of being parented. Parents who are confident and are not under stress are therefore more likely to cope with a demanding baby; they may be able to respond more positively and thus moderate the baby's original disposition.

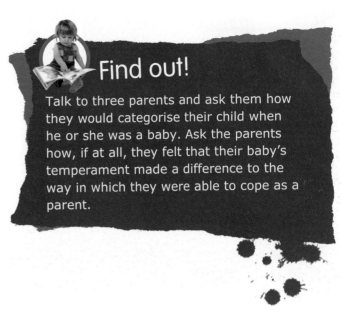

Find out!

Talk to three parents and ask them how they would categorise their child when he or she was a baby. Ask the parents how, if at all, they felt that their baby's temperament made a difference to the way in which they were able to cope as a parent.

Section 2

The role of the professional in promoting development

In practice

It is Matthew's first day with you as his carer. Matthew is 6 months old and his parents are a little nervous because this is the first time that Matthew will be with you all day.

By the end of this section you will know how to work effectively with Matthew and his parents.

How to work in partnership with parents/carers and families

It is hard for parents and carers to leave their baby in the care of someone they do not know – it often feels strange and can make parents very anxious. This is because attachments between babies and their carers are reciprocal (see page 577). It is therefore important to work effectively with parents and carers to develop a strong partnership with them. They need to know that their baby is going to be nurtured, not just looked after. To do this well you will need to gain information from parents and carers about their baby's needs, interests and 'little ways'. You will also need to know about any medical condition or allergy the baby has. This type of information is recorded so there is no confusion and the key worker can use it when planning activities and carrying out care routines such as feeding.

Sharing information

One of the ways that you can successfully build a partnership with parents and carers is by thinking about settling-in procedures. Parents will find it easier to leave their baby with you if they can see that you have made an effort to get to know them and their child. Spending time on initial visits sharing information and sharing the care of their baby is essential. Parents may show you how they settle their baby to sleep or explain how they know when their child is tired or hungry.

Once you have begun to take care of their baby, parents will want and need information about what has happened during the session. Details of naps, food and nappy changing are very important and it is usual for this information to be written down. Parents and carers also need to know what their baby has been enjoying and about their day. In the same way, you will need to know what the baby has been doing while in their care.

⇧ **Babies enjoy opportunities to discover how things work**

U18

2

The role of play in development when working with babies

Babies are playful but need a partner to play with. The adult is usually this partner and from early play experiences, babies learn a significant amount.

Physical development

Play naturally encourages babies to use their body – they may try and reach out for toys or wave their arms in excitement. A range of movements is thus promoted, including fine motor and gross motor development. If babies are also given opportunities to play on the floor by, for example, rolling balls or putting out treasure basket play (see pages 583–4), large movements known as locomotive movements are encouraged.

Intellectual development

Stimulation is important to babies' early brain activity and thus cognitive development, and play is a major way in which babies are stimulated. You can see examples of cognitive development in the way in which babies can often remember toys, games and the patterns to rhymes. Play also provides babies with opportunities to problem solve – you will often see them repeat things in order to discover how something works or use a piece of knowledge and try it in a range of circumstances, for example once babies find that they can post things they often drop a range of different objects into containers or gaps.

Communication and language development

The majority of play opportunities for this age range should be accompanied by interaction with adults. This means that play can help to promote the language development of babies.

Social, emotional and behavioural development

Play provides children with early social skills. Babies learn to join in games and to take turns. At first their contribution to the play may simply be to smile or show enjoyment, but as their physical development increases they will actively join in. A good example of this is a finger rhyme such as 'Round and Round the Garden'; at first the baby smiles and laughs when he knows he is about to be 'tickled under there', but as the baby develops he is likely to put the adult's hand on to his own to encourage the adult to play the little game again. Babies also learn through this early play how to respond to others and will often imitate facial expressions and gestures.

Play is enjoyable and pleasurable so is important to babies' emotional well-being and development. Through play and other activities, babies will develop a strong attachment to their parents and the adults who care for them, which helps them to feel secure. Early play is often highly repetitive. While this can feel limiting for adults, it is important to encourage this repetition as it is another way in which babies can feel secure.

⇧ **Through play and other activities, babies will develop a strong attachment to their parents and carers**

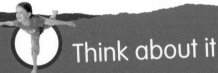

Think about it

Observe an adult playing with a baby.

1. What do you notice about the baby's facial expression?

2. What skills do think this baby is learning?

3. How is playing helping the baby to feel secure?

Examples of play activities for babies

There are many simple games and play activities that babies enjoy; some of these are described below.

Posting and dropping

Once babies reach about 8 months, they enjoy watching things drop and posting things. They may throw a spoon down from the highchair, watch you pick it up and once it is returned to them throw it down again. This is a simple game and many babies will enjoy playing it ten times or more! You can also provide tubes, tins and containers for babies to drop objects into. Again, they will drop an item into the container and then a few moments later retrieve it. Look out for containers that make a noise such as a metal tin or for objects that make a sound as they land, for example a bunch of keys.

Peepo

From around 7 or so months, babies enjoy finding things that are hidden but they know to be there. You might, for example, pull a hat down over your face then pull it back up and smile. If you do this repeatedly, the baby will start to learn that you are there. At first they may just look, but eventually they will start to join in by pulling off the hat and 'finding you'. From this you can start to hide the baby. Gently pull the hat over their eyes (not their whole face), wait a moment then pull it back up to 'find them'. As with other simple games, repeat this several times. You will probably find that babies then begin to show you that they like hiding by pulling the hat over themselves.

Knocking down

Knocking down is a simple game where a pile of objects is built up so that the baby can watch this and then eventually join in knocking them down. Stacking beakers, small boxes and wooden bricks can all be used. Begin by piling up the objects then show the baby how they can be knocked down. As with many simple games, you will probably need to repeat it a couple of times so the baby understands the game. Then look out for signs that the baby is ready to do the knocking down.

Cold cooked spaghetti

Cook some spaghetti, drain it then add a couple of drops of food colouring. Leave it until it is cold. Put it out either on a large sheet of plastic on the ground or on the tray of the highchair. Touch it for the baby to see and then encourage the baby to enjoy touching and playing with it. Note that this is not suitable for babies who have a wheat allergy as some babies may try to eat it!

Treasure basket play

A particular type of play known as treasure basket play is usually recommended for babies. This is easy to prepare and plan for. It has its origins in traditional ways in which babies were cared for, but has been brought to modern-day attention by Elinor Goldschmied.

A range of natural materials, objects and artefacts are put together in a basket that the baby can easily reach into. The aim is that the baby can take things out and explore them using all the senses including the mouth. This means that objects need to be kept clean but also checked as a choking hazard. Examples of items that might be included in a treasure basket include the following:

- Ball of string
- Cardboard tubing
- Natural sponge
- Orange
- Wooden spoon
- Coconut
- Metal biscuit tin
- Metal teaspoon
- Rubber plunger
- Leather purse
- Corks
- Rubber plug

Babies enjoy this activity as it satisfies their curiosity and gives them plenty of stimulation. During the activity they learn about textures, shape, size and how to make connections. Interestingly, babies will often spend quite long periods engaged in this play. The role of the adult is unusual – instead of interacting or showing the baby objects, the adult stays close by and is there for reassurance rather than to be active in the play. This is a good time to observe babies' development as well as notice what type of things fascinate or intrigue them.

In order to maintain interest in the activity it is important that new objects appear in the basket, especially those that will support any play themes the child has shown interest in, for example trying to stack objects or posting them.

Supporting play with communication and language

A major task for babies in their first year is to break into communication and language. Babies seem instinctively primed to do this but can only achieve it with adults' help. They need adults to talk and interact with them. This is an essential role for adults who work with babies as it makes a significant difference to babies' later cognitive development and behaviour (see also page 582).

Cuddling and talking

Most adults adapt their style of speech to suit babies almost instinctively. The pitch of the voice becomes higher, key words are emphasised and the facial expression is exaggerated. This is sometimes dubbed 'parentese'. Physical interaction such as cuddling and holding is also important. For the adult, this makes it easier to switch into 'parentese'; it also helps the baby to feel reassured.

It becomes easier to talk to a baby when you both 'know' each other. This is why it is essential for language development that babies have their own key worker with whom they develop a special relationship.

Running commentary

One of the ways in which adults can support early language is by talking to babies, even though their responses may seem limited. This type of talk is sometimes referred to as a running commentary – the adult talks to the baby about what they are doing and tries to include the baby. You may find yourself doing this while involved in some of the routine physical care aspects of working with babies such as nappy changing and feeding.

Acknowledging babies

One of the key ways to support babies' language and communication development is by acknowledging facial expressions and any vocalisations. You can do this by smiling, laughing and talking back. It does not matter that you do not always understand what is 'said', as long as the baby's efforts are acknowledged positively. In this way adults can have 'conversations' with very young babies. Where vocalisations are acknowledged and positive responses are given, babies learn that they are valued.

Drawing babies' attention to objects and games

Another way of helping babies to break into the code of language is by drawing their attention to things. You may, for example, hold a rattle in front of the baby and shake it while talking about it. In the same way, you might carry a baby over to a window and point out a passing cat and talk about the cat. From around 10 months, most babies who have had their attention drawn to things begin to reciprocate this movement; they will start to point out things to you such as a favourite toy on a shelf or their bib.

Rhymes and songs

Singing to babies and saying rhymes is a traditional way of providing emotional reassurance to babies; it also helps them to develop language. It is important that babies have individual times when their key worker holds them and uses songs and rhymes. These should be often repeated so that the baby can predict what is going to happen and become familiar with the sounds, rhythms and tunes.

Good practice checklist

Supporting communication and language
- ✓ Sing and say rhymes and songs.
- ✓ Use finger play.
- ✓ Make eye contact.
- ✓ Hold the baby.
- ✓ Respond to facial expressions.
- ✓ Acknowledge babbling.
- ✓ Use a running commentary.
- ✓ Point and draw attention to objects.
- ✓ Use simple picture books.

How to use observation methods to assess development

As part of your work with babies you need to assess their development and interests. This is important so that you can be sure that activities and your way of working meet their needs; for example, when a baby can roll over you will need to be vigilant when changing his or her nappy. Observation and assessment is also essential as a way of checking that babies are meeting expected developmental milestones; early identification of developmental delay and subsequent support is known to be beneficial.

Observations needs to be regular

The pace of babies' development in the first year is incredible, so observations need to be carried out regularly in order to make accurate assessments of development. It is usual for the key worker to carry out such observations. This makes sense as the key worker needs to develop a strong understanding and awareness of the baby.

Observation methods

In Unit 2, you looked at various methods of observing children (see pages 89–98). Most settings observe babies using two styles: checklists and snapshots.

Checklists

Checklists are usually based on the milestones of expected development and can be helpful in reminding practitioners of these in relation to the babies in their care. It is important that checklists are completed accurately so that a picture of the child's rate of development can be built up. Remember that it is usual to find that the developmental picture is not uniform; babies may reach milestones in advance of their chronological age in some areas of development but not in others.

Snapshot observations

Many settings use a system of noting down odd incidents or glimpses of development throughout a session. These notes are used to build up a picture of development and record a baby's play interests. Snapshot observations are popular with parents as they seem less clinical than checklists.

Photographs and film

Photography and filming has become a cheap and easy way of visually recording babies. It is also a lovely way of sharing information with parents as they can see what their baby has been doing and enjoying. As with all observation and recording methods, it is important that care is taken about obtaining permission from parents and that photographs and films are properly stored. Permission is also needed from other parents as it is hard to film only one baby without others coming into view.

Recording speech

You have seen that language development is a critical area for babies, so language development needs to be recorded in order that it can be easily assessed. To do this you can use an MP3 player, Dictaphone or tape recorder. Catching babies' vocalisations on a recording means that you can listen to their changing vocalisations and check their development. This can be a useful tool in identifying sensory impairment (see page 587).

Using observations

There is no point in carrying out observations if the information generated from them is not used. There are three key ways in which observations need to be used:

→ to build a partnership with parents and carers
→ assessment of development
→ planning.

These three ways are interrelated.

Partnership with parents and carers

Observations are a key way in which you can work well with parents and carers. Parents and carers should see any observations that have been carried out and be given regular feedback about their baby's interests and development achievements. This allows parents to follow up their baby's interests at home and to be aware of some of the safety implications, for example a key worker might report that the baby has shown an interest in doors and often sits in front of them. In some settings, parents add notes to observations about what their baby has been doing at home so that records are more rounded and complete.

It is important that any concerns about a baby's progress, health or interests are talked through with the child's parents or carers.

How to plan care and activities to promote development and support the welfare of the child

Looking after babies requires good organisation and planning. The planning of care and activities should act as a framework for your day-to-day work with babies and be based around individual babies' needs.

The starting point for developing plans should be the information that you gain from parents and carers about their children and the ongoing observations that you carry out.

As babies develop quickly during their first year, so too will the routines and plans change. What is suitable for a baby of 3 months will not be appropriate for a mobile and active 11-month-old child. The spider diagram below shows the factors that need to be taken into consideration when planning for babies.

Spider diagram: Factors to consider when planning for babies — Stage of development, Play preferences, Nap times, Nappy changes, Mobility, Bathing, Feeding.

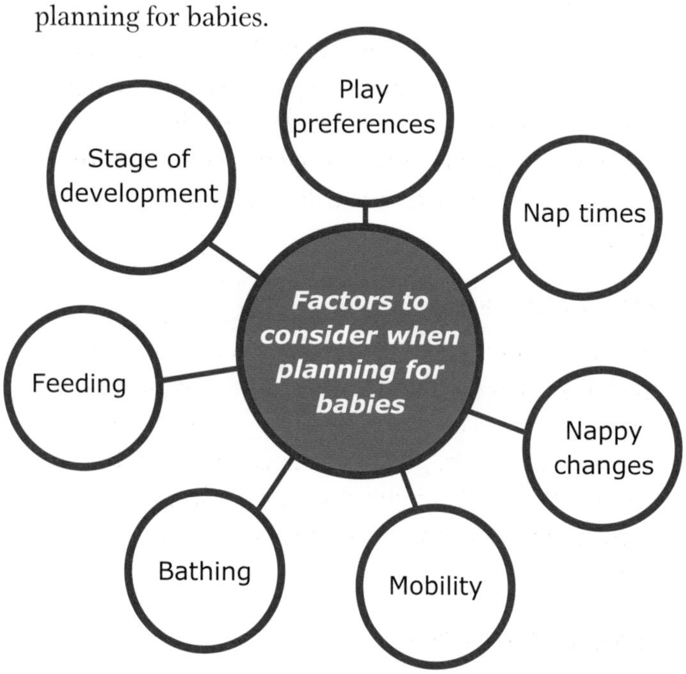

Nap times

It is important to find out how much sleep the baby needs and at what time of day he or she naps. The amount of naps a baby needs will change as he or she gets older and so will the timings.

Bathing

In many situations parents enjoy bathing their baby, but in some settings this will be the responsibility of the carer. It is usual for bath times to be built into an overall routine. Some parents prefer their baby to be bathed in the morning while others prefer this to happen just before bed. Note that some families will want their baby to be washed in running water (see also Unit 8, page 337).

Nappy changes

Nappy changes must be regular to avoid nappy rash and nappies must be changed immediately after they have been soiled.

Feeding

Babies need to be fed regularly and it is important to be organised so they are not kept waiting and hungry. Once babies reach 6 months of age, they will need to be weaned (see Unit 12, pages 465–6). It is important to find out from parents about any food preferences or dietary needs their child has. Advice about feeding babies can change, so you will also need to keep up to date with the latest guidance.

Mobility

It is important when planning for babies that they are given sufficient time and space in order to move freely. The physical development of babies affects the type of play they can engage in and, therefore, the safety precautions you will need to take (see page 588).

Play preferences

When planning activities it is important to consider the baby's play preferences as babies will quickly develop a memory for their favourite games, songs and toys. However, play preferences will change over time as the baby develops so it is important to introduce new activities in order to keep the child stimulated.

Stage of development

It is essential to observe a baby's development and to understand what the baby will be mastering next. In this way you can ensure that the right toys, games and equipment are provided.

Using observations to support planning

Observations should be used to support planning. You may need to adjust a baby's care routine as a result of what you have noticed, for example a baby trying to feed herself will need more finger foods. Sometimes observations can make practitioners aware of safety issues that should be shared with parents, such as a baby pulling up on furniture to help him stand. Observations should also be used to plan activities, resources and games for the baby. Changing needs, interests and development mean that resources and games might need to be adapted or new ones considered.

How to recognise developmental delay or sensory impairment

It is important that observations are used to consider whether babies are making sufficient developmental progress given their age; the expected milestones of development should be used here to underpin any assessment. It is also essential that you refer to previous assessments to ascertain how the baby is developing. As part of assessing development it is good practice to involve parents and carers, who will see their baby at different times; this is because babies sometimes respond in different ways depending on whom they are with.

Where babies are not meeting the expected milestones, it is important that parents are encouraged to visit their family doctor or see a health visitor for further advice. Recognising developmental delay is important as prompt referral can sometimes change the longer term outcomes.

Recognition of sensory impairment

It is important to be aware of the signs that a baby may have sight or hearing loss. Sensory impairment can impact significantly on a child's later development so needs to be identified as quickly as possible. This is one reason why it is important to encourage parents to take up the offer of health screening that is provided by the health professionals in your local area (see also Unit 11, pages 399–400).

Checking for visual impairment

Babies cannot tell you that they do not see so it is important that you actively assess their vision. To consider whether a baby's vision is developing you need to know what should be happening at different ages in the first year; this is shown in the table on the next page. Using this knowledge you can then consider whether a baby may need further checks.

⏳ Developmental milestones for babies' vision

Age	Developmental milestone
By 2 months	Looks at a person Follows moving faces Smiles in response to a smile Eyes move together
By 6 months	Looks around with interest Reaches out for small objects
By 9 months	Can see and pick up tiny objects such as crumbs
By 12 months	Points to things when asked Recognises people's faces

Checking for hearing impairment

Being able to hear is crucial for the development of language. Since all babies vocalise even when they are not hearing, it is important to look out for other signs that a baby has a hearing impairment. As with vision you will need to be familiar with the developmental milestones for hearing (see table below) and then use this information to consider whether the baby's development accords with this. Hearing will need to be checked by a professional as soon as concerns are raised.

⏳ Developmental milestones for babies' hearing

Age	Developmental milestone
By 1 month	• Notices sudden sounds by pausing and listening
By 4 months	• Smiles or quietens when hears voice of parents and carers or key worker, e.g. awake in cot and crying but stops when called out to • Turns head in response to hearing a voice immediately behind them
By 7 months	• Turns head in response to hearing a voice or sound on the other side of the room
By 9 months	• Babbling is plentiful and tuneful; listen out for a 'sing-song' quality
By 12 months	• Responds to own name and other familiar words • Makes gestures when hears familiar words such as 'bye bye'

How to provide a safe, hygienic environment in a variety of settings

Providing a safe environment

Safety is a key responsibility of adults regardless of the age of children they are working with. With babies there are particular safety issues that must be addressed in your working practice.

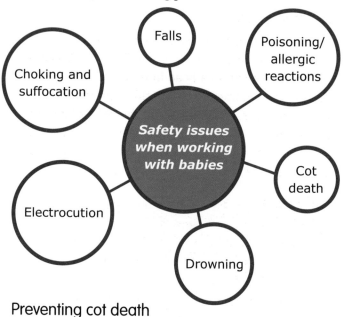

Preventing cot death

The way in which babies are put down to sleep can reduce the risk of cot death. This is an area of ongoing research so it is important to seek out the latest guidance. At the time of writing the following is recommended:

→ Babies should be put down to sleep on their back with their feet touching the base of the cot (the 'feet to foot' position).

→ Do not allow the baby to become too hot or too cold. Room temperature should be between 16 and 20 degrees Celsius (ideally 18 degrees Celsius).

→ Cot bumpers, duvets and pillows should not be used.

→ Settling a baby to sleep with a dummy can reduce the risk of cot death.

→ Young babies should not be exposed to smoky environments or placed in rooms where adults have previously smoked. Adults should not smoke and then shortly afterwards handle babies. This is because the oxygen levels in the environment/adult's breath are lower and the baby will therefore inhale slightly less oxygen than otherwise.

Preventing falls

It is essential that you are aware of areas in the environment where a baby might fall, as falls can be fatal if they result in a head injury. You will need to use safety equipment and carefully supervise babies to prevent falls. When assessing the risk of falls, it is important not to underestimate babies – a baby who can walk may quickly try and climb on to a surface or go over to a small step and fall over.

Good practice checklist

Preventing falls

- ✓ Never leave a baby unattended on a raised surface such as a changing area.
- ✓ Do not use baby walkers.
- ✓ Always use the available harnesses and straps on equipment such as highchairs or pushchairs.
- ✓ Install and use safety gates.
- ✓ Keep the floor area fairly tidy.
- ✓ Remember that non-mobile babies can often roll or wriggle.
- ✓ Supervise toddlers who may sometimes try and tip out a baby from a piece of equipment.

Preventing choking and swallowing objects

As part of their development, babies put objects into their mouth in order to explore them. This increases the risk of a choking incident. Babies from around 9 months are also prone to looking out for and picking up tiny objects that they spot, such as pins or buttons, which they may then put into their mouth.

This means that you need to take preventative measures to avoid accidents. Many 'harmless' objects have the potential to cause suffocation or choking in babies, including carrier bags, soft toys and pillows.

Good practice checklist

Preventing choking and swallowing

- ✓ Make sure that toys and equipment are age appropriate by reading the manufacturer's advice.
- ✓ Keep floor areas properly clean and vacuumed.
- ✓ Check that objects in the environment do not pose a choking hazard.
- ✓ Keep pins, needles and other sharp items in separate areas.
- ✓ Make sure that home-made garments are strong and well made – check that buttons are properly sewn on.
- ✓ Keep plastic bags and wrapping away from babies and toddlers.

Feeding

When they are first weaned at 6 months, babies tend to choke a little on their food. It is therefore important to put only small amounts of food on to the spoon and be ready to remove a baby quickly from the harness in a highchair. You should also learn the first aid technique to prevent choking. It is also important that the choice of foods given to babies is suitable for their stage of weaning. For example, babies can easily choke on a grape or piece of apple until such time as they are chewing well. Cutting up fruit into smaller pieces can therefore be a preventative measure.

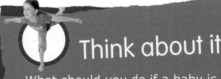

Think about it

What should you do if a baby is choking on food? (You may wish to refer to Unit 11, page 444.)

Preventing burns, scalds and electrocution

Once babies are mobile they become extremely adventurous and interested in the environment. They will, for example, start to look into bags and notice what adults do with objects, and will start to pull themselves up using furniture. They will also become interested in turning things on and off, so may try and poke things into electrical appliances or plugs. This increases the risk of many types of accidents including burns, scalds and electrocution. It is therefore important to supervise babies extremely carefully and to not underestimate their abilities.

Scalding incidents sometimes occur because adults miscalculate the temperature of food when feeding a baby or of water when preparing a bath. Babies' skin is significantly more sensitive than adults' so a temperature that seems fine for an adult might cause scalding for a baby. It is therefore important to check the temperature of food and water carefully and to use a temperature gauge when bathing a baby.

Good practice checklist

Preventing burns, scalds and electrocution

✓ Never leave hot drinks or liquids in the same room as a baby.

✓ Do not leave matches or lighters in the same area as a baby, for example in a handbag that a baby might reach into.

✓ Check the temperature of feeds and food carefully.

✓ Use a temperature gauge to check the water when bathing a baby.

✓ Use safety gates to avoid babies straying into the kitchen area.

✓ Use safety covers to protect babies from electrical sockets.

✓ Do not encourage babies to touch or become interested in electrical appliances such as the television or stereo. Make sure they cannot see how you are operating them.

Preventing drowning

It may seem hard to believe but babies and toddlers can drown in water that is only 2.5cm (1 inch) deep. This means that babies must never be left unsupervised when there is water around. Bath time has the potential to be dangerous as adults can be tempted to 'pop' out and get something such as a towel that they have forgotten while the baby is sitting happily and playing. These moments have sadly resulted in many babies' deaths. This means that before bathing a baby it is sensible to have everything you need to hand and to remain with the child at all times.

Preventing poisoning and dealing with allergic reactions

Extreme vigilance is required to remove any chemicals or medicines out of the reach of babies. It is also essential to be aware that some babies can have allergic reactions and to always check that you are giving the correct food and feeds to babies. If you think that a baby has come into contact with something that is potentially poisonous or may provoke an allergic reaction, you should seek medical attention immediately. It is also important to take with you the substance that the baby has ingested. It is essential that you take a paediatric first aid course so that you can resuscitate a baby.

Good practice checklist

Keeping babies safe

✓ Supervise babies carefully – be vigilant at all times.

✓ Always use the safety equipment that is provided.

✓ Do not underestimate babies' mobility or ability to copy movements.

✓ Follow manufacturer's instructions when using toys and equipment.

✓ Follow the latest guidance when putting babies down to sleep.

✓ Use harnesses when babies are in highchairs and pushchairs.

✓ Attend a paediatric first aid course.

Providing a hygienic environment

Babies are at greater risk of infection than older children because their immune system is immature. A baby's immune system is also less effective at coping with infection so illnesses that might be considered fairly harmless in the general population, for example food poisoning, can be a serious risk in babies.

Personal hygiene

In some ways hygiene begins with you: a good standard of personal hygiene will help to prevent the spread of infection. (See also Unit 9, page 366.)

Handwashing

Handwashing is essential when working with babies as many infections are passed on via direct contact. It is also important that your nails are kept short and clean so they are easier to wash and to prevent babies from getting scratched. Key times when hands must be washed include:

→ before touching babies if you have been playing with older children
→ before preparing feeds or feeding babies
→ after using the toilet
→ after nappy changes.

Clothing

Adults' clothing must be kept clean, so most people working with babies choose clothes that can be washed and dried easily. In many settings a uniform is provided, although it may still be the responsibility of staff to wash it.

Disposable aprons and gloves

To prevent the spread of infection, disposable gloves and aprons must be worn when coming into contact with bodily fluids, for example during nappy changing. Aprons and gloves must be discarded immediately afterwards.

Hair

It is good practice to keep long hair tied back so that it does not touch babies or end up in food. It also makes practical sense as in settings caring for young children there is often a risk of catching head lice. Babies also have the tendency to pull hair, which can be painful.

Bottles and feeding equipment

Bottles and feeding equipment must be properly washed and then sterilised. This is to avoid babies swallowing germs and developing food poisoning. There are several systems of sterilisation although there are three principal methods: chemical, steam and boiling. It is important that you find out how the sterilisation system in your setting works and read the instructions carefully. Never be tempted to take short cuts as food poisoning can be fatal.

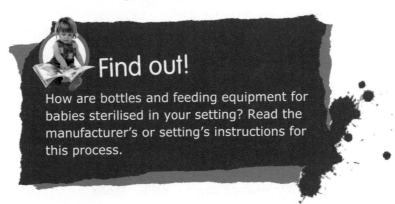

Find out!

How are bottles and feeding equipment for babies sterilised in your setting? Read the manufacturer's or setting's instructions for this process.

Toys and equipment

Toys and equipment can carry infection so it is important that babies are provided only with materials that can be easily cleaned and washed. In group care settings, some toys that are mouthed need to be washed or kept aside for individual children, to avoid cross-infection. Where toys or equipment cannot be physically washed, they should be carefully wiped down with a sterilisation solution.

Nappy changing

Nappies need to be changed promptly and regularly so that babies do not develop a rash. It is important that you carefully follow the procedures in your setting for changing nappies to prevent cross-infection. Disposable gloves and aprons should be worn and then taken off when finished. This is to avoid any traces of urine or stools being passed to babies via your hands or clothes. Dirty nappies must be immediately disposed of; in many settings there will be bags or a special bin for their disposal. The area where you have changed the baby needs to be cleaned thoroughly so that it is ready for the next change.

⬇ **It is important to clean the nappy changing area thoroughly after each use**

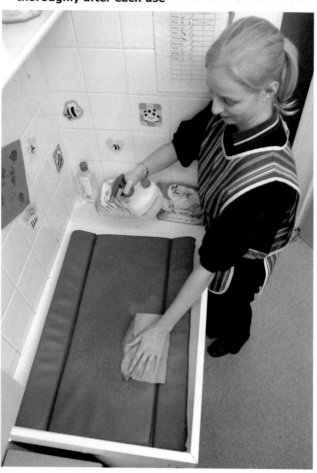

Further information on nappy changing, including the procedure for changing a nappy, is provided in Unit 4, pages 207–8.

Bathing

Keeping skin clean is a key way to reduce the risk of cross-infection. Not all settings take responsibility for bathing babies, but if you work in home-based care you may need to do this. It is important to check with parents about any products they would like you to use or ways of bathing the baby.

A step-by-step procedure for bathing a baby, together with a list of the various items you will need, is given in the chart below.

⬇ **Procedure for bathing a baby**

Checklist	Step-by-step procedure
Essential items: • Clean nappy • Clean clothes, including vest • Cotton wool or baby wipes • Bag or bucket for waste materials such as dirty nappy and wipes • Towels • Shampoo *Non-essential items:* • Thermometer to check temperature of water • Barrier cream • Soap or bubble bath • Talcum powder (Skin products should be used only after checking with parents as the baby may have a skin allergy.)	1. Prepare all the equipment and fill the baby bath with warm water. 2. Put the baby on a flat surface, undress him/her and take off the nappy. Clean the nappy area. 3. Wrap the baby gently but securely in a towel, so that the arms are tucked in. Wash the face with moist cotton wool. 4. Hold the baby over the bath and wash the head and hair. 5. Take off the towel. Holding the baby securely under the head and round the arm, lift him/her into the water. 6. Use your spare hand to wash the baby. 7. Lift the baby out of the bath, supporting under the bottom, and quickly wrap him/her in a warm towel.

Parenting and child-rearing practices

In addition to sharing information about babies' needs, interests and development, you also need to find out from parents and carers about their preferences for caring for their child. Some parents may, for example, want their baby to have a dummy to go to sleep, while others may wish for barrier cream to be applied at nappy changes. Some parenting and child-rearing practices are cultural or religious while others might be social; a parent may, for example, want their child to eat only organic and free-range meat because of their social conscience. It is important that these preferences are respected as you should be aiming to work alongside parents and carers.

However, the main exceptions to this rule are if parents' and carers' wishes run counter to professional practice and are detrimental to the health of the children in your care. For example, if parents insist that their 4-month-old baby is put down to sleep on her front, this would contradict professional advice on how to avoid cot death (see page 588). In such cases, it is usually possible to talk through the reasons why you cannot respect the parents' or carers' requests.

Below are examples of the questions that you might need to ask parents and carer about how to care for their child:

→ Do you use barrier cream, oil or any particular skin product on your baby?
→ Does your baby have a particular comforter or toy at nap time?
→ Do you have a particular method of helping your baby to sleep, for example music, stroking, massage?
→ Do you use a dummy with your baby? If so, in what situations?
→ Are there any specific dietary requirements, for example halal, kosher, organic or vegetarian foods?

Section 3

The roles and responsibilities of professionals working with babies

In practice

The nursery you are working with is reviewing its policies as it has recently begun to accept babies. You have been asked to look at the existing policies and consider how they might be extended to incorporate the needs of babies.

By the end of this section you will know about what constitutes overall good practice when working with babies and their families.

The importance of the key worker system in a variety of settings

One of the most important ways in which you can work effectively with babies and their families is to provide a robust key worker system. A key worker is someone who has a special and consistent relationship with the baby. The quality of the relationship is important as the baby needs to form a bond or attachment to their key worker. This is essential for babies' emotional well-being and is considered a key factor in providing quality care for young children.

The role of the key worker

Regardless of the setting, the role of the key worker remains the same: the key worker must effectively act as a substitute 'parent' and the baby should spend most if not all of their time in the key worker's company. The key worker should also be the person who carries out the routine physical care for the baby such as nappy changing, feeding and cleaning. This is important as these moments provide opportunities for close one-to-one interaction. In addition, the key worker needs to provide plenty of physical contact, reassurance and warmth. This means holding the baby, pointing things out to the baby and interacting well. The key worker also needs to help the baby settle to sleep and be there when

the baby awakes. This is important as at these times babies can feel disorientated and vulnerable.

Being a key worker is an enormous responsibility and should not be undertaken lightly. The baby's need to attach is of paramount importance so the adult must be consistently present for the child as well as emotionally available. In addition, the key worker should liaise with the child's parents and carers so that information can be properly shared and developmental changes noted alongside the baby's needs. Observations, records and plans also need to be shared with parents and carers so they can contribute and work in partnership (see also page 586).

Providing backup for a key worker in group care settings

In group care settings where staff may go on holiday, gain promotion or take a break from work, babies will need an additional person with whom they can feel safe and comfortable. This provides backup for the baby in situations where their key worker may not be available, for example because of illness. It is important, however, to stress that this additional adult does not play the same role in the baby's day-to-day life as the key worker – it is important that the baby has one strong attachment rather than several weaker ones.

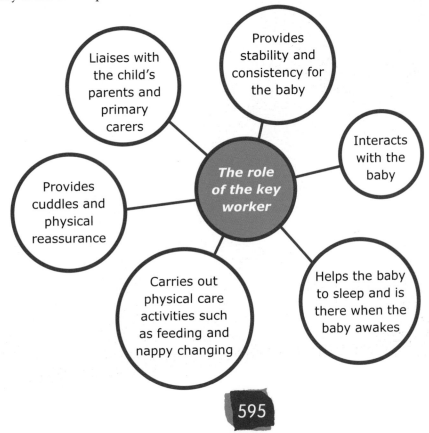

Policies and procedures for the care of babies and legal and ethical responsibilities

Policies are guidelines that set out the aims of how practitioners intend to work with children. From these policies, procedures are established so that everyone knows what they should do in any given situation. It is important that policies and procedures consider the needs of babies and their families.

Procedures can change from setting to setting in order to reflect the different organisational structures and facilities. Policies and procedures will also reflect both legal and ethical responsibilities towards babies and their families; legal responsibilities will be based on the current legislation in place in a country. In England, for example, settings including childminders will have to follow the standards in the new Early Years Foundation Stage from September 2008. In other countries, standards for care are set by national inspectorates. Examples of ways in which legal responsibilities affect day-to-day practice include the staff to baby ratio and the way in which babies' physical needs are met.

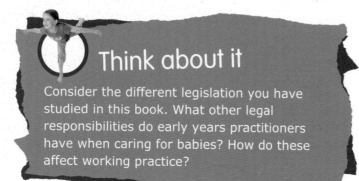

Think about it

Consider the different legislation you have studied in this book. What other legal responsibilities do early years practitioners have when caring for babies? How do these affect working practice?

In addition, professionals have ethical responsibilities towards babies and their parents. This might include providing a family with advice and support or letting them know of local and national services that might help them. By supporting families in this way, settings will be indirectly helping the baby.

Key procedures that you must be aware of when working with babies include:

→ settling-in
→ nappy changing
→ bathing
→ putting babies down to sleep
→ preparing food and feeding babies
→ reporting health and safety concerns
→ what to do if you have concerns about a baby's well-being.

The organisation of care in a variety of settings

Today, babies are cared for in group settings and non-group settings, which is often referred to as home-based care. Babies' requirement for loving interactions, stimulation and physical care is a constant wherever they are cared for. In this section you will look at the organisation of care in group settings; on pages 597–8 you will consider good practice in non-group settings.

Providing personalised care

One of the key issues when working with babies in group care is to avoid situations whereby a baby is seen as part of a 'group' rather than as an individual. You have read that attachment is vital for babies' emotional well-being (see page 576); hence routines such as feeding, nappy changing and sleeping must be personalised. This means that each baby should have their own routine rather than one that is organised for the benefit of the setting. Babies should be fed individually rather than in groups and the same goes for nappy changing – it is essential that these are points of contact with the key worker. It is also vital that thought is given to how babies will have plenty of individual time with their key worker so they can establish a genuine bond.

Many group care settings try to personalise the equipment and resources they use. For example, a baby may always go into the same cot and have the same blanket, or when it is time for feeding be given the same patterned bowl, spoon and bib. Personalising care helps babies to realise that they are individual and is considered another aspect of good practice.

Layout

The layout and furnishing of day care settings is an interesting consideration. Should babies be in environments that resemble miniature nurseries or should the environment look homely? Most experts believe that the latter is best so that babies and the staff caring for them are in a relaxed and cosy environment. This means that many settings provide sofas and comfortable armchairs in the rooms alongside essential equipment such as cots and highchairs.

Changing rooms

Many babies spend significant amounts of time in day care – it is not unusual for babies to be there longer than the staff! In order to meet their need for stimulation, it is important that babies spend time in different environments rather than just one room. This is why it is good practice for babies to be taken outdoors and into other areas within the setting.

Stimulation

You have seen that toys and equipment are important, but in some ways the most significant stimulation is the interaction between key worker and child. In this respect a 'running commentary' style of working is important (see page 584). Adults always find this easier to achieve when they are doing something or there is something they can draw babies' attention to. This is important to think about as otherwise there is a danger that you can become bored and the quality of your interactions will decrease. Day care settings have different answers as to how to maintain a stimulating environment for both babies and adults so that the time spent does not become monotonous. Going outside, planning activities or inviting a sibling down to play are all ways of creating a varying and stimulating environment.

Attachments to siblings

Caring for babies and children for extended periods in day care settings is a relatively new phenomenon. One thing that should be thought about is the relationship that siblings need to develop with each other. Many day care settings group children according to their age so there is a danger that unless a system is in place, siblings might not play together. This is important because family relationships are central in children's lives, beginning as early attachments. This means that where a baby has an older brother or sister, you should think about encouraging them to small but frequent amounts of time together. Some settings bring siblings together at mealtimes but it is also possible for them to be brought together so they can learn to play.

Good practice in non-group settings

The need to find ways of personalising care becomes much easier in home-based care where nannies, childminders or foster carers may work. Essentially the nanny or childminder becomes the key worker and a strong relationship can quickly be built, as they will have sole care of the baby.

Coping with children of different ages

In some situations, babies will be looked after alongside older siblings or children. It is important that sufficient thought is given to how the babies' needs are met alongside those of the other children, for example the baby will need time on the floor but older children may want to play outdoors. Most home-based carers find that they are able to juggle the demands by developing strong routines and managing time well. For example, an older child might have a drink and snack when he comes home from school which coincides with the baby being given her feed.

⬆ **Children of different ages, including siblings, are more likely to play together in home-based childcare**

Safety

Safety is a major consideration in all settings, but in home-based care there may be additional hazards that need risk assessing. Hazardous environments may include the kitchen, stairs and living room. Additional safety equipment will be required and good habits in terms of supervising children will need to be adopted. It is also important to be aware that older children's behaviour and activities can pose a danger, for example they may leave small toys around or become boisterous in their games around a baby. It is therefore essential that the adult supervises activities well and is able to anticipate potential dangers and eliminate them.

Working with parents

As with day care settings, working with parents is essential. Working with parents in home-based care can be more intense but this can also create a strong partnership. It is essential that the relationship with parents remains friendly yet professional. This is important as otherwise it can become difficult to discuss sensitive issues such as finance. As in day care settings, it is important to share information at the start and end of a session. Many home-based carers keep a diary which includes observations and notes.

How to work with other professionals in a multi-agency team

As part of your work with babies and their families, you may work with other professionals. This will to a large extent depend on the needs of the child and the family, as well as the type of setting in which you work.

For more information on the types of professionals who work with children and guidance on how to work with them in a multi-agency approach, you should revisit the following units:

➔ Unit 3 page 128
➔ Unit 5 pages 215–17
➔ Unit 8 pages 347–57
➔ Unit 9 page 381
➔ Unit 11 pages 450–1
➔ Unit 14 pages 530–3

Safeguarding and protecting children from harm

Child protection, which is increasingly referred to as safeguarding children, is an important aspect of working with children. As you have seen in Unit 3, it is essential that you understand the policy and procedures for protecting children in your setting. Caring for a baby is a demanding task; sometimes parents and other adults caring for a baby can fail to meet the baby's needs and in rare cases may even deliberately set out to harm a baby. The reasons why babies are vulnerable to abuse are complex; difficulties with attachment, substance abuse, depression and the acceptance of responsibility can all play a part. (See also Unit 3, pages 123–4.)

Recognising signs of abuse

It is important to be aware of the signs of abuse or difficulties with parenting so that advice, support or if necessary intervention can be sought. The categories of abuse that you looked at in Unit 3 (pages 124–6) are the same when working with babies and many of the indicators remain the same. Below are some specific points that relate to the care of babies.

Bruises or injuries in non-mobile babies

Any marks or injuries in non-mobile babies need to be taken seriously. Non-mobile babies rarely bruise themselves even when playing with toys or having their nappy changed. Marks may therefore indicate that a baby has been deliberately harmed or that the adult responsible for the baby has not been taking proper care of him or her.

Injuries in mobile babies

Once babies become mobile, the potential for accidents increases. Below is a list of signs that may indicate non-accidental injury:

➔ finger bruising on the chest
➔ burns and scalds on the back of hands
➔ burns and scalds on the back
➔ bruises on the back or buttocks (babies usually fall forwards)
➔ black eyes
➔ bite marks
➔ striped bruising – indicating a baby may have been slapped
➔ fractures – most babies' falls do not result in fractures.

Where a baby frequently sustains minor accidental injuries, concerns may be raised as to whether there is some neglect, for example the failure to supervise or use safety equipment. In some cases this may indicate that the adult responsible is unaware of the dangers in the environment or is not coping with the responsibility of caring for a baby.

Growth and development

The overall growth and development of babies may also indicate whether a baby is getting sufficient care and attention. Babies who are not being fed sufficiently will not put on weight and will be more vulnerable to infections; they may also fail to meet the expected developmental milestones. Babies whose nappies are not being changed are likely to have skin infections.

Shaken baby syndrome

As a result of CT scanners it is now possible to see whether a baby has received a head injury even when the head itself has no physical signs of trauma. Shaking a baby can cause injuries to the brain resulting in death. It is therefore important that parents and adults working with babies understand that shaking a baby can cause brain damage or death. Signs that a baby has been shaken include lethargy, floppiness, irritability, difficulty in breathing and drowsiness, although these symptoms can also be the result of other medical conditions including a serious infection. As these are signs that a baby is not well, a baby should always be seen by a doctor in such circumstances.

Post-natal depression

As part of preventing child abuse, it is important to recognise signs that a mother may need additional support. Post-natal depression can affect women in the months after birth and can be a serious condition, affecting the mother's ability to look after the baby and/or herself. While most women report feeling miserable and having mood swings in the early days after giving birth (known as the 'baby blues'), this is a natural consequence of hormonal changes in the body. Post-natal depression is longer lasting and can be more severe. While it is common for it to occur in the first few weeks following the 'baby blues', it can appear later and develop gradually. Few women with post-natal depression

harm their baby, although they may contemplate harming themselves, but it can affect their enjoyment and ability to respond to their baby. This in turn can affect the mother–baby attachment.

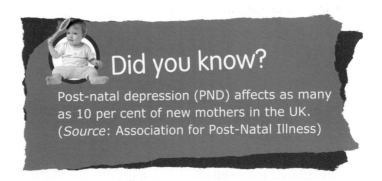

Did you know?

Post-natal depression (PND) affects as many as 10 per cent of new mothers in the UK. (*Source*: Association for Post-Natal Illness)

Signs that a woman may be suffering from post-natal depression include:

→ sleeplessness and insomnia, even though the mother may be very tired
→ tiredness
→ irritability
→ lack of interest and enjoyment in the baby, their partner or in life
→ panic attacks
→ lack of appetite
→ irrational thoughts such as the baby not liking them
→ fear of harming the baby
→ suicidal thoughts.

Supporting women with post-natal depression

Women with post-natal depression can feel guilty that they are not enjoying being with their baby, so may not seek help. They often do not realise that their feelings are caused by a depression and this may prevent them from talking to friends and family about how they are feeling. Many women, therefore, do not get the support they need; it is estimated that only 1 in 4 women seek treatment. It is important, wherever possible, to encourage women to visit their family doctor to be assessed. Treatment can include a course of anti-depressants but sometimes just identifying that depression is the cause and gaining extra support from friends and professionals is sufficient. Recovery from post-natal depression can take some time but the overall outlook is very positive.

What to do if you suspect that a baby is at risk of harm or neglect

If you suspect that there may be a problem, it is essential that you report your concerns quickly. Babies cannot seek help nor can they modify their behaviour to keep themselves safe, for example by stopping crying. You should contact the member of staff designated in your setting's child protection procedure.

Find out!

1. Find out about your setting's policy in regard to safeguarding babies.
2. To whom would you pass on your concerns if you suspected that a baby was at risk?

Sources of support for families

Becoming a parent is no easy task. Many parents therefore find it useful to gain information and support from others. There are many groups that help parents in this way. Some groups provide general information while others help parents deal with specific problems such as crying. In recent times the Internet has become a popular tool as parents who may not be able to physically 'go' somewhere to meet others can do so online. The Internet also allows parents to get advice and support without anyone knowing their identity. This anonymity can help parents feel less judged and more secure, especially if they are embarrassed at having problems. Below are some examples of support groups who help families.

Examples of support groups for families

Name	Purpose	Website address
National Childbirth Trust	Helps parents gain advice and support before and after the birth of their child.	www.nct.org.uk
Home-Start	An organisation that helps parents of babies and young children. As part of their work, volunteers will visit and support parents.	www.home-start.org.uk
Cry-sis	An organisation that supports parents with demanding, sleepless and crying babies.	www.cry-sis.org.uk
Veritee's Post Natal Illness Web Site	Website for women experiencing post-natal depression (post-natal illness) run by sufferers and survivors of the condition.	www.pni.org.uk
Gingerbread	An organisation for lone parents and their children. Provides advice and support for lone parents.	www.gingerbread.org.uk
BBC Online –Parenting	A website providing advice on parenting and preparing for parenthood.	www.bbc.co.uk/parenting
Fathers Direct	Provides advice and training for supporting fathers and their families.	www.fathersdirect.co.uk
Netmums	A website that provides mothers with local information and puts local mothers in contact with each other.	www.netmums.com
Parentlineplus	Advice for parents who are feeling stressed and who need advice and support.	www.parentlineplus.org.uk
Raising Kids	An online magazine that has advice, support and ideas for parents.	www.raisingkids.co.uk

Find out!

Research two of the support groups listed on page 600 for families. How easy would it be to gain information and support from the websites?

Case study

New parents may need support

Fergus and Amanda are starting to feel weary and stressed. Their daughter, Millie, is 3 months old and cries for long periods. They have been to their doctor who can find nothing medically wrong with her. Their health visitor has reassured them that it is nothing they are doing and that most babies who cry like this eventually grow out of it. They have tried a range of different things, hoping to find a way of stopping her from crying – they have rocked her, taken her outside in the buggy and bought dummies. The stress is starting to show as they have had very little sleep and rest. The other night Amanda came close to shaking her daughter and this incident really frightened her. They already have a son who is at nursery and with whom they had no problems.

Today Amanda has come to a support group that she has been told about by her friend. After a coffee, a few tears and a break from looking after Millie, Amanda feels much better. She starts to realise that she is not the only parent who is having problems and feels much calmer. She says that the group has made her feel better and not so guilty. She says it is good to hear how other mums have also felt angry with their babies. She decides to go back to the doctor and to find out more about milk allergy.

1. Explain how support groups can help parents.

2. Why is it important that groups are non-judgemental and accepting?

3. How might support groups play a role in child protection?

How to promote and maintain a non-judgemental and anti-discriminatory approach when working with babies and their families

One of the main ways in which you can help parents adjust to the role of being a parent is by being non-judgemental. Parents often need someone to turn to who will be able to listen to them without judging them. It is normal for most parents to have mixed and intense emotions; the strength of these emotions may take some parents by surprise. They may, for example, be concerned that they can feel angry towards their baby when at other times they will feel intense love or pride for their child. It is important that they can express this ambivalence without fear of being judged as a 'bad parent'. Tiredness is also a feature of the first few months of parenting and many parents find this puts a strain on their relationships with partners and close family members.

You may discover as you listen that there are a range of ways in which parents care for their children. In some cases these will be linked to cultural and social influences, for example some parents believe it necessary to keep their baby in bed with them. Recognising that there are variances in child-rearing practices is important when listening to and supporting parents. Where parents feel that someone is judging them or criticising them, they quickly become reluctant to share their problems.

Getting ready for assessment

Below are some questions that you can use to check your understanding and recall of this unit.

1. Outline the physical development that might be expected of babies from birth to 12 months.

2. Explain the different factors that might affect the progress of development in the first year of life.

3. Describe the ways in which play can support babies' development in the first year of life.

4. Analyse the role of the key worker when working with babies and their families.

5. Evaluate the role of the practitioner when working with babies and supporting families.

Further reading

Unit 1: An introduction to working with children

→ Squire, G. (ed.) (2007) *Children's Care, Learning and Development*. Oxford: Heinemann

Websites

→ Every Child Matters: www.everychildmatters.gov.uk
→ SureStart: www.surestart.gov.uk

Unit 2: Development from conception to age 16 years

→ Bee, Helen (2000) *The Developing Child* (9th ed.). London: Allyn and Bacon
→ Gross, Richard D. (2001) *Psychology: the science of mind and behaviour*. London: Hodder & Stoughton
→ Hobart, Christine & Frankel, Jill (2004) *A Practical Guide to Child Observation and Assessment* (3rd ed.). Cheltenham: Nelson Thornes
→ Meggitt, Carolyn & Sunderland, Gerald (2000) *Child Development: an illustrated guide*. Oxford: Heinemann
→ Sheridan, Mary D. (1997) *From Birth to Five Years: children's developmental progress*. London: Routledge
→ Squire, G. (ed.) (2007) *Children's, Care Learning and Development*. Oxford: Heinemann
→ Sylva, Kathy & Lunt, Ingrid (1982) *Child Development: A first course*. Oxford: Blackwell

Unit 3: Supporting children

→ Department of Health, Home Office, Department for Education and Employment (1999) *Working Together to Safeguard Children: A guide to inter-agency working to safeguard and promote the welfare of children*. London: HMSO
→ Nutbrown, Cathy & Clough, Peter (2006) *Inclusion in the Early Years*. London: Sage
→ Squire, G. (ed.) (2007) *Children's, Care Learning and Development*. Oxford: Heinemann

Websites

→ Every Child Matters: www.everychildmatters.gov.uk
→ Commission for Equality and Human Rights: www.cehr.org.uk
→ UNICEF UK: www.unicef.org.uk

Unit 4: Keeping children safe

Websites

→ Child Accident Prevention Trust: www.capt.org.uk
→ Countryside Foundation for Education: www.countrysidefoundation.org.uk
→ Department of Health: www.doh.gov.uk
→ Food Standards Agency: www.food.gov.uk
→ Health and Safety Executive: www.hse.gov.uk
→ Learning Through Landscapes (organisation that specialises in showing ways in which nursery and schools can use the outdoor area to promote learning): www.ltl.org.uk
→ Ofsted (for regulations and safety in early years settings): www.Ofsted.gov.uk
→ RoSPA (The Royal Society for the Prevention of Accidents): www.rospa.com/homesafety/advice/child/accidents.htm
→ Safe Kids: www.safekids.co.uk
→ Teachernet website on Growing Schools programme: www.teachernet.gov.uk/growingschools/resources/teachingresources/detail.cfm.
→ Teachernet website on learning outside the classroom: www.teachernet.gov.uk/learningoutsidetheclassroom
→ Think! Road Safety Website: www.thinkroadsafety.gov.uk

Unit 5: The principles underpinning the role of the practitioner working with children

→ Adams, S., Alexander, E., Drummond, M.J. & Moyles, J. (2004) *First Hand Experience: What matters to children. Rich Learning Opportunities*
→ Department for Education and Skills (2007) *Statutory Framework for the Early Years Foundation Stage*. Nottingham: DfES Publications

Websites

- → Children and Young People Now: www.childrennow.co.uk
- → Every Child Matters: www.everychildmatters.gov.uk
- → Montessori International Magazine: www.montessorimagazine.com
- → Nursery World: www.nurseryworld.co.uk
- → Ofsted: www.ofsted.gov.uk
- → SureStart: www.surestart.gov.uk
- → 4Children: www.4children.org.uk

Unit 6: Promoting a healthy environment for children

- → Hobart, Christine & Frankel, Jill (2004) *A Practical Guide to Child Observation and Assessment* (3rd ed.). Cheltenham: Nelson Thornes
- → Meggitt, Carolyn & Sunderland, Gerald (2000) *Child Development: an illustrated guide*. Oxford: Heinemann
- → Squire, G. (ed.) (2007) Children's, *Care Learning and Development*. Oxford: Heinemann
- → Tassoni, Penny & Hucker, Karen (2006) *Planning Play and the Early Years*. Oxford: Heinemann
- → Tassoni, P. (2002) *Planning for the Foundation Stage: Ideas for themes and activities*. Oxford: Heinemann

Websites

- → Every Child Matters: www.everychildmatters.gov.uk
- → Nursery World: www.nurseryworld.co.uk

Unit 7: Play and learning in children's education

- → Bruce, Tina (1997) *Early Childhood Education*. London: Hodder & Stoughton
- → Department for Education and Skills (2007) *Statutory Framework for the Early Years Foundation Stage*. Nottingham: DfES Publications
- → Tassoni, Penny & Hucker, Karen (2006) *Planning Play and the Early Years*. Oxford: Heinemann

Websites

- → Every Child Matters: www.everychildmatters.gov.uk
- → I Can (helps children communicate): www.ican.org.uk
- → National Deaf Children's Society: www.ndcs.org.uk
- → Nursery World: www.nurseryworld.co.uk
- → The Standards Site: Department for Children, Schools and Families: www.standards.dfes.gov.uk
- → SureStart: www.surestart.gov.uk
- → Teachernet: www.teachernet.gov.uk

- → World Organisation for Early Childhood Education: www.omep-ong.net

Unit 8: Caring for children

- → Squire, G. (ed.) (2007) *Children's, Care Learning and Development*. Oxford: Heinemann

Websites

- → Children's Workforce Development Council: www.cwdcouncil.org.uk

Unit 9: Development of professional skills within children's education

- → Hobart, Christine & Frankel, Jill (2004) *A Practical Guide to Child Observation and Assessment* (3rd ed.). Cheltenham: Nelson Thornes
- → Squire, G. (ed.) (2007) *Children's, Care Learning and Development*. Oxford: Heinemann

Unit 11: Care of sick children

Websites

- → Action for Sick Children: www.actionforsickchildren.org
- → Association for Spina Bifida and Hydrocephalus (ASBAH): www.asbah.org
- → Association of Children Hospices: www.childhospice.org.uk
- → Asthma UK: www.asthma.org.uk
- → BBC Health website: www.bbc.co.uk/health
- → Cabinet Office: Social Exclusion Taskforce: www.cabinetoffice.gov.uk/social_exclusion_task_force
- → Child and Adolescent Mental Health Services (CAMHS): www.youngminds.org.uk/camhs
- → Diabetes UK: www.diabetes.org.uk
- → Department of Health: www.dh.gov.uk
- → Epilepsy Action: www.epilepsy.org.uk
- → Health Protection Agency: www.hpa.org.uk
- → NCH (National Children's Home): www.nch.org.uk
- → National Eczema Society: www.eczema.org
- → National Institute for Health and Clinical Excellence: www.nice.org.uk
- → NHS Immunisation Information: www.immunisation.nhs.uk
- → NHS Newborn Hearing Screening Programme (NHSP): hearing.screening.nhs.uk
- → Shelter: england.shelter.org.uk
- → Sickle Cell Society: www.sicklecellsociety.org
- → UK Air Quality Archive (Department for Environment, Food and Rural Affairs): www.airquality.co.uk

Unit 12: Nutrition and healthy food for children

Websites

→ 5 a day: www.5aday.nhs.uk
→ Allergy in Schools: www.allergyinschools.org.uk
→ British Nutrition Foundation: www.nutrition.org.uk
→ Cystic Fibrosis Trust: www.cftrust.org.uk
→ Diabetes UK: www.diabetes.org.uk
→ Food Standards Agency: www.foodstandards.gov.uk
→ Food Standards Agency, Eat Well campaign: www.eatwell.gov.uk
→ The Information Centre: Infant Feeding Survey 2005: www.ic.nhs.uk/pubs/breastfeed2005
→ National Childbirth Trust, Breastfeeding Awareness: www.nct.org.uk/breastfeeding
→ NHS Breastfeeding website: www.breastfeeding.nhs.uk
→ School Food Trust: www.schoolfoodtrust.org.uk
→ Social Issues Research Centre: www.sirc.org
→ Vegetarian Society: www.vegsoc.org

Unit 14: Working with children with special needs

→ Tassoni, Penny (2003) *Supporting Special Needs: Understanding inclusion in the early years.* Oxford: Heinemann

Websites

→ Contact a Family (information and support for families and professionals about a range of medical conditions, disabilities and special needs): www.cafamily.org.uk
→ I Can (specialises in promoting the communication development of all children, especially those who may need additional support): www.ican.org.uk

Unit 16: Developing children's (3–8 years) communication, language and literacy skills

→ Makin, Laurie & Whitehead, Marian (2004) *How to develop children's early literacy: a guide for professional carers and educators.* London: Paul Chapman
→ Squire, G. (ed.) (2007) *Children's, Care Learning and Development.* Oxford: Heinemann

Websites

→ British Dyslexia Association: www.bdadyslexia.org.uk
→ Department for Children, Schools and Families: www.dcsf.gov.uk
→ National Literacy Trust (provides up to date information about all aspects of literacy and language): www.literacytrust.org.uk
→ Teachernet (online resources for teachers and teaching assistants, including good practice video clips): www.teachernet.gov.uk

Unit 18: Working with babies from birth to 12 months

→ Abbott, L. & Moylett, H. (eds.) (1997) *Working With the Under-Threes: Responding to children's needs.* Buckingham: Open University Press
→ Meggitt, Carolyn & Sunderland, Gerald (2000) *Child Development: an illustrated guide.* Oxford: Heinemann
→ Sheridan, Mary D. (1997) *From Birth to Five Years: children's developmental progress.* London: Routledge
→ Squire, G. (ed.) (2007) *Children's, Care Learning and Development.* Oxford: Heinemann

Websites

→ BBC Parenting (resources and information for parents): www.bbc.co.uk/parenting/having_a_baby/
→ The Foundation for the Study of Infant Deaths (FSID): www.sids.org.uk
→ National Childbirth Trust (information about pregnancy, childbirth and parenting): www.nct.org.uk
→ Tommy's the Baby Charity (provides information about conception, pregnancy and early development): www.tommys.org

Index

bladder and bowel control 340-1
body language 13, 140
bonding see attachment
book corners 306
bowel and bladder control 340-1
Bowlby, John 80, 82-3, 576
brain development 40
breastfeeding/breast milk 260, 399, 417, 458, 464-5, 471, 574-5
British Sign Language (BSL) 529
Bruner, Jerome 285
bullying 155

CACHE Statement of Values 367
care needs 204-8
    encouraging independence 210-11, 344-6
    identifying individual 343
    planning care routines 208-10
    recognising basic needs 336-42
Care Standards Act (2000) 250
centile charts 37
central nervous system (CNS) 40
chicken pox 408, 423
Child and Adolescent Mental Health Services (CAMHS) 422-3, 451
Childcare Act (2006) 117, 163, 288
Childcare Commission 239-40
child-centred vs adult-led practice 234
child development
    factors affecting 27-8
    nature versus nurture debate 34
    theories of 575-6
        applying in practice 369
        linking to observations 372
        understanding stages of 291-2
Child Health Promotion Programme 397-400
childhood illness, responding to 432-6
    basic hygiene routines 438-9
    emergencies, dealing with 442-6
    medication, administering 440-1
    reporting and recording illness 437-8
    see also illnesses; sick children
child protection
    acting professionally 10-11, 211
    legislation covering 7, 116, 117
    planning outings 133

policies and procedures 128, 218, 387, 388
    see also abuse; accidents
Children Act (1989) 7, 15-16, 116, 495, 508
Children Act (2004) 116, 239, 250, 288
Children's Centres 332-3
Children's Minds (Donaldson) 86
Children's Workforce Development Council (CWDC) 240-1
Children and Young Peoples Plan (CYPP) 241-2
choices, giving children opportunities to make 136
Chomsky, Noam 72, 576
circle time 141
citizenship, promoting 149
clay, learning from using 307-8
cleanliness see hygiene
clothing for children 336-7
codes of practice 216-17
cognitive development 35, 66
    abstract concepts 48-50
        stages of learning 50-1
    concentration 52, 529
    and intelligence 48
    memory 52-3
    Piaget's theory 66-70
    and play 272
    ways of supporting 529-30
    see also intellectual development; learning theories
colds and coughs 411, 412
Commission for Equality and Human Rights 116
Common Assessment Framework 240, 298, 348
communication difficulties of children
    alternative and augmentative methods for 527-9
    I CAN charity, Early Talk programme 244
    language partners 139, 525-6
    Picture Exchange Communication System (PECS) 528
    sign language/representations 528-9
    stammering 527
communication skills
    children's
        development of 35, 43-6

        multilingual children 46-8
        effect of illness on 429
        factors hindering 549-50
        importance of 138-9
        see also language development
    of professionals 12-13, 364-6
        with children 220-2, 365
        with colleagues 223, 353-5
        with parents 222
    see also language development; literacy
comparison to others 60
computers, enhancing learning 309, 564
concentration 52, 529
concepts, learning 48-52
confidence of children 550-1
confidentiality 11, 98-9, 127, 355-6, 365-6, 370-1
consent, obtaining parental
    for medicines/treatments 183, 205, 206, 440
    for outings 131
    for photographs and videos 91
consistency, importance of 12, 85, 86, 137, 142, 224, 349-50, 595
construction areas 309
continuity, importance of 148
coordination 39
COSHH Regulations 162
cot death, preventing 588
creative play 274-5, 278
cross-infection, preventing 185, 186, 412, 438, 591, 592
cross-sectional information, growth 37, 38
cultural differences 209-10, 478
curriculum planning 191, 293-5
    creating plans 313-14
    curriculum frameworks 301-4
        influence on early years provision 304-10
        planning activities to meet 375
    effectiveness of different approaches 310-11
    examples of planning 314-17
    group planning 319
    implementing plans and activities 317-19
    Individual Education Plans (IEPs) 299
    Individual Learning Plans (ILPs) 295-7